THE MAPS OF ANTIETAM

*An Atlas of the Antietam (Sharpsburg) Campaign,
Including the Battle of South Mountain,
September 2 - 20, 1862*

Bradley M. Gottfried

SB

Savas Beatie
New York and California

The Maps of Antietam: An Atlas of the Antietam (Sharpsburg) Campaign, Including the Battle of South Mountain, September 2 - 20, 1862

Cataloging-in-Publication Data is available from the Library of Congress.

ISBN-13: 978-1-61121-086-6

Second Edition, First Printing

SB
Published by
Savas Beatie LLC
989 Governor Drive, Suite 102
El Dorado Hills, CA 95762

Editorial Offices:

Savas Beatie LLC
P.O. Box 4527
El Dorado Hills, CA 95762
Phone: 916-941-6896
(E-mail) editorial@savasbeatie.com

Savas Beatie titles are available at special discounts for bulk purchases in the United States by corporations, institutions, and other organizations. For more details, please contact Special Sales, P.O. Box 4527, El Dorado Hills, CA 95762. You may also e-mail us at sales@savasbeatie.com, or click over for a visit to our website at www.savasbeatie.com for additional information.

To my darling wife, Linda

Contents

Contents (continued)

Map Set 3. South Mountain: Fox's Gap (Morning)

Map Set 4. South Mountain: Fox's Gap (noon - 8:00 p.m.)

Contents (continued)

Map Set 5. South Mountain:
Frosttown Plateau (2:00 - 9:00 p.m.)

Map Set 6. South Mountain:
Turner's Gap (3:30 - 9:00 p.m.)

Map Set 7. South Mountain:
Crampton's Gap (11:00 a.m. - 7:00 p.m.)

Contents (continued)

Map Set 8. *The Capture of Harpers Ferry* *(September 12 - 15)*

Map Set 9. *To Sharpsburg* *(September 14 - 16)*

Contents (continued)

Map Set 10. The Eve of Battle (September 16)

Map Set 11. Antietam:
Hooker Opens the Battle (5:15 - 7:00 a.m.)

Contents (continued)

Contents (continued)

Contents (continued)

Map Set 17. Antietam: The Lower (Burnside's) Bridge (9:00 a.m. - 2:00 p.m.)

Map Set 18. Antietam: Burnside Advances on Sharpsburg (Afternoon, September 17)

Contents (continued)

Map Set 19. Antietam: A. P. Hill's Division
Arrives from Harpers Ferry (3:00 a.m. - 5:30 p.m.)

Map Set 20. Antietam:
Evening Stalemate (September 17 - 18)

Map Set 21. Aftermath: The Battle of
Shepherdstown (September 19 - 20, 1862)

Contents (continued)

Introduction

What began several years ago with an idea to better visualize and understand the Battle of Gettysburg and the major campaigns in the Eastern Theater has developed into several volumes that are now part of the Savas Beatie Military Atlas series—a significant effort to research and illustrate the major campaigns of the Civil War in an original and useful manner. My initial effort in 2007 resulted in *The Maps of Gettysburg*, which spawned a second book two years later entitled *The Maps of First Bull Run*. Soon after the Gettysburg volume appeared my publisher expressed an interest in expanding the series to the Western campaigns. I agreed it was a good idea, but because my interest lies in the East, other historians would have to be brought aboard to assist. The first two were David Powell and David Friedrichs, who collaborated to produce *The Maps of Chickamauga* in 2009, the same year my First Bull Run study appeared. Other Western Theater campaign studies for this series are in the works, as are atlas books dealing with Napoleon's 1812 invasion of Russia and various World War II campaigns. This is personally pleasing, for as so many people have shared with me, the only way you can really understand a military campaign is through maps, and this presentation unlocks other books on the same subjects.

All this explains why the book you hold in your hands, *The Maps of Antietam: An Atlas of the Antietam (Sharpsburg) Campaign, Including the Battle of South Mountain, September 2 - 20, 1862*, is my third effort but the fourth volume in this ongoing atlas series. My next volume, much of which is complete as of the date of this writing, covers the interesting but usually overlooked months following Gettysburg through the end of 1863 and into early 1864, including the campaigns of Bristoe Station and Mine Run and the various ancillary operations that took place during that period. The volume thereafter opens the Overland Campaign, with coverage of the Wilderness and Spotsylvania. Although I am not producing these in chronological order, it is my sincere hope that I will one day complete the major Civil War campaigns in the Eastern Theater of the Civil War from 1861-1865.

The Maps of Antietam is neutral in coverage and includes the entire campaign from both points of view. The text and maps cover the movement of the armies from the beginning of the campaign in early September to the battlefields in the various gaps slicing through South Mountain, the fascinating siege of Harpers Ferry, the maneuvering to the vicinity of Sharpsburg, and to the dramatic climax of the operation along Antietam Creek on September 17. The final segment of the book covers the withdrawal of Lee's army into Virginia and the fighting at Shepherdstown on September 19-20. As anyone who is familiar with this series will attest, the purpose of these atlas books is to offer a broad and full understanding of the complete campaign, rather than a micro-history of a particular event or day.

To my knowledge, no single source until now has pulled together the myriad of movements and events of this mammoth campaign and offered it in a cartographic form side-by-side with reasonably detailed text complete with endnotes. Like the books that have come before, *The Maps of Antietam* dissects the actions within each sector of a battlefield for a deeper and hopefully more meaningful understanding and reading experience. Each section of this book includes a number of text and map combinations. Every left-hand page includes descriptive text corresponding with a facing original map on the right-hand page. One of the key advantages of this presentation is that it eliminates the need to flip through the book to try to find a map to match the text. Some sections, like the preliminary operations (September 13-14) immediately leading up to the fighting at South Mountain are short and required only two maps and two text pages. Others, like the fighting for the Sunken Road on September 17 at Antietam, required eight maps and their corresponding eight text pages. Wherever possible, I utilized firsthand accounts to personalize the otherwise straightforward text. I hope readers find this method of presentation useful.

As I have written in previous introductions, the plentiful maps and sectioned coverage make it much easier to follow and understand what was happening each day (and in some cases, each hour) of this complex campaign. The various sections may also trigger a special interest and so pry open avenues ripe for additional study. I am hopeful that readers who approach the subject with a higher level of expertise will find the maps and text not only interesting to study and read, but truly helpful. If someone, somewhere, places this book within reach to refer to it now and again as a reference guide while reading other studies on the campaign, the long hours invested in this project will have been worthwhile.

And now, a few caveats are in order. *The Maps of Antietam* is not the last word or definitive treatment of the campaign, the various battles, or any part thereof—nor did I intend it to be. Given space and time considerations, I decided to cover the major events of the campaign and battles, with smaller transition sections to flesh out the full campaign story. As a result, many aspects of the campaign are purposely not fleshed out deeply. For example, I included a light overview of the loss and discovery of General Lee's Special Orders No. 191, but not a detailed explanation of how they were lost and who might have mishandled them. The importance to this book is that these important orders were written, lost, found, and utilized. The endnotes offer additional avenues of study on this and other interesting but tangential matters.

Original research was kept to a minimum. My primary reliance was upon firsthand accounts and battle reports, followed by quality secondary scholarship. Therefore, there are no new theories or evaluations of why the campaign or battles unfolded as they did. I am also very familiar with the battlefields described in this study and have walked them many times over the years, often in the company of other students of the war. Whenever a book uses short chapters or sections, as this one does, there will inevitably be some narrative redundancy. I have endeavored as far as possible to minimize this.

The sources can and often do conflict on many points, including numbers engaged, who moved when and where and why, what times specific things happened and, of course, casualties. I have tried to follow a generally accepted interpretation of the campaign and battles (I hope with some success) and portray the information accurately and with an even hand. Because of all these discrepancies, I have pieced the evidence together, discussed it with other historians, and reached my own conclusions. It is common to be confronted with multiple recollections by the men who were present of when and where events occurred. The simple fact is that we will never know or fully understand everything exactly how and when it transpired.

Inevitably, a study like this makes it likely that mistakes of one variety or another end up in the final text or on a map, despite endless hours of proofreading. I apologize in advance for any errors and assume full responsibility for them.

*   *   *

Everyone today studying the Maryland Campaign is indebted to Ezra A. Carman, who was a colonel in command of the 13th New Jersey infantry during the campaign (Brig. Gen. George Gordon's brigade, Brig. Gen. Alpheus Williams' division, Maj. Gen. Joseph Mansfield's XII Corps). Carman witnessed fighting in and around the Miller cornfield and the East Woods. After the war he devoted his life to researching the entire campaign. He spoke to and corresponded with hundreds of veterans on both sides and frequently walked the fields, compiling an impressive collection of notes and letters he eventually utilized to write a long and monumentally important history of the campaign. Carman's manuscript has only recently been published.

The Maps of Antietam could not have been written without the assistance of a host of people. As always, Theodore P. Savas of Savas Beatie heads the list. A good friend and effective editor, he has always supported my efforts. Because Ted is also a distinguished historian and author in his own right, he understands the researching and writing process and is always supportive.

I am also indebted to Dr. Tom Clemens, who has superbly edited Carman's manuscript for publication in two large volumes, and to Antietam park ranger John Hoptak. Both read the manuscript and provided invaluable suggestions on how to make it better. Steve Stotelmyer, an engineer by trade, has devoted much of his life to studying the South Mountain battles in general, and the action at Fox's Gap in particular. Steve was very generous of his time and materials, tramped over the fields with me, and shared many of his resources.

Ted Alexander, the Chief Historian of the Antietam National Battlefield, allowed me to use the battlefield library on numerous occasions and patiently answered all of my questions. Ted is a good friend to historians everywhere.

Finally, I would like to thank Linda, my friend, my partner, and my wife. Linda traveled with me on my many trips to the battlefields, patiently listened to my endless stories, and allowed me the time to complete this important effort.

Bradley M. Gottfried

La Plata, Maryland

Foreword

The late summer and fall of 1862 was, by any measure, the most critical time of the Civil War. After achieving significant victories in the spring, the summer found Union armies bogged down or in retreat across the country. Conversely the Confederates, reaping the benefit of their Conscription Act, mounted several campaigns destined to create a thousand-mile offensive from the Mississippi River in the west all the way east to the Chesapeake Bay. The most important of these was Robert E. Lee's Maryland Campaign, whose failure north of the Potomac River foreshadowed the outcome of the others.

In July of 1862, Gen. Lee's Army of Northern Virginia was tethered to Richmond by Maj. Gen. George B. McClellan's Army of the Potomac at Harrison's Landing barely twenty miles from the city. Lee did not dare abandon his capital to venture northward, yet his impatience grew with the knowledge that the South could not win independence by defending their key cities. Lee's agitation increased in late July when President Abraham Lincoln sent a new army under Maj. Gen. John Pope to threaten Richmond from the north. Lee sent his able lieutenant Thomas J. "Stonewall" Jackson with a small force to confront Pope, and was soon relieved to learn that Union Maj. Gen. Henry Halleck ordered McClellan to withdraw from the James River and join forces with Pope in northern Virginia. Lee boldly set out with most of his army to destroy Pope prior to any unification with McClellan's forces.

Through a series of maneuvers, Lee turned Pope's western or right flank and forced the Federals back toward their own capital. Lee then confronted Pope on the same ground near Manassas where many of these men had struggled thirteen months ago, and with similar results: a routed Union army flooding toward Washington, DC. After an unsuccessful attempt to cut off the retreat, Lee received reinforcements and turned his aspirations northward to Union-held Maryland and perhaps Pennsylvania.

Now with an unfettered opportunity, Lee sent his ragged troops splashing across the Potomac on September 4 with the crossroads town of Frederick as their primary objective. Although the weak and unfit were sent to Winchester to recoup and re-supply, the Army of Northern Virginia still numbered 55,000 to 60,000 men. Many and varied are the reasons ascribed to Lee for this daring campaign. He explained to his president, Jefferson Davis, that threatening Pennsylvania and occupying Maryland would yield numerous advantages to the South. Beyond the mundane but necessary requirement to provision his army and its thousands of horse and mules, Lee believed political and morale advantages could be gained in Maryland, a state of divided loyalties and sympathies. By feeding his army on Northern foodstuffs Lee ensured Virginia farmers could harvest and store their crops as occupying Union troops would vacate Virginia to follow his bold move. Beyond these logistical considerations Lee believed threatening Washington, DC would negatively impact Northern morale and politics. With mid-term elections on the horizon, Lee thought a Southern victory on Northern soil might result in a "peace" Congress capable of forcing Lincoln's hand and creating a negotiated settlement to end the war. In an effort to win the hearts of Marylander's, Lee ordered his army to respect private property and issued a proclamation casting his army as liberators of a state oppressed by Union tyranny. On September 8 Lee wrote to Davis from Frederick suggesting the latter open discussions of peace with the Lincoln administration.

Never were Confederate hopes higher. Lee had under his command a mostly veteran force, with a larger percentage of all Confederate soldiers in service than any other time during the war. After assuming command a scant three months earlier Lee had advanced the war's frontier from the James River north to the Potomac River, and now hoped to checkmate Lincoln's beleaguered call for 300,000 more troops to suppress the rebellion. As his troops basked in the sun outside Frederick, all things seemed possible.

Meanwhile, Washington DC remained in chaos, the defeated and demoralized Federal troops gathered at fortifications surrounding the city and suffering in wants physical as well as spiritual. Lincoln swiftly reacted by sacking Pope and giving McClellan authority to defend the capital. When it became clear that Lee had crossed into Maryland east of the Blue Ridge and was a scant forty miles from the city, Lincoln and Halleck determined to send a field army to confront him. After offering this command to two other generals they approached McClellan, putting him in command of the field army he created at their behest. This decision was far from popular with political leaders. Two of Lincoln's cabinet conspired to challenge the appointment, but Lincoln when avowed that no other leader could organize an army and move it toward the enemy as quickly as McClellan could, the cabinet acquiesced. McClellan hastily assembled some 70,000 men and on September 6 moved them toward Confederate-occupied Frederick. Given the exigency of the situation, Maj. Gens. Fitz John Porter and William B. Franklin were released from arrest to go with the army. Not only was this hastily composed army disorganized and poorly supplied, but nearly 19,000 men were new to military life, having served no more than two months in the ranks.

The goals and objective given to McClellan were twofold: protect and defend Washington and Baltimore and drive the Confederates from Maryland. Knowing the tenuous nature of his relationship with President Lincoln, McClellan was in no position to take risks with his new army. His primarily defensive mission was further hampered by the constant cautioning of Halleck, who routinely warned McClellan that Lee would swiftly re-cross the Potomac and attack Washington from the south. True to his word, Lincoln ordered Halleck to forward more troops and supplies to McClellan as they became available. By September 17, the Army of the Potomac fielded more than 87,000 men.

Unbeknownst to McClellan, Lincoln had decided to appease the radical wing of his party by escalating the conflict from a war to restore the Union to a war to also end slavery. Lincoln recognized the economic and military advantages slavery provided the South and moved to end them. He wrote a proclamation based on his authority from the Confiscation Act of 1862 that called upon Southern states to end their affiliation with the Confederacy and rejoin the

Union, promising they could retain their slaves by doing so. It was a hedged bet. Lincoln realized compliance was unlikely, but his proclamation would weaken the war effort and economy in the South while making it unlikely that foreign powers would support a nation fighting to retain slavery. Ironically, if McClellan was successful in his mission, he would (unwittingly) create the victory that would allow Lincoln to announce a major shift in war policy that McClellan himself opposed.

Lee's complacency was soon unsettled by the fact that the Union garrison at Harpers Ferry, which was closer to his supply depot at Winchester than Lee, did not evacuate its position. After deliberation with his subordinates, Lee moved to neutralize this Union threat side by dispatching Stonewall Jackson's wing of the army to gain control of the vital gateway to the Shenandoah Valley. McClellan was requested to rescue the threatened Harpers Ferry garrison. He was fortuitously aided in this endeavor when a Union soldier resting on the site of an abandoned Confederate camp discovered a misplaced copy of Special Orders No. 191 delineating this operation. Moving to strike the scattered portions of Lee's army on September 14, McClellan pushed through the various passes and gaps along South Mountain, triggering a series of battles that defeated the Southern defenders and triggered a desperate night retreat by Lee. After suffering nearly 3,000 losses at South Mountain Lee retired to concentrate his army with the hope that he could continue the campaign. McClellan's victory at South Mountain sparked his pursuit, and he found Lee drawn up on the heights of Sharpsburg. Once again, McClellan moved to attack him.

The fighting at Sharpsburg on September 17, 1862, was the bloodiest struggle experienced by either army up to that time, nearly twelve hours of unrelenting bloodletting that still represents the bloodiest day in American history. The next day, September 18, the armies remained in position, but neither commander reopened the combat. With his Maryland offensive undone, Lee was once again forced to retire, this time south of the Potomac and back into Virginia. Active operations ended following Lee's rebuff of an aggressive Union pursuit beyond the river at Shepherdstown on September 20.

The seizure of the South Mountain passes and long bloody struggle along Antietam Creek ended Lee's high hopes for a long stay north of the river. His army rested and recuperated near Winchester while McClellan was content to guard against further invasion. Lincoln used McClellan's strategic victory to issue his Emancipation Proclamation, which ensured a bitter and debilitating war for both sides. Although Lee would rebuild his army and go on to earn a reputation virtually unmatched in American history, his lack of success in Maryland that September, coupled with Confederate failures in Kentucky and Mississippi, doomed any chance the Southern cause had for independence. The Army of Northern Virginia would march farther north the following summer, but changed circumstances and fewer opportunities rendered the Gettysburg Campaign strategically less important than the events of September of 1862.

Dr. Thomas G. Clemens
Hagerstown, Maryland

THE MAPS
OF ANTIETAM

*An Atlas of the Antietam (Sharpsburg) Campaign,
Including the Battle of South Mountain,
September 2 - 20, 1862*

Map Set 1. The Invasion of Maryland (September 2-13, 1862)

Map 1.1: September 2-4, 1862

During the final days of August 1862, Gen. Robert E. Lee's ascendant Confederate Army of Northern Virginia outmaneuvered, outfought, and routed from the field Maj. Gen. John Pope's Federal Army of Virginia at the Battle of Second Manassas (Bull Run). Pope's modest victories in the West had triggered his call to Washington to lead the new Federal army, an array of units lashed together for yet another campaign against Richmond. As Pope organized and planned, Maj. Gen. George McClellan's Army of the Potomac remained inactive along the James River below the Southern capital. Given the size of his army and his audacious plan to capture Richmond, McClellan's forced withdrawal during the series of heavy combats known as the Seven Days' Battles (June 25 - July 1, 1862) was bitterly disappointing. Unwilling to allow McClellan to sit along the river and turn the initiative over to Lee, President Abraham Lincoln ordered him to abandon the peninsula and return his army to Washington that August. Using his interior position to advantage, Lee left a small force to watch McClellan and moved north to engage Pope. McClellan shuttled his units northward as ordered, but they did not arrive in time or in sufficient strength to prevent Lee's stunning victory on the plains of Manassas.

With yet another army in disarray and plagued with low morale, Lincoln reluctantly (and against the advice of many in his Cabinet) consolidated the two armies under McClellan. An enlisted man's general and outstanding organizer, "Little Mac" prepared the troops so they could fight again as soon as possible.[1]

A panicked Washington, meanwhile, prepared for the onslaught of Lee's army. Government workers were armed and valuable papers and supplies packed up and shipped away. Even a steamer stood ready to whisk Lincoln and other high-ranking officials to safety should such an event prove necessary.[2]

Foreign discontent with the war was approaching its zenith. The Federal blockade of Southern ports was choking off the flow of vital southern commodities, including cotton and tobacco, to England and France. Because of the reduction in cotton exports, large numbers of British textile workers were either out of work or working reduced hours. Talk of recognizing the fledgling Confederacy on some level was commonplace in many foreign capitals.[3]

Although rebuffed at Ox Hill (Chantilly) on September 1, Lee was still prepared to give battle the next day. The Federals, however, fell back to the safety offered by the ring of forts protecting Washington. Riding the wave of two major field victories that had carried his army from the James River all the way north to the Potomac, Lee found himself facing one of the most important decisions in his career: What to do next? Washington was too strong to attack, and falling back and giving up large swaths of Virginia was unthinkable. Remaining stationary in northern Virginia was also not viable because food and forage was scarce in that part of the state. Aggressive by nature, Lee believed that only field victories could win the war, by reducing the will of the North to continue fighting. Given the possibility of foreign recognition, Lee believed maneuvering and foraging for as long as possible above the Potomac River offered the best course of action. Lee broached the idea in a September 3 dispatch to President Jefferson Davis. A move into Maryland from Dranesville could supply the army with needed supplies, perhaps bring the state into the Confederacy's fold, and keep Federals away from Richmond. A significant victory in Maryland might convince the North to sue for peace.[4]

On September 4, 1862, Federal troops were dispersed in and around Washington. The II Corps and XII Corps, with Darius Couch's division of the IV Corps, ended the day in Tennallytown just northwest of the capital. The VI Corps was near the Alexandria Seminary, while the I Corps and V Corps camped near Upton's Hill northwest of Washington; the IX Corps was in Washington. Lee's army was on the move toward the Potomac to cross into Maryland. In fact, Daniel H. Hill's division was already crossing the river at multiple sites (e.g., at Point of Rocks, at Noland's Ferry, and near the mouth of the Monocacy River). Thomas J. "Stonewall" Jackson's wing of the Southern army halted for the night between White's Ford and Leesburg, with James Longstreet's wing of divisions a few miles south of Leesburg at Newton Hall.[5]

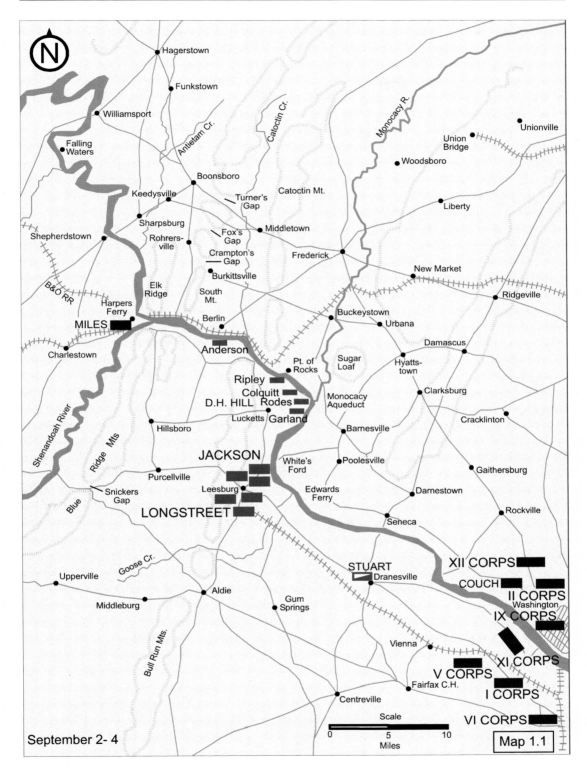

September 2- 4

Map 1.1

Map 1.2: September 4-5, 1862

Both armies were reinforced prior to the opening of the Maryland Campaign. McClellan's Army of the Potomac absorbed two of John Pope's corps. McClellan's army was well equipped and officially numbered nearly 160,000, but its men were demoralized by the string of recent defeats. Lee's Army of Northern Virginia had been substantially reinforced while the Army of the Potomac stood on the doorstep of Richmond when units from other regions rode the rails to help save the capital. These units were not returned to their original armies and states, but instead incorporated into Lee's army. With Lee poised to move north of the Potomac River, additional combat commands were shuttled north to swell his numbers to more than 70,000 men. However, excessive straggling, illness, and other reasons would trim tens of thousands from his ranks by the time the pivotal battle of Sharpsburg (Antietam) was fought.[6]

Once Lee's army began moving north toward Leesburg, it largely disappeared from McClellan's view. Federal cavalry from the Virginia peninsula provided McClellan with the intelligence he needed to make an educated guess about Lee's plans, but little else. McCllellan knew Lee was in Leesburg on the evening of September 3, and his cavalry commander, Brig. Gen. Alfred Pleasonton, correctly surmised that a Southern cavalry attack on the forts near the Chain Bridge was merely a distraction from the main issue: Lee was crossing the Potomac into Maryland. Because of the Lincoln's concerns about losing Washington, McClellan marched north with only about half of his men (some 70,000) by the end of September 4, leaving the remainder (including the III Corps, V Corps, and XI Corps) behind to guard the capital. Apparently, Lee did not decide on a full-blown thrust into Maryland until that morning, when he wrote to President Davis, "should the results of the expedition justify it, I propose to enter Pennsylvania, unless you should deem it unadvisable upon political or other grounds." Two of Lee's concerns were making sure he had adequate ammunition and subsistence to make the invasion. After deciding on this daring action he drafted General Orders No. 102, which dictated how the army was to behave while operating in Maryland.[7]

After committing to insert his army into Maryland, Lee had to determine where he would cross the Potomac. He had already sent D. H. Hill across the river south of Harpers Ferry. Crossing of the rest of the army in that sector would put considerable pressure on the Federals to leave the safe confines of the Washington defenses and march out to give battle. A crossing father north near Shepherdstown would safeguard Lee's line of communications, but not provide the same impetus to pull McClellan's army away from Washington. Lee decided by the evening of September 4 to take his chances on a more southerly crossing at White's Ford.[8]

Lee met with Stonewall Jackson and James Longstreet at his headquarters in Leesburg on the night of September 4 and told them of his plans to cross the Potomac River and enter Maryland. After crossing at White's Ford opposite Leesburg, he explained, the army would march north to Frederick. Both subordinates greeted the news with optimism.[9]

By the end of September 5, the three infantry divisions under Jackson's command led by John R. Jones (Jackson's former division), A. P. Hill, and Alexander Lawton reached Buckeystown, Maryland, about nine miles south of Frederick. Although the first to cross the Potomac River, D. H. Hill's division now brought up the rear of the column. James Ewell Brown (Jeb) Stuart's cavalry division followed Jackson's men across the Potomac and rode to Poolesville, where Fitzhugh Lee's cavalry brigade routed a Federal cavalry regiment. Longstreet's four divisions under David R. Jones, Lafayette McLaws, Richard Anderson, and John B. Hood moved through Leesburg and approached the Potomac, camping on the same ground Jackson's men had occupied the night before. John Walker's small infantry division reached Leesburg by the end of the day.

McClellan, meanwhile, continued moving his corps slowly through Maryland. The II Corps and XII Corps marched north to Rockville, while the IV Corps' only division under Maj. Gen. Darius Couch moved to Offutt's Crossroads (now Potomac), Maryland. Pleasonton's cavalry made its way north of Seneca in an attempt to discover Lee's position and intentions.[10]

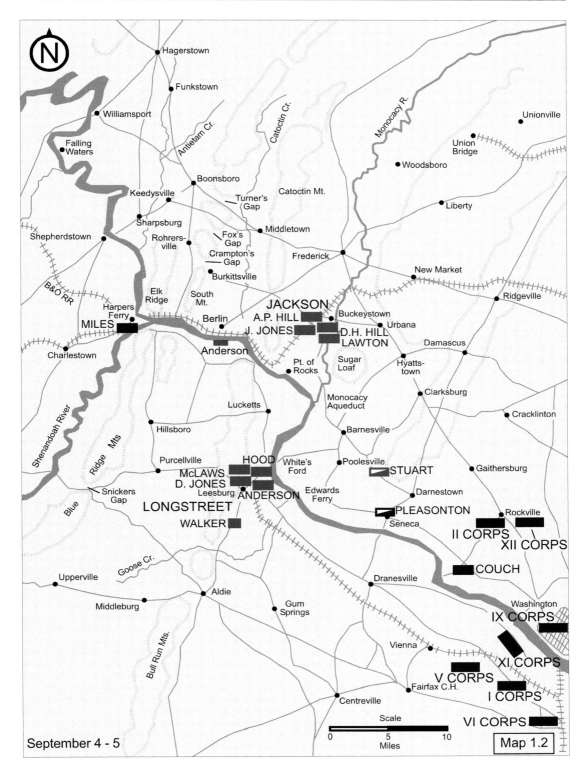

September 4 - 5

Map 1.2

Map 1.3: September 6, 1862

The recent rains had swelled the Potomac River at White's Ford to about one-half mile wide and chest deep. Most of the men took off not only their shoes, but also their trousers and undergarments. Rather than drive straight across the river, the wading column bowed to the right to take advantage of Mason's Island, which broke up the trip, before veering back to the left to finish the journey. The steep banks on the Virginia side of the ford made it difficult for wheeled vehicles to cross, so the earth was dug down to provide a more gentle grade. Generally exuberant about the crossing, the men waded the broad river singing "Maryland, My Maryland." The route took the Confederates through Poolesville, where Southerners found many residents less than overjoyed at the sight of the bedraggled invaders.[11]

Jackson's march began again early on September 6. The divisions under Lawton and A. P. Hill (the latter under Brig. Gen. Lawrence Branch because of Hill's recent arrest) halted at Monocacy Junction with orders to capture the important Baltimore and Ohio Railroad bridge over the Monocacy River. J. R. Jones halted his brigades just outside of Frederick. Colonel Bradley Johnson's brigade was thrown into the town to act as a provost guard. "This morning about 10 o'clock the Rebels took possession of our good city of Frederick without opposition— no soldiers of the U.S. being there," recalled one resident. "No commotion or excitement, but all peaceably and quiet the soldiers are around the town purchasing clothing—shoes, caps and eatables. . . . Many of our citizens left town last night." The locals were unimpressed with the Southern warriors. According to a physician's diary, they did not have "uniforms" but "multiforms" which were uniformly filthy; their faces "had not been acquainted with water for weeks," their hair was "shaggy and unkempt." The men did not march through the town, he continued, but "strolled . . . marching it could not be called without doing violence to the word." Their bands tried to play "Dixie" and "Maryland" in "execrable style." Many of the men carried watermelons under their arms, recently liberated from a B & O Railroad depot.[12]

Longstreet's wing, which had camped just short of the Potomac River on the evening of September 5, crossed at White's Ford and followed Jackson's route toward Frederick. The men camped in the area vacated by Jackson that morning at Three Springs near Buckeystown. Walker's division brought up the rear and camped at Big Spring on the Virginia side of the Potomac, which had served as first Jackson's and then Longstreet's camp for the past two nights. The weather was hot and dry, and the thousands of feet, hooves, and wheeled vehicles kicked up considerable dust clouds, reducing visibility at times to less than fifty feet.[13]

Jeb Stuart led his troopers out of Poolesville during the morning and headed to Urbana. Lee ordered him to divide his command and threaten both Baltimore and Washington, reporting on Federal movements all the while.[14]

Unfortunately for the Southern cause, the three top commanders began the campaign in various levels of pain and immobility. Lee was holding the reins of his horse on August 31 when something spooked the animal. He reached for the reins, tripped, and fell forward, breaking a bone in one wrist/hand and badly spraining the other; both were splinted. Unable to hold the reins or even dress himself, Lee was forced to travel in an ambulance. Stonewall Jackson also had a mishap and was riding in an ambulance after an admirer gave him a horse that reared and fell on top of him. Although his aides were worried that he may have broken his back, it was only badly bruised. As for Longstreet, "A boot chafed his heel, which took on an ugly look and refused to heal," recalled his staff officer Moxley Sorrel. He was forced to "don a slipper, and at Sharpsburg he was in no good humor at such footwear. . . . In fact," Sorrel continued, "a wobbly carpet slipper was not a good looking thing for a commander on the field.[15]

As Lee's army moved north, most of the Federal army remained in its camps. The I Corps and IX Corps marched through Washington to Leesborough (now Wheaton) and the VI Corps and George Sykes' division of the V Corps marched to Tennallytown. By the end of September 6, McClellan had sixty percent of his army arrayed in a vast arc about ten miles north and west of the capital of Washington.[16]

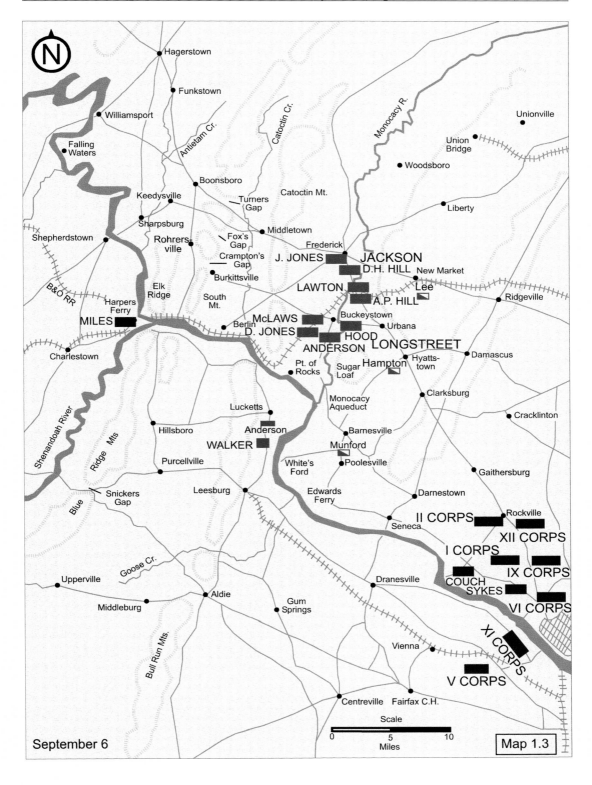

September 6

Map 1.3

Map 1.4: September 7-8, 1862

The Army of the Potomac became stronger by the day with the arrival of reinforcements. About twenty regiments of green troops joined prior to the campaign, but there was little time for orientation or drilling. Each was assigned to an existing brigade with the hope its men would learn their new trade from the veterans around them. The army also regained some of its confidence with McClellan in overall command. According to some historians, the troops were not as demoralized by the defeats as they were angry with their commanders at all levels for the poor strategic and tactical decisions they had demonstrated on several battlefields. Despite his poor showing at the gates of Richmond, only a small percentage of the enlisted men personally blamed McClellan. He still had their confidence. Little Mac personally quit Washington and joined his troops in the field on September 7.[17]

The arrival of Longstreet's divisions at Frederick on September 7 united most of the Rebel army. After marching and fighting for weeks, the exhausted men savored their respite by bathing, organizing their belongings, and foraging for something to eat. Once Walker forded his division across the Potomac at Cheek's Ford, the entire Army of Northern Virginia was in Maryland. Walker's men halted for the night just south of Buckeystown.[18]

Although not designed to unfold in tandem, Lee's move into Maryland coincided with a Confederate thrust into Kentucky by two armies under Braxton Bragg and Kirby Smith. Success in the latter campaign required the eventual convergence of the two armies (as well as smaller columns) in a complicated plan that was beyond the ability of the men conducting the effort. Other Confederate troops were poised to reclaim what is now West Virginia.[19]

One of Lee's goals in crossing the Potomac River was to swell his ranks with young Maryland recruits. In this regard he would be sorely disappointed. Lee released a proclamation (studded with exclamation points) on September 8 decrying "sixteen months of oppression more galling than the Austrian tyranny," and urged that the time was right to "strike for liberty and right." The proclamation failed to win over the hearts of more than a few hundred Marylanders.[20]

As evident from army dispatches to Richmond during this time, Stuart's cavalry was not providing Lee with the quality and quantity of intelligence he required. Instead, Lee's young cavalry leader appeared to be spending more time planning and hosting a large ball the following day (September 8). The gala came off as planned, but the Yankees did not cooperate. Just as the dance was picking up steam, a breathless courier arrived with word that the enemy had attacked Stuart's outposts. Forced to leave the ladies behind, Stuart and his men mounted their horses and galloped away. Much of Lee's intelligence about the Federal army was gleaned from Northern newspapers. Lee believed the Federal infantry was still huddling within the Washington defenses, but in reality the foot soldiers were north of town in Maryland, ready to advance in his direction from the south and southeast.

There was only one major Federal troop movement on September 7, when the VI Corps marched to Rockville to join the II Corps and XII Corps resting in camps there. McClellan turned over command of Washington to Maj. Gen. Nathaniel Banks and rode north to join his army. He halted at Rockville and established his headquarters there.[21]

While the Confederate army rested on September 8 (except for Walker's division, which completed its march to Frederick), the Federals marched after Lee's army in three separate columns. McClellan's plan was for the left wing, composed of the VI Corps and Sykes' division of the V Corps, to move via Seneca, keeping the Potomac River on their left. The center wing, composed of the II Corps and XII Corps, would travel from Rockville to Frederick via Hyattstown, while the right wing, composed of the I Corps and IX Corps, reached New Market via Brookville and Urbana. The VI Corps began its march just south of Rockville and halted about a mile north of it. After resting several hours, it continued its march before halting about four miles south of Darnestown at Muddy Branch. The IX Corps began its seven-hour march from Leesborough about 6:00 p.m. The II Corps and XII Corps left Rockville and camped at Middlebrook that evening. The remaining Federal troops spent September 8 resting.[22]

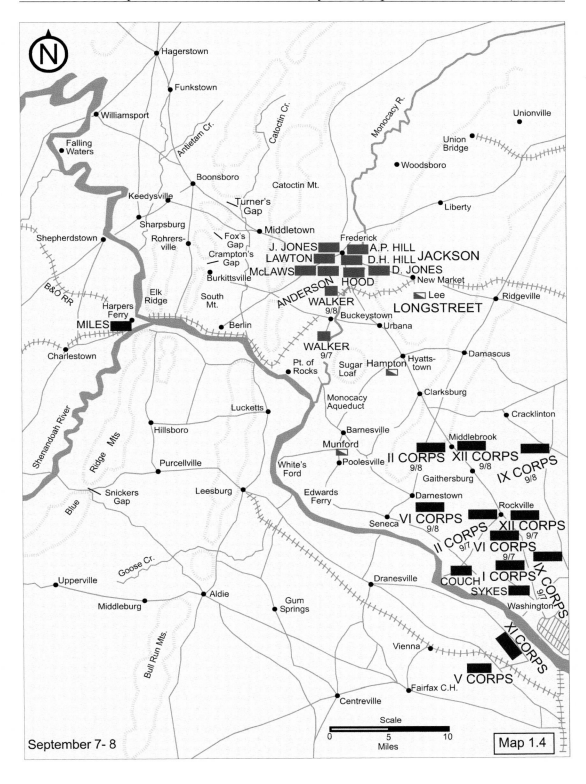

September 7- 8

Map 1.4

Map 1.5: September 9, 1862

After several days of reassuring President Davis about the adequacy of his provisions, Gen. Lee reversed himself. Farmers were driving their herds north out of the reach of his foraging commissary, and those who remained demanded inflated prices. To avoid confiscating supplies without recompense, and to establish a more secure line of communications, Lee moved north to open a clear route into the abundant Shenandoah Valley. He believed this move would also force the Federal garrisons in Martinsburg and Harpers Ferry to withdraw.

Lee now also knew that at least four Federal corps had left Washington, with one as near as Poolesville just fifteen miles away. This did not cause Lee undue concern. He had been in the state for several days and the enemy had barely moved. What Lee seems not to have realized was that the Federals had spent most of that time reorganizing, and were only now free to march as rapidly in his direction as they desired. If Lee had any real concern, it was about a column of Federals pushing north along the Potomac River that had the potential to get between his army and Virginia.[23]

The first major problem of the campaign became apparent by the afternoon of September: the sizeable enemy garrisons at Martinsburg and Harpers Ferry, which were blocking Lee's line of communications with the Shenandoah Valley, had not retreated as he expected. Lee's options were limited. He could continue with his invasion, moving the army northwest to Hagerstown and ignore the Federal garrisons; divide the army and send part of it to capture Harpers Ferry; or, turn to stand and fight McClellan's approaching army. Jackson liked the third option, but Lee selected the second and outlined his plans in Special Orders No. 191. Lee believed he could conduct a rather complex marching assignment to neutralize the Federal garrisons and then reunite his divisions before McClellan's slow-moving Union army became a serious threat. Longstreet objected to the plan, arguing that dividing the army under such circumstances with tight time constraints was a hazardous undertaking. Lee knew the risks and offered some compromises that mollified his senior lieutenant.[24]

According to S.O. No. 191, the army would resume its march the next day, September 10, along the Hagerstown Road. Jackson had the longest march and would take the lead. After passing Boonsboro, he would veer to Sharpsburg, cross the Potomac River, and head for Martinsburg, drive the enemy away, and move down the south side of the Potomac to Harpers Ferry. Longstreet would follow to Hagerstown to guard the supply and wagon trains gathered there. D. H. Hill's division formed the army's rearguard at Boonsboro. Two other divisions under Lafayette McLaws and Richard Anderson would march to Middletown and thence to Harpers Ferry, where a portion of the two divisions would scale Maryland Heights while the rest remained in Pleasant Valley. Walker's division would return the way it came, re-crossing the Potomac at Cheek's Ford for its march to Loudoun Heights, where it would cooperate in the reduction of the Harpers Ferry garrison. After completing their missions, the widely separated divisions would reunite as soon as possible at Boonsboro or Hagerstown.

Lee did not know either the exact strength of the two garrisons (Martinsburg had 2,500 men; Harpers Ferry had 10,400) or their orders to "Be energetic and active, and defend all places to the last extremity." Lee expected them to flee on his approach—a reasonable expectation. If he was correct, it would avoid entangling a large portion of his army in a siege operation. The Harpers Ferry garrison was commanded by Col. Dixon Miles, who lingered under the accusation of being drunk at First Bull Run. Although a court found him innocent, Miles had been banished to Harpers Ferry, what had once been considered a backwater assignment.[25]

While Lee was dividing his army McClellan was completing his deployment, with orders to interpose his army between Lee and the capital. The I Corps moved north from Leesborough to Brookville to get closer to its right wing sister, the IX Corps, camped at Cracklintown. The center wing remained at Middlebrook just north of Gaithersburg. The left wing's VI Corps finished its march to Darnestown as Couch's division moved to Seneca and Sykes' occupied Rockville.[26]

Walker's division was the only Rebel unit on the march this day, ordered south to destroy the Monocacy Aqueduct.[27]

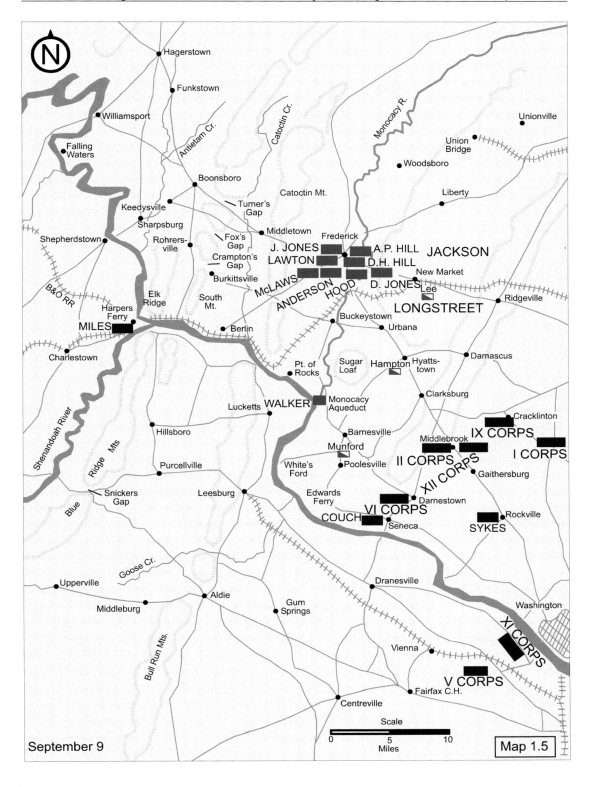

September 9

Map 1.5

Map 1.6: September 10, 1862

Stonewall Jackson's men were on the road by 4:00 a.m. on September 10. The citizens of Frederick lined their streets to watch the Confederates march through town, one division after another. Even though the Rebels had thus far conducted themselves reasonably well, few were sorry to see them leave. Many Marylanders would always remember the intense and almost overwhelming smell that permeated Lee's veterans. The heat only made it worse. Once out of town Jackson's column followed the National Road toward South Mountain.[28]

After marching northwest across South Mountain at Turner's Gap, Jackson halted his column about 10:00 a.m. one mile south of Boonsboro and ordered his men into camp. Dividing the army in enemy territory was a risky proposition, and it was critical that Martinsburg and Harpers Ferry be taken as quickly as possible. Instead of marching hard, however, Jackson, a mere twelve miles northwest of Frederick, went into an early bivouac before noon. One historian of the Maryland Campaign hypothesized that Jackson learned the road he was on was about to become more difficult for his troops, so he allowed his men to rest while he considered his options. Longstreet's command, which was marching behind Jackson, only made it ten miles out of Frederick to Middletown. D. H. Hill's division, at the tail of the column, barely budged from its campsite and made it only to Frederick. Generals McLaws and Anderson, whose divisions would play a significant role in capturing Harpers Ferry, marched thirteen miles through the hot and dusty day before camping near Middletown around midnight.

Meanwhile, Walker's division, which was near the Monocacy Aqueduct, withdrew and was marching north. Walker received orders to re-cross the Potomac River at Cheek's Ford and join the operation against Harpers Ferry. The assignment was not to Walker's liking because he was convinced it was now strongly defended. He put his men back on the road about 2:00 p.m. and, taking a circuitous route, marched to Point of Rocks, which he reached about midnight. The men were ready to sleep, but Walker would hear none of it. He worked them through much of the night, bridging the canal with railroad ties so they could cross the river at first light on September 11. Once across, the men grabbed some sleep about one mile south of the river. While the infantry moved about, Jeb Stuart and most of his cavalry spent most of September 10 resting, a decision that deprived Lee of any additional information about McClellan's activities.[29]

While Lee pushed his men north and west from Frederick, McClellan worried Lee's ultimate goal was Baltimore (in the opposite direction). This concern was reinforced by a report that Jackson's men were east of Frederick in New Market. As a result, McClellan on September 10 decided to move his men toward Parr's Ridge between Frederick and Baltimore to form a Union line from Ridgeville on the right to Barnesville on the left. The movement began at the appointed time in the morning, but soon thereafter McClellan received a report that the enemy was still in and around Frederick and was not moving toward Baltimore as first believed. McClellan stopped his army after a short march and decided a reconnaissance was in order before continuing to march. On the right, Ambrose Burnside had pushed Reno's IX Corps northward, halting between Damascus and Cracklinton. Joseph Hooker's I Corps marched a short distance toward Poplar Spring from Brookville, halting near Triadelphia at about the midway point. On the left, William Franklin's VI Corps marched ten miles to Barnesville, which was about twelve miles southeast of Frederick. Darius Couch's division of the IV Corps marched from Seneca to Poolesville. In the center, Edwin Sumner's II Corps approached within three miles of Clarksburg, while Joseph Mansfield's XII Corps moved north, camping within two miles of Damascus.[30]

These Federal movements convinced Col. Thomas Munford to move his small Confederate cavalry brigade back to Sugar Loaf Mountain, where a small Federal cavalry force tried to expel it. Realizing the mountain's strategic value, McClellan ordered Gens. Franklin and Couch to provide infantry support to the cavalry, but neither appeared to take the order seriously.[31]

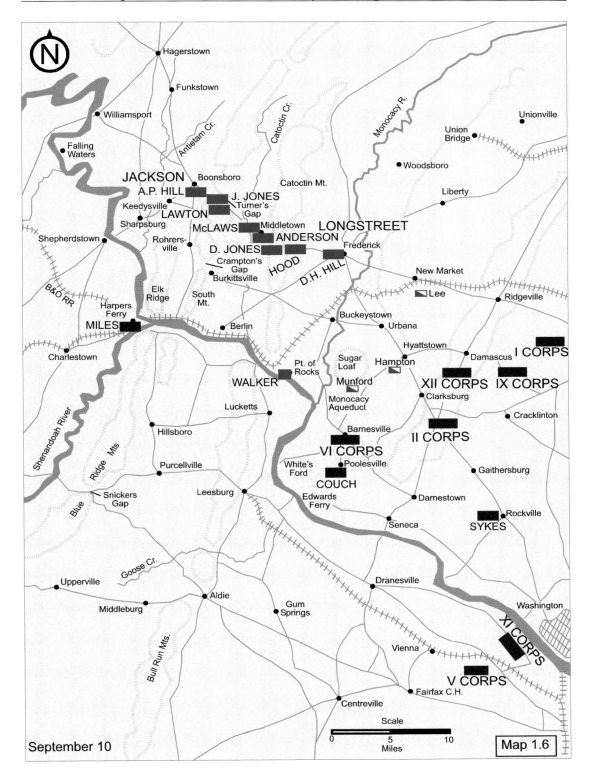

September 10

Map 1.6

Map 1.7: September 11, 1862

Both armies were on the march on September 11. Lee's men were moving to implement Special Orders No. 191, while McClellan tried to figure out what the invading Rebels were doing and where they were doing it.

Jackson was up and about long before first light. Lee hoped that Washington would order the evacuation of the garrisons at Harpers Ferry and Martinsburg, but Jackson's aides reported both places manned and ready. Both locations would have to be reduced. Jackson decided against the most direct route through Shepherdstown, choosing instead a circuitous route through Williamsport that added ten miles to his march. His decision allowed him to interpose his men between Martinsburg and safety. His goal was North Mountain Depot, a station on the B & O Railroad about seven miles west of Martinsburg.[32]

J. R. Jones led the "Stonewall Division" through Boonsboro about 4:00 a.m. and continued toward Williamsport. Lawton's and A.P. Hill's divisions followed. When the grayclad veterans re-crossed the Potomac at Light's Ford, the bands struck up "Carry Me Back to Old Virginia." Many in the ranks believed the brief excursion into Maryland was over. Jones and Lawton ended their march at Hammond's Mill, about a mile and a half from North Mountain Depot. A. P. Hill had taken a more direct approach and was closing in on Martinsburg on the road from Williamsport. These were handsome marches, with each division averaging twenty-three miles. When they halted, the men dropped to the ground in exhaustion.[33]

With Jackson finally making good progress, Longstreet's path along the National Turnpike was now clear. Hood's and D. R. Jones' divisions were on the road by 5:00 a.m. They moved through Turner's Gap and arrived at Boonsboro by 8:00 a.m. This was Longstreet's original destination, but intelligence indicated that Federals were attempting to secure large supplies of flour from Hagerstown, and that twenty miles farther north in Chambersburg, Pennsylvania, enemy troops were massing for a possible advance into Lee's rear. As a result, Longstreet continued marching his divisions toward Hagerstown, but stopped for the night at Funkstown. Longstreet was unhappy with his current orders and the way the campaign was unfolding. "General," Longstreet told Lee, "I wish we could stand still and let the damned Yankees come to us."[34]

Without information from Jeb Stuart to the contrary, Lee had no reason to believe that McClellan's infantry posed a threat to the safety of his army. Lee set about dividing his army yet again, sending D. H. Hill's 8,000-man division toward the South Mountain range. Hill broke camp on the morning of September 11 and marched through Frederick before stopping for the day about two miles from Turner's Gap. The Army of Northern Virginia was now operating as five independent columns.[35]

McLaws and Anderson, meanwhile, had their men up early marching south from Middletown. They halted for the night near Burkittsville, where local women heckled the men for their tattered appearance. Both divisions were under orders to cross South Mountain and enter beautiful Pleasant Valley, which ran north of Harpers Ferry. Walker rested his exhausted troops in Virginia across from Point of Rocks.[36]

The methodical uncoiling of the Federal army from around the Union capital city continued. The IX Corps marched to Ridgeville southwest of Frederick and halted just beyond on the road to New Market; the I Corps completed its march to Poplar Springs, and the II Corps stood its ground at Clarksburg. The XII Corps did not move, but Gen. Sumner ordered it to "select the strongest position in the vicinity" of Damascus. The left wing waited until Col. John F. Farnsworth's cavalry brigade, supported by Brig Gen. Winfield Hancock's brigade of infantry, advanced and drove Munford's small Confederate cavalry brigade from the base of Sugar Loaf Mountain that afternoon. The slow but steady advance of corps-sized pieces of the Federal army forced Stuart's other brigades to also fall back. Fitz Lee's brigade left New Market and headed for Liberty and the Monocacy River, while Wade Hampton rode his men to Frederick.[37]

Realizing that Jackson was making an encircling movement, Brig. Gen. Julius White marched his 2,500 men out of Martinsburg to consolidate his command with that of Col. Dixon Miles at Harpers Ferry.[38]

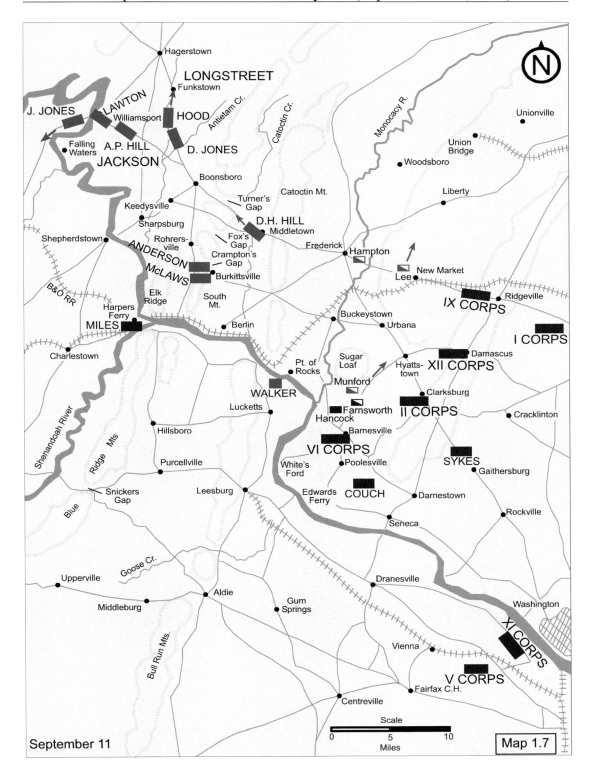

Hagerstown

LONGSTREET

Funkstown

J. JONES   LAWTON

Williamsport   HOOD

Falling   A.P. HILL   D. JONES
Waters   JACKSON

Antietam Cr.

Catoctin Cr.

Monocacy R.

Unionville

Union
Bridge

Woodsboro

Boonsboro

Catoctin Mt.

Liberty

Keedysville

Turner's
Gap

Sharpsburg

D.H. HILL

Shepherdstown   Rohrers-   Fox's   Middletown
ville   Gap

ANDERSON   Crampton's   Frederick   Hampton
McLAWS   Gap

Burkittsville   New Market

Elk   South   Lee
Ridge   Mt.

B&O RR   Harpers   Buckeystown   IX CORPS   Ridgeville
Ferry

MILES   Berlin   Urbana   I CORPS

Charlestown   Sugar   Damascus
Loaf   Hyatts-   XII CORPS

Pt. of   town
Rocks   Munford   Clarksburg

WALKER   II CORPS   Cracklinton

Lucketts   Farnsworth
Hancock   Barnesville

Shenandoah River   Hillsboro   VI CORPS   SYKES
Poolesville   Gaithersburg

Ridge Mts   Purcellville   White's
Ford   COUCH   Darnestown   Rockville

Snickers   Leesburg   Edwards   Seneca
Gap   Ferry

Blue   Goose Cr.

Upperville   Dranesville

Aldie   Washington

Middleburg   Gum
Springs

Bull Run Mts.   Vienna   XI CORPS

V CORPS

Fairfax C.H.

Centreville

Scale

September 11   0   5   10   Map 1.7
Miles

Map 1.8: September 12, 1862

Rain that began the previous day and stopped during the night reduced the dust and the temperature settled in the seventies. Lee believed the enemy would vacate Harpers Ferry and there would be no siege. Col. Miles and his garrison, however, held fast. Lee's columns were not yet in position to reduce Harpers Ferry. McClellan wanted Miles to pull out and join his army, but Maj. Gen. Henry Halleck, the Union General-in-Chief, rebuffed him because that would expose the garrison to attack and possible destruction or capture.[39]

Two-thirds of Lee's army was now approaching Harpers Ferry. To the east, Gen. McLaws threw his brigades out as a net to prevent an escape and deploy his guns on Maryland Heights, the southernmost extension of Elk Ridge, to rain iron into Harpers Ferry. McLaws had his and Anderson's men in motion at 6:00 a.m. His two most reliable brigades under Joseph Kershaw and William Barksdale moved across Pleasant Valley to Elk Ridge while Howell Cobb's brigade marched along the base of the ridge. Ambrose Wright's brigade scaled South Mountain to the east and marched south toward Weverton Cliffs on the Potomac River while Roger Pryor moved his regiments south along the base of the mountain toward Weverton armed with orders to capture it. McLaws sent Lewis Armistead's, Cadmus Wilcox's, and Winfield Featherston's brigades south in Pleasant Valley to connect with Cobb's men on one side and Pryor's men on the other. McLaws ordered his remaining brigades under Paul Semmes and William Mahone to guard Crampton's Gap and Brownsville Gap on South Mountain. When Kershaw's infantry met resistance from Federal skirmishers while scaling Elk Ridge, Kershaw pulled back and reformed his regiments for another effort the next morning. (A more detailed account of these actions is found in Map Sets 8.3 and 8.4.)[40]

Stonewall Jackson and his three divisions marched into a deserted Martinsburg, which Gen. White had vacated the day before. Mobs of citizens cheered the new arrivals, who set about finding supplies left behind by the departing enemy. While Jones' division remained on the outskirts of Martinsburg, Lawton's and A. P.

Hill's men marched three miles east to camp on the banks of the Opequon River. To the south, Walker's division, refreshed from a day off from marching, moved toward its assigned position on Loudoun Heights south of the Shenandoah River. Leaving his camping area just across the river from Point of Rocks, Walker moved north to Lovettsville, where he turned left (south) on the Berlin Turnpike to swing in a loop toward Loudoun Heights. His men were eight miles from the heights when they bivouacked for the night.[41]

Farther north, Longstreet had his pair of divisions on the road by 7:00 a.m. and quickly covered the easy five miles to Hagerstown. Three brigades in D. R. Jones' division marched through town to guard the road to Chambersburg, Pennsylvania, while the other two marched west to Williamsport. An independent brigade under Brig. Gen. Nathan Evans moved to the right to cover the sector east of Hagerstown while Robert Toombs' brigade marched into the town. John Hood's division remained just to the south.[42]

D. H. Hill had his men on the road early and climbed South Mountain at Turner's Gap with orders to guard the trains near Boonsboro and capture Federals fleeing from Harpers Ferry. His position is not known with certainty, but it appears Hill deployed south and west of Boonsboro.[43]

McClellan continued his attempts to piece together the disparate and often contradictory information on the Lee's movements. By the end of the day, Reno's IX Corps was closest to the enemy, camped in and near Frederick. John Reynolds' division of the I Corps marched from Poplar Springs to Monocacy Bridge while King's division reached New Market, and Ricketts' arrived in Ridgeville. The II Corps marched seven miles from Clarksburg to Urbana. The XII Corps marched six miles from Damascus to Ijamsville Crossroads. On the left, Farnsworth's cavalry pushed north through Urbana to Frederick. Far behind was the VI Corps, which moved a mere five miles from Barnesville to Licksville Crossroads. Couch's division (IV Corps) marched from Poolesville to Barnesville. McClellan was finally able to completely extract the V Corps from the Washington defenses and Sykes' division of Regulars marched eleven miles from Middlebrook to Urbana; Morell's division crossed the Potomac River at Arlington and made a strong twenty-mile march to Brookeville.[44]

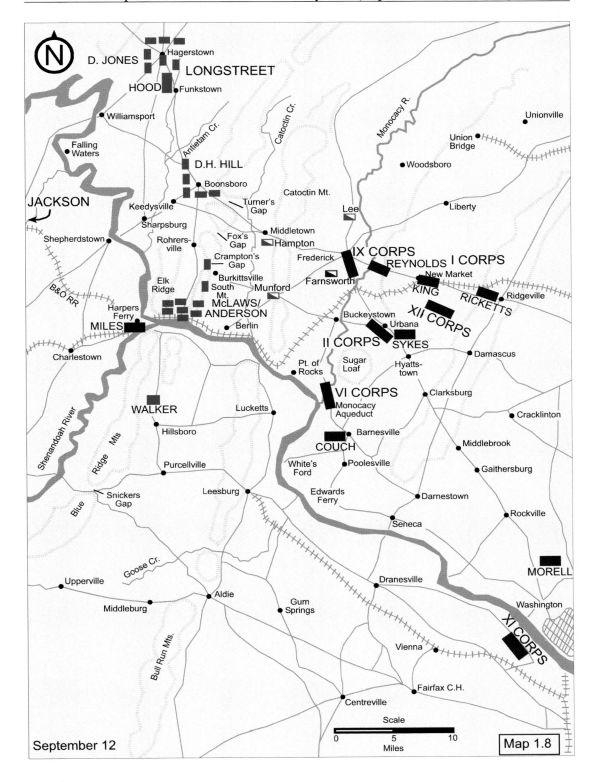

September 12

Map 1.8

Map 1.9: September 13, 1862

The Army of the Potomac was on the move as the sun's morning rays broke through the dark sky. The IX Corps marched through Frederick to the mass hysteria of its residents. McClellan also pushed out his cavalry, supported by a detachment from Rodman's division of the IX Corps, toward Middletown to scout the enemy's movements. The remainder of the IX Corps followed, camping for the night within two miles of Middletown. Most of the rest of the army was closing in on Frederick. The II Corps, which started the day at Urbana, finished it on the outskirts of Frederick. The XII Corps could see its steeples at the end of its march from its bivouac point south of town. The I Corps had an easier time of it, reconsolidating at the Monocacy River about two miles from Frederick. Sykes' division of the V Corps also made its way to Frederick, while Morell's division halted at Licksville. To the south, the VI Corps advanced to Buckeystown, its former position being taken by Couch's division.[45]

Lee began his day determined to minimize the growing threat to his exposed army. Precise information as to McClellan's movements and reasonable projections as to his intentions should have been available to Lee, but Jeb Stuart and his cavalry commanders were not providing it. Reports were filtering in that suggested the entire Yankee army was on the move, and that some units had thrust as far as Frederick—just a short march away from the South Mountain gaps. The news surprised and frustrated Lee, who now realized the peril facing his widely scattered army. Stuart believed McClellan would march south from Frederick to relieve the Harpers Ferry garrison and not to and through the northern gaps (Fox's and Turner's) slicing across South Mountain. What Lee did not know is that Alfred Pleasonton's Union cavalry division, followed by Reno's IX Corps, was already approaching these vulnerable passes and by mid-afternoon had chased Stuart's cavalry screen away. Lee would later write Jefferson Davis that the enemy on September 13 was advancing "more rapidly than convenient."[46]

Jeb Stuart served as Lee's eyes and ears, but on the day before the critical battle for South Mountain the army commander was operating almost blind and deaf. Stuart had dispatched one of his three brigades under Fitzhugh Lee on what some considered to be a senseless mission to Westminster, leaving Stuart with only Hampton's and Munford's brigades. Although he knew from prisoners that the Federal IX Corps was heading toward Middletown, Stuart downplayed the potential threat. The two Confederate cavalry brigades held several positions on and around Catoctin Mountain and skirmished fitfully with the probing enemy. One of Stuart's important tasks was to defend the South Mountain gaps. When he realized it was all but impossible for him to do so with his small force, Stuart requested infantry support from D. H. Hill at Boonsboro. Hill complied by sending Alfred Colquitt's brigade to man Turner's Gap, and later Samuel Garland's brigade and four batteries of Cutts' battalion (Lane's, Patterson's, Ross', and Bondurant's) as well.[47]

It was on this 13th day of September that one of the most fascinating events of the entire campaign transpired. While resting in a meadow a short distance from Frederick, several men of the 27th Indiana (XII Corps) spied a bulky envelope lying on the grass. Inside were several cigars and what looked to be a message from the Confederate army commander to D. H. Hill. They forwarded the envelope, minus at least one cigar, up through the chain of command. A copy of Special Orders No. 191 was now in Union hands.[48]

With Lee's master plans in his possession, McClellan knew the Army of Northern Virginia was divided and vulnerable to defeat in detail. He also realized that the demise of the Harpers Ferry garrison grew more likely with every passing hour. McClellan fired off a message at 6:20 p.m. to VI Corps commander Gen. Franklin to have his command on the road by daybreak the next day; his destination was Rohrersville and his objective was the destruction of McLaws' command. Once this was accomplished, Franklin was to march along the road to Sharpsburg to cut off Jackson's command and keep him from re-crossing the Potomac back into Maryland. Couch's division would march to link up with Franklin. "My general idea is to cut the enemy in two and beat him in detail," explained McClellan.[49]

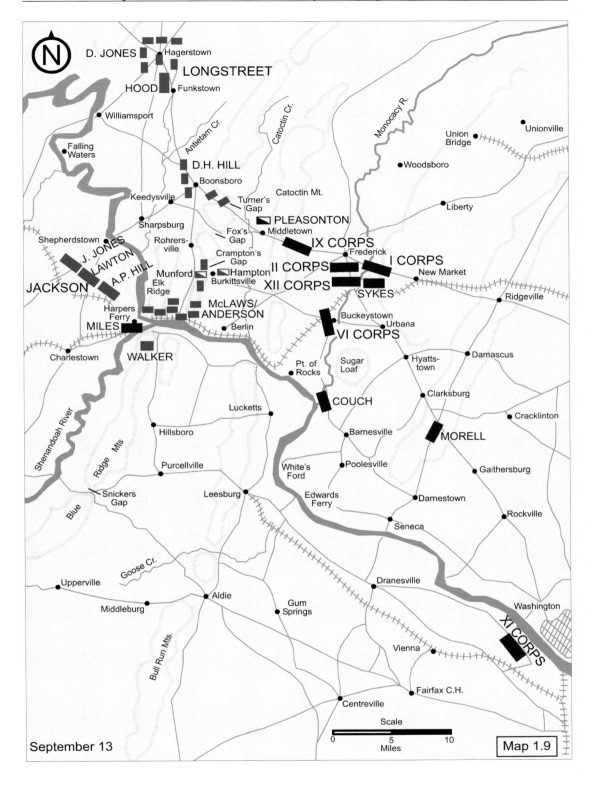

September 13

Map 1.9

Map Set 2. Preparing for Battle: The South Mountain Gaps
(September 13 - 14, 1862)
Map 2.1: September 13

Some historians have characterized Gen. McClellan's movements up to September 13 as slow and overly cautious, but many factors dictated the pace and scope of his actions. Maj. Gen. Henry Halleck believed that Gen. Lee was marching toward Pennsylvania to draw the Union army away from Washington and strike it in the open. The farther McClellan's columns moved, the more concerned Halleck became. The discovery of Lee's Special Orders 191 changed this. Now, the Union high command knew the general location of the various columns of the Army of Northern Virginia, though not their strength. Whether Lee ever learned during the campaign that a copy of his orders had fallen into McClellan's hands is unclear.[1]

Because Dixon Miles was still holding Harpers Ferry, Lee was confident McClellan would move to save the Federal garrison, which would in turn put Maj. Gen. Lafayette McLaws' command in Pleasant Valley in extreme danger. Only Maj. Gen. Jeb Stuart's small cavalry force stood between McLaws' two infantry divisions and the enemy. Lee was dealt another blow when he read Maj. Gen. D. H. Hill's dispatch indicating that a large Federal infantry force (McClellan's right wing) was moving toward Turner's Gap. Lee's options were limited. When he learned that Maj. Gen. Thomas "Stonewall" Jackson's divisions were closing in on Harpers Ferry and that its garrison could surrender as early as September 14, Lee decided to maintain his current course. Holding the South Mountain gaps loomed large in that equation. D. H. Hill's division and a couple of brigades from McLaws' command would move into position to hold the passes throughout the day. Lee was gambling McClellan would not aggressively force the South Mountain range before the fall of Harpers Ferry. He discussed the matter with Maj. Gen. James Longstreet and ordered him to move his command along Beaver Creek, about three miles northwest of Boonsboro and five miles beyond Turner's Gap. Longstreet argued that the gamble put the army at dire risk. A better strategy, he insisted, would be to withdraw and await the enemy in a strong defensive position. Lee disagreed and issued a stream of dispatches to his generals. Jackson and McLaws were reminded about the importance of reducing Harpers Ferry as soon as possible, and Hill was ordered to Turner's Gap to supervise its defense. Hill put Brig. Gen. Roswell Ripley's brigade on the road to the gap.[2]

Lee may have been less anxious had he realized McClellan would not immediately exploit the good fortune of S. O. 191. There was still about seven hours of daylight left and his troops had marched but little that day when McClellan received the orders. Even after S. O. 191 was verified he hesitated. His reasons are understandable. First, the orders were drafted four days earlier on September 9. Had they been cancelled or modified? Where were the columns now? (Longstreet, for example, was at Hagerstown and not Boonsboro.) Second, the orders did not include the strength of each column. Whether justified or not, it would be a full eighteen hours after receiving the orders before Federal soldiers began moving in earnest to take advantage of the intelligence. As a result, no Federal troops were on the road on September 13.[3]

McClellan assigned two wings of his army with the task of pushing through South Mountain and into Pleasant Valley to relieve Harpers Ferry. Maj. Gen. William Franklin's left wing would force its way through the southernmost pass at Crampton's Gap. McClellan thought that Franklin exhibited "little energy," and his "efficiency is very little," so he crafted and sent precise orders to Franklin prior to 6:30 p.m. on the 13th. A more forceful commander might have put his men on the road for the short twelve-mile march to Crampton's Gap, but Franklin waited until the next morning. His men moved out about 6:00 a.m. on the 14th.

Farther north, Maj. Gen. Ambrose Burnside's right wing was ordered to march against Turner's Gap. Burnside placed Maj. Gen. Jesse Reno's IX Corps in the lead. Because part of his IX Corps had reached Middletown on September 13, it was considerably closer to its destination than Franklin's left wing. At that time, Turner's Gap and Fox's Gap (one mile south) were only lightly defended, with Col. Alfred Colquitt's and Brig. Gen. Samuel Garland's brigades holding the former, and the 5th Virginia Cavalry and two guns under Capt. John Pelham defending the latter.[4]

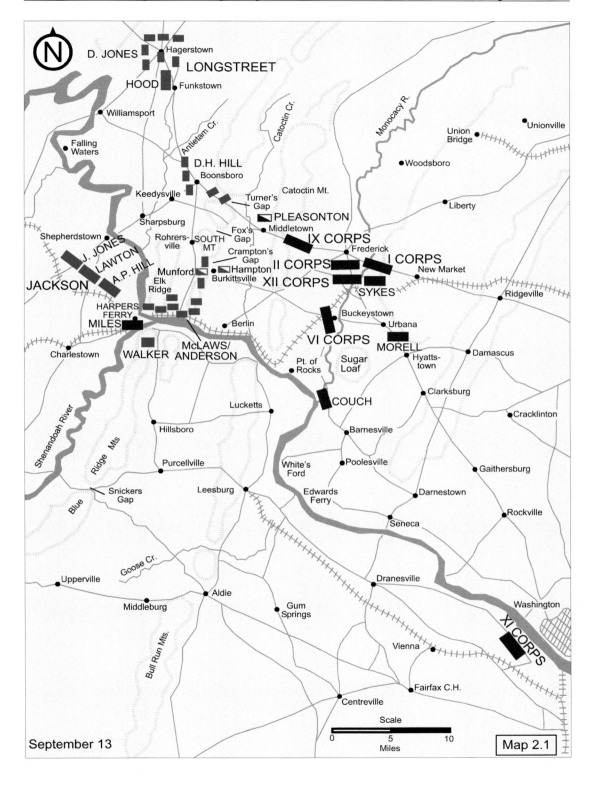

September 13

Map 2.1

Map 2.2: September 14

The chilly night of September 13 gave way to a bright and hot September 14. Intense heat and dusty roads plagued the marching Federal troops. At 6:00 a.m., Brig. Gen. Jacob Cox sent Col. Eliakim Scammon's brigade of his Kanawha Division west toward Turner's Gap from the division's bivouac area west of Middletown. Scammon's Ohioans would support Brig. Gen. Alfred Pleasonton's cavalry division, which was tasked with clearing the gap. Pleasonton did not expect much of a fight, but he wanted infantry with him just in case. When a chance meeting with a paroled Federal officer suggested the Rebels were waiting for them in greater force than anyone expected, Cox also ordered up Brig. Gen. George Crook's brigade and sent word to Reno that the mountain might be heavily defended. Maj. Gen. Joseph Hooker's I Corps, part of Burnside's right wing, marched behind the IX Corps, tramping across the Middleton Valley between Catoctin Mountain and South Mountain.[5]

Farther south near Buckeystown, Franklin's VI Corps tramped for Crampton's Gap. Like Cox's men, they were on the road about 6:00 a.m. for the twelve-mile march to the pass. The pace was slow. The men climbed Catoctin via the Mountville Pass and marched a short distance to Jefferson, which they reached between 10:00 a.m. and 11:00 a.m. Even though he was ordered not to do so, Franklin rested his men to await the arrival of Maj. Gen. Darius Couch's division. Couch's men were still miles behind him, so after waiting about an hour Franklin put his corps back on the road. It was about this time that Confederate scouts atop South Mountain caught sight of long lines of Federal infantry snaking in their direction.[6]

With the departure of Jeb Stuart's cavalry screen, the task of holding the northern gaps of South Mountain (Orr's, Frosttown, Fox's, and Turner's) fell solely to D. H. Hill and his 8,000-man division. Hill, who was on his horse riding south toward Turner's Gap by 5:30 a.m., knew he could not defend all four gaps, so he decided to concentrate on Turner's because it was traversed by the National Road and therefore the most likely Federal target. Colquitt's and Garland's infantry brigades were already there,

while the 4th Georgia from Ripley's brigade moved to man Orr's Gap. The rest of Ripley's brigade, along with Brig. Gen. Robert Rodes' brigade, remained near Boonsboro to watch the road from Harpers Ferry. Hill's last brigade under Brig. Gen. George B. Anderson was also summoned to the mountain.[7]

James Longstreet had his men ready to march from Hagerstown about 5:00 a.m. The march, however, did not begin for another three hours, and the rearguard under Brig. Gen. Nathan Evans did not leave town until 1:00 p.m. Ordnance trains and the army's reserve artillery followed Longstreet's column. The mountainous terrain, combined with the heat and dense clouds of dust, slowed the march to less than three miles an hour. Exhaustion and heat stroke knocked hundreds from the ranks. "We marched as hurriedly as we could over a hot and dusty road," Longstreet later explained. The vanguard of Brig. Gen. David R. Jones' division completed the ten-mile march to Boonsboro about noon.[8]

To the south, Brig. Gen. Paul Semmes' brigade of infantry guarded the Brownsville Pass and Crampton's Gap. Separated by one mile, Semmes did not know which pass the Federals would attempt to force. He suspected it would be the former, so that is where he kept most of his brigade. Col. William Parham, in command of Brig. Gen. William Mahone's small brigade, was sent hustling to Crampton's Gap just in case Semmes was wrong. Col. Thomas Munford's small cavalry brigade of about 275 men was also in the Crampton's Gap sector.[9]

The terrain on and around South Mountain did not make for easy marching or maneuvering for either side. The mountain towered about 1,300 feet above the valley, with its valuable gaps about 200-300 feet lower than its rounded peaks. The mountainside was deeply rutted by ravines and hollows, which laced the heavily wooded slopes clotted with thick mountain laurel. Farms dotted the mountainside on the occasional patches of flat ground nearer the crests, their fields usually lined by fences and low stone walls. All of these features, both manmade and natural, aided the defenders, but the road system aided flanking movements and thus forced the Confederate defenders to man a wide expanse of the hillside.[10]

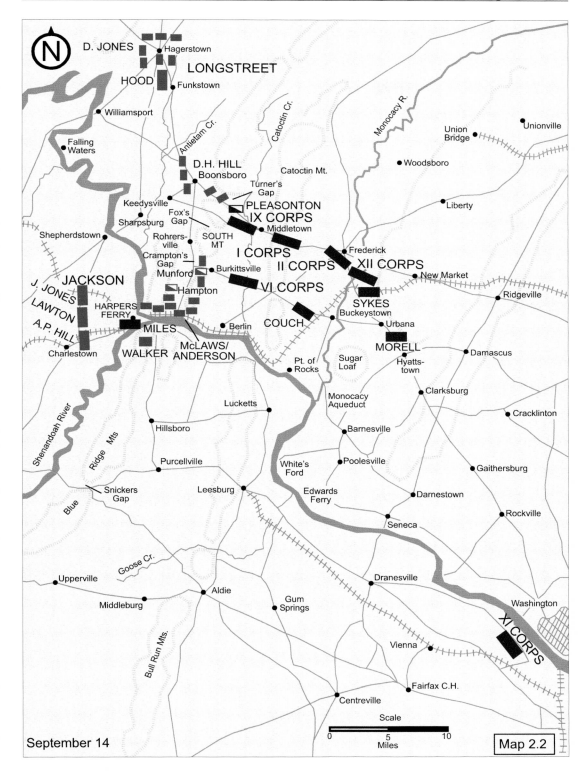

September 14

Scale

0   5   10
        Miles

Map 2.2

Map Set 3. South Mountain: Fox's Gap (Morning)

Map 3.1: Preliminary Movements (6:00 - 8:00 a.m.)

Col. Eliakim Scammon's nearly 1,500-man Federal brigade, composed of the 12th, 23rd, and 30th Ohio and a battery of six 10-pounder Parrotts, was marching at 6:00 a.m. toward Turner's Gap to support Maj. Gen. Alfred Pleasonton's cavalry. Brig. Gen. Jacob Cox, Scammon's division commander, accompanied the column. Cox was surprised to find brigade commander Col. Augustus Moor standing by the side of the road. Moor had been captured at Frederick and exchanged, and was now heading for the rear. All the paroled officer could tell Cox was "My God! Be Careful!" The warning convinced Cox to order up George Crook's brigade and direct each regimental commander to exercise caution.[1]

The engagement at Fox's Gap began when Capt. Horatio Gibson's and Lt. Samuel Benjamin's Federal batteries dropped trail on a hill just west of Bolivar and opened fire on the pass. The shelling drew an almost immediate response from Capt. John Lane's six-gun battery deployed on a hill just east of the gap. Overpowered by the dozen Federal pieces, Lane's dispersed guns were forced to change positions several times.[2] When Pleasonton told Cox that Confederates were holding Turner's Gap in strength, the division leader decided a more prudent approach would be to force Fox's Gap and take Turner's Gap from the flank and rear. Pleasonton's troopers would demonstrate before the latter gap to distract the enemy while Scammon's infantry marched to Fox's Gap along the Old Sharpsburg Road.[3]

As Scammon's men struggled up the side of the mountain, stopping often to rest and keep their ranks closed, Cox added two more batteries under Capt. Seth Simmonds and Capt. James McMullin to the hill near Bolivar, raising the number of guns there to twenty-two. Crook's brigade, meanwhile, made good time and arrived behind Scammon. The column left Bolivar and marched southwest on a small road, then turned right on the Old Sharpsburg Road to continue their ascent. It was about this time when the Buckeyes were hit by artillery fire, probably from a section of horse artillery under Capt. John Pelham deployed in support of Col. Thomas Rosser's 5th Virginia Cavalry. Scammon decided to flank the enemy and ordered the 23rd Ohio, under the command of future president Lt. Col. Rutherford Hayes, to march along the Loop Road.[4]

From a bird's-eye view, it appeared as though the Confederates did not stand a chance because only some 200 dismounted cavalrymen and a few artillery pieces were defending Fox's Gap. Help, however, was on the way. A messenger from Gen. Lee had ordered Maj. Gen. D. H. Hill at midnight to help defend the pass the next morning. Hill complied by moving from his camp west of Boonsboro about 4:00 a.m. to scout the gap for himself. He found Brig. Gen. Samuel Garland's regiments positioned at the top of the heights, and was told Alfred Colquitt's brigade was farther down the mountain. To Hill's surprise, when he rode down the slope he found Colquitt was "without vedettes and without information of the Federals, but believ[ed] they had retired." Hill was not so certain. He was also upset about a message he received from Jeb Stuart that he had shifted his screen of troopers south to watch Crampton's Gap. Hill, of course, was in desperate need of information that only Stuart's mounted men could provide.[5]

Once Colquitt's men were posted in a swale about one-half mile east of the Mountain House, Hill rode to the right to check on Fox's Gap. About three-quarters of a mile into his ride Hill heard the sounds of troops on the move. The enemy was approaching, and Fox's Gap was about to be attacked. Federal artillery commenced firing soon thereafter, sending Hill galloping back to Turner's Gap for reinforcements. What he did not yet know was that the 5th Virginia Cavalry and Pelham's horse artillery were holding the gap against Scammon's skirmishers.[6]

The 5th Virginia Cavalry played a key role that day by vigorously opposing Scammon, who decided to move west along the Loop Road rather than advancing directly on Old Sharpsburg Road. The result bought valuable time for Hill to rush reinforcements to the sector.[7]

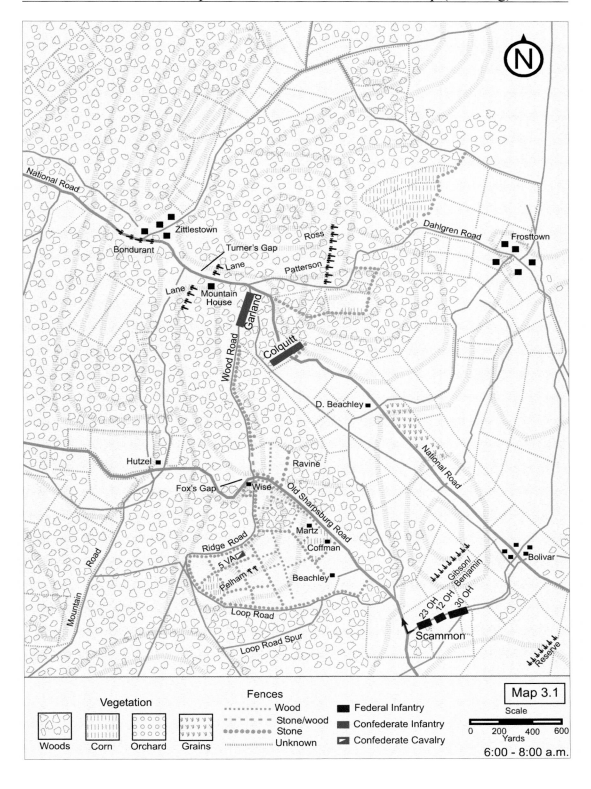

Map 3.2: Scammon and Garland Deploy (9:00 - 9:30 a.m.)

Before riding south toward Fox's Gap, D. H. Hill had ordered Brig. Gen. George B. Anderson's brigade to head to South Mountain from its camp west of Boonsboro. Hill was also worried about Orr's Pass about three miles north of Turner's Gap on the left of the Confederate line. He sent the 4th Georgia of Ripley's brigade to man the pass while the rest of the brigade remained behind to watch the approaches to Hagerstown. Brig. Gen. Robert Rodes' brigade remained with Ripley's main body.[8]

Returning to Turner's Gap after his ride to Fox's Gap, Hill found Samuel Garland's brigade under arms and ready to march. Hill explained the unfolding situation and the vulnerability of the army's wagon trains should the enemy punch through the pass. Once he was sure Garland understood the gravity of the situation, Hill ordered the brigadier to sweep through the woods and hold the road at all costs. "He went off in high spirits and I never saw him again," Hill recalled long after the battle.[9]

Fairly confident Colquitt could defend Turner's Gap, Hill set about aligning his regiments on either side of the National Road so they could pour a concentrated fire into any Federals attempting to force the gap via that route.[10]

By now it was almost 9:00 a.m. and Col. Scammon was deploying his Federals marching along the Loop Road Spur. Lt. Col. Hayes' 23rd Ohio was first in line, with the 12th Ohio behind it. The next regiment in line, the 30th Ohio, turned right from the Loop Road and headed toward the Confederate left. Its goal was to push the flank back into Fox's Gap and then hold the gap until reinforced. The 23rd and 12th Ohio regiments, meanwhile, aimed for the Confederate right flank and center from the Loop Road Spur. Scammon hoped these thrusts would force the enemy (whose strength was not known) from the sector. Cox received a message from Maj. Gen. Jesse Reno, commanding the IX Corps, with reassurances that his actions were approved and that the rest of the powerful corps was on its way. As Scammon deployed his men, he could see the van of George Crook's brigade swing into view behind him.[11]

Most of Cox's men were probably unaware that Garland's Confederates had arrived to reinforce Rosser's Virginia cavalrymen. Garland only had about 1,100 trigger-pullers—far too few for the important task assigned to them. The small command had sustained heavy losses during the Peninsula Campaign earlier that year and the addition of conscripts had not fleshed out the brigade to its prior strength. These new troops were poorly trained and some did not even know how to properly load and fire a rifled musket. Garland's first regiment in the column, the 400-man 5th North Carolina, deployed behind a stone wall. Two more regiments, the company-sized 12th North Carolina and the 23rd North Carolina, followed close behind. Garland's final two regiments, the 20th and 13th North Carolina, were farther up the road and would not arrive for some time. Capt. James Bondurant's Alabama battery galloped down Ridge Road and deployed in an exposed position at the top of the heights left of the 5th North Carolina. Apparently, none of Garland's regimental commanders knew that the 5th Virginia Cavalry and Pelham's section of guns were manning the far right. Garland had moved them to this position to guard his exposed flank.[12]

The infantry fight for Fox's Gap got underway when a company of Lt. Col. Hayes' 23rd Ohio moved onto the skirmish line and collided with skirmishers from the 5th North Carolina. Hayes upped the ante by throwing in two more companies. The strong Federal skirmish line did not expect what happened next when Col. Duncan McRae launched his entire 5th North Carolina down the slope, into a cornfield, and toward the Loop Road. Although these Tar Heels were new to the army and had learned their craft during the march into Maryland, they somehow managed to fire effective volleys into Hayes' surprised Buckeyes.[13]

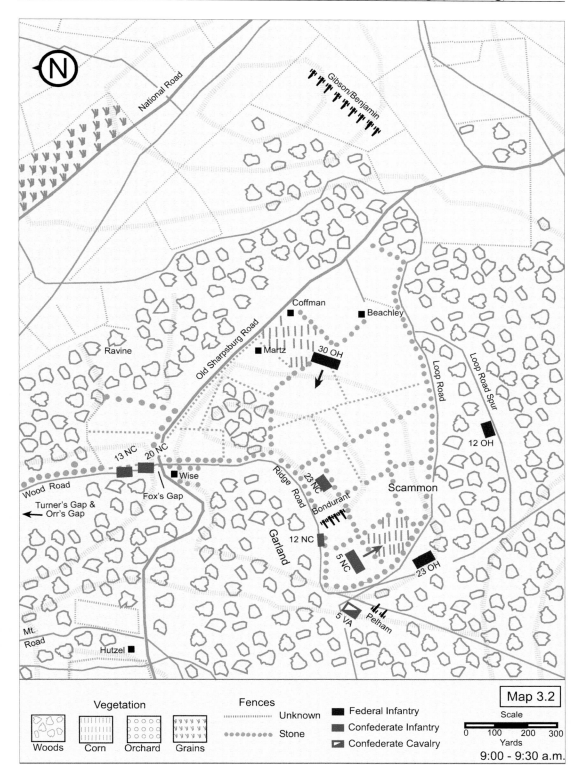

National Road

Gibson/Benjamin

N

Coffman

Beachley

Old Sharpsburg Road

Ravine

Martz

30 OH

Loop Road

Loop Road Spur

12 OH

13 NC   20 NC

Wise

Ridge Road

23 NC

Scammon

Wood Road

Fox's Gap

Bondurant

Turner's Gap &
Orr's Gap

12 NC

Garland

5 NC

23 OH

Mt.
Road

Hutzel

5 VA   Pelham

Vegetation

Woods   Corn   Orchard   Grains

Fences

··········· Unknown

●●●●●●●● Stone

■ Federal Infantry

■ Confederate Infantry

◥ Confederate Cavalry

Map 3.2

Scale

0   100   200   300
Yards

9:00 - 9:30 a.m.

Map 3.3: The Buckeyes Attack
(9:30 - 10:00 a.m.)

The 23rd Ohio and 5th North Carolina stood firm and poured volleys into one another with neither side willing to retreat. Lt. Col. Hayes decided that a counterattack was his best course of action, so he worked to realign those of his men still facing in the wrong direction because of the route of their approach. The mountain laurel and topography weighed heavily against his success, but the stubborn Hayes persisted. "[B]ullets pattered around us like raindrops on the leaves," recalled one Buckeye. "Then we heard the voice of Colonel Hayes saying, 'Men of the Twenty-third, when I tell you to charge, you must charge." When Hayes yelled "Charge bayonets!", the men of the 23rd Ohio dashed in the direction of the North Carolinians. The Tar Heels managed a destructive volley that killed and wounded many Ohioans, but the Buckeyes were not to be denied. As they drew closer, some of Col. McRae's new recruits drifted to the rear, others soon followed, and before long the entire regiment was in retreat. When Hayes stopped his advance to reform his regiment, McRae got his regiment under control and opened fire once again. Worried whether his men could take the renewed punishment, Hayes nonetheless ordered another advance that once again pushed the enemy into retreat, this time back across the cornfield toward Ridge Road and the rest of Garland's brigade.[14]

Hayes' men dashed after the North Carolinians. After they were hit by small arms fire from ahead and to their right from the 12th and 23rd North Carolina, he ordered his men to take cover behind a stone wall bounding the cornfield. "Most of our losses occurred at this point," recalled a Federal officer. The aggressive Hayes decided on yet a third attack, this one uphill, but a bullet shattered his left arm and forced him to the ground behind his men. The wounded regimental commander could clearly hear the sounds of battle echoing all around him and knew his men were in a difficult spot. Garland's Confederates had been pouring in fire from the front and right, and now from the left, probably from dismounted troopers from the 5th Virginia Cavalry. In an effort to defend against this latter fire, Hayes refused his left company, bending his line at an angle to avoid the fire and minimize the chance of being flanked. The order was misunderstood in the confusion of battle and the entire regiment began to follow suit until Hayes stopped it. The regimental shift, however, left the prostrate Hayes exposed in no-man's-land. The firing continued for perhaps another quarter-hour before falling off. The lull ended when some of Hayes' men ventured forward to attempt to carry their commander to safety. After several attempts and flare-ups, the Ohioans finally pulled the future president to safety.[15]

Although the 5th and 23rd North Carolina regiments were holding their own on the firing line, the small 70-man 12th North Carolina originally stationed between them was gone. When the 23rd Ohio launched its attack, Capt. Shugan Snow, the 12th's young and inexperienced commander, ordered his men to "Fire and fall back." About half of them joined the ranks of the 13th North Carolina, but the rest retreated out of the fight. With his left flank exposed, Col. McRae pulled the 5th North Carolina back toward Ridge Road. The withdrawal exposed Bondurant's gunners to the Ohioans, whose fire forced the Southern battery to redeploy farther north.[16]

When McRae told Garland that the enemy could turn his right flank, the brigade leader rode left up Ridge Road to bring down his remaining two regiments (the 20th and 13th North Carolina) to reinforce his endangered right flank. Neither regiment made it beyond the 23rd North Carolina because during their approach march the 30th Ohio's skirmish line appeared without warning. The most immediate threat was now against Garland's left flank. The brigadier ordered the 20th to slide into position left of the 23rd North Carolina, but a lack of cover forced its commander, Col. Alfred Iverson, to order his men to remain on the Ridge Road. The 13th North Carolina deployed near Bondurant's guns.

A skilled tactician, Garland was doing the best he could under a difficult situation, but his front was about 1,300 yards long with large gaps between the regiments. Under ideal circumstances, it should have been no more than 350 yards long and tightly aligned.[17]

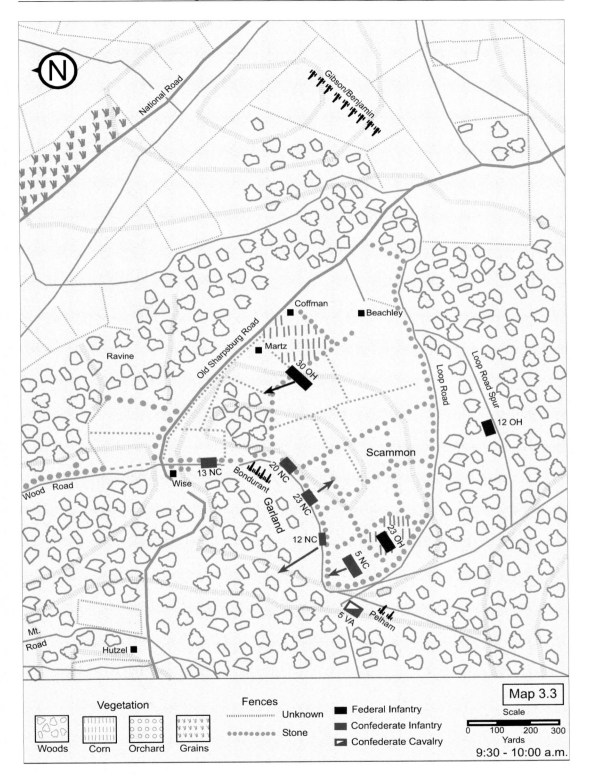

Map 3.3

9:30 - 10:00 a.m.

Map 3.4: The Death of Samuel Garland (10:00 - 10:15 a.m.)

During the march behind the 30th Ohio along the Loop Road Spur, the 12th Ohio spied the 23rd North Carolina deployed to the right in line of battle on the top of the plateau. While the 23rd Ohio moved against Garland's right and the 30th Ohio advanced against his left, the Buckeyes of the 12th descended toward the Loop Road and into the open fields beyond. Even from 400 yards away the North Carolinians' fire was heavy, and the Buckeyes moved forward through it as quickly as possible until they reached the edge of a bluff that provided a measure of protection from the hail of enemy bullets. The 12th Ohio was in a difficult position and vulnerable to a counterattack. (The small 12th North Carolina that had been in line between the 23rd North Carolina and the 5th North Carolina had fallen back.)[18]

Meanwhile, Col. Hugh Ewing's 30th Ohio continued advancing up the hill on the far right of Col. Scammon's brigade line. Artillery fire from both Lane's battery to the north and other guns halted the advance on the side of the hill. "The storm of iron hail that went whizzing and shrieking through the air over our heads was terrific," was how one Union private recalled it. "Sometimes a shell would come tearing through the woods and explode near us with a terrible clash." Unable to keep his men where they were, Col. Ewing pushed them to the top of the hill. The first thing Ewing saw when he reached the summit was Bondurant's Southern battery to his left. His men opened fire on the cannoneers, but the Alabamians continued firing canister into Ewing's ranks. Small arms fire from the left of the 20th North Carolina and the newly arrived 13th North Carolina killed and wounded more of Ewing's exposed men.

The 13th North Carolina's commander, Lt. Col. Thomas Ruffin Jr., could see a Federal skirmish line posted behind a fence to his left front, but he could not see the enemy infantrymen who were firing from the woods behind the line because the ground dropped off in that direction. Ruffin directed his men to concentrate their fire against the troops behind the fence. "Our men were cool and fired with

precision and effect," Ruffin noted in his report.[19]

Sam Garland, meanwhile, remained behind the left side of his line urging his men to continue their deadly work. The native of Lynchburg, Virginia, and graduate of the Virginia Military Institute was worried about his exposed and unanchored left flank. His command style was simple: lead from the most vulnerable points of his line. That habit had earned Garland a bullet in the elbow at Williamsburg on May 5, 1862, and on this day his desire to command from the front would kill him.

When he spotted the exposed Garland near the front, Lt. Col. Ruffin yelled, "General, why do you stay here? You are in great danger!"

Garland calmly relied, "I may as well be here as yourself."

This reply didn't sway Ruffin, who told the brigadier that it was the role of the regimental commander to remain with his men and for the brigade commander to command his regiments from a safe distance behind the line. Just then, a bullet struck Ruffin in the hip and spun him around. Almost immediately thereafter another round struck Garland. Several soldiers placed the brigade leader in a blanket and ran north along Ridge Road seeking medical assistance. It was already too late to save the mortally wounded Garland; he expired on the field. The 5th North Carolina's Col. Duncan McRae assumed command of the brigade.[20]

The wounded Ruffin remained with his men and pulled them back about fifty yards to the safety of Ridge Road, where his right flank connected with the 20th North Carolina. Col. Ewing, meanwhile, moved his Federals left to take on Bondurant guns, but the gunners withdrew and the Buckeyes stopped their advance.[21]

With pressure mounting all along the brigade line, Col. McRae felt overwhelmed by the responsibility now resting on his shoulders. "I felt all of the embarrassment the situation was calculated to inspire," was how he explained it in his after-action report. Realizing he needed help and needed it quickly, McRae dispatched an aide to find D. H. Hill with a plea for reinforcements.[22]

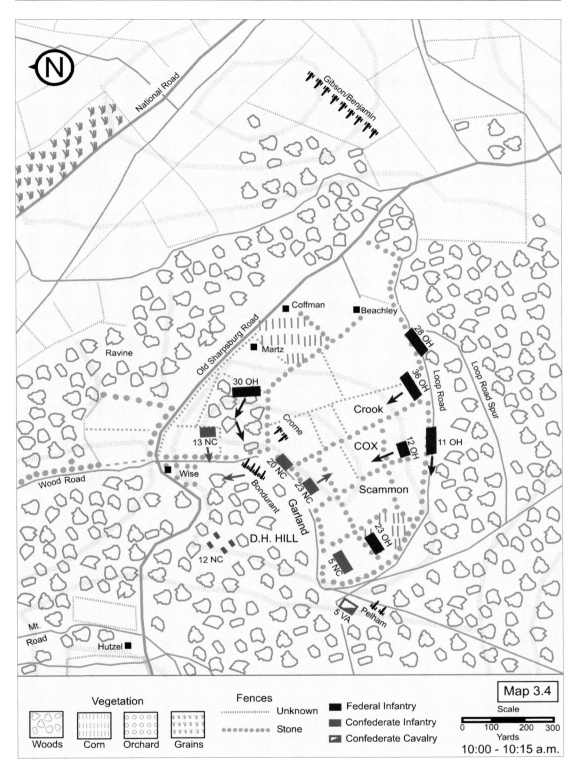

Map 3.4

Scale

0   100   200   300
Yards

10:00 - 10:15 a.m.

Vegetation

Woods   Corn   Orchard   Grains

Fences

Unknown

Stone

Federal Infantry

Confederate Infantry

Confederate Cavalry

Map 3.5: Confederate Reinforcements Arrive (10:15 - 11:00 a.m.)

Division leader Jacob Cox was frustrated. Despite his numerical advantage, his men had thus far been unable to push the Tar Heels from their defensive positions near Ridge Road. Cox decided to call up artillery to blast the Rebels from their hiding places. When orders to move up filtered down to Capt. James McMullin, the artillerist was unsure whether there was a suitable place to unlimber his guns. According to an eyewitness, McMullin "at first demurred, complaining that Old Granny (as Scammon was called) did not know what he was about." Reassurances that the 12th Ohio would protect his pieces finally convinced McMullin to comply, and he dispatched a section of guns under Lt. George Crome.

Pulling and pushing the guns up the side of the mountain was tough work, but with help from the members of the 12th Ohio, the gunners succeeded in deploying the two 10-pounder Parrotts in an open field. The artillerists dropped double charges of canister down the tubes and opened fire. With the line of the 20th North Carolina deployed behind a stout stone wall a mere forty yards away, however, the gunners stood no chance at all. The men stood by their pieces and fell one by one until Lt. Crome ran forward to serve one of the guns. When he dropped with a mortal wound, the guns fell silent after having fired some four rounds. The bloody event was still fresh in the mind of a veteran four decades later when he recalled, "[I]t was a tragic scene that I shall never forget." The remaining gunners abandoned the pair of cannon, but the Confederates were unable to capture them because of the heavy small arms fire from Federal troops in that sector.[23]

The guns were moving up the mountain when Cox ordered the 23rd Ohio on the left of the line to move by the right flank and link up with the 12th Ohio on its right. The Buckeyes stopped so close to the Confederate line that they could hear enemy officers shouting orders. Concerned about his left flank, and with Gen. Crook's brigade now up, Cox shifted the 11th Ohio to the left of the 23rd Ohio to protect his flank from the 5th Virginia Cavalry. When they spotted this move, the 5th and 23rd North

Carolina regiments opened a deadly flank fire against 11th Ohio. The 23rd North Carolina had been coaxed back into the open field in front of the cornfield prior to the 11th Ohio's sudden appearance. Next in was the 800-man 36th Ohio, sent by Cox to fill the gap between the 12th and 30th Ohio. Another large regiment, the 28th Ohio, remained on the opposite side of the Loop Road Spur to support the right side of Cox's line. Both sides were inserting troops into the spreading fight in a piecemeal fashion, but the Northern advantage in numbers was beginning to tell. Cox's pair of brigades numbered some 3,500. Standing against them was only Garland's brigade (now under McRae), which numbered less than one-third that number. Even worse for the defenders, many Federal regiments had worked their way very close to the Confederate line. A determined attack from that position could overwhelm the thin rank of the defenders along Ridge Road. Finally, it was only 11:30 a.m. Many long hours of daylight remained for the Federals to finish the job.[24]

Help, however, was on the way for Garland's beleaguered brigade. When news reached him about a looming disaster, D. H. Hill dispatched the 2nd and 4th North Carolina regiments from G. B. Anderson's brigade under the command of Col. Charles Tew. The reinforcements streamed up the side of the mountain on Wood Road at the double-quick. The Tar Heels passed a steady stream of wounded including Garland, whose body was being carried to the rear. Tew rode ahead to report his arrival to McRae, who was happy for the reinforcements and because Tew outranked him. McRae offered Tew command, but the colonel declined, asking instead where to position his two regiments. McRae directed the arrivals to his left flank next to Lt. Col. Ruffin's 13th North Carolina.[25]

While Tew was marching to reinforce McRae, the 11th Ohio was advancing along the Loop Road. Heavy fire from the dismounted 5th Virginia Cavalry troopers in its front and left flank, and the 5th North Carolina on its right, tore through the ranks of the Buckeyes. Col. Tom Rosser had skillfully dispersed his cavalrymen to give the illusion of larger numbers, while John Pelham's two guns fired canister into the approaching Ohio infantry. The commander of the 11th Ohio ordered most of his regiment to slide to the right in an effort to avoid this fire.[26]

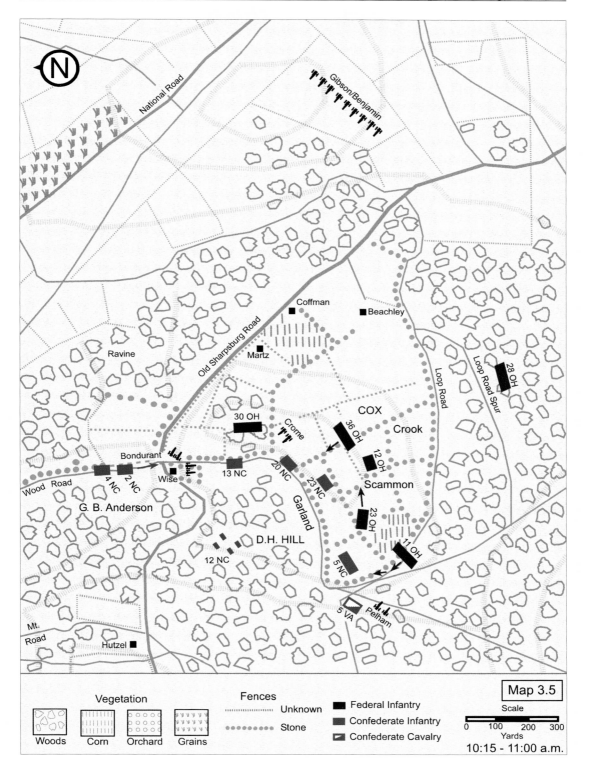

National Road

Gibson/Benjamin

Coffman

Beachley

Loop Road Spur

28 OH

Ravine

Old Sharpsburg Road

Martz

Loop Road

COX

30 OH

Crome

36 OH

Crook

Bondurant

Wood Road

4 NC

2 NC

Wise

13 NC

20 NC

23 NC

12 OH

Scammon

23 OH

11 OH

G. B. Anderson

D.H. HILL

12 NC

5 NC

Mt.
Road

Hutzel

5 VA

Pelham

Map 3.5

Scale

Vegetation

Fences

Unknown

Woods   Corn   Orchard   Grains

Stone

Federal Infantry

Confederate Infantry

Confederate Cavalry

0   100   200   300
Yards

10:15 - 11:00 a.m.

Map 3.6: Most of Garland's Brigade is Defeated (11:00 - 11:30 a.m.)

Sliding into position on the left of Lt. Col. Ruffin's 13th North Carolina, Col. Tew ordered the 2nd and 4th North Carolina to open fire on the 30th Ohio skirmish line a mere 100 yards distant. Worried about the large open area on his left, Tew sent a message to Gen. G. B. Anderson requesting reinforcements. Tew interpreted Anderson's odd response—"flank to the left"—as an order to shift his two regiments in that direction, which would break their link with the 13th North Carolina on their right. A baffled Tew shared Anderson's communication with McRae, who sent an aide galloping north to find D. H. Hill and explain the situation to him. Because he was confident additional reinforcements would soon arrive, McRae ordered Ruffin to move his 13th North Carolina to the left to reconnect with Tew, which in turn left a gaping 200- to 300-yard hole in the line (No. 1). McRae decided to fill this new gap with the 5th North Carolina on the right side of his line. It was a bold and dangerous gamble because the withdrawal of the 5th North Carolina would leave the right flank vulnerable to an attack by the 11th and/or 23rd Ohio. When he rushed to the right of his line and realized the 5th North Carolina was too advanced to be pulled back and shifted elsewhere, McRae left the regiment in place and hoped Hill was sending enough reinforcements to close the gap before the Federals learned of its existence.[27]

The Garland-McRae line had managed to hold all morning against overwhelming odds, but it was just a matter of time before Scammon's and Crook's 3,500 men overwhelmed the outnumbered North Carolinians aligned on or near Ridge Road. The 11th Ohio blazed away at the 5th North Carolina (No. 2) while the Buckeyes of the 23rd Ohio eased their way forward to the crest of the plateau. When they heard an officer scream "Up and at them!" (No. 3), they moved aggressively ahead and closed the distance to the 23rd North Carolina. Seeing their comrades rushing forward, the men of the 12th Ohio—who had also been fighting their way toward the Southern line—jumped to their feet only to be ordered to lie back down. Many of those slow to respond were knocked off their feet by a volley from the 23rd North Carolina. Unwilling to be denied, the Buckeyes jumped to their feet a second time and stormed the Tar Heel position, screaming at the top of their lungs as they advanced. The 30th and 36th Ohio on the right joined the attack.[28]

The North Carolinians opened a blistering fire from their advanced position behind a stone wall in a gallant effort to hold the line. The long line of Buckeyes lapped around both flanks, however, and before the Tar Heels knew it the Ohioans were among them with fixed bayonets. Col. Daniel Christie realized the game was up and ordered his 23rd regiment to the rear to avoid its all but certain destruction. Frustrated by their lack of progress and heavy losses that morning, the Ohioans were not inclined to show mercy. Bayonets and clubbed muskets were used on many of the North Carolinians who remained in position. Some Tar Heels were run down and bayoneted. Within minutes the entire Confederate right had disintegrated, which also forced the 5th North Carolina and 5th Virginia Cavalry into retreat.[29]

While the 11th, 12th, and 23rd Ohio crushed the right side of Garland's brigade, the 36th Ohio took on its center (No. 3). The 20th North Carolina delivered a heavy fire that was returned by the surging attackers, who surged forward and overwhelmed the Confederate position. As Col. Alfred Iverson would later report, "there was nothing to do but to get away or surrender." The Federals pursued, shooting many of the rebels as they fled for safety. "We let into their backs and did great execution," admitted one Federal. Iverson offered an honest assessment of the condition of his command when he wrote, "my regiment was scattered in every direction and it took the remainder of the day to get them together." McRae reported that the enemy, "with long-extended yell, burst upon our line . . . the enemy's strength was overpowering, and could not be resisted."[30]

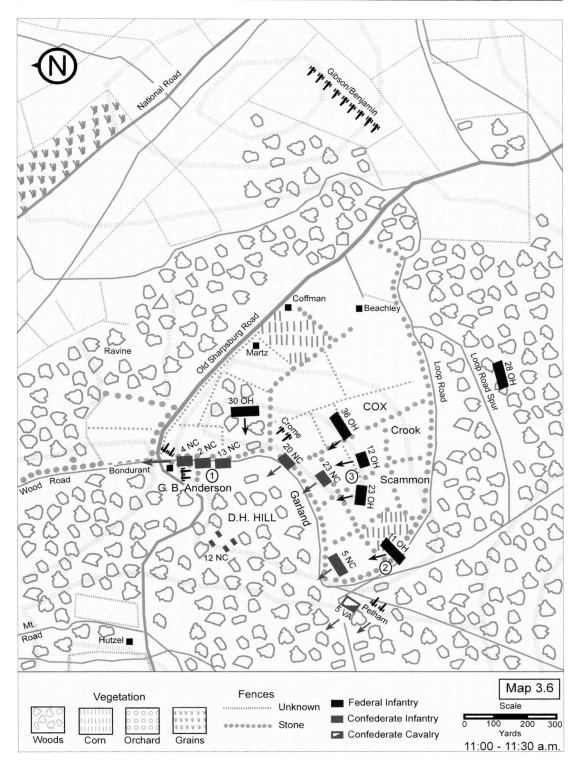

Map 3.6

11:00 - 11:30 a.m.

Map 3.7: The Buckeyes Battle the 13th North Carolina (11:30 a.m. - noon)

By now, the only organized force left from Garland's decimated brigade was Lt. Col. Ruffin's 13th North Carolina and Bondurant's supporting battery.

Seeing the 30th Ohio advance against their front, the North Carolinians fired volley after volley in a desperate effort to stop it. The 13th North Carolina's right flank once again came under small arms fire from the 36th Ohio. Ruffin intended to turn his men left and head toward Tew's regiments of Brig. Gen. G. B. Anderson's brigade, but Anderson had already shifted the 2nd and 4th North Carolina farther north, creating yet another gap between those units and the 13th. Ruffin only learned about this gap when members of the 30th Ohio penetrated it and fired into his left flank. Although they had moved north, the 2nd and 4th North Carolina were able to fire into the left side of the charging 30th Ohio. Nevertheless, Ruffin was now taking fire on three sides. His men had fought valiantly but it was time to pull back. There was only one escape route open to them, and Ruffin ordered his men to use it—fast. The Tar Heels encountered still more Yankees as they moved to the rear. These Federals belonged to the 12th Ohio, which had already crushed Garland's center and was moving to capture Bondurant's pesky guns. Unfortunately for Ruffin and his command, the Buckeyes were cutting across their only clear avenue of withdrawal.[31]

When the 12th Ohio opened fire on Bondurant's battery, the gunners limbered their pieces and rolled them out of harm's way, escaping on the road to the Mountain House. The same can not be said for Ruffin's men. With Ohio troops all around them Ruffin was convinced all was lost, but he determined to fight on as long as possible. He and many of his men made a stand near the Wise cabin, about where Bondurant's battery had been deployed. Desperate situations require desperation actions, and Ruffin ordered his men to attack to the east, taking on the unsuspecting 30th and 36th Ohio regiments. The counterattack had the desired effect, halting the surprised Buckeyes in their tracks. Ruffin, a keen tactician, changed front to the south (right) and attacked the 12th Ohio and

part of the 36th Ohio. While slugging it out with the 12th, parts of the 30th Ohio shook off Ruffin's counterattack and continued their advance west. The aggressive Ruffin once again turned his men and attacked. With the Ohioans in turmoil, Ruffin ordered a retreat north out of immediate danger. The Tar Heels were approaching the Old Sharpsburg Road when they met men from G. B. Anderson's brigade. D. H. Hill was also there and, as Ruffin later related to him, "I shall never forget the feelings of relief which I experienced when I first caught sight of you."[32]

With Ruffin out of the fight, the full fury of the Federal onslaught fell upon Col. Tew's two regiments, which gamely attempted to hold off the enemy. Given their position and the lopsided nature of the fight, annihilation seemed a distinct possibility. To their immense relief, Anderson appeared with his two remaining regiments, stabilizing the fighting and effectively ending it.[33]

It was just about noon when the combat finally ended and a fitful quiet descended upon the battlefield. Garland's brigade had held its position for about three hours against overwhelming numbers. Losses on both sides were heavy. Col. Scammon's brigade, which had done most of the fighting on the Northern side, sustained 262 losses including 62 dead, or about 17 percent of the brigade's strength. The 12th and 36th Ohio of George Crook's brigade lost a combined 62 men killed, wounded, and missing. Garland's losses were especially severe at 43 dead, 168 wounded, and a similar number missing or captured, for nearly 37 percent of its strength.

Gen. Jacob Cox was now in a splendid position. If he moved quickly, he could hit D. H. Hill's flank and rear and drive him from Turner's Gap—the ultimate objective of the day's fighting. His men, however were spent after some three hours of fighting and the associated exertions that came with it. Cox was also unaware of the enemy's strength. Without fresh troops, he decided to rest his men, consolidate his position, and await the arrival of the remainder of the IX Corps. D. H. Hill, meanwhile, pushed up as many artillery pieces as possible to discourage any movement the enemy might make. The lull also bought time for Maj. Gen. James Longstreet to move units south to assist the beleaguered Hill.[34]

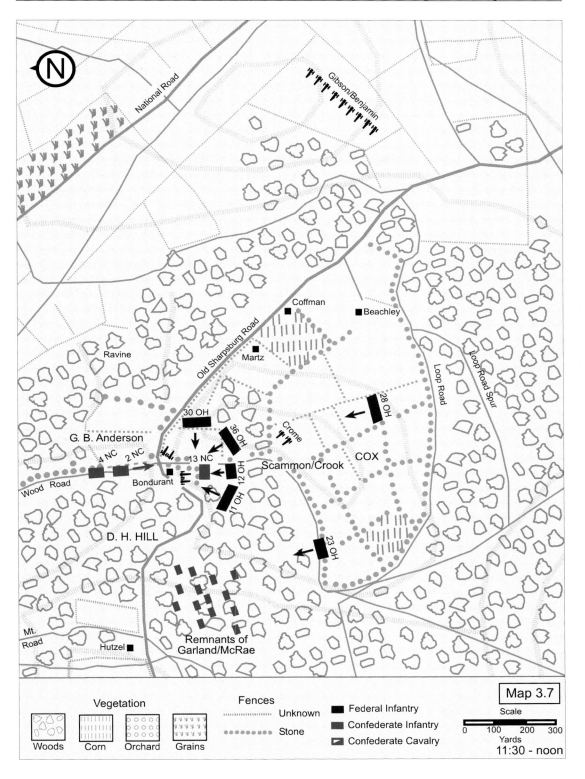

Map 3.7

11:30 - noon

Map Set 4. South Mountain: Fox's Gap (noon - 8:00 p.m.)

Map 4.1: Midday Lull (noon - 2:00 p.m.)

The situation looked bleak for D. H. Hill and the Army of Northern Virginia. One of his brigades (Garland) had been nearly destroyed and the Federals had an important foothold near Fox's Gap with reinforcements pouring into the area. Federal division leader Brig. Gen. Jacob Cox consolidated his position on the heights, forming a diagonal line following the mountain's contours. The 11th and 23rd Ohio held the left, almost parallel to the Old Sharpsburg Road. The 12th Ohio, with the 36th Ohio in reserve, occupied the center. The 30th Ohio, supported by the 28th Ohio, held the right looking north toward the Wise cabin. Cox believed his left and center were "strongly posted," but was less confident about his right, which was closest to the enemy. Two more guns from Capt. Seth Simmonds' battery under Lt. Daniel Glassie arrived and were pushed forward to an open area in front of the 30th Ohio. They opened fire on Bondurant's Alabama battery, which had redeployed just north of the Wise cabin.[1]

D. H. Hill had portions of two brigades available to help seal the breach. Brig. Gen. George B. Anderson's 1,250-man brigade was already in the sector and some of its regiments had exchanged gunfire with the enemy. The second brigade under Brig. Gen. Roswell Ripley numbered slightly more than 1,000 men and had been ordered to move to Turner's Gap at 9:00 a.m. Ripley followed Anderson to the Mountain House at Turner's Gap and probably arrived about 2:00 p.m. Hill ordered Ripley south to reinforce Anderson, whom Ripley found on the Old Sharpsburg Road with his left at the Wise farm. After some discussion, Anderson agreed to move his command to the right (west) to make room for Ripley's regiments. Two additional brigades from James Longstreet's command (Brig. Gen. G. T. Anderson's small 500-man organization and Brig. Gen. Thomas Drayton's 1,300 men) arrived at the Mountain House about 3:30 p.m. D. H. Hill accompanied them south with the intent of deploying them on Ripley's left, but he first had to shift that brigade and

Anderson's farther right to make room for the new arrivals. G. T. Anderson arrived first and moved right to deploy next to Ripley. Drayton's infantry were still in the rear making their way south. Hill hoped these four brigades, about 4,000 men all told, could launch a coordinated attack against Cox's foothold and drive the Federals down the slope.[2]

When he learned that Cox was moving to attack the Confederates on South Mountain, Maj. Gen. Jesse Reno mobilized the remainder of the IX Corps. Brig. Gen. Orlando Willcox's division (the brigades of Col. Benjamin Christ and Col. Thomas Welsh) moved out first from its bivouac a mile and a half east of Middletown, beginning its march at 8:00 a.m. along the National Road. Just as Cox had done earlier, Willcox consulted with Maj. Gen. Alfred Pleasonton when the head of the column reached Bolivar. When the cavalry commander suggested an attack along the National Road, Willcox moved in that direction. He halted just southeast of the Mountain House and deployed his two brigades. Wing commander Maj. Gen. Ambrose Burnside arrived to inform Willcox that his planned attack was too far north, and that he did not want a yawning gap between his two divisions. Burnside ordered Willcox to countermarch down the National Road and then up Old Sharpsburg Road to put his brigades on the right side of Cox's division. Once Brig. Gen. Samuel Sturgis' division arrived, Burnside believed he had a good chance of driving the Rebels from their perch at Fox's Gap.[3]

Because of his wasted march, Willcox did not arrive on Cox's right flank until about 2:00 p.m. Cox's men were about 200 yards left of Old Sharpsburg Road skirmishing with the enemy on the wooded slopes. Willcox sent the 8th Michigan and 50th Pennsylvania along the left side of the road to link up with Cox's right. Willcox intended to position the rest of his division across the road in a roughly north-south orientation. Before he could do so, Reno ordered him to take advantage of the stone walls by deploying along Old Sharpsburg Road facing the National Road. This decision put the division at roughly right angles to Cox's position.[4]

Willcox's initial deployment did not go well when Bondurant's artillery spotted the move and sent shells into the 8th Michigan. The Wolverines stampeded to the rear, directly into the ranks of the trailing 50th Pennsylvania.[5]

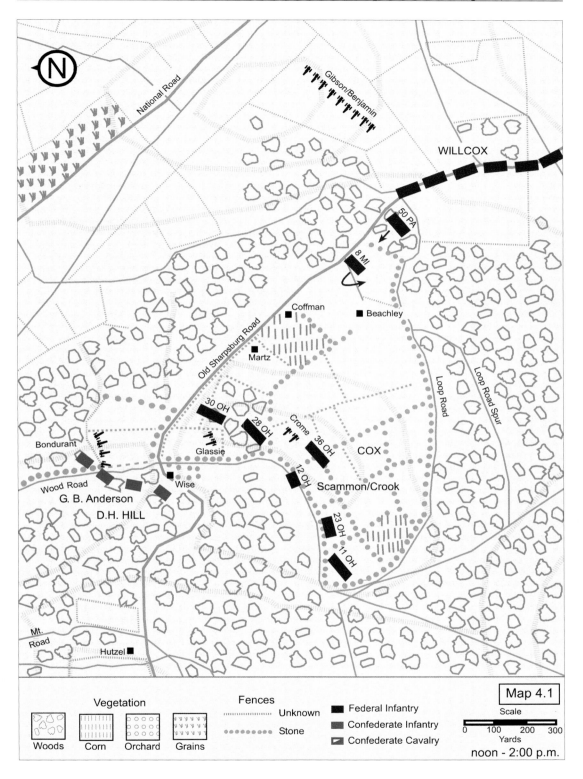

N

Gibson/Benjamin

National Road

WILLCOX

50 PA

8 MI

Coffman   Beachley

Old Sharpsburg Road

Martz

Loop Road

Loop Road Spur

30 OH

28 OH

Crome   36 OH

Glassie   COX

Bondurant

Wood Road   Wise   12 OH   Scammon/Crook

G. B. Anderson

D.H. HILL   23 OH

11 OH

Mt.
Road

Hutzel

Vegetation

Woods   Corn   Orchard   Grains

Fences

.... Unknown

●●●●●●●● Stone

■ Federal Infantry

■ Confederate Infantry

◼ Confederate Cavalry

Map 4.1

Scale

0   100   200   300
Yards

noon - 2:00 p.m.

Map 4.2: Additional Confederate Reinforcements Arrive
(2:00 - 4:00 p.m.)

In accordance with Gen. Reno's order, Willcox shifted the balance of his division to Cox's right flank. A section of Capt. Asa Cook's battery arrived and took position on the right side of the Old Sharpsburg Road, with the 17th Michigan deploying behind and to the right of the guns. The 79th New York deployed on the 17th's left beyond the road, with the 45th Pennsylvania and 46th New York moving up closer to Cox's right flank. The 17th Michigan, only three weeks from their departure from Detroit, deployed on the right side of Old Sharpsburg Road, and was supported by the 28th Massachusetts. Capt. Joseph Clark's battery, meanwhile, moved along the Loop Road on the left of Cox's division and dropped trail near the 11th Ohio with the 50th Pennsylvania, which had been on the right of Cox's line, tramping behind the lines to support the guns.[6]

Bondurant's Confederate guns north of the Wise cabin, together with Lane's battery farther north near Turner's Gap, killed and wounded many of Willcox's men and forced them to take cover wherever they could. The Highlanders of the 79th New York did not find much reassurance behind their stone wall of choice, especially when iron shells repeatedly hit the protective barrier and sent deadly chunks of rock flying in every direction. When Willcox received orders to silence Bondurant's guns, the Highlanders looked to be in the best position to accomplish the difficult task. The 79th New York had a history of hard fighting that began at First Bull Run, and the combat and exertions had dramatically thinned their ranks. Confederate infantry supported the battery, but no Federals knew how many were waiting for them. As a result, Willcox used the larger 45th Pennsylvania, which switched places with the New Yorkers. The 17th Michigan on the 45th's right and the 46th New York on its left would join in the attack. Willcox was so concerned about the destructive nature of Bondurant's fire that he was prepared to launch his entire division against the Rebel guns, if necessary.[7]

While Willcox was preparing to attack Bondurant's battery and the Rebel infantry supporting it, Cook's two Federal pieces in their advanced position on the Old Sharpsburg Road had been suffering under the rain of shells from the time they deployed. Within a few minutes one of the two Federal guns was hit and knocked out of action. Cook called for a fresh gun from the rear as his gunners rolled the disabled piece out of harm's way—but not before his position was hit again, this time with iron canister balls that killed one cannoneer and wounded four others. The Confederate artillery fire was so accurate that Cook decided to quit his position altogether. Bondurant's gunners shifted to solid shot and sent some bounding down the Old Sharpsburg Road. The bouncing balls took out several Union infantrymen and sent scores more scampering to for safety.[8]

By this time D. H. Hill was prepared to halt the Federal advance with four brigades along the Old Sharpsburg Road, aligned east to west as follows: Drayton, G. T. Anderson, Ripley, and G. B. Anderson. Brig. Gen. Thomas Drayton's mixed brigade of the 50th and 51st Georgia, 3rd South Carolina Battalion, 15th South Carolina, and Phillip's Legion had marched down the Wood Road from Turner's Gap to deploy near the Wise cabin. The unit was part of Brig. Gen. David R. Jones' division, which together with G. T. "Tige" Anderson's brigade was marched hurriedly south to reinforce Fox's Gap. Drayton deployed in a rough "L"-shaped alignment with his two South Carolina units running along Old Sharpsburg Road facing south with the 15th South Carolina on the right and the 3rd South Carolina Battalion next to it. The three Georgia units continued the front and comprised the bottom of the "L" with the Phillip's Legion and 51st Georgia facing east and the 50th Georgia facing generally northeast.

Once Drayton maneuvered his brigade into line, the weakness of his position became obvious. Neither of Drayton's flanks was anchored nor protected in any way, and a 300-yard gap yawned between his right flank and G. T. Anderson's left flank. These problems made Drayton's command the most vulnerable of any of the four brigades defending Fox's Gap.[9]

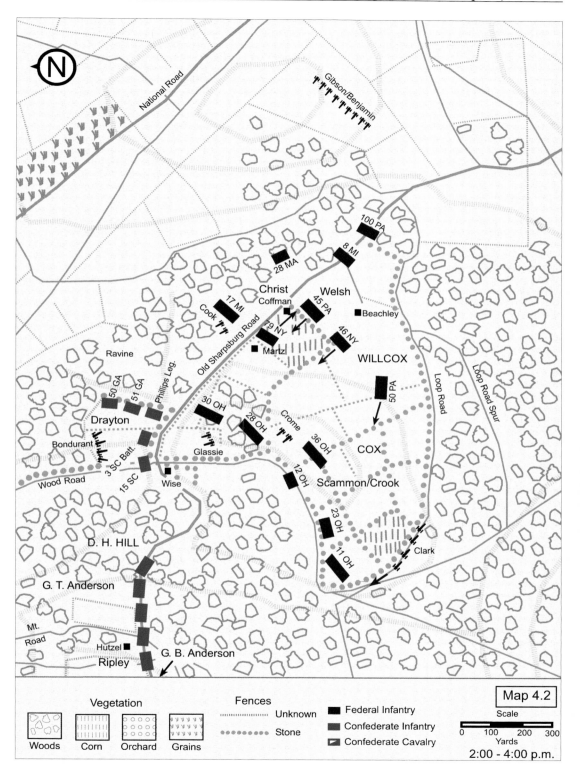

N

Gibson/Benjamin

National Road

100 PA

8 MI

28 MA

Christ

Welsh

Coffman

17 MI

45 PA

Cook

Beachley

79 NY

Old Sharpsburg Road

46 NY

Ravine

Martz

WILLCOX

50 GA

51 GA

Phillips Leg.

30 OH

50 PA

Drayton

28 OH

Crome

Bondurant

36 OH

COX

Glassie

3 SC Batt.

12 OH

15 SC

Wise

Scammon/Crook

Wood Road

23 OH

Loop Road

Loop Road Spur

D. H. HILL

11 OH

Clark

G. T. Anderson

Mt.
Road

Hutzel

G. B. Anderson

Ripley

Vegetation

Fences

Unknown   ▬ Federal Infantry

Stone   ▬ Confederate Infantry

Woods   Corn   Orchard   Grains   ⟋ Confederate Cavalry

Map 4.2

Scale

0   100   200   300
Yards

2:00 - 4:00 p.m.

Map 4.3: Thomas Drayton's Brigade Redeploys (4:00 - 4:30 p.m.)

Charged with defending several mountain gaps with too few men, D. H. Hill left Brig. Gen. Ripley in charge of the four brigades now deployed and tasked with defending Fox's Gap. Although Ripley was a West Pointer, a contemporary would later write that he "appears to have been unequal or disinclined to the task." Future events would bear out this opinion.[10]

Deeply worried about the vulnerable gap between his right and Anderson's left, Drayton ordered his men to close the space. The Phillip's Legion turned to face south while the 50th Georgia and 51st Georgia continued facing east. When Drayton discovered the gap was too wide to fill in this manner, he threw a company of the 3rd South Carolina Battalion across Wise's field to reconnoiter the location of the enemy. Messengers returned with news that the Federals were present in large numbers in the woods just to his front. Although Ripley was technically in charge of all four brigades, Drayton knew D. H. Hill wanted to attack the Federals and dutifully ordered all his regiments to face south to do so. His Confederates had barely moved out into the open fields east of the Wise cabin when heavy small arms fire by the 12th, 28th, and 30th Ohio regiments ripped through their ranks. Within a short time, hand-to-hand combat on a small scale erupted at various points along the disjointed line. When the Buckeyes proved too numerous, Drayton withdrew to his original position along the road. His losses were heavy and many questioned Drayton's judgment in ordering his men to leave the protection of the sunken Old Sharpsburg Road for an offensive into the open. What they did not know was that the order to charge originated with D. H. Hill.[11]

When he did not see any enemy troops to his east, Drayton wheeled his 50th and 51st Georgia south and aligned them behind a stone wall facing the Old Sharpsburg Road. Somehow he missed seeing the large 17th Michigan, which was in line of battle in the ravine. It originally fronted Drayton's two Georgia regiments; now it was poised directly on their flank. Once this new alignment was complete, all of Drayton's men faced in the same general southerly direction (No. 1).[12]

Redeployed near the Wise cabin, Bondurant's guns opened fire on the large bodies of enemy soldiers moving into position. "The enemy's guns continued to play on us, killing and wounding at all points," reported Willcox. "[W]e lay silent and kept concealed." According to the commander of the 46th New York, his men made good use of the fence to their front for cover. With his three regiments in place to attack Bondurant's battery, Willcox ordered the 45th Pennsylvania and 46th New York to play bait and distract the gunners by advancing against the battery's front while the 17th Michigan approached Bondurant's left flank to knock it out of action. Winded after their exhausting movement to South Mountain and knowing they would soon to be thrown into battle against an unseen enemy unsettled nerves. When a portion of the 8th Michigan moved forward to counter aggressive Confederate skirmishers, the men of the 46th New York thought they were also to move to the left and began doing so before being ordered back. Federal reinforcements from Brig. Gen. Samuel Sturgis' division were arriving at this time, including another battery under Capt. George Durell. Its appearance pleased Willcox's foot soldiers, who looked forward to anything that could help neutralize the Rebel guns.[13]

Willcox's attackers stripped off their knapsacks, loaded their muskets, and fixed bayonets. When the order to attack arrived, they leaped stone walls and any other obstacles and charged ahead. The 45th Pennsylvania headed straight toward the battery and Drayton's men in front of it (No. 2). The 46th New York advanced a short distance behind the Pennsylvania troops on their left and formed one united front. Both regiments ran into Drayton's blazing skirmish line. After lying impatiently in a ravine north of the Old Sharpsburg Road while listening to the battle erupting on their left, the Wolverines of the 17th finally received orders to rise and advance against Drayton's exposed left flank (No. 3). The anxious Michiganders rushed forward with a shout, experiencing their first taste of combat.[14]

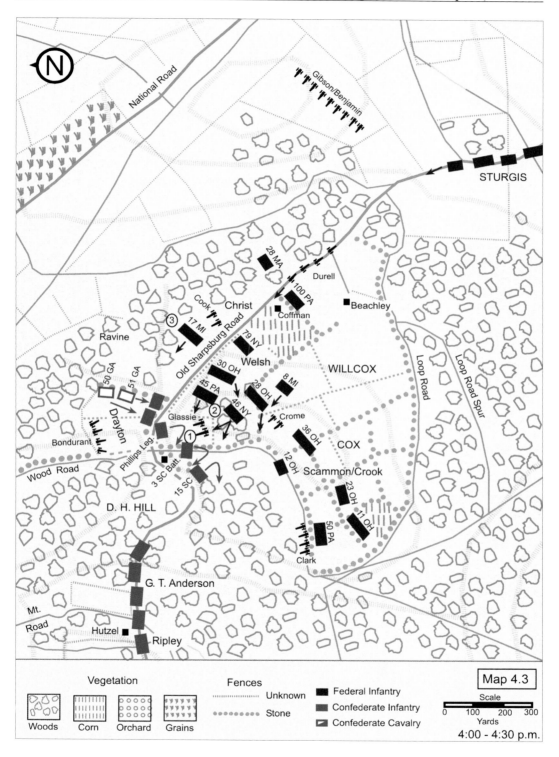

Vegetation

Woods   Corn   Orchard   Grains

Fences
.... Unknown
●●●●●●●● Stone

■ Federal Infantry
■ Confederate Infantry
⚑ Confederate Cavalry

Map 4.3

Scale
0   100   200   300
Yards

4:00 - 4:30 p.m.

Map 4.4: Scammon and Willcox Attack Drayton's Brigade (4:30 - 5:00 p.m.)

A deeply concerned D. H. Hill watched the determined Federal attack from a vista near the top of Turner's Gap. The enemy approached in an inverted "V" formation heading straight for Thomas Drayton's exposed and now vulnerable brigade. The tangled underbrush, however, broke apart the Federal formation, but not the forward momentum of the charge itself.

When the 17th Michigan infantry reached a clearing, its members spotted the 50th and 51st Georgia regiments on the far side. The Rebels opened fire on the exposed Wolverines, who continued driving ahead. Firing from the vicinity of the Mountain House, Lt. Col. Allen Cutts' Confederate artillery battalion pounded their right flank, killing and wounding groups of men with each discharge that opened gaps in the 17th Michigan's line. The iron fragments forced the Michiganders to crowd left across the Old Sharpsburg Road and into the advancing 45th Pennsylvania (No. 1). The artillery also played on the wall protecting the supporting troops. The Highlanders of the 79th New York thought they were safe until solid shot "rattled over the tops of the stone wall, knocking the stones about and making great gaps here and there."[15]

The 900 men of the 3rd South Carolina Battalion, Phillip's Legion, and the 15th South Carolina of Drayton's brigade who had advanced in their own charge halted in line of battle just south of the Wise cabin. Somehow, they held their ground despite mounting losses suffered by the entire brigade, which was facing elements of four Federal brigades from Cox's, Willcox's, and Sturgis' divisions. If D. H. Hill's aim was to delay the Federals from marching on Harpers Ferry, then Drayton was certainly doing his part to achieve that goal. Brig. Gen. John Hood's division of two brigades, meanwhile, had arrived at the Mountain House and was now on its way south to reinforce Fox's Gap.[16]

By this time, Brig. Gen. Samuel Sturgis' division was fully deployed and ready for action. Some of its members had never been in battle before, so the long line of the wounded passing by on the way to the rear was a bit unnerving for many. One young drummer being carried on a stretcher yelled at the top of his lungs, "Forward boys, forward! We're driving them! Don't let this scare you; give 'em hell! They can't stand cold steel!" Sturgis spun off the 2nd Maryland and 6th New Hampshire toward Turner's Gap and ordered Clark's battery to reinforce Jacob Cox's vulnerable left flank. Col. Edward Ferrero's brigade deployed first as Durell's battery was ordered into action, dropping trail just to the right of the Old Sharpsburg Road (No. 2). Supported by the 51st New York and 51st Pennsylvania, Durell's guns together with Clark's pieces opened fires on Lane's Southern artillery by Turner's Gap and quickly silenced it. This allowed the 17th Michigan to shift back to the right, much to the relief of the cramped 45th Pennsylvania.[17]

Short of ammunition, the commander of the 46th New York, Lt. Col. Joseph Gerhardt, asked permission to vacate the front line. He was leading his men to the rear when the inexperienced 9th New Hampshire of Col. James Nagle's brigade (Willcox's division) advanced to the front where, according to Lt. Col. Gerhardt, "it commenced firing before they had taken our position . . . our soldiers . . . only saved themselves by throwing themselves down on the ground." The 100th Pennsylvania of Col. Thomas Welsh's brigade (Willcox's division) and the 48th Pennsylvania of Nagle's brigade also moved up to the front (No. 3).

The 9th New Hampshire formed itself on the left of the 48th Pennsylvania. The 35th Massachusetts also advanced on the left side of the Old Sharpsburg Road to provide support. Like their comrades, they were tired after their march to the battlefield that included scaling the rough slopes of South Mountain. One Bay Stater recalled what it was like to march into battle for the first time: "The crackling rattle of musketry grows nearer and nearer, the bellowing guns are louder, and just over their heads is heard the swift sailing song of the Minie, with its devilish diminuendo." Among the fortunate that day were the men of the 21st Massachusetts, who were placed in reserve.[18]

Perhaps the most exhausted men of all belonged to the 28th and 30th Ohio, who after battling Samuel Garland's veterans for much of the morning continued fighting during their fitful advance along the Wood Road.[19]

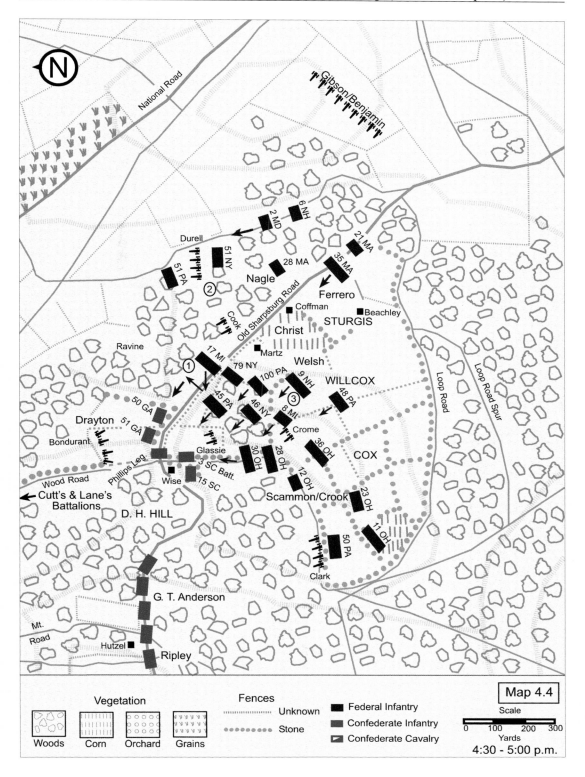

Map 4.4

Scale

0 100 200 300
Yards

4:30 - 5:00 p.m.

Vegetation

Woods | Corn | Orchard | Grains

Fences

Unknown

Stone

Federal Infantry

Confederate Infantry

Confederate Cavalry

Map 4.5: Drayton's Brigade Collapses (5:00 - 5:30 p.m.)

Once Durell's guns had helped silence Lane's pieces near the Mountain House, they turned their iron against Bondurant's battery deployed north of the Wise cabin. One of its initial shots dismounted a Napoleon. It was now obvious to Bondurant that this new threat, combined with the increasing pressure from Federal infantry, made his exposed position untenable. Bondurant's withdrawal concerned many of Drayton's men, who were now more concerned than ever about holding their exposed positions against such overwhelming odds.

The 50th and 51st Georgia regiments on Drayton's line were among the first to fall back. They had no real choice because without the artillery support, the 17th Michigan had obliqued to the right and was coming in behind them. At the same time, their front was also being fired into by troops on the opposite side of Old Sharpsburg Road, which was now heaped with dead and dying Georgians. The 48th and 100th Pennsylvania and 9th New Hampshire took on the rest of Drayton's hard-hit regiments while the 12th and 30th Ohio from Cox's division fired into the right side of Drayton's beleaguered line. The withdrawal of the Georgians triggered a domino effect when Phillip's Legion and the 15th South Carolina followed them to the rear.[20]

Unwilling to show his men's backs to the enemy, regimental commander Lt. Col. George James of the 3rd South Carolina Battalion ordered his troops to seek protection behind stone walls in the hope they could hold out against the approaching enemy infantry. Losses mounted quickly, however, and when a bullet drilled into James' chest and another felled his second in command, the surviving Palmetto soldiers headed for the rear.[21]

An ever-growing number of Federal troops were joining the action by the time Drayton's line collapsed. The 17th Michigan and 45th Pennsylvania played a major role throughout the fighting. The 46th New York, which fell back to replenish its ammunition, returned to action and the 48th and 100 Pennsylvania, along with the 9th New Hampshire, helped finish off the defenders. Plenty of other fresh Federal troops were ready to take a crack at the enemy, including the 21st, 28th, and 35th Massachusetts, 51st Pennsylvania, and 51st New York. Although spent from the morning's fighting, Cox's division was also available, if necessary.

Gen. Sturgis offered a succinct and generally accurate account of the fighting when he wrote: "The enemy made several charges with the hope of driving our brave troops from their position, but were driven back with great slaughter behind a stone fence, where he reformed, but was driven again even from that shelter, and we occupied the highest point of the mountain."[22]

Drayton's losses were exceptionally heavy. More than half his command (51%) fell with 206 killed, 227 wounded, and 210 captured or missing. The 3rd South Carolina Battalion, which had valiantly held the center of Drayton's line, was nearly surrounded and paid the price by losing 85% of its effectives; the 50th Georgia on the left of the line (which took fire along its front, flank, and rear) lost three of every four men (76%) on the slopes of South Mountain. Lt. Peter McGlashen of the latter regiment wrote home that "a man could have walked from the head of our line to the foot on their bodies." The situation was quite different on the right side of Drayton's line, where the 15th South Carolina lost 25% of its men—a figure that in most battles would have been considered substantial. Drayton's survivors were upset with their commander. They knew their losses would have been significantly smaller and their chances of success significantly greater had they remained in their defensive positions behind the stone walls flanking the Old Sharpsburg Road.[23]

Federal losses paled in comparison. Willcox's entire division lost 355 men from all causes (12%) while Sturgis' division lost 157 (5%) for a total of 512 of those engaged (9%). The heaviest losses were sustained by the 17th Michigan (132 killed, wounded, captured/missing, or 25%) and 45th Pennsylvania (134, or 24%). Both units had been involved in most or all phases of the afternoon attack. (Most of Cox's losses occurred in the morning, as set forth in Map 3.7.)[24]

John Hood's Confederate division, composed of the brigades of Cols. William Wofford and Evander Law, was now deployed on the left of the Wood Road, preparing to provide support for Drayton's routed brigade.[25]

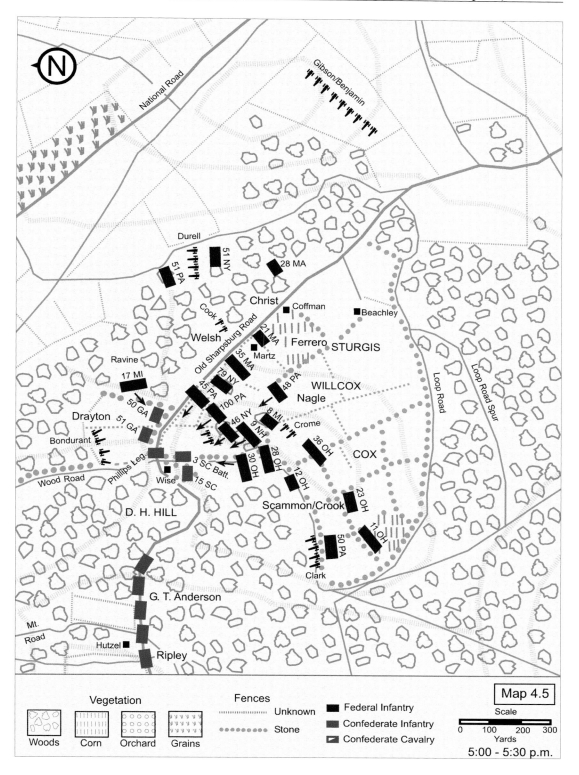

N

National Road

Gibson/Benjamin

Durell

51 PA   51 NY   28 MA

Christ

Cook   Coffman   Beachley

Welsh   Old Sharpsburg Road   21 MA   Ferrero   STURGIS

Ravine   35 MA   Martz

17 MI   79 NY   48 PA   WILLCOX

45 PA   Nagle

50 GA   100 PA   8 MI   Crome

Drayton   51 GA   46 NY   Loop Road   Loop Road Spur

Bondurant   9 NH   36 OH   COX

3 SC Batt.   28 OH

Phillips Leg.   30 OH   12 OH

Wood Road   Wise   15 SC   Scammon/Crook   23 OH

D. H. HILL   11 OH

50 PA

Clark

G. T. Anderson

Mt.
Road   Hutzel   Ripley

Vegetation

Woods   Corn   Orchard   Grains

Fences

Unknown

Stone

Federal Infantry

Confederate Infantry

Confederate Cavalry

Map 4.5

Scale

0   100   200   300
Yards

5:00 - 5:30 p.m.

Map 4.6: G. T. Anderson's Dilemma (5:30 - 6:00 p.m.)

The attack on Drayton's brigade was in many ways a textbook example of how to (almost) annihilate a defender: press the front, find a weak flank, and turn and crush the enemy. With Drayton's defeat, Jesse Reno's IX Corps effectively commanded Fox's Gap even though the fighting in this area was not yet over.

A Georgia brigade under Col. George T. ("Tige") Anderson composed of the 1st Georgia Regulars, and the 7th, 8th, 9th, and 11th Georgia, had preceded Drayton's command down the Old Sharpsburg Road that morning and was again in motion during Drayton's fight on the left of the line. Anderson moved by the right flank in an effort to locate Brig. Gen. Roswell Ripley's left flank. When the fighting erupted in Drayton's sector, Ripley (the officer D. H. Hill put in command of all four brigades defending Fox's Gap) ordered G. T. Anderson to halt his westward move and instead slide east (to the left) to find and reinforce Drayton. Anderson complied immediately, but no one remembered to inform his skirmish line, which failed to sidle left with the main body. As a result, the move left Anderson's entire front uncovered. With the sound of the fighting escalating to the left, Anderson hastened his men in that direction by changing front forward on the left. He also threw out half of the 1st Georgia Regulars as a new skirmish line and ordered it forward to feel for the enemy. The Regulars did not cover much ground before they caught sight of Drayton's defeated men fleeing to the rear. The Federals were now threatening Anderson's left and rear.[26]

Tige Anderson decided to move his brigade to the left and re-cross the Old Sharpsburg Road. Another aide arrived with news that the enemy was already on his left flank, so Anderson continued sliding his brigade obliquely to the left. The Federal troops observed by his scouts probably included elements of six regiments, mainly the 9th New Hampshire and 35th Massachusetts, which were advancing to mop up enemy resistance. Alone in the fading light and ignorant of the enemy's strength or disposition, Anderson decided not to attack. The Federals his Georgians saw were exhausted from their journey up the side of the mountain and subsequent fight with Drayton, and their advance sputtered to a halt with most of the men heading back to the safety of the rear.

Determined to find Ripley's left flank now more than ever, Anderson reversed course a second time. His men had not covered much ground when Anderson received another report that unknown troops were heading in his direction through the thickets covering his left flank. If true, enemy troops in his front and to his left meant the Georgians were in a precarious situation. Luckily, the unknown troops proved to be reinforcements from Longstreet's command in the form of two brigades from Maj. Gen. John Hood's division. Rather than seek out Ripley, Anderson requested instructions from Hood. The exchange prompted Anderson to move around Hood's rear in order to reach his vulnerable left flank. About this same time, Hood was ordered to shift his entire division to the right to help plug the gap caused by Drayton's defeat.[27]

Tige Anderson was not the only Anderson trying to help Drayton. Brig. Gen. George B. Anderson on the right end of the line also heard the gunfire far to his left and responded by moving his command (the 2nd, 4th, and 30th North Carolina, and the 13th North Carolina of Garland's brigade) in that direction. He did so without orders from Ripley, who could not be located. Because of the confusion on this part of the field and the difficult terrain, Anderson's own 14th North Carolina had attached itself to Ripley's command, which was on its own strange odyssey that day. "We were marched forward and backward across the mountain and were marched to the top of it by the left flank in a line of battle, waited there till near sundown, then back again," Calvin Leach of the 1st North Carolina, part of Ripley's brigade, complained in his diary. Ripley lost his way and took himself and his brigade out of the fighting. (See Map 4.7 for more information.)[28]

Meanwhile, the 35th Massachusetts was thrown out on the skirmish line about sunset to reconnoiter the woods north and west of the Wise cabin. The Bay Staters, explained one historian of the battle, "went some distance, came back, reported that no enemy was in the immediate front, and resumed its place in the third line of the brigade."[29]

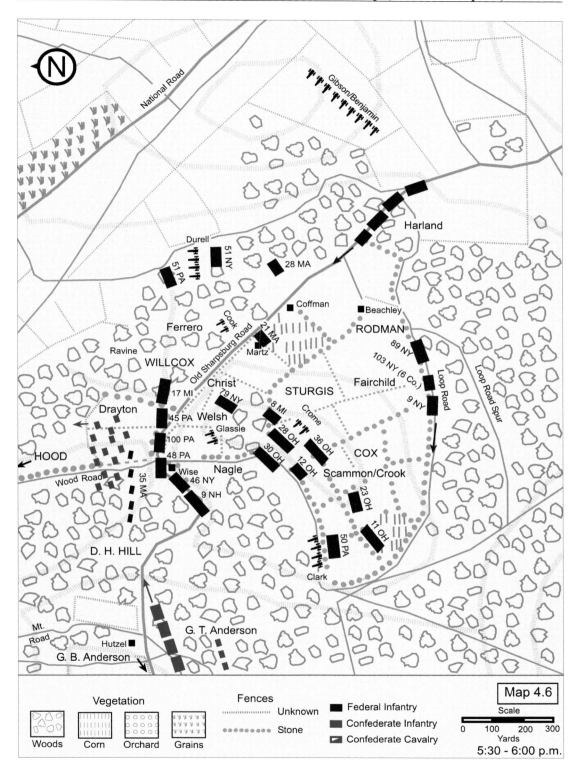

Map 4.6

5:30 - 6:00 p.m.

Map 4.7:
George B. Anderson's Failed Attack
(6:00 - 6:45 p.m.)

Around this time, Roswell Ripley received a report that a mass of Federals was moving along his front. In reality, the troops belonged to George B. Anderson's Rebel brigade, which was moving south to attack the enemy. Worried that his own brigade would be overwhelmed, Ripley ordered his men up the mountain and then down its west side. They would not return until the fighting for Fox's Gap was over. In fact, Ripley's men would not pull a trigger the entire day. As the disgusted D. H. Hill sarcastically put it, "I received a note from Ripley saying that he was progressing finely; so he was, to the rear of the mountain on the west side." Ripley defended his actions in his report: "The natural difficulties of the ground and the condition of the troops prevented these movements from being made with the rapidity which was desirable, and the enemy forced his way . . . between General Drayton's force and my own."[30]

Gen. Lee's Army of Northern Virginia was now in a precarious position, with only a handful of brigades clinging to the vital mountain passes at Fox's and Turner's gaps. Losing the gaps would cleave his army in two and possibly result in the piecemeal destruction of its individual segments.

The arrival and deployment of Brig. Gen. Isaac Rodman's division fully unified the powerful Federal IX Corps facing Fox's Gap. The division left Frederick at 3:00 a.m. that morning, rested four hours near Middletown, and continued apace at 2:00 p.m. to reach the field between 4:00 and 5:00 p.m. Col. Edward Harland's brigade, composed of the 8th and 11th Connecticut and 4th Rhode Island, moved to the right of the Old Sharpsburg Road to support Willcox's and Sturgis' divisions; Col. Harrison Fairchild's brigade moved left to support Cox's men and deployed behind Clark's battery, from left to right as follows: 89th New York, 103rd New York (six companies), and 9th New York.[31]

G. B. Anderson's brigade finally made it to the top of the boulder- and thicket-strewn mountain. Because he could not see anything below him, a skirmish line was thrown forward to ascertain the location of the enemy. An aide returned with the exciting news that the Rebel brigade was on the enemy's left flank and if it moved swiftly to the attack, could capture a battery there (Clark's) and possibly roll up the Federal line. Marching down the Mountain Road as quickly as possible, Anderson deployed and launched his men against the Federals. The 4th North Carolina, which formed on Anderson's left, veered left and struck the left flank of the 9th New Hampshire. The Federals initially took flight with the Rebels right behind them, but soon enough stopped and stood their ground with both sides exchanging fire until darkness ended the fight. The rest of Anderson's line of battle, composed of the 2nd and 13th North Carolina, bore down on Clark's guns and opened fire.

What Anderson's Tar Heels did not see was Col. Harrison Fairchild's brigade of Rodman's division arriving at the same time and taking its place behind and to the left of Clark's battery on the extreme left of the Federal line. The initial Confederate volleys convinced the cannoneers and infantry to hit the ground. The sudden appearance of the Tar Heels was too much for Fairchild's new 103rd New York and it stampeded for the rear. Raising the "Rebel Yell," the 2nd and 13th North Carolina pitched downhill toward the battery. They were closing the distance when Fairchild's remaining two regiments took to their feet and hit the surprised Tar Heels with devastating volleys while Clark's men opened fire with double canister, the flames shooting out of the barrels and illuminating the area around them in the growing darkness. A soldier in the 89th New York wrote home, "after they fired the first round we rose up and let it into them . . . and they skedaddled." The 50th Pennsylvania on the right of Clark's guns also added its weight to the encounter.

Caught out in the open, Anderson's attacking line simply melted away. The North Carolinians clambered back up the mountainside as fast they as could. In their wake was a Maryland slope strewn with their dead and their dying.[32]

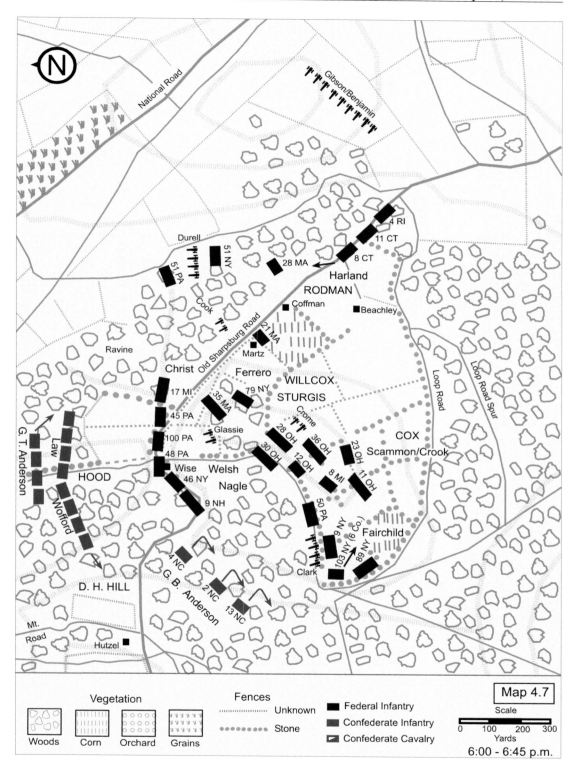

Map 4.7

Scale

0   100   200   300
Yards

6:00 - 6:45 p.m.

Vegetation

Woods   Corn   Orchard   Grains

Fences

.... Unknown
●●●●●●●●● Stone

■ Federal Infantry
■ Confederate Infantry
◤ Confederate Cavalry

Map 4.8: The Death of Jesse Reno
(6:30 - 8:00 p.m.)

Once Brig. Gen. John Hood's two-brigade division reached the Mountain House about 4:00 p.m., it assumed a position north of the National Road before Hood ordered it to cross the road and move south to support the beleaguered Confederate defenders. They encountered survivors from Drayton's brigade during the march to Fox's Gap who told them about the plight that had caused their defeat and about the thousands of enemy soldiers in the fields behind them. Hood shifted his troops to the right as G. T. Anderson's fresh brigade, which had marched behind the division, attached itself to Hood's left flank. (See Map 4.7). The three brigades continued a slow southward advance toward the Wise cabin. Hood expected an attack, but when it did not occur he ordered his men to fix bayonets and launched his own assault.[33]

While Hood's division was moving south, Gen. Orlando Willcox ordered Col. Edward Ferrero to lead his brigade to the front. Its units had been scattered along the right of the line, but were now rushed to the front to end any thought of a Confederate attempt at pushing the IX Corps from its foothold near Fox's Gap. The new large 800-man 35th Massachusetts was thrown forward to form a front of skirmishers and disappeared into the dark woods. Ferrero deployed the remainder of his brigade in line of battle with the 51st Pennsylvania on the right and the 51st New York to its left along the Old Sharpsburg Road. The 21st Massachusetts went to ground between them to provide support.[34]

Hood halted in the woods just north of Drayton's original position, having reclaimed almost all of the lost Confederate ground with relatively few casualties and very little fighting. The Pennsylvanians of the 51st in the first line were not happy with the green men of the 35th Massachusetts behind them. The Bay Staters had opened fire when they spotted Hood's men, forcing the Pennsylvanians to their front to the ground to avoid being hit.[35]

Thousands of men fell at Fox's Gap on September 14, and one of the last was the highest ranking to die. IX Corps commander Maj. Gen. Jesse Reno approached the front on the Old Sharpsburg Road in the gathering darkness.

Beginning with the Ohioans on the left of the line, Reno—who was known to his men as a "soldier's soldier"—congratulated each unit as he rode north. When he perceived movement in the woods to the front, Reno ordered the 51st Pennsylvania to cross the Old Sharpsburg Road while the 51st New York advanced on its left. Hood's men opened fire and the Union troops responded. One bullet hit Reno's scabbard and slammed into his chest just below his heart. He tilted slightly in his saddle, dismounted slowly, and exclaimed that he was wounded and he feared badly. Stretcher bearers carried him down the mountain and placed him under a large oak tree along the road. Reno died at 7:00 p.m. He was thirty-nine years old.[36]

The fight for Fox's Gap was finally over. The entire IX Corps, about 12,000 men, had spent much of the day trying to force the gap and enter Pleasant Valley. Hard and prolonged fighting that morning ended with the defeat of Samuel Garland's Southern brigade and his death, and later that afternoon the crushing defeat of Thomas Drayton's brigade. Only seven undersized Rebel brigades, or about 7,500 men, held this sector and one of them, Roswell Ripley's, didn't see any action.

According to Maryland Campaign historian Ezra Carman, the IX Corps lost 157 killed, 691 wounded, and 41 missing. Confederate losses are harder to specifically determine, and Carman estimated them to be about 600 killed and wounded, with hundreds more missing or captured. "The IX Corps had fought all day for nothing," was how one modern author summed up the Federal effort. "They had not defeated the Confederates who they outnumbered and had lost a general whom they loved. They had nothing to feel elated about."[37]

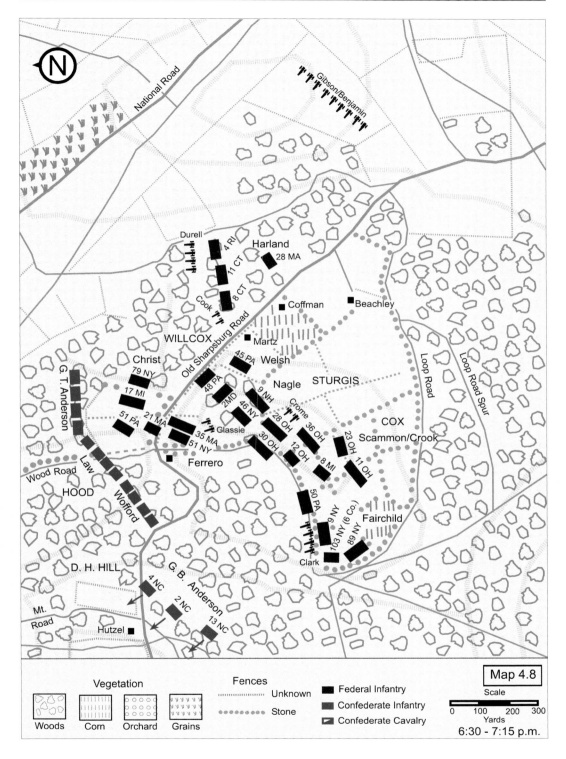

Map 4.8

Scale

0   100   200   300
Yards

6:30 - 7:15 p.m.

Vegetation

Woods   Corn   Orchard   Grains

Fences

Unknown

Stone

Federal Infantry

Confederate Infantry

Confederate Cavalry

Map Set 5. South Mountain: Frosttown Plateau (2:00 - 9:00 p.m.)

Map 5.1: Hooker's I Corps Approaches the Field (2:00 - 3:45 p.m.)

At daybreak on September 14, Maj. Gen. James Longstreet began moving his command south from Hagerstown to help hold the all-important Turner's Gap. It promised to be a long day, for a large portion of the Federal army was also snaking its way toward South Mountain, determined to force the passes and divide Gen. Robert E. Lee's invading army.

On the opposite side of the mountain, Maj. Gen. Joseph Hooker's 12,000 men of the Federal I Corps rose at 3:00 a.m., ate hardtack and coffee, and got onto the road about 6:30 a.m. Hooker had only been in command since September 5, so he was not well known to the men. Brig. Gen. George Meade's Pennsylvania Reserve division led the three-division column. The corps reached Frederick about 8:00 a.m. to a hero's welcome. There was no time to savor the reception and the corps continued on. It finally rested by the side of Catoctin Creek a mile west of Middleton at 1:00 p.m. while Hooker rode west to examine the countryside. Many of Frederick's civilians ventured along with the troops, hoping to catch a glimpse of a real battle.[1]

Hooker's four-mile column commenced its trek up the side of South Mountain at 2:30 p.m. The men turned right at Bolivar on the Old Tabor Road to Mount Tabor Church, where they moved off the road to march left into the scenic fields. Lane's Southern battery near the Mountain House and batteries under Capts. George Patterson and Hugh Ross along Dahlgren Road opened fired on them. Capt. James Cooper's Federal battery galloped to the front, unlimbered by the base of the Frosttown Road, and returned fire. As Samuel Sturgis' division moved west along Old Sharpsburg Road, Meade's division continued northward toward Turner's Gap on the National Road. Brig. Gen. Truman Seymour's brigade (the 1st, 2nd, 5th, 6th, 13th Pennsylvania Reserves) led the column, followed by Col. Thomas Gallagher's (the 9th, 10th, 11th, 12th Pennsylvania Reserves). Col. Albert Magilton's brigade (the

3rd, 4th, 7th, and 8th Pennsylvania Reserves) brought up the rear of Meade's division.[2]

When he reached Bolivar, Seymour turned his column right on the Old Hagerstown Road and marched north. The 13th Pennsylvania Reserves was thrown out on the skirmish line when the column reached the Garber house with orders to ascertain the enemy's position. Finding the sector occupied in some strength, Hooker continued beyond what is now the Dahlgren Road and halted Seymour when he moved his division just north of the Frosttown Road. Col. Gallagher's Pennsylvania brigade halted just as its van reached the road, and Col. Magilton's brigade straddled the Dahlgren Road. Magilton's 3rd Pennsylvania Reserves moved north to protect the division's right flank. Meade's right now rested about one and a half miles north of the National Road. Facing left (west), the men could see a series of parallel ridges with valleys between them as South Mountain rose in the distance. The ridges became increasingly higher and steeper closer to the crest. Gorges and ravines bisected the ridges in several places, and trees and rocks studded the mountainside. Confederates held strong defensive positions on these ridges.[3]

Opposing Hooker's I Corps were two brigades under Brig. Gen. Robert Rodes and Col. Alfred Colquitt. The latter command occupied high ground south and east of Turner's Gap blocking the National Road, with Rodes deployed about three-quarters of a mile father north. Halting Meade's 4,000 Pennsylvanians would be Rodes' tall responsibility. The Virginian's front stretched 3,500 feet, much too long to defend with his 1,200-man brigade even with the advantage of defensible terrain. The 12th Alabama deployed on the right at the gorge surrounding the Dahlgren Road near Patterson's guns in an attempt to close the gap with Colquitt's men farther south. The 6th Alabama at the opposite end of the line was south of Frosttown Road. In between Rodes deployed the 5th Alabama near a deep ravine, the 3rd Alabama north of the Haupt house, and the 26th Alabama behind the O'Neil house with its right flank in a gorge between two high hills. Because of the distances involved, heavy woods, and the many hills and ravines, none of the regiments were within eyesight of one another. When Rodes asked for artillery assistance, Capt. Lane sent one of his guns forward along Dahlgren Road.[4]

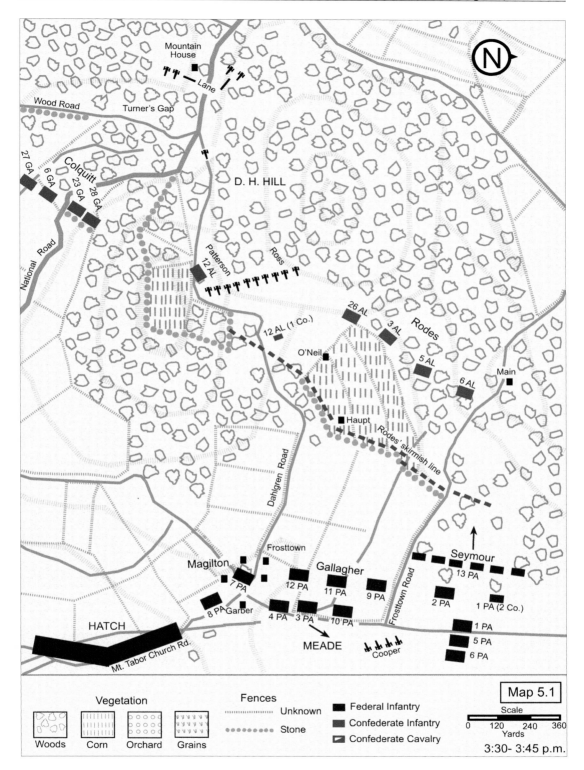

N

Mountain House

Lane

Wood Road

Turner's Gap

27 GA
6 GA
Colquitt
23 GA
28 GA

National Road

D. H. HILL

Patterson
12 AL
Ross

12 AL (1 Co.)

26 AL
3 AL
Rodes
5 AL
6 AL
Main

O'Neil

Haupt

Rodes' skirmish line

Dahlgren Road

Frosttown

Seymour

Magilton
7 PA
Gallagher
12 PA
11 PA
9 PA
13 PA
2 PA
1 PA (2 Co.)

8 PA
Garber
4 PA
3 PA
10 PA
Frosttown Road
1 PA
5 PA
6 PA

HATCH

Mt. Tabor Church Rd.

MEADE
Cooper

Vegetation

Woods   Corn   Orchard   Grains

Fences

Unknown

Stone

Federal Infantry

Confederate Infantry

Confederate Cavalry

Map 5.1

Scale

0   120   240   360
Yards

3:30- 3:45 p.m.

Map 5.2. Meade's Division Engages Rodes' Brigade (4:00 - 6:00 p.m.)

Meade had his division deployed and moving forward by about 4:00 p.m. He intended to launch a coordinated attack along a three-brigade front (Seymour, Gallagher, and Magilton), but the rough terrain had other ideas. Within minutes the brigades lost contact with one another and ended up fighting separately.

Seymour's brigade on the right flank was guided by the 13th Pennsylvania Reserves on the skirmish line. During part of its advance, the Pennsylvanians could look down upon the 5th Alabama in the gorge to their left front. They could also see the 6th Alabama to their right front waiting on the heights. The 3rd and 26th Alabama were out of sight to their left. It did not take Seymour long to realize he could flank the enemy's left and perhaps roll up the entire line. He sought permission from Meade to do so and was given the go-ahead about 5:00 p.m.[5]

On the other side of the battle line, Robert Rodes watched with growing apprehension as the Federal infantry tramped toward his line. He had ordered skirmishers from each regiment to descend the hill to help stall the Federal onslaught until darkness could end the threat. Realizing the vulnerability of his left flank, Rodes moved the 6th Alabama farther left on the high ground near the Widow Main house north of Frosttown Road. Fighting broke out when the Alabamians encountered some of Seymour's men during the move. The 6th Alabama brought the Federal advance in this sector to a halt with solid musketry and artillery support.[6]

Meanwhile, Gallagher's brigade in the center of Meade's line also was pushing forward at a slight oblique angle in an effort to maintain contact with Seymour's left flank. The 9th Pennsylvania Reserves, on the right of Gallagher's brigade line, drove to a stone wall at the foot of the mountain to engage Confederate skirmishers near a log cabin. After exchanging fire for about twenty minutes the Pennsylvanians charged, driving the Alabamians from the house. The 11th Pennsylvania Reserves in the middle of Gallagher's line was approaching a ravine when a series of volleys (likely from the 3rd Alabama)

exploded across their front and killed and wounded half of the commissioned officers and about thirty men. Rodes had ordered his troops to hold their fire until the enemy was within 100 yards to increase the deadliness of the volleys. The 12th Pennsylvania Reserves, on the left of the 11th, was hit by the same volley, though fewer men fell. When Col. Gallagher was wounded in his right arm during this initial fighting, he passed command of the brigade to Col. Robert Anderson of the 9th Pennsylvania Reserves and headed to the rear. The 12th Pennsylvania Reserves on the left of Anderson's line engaged the 26th Alabama and put up a good fight, but could not gain traction to make any significant headway.[7]

Meade watched his three brigades approach the enemy's position from behind the center of his divisional front near the 10th Pennsylvania Reserves in Gallagher's second line. When he saw what looked to be an effort by the Rebel to turn Seymour's left flank, Meade sent the 10th Pennsylvania Reserves northward to stabilize the line. On the right of the Federal line, the 6th Alabama mauled Seymour's 13th Pennsylvania Reserves when it stepped into an open field. Behind the 13th in the main line, the 2nd Pennsylvania Reserves moved forward to support it while the commander of the 6th Pennsylvania Reserves, on the right side of Seymour's line, spun out two companies northward to find the Rebel left flank. At the same time, Seymour ordered the commander of the 5th Pennsylvania Reserves in the middle of rear third line to "Put your regiment into that corn-field and hurt somebody!"[8]

On the left side of Meade's line, meanwhile, the 8th Pennsylvania Reserves had some difficulty making headway against a stubborn company-strength skirmish line from the 12th Alabama. Forty men against six times their number can only hold out for so long, however, and it didn't take too long before the Pennsylvanians forced the tenacious skirmishers out of their positions. Still full of fight, these Southerners stopped several times to fire into their pursuers during the mad scramble up the rough mountainside. Most of these 12th Alabama skirmishers were eventually killed, wounded, or captured (including their commander Lt. Robert Park) during their gallant effort to slow the inexorable Federal advance.[9]

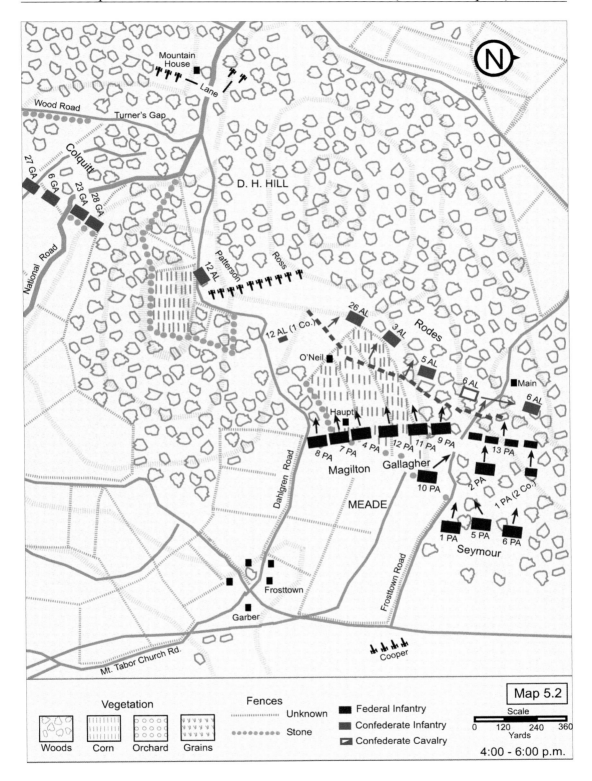

Mountain House

Lane

Wood Road

Turner's Gap

Colquitt

27 GA

6 GA

23 GA

28 GA

National Road

D. H. HILL

Patterson

Ross

12 AL

12 AL (1 Co.)

26 AL

3 AL

Rodes

O'Neil

5 AL

6 AL

Main

6 AL

Haupt

8 PA

7 PA

4 PA

12 PA

11 PA

9 PA

13 PA

Magilton

Gallagher

10 PA

MEADE

2 PA

1 PA (2 Co.)

Dahlgren Road

Frosttown Road

1 PA

5 PA

6 PA

Seymour

Frosttown

Garber

Mt. Tabor Church Rd.

Cooper

Vegetation				Fences			Map 5.2

Woods   Corn   Orchard   Grains

Unknown

Stone

Federal Infantry

Confederate Infantry

Confederate Cavalry

Scale

0   120   240   360
Yards

4:00 - 6:00 p.m.

Map 5.3: Rodes is Defeated
(6:00 - 7:00 p.m.)

With the sun sinking behind them, Rodes' men knew if they could hold on until darkness they would successfully keep the enemy from marching through Turner's Gap. Across many parts of the hill, however, there were no Confederate infantry at all, though few if any Federals fully appreciated that fact. Magilton's men inched forward to the left front, unsure what the next thicket or clump of trees or slope of ground held for them with numerous enemy guns in view. To their right, however, Gallagher's regiments slammed into the middle of Rodes' line, where the 11th and 12th Pennsylvania Reserves battled the 3rd and 26th Alabama. Farther right, when the 9th Pennsylvania Reserves ran out of ammunition, Meade ordered the 10th Pennsylvania Reserves to scuttle its movement right to replace its sister regiment. "Go in and help our men in there," Meade yelled to the 10th's commander.[10]

Seymour's brigade, meanwhile, was also meeting with success. The 1st and 5th Pennsylvania Reserves veered left and advanced through a cornfield to strike the 5th Alabama, which in turn forced its left side up the mountainside. This group from the 12th attempted to form on the right side of the 6th Alabama. The remainder of the regiment held its ground until the Reserves stepped within 100 yards before firing a killing volley that knocked down a score of men. Realizing they could no longer hold their position, and being struck by fire from the 2nd, 6th, and 13th Pennsylvania Reserves, the Alabamians bolted up the mountainside with the Pennsylvanians in hot pursuit. Many fell into Yankee hands.[11]

The Confederates occupied a naturally strong position, but they were far too few in number to hold the entire line that needed defending without leaving large gaps between the thinly stretched regiments. One such breach yawned wide between the 3rd and 5th Alabama. The 10th Pennsylvania Reserves exploited this gap by driving through it. The 3rd Alabama fought gallantly during this encounter, and at one time showed remarkable presence of mind to form an inverted "V" to fight the Pennsylvanians from two directions. According to its commander, "The 3d Alabama changed position no less than seven times on that mountain, and always in perfect order." Hand-to-hand fighting, which was much rarer during the war than commonly believed, was commonplace in this part of the fighting. The right wing of the 5th Alabama was cut off and almost captured. Just to the south, the 11th and 12th Pennsylvania Reserves swarmed the 26th Alabama and forced its retreat. After a stout defense whose result was nearly foreordained, four of Rodes' regiments were retreating for their lives. Only the 12th Alabama, which was fighting farther south near the line of flaming Southern guns along the Dahlgren Road, remained in position.[12]

"In the first attack of the enemy up the bottom of the gorge, they pushed on so vigorously . . . separating the Third from the Fifth Alabama Regiment," was how Rodes described the matter in his after-action report. "The Third made a most gallant resistance at this point, and had my line been a continuous one it could never have been forced."[13] But his line was not "a continuous one" and forced it indeed was. Dispersed, outnumbered, and with regimental flanks in the air and turned, Rodes had no chance against a determined enemy intent on seizing the high ground away from the Southerners. According to historian Ezra Carman, "Meade's men were very persistent . . . they followed them closely up the mountainside, pushed them from every point of vantage . . . penetrated their thin and broken line, worked in and on their flanks, and continued swinging around their left.[14]

Meade was justifiably pleased when he realized his men were driving the enemy along his entire front. "In a short time, the action became general through the whole line," he reported after the battle. "Steadily the line advanced up the mountain side, where the enemy was posted behind trees and rocks, from whence he was slowly, but gradually, dislodged, Seymour first gaining the crest of the hill, and driving the enemy to the left along the ridge, where he was met with the fire of the other two brigades."[15]

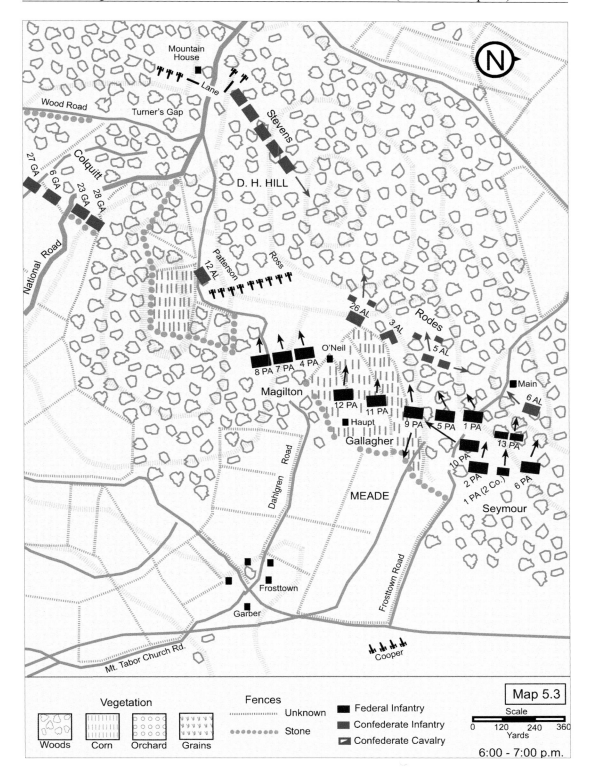

Map 5.3

6:00 - 7:00 p.m.

Map 5.4. The Arrival of Stevens' South Carolina Brigade (7:00 - 9:00 p.m.)

Success was obvious, but the careful Meade was still concerned. Was the Rebel line being extended left (toward Meade's right) in an effort to flank Seymour? Meade sought assistance from Gen. Hooker, who sent Brig. Gen. Abram Duryee's brigade (Ricketts' division) forward from its reserve position.

When he realized Rodes could not hold his position, D. H. Hill sent his own reinforcements. Brig. Gen. Nathan "Shanks" Evans' small 550-man brigade under Col. Peter Stevens arrived first. The South Carolinians appeared just as Rodes' men began streaming from their positions with the Pennsylvanians, flushed with victory and their ranks disordered, giving chase. The South Carolinians were moving up when Rodes reformed his shattered brigade near the top of the mountain. Stevens, who had never led a brigade, had received conflicting orders while moving into position. Evans, who led an unofficial small division in Maryland, ordered Stevens to halt during his advance, but a messenger from Rodes urged him on to support the embattled command. Before he had a chance to seek clarification from Evans, Stevens spotted the Yankees approaching in the valley below. He threw out the Holcombe Legion as skirmishers and deployed the rest of the brigade on the brow of the mountain, from right to left: the 17th South Carolina, 18th South Carolina, 22nd South Carolina, and 23rd South Carolina.[16]

"I heard that some Confederate troops [Stevens] had joined my right very nearly," Rodes recalled in his report, a telling observation that confirmed how the terrain made it difficult to operate and how the swirl of combat produced a true fog of war. The pressure on his brigade was so intense that Rodes realized his only hope was to order a withdrawal to reorganize his front. This could only occur if the Federals slowed down or halted their aggressive pursuit. "Finding that the enemy were forcing my right back, and that the only chance to continue the fight was to change my front so as to face to the left," reported Rodes with the benefit of hindsight, "I ordered all the regiments to fall back up the . . . mountain, fighting." The units moved up the mountain from right to left as follows: 12th Alabama – 26th Alabama – 3rd Alabama – 5th Alabama – 6th Alabama. Rodes refused the latter regiment and the left wing of the 5th to counter Seymour's move northeast. The regiments looked good on paper but reality was something different. The 26th Alabama, for example, "was by this time completely demoralized; its colonel was wounded, and the men mingled in utter confusion with some South Carolina stragglers on the summit of the hill." The others were in a similar difficult state.[17]

With the 17th South Carolina on his right holding its own, Stevens rode to his left and found the 22nd and 23rd South Carolina regiments being driven by the 4th and 7th Pennsylvania Reserves of Magilton's brigade. Within minutes the 18th South Carolina farther right was also retreating. The men of the 17th South Carolina had no idea their left was exposed, and the 8th Pennsylvania Reserves "mowed them down" and forced their retreat. "From that time the fight was a retreating one until the enemy occupied the mountain and we were driven from it," admitted Stevens, who attributed the defeat to the poor behavior of his troops rather than the persistence of the enemy. "I cannot commend the behavior of the men," he added. "Some two or three bravely faced the foe [during the retreat], but a general lack of discipline and disregard for officers prevailed all around me." How long Stevens' command fought is open to debate, but no one can contest the magnitude of his losses at almost 50%. So few men were left that Rodes confused this brigade with "some South Carolina stragglers on the summit of the hill."[18]

With the Pennsylvania Reserves moving around each flank and assaulting along the front, and with their losses mounting rapidly, Rodes' men continued defending the mountaintop. Brig. Gen. Abram Duryee's Federal brigade arrived and deployed behind the Reserves, ready to relieve them if necessary. Darkness, however settled the issue. "It was so dark that it was difficult to distinguish objects at short musket range, and both parties ceased fighting," noted one of the combatants. Rodes achieved his goal of holding the mountain north of the gap, but he lost about one-third of his command (about 422 men). D. H. Hill had nothing but praise for Rodes and his brigade, which "fighting, for hours, vastly superior odds, and maintaining the key-points of the position until darkness rendered a further advance of the Yankees impossible."[19]

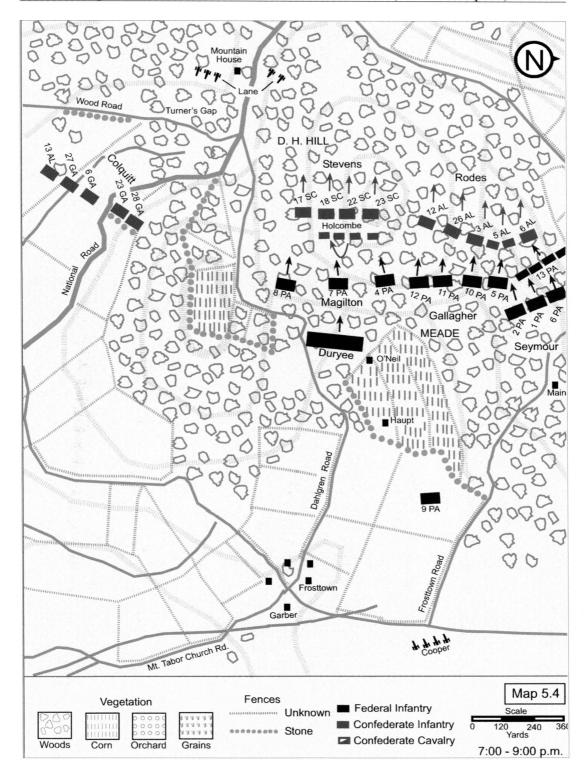

Woods
Corn
Orchard
Grains

Vegetation

Fences
.... Unknown
●●●●●●● Stone

■ Federal Infantry
■ Confederate Infantry
◪ Confederate Cavalry

Map 5.4

Scale
0   120   240   360
Yards

7:00 - 9:00 p.m.

Map Set 6. South Mountain: Turner's Gap (3:30 - 8:30 p.m.)

Map 6.1: Hatch's Division Advances (3:30 - 5:30 p.m.)

While George Meade's division battled Confederates north of Turner's Gap, Brig. Gen. John Hatch's 3,500-man Federal division moved toward the gap itself in an effort to capture the "south spur" of the mountain. A deep ravine separated the two divisions.

Hatch reached Mount Tabor Church about 3:30 p.m., where he met corps commander Maj. Gen. Joseph Hooker (who would be elevated to command the Army of the Potomac in less than six months). Hooker had just finished deploying Meade's division and was ready to throw Hatch into the fight. Brig. Gen. Marsena Patrick's New York brigade was in the van. The brigadier threw out the 21st New York as a skirmish line, which moved forward slowly along the south side of what is now the Dahlgren Road. A short time later orders arrived for Patrick to push out the remainder of his brigade (the 23rd, 35th, and 80th New York). The 21st continued its careful advance on the right.[1]

During the advance the New Yorkers encountered an elderly woman who asked an officer about his orders. "Only going up the hill," came his reply. "Don't go there," she cautioned. "There are hundreds of 'em up there. Don't you go. Some of you might get hurt." Those within earshot smiled and continued picking their way forward up the slope.

The old woman was right. Several Confederate brigades belonging to Brig. Gen. David R. Jones' division were moving into position. Brig. Gen. James Kemper's small all-Virginia brigade (the 1st, 7th, 11th, 17th, and 24th) numbering perhaps all of 400 men led the column and reached Turner's Gap about 4:00 p.m. Kemper moved his men along the Dahlgren Road to bolster that part of the line. Another small brigade of Virginians under Brig. Gen. Richard Garnett (the 8th, 18th, 19th, 28th, and 56th) followed Kemper, while Col. Joseph Walker's South Carolina brigade (the 1st, 2nd Rifles, 5th and 6th South Carolina, 4th South Carolina Battalion, and Palmetto Sharpshooters) brought up the rear.[2]

The Confederates were tired long before they arrived on South Mountain. The three small brigades, which had left Hagerstown that morning with instructions to help D. H. Hill hold Fox's Gap, spent a considerable amount of time marching and countermarching. The weather was exceedingly hot and the roads dusty. Scores of men fell from the ranks, further reducing the strength of the already undersized units. By the time those still in the ranks reached the area around Turner's Gap, their presence was sorely required. "I had now become familiar with the ground, and knew all the vital points," explained a frustrated Hill, "and had these troops reported to me, the result might have been different. As it was, they took wrong positions, and in their exhausted condition after a long march, they were broken and scattered."[3]

"It was now about 5 o'clock and the shells of the enemy come whistling over our heads fast and furiously as we ascend the mountain," Pvt. John Dooley of the 1st Virginia, part of Kemper's brigade, recorded in his journal. "Scarcely are we at the summit . . . that a battery but a short distance away opens [with] ball and shell against our ranks from the spur of the mount nearly opposite, and as it sweeps every yard of the road over which we are passing the greatest confusion for a time prevails." Dooley was writing about Capt. George Durell's Federal battery south of the Virginians. "I tell you, I was frightened!" admitted Dooley, a veteran of several campaigns. What concerned him almost as much as the incoming shell fire was the fact that their muskets were not loaded and there was no officer in sight.

When the enemy artillery opened on his men, Kemper ordered his Virginians into position straddling the Dahlgren Road facing Magilton's Federal brigade. Although they were not far from the enemy troops, the rugged terrain prevented the Virginians from seeing the Pennsylvanians advancing off to their left—but they could hear the sounds of battle along their left flank creeping a bit to their rear. Kemper aligned his troops from left to right as follows: the 24th Virginia, 7th Virginia, 1st Virginia, 11th Virginia, and 17th Virginia. The straggling had reduced Kemper's brigade to the size of a well-used regiment.[4]

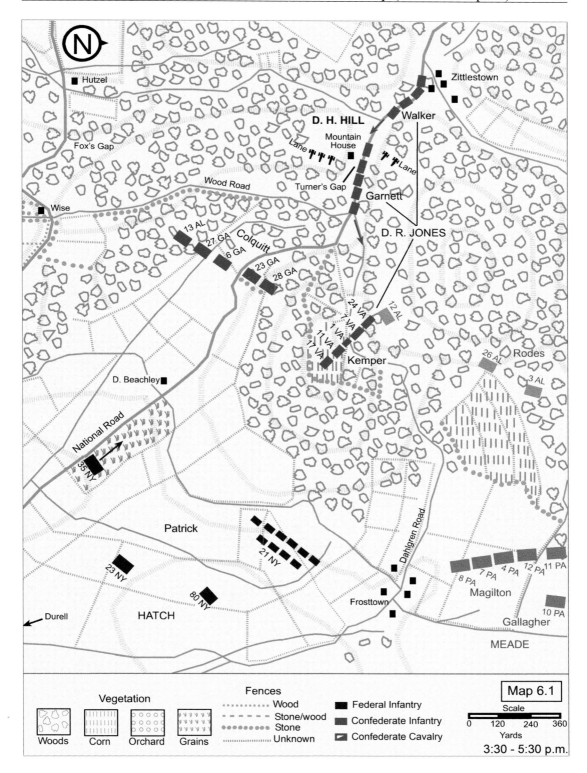

N

Hutzel

Zittlestown

D. H. HILL

Walker

Fox's Gap

Lane

Mountain House

Turner's Gap

Wood Road

Lane

Wise

Garnett

D. R. JONES

13 AL

27 GA   Colquitt

6 GA

23 GA

28 GA

24 VA

12 AL

1 VA

11 VA

17 VA   Kemper

26 AL   Rodes

3 AL

D. Beachley

National Road

35 NY

Patrick

Dahlgren Road

21 NY

7 PA   4 PA   12 PA   11 PA

23 NY

8 PA

Magilton

80 NY

Frosttown

10 PA

Durell   HATCH

Gallagher

MEADE

Vegetation

| Woods | Corn | Orchard | Grains |

Fences

.... Wood
— — — Stone/wood
●●●●●●● Stone
.... Unknown

■ Federal Infantry
■ Confederate Infantry
▰ Confederate Cavalry

Map 6.1

Scale

0   120   240   360

Yards

3:30 - 5:30 p.m.

Map 6.2: Patrick's Brigade Attacks Garnett's Virginians (5:30 - 6:30 p.m.)

Riding back and forth along his front, Brig. Gen. Patrick seemed to be everywhere that evening. When the 35th New York settled into position on the left of the line, Patrick realized it had moved too far left, with its flank across the National Pike. He tried to remedy the situation by pushing the 23rd New York left to support the 35th and the 80th New York farther right to support the 21st New York on the far right. With his men moving into position, Patrick rode north to reconnoiter and encountered a company of the 17th Virginia (Kemper). Sizing up the situation within a few seconds, Patrick and his aide bolted east back to the main line and ordered the 21st and 80th New York regiments forward. Brig. Gen. Hatch, meanwhile, pushed his other two brigades under Col. Walter Phelps and Brig. Gen. Abner Doubleday forward to support Patrick's advancing lines of battle.[5]

By this time Richard Garnett's Confederate brigade was moving toward the front from the opposite side of the mountain, albeit very slowly. An aide tasked with positioning his command could only tell the frustrated Garnett to "about-face . . . return the way I came until I reached a path, which I must take." Garnett requested clarification, but the aide was unable to offer more specific directions. The brigadier marched his men rather aimlessly until another aide arrived with more complete information. By this time, reported Garnett, "my men were almost exhausted. I consequently lost the services of a number of men by straggling." With the help of the second guide he eventually deployed his brigade at a forty-five degree angle to Kemper's command, facing southeast, from right to left as follows: 8th Virginia – 18th Virginia – 19th Virginia – 28th Virginia – 56th Virginia. According to Garnett, heavy woods blanketed his right flank and a cornfield spread out on his left. Like Kemper's small command, Garnett's Virginians numbered only about 400 or so effectives and suffered under the shot and shell pouring out of Durell's battery.[6]

Meanwhile, the sounds of battle continued to grow in the valleys and heights north of Kemper's prone men straddling the Dahlgren Road. Because of the heavy terrain, they could not see the combatants (Meade and Rodes). The battle increased in intensity with the arrival of Brig. Gen. Nathan Evans' brigade (under Col. Peter Stevens) just to their left. Sunset was approaching when Garnett, finally satisfied with his brigade's deployment, threw out a skirmish line to feel for the enemy. Just as he sent them forward, Garnett received a message from division leader D. R. Jones ordering him to push the 56th Virginia toward Kemper's right flank and move the rest of his brigade to a wooded ridge to his left-rear. Garnett was about to implement these orders when a Federal skirmish line appeared in front of his brigade, followed closely by a large body of infantry. The action, Garnett reported, "at once became general."[7]

Exactly which Federal troops advanced against Garnett's front is not clear. It may have been the 21st and 80th New York moving against the left of his line along a ravine, or perhaps it was the 23rd and 35th New York advancing against his right. Regardless of who it was, all of Patrick's New Yorkers were frustrated by their slow progress up the steep, rocky, and wooded hillside that wreaked havoc on their regimental lines of battle. The men had to stop every fifteen to twenty paces just to realign their formation and stay semi-organized. According to one historian, Patrick's brigade halted more than forty-eight times to realign its ranks as it advanced through 1,800 feet of woods. Garnett's men probably did not see the 2nd U.S. Sharpshooters from Phelps' brigade. The blue marksmen had been thrown over to the right of the 21st New York because Hatch believed Patrick's men were advancing too far southeast of the Rebel line.

Patrick was also worried—not about his general direction, but about the gaps growing in his brigade line. The two regiments on his left were veering west (left) toward the National Road, widening the gap between his two wings. Phelps' men filled the gap. As a result, Patrick was forced to ride around Phelps' brigade to get from one wing of his own brigade to the other.[8]

This was not an ideal tactical situation when your men are about to engage in heavy combat.

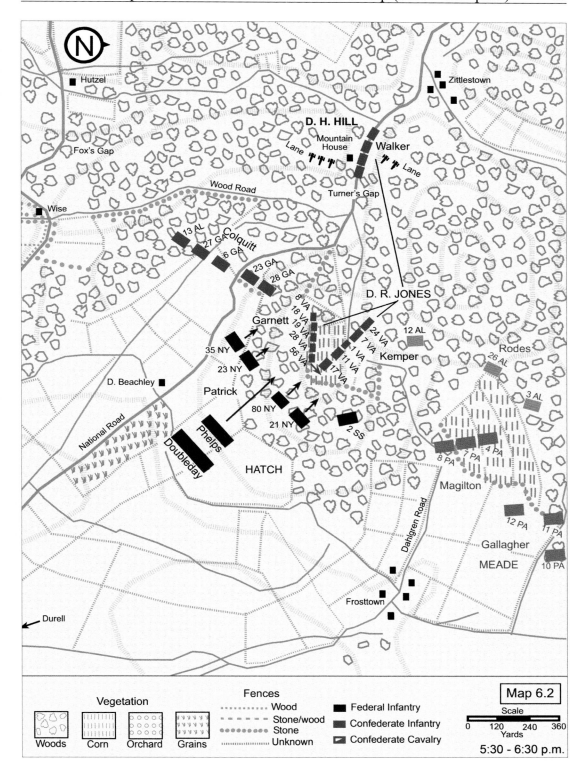

Map 6.3: Hatch's Division Closes on Garnett and Kemper
(6:30 - 7:00 p.m.)

When he observed the danger spearheading its way toward the center of his line, D. H. Hill attempted to blast Patrick's approaching infantry with artillery fire from his guns near the Mountain House. The effort failed abysmally. The artillery fire, complained Hill, was "as harmless as blank-cartridge salutes in honor of a militia general . . . the enemy did not honor by so much as a dodge." Hill attributed this to "little practice of the gunners and to the large angles of depression." The military bearing demonstrated by Hatch's division impressed Hill. "[H]is colors were all flying, and the alignment of his men seemed perfectly preserved," he recalled. "From the top of the mountain the sight was grand and sublime."[9]

The offensive effectiveness of Patrick's brigade deteriorated as the gap between his two wings widened during his increasingly difficult advance up the slope. Simply put, Patrick had lost his ability to keep both wings moving in a coordinated manner. The delay in the advance frustrated Hatch, who rode forward to determine what was happening. The division leader encountered the 35th New York on Patrick's left, but was unable to determine the location of the rest of the brigade. Garnett's position behind a stone fence on the summit of the spur, however, with a band of woods to the front and a cornfield behind it strewn with rocky ledges, was clearly evident.

One of Col. Phelps' aides found Hatch and requested orders for the brigade, which had passed through a gap in the skirmish line and was now bisecting Patrick's widely divided line of battle. Hatch ordered Phelps to advance behind the skirmish line and make for the Rebel lines. In other words, Hatch was ordering Phelps to strike the enemy, even if his attack drove between the wings of Patrick's brigade. The intensity of the fighting increased rapidly thereafter. "The firing was very heavy, the enemy making a desperate resistance, and our troops advancing, with determined courage," confirmed Hatch.[10]

The sudden appearance of so many Yankees rattled Garnett's exhausted and understrength Virginia command. Although their initial volleys were ragged and poorly aimed, the Virginians regained their composure and Yankees were soon falling with regularity. Capt. Henry Owen of the 18th Virginia watched grimly as the Federals approached his line. "A heavy fire was soon opened upon the enemy," he wrote, "but they neither paused nor faltered, and a brief, fierce contest took place along the ridge until the enemy brought up a second line of reinforcements [Phelps' Brigade]." The two sides slugged it out for at least fifteen minutes. Out in the open, Phelps' men were especially hard hit and lost about thirty-five percent of their number during this short but especially intense encounter. With his men caught in this maelstrom of fire, Phelps had two options: retreat or attack. He chose the latter, even though he was convinced he was facing overwhelming numbers.[11]

Two events transpired to change the complexion of the encounter. The first occurred when Hatch was painfully wounded in the leg while riding along Phelps' brigade and was replaced by Brig. Gen. Abner Doubleday. Hatch's fall could have demoralized the men, but instead they were "encouraged by his valor and inspiriting orders," wrote Phelps. The infantry "moved forward with unbroken front, and the engagement became general through my entire line." Phelps may have exaggerated a bit for patriotic purposes, because Hatch later believed he was wounded "at the moment of carrying the fence." The second event that helped turn the tide of battle was when Patrick shifted his left regiments, which had wandered too far to the left, back into the fighting around this same time. The wing composed of the 23rd and 35th New York approached the right side of Garnett's line, which was held by the 8th and 18th Virginia regiments.[12]

Despite Patrick's divided command and Hatch's wounding, the outcome of the fighting was probably never really in doubt as long as the Yankees kept advancing. Garnett's small 400-man brigade was facing Hatch's division of 3,500 men. The determined Federals were simply smothering Kemper and Garnett. According to Phelps, "the conflict at the fence became desperate, many of the enemy at this time being less than 8 rods in our front."[13]

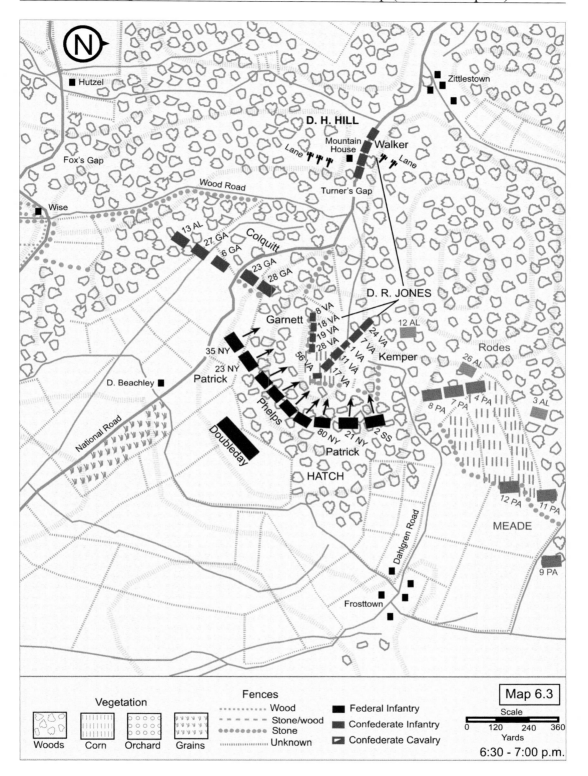

Hutzel

Zittlestown

D. H. HILL

Fox's Gap

Mountain
House   Walker

Lane   Lane

Wood Road

Turner's Gap

Wise

13 AL

27 GA   Colquitt

6 GA

23 GA

28 GA

8 VA   **D. R. JONES**

Garnett   18 VA

19 VA   12 AL

28 VA   7 VA   24 VA

35 NY   56 VA   1 VA   Rodes

23 NY   17 VA   11 VA   Kemper   26 AL

Patrick   D. Beachley   8 PA   7 PA   4 PA   3 AL

Phelps

Doubleday   80 NY   21 NY   2 SS

Patrick   12 PA   11 PA

HATCH   MEADE

National Road

Dahlgren Road

9 PA

Frosttown

Vegetation				Fences		Map 6.3

Fences
.... Wood
- - - - - Stone/wood
●●●●●●● Stone
.... Unknown

Vegetation
Woods   Corn   Orchard   Grains

■ Federal Infantry
■ Confederate Infantry
▨ Confederate Cavalry

Map 6.3

Scale
0   120   240   360
Yards

6:30 - 7:00 p.m.

Map 6.4: Garnett and Kemper are Defeated (7:00 - 7:30 p.m.)

The long line of charging Federal troops blanketing their front told the Virginians that it was time to skedaddle. The right side of Garnett's line, composed of the 8th and 18th Virginia, watched the approach of the 23rd and 35th New York (Patrick's brigade) against their right flank and Phelps' brigade moving against their front. Some of the Virginians began drifting to the rear. They had already sustained almost forty-five percent casualties and, together with their exhausted condition, they had little more left to give. Before long the line was melting away entirely. Capt. Henry Owen of the 18th Virginia remembered the chaotic nature of the retreat: "being greatly outnumbered, [we] suddenly gave way and rushed back down the hill and out in the open field. There was great confusion, and the broken ranks were hard to rally and re-form, so that had the enemy followed up closely behind they could have taken the gap [Turner's] without any difficulty." According to Garnett, it was the left side of his line that retreated first, probably stung by the small arms fire from the right front of Phelps' brigade and men from the 21st and 80th New York of Patrick's brigade.[14]

The 56th Virginia, which had been on the left of Garnett's line, did not join in the retreat because it had been sent father left to keep an eye on Kemper's exposed right flank. Despite its proximity to the attacking Yankees, Kemper's front did not face the assaulting enemy at this time and so was not heavily involved in this part of the fighting.

Some of Garnett's men still had some fight in them, as Owens of the 18th Virginia recalled scattered groups "falling back and fighting as we retreated." He continued: "we reached a fence across the field, and although half of the brigade had disappeared, the survivors made a stand along the fence and endeavored to hold the enemy back until reinforcements could be brought up." The men fought in squads of a dozen or more with large gaps between them, all from behind a fence that provided some protection from Federal bullets. "Many renewed the contest a little farther to the rear," reported Garnett, "but it had now become so dark it was impossible to distinguish objects, except at a

short distance." Many of these Virginia defenders, who by this time probably numbered fewer than 150, were surprised the Federals did not press their victory as aggressively as they otherwise might have done.[15]

Perhaps in an attempt to explain why his brigade did not perform well near Turner's Gap on South Mountain, Garnett added the following to his report: "it had marched (a portion of the time rapidly) between 22 and 23 miles before it went into action; much oppressed by heat and dust; reached its position a short time before sunset under a disheartening fire of artillery, and was attacked by a much superior force as soon as it was formed in line of battle."[16]

Farther west up the slope near the Mountain House, Capt. John Lane watched the retreating Confederate infantry and shifted the orientation of his battery to open fire on the right side of the advancing Federal line. The men of the 21st New York saw the muzzle flashes in the growing darkness and opened fire on the gunners, forcing them to take cover as often as they could. The accuracy of this fire helped silence Lane's guns.[17]

The left three regiments of Kemper's brigade also abandoned their positions, but no one told the men farther to the right and closest to the enemy. The latter quickly crossed the Dahlgren Road and took position behind a fence to await the advance of the Federals. They held this new position until 7:30 p.m., when they fell back.[18]

After their long slog to and up South Mountain and the subsequent fight, Patrick's and Phelps' men were now spent. Doubleday's brigade was called up to relieve them. "[T]he resistance of the enemy being so much more determined than had been anticipated," explained the wounded Hatch, "Doubleday was ordered up." Before leaving the field to seek medical attention, Hatch also requested assistance from Brig. Gen. James Ricketts' division, and before long his two brigades under Col. William Christian and Brig. Gen. George Hartsuff advanced behind Phelps.

The Rebels also received reinforcements about this time in the form of Jenkins' brigade under Col. Joseph Walker. This small South Carolina command also made the long march to the South Mountain battlefield with Kemper's and Garnett's brigades. It was coming up behind Kemper's left flank.[19]

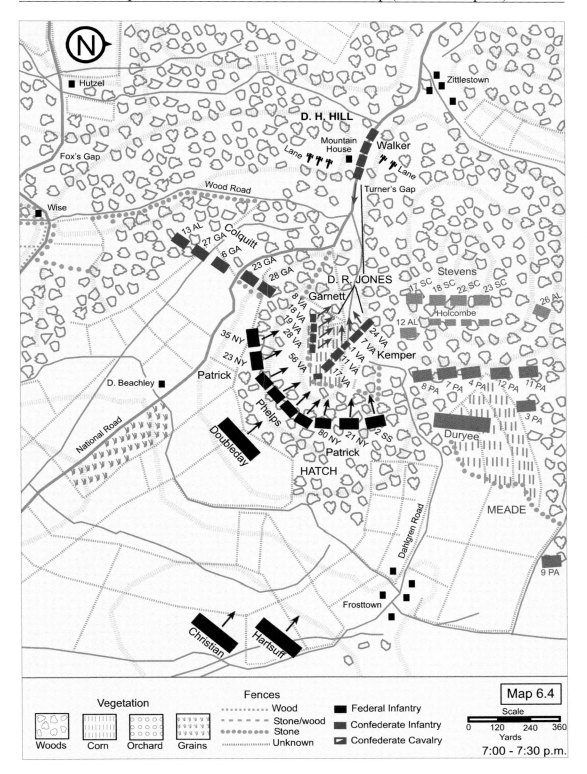

Map 6.4

Scale

0   120   240   360

Yards

7:00 - 7:30 p.m.

Vegetation

Woods   Corn   Orchard   Grains

Fences

·········· Wood

– – – – Stone/wood

●●●●●● Stone

············ Unknown

■ Federal Infantry

■ Confederate Infantry

◪ Confederate Cavalry

Map 6.5: Doubleday Attacks, Walker's Brigade Arrives (7:30 – 8:30 p.m.)

"Our brigade cannot sustain itself much longer as we are nearly out of ammunition. For God's sake, to the front!" screamed the adjutant of Phelps' brigade's when he found Doubleday's brigade resting in the rear. While their colleagues were slugging it out with the enemy on the heights, Doubleday's men were eating or roaming about looking for food. Officers yelled commands and the troops formed and moved to their jumping-off point. The slope was so steep that at times they had to grab saplings and stumps to pull themselves forward.

Doubleday's brigade (now under Lt. Col. Hoffman) knew the enemy's position had been breached, and hoped the Southern defenders were making their way down the far side of the mountain. When the newly arrived infantry moved through Phelps' and Patrick's bloodied and disorganized men in the gathering darkness, however, several volleys passed through their ranks. When the order to "Fix bayonets" arrived the fresh troops complied and their exhausted comrades melted to the rear.[20]

Although Doubleday's men did not know it, they outnumbered the survivors of Kemper's and Garnett's brigades by almost three to one. The darkness, intensity of gunfire, and the fact that the defenders were behind stone walls and fences prevented anyone from grasping the true tactical situation. Some of the Federals reported an initial panic; these were not ideal fighting conditions. Officers helped calm the men and prepare them for the fighting.[21]

Sensing it was now or never, Col. William Wainwright ordered his small 76th New York forward to chase the enemy from their defenses along the Dahlgren Road. When the New Yorkers hesitated, Sgt. Charles Stamp, their disgusted flagbearer, rushed forward alone until he was only sixteen yards from the enemy line. "There, come up to that!" he yelled back to his comrades. Before they could comply, scatterd shots tore through the darkness and Stamp fell dead. His death was followed by a volley directly into the unsuspecting Yankees. According to one of the New Yorkers, "as we neared the summit we . . . receive[d] a well-directed volley full in our faces." Several men bolted for the rear until

officers stopped their flight. Col. Wainwright and his horse went down together in a heap. To the utter shock of most of the onlookers, the remnants of 18th and 19th Virginia regiments hopped over their defenses and advanced to within sixty feet of the Federal line. Shot in the arm, Wainwright emptied his revolver into the approaching enemy as he ordered his men to fire (No. 1).[22]

The rest of Doubleday's brigade opened fire on the determined Virginians, felling a number of them. Some of the 8th Virginia trotted southwest to take up a position along the National Pike to watch for a flank attack.[23]

The impetuous Rebels were withdrawing from their advanced positions when Col. Joseph Walker arrived with his South Carolina brigade. Standing in his stirrups, Walker yelled, "By brigade, right wheel! Forward, charge bayonet!" This movement put the South Carolinians on Garnett's right flank (No. 2).

It was now about 8:00 p.m. Doubleday's brigade was moving to the rear as two of Ricketts' infantry brigades (Col. Christian's and Brig. Gen. Hartsuff's) maneuvered into position. (No. 3) Seeing the approach of the South Carolinians and thinking they were going to flank the Federal left, Col. Wainwright turned his 76th New York and the 7th Indiana next to him and marched them back into the fight. (No. 4) Christian's brigade arrived, relieving Wainwright's men. Several deliberate volleys fired by these fresh troops brought Walker's advance to a halt (No. 5). A fitful firing followed, after which the Confederates withdrew about thirty minutes later.[24]

Hatch's three brigades under Patrick, Phelps, and Doubleday lost a combined 177 men killed, wounded, captured, and/or missing during the fight for Turner's Gap. (Ricketts' division, which played a supporting role, lost only 64 men.) Southern losses were much higher. Garnett lost 196 men, or about one-half of the bayonets he carried to the field. Stevens' losses totaled 210, Kemper's 75, and Walker's 32.

D. H. Hill was right. These troops had taken up the wrong positions, and they paid the price: "in their exhausted condition after a long march, they were broken and scattered."[25]

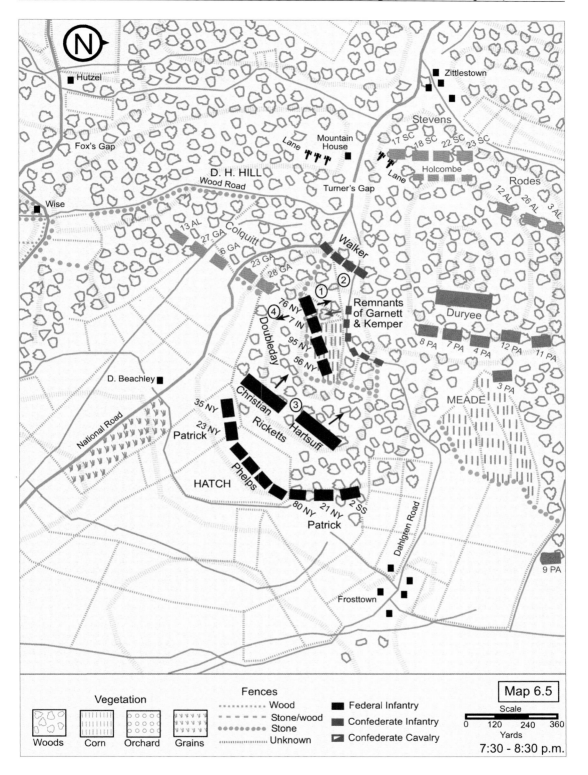

Map 6.5

Scale

0   120   240   360
Yards

7:30 - 8:30 p.m.

Vegetation

Woods   Corn   Orchard   Grains

Fences

··········· Wood
‒ ‒ ‒ ‒ Stone/wood
●●●●●● Stone
············ Unknown

■ Federal Infantry
■ Confederate Infantry
▱ Confederate Cavalry

Map 6.6: Gibbon's "Iron" Brigade Enters the Fight (5:15 - 6:30 p.m.)

While three brigades from Hatch's division (Patrick, Phelps, and Doubleday) maneuvered toward and then attacked Kemper and Garnett north of the National Road, Hatch's fourth and final brigade under Brig. Gen. John Gibbon moved toward Turner's Gap farther south (on the far left) between 5:00 and 5:30 p.m. After leaving Bolivar Gibbon marched astride the pike. The 19th Indiana advanced in a line of battle through the fields left of the road and the 7th Wisconsin on the right, while the 2nd and 6th Wisconsin, left and right of the road respectively, marched behind them in double column (No. 1). A couple of companies were out on the skirmish line. A section of Capt. Joseph B. Campbell's Battery B, 4th U.S. Artillery, brought up the rear. The brigade had been resting along the road for about two hours when Maj. Gen. Ambrose Burnside ordered it to move forward.[26]

Col. Alfred Colquitt watched the Union advance with trepidation while his Southern brigade deployed on a spur astride the National Road. He requested aid from D. H. Hill but, "being pressed at other points, he had none to give me." The Georgian inspected his line, which was bisected by the National Road. His far left was held by the 28th Georgia with the 23rd Georgia extending the line toward to the pike. Each boasted about 300 men. A stone wall covered the front of the 23rd and about one-quarter of the 28th's; both regiments were deployed in the woods. The 23rd Georgia's position was exceptionally strong, commanding a rise in the road about forty yards in its front, and the 28th Georgia could enfilade any Federal troops marching along the road. Two companies from each regiment were thrown forward as skirmishers.

Three of Alfred Colquitt's regiments were deployed to the right of the National Road and extended the line generally southwest toward Fox's Gap in a vain attempt to connect with Confederates there. The 13th Alabama, on Colquitt's far right, had orders to connect with Garland's brigade, but there were not enough men and a 400-yard gap yawned between the two brigades. Next to the Alabamians was most of the 27th Georgia, with the balance (two companies) in line next to the pike. In between was the 6th Georgia. Four infantry companies from the various regiments under Capt. William Arnold were thrown out in the thick woods on the right side of the pike. Although oddly aligned, Colquitt's 1,350 men were rested and ready for action. Lane's battery was in position behind the brigade near the Mountain House. One witness was unimpressed with Lane's artillery: "his shot fly wild, making a good deal of hissing, but doing no harm."[27]

Gibbon's skirmish line encountered a smattering of gunfire from the upper stories of the Beachley house along the pike. When the commander of the 19th Indiana called for artillery support, Stewart's guns unlimbered and fired three times across the gorge, quickly emptying the house of its Southern occupants. Gibbon continued advancing. The left side of his line soon came under fire from Arnold's swarm of skirmishers hidden in the woods. According to Colquitt, Arnold's "sudden and unexpected fire" caused the enemy to fall back in confusion. This was not correct. When he detected enemy soldiers to his left, Gibbon ordered Col. Solomon Meredith of the 19th Indiana to send skirmishers and reconnoiter. Meredith misunderstood the orders and sent his entire regiment angling in that direction (No. 2). Gibbon rectified the situation, but the Hoosier's right flank no longer connected with the National Road, leaving a space that would later be filled by the 2nd Wisconsin.[28]

According to Meredith, "their skirmishers soon opened a sharp fire upon ours, which made it necessary for us to push forward. We then opened fire on the enemy at short range, who were concealed . . . under cover. The fire became general on both sides. The Nineteenth gave a shout, and pressed forward . . . cheering all the time." After driving the enemy about three-quarters of a mile, added Meredith, "I discovered a stone fence in front, which the enemy had fallen back to." Meredith was describing the center-right of Colquitt's front held by the 6th Georgia.[29]

On the right side of the road, meanwhile, the 7th Wisconsin came under an oblique fire on its left from the 23th Georgia and the enemy across the National Road. The Badgers quickly swung around to face this new threat, but the movement presented the regiment's right flank and rear to the 28th Georgia, which quickly obliged and poured a devastating fire into it (No. 3).[30]

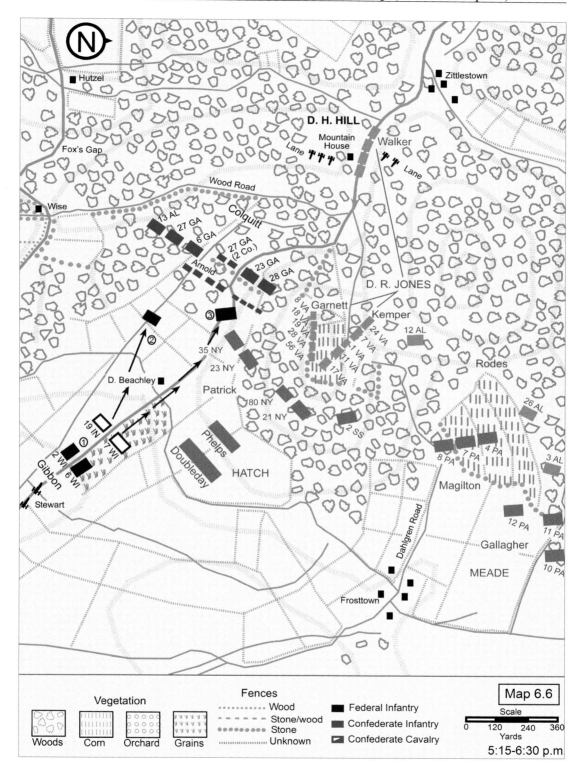

Hutzel

Zittlestown

D. H. HILL

Mountain
House

Walker

Lane

Lane

Fox's Gap

Wise

Wood Road

Colquitt

13 AL

27 GA

6 GA

27 GA
(2 Co.)

23 GA

28 GA

Arnold

D. R. JONES

Garnett

Kemper

8 VA
18 VA
19 VA
28 VA
56 VA

24 VA

7 VA

12 AL

③

1 VA

11 VA

35 NY

17 VA

23 NY

Rodes

D. Beachley

Patrick

②

80 NY

26 AL

21 NY

2 SS

19 IN

7 WI

①

Phelps

8 PA

7 PA

4 PA

3 AL

2 WI

6 WI

Gibbon

Doubleday

HATCH

Magilton

Stewart

12 PA

11 PA

Dahlgren Road

Gallagher

MEADE

10 PA

Frosttown

Vegetation

Woods   Corn   Orchard   Grains

Fences

.... Wood
– – – – – – Stone/wood
●●●●●●● Stone
.... Unknown

■ Federal Infantry
▬ Confederate Infantry
▰ Confederate Cavalry

Map 6.6

Scale

0   120   240   360
Yards

5:15-6:30 p.m

Map 6.7: The "Iron" Brigade Defeats Colquitt's Brigade (6:30 - 9:00 p.m.)

The 7th Wisconsin on Gibbon's right was in trouble. An aide rode for the rear and found help in the form of Lt. Col. Edward Bragg's 6th Wisconsin. Half of that regiment took up a new position on the right of the 7th Wisconsin (No. 1). The left wing of the 6th Wisconsin, however, was unable to fire because it was behind the right side of the embattled 7th Wisconsin.[31]

Lt. Col. Bragg ordered the right wing to move forward to prevent a flanking movement on the 7th Wisconsin, and then ordered his left wing to move behind it. "Have your men lie down on the ground, I am going over you!" Bragg yelled to Maj. Rufus Dawes, his second in command leading the right wing. The left wing moved through the prone right wing and fired a volley into the woods, hit the ground, and waited while the right wing moved through them and fired another volley. This outstanding tactical movement occurred several times as the 6th Wisconsin leapfrogged its way closer to the enemy position.[32]

The 19th Indiana and 2nd Wisconsin on the left of the road, meanwhile, continued their approach toward the Rebel lines as Colquitt's men opened fire on them. "At that point they were annoying us very much," admitted the 19th Indiana's Col. Meredith, who rode over to the commander of Company G and told him to "wheel his company to the left, and move by the right flank until he could command the line of battle lying directly behind the stone fence." The move worked and the two companies of the 27th Georgia behind the wall were driven back. My men, reported Meredith, "opened a flank fire upon the enemy, causing them to retreat precipitately" (No. 2).[33]

With their immediate front clear of enemy soldiers, the right side of Col. Lucius Fairchild's 2nd Wisconsin was ordered to oblique to the right and throw an enfilade fire into the right flank of the 23rd Georgia as the 7th Wisconsin raked its front. When the right wing's ammunition ran low, Fairchild ordered his left wing to pour fire into the Georgians. They were replaced by the right side of the 19th Indiana and then the companies holding the left side of that regiment. Despite the tremendous firepower

brought to bear against them, the 23rd and 28th Georgia regiments used their stone walls to advantage and refused to budge (No. 3).[34]

Watching from the north side of the road, Col. Colquitt wrote, "Confident in their superior numbers, the enemy's forces advanced to a short distance of our own lines, when, raising a shout, they came to a charge . . . they were met by a terrific musketry . . . this gave a sudden check to their advance. They rallied under cover of the uneven ground, and the fight opened in earnest. They made still another effort to advance, but were kept back by the steady fire of our men." Col. Bragg tried to move his wing farther up the hill to flank the 28th Georgia, but it was just too dark to drive the enemy from their stone wall.[35]

By now it was almost 9:00 p.m. and the firing had all but ended. When Gibbon heard that his men were out of ammunition, he ordered them to hold their segment of the mountainside with their bayonets. Somehow the Rebels still held Turner's Gap despite the firepower of a large division thrown against three small and one average-sized Rebel brigades. "The fight continued with fury until after dark," Colquitt wrote at the end of his official report. "Not an inch of ground was yielded. The ammunition of many of the men was exhausted, but they stood with bayonets fixed." In reality, Colquitt's men had fallen back up the hill in disarray at the end of the combat. The fight for Turner's Gap was over.[36]

Despite Colquitt's retreat, the gallant effort to hold the pass throughout that long afternoon and evening had prevented the Federals from entering Pleasant Valley. Losses were heavy on both sides. During the short but sharp fighting at Turner's Gap Gibbon's brigade lost 37 killed, 252 wounded, and 30 missing for a total of 319 against Colquitt's losses from all causes of 110.[37]

D. H. Hill was justifiably proud of his men. The action, he wrote in his report, was "one of the most remarkable and creditable of the war. The division had marched all the way from Richmond, and the straggling had been enormous in consequence of heavy marches, deficient commissariat, want of shoes, and inefficient officers. . . . [T]he division numbered less than 5,000 on the morning of September 14, and had five roads to guard, extending over a space of as many miles."[38]

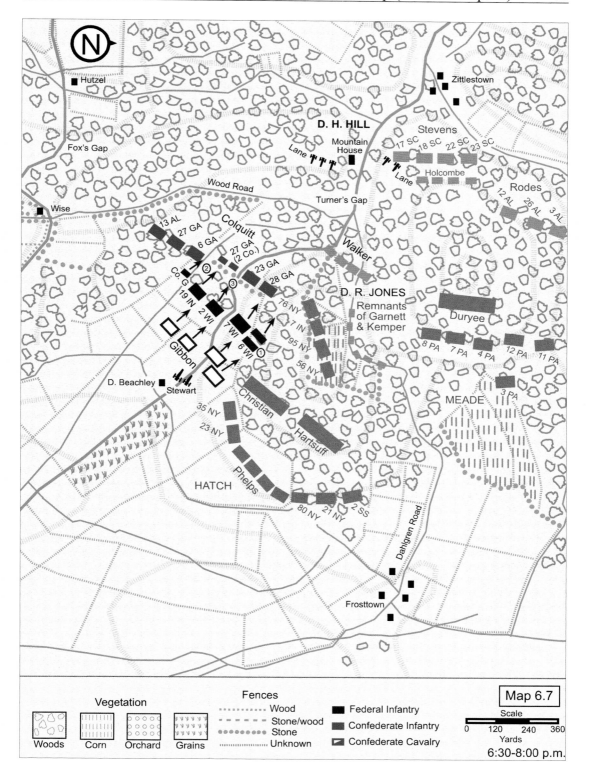

N

Hutzel

Fox's Gap

Wise

Wood Road

D. H. HILL

Mountain House

Lane

Turner's Gap

Zittlestown

Stevens

17 SC   18 SC   22 SC   23 SC

Holcombe

Rodes

12 AL   26 AL   3 AL

13 AL

27 GA

6 GA

Colquitt

27 GA (2 Co.)

Co. G

② ①

③

19 IN   2 WI   7 WI   6 WI   ①

23 GA

28 GA

76 NY

7 IN

95 NY

56 NY

Walker

D. R. JONES
Remnants of Garnett & Kemper

Duryee

8 PA   7 PA   4 PA   12 PA   11 PA

Gibbon

D. Beachley   Stewart

35 NY

23 NY

Christian

Hartsuff

3 PA

MEADE

Phelps

HATCH

80 NY   21 NY   2 SS

Dahlgren Road

Frosttown

Fences

.... Wood

– – – – Stone/wood

●●●●●●● Stone

.... Unknown

Vegetation

Woods   Corn   Orchard   Grains

■ Federal Infantry

■ Confederate Infantry

◤ Confederate Cavalry

Map 6.7

Scale

0   120   240   360
Yards

6:30-8:00 p.m.

Map Set 7. South Mountain: Crampton's Gap
(11:00 a.m. - 7:00 p.m.)

Map 7.1: The Confederates Deploy
(11:00 a.m. - 12:30 p.m.)

While the Federal I Corps and IX Corps assaulted Fox's and Turner's gaps, the Federal VI Corps under Maj. Gen. William Franklin advanced toward Crampton's Gap farther south. After forcing its way through the pass, the VI Corps had orders to march on Rohrersville in Pleasant Valley to cut off Lafayette McLaws' Confederate division, which was participating in the reduction of Harpers Ferry.

Maj. Gen. Henry Slocum's division led Franklin's advance. The corps left Buckeystown at 6:00 a.m. on the morning of September 14 for Burkittsville but halted just beyond Jefferson to wait for Darius Couch's division of the IV Corps. When Couch failed to show up, Franklin put his column on the march again between 10:00 a.m. - 10:30 a.m. Known as a cautious general, Franklin knew he could not linger any longer. Slocum's Second Brigade under Col. Joseph Bartlett was the first to enter Burkittsville. Capt. Basil Manly's Rebel rifled guns deployed near Brownsville Pass opened fire on the 96th Pennsylvania as it marched forward with two companies on the skirmish line. The accurate firing convinced the Federal high command that their attack should be made against Crampton's Gap and not the pass at Brownsville.[1]

Brig. Gen. Paul Semmes, who led a brigade in McLaws' division, was tasked with holding Crampton's Gap and the Brownsville Pass with two understrength brigades (his own and another under Col. William Parham). Numbers were not the only problem the Rebels faced. Semmes had never led a brigade in battle. The native Georgian believed the main Federal push would be against Brownsville Pass, so he stationed most of his brigade there. The 10th Georgia was on picket duty along the Rohrersville Road, keeping an eye on the routes coming out ofrom Harpers Ferry. Cavalry commander Jeb Stuart assigned Col. Thomas Munford to defend Crampton's Gap, and he was now in command of that sector. There was not much to command. In addition to his own 2nd and 12th Virginia Cavalry and Capt. R. Preston Chew's three-gun battery of horse artillery, Munford was given Parham's 16th Virginia infantry. Two other regiments in Parham's command, the 6th and 12th Virginia, occupied Brownsville Pass supported by two guns from Capt. Cary Grimes' battery and four more belonging to Capt. Basil Manly. In all, fewer than 1,000 men spread across a mile and a half were about to be called upon to halt the passage of nearly 13,000 Yankees.[2]

By now it was about 12:30 p.m. Army commander Maj. Gen. George B. McClellan wanted immediate action, but Franklin was content to rest Slocum's division while Maj. Gen. William Smith's division approached Burkittsville. Only two Federal batteries met Manly's initial artillery challenge. While the Federals lingered, the Rebels sprang into action. Munford deployed Parham's Virginia regiments (the 6th, 12th, and 16th) in an unusual manner. Rather than using South Mountain's steep slope to his best advantage, the cavalryman deployed the infantry at the base of the hill along Mountain Church Road, where he did enjoy a wider field of fire. The 16th was aligned astride the road leading to Burkittsville (West Main Street). The 2nd Virginia Cavalry dismounted and formed on either side of the Virginia infantrymen. The 12th Virginia, which numbered just 75 men for the entire regiment, crouched behind a stone wall just north of the Grams house. Because of the long front that needed to be defended, there was about eight feet between each man. The 6th Virginia formed on the left of the 12th. Because of terrain irregularities, no one in the 12th Virginia could see anyone in the 16th Virginia. The small 12th Virginia Cavalry was deployed on the left along the Arnoldstown Road.

Semmes, who was still at the Brownsville Pass, released a 6-pounder from the Richmond Fayette Battery and another from the Magruder Light Artillery. Chew's and Grimes' batteries dropped trail about halfway down the Gapland Road. Munford had covered his half-mile defensive line with strength on both ends while leaving the middle weak. The left flank was made stronger by the arrival of eight companies of the 10th Georgia of Semmes' brigade, which formed on the left of the 6th Virginia; the last two companies stayed in the rear by the A. M. E. Church.[3]

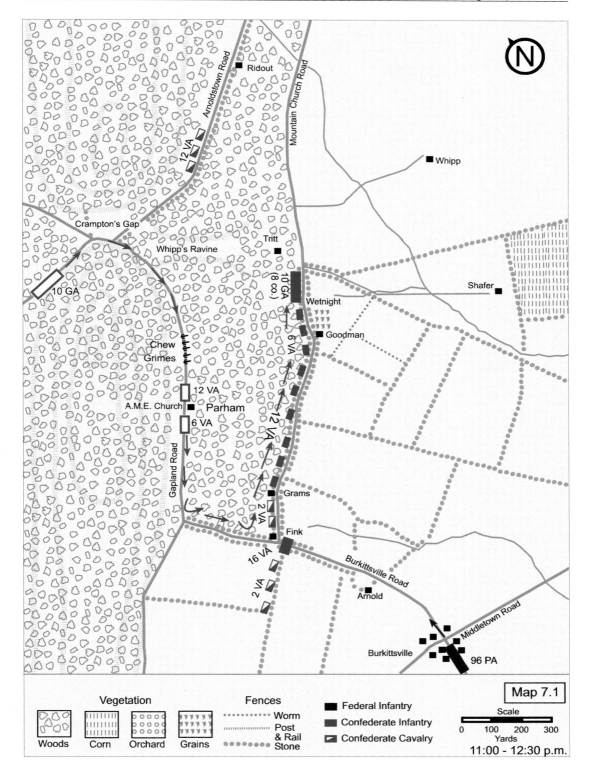

Map 7.1

11:00 - 12:30 p.m.

Map 7.2: Federal Troops Deploy (4:00 - 5:00 p.m.)

The decision on how to force the passage through Crampton's Gap was apparently made by Col. Joseph Bartlett, one of Slocum's brigade commanders.

The inexperienced brigadier and former lawyer from New York must have had misgivings when he was ordered to see Gen. Franklin, who was pleasantly conversing with two division commanders as well as several brigade commanders when Bartlett arrived. The men, wrote the young officer, were "grouped there, resting upon the ground, in as comfortable positions as each one could assume, after lunch, smoking their cigars." The group had discussed its options and cast an informal vote, which ended in a tie. Bartlett was called in to cast the deciding vote, even though he was the only non-West Pointer of the bunch. "Without a moment's hesitation I replied, 'On the right [of the road].'" Bartlett was at first incredulous about this encounter, and then his emotions changed. "I was naturally indignant that I should be called upon to give even an opinion upon such an important matter without previously hearing the views of such old and experienced officers upon such an important question." The other officers explained that Bartlett was the only one among them who had studied the ground over which the attack would be made. When division commander Slocum asked for additional advice, Bartlett replied, "[I]t is no more than fair that I should leave to you the formation." Still, Bartlett "suggested the formation of the three brigades in column of regiments deployed, two regiments toward a point I indicated to him, at nearly right angles to the road which crossed the mountain."[4]

Slocum's division entered Burkittsville with Bartlett's brigade in the van, which deployed to the right of West Main Street. Brig. Gen. Alfred Torbert's First New Jersey Brigade moved up on his left, with his own left near the Burkittsville Road. Brig. Gen. John Newton's brigade deployed between the two units.[5]

Bartlett unleashed his skirmish line, composed of the 27th New York, about 4:00 p.m. "[A]s secretly as possible [I was to advance] to a large field near its base, where the column of attack was to be formed," he later reported,

"each brigade in two lines, at 200 paces in the rear." Bartlett threw the rest of his brigade forward at quick time. The 5th Maine was on the left of the first line and the 16th New York was on its right. Newton's brigade had orders to advance behind Bartlett to provide support. When he looked back, however, Bartlett saw Newton's men, "by some unexplained and accountable mistake," more than 1,000 yards in his rear. He ordered in his 27th New York skirmish line, the 5th Maine and 16th New York to sweep forward. They halted at a rail fence on a rise about 300 yards from the Virginians manning the stone wall at the base of the mountain. Because of their exposed position, these Federal regiments lost heavily. Bartlett later complimented his men for their "most undaunted courage and steadiness" for attacking alone against what he thought were overwhelming numbers holding a strong position.[6]

Bartlett had two other regiments to utilize that afternoon. The 96th Pennsylvania, which had led the column to Burkittsville, was now to the left, as it had followed Torbert's First New Jersey Brigade when it left the town. The other regiment, the 121st New York, was so green that Bartlett decided to retain it in the rear as a reserve.[7] Torbert's New Jersey troops deployed just to the right of the Burkittsville Road in two lines with the 1st New Jersey on the right of the first line and the 2nd New Jersey on its left. The second line, about 150 yards behind the first, was composed of the 3rd and 4th New Jersey regiments.[8]

As the Federals deployed, Company C of the 16th Virginia ventured boldly forward and attacked the Federal left flank. This movement was quickly repulsed, but it convinced Franklin to deploy Brig. Gen. William Brooks' Vermont brigade on the left side of the Burkittsville Road to watch that exposed part of the line.[9]

The Confederates were heavily outnumbered that afternoon, and were about to be outgeneraled. While most of the Union brigade and divisional commanders were West Point graduates, two Southern brigade leaders who would play a large role defending Crampton's Gap were not. Howell Cobb was a lawyer and a politician, and Paul Semmes had been a Georgia banker and plantation owner.[10]

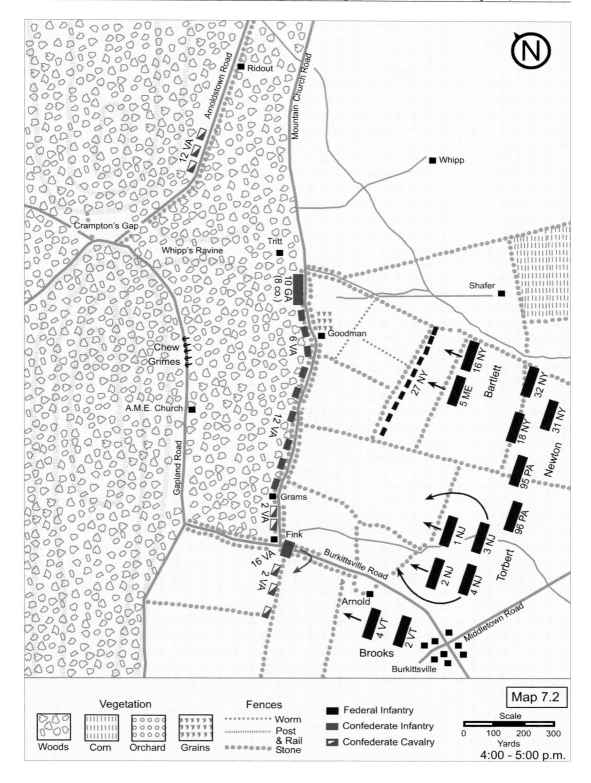

Map 7.2

Vegetation

Woods   Corn   Orchard   Grains

Fences
.... Worm
.... Post
& Rail
●●●●●● Stone

■ Federal Infantry
■ Confederate Infantry
◪ Confederate Cavalry

Scale
0   100   200   300
Yards

4:00 - 5:00 p.m.

Map 7.3: Pre-Battle Positioning
(5:00 - 5:30 p.m.)

After an anxious wait, Newton's men moved up behind Bartlett. The 18th New York advanced on the left and the 32nd New York was on the right, followed by the 95th and 31st New York. With reinforcements up and his ammunition almost expended, Bartlett withdrew and reformed his two regiments about twenty paces behind Newton's brigade. Bartlett's 96th Pennsylvania, meanwhile, moved from the left of the brigade, near Torbert's New Jerseyians, to the right of where his brigade had been deployed.[11]

More reinforcements for the heavily outnumbered Confederates were on the way. Brig. Gen. Howell Cobb received orders at 1:00 p.m. to move his brigade back to Brownsville Pass from Sandy Hook to reinforce Semmes. His troops arrived about 4:00 p.m. About an hour later, a horseman from Col. Tom Munford pulled up his mount to plead for reinforcements for Crampton's Gap: the Federals were deploying opposite that point in heavy numbers. Cobb dispatched his two largest regiments, the 24th Georgia and 15th North Carolina, but they were barely underway when Cobb received another message from Gen. McLaws ordering the rest of Cobb's brigade to hoof it immediately to Crampton's Gap. The remainder of McLaws' command was well to the south reducing Harpers Ferry. He could not allow the Federals to get into his rear. McLaws adamantly instructed Cobb that he must "hold the gap if it cost the life of every man in [your] command."[12]

When Cobb reached the gap about thirty minutes later, Munford relinquished command of the sector to the politician-turned-general and returned to brigade command. Unsure of the lay of the land, Cobb asked Munford to place his arriving infantry to their best advantage. By this time the Federal attack (see Map 7.4) was underway in earnest. The 24th Georgia and 15th North Carolina moved to the left of the line. The 15th North Carolina deployed itself along the Arnoldstown Road and the 24th Georgia moved down the slope to form a new line in the woods behind the 10th Georgia. The 16th Georgia and Cobb's Legion formed on the right of the 24th when they arrived a short time later. Again, Cobb

had asked Munford to place his men in position when they arrived. Munford was anything but pleased with Cobb and his Georgians, and he let it be known in his report when he wrote, "they [16th Georgia and Cobb's Legion] behaved badly and did not get in position before the wildest confusion commenced." These regiments deployed near where Chew's guns had been posted before moving back up to the summit of the mountain.[13]

When he heard distant cheering from beyond Mountain Church Road, Col. Bartlett realized reinforcements had joined the Rebel defenders. It was with some trepidation that he prepared to kick off the charge. Before all three brigades could be launched in unison, however, Torbert's brigade broke from cover about 5:30 p.m. to initiate the attack. The New Jersey brigade had participated in several battles but had yet to taste the fruits of victory. Worse, its 4th New Jersey had been captured almost en masse at Gaines' Mill during the Seven Days' Battles earlier that summer in Virginia. Recently exchanged, its members sought to redeem their reputation. In their enthusiasm, many Jerseymen mounted the wall to shout a volley of oaths against the Virginians, who leveled their rifles and picked off several of the careless blueclad infantrymen.[14]

Torbert ordered his 3rd and 4th New Jersey, which formed his brigade's second line, to move forward to spearhead the attack against the Virginians, and then launched his original first line forward as well. The 1st and 2nd New Jersey in this new second line may have been upset about not being in the lead, so they closed quickly on the first line in what can only be described as a dense formation. If the Confederates had deployed artillery along the Mountain Church Road, the guns would have devastated Torbert's men. But no guns were there, and the Union infantry came on in what looked to be an unstoppable fashion. Some of Manly's Southern guns positioned between the two gaps opened fire on the New Jersey troops, but the distance was long and the shots largely harmless.[15]

The battle of Crampton's Gap, and by extention the fate of Lafayette McLaws' command operating beyond against Harpers Ferry, was now underway.

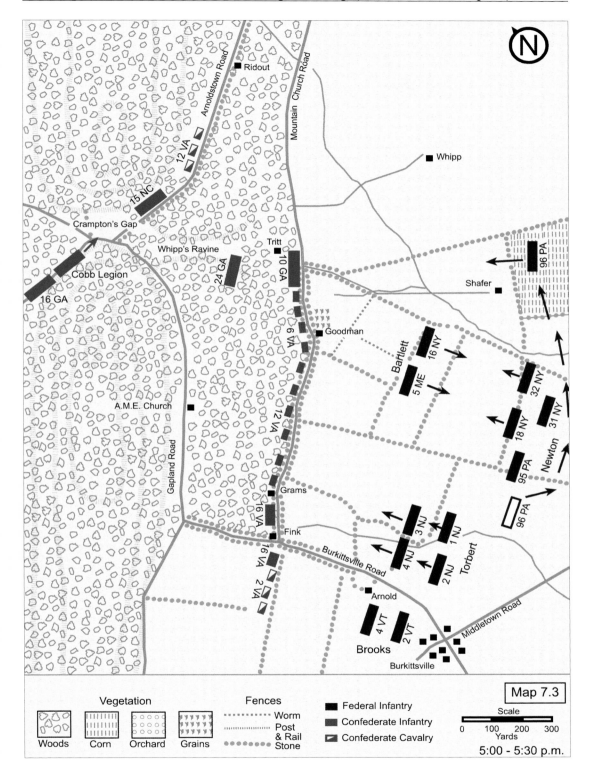

Vegetation

Woods   Corn   Orchard   Grains

Fences

········ Worm
········ Post
& Rail
●●●●●● Stone

■ Federal Infantry
■ Confederate Infantry
▨ Confederate Cavalry

Map 7.3

Scale

0   100   200   300
Yards

5:00 - 5:30 p.m.

Map 7.4: The Confederates Abandon their Defenses (5:30 - 5:45 p.m.)

Rushing across the open fields toward the stone wall, Torbert's New Jerseymen screamed, "Remember Manassas and Gaines' Mill!" referencing two of their more notable defeats. These soldiers had been beaten in every prior engagement in which they had participated; this time they would not be denied. The Virginians of the 16th regiment and most of those in the small 12th Virginia opposite the attack by the Union left knew there was no stopping the onrushing waves of infantry and began falling back up the rough slope of South Mountain.[16]

Tasked with coordinating the attack on the Rebel positions at the base of Crampton's Gap, Col. Bartlett ordered the rest of the division into action. He rode over to the 96th Pennsylvania of his own brigade, which had moved from the far left to the extreme right flank, and told its commander Col. Henry Cake, "We have no artillery . . . we can do nothing without it. If you will take the 96th into that field to the right and charge the wall it would be glorious work." Cake agreed and later noted, "Brisk musketry firing was in progress on our left, but the good cover in possession of the enemy and the distance at which we stood rendered it quite certain that we could gain nothing at a stand-off fight . . . it was evident that nothing but a rush forward would win." With a shout, Cake's Pennsylvanians launched their charge across open grassy fields.

Obstructions forced Cake to halt his men twice to reform their ranks. Well-aimed volleys from the 10th Georgia crouching behind a stone wall along Mountain Church Road ripped through the Pennsylvanians when they emerged from a large cornfield. Higher up the side of the mountain, the 24th Georgia also opened fire. According to Cake, his men were "shocked, but not repulsed [and] the men bounded forward, determined to end it with the bayonet." The Georgians were just as determined to stand fast, knowing they occupied the vulnerable left flank of the line defending Crampton's Gap. Hand-to-hand fighting broke out along parts of the wall and for a few moments the issue was in doubt. Within a short time, however, the longer Pennsylvania line wrapped around the Georgians' exposed left flank and their defensive

effort unraveled. The Southerners began withdrawing toward Whipp's Ravine, their role in the battle already at an end.[17]

If the Pennsylvanians of the 96th had looked to their left and rear they would have seen the 32nd New York of Newton's brigade huffing toward the Rebel line. On their left was the 18th New York, with the 31st New York and 95th Pennsylvania extending the line toward the Burkittsville Road. The 16th New York and the 5th Maine of Bartlett's brigade advanced with fixed bayonets behind Newton's front. The five Confederate artillery pieces deployed at Brownsville Pass continued taking a toll on the attacking line. Confederate troops supporting these guns had a grand view of the battlefield. None of them had ever seen so many Yankees in one place before. "It was a grand sight," admitted one of them. "I will never forget it." Light gunfire, meanwhile, erupted beyond the right-front of the 96th Pennsylvania, where several Georgians had barricaded themselves in the stone Tritt house. Col. Cake cleared the house, eyed the daunting mountain looming above him, and ordered his men up the side of it.[18]

The men of the 6th Virginia and remnants of the 12th Virginia holding the stone wall along the Mountain Church Road just to the right of the 10th Georgia were stretched to the breaking point. Many did their best, remaining in place and firing at Newton's approaching troops. Farther south below the Burkittsville Road, troopers of the 2nd Virginia Cavalry had dismounted and were fighting as infantry against the Vermonters of Brooks' brigade. The Federal troops, "roaring like bulls . . . and howling like devils let loose from the infernal regions," wrote one Virginian, were simply unstoppable. Like the Georgians farther north, the remaining Virginians realized it was a lost cause and turned and rushed up the side of the mountain. By the time the Federal troops reached the wall, there were no Virginians there left to vanquish.

The Federal attackers stopped to take stock of what they had just accomplished and reorganize their ranks, firing at any Confederates still within view. Howell Cobb and Tom Munford, meanwhile, were scrambling as fast as they could to deploy the newly arriving reinforcements from Cobb's Georgia command.[19]

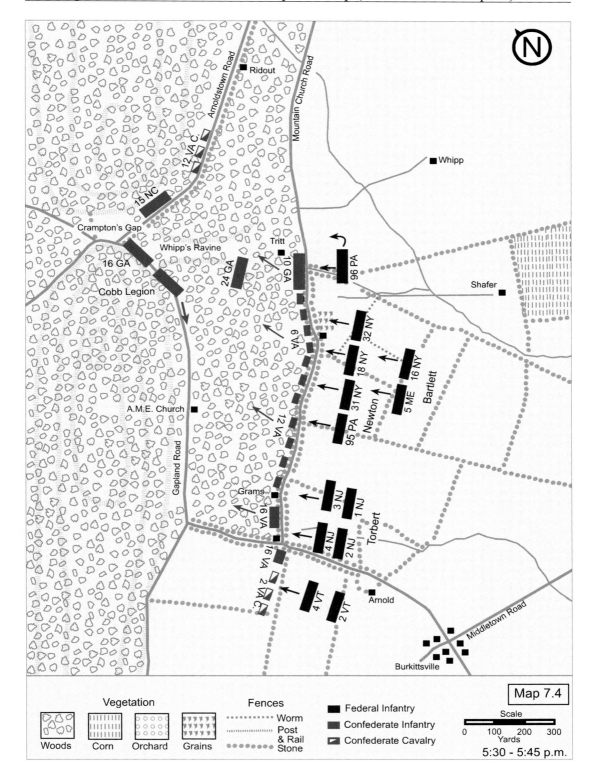

Woods Corn Orchard Grains

Vegetation

Fences
········· Worm
············· Post
& Rail
●●●●●●●● Stone

■ Federal Infantry
█ Confederate Infantry
▨ Confederate Cavalry

Map 7.4

Scale
0   100   200   300
Yards

5:30 - 5:45 p.m.

Map 7.5: The Destruction of Cobb's Legion (5:45 - 6:15 p.m.)

While the Federal right and center crushed the Confederate units behind the stone walls in their front, Brooks' brigade on the far left of the line launched its attack against the Confederate right flank. The results were the same; only the units were different.

The 4th Vermont, followed closely by the 2nd Vermont, moved forward against the remainder of the 16th Virginia and 2nd Virginia Cavalry to the right of West Main Street (also called the Burkittsville Road). Col. William Irwin's brigade advanced in the rear of Brooks' Vermont troops. Realizing the futility of trying to hold an untenable position, the two Virginia units pulled back in search of a safer defensive position.

From his position at Brownsville Pass, Brig. Gen. Paul Semmes watched the Vermont troops breach the front and then scamper up the hillside. He ordered Manly's battery to open fire on them, but the Green Mountain boys were moving too fast and any casualties the guns inflicted were inconsequential. With the determined Federals scrambling up the hill in front of them, and with both of his flanks in the air, Maj. Robert E. McMillan of the 24th Georgia, part of Howell Cobb's brigade, pulled his regiment back along the Gapland Road toward the pass.[20]

By this time the men of Torbert's First New Jersey Brigade had caught their breath and set out to pursue the defeated enemy in earnest. This meant scaling the steep side of South Mountain. Less than halfway up the slope, the Jerseymen spotted a fairly large group of enemy soldiers to their right, so they swung in that direction. These Confederates belonged to Lt. Col. Jefferson Lamar's Cobb's Legion, which formed the new Confederate right flank after the rapid exit of the 16th Virginia. As Tom Munford noted in his after-action report, the small 250-man Legion arrived and began deploying just as the Virginians were retreating from the wall. These troops, Munford confirmed, were tardy getting into position and could have been ready for the onslaught. Instead, they found themselves in a very vulnerable condition and position at the worst possible moment.

The Legion's Georgians opened fire on the 4th New Jersey approaching their front, and seemed to be holding their own for a time when a cry from the right of the line announced that enemy soldiers were attacking from that quarter as well. The 1,200 victorious soldiers from the New Jersey brigade heavily outnumbered the small Georgia unit and their front overlapped the Legion when the 1st, 2nd, and 3rd regiments turned and struck its right flank.

Despite the disparity in numbers and his tenuous tactical position, Lamar decided to stand tall and take on the Jerseymen. He knew he needed to buy time for the Virginians on his right to get away from the enemy troops who had driven them up the side of the mountain, and that the pass had to be held. Perhaps Cobb had conveyed Gen. McLaws' admonition that Cobb and his men were to "hold the gap if it cost the life of every man in [your] command." The Georgians would pay dearly for Lamar's decision.

Lamar refused his right flank and took on the enemy attacking his command from two sides. The 3rd New Jersey circled around to the Legion's rear. The bullets flew from several directions and killed and wounded large numbers of Georgians. The steep slope made it difficult to mount a defense, restricted movement, and caused many to lose their balance and fall. Some in the Legion had the good sense to seek safety in the rear, but Lamar stopped them with plaintive cries to help him. After several minutes even Lamar realized the futility of his actions and ordered a retreat by the left flank. Lamar fell with a mortal wound and scores of men were captured. Some of the New Jersey soldiers realized their actions bordered on murder and tried to end the killing by closing the trap. The only avenue open for the surviving Georgians was up the side of the mountain toward Crampton's Gap. When the fighting ended, Lt. Col. Lamar's small command had lost nearly 80% of its men on the mountainside.[21]

With the entire line crumbling in the face of overwhelming strength, Howell Cobb sent an urgent message to Semmes to send reinforcements to Crampton's Gap. Semmes complied by putting the 15th and 32nd Virginia and 53rd Georgia on the road before galloping ahead to see what he could do to help the deteriorating situation.[22]

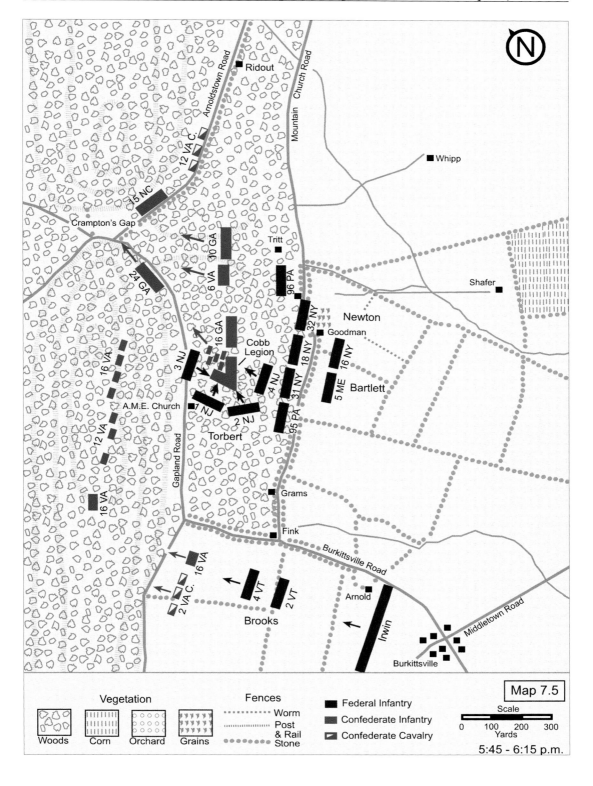

Map 7.5

5:45 - 6:15 p.m.

Map 7.6: The Federals Continue up the Mountainside (6:15 - 6:30 p.m.)

As the 96th Pennsylvania began its sweep up the side of the mountain, the 18th and 32nd New York on its left lagged a bit behind and obliqued to their right to follow the 96th Pennsylvania toward Whipp's Ravine. The 16th New York, which had been following the attack on the Mountain Church Road in the second line, now surged forward and climbed the side of the mountain, taking the route the 18th New York would have taken had it not veered to the right. Those who had once manned the Mountain Church Road line were not the only Rebels in flight at this time. Seeing the determined Federal advance up the side of the mountain, the 12th Virginia Cavalry along Arnoldstown Road galloped to safety.[23]

When the 15th and 32nd Virginia and 53rd Georgia dispatched by Gen. Semmes arrived, their officers realized they were now behind enemy lines and headed back toward the Brownsville Pass as quickly as possible.[24]

The Green Mountain boys continued their ascent up the steep slope on the Federal left without encountering any resistance. Near the crest, the adjutant of the 4th Vermont, Lt. George Hooker, was ordered to take four companies and move to the left to silence Manly's battery. On the way, the men encountered a large group of exhausted Confederate soldiers. When Hooker realized the number of enemy soldiers exceeded 100, he boldly proclaimed that a large force of Federal troops was nearby and they had best surrender to him. They did, and thirty years later he received the Medal of Honor for his gallantry.[25]

The 16th Georgia had taken a position on a ledge on the side of the mountain on the left of the Cobb Legion, but was now in a precarious situation. The retreat of the 6th Virginia along Mountain Church Road exposed the front of the Georgia regiment, and the 18th New York was approaching rapidly. The destruction of Cobb's Legion opened the way for Torbert's First New Jersey brigade to strike the 16th Georgia's right flank and rear. "They fell back on our right and let the enemy flank us," Eli Landers of the 16th Georgia wrote to his mother. "They come near taking all of our regiment prisoners." Many of

Torbert's men were advancing on the Gapland Road above the Georgians, firing down into the beleaguered defenders. It was now every man for himself. Those Georgians making their way to the left, toward Whipp's Ravine, were shot down by members of the 96th Pennsylvania and the 18th and 32nd New York. Most of the men merely turned to their left and ascended the mountain's steep shoulder. The 16th New York joined in the mopping-up process, and small knots of exhausted Confederates were captured. A ruse by a single Federal soldier, James Allen, convinced fourteen Confederates to surrender. For this act of heroism, Allen was promoted to corporal that same day and in 1890 received the Medal of Honor. The New Yorkers also came away with the 16th Georgia's battle flag.[26]

Seeing the approach of the 96th Pennsylvania in and around Whipp's Ravine in their front, and the New Jersey regiments from Torbert's brigade moving along Gapland Road to the right, the 24th Georgia, which was deployed along this road, wisely opted to scale the heights to safety.[27]

With the defeat of the 16th Georgia, the 96th Pennsylvania and 16th, 18th, and 32nd New York continued their ascent up the side of the mountain through Whipp's Ravine. The 15th North Carolina, deployed behind a stone wall along the Arnoldstown Road fronting the ravine, was the last of Cobb's Brigade still in position. Although the Federal regiments were fairly jumbled up at this time, the North Carolinians could count battle flags and knew they were tremendously outnumbered. Worse, they were now receiving fire from three sides. They all felt a sense of relief when they heard their officers yelling orders for their retreat.[28]

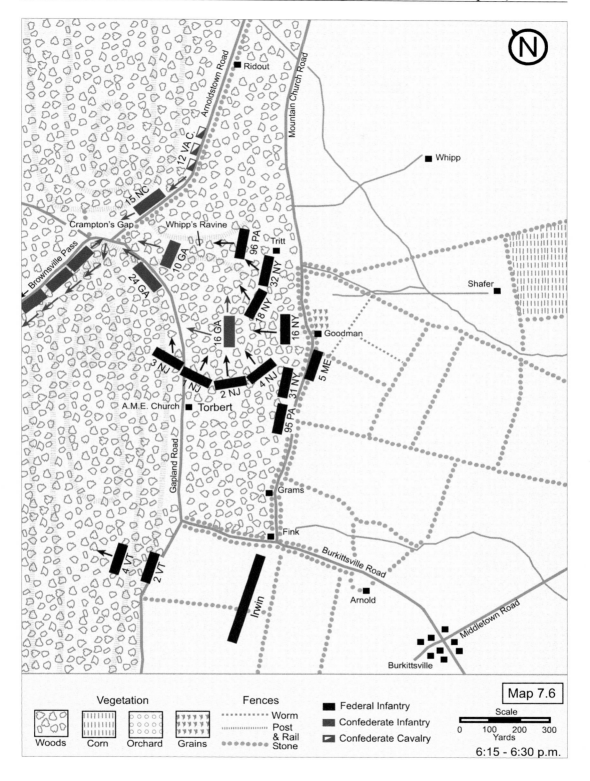

Map 7.6

6:15 - 6:30 p.m.

Map 7.7: The Fight at Padgett's Field (6:30 - 7:00 p.m.)

Although most of the Confederate troops were in full retreat, Howell Cobb was still full of fight. From the summit of South Mountain in a clearing called Padgett's Field, Cobb rallied the remnants of the 10th and 16th Georgia, or at least those who stopped because of his persistent pleas. The 24th Georgia arrived in a more cohesive formation. Grabbing its flag, Cobb exhorted them to halt and stand firm. Many did as ordered, but others had had enough fighting for the day and continued their retreat. Those who decided to stay took up defensive positions behind a stone wall bordering the field, despite the pleas of Cobb to come out and form along a worm fence closer to the enemy approach. When a section of the Troup Artillery under Lt. Henry Jennings arrived, Cobb deployed the guns in advance of the infantry so that one could fire along Gapland Road and the other along the Arnoldstown Road. The cannoneers were justifiably uneasy because they had no ready infantry support.[29]

By now it was getting dark. The artillerists standing by their guns could barely discern the advancing Federal troops. There was no such thing as separate Federal regiments now, for all order had been lost during the attack and mad dashes and fighting up the side of the mountain. A mob of Federals from Torbert's First New Jersey Brigade approached the guns from along Gapland Road while pieces of the 16th, 18th, and 32nd New York approached from the direction of Whipp's Ravine.[30]

Each of Jennings' guns had a special name. "Sallie Craig" was on the right, facing the New Jersey troops, while "Jennie" was on the left facing the mass of approaching New Yorkers. Both guns discharged canister into the masses of disorganized Federal troops. The New Jersey men halted, raised their rifles, and fired into the gun crew, felling several gunners. Bullets ricocheted off the wheels, cannon barrels, and trails. "Sallie Craig" fired at least seven times, but the rounds failed to stop Torbert's determined infantry. Some had left the road to make their way around the gun to its right to enfilade the artillerymen. When the Federals were a mere seventy-five yards away, the two guns limbered

up and made their way to safety. Cobb's men in Padgett's Field remained, however, blazing away at the approaching Federals. The Yanks returned the fire and many of Cobb's men threw themselves to the ground. Thereafter, most of them jumped up and headed for safety. The last vestiges of Cobb's defense melted away at Padgett's Field.[31]

The Jerseymen's stamina finally gave way after crushing the last Confederate resistance in the fight for Crampton's Gap. Over to their right, the 95th Pennsylvania and 31st New York of Newton's brigade passed through to continue their pursuit of the beaten Rebels. Jennings' pair of guns had redeployed farther down the road and opened fire on their pursuers. As the latter closed the distance, the guns limbered up again, but this time they were not so fortunate. "Jennie" broke an axle during the attempt to roll away and had to be abandoned. The Pennsylvanians halted and they celebrated the capture of the gun.[32]

Over to the left, the 2nd Vermont, which had been following the 4th Vermont up the slope, was denied an opportunity to engage the enemy. While the 4th remained near the summit, the 2nd drove down the western slope looking for a fight. The Green Mountain boys did not find one, but they did find the abandoned "Jennie" and claimed the piece for their own. They had no way of knowing that its actual captors, the 95th Pennsylvania, had been ordered back up to the summit of the mountain. It was now about 7:00 p.m. and the battle of Crampton's Gap was over.[33]

Although two Rebel brigades (Parham's and Howell Cobb's) had been thoroughly beaten and almost destroyed, they had accomplished what was asked of them: defend the gap as long as possible and delay the powerful Federal VI Corps from gaining entry into Pleasant Valley where it could trap McLaws' and R. H. Anderson's divisions operating against Harpers Ferry. Although the corps would cross into Pleasant Valley the following day, Cobb's stubborn defense bought valuable time.

All told, the Confederates lost 873 men to all causes compared to the Federals' 441.[34]

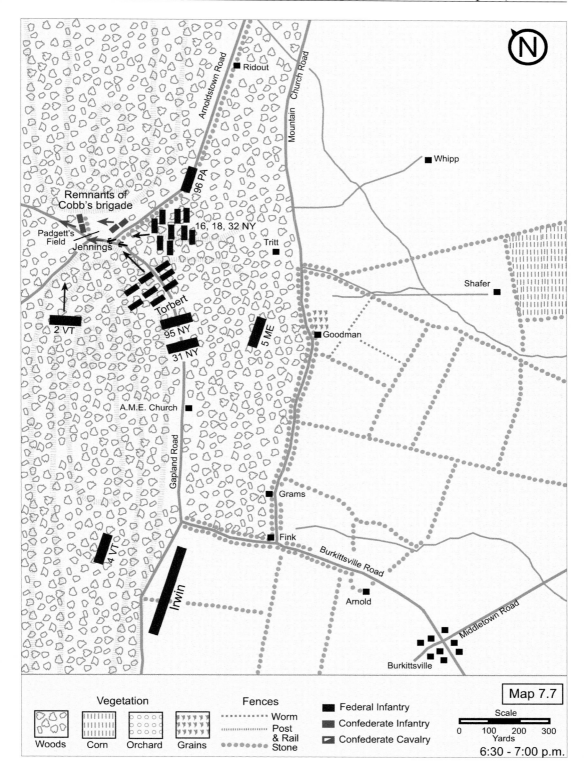

Map 7.7

6:30 - 7:00 p.m.

Map Set 8. The Capture of Harpers Ferry (September 12 - 15)

Map 8.1: Strategic Complications (September 12: Morning)

As discussed and portrayed in Map 1.8, the trap around Col. Dixon Miles and his garrison at Harpers Ferry began closing in earnest on September 12. Gen. Robert E. Lee's plan did not envision laying a true siege and he did not think one would be needed. "I have no doubt that they will leave that section as soon as they learn of the movement across the Potomac," Lee wrote Jefferson Davis on September 5. His Special Orders 191 was predicated on the belief that the Federal garrisons (Harpers Ferry and Martinsburg) would withdraw. When they did not, Lee decided he could not leave strong enemy forces in his rear. The garrisons stayed put because of General-in-Chief Maj. Gen. Henry Halleck, who believed that Maj. Gen. George McClellan's Army of the Potomac could protect Harpers Ferry's strategic position. "Defend all places to the last extremity," department commander Maj. Gen. John Wool telegraphed Miles. "There must be no abandoning of post, and shoot the first man that thinks of it."[1]

One cannot understand the Harpers Ferry campaign without understanding the geography of the region. Harpers Ferry sits in a bowl at the confluence of the Potomac and Shenandoah rivers surrounded by three heights: Maryland Heights (an extension of Elk Ridge) on the northeast, Loudoun Heights to the south, and Bolivar Heights to the west.

Pushing up about 1,400 feet, Maryland Heights was by far the tallest of the three. Blasting to make space for a railroad, road, and canal had pushed the high ground away from the Potomac River and created an imposing cliff. While all three heights would play a role, the control of Maryland Heights would determine the fate of the Harpers Ferry garrison. Loudoun Heights to the south was less imposing but was still some 1,100 feet above sea level. Although too far from Harpers Ferry for effective small arms fire, artillery deployed on these heights could rain destruction on the town. About a mile west of town stood the 300-foot Bolivar Heights, described in part as a "superb bastion against a Confederate incursion from the west" because it stretched from the Potomac to the Shenandoah, and if properly defended could prevent a flanking movement.[2]

Improvising from his general orders, Lee sent two-thirds of his army against Harpers Ferry in three wings. The first part, under Maj. Gen. Lafayette McLaws (which included his division and another under Maj. Gen. Richard Anderson) was ordered to deploy north of the Potomac River. On the morning of September 12, brigades under Joe Kershaw and William Barksdale marched down Elk Ridge toward Maryland Heights while Howell Cobb's brigade moved on their left through Pleasant Valley (between Elk Ridge and South Mountain) following the eastern slope of the ridge. McLaws' final brigade under Paul Semmes, together with William Mahone's brigade had the unenviable task of defending three mountain gaps through which enemy troops could march: Solomon's Gap in Elk Ridge, and Crampton's Gap and Brownsville Pass in South Mountain. Anderson's remaining brigades approached the Potomac River. Ambrose Wright's moved south atop South Mountain to Weverton Cliffs overlooking the Potomac River (Maryland Heights was visible to the west across Pleasant Valley). The balance of Anderson's brigades moved south through Pleasant Valley: Roger Pryor's below Wright's command with orders to capture Weverton; Lewis Armistead's men headed toward Sandy Hook, and the brigades of Cadmus Wilcox and Winfield Featherson aligned and moving between Armistead and Pryor. Brig. Gen. John Walker's small division, the operation's second wing, approached Loudoun Heights from the direction of Lovettsville. Stonewall Jackson's three divisions, marching up from Martinsburg for Bolivar Heights, would close the trap.[3]

Federal Brig. Gen. Julius White arrived at Harpers Ferry with his Martinsburg garrison. Although he outranked Col. Dixon Miles and could have assumed command, White followed usual military convention and left the officer in charge who was already overseeing the operation. Few men, however, had confidence in Miles. He had sworn off drinking, but its aftereffects were plain to see: "a mental dullness, a lack of decision, and a mulish stubbornness." Miles, one recent historian noted, "displayed little initiative in planning to meet an attack, and none when it came."[4]

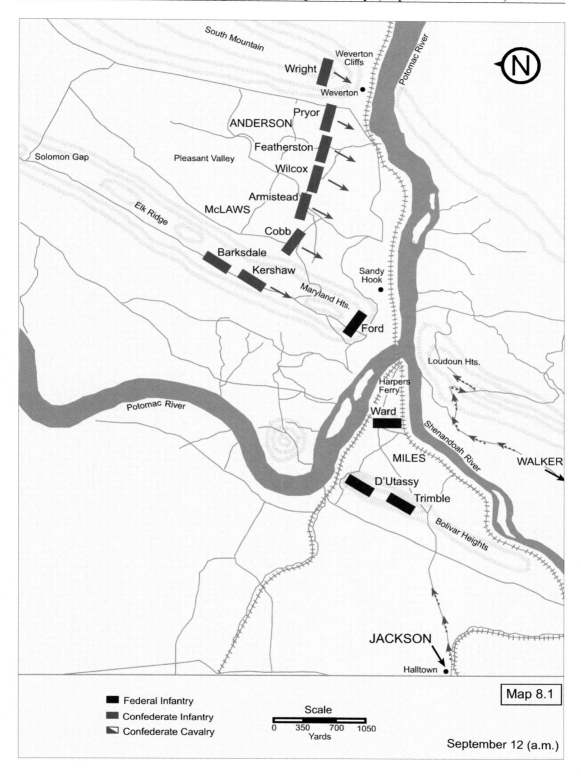

September 12 (a.m.)

Map 8.1

Map 8.2: The Federal Deployments (September 12: Afternoon)

While Miles may not have been the aggressive and clear-thinking leader the garrison needed, he did have the advantage of experience. During the summer of 1862, Miles served as chief-of-staff to Brig. Gen. Rufus Saxton, who commanded the garrison at Harpers Ferry. During the 1862 Shenandoah Valley Campaign, Stonewall Jackson spent two days demonstrating in front of the town before pulling back. This experience imparted upon Miles the importance of holding Bolivar Heights to defend Harpers Ferry from an enemy approaching from the west—just as Jackson had done during 1862. The steep 300-foot bluff stretched for more than a mile from the Potomac River on the north to the Shenandoah River on the south. Miles did not fully appreciate the effectiveness of enemy artillery and small arms fire from Loudoun Heights, but he did realize the danger posed by Confederates on Maryland Heights, and so he posted a brigade there. Its slopes were steep and rocky and wooded, so he did not believe the Rebels could get guns on its crest.[5]

The Federal dispositions in and around Harpers Ferry were complete by September 11. Miles created four brigades to defend the key logistics center. The First Brigade under Col. Frederick D'Utassy was composed of the colorful 39th New York, and the 111th and 115th New York. Miles placed this brigade on the right side of Bolivar Heights with its right near the Potomac. On its left was Col. William Trimble's Second Brigade composed of the 60th Ohio, 9th Vermont, and 126th New York. The Fourth Brigade under Col. William Ward occupied Camp Hill, an earthwork in the upper part of Harpers Ferry itself. Ward's command was composed of the 12th New York (militia), 87th Ohio, 1st Potomac Home Guard, and 8th New York Cavalry. Miles' final brigade was the only one not situated in or near the town. Col. Thomas Ford's command occupied Maryland Heights with its 32nd New York, three companies of the 1st Maryland Potomac Home Guard Brigade, and several cavalry units.[6]

Miles knew that the Confederates were approaching long before they scaled the heights around the town. A Federal infantry outpost encountered enemy infantry near the Point of Rocks and Federal cavalry encountered Jackson's men near Boonsboro on September 10. Gen. White and his men vouched for the Confederate move on Martinsburg (farther to the west) soon thereafter.

Miles, however, followed the recipe for success that had earlier worked for Gen. Saxton even though the differences between that time and now were substantial. Unlike his prior excursion, Jackson was dead set on capturing Harpers Ferry. He arrived in much greater numbers and approached the town on three sides instead of just one. Despite being ordered by Gen. Wool to build fortifications in June and again in August, Miles had not done so. His main line of defense would be posted on Bolivar Heights, as Saxon had done, but Miles did not put any troops on Loudoun Heights. When he learned the enemy was moving along the Potomac River, Miles established a defensive perimeter on Maryland Heights on September 5 under the command of Col. Ford of the 32nd Ohio. In addition to his own brigade, Ford was sent reinforcements including the 126th New York, a regiment that had been in the army all of three weeks. All told, Ford had about 1,600 men and seven guns under Capt. Eugene McGrath on these decisive heights that could determine the fate of the garrison because they overlooked the town and the Federal defenses.

After reconnoitering, Ford decided the best way to keep the Rebels off Maryland Heights was to establish a strong defensive position farther north at Solomon's Gap. When Miles overruled him, Ford put his men to work building primitive breastworks on the heights themselves. The men were aided by a path that shot northward from Sandy Hook Road to the top of Maryland Heights. Ford ordered his men to build the breastwork on the crest about 300 yards north of a small log hut called "The Lookout," and a line of abatis about eighty yards in front of that. The east side of the heights was precipitous and deemed too steep for enemy infantry to climb, and the west side was covered in woods and dense mountain laurel. Thickets on either side of the path made any organized movement there difficult. Ford also sent a picket line out about one-quarter of a mile toward Solomon's Gap, through which the Confederates would soon flood.[7]

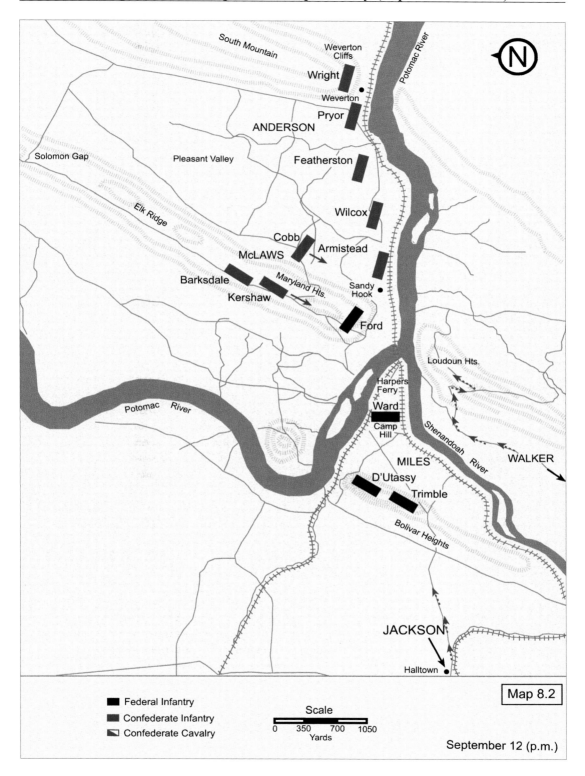

Map 8.2

September 12 (p.m.)

Federal Infantry
Confederate Infantry
Confederate Cavalry

Scale

0   350   700   1050
Yards

Map 8.3: The Opening Fight
for Maryland Heights
(September 13: 6:30 - 11:30 a.m.)

McLaws knew he must capture Maryland Heights in order to reduce Harpers Ferry. To do so, he sent Kershaw and Barksdale, his two best brigades, up against what would prove to be an inexperienced and ill-prepared Federal defense.

Kershaw's men encountered the Federal skirmish line on September 12 during their difficult slog up the tangled heights. After slowly pushing the skirmishers back toward Ford's main body, Kershaw realized the Federals were deployed in strength and halted for the night. At this point the Confederates outnumbered the Federals about 2,000 to 1,200. Worried about his vulnerable position, Ford sent a stream of urgent messages to Miles during the evening hours of September 12 pleading for reinforcements. Miles promised to send three regiments and two guns to his support. A pair of Kershaw's regiments, the 7th and 8th South Carolina, advanced between 6:30 a.m. and 7:00 a.m.; Kershaw's other two regiments, the 2nd and 3rd South Carolina, moved up behind them. The 8th South Carolina on the Confederate right encountered a rock ledge that barred its progress, but the 7th South Carolina pushed on and spotted Federal defenders to their front. William Barksdale's Mississippians, meanwhile, moved to hit the Federal right flank and rear, but the rugged terrain hindered their movements.

The Federal line of battle was first formed about 300 yards in front of the breastworks. Seventy-five men of the 39th New York were deployed on the left, with three companies of the 32nd Ohio on their right. Next came nine companies of the 126th New York. Two of the 1st Maryland Cavalry held the right flank. When they heard the command "charge bayonets," the Maryland cavalry skedaddled to the rear (No. 1).

The Federal line moved behind the abatis with the fleeing of the 1st Maryland Cavalry's two companies. After about fifteen to twenty minutes of additional fighting, the Federals retreated to their more substantial breastworks (No. 2). By this time, the 8th South Carolina had bypassed the rock barrier in its front and swung into position on the right side of the 7th South

Carolina. The Confederate line reached the abatis, about eighty yards from the Federal line, and the two sides exchanged a heavy fire. Try as they might, Kershaw's regiments could not pry Ford's men from their breastworks. The frustrated South Carolina brigadier called up the 3rd South Carolina from the rear while some of the promised Federal reinforcements appeared in the form of the 3rd Maryland about 10:00 a.m. These troops were split up, with four companies heading to the "Lookout" on the heights, and the other four moving forward to the west side of the heights. Three additional companies of the 32nd Ohio accompanied the latter Marylanders (No. 3).[8]

By this time, Barksdale had his Mississippians in position to join Kershaw's attack. They were on the flank and rear of Ford's line, however, so Kershaw's fire would hit them if they advanced. Kershaw ordered his men to cease fire, hoping that Barksdale might bag the entire defensive line, but some of the Mississippians fired prematurely into the right side of the 126th New York, severely wounding its well-respected commander Col. Eliakim Sherrill. "After Colonel Sherrill was wounded," recalled one observer, "there appears to have been no field officer in responsible command on the heights, and contradictory and confusing orders followed one another. . . . [I]t was a bad place in which to match green troops against veterans." Panic spread through the Union ranks and many of the men abandoned their positions and fled down the hill.[9]

No one was responsible for the defense after Sherrill fell because Col. Ford was ill that day and did not scale the heights to watch the action or direct the defense. Ford sent Maj. Sylvester Hewitt of his own regiment up the hill to act on his behalf. Hewitt, a physician by training and without much military experience, did not go up to the barricade to see the fighting. When large numbers of troops began streaming for the rear about 11:00 a.m., however, Hewitt thought all was lost and ordered the barricade abandoned. What he did not realize was that some of his troops, including portions of the 126th New York, 3rd Maryland Regiment, and 32nd Ohio, were still holding their own against the Rebels in a gallant defense of the high ground. The Buckeyes were not that sorry to see Ford's men abandon the works in front of them, for they had already lost 35 killed and nearly 200 wounded.[10]

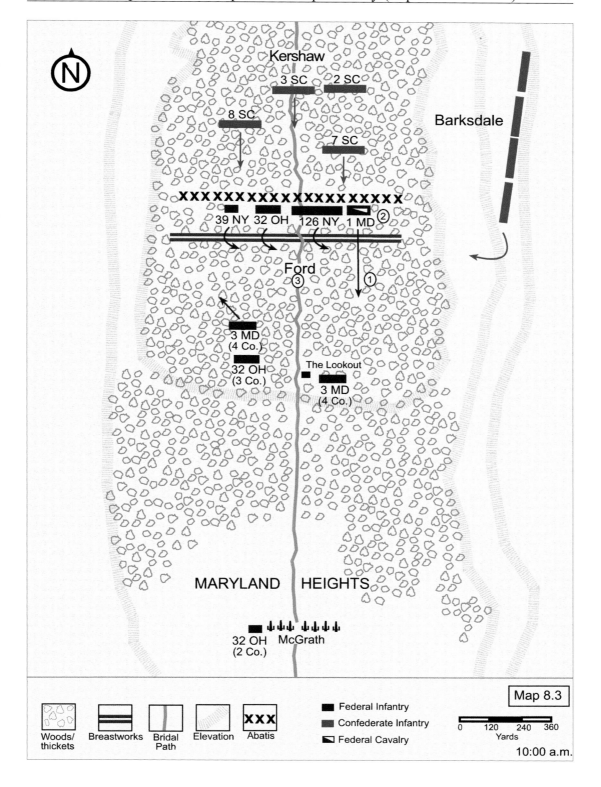

Kershaw

3 SC   2 SC

8 SC

Barksdale

7 SC

XXXXXXXXXXXXXXXXXXXXXXX

39 NY 32 OH 126 NY 1 MD ②

Ford
③

①

3 MD
(4 Co.)

32 OH
(3 Co.)

The Lookout

3 MD
(4 Co.)

MARYLAND   HEIGHTS

32 OH
(2 Co.)   McGrath

Map 8.3

Woods/
thickets   Breastworks   Bridal
Path   Elevation   Abatis

■ Federal Infantry
■ Confederate Infantry
◤ Federal Cavalry

0   120   240   360
Yards

10:00 a.m.

Map 8.4: Maryland Heights Falls (September 13: 11:30 a.m. - 4:30 p.m.)

Col. Miles learned that his troops had abandoned the high ground when he crossed the river to Maryland Heights to determine the course of the fighting. Col. S. W. Downey, the commander of the 3rd Maryland, was upset about the orders to abandon the breastworks and confronted both Miles and Ford to demand whether they were involved in the decision to withdraw. Both officers denied it and ordered Downey to retake the crest. When he asked for reinforcements, Downey was told to use the 126th New York, along with his own regiment.

By this time the stream of retreating soldiers had become a flood. According to Col. Ford, "as fast as we forced them up one mountain path they returned by another until all seemed to be lost." It was hard work, but Miles and Ford patched together a sizable force and ordered it back up the hill to retake the critical barricade. Downey pushed his Marylanders up the western side of the heights. Portions of other commands, including the 126th New York and the 32nd Ohio, were to the right of the Maryland men. To their dismay, the Union officers discovered the Confederates already occupied the breastworks, from which point they threw a merciless small arms fire against the already wary and shaken Federals. Col. Miles had already left Maryland Heights under the mistaken belief that he had stabilized the situation. He left Col. Ford in charge on the crest. Ford, however, was under the impression that he had discretionary orders to abandon Maryland Heights if he decided it was necessary. This critical misunderstanding did not bode well for holding on to Harpers Ferry and its besieged garrison.[11]

Ford was cheered about noon by the addition of seven companies of the 115th New York. Exactly how he made the decision to use these New Yorkers remains something of a mystery. Rather than pushing all of these badly needed reinforcements up the hill in one strong thrust, Ford held back five of the companies near the side of the hill just beyond McGrath's battery, and only sent the two remaining companies farther up the mountain to provide direct support to the men fighting there.

The two sides skirmished for several hours in what appeared to be a stalemate. Ford likely did not know it, but with the recent Federal reinforcements he outnumbered Kershaw and Barksdale about three to two. The Confederates appeared to be content with a slow advance rather than a direct attempt to force the issue. By 3:30 p.m., the Mississippians were lapping around the Union right flank while the South Carolinians pressed against the front. Thinking back on Miles' discretionary orders, which were to withdraw his forces if they "gave way once again," Ford finally ordered the guns spiked and his infantry to fall back across the Potomac River. One of the worst fates for an artillery commander was the loss of his guns, and McGrath fought the order to spike his precious pieces. Many of Ford's infantry voiced disbelief when orders to withdraw reached them, but they obeyed when a second order to fall back arrived. From his distant vantage point Miles watched in stunned disbelief as Ford's command snaked its way down the mountainside. "God Almighty!" he yelled. "They are coming down! Hell and damnation!" Once they reached Harpers Ferry, Ford's men were put into position on Bolivar Heights, where they prepared their evening meal and waited for an attack on the morrow, which they knew would surely come.[12]

Although his forces were sealing off Harpers Ferry, time was running out for General Lee and his widely dispersed army. With the knowledge of Lee's plans in Special Orders No. 191 firmly in his grasp, General McClellan was aggressively pushing his troops north and west. With Harpers Ferry in grave danger, he directed I Corps, VI Corps, and IX Corps (with the II Corps following in reserve) toward the mountain passes at Crampton's, Fox's, and Turner's gaps. If at least one punched through into Pleasant Valley, Lee's army would be divided and the column under Lafayette McLaws trapped. From there, it was but a short march to Harpers Ferry.[13]

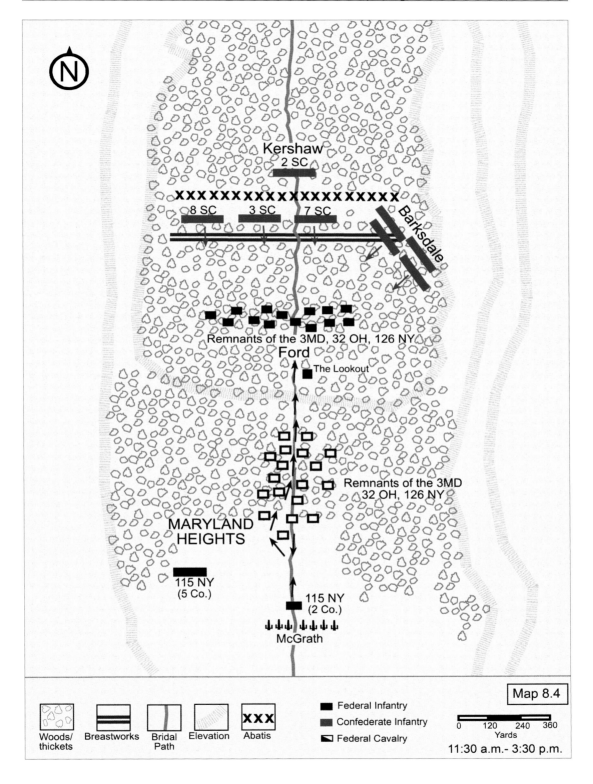

Kershaw
2 SC

XXXXXXXXXXXXXXXXXXXXXXXXXX

8 SC   3 SC   7 SC   Barksdale

Remnants of the 3MD, 32 OH, 126 NY
Ford

The Lookout

Remnants of the 3MD
32 OH, 126 NY

MARYLAND
HEIGHTS

115 NY
(5 Co.)

115 NY
(2 Co.)

McGrath

Map 8.4

Woods/   Breastworks   Bridal   Elevation   Abatis
thickets   Path

XXX

■ Federal Infantry
▬ Confederate Infantry
◣ Federal Cavalry

0   120   240   360
Yards

11:30 a.m.- 3:30 p.m.

Map 8.5: Jackson Closes the Loop (September 13)

The commanders directing Gen. Lee's far-flung columns (Jackson, McLaws, and Walker) had to move quickly to reduce the town. With Maryland Heights now in Confederate hands, the situation had gone from bad to worse for the Federal defenders. Still, there was some hope for Miles and his men because the enemy had to get their guns up both Maryland and Loudoun heights in order to subdue the town.

John Walker's small division arrived first, reaching the base of Loudoun Heights about 10:00 a.m. He sent two regiments scrambling up the steep slopes about noon, while the rest of his division guarded the roads from Harpers Ferry. Because Walker's men were instructed to not reveal their presence, they left the roads periodically to hack paths through the dense vegetation. As a result, they did not reach the top of Loudoun Heights until about 5:00 p.m. What greeted them was a stunning panoramic view of the countryside. Some of McLaws' troops on Maryland Heights may have been visible, but they definitely saw the Federal camps below them. Some of the men estimated that the garrison numbered about 10,000, which was not far off the mark.[14]

Stonewall Jackson began the day with the knowledge that the planned-for swift surgical extraction of the Federals from the lower Shenandoah Valley was at least one good day behind schedule. Old Jack also learned the three Confederate columns were up against about 13,500 men in Harpers Ferry, the place of Jackson's first command the year before. He had spent considerable time thinking about its defense. As one prominent historian of the campaign concluded, "no general of the Confederacy was better suited to conduct operations against Harpers Ferry than Jackson." Given his intimate knowledge of the place, Jackson was probably surprised that Miles had decided to stake the defense of the town on holding Bolivar Heights at the bottom of a "topographical bowl" without adequate breastworks on the other surrounding heights.

Jackson's command began the 13-mile march to Harpers Ferry at daylight. A. P. Hill's division took the van, followed by those under J.

R. Jones and Alexander Lawton. The roads were clear and the troops made good progress. The head of Jackson's column reached Halltown about 11:00 a.m. Riding ahead, Jackson spotted the enemy's defenses on Bolivar Heights. With all three columns at their assigned positions, it was time to bring up the artillery, which would convince the Federals that mounting any further defense was folly.[15]

The loss of Maryland Heights weighed heavily upon Col. Miles. He seems not to have ever seriously considered giving up the town—especially after Gen. Halleck messaged him, "The Government has the utmost confidence in you, and is ready to give you full credit for the defense it expects you to make." Miles learned soon enough that Rebels were now on Loudoun Heights and in front of the main defenses on Bolivar Heights. His only hope was that reinforcements would appear sooner rather than later to break up the Confederate effort.

Miles ordered Capt. Charles Russell of the 1st Maryland Cavalry to attempt to break through the enemy lines with a handful and men to "try to reach somebody . . . anybody . . . [about] the condition of Harpers Ferry." Miles indicated that he could probably hold out for forty-eight hours, but no more. Russell made a successful breakout and delivered his message to Jesse Reno, the commander of the Federal IX Corps, and then to McClellan himself about 9:00 a.m. The army commander sent three different couriers to Miles with word to hold on: help was on the way.[16]

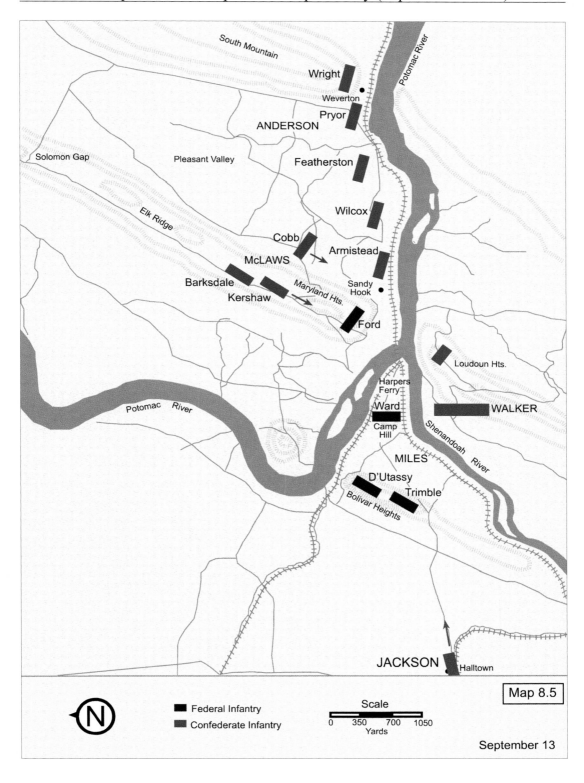

Map 8.5

Federal Infantry
Confederate Infantry

Scale

0   350   700   1050
Yards

September 13

Map 8.6: Both Sides Prepare for Action (September 14: 7:00 a.m. - 2:00 p.m.)

While Miles pondered his options during the evening of September 13, the Confederates continued moving into position. The Federal garrison commander was not concerned about Loudoun Heights because the distance was too great for small arms fire and he did not believe the enemy could move artillery up its nearly vertical slopes that rose 700 feet above the Shenandoah River. Maryland Heights posed a more significant problem; although its slopes were not as steep, its crest was much higher.

Back on Loudoun Heights, meanwhile, Walker ordered his men to work through the night to get a passable road in place. By 8:00 a.m., the fruits of their efforts manifested themselves in the form of five rifled guns frowning in the direction of Harpers Ferry. Walker asked Stonewall Jackson whether he should open fire or wait for McLaws to position his guns on Maryland Heights. Jackson sent word to "wait."

McLaws' men were also at work cutting a road to the top of Maryland Heights during the morning of September 14. It took 200 men pulling on heavy ropes to haul each gun up the steep slopes. By 2:00 p.m. a pair of rifled pieces dropped trail to overlook Harpers Ferry. Others would soon join them there.

That morning, Jackson sent McLaws very specific orders: "As soon as you get your batteries planted . . . I desire . . . to send in a flag of truce for the purpose of getting out the non-combatants, should the commanding officer refuse to surrender. Should we have to attack, let the work be done thoroughly; fire on the houses when necessary. The citizens can keep out of harm's way. . . . Demolish the place if it is occupied by the enemy and does not surrender." Jackson also indicated that the Federal defenses on Bolivar Heights were very strong, so he intended "to remain quiet" until the guns could open fire, drawing enemy attention away from his infantry. Jackson knew by 2:00 p.m. that powerful Federal reinforcements were approaching and that he could not delay another minute. The Confederate artillery was well positioned to make Harpers Ferry untenable for the Federal garrison, but how quickly they could force a surrender was not clear. Any extensive

delay offered McClellan the time he needed to shove troops through the South Mountain passes and lift the siege. [17]

Miles' defensive position on Bolivar Heights was indeed substantial on the morning of September 14. Col. F. G. D'Utassy's brigade held the right side of the ridge with his own right flank extending to the Potomac River. Three heavy guns from Graham's battery anchored the right side of the line. The 65th Illinois extended the line left in the direction of the meandering Shenandoah River, continued by the 39th New York, 115th New York, and 111th New York. Phillips' six-gun battery anchored the left side of D'Utassy's brigade and von Sehlen's pieces solidified its center.

Col. William Trimble's brigade held the left side of Bolivar Heights. Bloodied from its fight on Maryland Heights the day before, the 126th New York now held the right of the brigade, with the 60th Ohio to its left and then Rigby's battery about fifty yards from the Charlestown Turnpike. Below the road was the 9th Vermont on the far left. All of the guns were protected by slight breastworks, but the men were exposed on the heights because Miles had not put the men to work chopping down trees and digging into the earth to strengthen the position. With the enemy now on full display before them on September 14, the men set about throwing up crude entrenchments. According to one contemporary, they were made of "logs and earth and filled in with tents, cast-off clothing, army blankets, and anything else that would break the force of a ball."

The area south of Bolivar Heights (between the ridge and the Shenandoah River) was heavily wooded and filled with ravines and guarded by a thinly spread 3rd Maryland. Miles also fortified Camp Hill, which was just south of Harpers Ferry. This reserve position contained the 12th New York Militia, Potts' battery, and part of Graham's battery.[18]

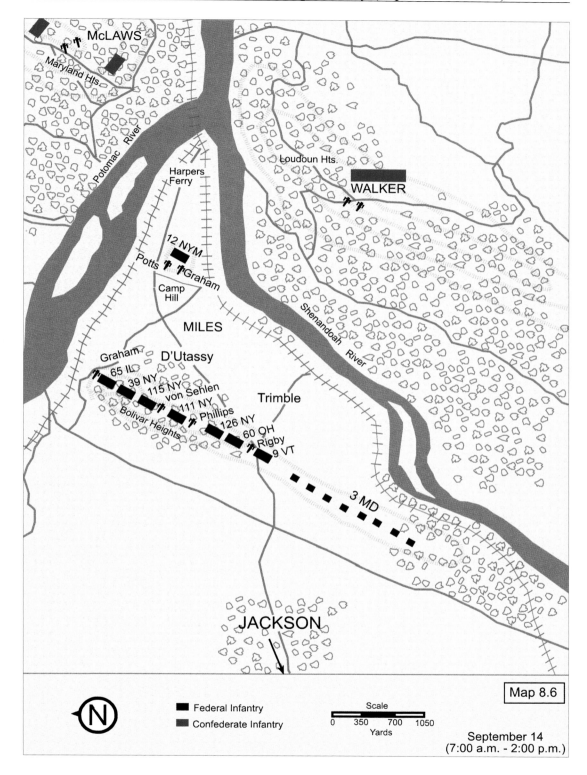

McLAWS

Maryland Hts.

Potomac River

Harpers Ferry

Loudoun Hts.

WALKER

12 NYM

Potts   Graham

Camp Hill

Shenandoah River

MILES

Graham   D'Utassy

65 IL

39 NY

115 NY

von Sehlen

111 NY

Trimble

Bolivar Heights

Phillips

126 NY

60 OH

Rigby

9 VT

3 MD

JACKSON

N

■ Federal Infantry

■ Confederate Infantry

Scale

0   350   700   1050

Yards

Map 8.6

September 14
(7:00 a.m. - 2:00 p.m.)

Map 8.7: Confederate Artillery Opens (September 14: 2:00 - 9:00 p.m.)

Once Jackson's guns were in position, the Confederate guns opened fire on the Federals. The first shots drove "the enemy from their works on the right of Bolivar Heights." After waiting impatiently for several hours, Walker decided he could no longer wait for McLaws to get his guns into position. Walker opened fire at 1:00 p.m. Some of his shells fell into the town. McLaws opened fire an hour later. This was an especially tense time for McLaws, who by now had received word that Gen. Franklin's Federal VI Corps was forcing Crampton's Gap in his rear. If Harpers Ferry did not fall quickly, his and Anderson's divisions would be trapped in Pleasant Valley.[19]

As expected, the Confederate artillery fire created panic within the ranks of the Federals in and around Harpers Ferry. Unable to withstand the cannonade, the men of the rookie 125th New York broke to the rear. "We were at their mercy," admitted one of its officers. "[T]o remain was to be slaughtered, so we ran like hounds to get under the cover of a hillside." A member of the 9th Vermont noted that the situation took on the "appearance of an overturned beehive. Artillery, infantry, and cavalry was mixed in an absurd melee."[20]

The Federal artillery on Bolivar Heights and Camp Hill swivelled to take on McLaws and Walker once their guns opened fire. It was a farcical mismatch from the start because the Federal guns could not reach their Confederate counterparts, which were too high and too far away. The Confederates pounded the town and the Federal defenders, knocking out four guns, blowing up two caissons, and destroying the morale of the infantry.[21]

While the guns extracted their toll, Stonewall Jackson's men deployed for battle in front of the Federal breastworks south of Harpers Ferry. Tasked with the major responsibility of capturing the town, A. P. Hill's division moved along the Shenandoah River on the Federal left to sweep around the defenses and force its way into Harpers Ferry. Jackson's other two divisions under Alexander Lawton and John R. Jones, meanwhile, would demonstrate in front of the Federal works. Jones planned to

send a brigade and a battery against the Federal right, while Lawton advanced his infantry up the turnpike from Hallstown.[22]

Jackson knew the artillery on Maryland Heights and Loudoun Heights would create havoc in the town, but he was less sure it would force its capitulation. Because "of the distance and range of their guns," Jackson reported, "not much could be expected from their artillery so long as the enemy retained his advanced position on Bolivar Heights."[23]

A. P. Hill's men advanced about 3:00 p.m. to the sounds of tremendous explosions tearing through the town and its defenses in front of them. The division initially followed the Shenandoah River in its move toward Harpers Ferry. As he approached Bolivar Heights, Hill divided his division into two wings. While Maxey Gregg's and Lawrence Branch's brigades continued following the river along the railroad bed, his three other brigades under Dorsey Pender, James Archer, and Charles Field (now under Col. John Brockenbrough) moved against the Federal defenses. Pender was put in charge of all three brigades. George Thomas' brigade followed as a reserve. Pender's men scattered the Federal skirmish line, forcing Miles to send relief to the beleaguered 3rd Maryland in the form of the 9th Vermont, which had comprised the left of Col. Trimble's brigade's defensive line. He would later be forced to send other reinforcements.[24]

Darkness hindered the Confederate push against Bolivar Heights. Another impediment to A. P. Hill's advance was J. R. Jones, who was slow to send Charles Winder's and William Starke's brigades ahead toward the Potomac River (the Federal right flank). These brigades did not slide into position until after dark. Lawton's division, which had orders to advance to School House Ridge, which straddled the Charlestown Pike in front of the main Federal line on Bolivar Heights, did not complete its movement until after dark.

Jackson now had no choice but to wait for the morrow to close the trap on the beleaguered garrison. He sent a message to Gen. Lee at 8:15 p.m.: "the advance which commenced this evening has been successful thus far, and I look to Him for complete success tomorrow."[25]

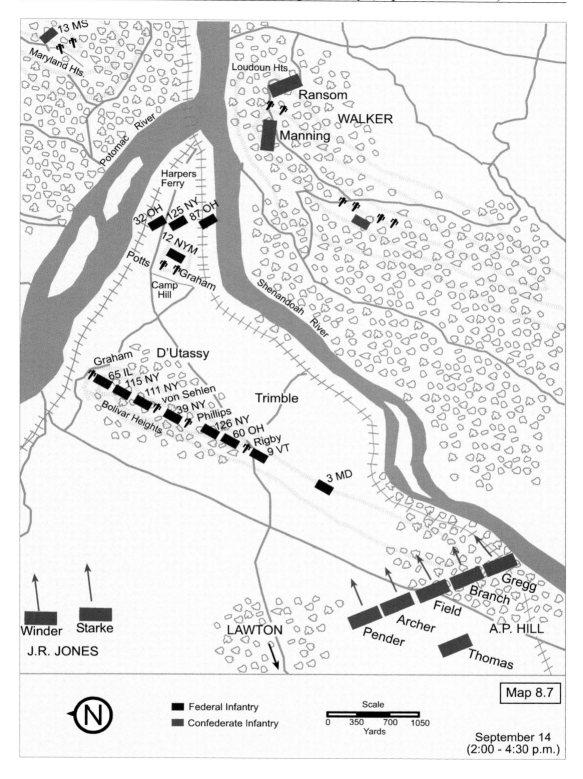

13 MS

Maryland Hts.

Potomac River

Loudoun Hts.

Ransom

WALKER

Manning

Harpers
Ferry

32 OH   125 NY   87 OH

12 NYM

Potts

Graham

Camp
Hill

Shenandoah River

D'Utassy

Graham

65 IL

115 NY

111 NY

von Sehlen

39 NY

Bolivar Heights

Phillips

126 NY

60 OH

Rigby

9 VT

Trimble

3 MD

Gregg

Branch

Field

A.P. HILL

Pender

Archer

Thomas

Winder   Starke

LAWTON

J.R. JONES

N

Federal Infantry

Confederate Infantry

Scale

0   350   700   1050

Yards

Map 8.7

September 14
(2:00 - 4:30 p.m.)

Map 8.8: The Confederate Vice Closes; Federal Cavalry Prepares to Escape (September 15: 3:00 - 7:00 a.m)

The officers who met with Col. Miles on the evening of September 14 verged on despair. Some felt Harpers Ferry should be evacuated as soon as possible. Others, like Gen. Julius White, pleaded with Miles to try to recapture Maryland Heights. He dismissed these very reasonable suggestions, claiming the heights were of no further consequence. "I am ordered to hold this place and God damn my soul to hell if I don't." The parameters were set: the fight would pit his own outnumbered forces on Bolivar Heights against whatever Stonewall Jackson could throw against them.[26]

Unable to convince Miles to retake Maryland Heights, White at least convinced him to mass all of his artillery on Bolivar Heights. Miles soon changed his mind, however, because he wanted to retain some of the guns near the river crossings. In the end it didn't matter anyway, because there were not enough horses to pull the heavy guns to the heights.[27]

The movement of A. P. Hill's division on the right of Jackson's line threatened to turn Miles' left flank on Bolivar Heights, forcing the Union commander to realign his troops into two wings essentially perpendicular to one another. Into the new wing he sent the 32nd and 87th Ohio, the 125th New York, and a section of Rigby's battery and a second section from Potts' battery.[28]

Jackson's men had not sat idle that night. While the infantry made final preparations for their early morning attacks, his artillery deployed all along the front. Col. Stapleton Crutchfield, Jackson's chief of artillery, ordered ten guns to splash across the Shenandoah River at Keys' Ford and head up to Loudoun Heights. The men hacked a path along the base of the heights and, soon after sunrise, ten guns were looking down on the left flank and rear of the Federal defensive lines. The seventy Confederate guns in front, on the flank, and behind the Federals opened fire about 6:00 a.m. for about one hour. The Federal guns replied, but one by one fell silent when they ran out of ammunition. After a short time only Rigby's and Potts' guns near the Shenandoah

River maintained an effective counter-battery fire. The Confederate infantrymen watched intently as these events unfolded. One soldier in the 21st North Carolina of Lawton's division recalled, "The bristling line of bayonets behind strong fortifications was a dangerous thing to approach and we knew that many of us would fall before we could hope to scale its ramparts and beat back its defenders." When an aide galloped into view, the men knew it was time to rise and take on the still formidable enemy defenses.[29]

Not all of the troops in the Harpers Ferry garrison, however, were content to wait around to be captured. During the afternoon of September 13, Col. Benjamin "Grimes" Davis of the 8th New York Cavalry and Lt. Col. Hasbrouck Davis of the 12th Illinois Cavalry approached Gen. White, who had been put in command of the garrison's cavalry. Both cavalry officers explained that they and their troopers were of very little use defending Harpers Ferry and that forage was running out for their mounts. They requested permission to cut their way out and attempt to reinforce McClellan. The capture of 1,500 horses by the enemy, they added, would help Lee's army substantially. White liked the idea and asked the two cavalry commanders to accompany him to Col. Miles' headquarters that evening. Miles listened as the cavalrymen made their case. He was not initially in favor of the idea, but announced he would consider it if they could all agree on a more concrete plan, including the escape route. Both officers raised the question about the desirability of including the entire garrison in the breakout plans. Miles dissented, adding that the infantry would be too slow and he did not have discretionary orders that would allow him to make such a bold decision.[30]

Col. Grimes Davis favored an escape along the Virginia side of the Potomac River, riding his troopers toward Kearneysville before crossing them into Maryland at Shepherdstown. Another route had the column crossing the Shenandoah River and following the Potomac toward Washington, or they could recross the river at or below Point of Rocks and ride to Frederick to join McClellan. Miles still had deep misgivings about the plan, but Grimes Davis was not going to give up so easily. He apparently indicated that he was leaving with or without orders. Sharp words were exchanged. Miles eventually relented.[31]

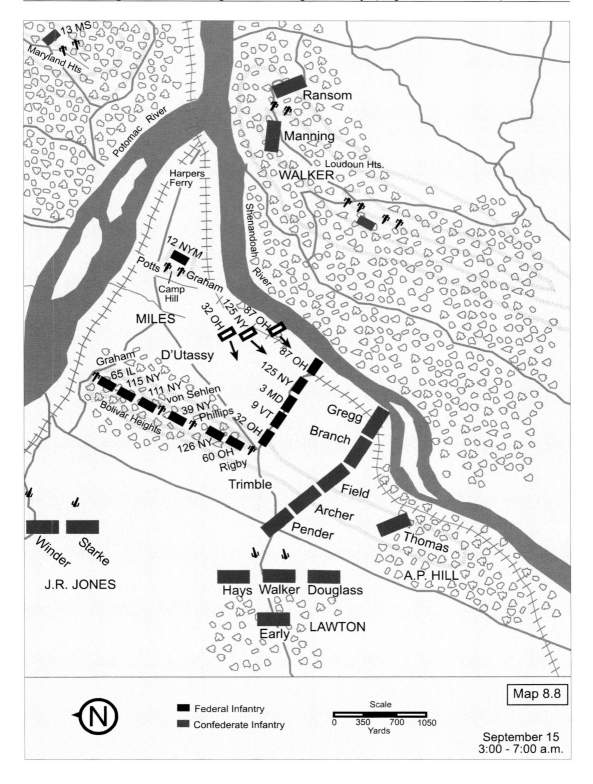

13 MS

Maryland Hts.

Potomac River

Ransom

Manning

Loudoun Hts.

WALKER

Harpers
Ferry

Shenandoah River

12 NYM

Potts   Graham

Camp
Hill

MILES

32 OH   125 NY   87 OH   87 OH

D'Utassy

125 NY

Graham   3 MD
65 IL   9 VT
115 NY
111 NY   von Sehlen   Gregg
39 NY   Phillips   Branch
Bolivar Heights   32 OH
126 NY   60 OH
Rigby   Field

Trimble   Archer

Winder   Starke   Pender   Thomas

J.R. JONES   A.P. HILL

Hays   Walker   Douglass

Early   LAWTON

Map 8.8

N

■ Federal Infantry
■ Confederate Infantry

Scale
0   350   700   1050
Yards

September 15
3:00 - 7:00 a.m.

Map 8.9: Federal Cavalry Breaks Out (September 15: 3:00 - 7:00 a.m)

The cavalry would ride north under Miles' Special Order No. 120, which set out the route of the column: a crossing of the pontoon bridge, a ride a short distance along the Potomac River, and a strike north to Sharpsburg. Although he was not part of the conference, the order named Col. Arno Voss of the 12th Illinois Cavalry as the commander of the mission. Miles designated the alignment of the column as follows: Cole's cavalry, 12th Illinois Cavalry, 8th New York Cavalry, 7th Squadron, Rhode Island Cavalry, and 1st Maryland Cavalry.[32]

The cavalry officers waited in anticipation for the sun to set on September 14. The men and horses were fed and before 8:00 p.m., the units rendezvoused in the main Harpers Ferry street close to the Shenandoah River. The men were ecstatic when they learned of their mission. "Although the enemy was believed to be in strong force on the road chosen and there were unknown dangers to be met in the darkness of night," explained one cavalryman, "it was an immense relief to be once more in motion with a chance for liberty." The men had been "hemmed in on all sides . . . harried by shot and shell without being able to strike back, and with the gloomiest forebodings for the future, the spirits of the officers and men had been depressed to the point of despondency; but all now recovered their cheerfulness, and pressed forward, full of hope and courage, and equal to any emergency."[33]

With an officer who knew the countryside at the head of the column, the cavalry rode out of town. The troopers crossed the pontoon bridge across the Potomac and turned left, passing between the C & O Canal and Maryland Heights. The breakout became more exciting when the column encountered a Rebel picket guard, which was dispersed with a wild charge. Shots were exchanged but no troopers were lost. When it reached the road leading to Sharpsburg, the column turned right and headed north. The pace was a rapid one in the dark night. The men were never really relaxed because fatal danger was a real potential at any point in the taxing journey. The column reached the sleepy little town of Sharpsburg about midnight, where the officers

stopped to allow the men and horses to rest and the column to close up.[34]

The stay in Sharpsburg was cut short when the officers learned a significant contingent from Lee's Army of Northern Virginia was assembling at Keedysville just three miles to the northeast. When a reconnoitering party confirmed this information, the ride toward Hagerstown continued. The column rested once again when it reached the road running east and west between Hagerstown and Williamsport just before daybreak. The men were preparing to continue their journey north when they heard the low rumbling of wagon wheels. Investigation revealed that a large wagon train was rolling along the road from Hagerstown. After a short discussion, the officers decided to capture the train. With the 8th New York and 12th Illinois deployed along the road and the rest of the units in support, Col. Davis moved into the road with a squadron of his 8th New York to block its progress. The trap was set. Davis and his men captured without incident the first wagon that appeared out of the darkness and ordered it to continue rolling northward. One by one the wagons were seized in this manner. Each wagon had four or five guards, but all were quickly captured. Two troopers climbed aboard each wagon to sit on either side of the driver to ensure compliance with their orders. The wagons belonged to James Longstreet's ordnance train.[35]

It was a dozen miles to Greencastle, Pennsylvania, and the captured wagon train and the troops rode there with abandon. Confederate cavalry was on hand to guard Longstreet's wagon train, but the gray troopers did not become involved until reinforced. By that time, the running clash with the rearguard of the Federal cavalry was too late to save the ordnance train. The wagons and Federal cavalry rumbled into Greencastle between 9:00 a.m. and 10:00 a.m. on September 15. Davis and his men captured at least forty wagons and hundreds of prisoners without the loss of a man.[36]

The loss of so many valuable ammunition wagons was a blow to the Southern army, but it could have been much worse. About an hour after their capture, the Army of Northern Virginia's artillery reserve rumbled along this same section of road and could have been captured just as easily.[37]

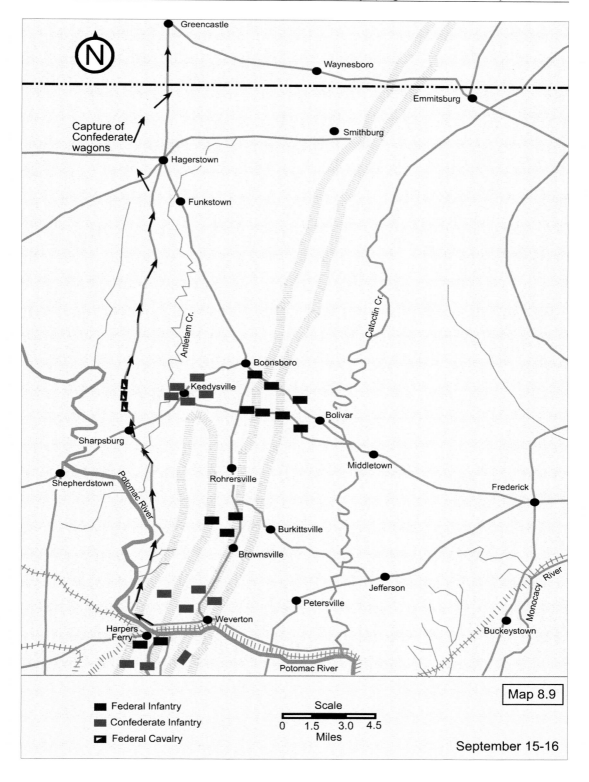

N

Greencastle

Waynesboro

Emmitsburg

Capture of
Confederate
wagons

Smithburg

Hagerstown

Funkstown

Antietam Cr.

Catoctin Cr.

Boonsboro

Keedysville

Bolivar

Sharpsburg

Middletown

Shepherdstown

Potomac River

Rohrersville

Frederick

Burkittsville

Brownsville

Jefferson

Monocacy River

Petersville

Weverton

Harpers
Ferry

Buckeystown

Potomac River

■ Federal Infantry
■ Confederate Infantry
▧ Federal Cavalry

Scale

0   1.5   3.0   4.5
Miles

Map 8.9

September 15-16

Map 8.10: The Garrison Falls
(September 15: 7:00 - 8:00 p.m.)

When the Federal artillery fire slackened, Stonewall Jackson ordered his three divisions forward against Bolivar Heights. The men knew they were heading toward a strong defensive line and that the cost might be severe. Suddenly, however, white flags of truce dotted the Federal front.

Intermittent Rebel artillery discharges still hit the area in and around Harpers Ferry. One exploded a few feet from Col. Miles and mortally wounded him. The colonel whispered to his aide-de-camp, "Well, Mr. Binney, we have done our duty, but where can McClellan be?" Miles died the following day. His last moments were recounted by Capt. Eugene McGrath: "He reached out his hand and took mine and pressed it; said he, 'Captain, I have done my duty to my country and I am ready to die; God bless you.'"[38]

Gen. White assumed command of the garrison and it was his chore to surrender it to Jackson. Donning his best uniform and mounted on a magnificent black charger, White rode out to capitulate. According to one of Jackson's aides, White "must have been astonished to find in General Jackson the worst dressed, worst mounted, most faded and dingy looking general he had ever seen anyone surrender to."[39]

With Harpers Ferry finally in his hands, Jackson knew he had no choice but to get the tired and dirty Confederates back on the road to reassemble the army. He informed Gens. Walker and McLaws by ten that morning to begin their march. Knowing just how desperate Lee's situation was, Jackson proposed leaving one division of his own wing to deal with the prisoners and collect supplies and march the remainder to Sharpsburg, where the Southern army was assembling. A. P. Hill's men were tapped to remain behind to gather the spoils of the significant victory and parole the officers and men. The Federal captives were issued two days' rations and told to march as quickly as possible in the direction of Washington.[40]

The captured booty was indeed immense: 73 cannon, 13,000 small arms, 200 wagons, and more than 12,000 men. No other capture of Federal men and hardware would exceed the taking of Harpers Ferry. Jackson achieved this feat with a minimal loss of just 39 killed and 247 wounded. The anger of the Federal troops toward Miles for his inept defense was substantial. Few bemoaned his mortal wounding or that he would be dead as they prepared for the long march to Washington. Jackson savored his victory as he rode through Harpers Ferry. The vanquished Federals crowded the streets to see what the victorious Confederate leader looked like. Most were surprised by his seedy appearance, but one yelled out to his comrades, "Boys, he is not much for looks, but if we'd had him we wouldn't have been caught in this trap."[41]

In the glory of the moment no one cared that Jackson had not reduced Harpers Ferry sooner. According to Special Orders No. 191, he was to be at or near the garrison on September 12. He left Frederick at dawn on September 10 and camped near Boonsboro near dusk after a march of just fourteen miles in twelve hours. September 11 was spent re-crossing the Potomac into Virginia and camping at Martinsburg. Jackson could have reached Harpers Ferry on the 12th with a forced march of twenty miles. Instead, he committed his men to a leisurely march of about seven miles. His divisions finally reached School House Ridge, just west of Bolivar Heights, on September 13. This was around the same time the Hoosier infantrymen found the copy of Lee's lost orders.[42]

McClellan's vigorous push against the South Mountain passes increased Lee's concern about the safety of his detached divisions, particularly McLaws' vulnerable command operating in Pleasant Valley. Lee knew his first incursion into the North was now all but derailed, and decided to concentrate his army near Sharpsburg before beginning an orderly withdrawal from Union soil. "It is necessary for you to abandon your position to-night . . . to unite with this command," Lee wrote McLaws at 8:00 p.m. The detached division commander decided against writing to Lee that his position was a strong one and that by leaving it, he would provide Miles with an escape route. Lee also sent word about the deteriorating situation to Jackson about the same time with a plea that the work be completed with haste.

Thus, great was Lee's relief when he read Jackson's message, which he transcribed at 8:00 a.m. on September 15: "Through God's blessing, Harpers Ferry and its garrison are to be surrendered.[43]

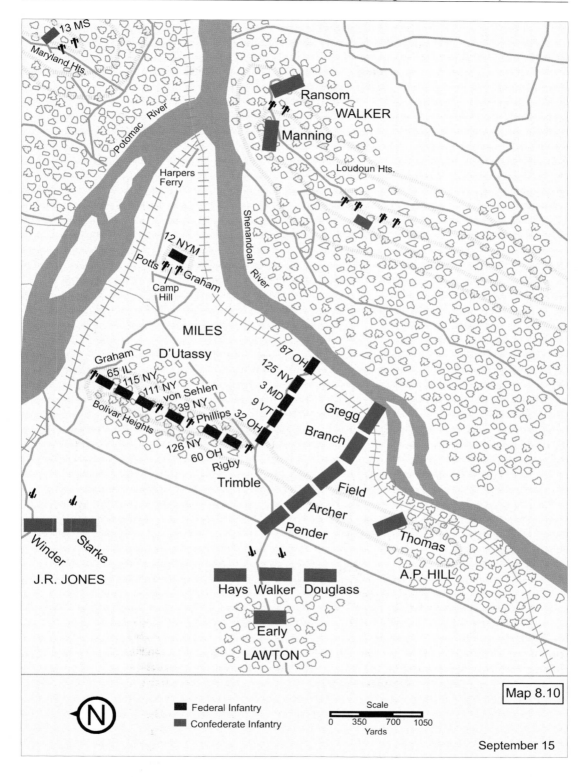

Map 8.10

Federal Infantry
Confederate Infantry

Scale
0   350   700   1050
Yards

September 15

Map Set 9. To Sharpsburg
(September 14 - 16)

Map 9.1: Pleasant Valley
(September 15: 8:00 a.m. - noon)

Maj. Gen. Lafayette McLaws knew he must do something about the growing menace of Maj. Gen. William Franklin's Federal VI Corps operating in his rear. Franklin's corps forced its way through Crampton's Gap on the evening of September 14 and was about to enter Pleasant Valley, which stretched between Elk Ridge and South Mountain. If Franklin moved his powerful corps into the valley and marched south, he would be in a position to break the siege of Harpers Ferry and trap McLaws and Anderson against the Potomac River. Ironically, both Franklin and McLaws believed he was outnumbered by the other. In reality, Franklin outnumbered McLaws by nearly three to one, and Darius Couch's 7,000-man Federal division was also approaching the sector. McLaws also had reinforcements he could call upon, about 4,000 men from brigades of his and Anderson's divisions near Weverton at the foot of South Mountain along the Potomac River.

McLaws decided to form a defensive line across Pleasant Valley about one and one-half miles south of Crampton's Gap. He deployed all of his artillery on this new line except for two rifled guns on Maryland Heights, and reinforced this new front with William Barksdale's, Joseph Kershaw's, and Cadmus Wilcox's brigades, together with the remnants of Howell Cobb's, Paul Semmes', and William Mahone's (Parham's) brigades, which had been roughly handled during the fight for Crampton's Gap. McLaws deployed his men in two ranks and tasked Richard Anderson with its command. Other brigades were available to reinforce the line if needed, but for the time being McLaws left them in position overlooking the Potomac River.[1]

When he learned the VI Corps had forced its way through Crampton's Gap, McClellan sent Franklin orders at 1:00 a.m. on September 15 to move into Pleasant Valley, send some troops to occupy Rohrersville, and the bulk to the road between the latter town and Harpers Ferry.

These troops were to force their way through the valley to reinforce the beleaguered garrison. Franklin was also to open communication with Col. Dixon Miles to let him know help was on the way. More detailed orders arrived before dawn directing Franklin to quickly seize control of Pleasant Valley, "attacking and destroying such of the enemy as you may find" before pressing on to Harpers Ferry. After lifting the siege, Franklin would move north to Boonsboro to rejoin the rest of the army. McClellan fully expected a major battle around Boonsboro, but if the Confederates were not thinking along the same lines, Franklin would be in position to descend upon Sharpsburg and fall upon the enemy's rear. McClellan ordered Franklin to leave a large force at Rohrersville should the detachment under Stonewall Jackson move up Pleasant Valley against the VI Corps' rear.

Franklin was well known for his caution, which was on full display on September 15. He viewed his aggressive orders with trepidation because he believed he was outnumbered. The corps commander looked down from South Mountain on the morning after his victory to see that "the whole breadth of the valley was occupied, and batteries swept the only approaches to the position." He moved his divisions down into Pleasant Valley about 9:00 a.m. and sent McClellan a report on his progress. He would not advance toward Harpers Ferry until Couch's division reached Rohrersville, which would take another two hours. Franklin was concerned that Henry Slocum's division was too bloodied after its fight for Crampton's Gap to be of much use. This left him with only Maj. Gen. William Smith's division of 4,500 men to force his way to Harpers Ferry. "If Harper's Ferry has fallen—and the cessation of firing makes me fear that it has—it is my opinion that I should be strongly reinforced," Franklin advised.

As Franklin temporized, another dispatch arrived from McClellan: "It is important to drive in the enemy in your front, but be cautious in doing it until you have some idea of his force. . . . Thus far our success is complete, but let us follow it up closely, but warily."[2]

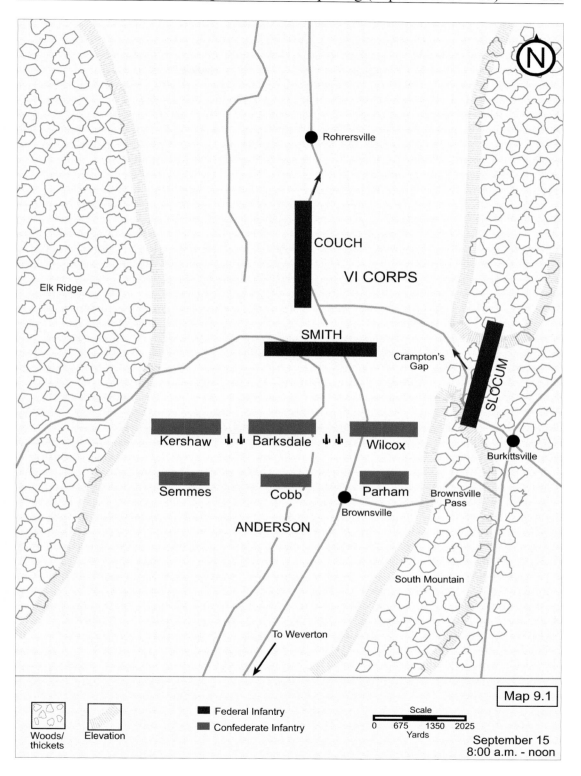

Map 9.1

September 15
8:00 a.m. - noon

Map 9.2: The Confederates Move to Sharpsburg (September 14-15)

Maj. Gen. D. H. Hill's battered Rebel division retreated off South Mountain about 10:00 p.m. on September 14. Once relieved by Micah Jenkins' brigade, Alfred Colquitt's men toiled back up the heights to the Mountain House and joined Robert Rodes and his bloodied regiments about 11:00 p.m. for their trek to and through Boonsboro. The column tramped southwest on the Boonsboro and Sharpsburg road and reached Keedysville about 1:00 a.m. on September 15.

Gen. Lee ordered Rodes to halt both brigades for an hour of rest before continuing on to Sharpsburg, where they were to push some Yankee cavalry out of the town. Another orderly arrived with a change in orders: only a portion of Rodes' command was to advance, so the brigadier selected the 5th and 6th Alabama. Yet another orderly drew in his mount, this one from Maj. Gen. James Longstreet, with orders that Rodes continue marching to Sharpsburg with his entire force. When no enemy cavalry was found in Sharpsburg, Rodes ordered his own men to occupy the high ground southwest of town while Colquitt's infantry made their way to Boteler's Ford (presumably to guard the important crossing). Jackson's command would cross the Potomac River there after its march up from Harpers Ferry.[3]

While Rodes and Colquitt marched on the main road from Boonsboro to Sharpsburg, Hill's remaining brigades—Samuel Garland's (now under Duncan McRae), Roswell Ripley's, and G. B. Anderson's—used country lanes to reach Boonsboro. Once in Boonsboro, they followed the same route to Sharpsburg. The column rested about an hour in and around Keedysville before continuing on. The men used the Middle Bridge to cross Antietam Creek just before sunrise, marched another mile or so, and took up a position above the Boonsboro Pike just north of town. Hill accompanied these three brigades and directed their actions. The division, he estimated, numbered about 3,000 men at Sharpsburg. What he lacked in infantry he made up in artillery: twenty-six of his own guns and another twenty or so from Cutts' battalion. Hill

wished he could attack the Yankees on September 16 as they cautiously crossed the creek, but he knew he was not strong enough to do so.[4]

Longstreet made the journey with D. R. Jones' division. Although everyone was anxious to leave the South Mountain area, they were forced to wait as the long wagon trains (quartermaster, ordnance, ambulance, and commissary) followed Hill's men south. Stephen D. Lee's six-battery reserve artillery battalion accompanied the wagon train and deployed near Hill north of the Boonsboro Road. The wagon train continued through the town and halted about half way to the Potomac River.[5]

The trains rolled slowly, and it was not until after midnight that Longstreet was able to get his infantry moving. Thomas Drayton's crippled brigade departed first, moving along lanes and fields to Boonsboro before using the Boonsboro-Sharpsburg road. James Kemper's and Richard Garnett's brigades, which had fought against portions of the Federal I Corps at Turner's Gap, were next in line, marching along the National Road. G. T. Anderson's brigade, also of Jones' division, was ordered to report to Maj. Gen. John Hood, whose own division formed the initial rearguard. It remained near Fox's Gap until ordered to join the retreat. Brig. Gen. Nathan Evans' brigade also joined the rearguard, giving Hood four brigades to contest any aggressive enemy follow-up actions. Soon thereafter Evans moved down the mountain to Boonsboro and made his way to Keedyville. The rest of Hood's men left Fox's Gap about 1:00 a.m. on September 15 and marched to Boonsboro, where they rested about a mile south of town until after daylight before continuing on to Keedysville.[6] Longstreet's rearguard was composed of Jenkins' brigade under Joseph Walker, which had relieved Colquitt at the Mountain House. Walker did not begin marching until 4:00 a.m. on September 15, and reached Sharpsburg via Boonsboro and Keedysville.

According to campaign historian Ezra Carman, the Confederate retreat from South Mountain "was not effected without much disorder and some demoralization, and the number of stragglers was very large—particularly in Longstreet's command, which had made a severe march from Hagerstown, been needlessly moved about the field, some of it very roughly handled by the enemy, and all of it much jaded."[7]

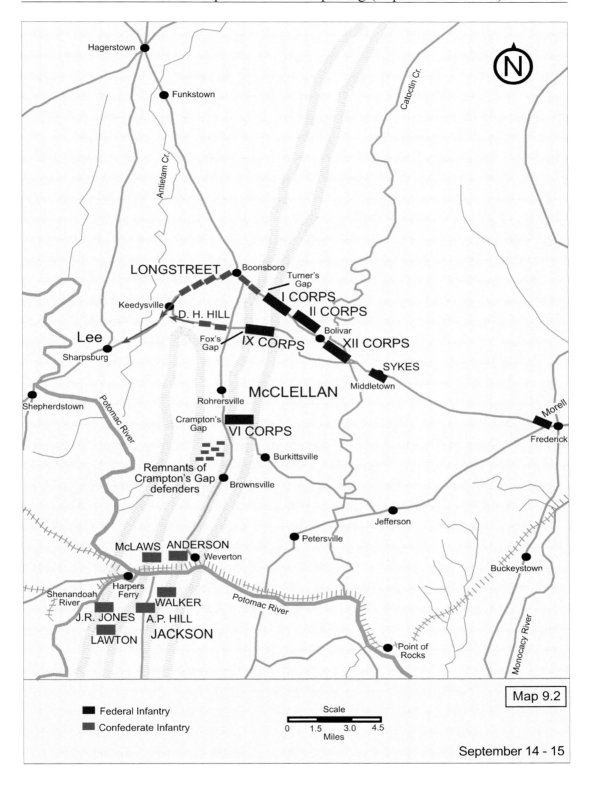

Hagerstown

Funkstown

Catoctin Cr.

N

Antietam Cr.

LONGSTREET Boonsboro
                      Turner's
                      Gap
Keedysville   I CORPS
         D. H. HILL   II CORPS
Lee   Bolivar
Sharpsburg Fox's IX CORPS XII CORPS
            Gap
                              SYKES
         Rohrersville McCLELLAN Middletown

Shepherdstown

Potomac River

Crampton's
Gap   VI CORPS   Morell

                  Burkittsville Frederick

Remnants of
Crampton's Gap
defenders Brownsville

                      Jefferson

McLAWS ANDERSON
              Weverton   Petersville
Shenandoah
River   Harpers
         Ferry   Buckeystown
J.R. JONES WALKER
         A.P. HILL   Potomac River
LAWTON JACKSON

                              Point of
                              Rocks

                      Monocacy River

■ Federal Infantry   Scale   Map 9.2
■ Confederate Infantry   0 1.5 3.0 4.5
                              Miles

                              September 14 - 15

Map 9.3: The Union Army Moves to Antietam Creek (September 15)

Federal pickets cautiously approached Turner's Gap at first light on September 15. When it was determined that the Rebels were gone, McClellan issued orders for a pursuit. The I, II, and XII corps would follow the National Road through Turner's Gap toward Boonsboro, while the IX Corps and Brig. Gen. George Sykes' division of the V Corps passed through Fox's Gap along the Old Sharpsburg Road. The Federals enjoyed a rare experience during this march: moving across and possessing a battlefield at the end of victorious combat.[8]

McClellan began the day at Bolivar on the National Road just east of Turner's Gap. One of his first acts was to order Maj. Gen. Edwin Sumner to march his II Corps past the bloodied and exhausted I Corps toward Boonsboro. Should the town be abandoned, McClellan explained, Sumner should find a strong position in the vicinity and stay put. McClellan was about to send off these orders when he learned the Confederates were in full retreat toward the Potomac River. He amended his orders to read that if Boonsboro was abandoned, Sumner should move toward the Potomac River with all haste. In fact, the town was abandoned and Sumner turned his II Corps left and headed for Keedysville, with the I Corps (now under Maj. Gen. Joe Hooker) trailing the II. The head of the column halted at Keedysville about 3:00 p.m.

Maj. Gen. Joseph Mansfield's XII Corps began the day at Bolivar and brought up the rear of the column. It reached the Nicodemus Mill, about two miles southeast of Keedysville on the Old Sharpsburg Road.[9]

Sumner's First Division under Brig. Gen. Israel Richardson was far in advance of the rest of the II Corps. Although it had been attached to Joe Hooker's I Corps the prior evening, Richardson's command was advancing toward Boonsboro on the Old Hagerstown Road early on September 15. The powerful division was confronted at Turner's Gap by Fitzhugh Lee's Southern cavalry brigade. The outgunned gray troopers were forced to withdraw, but halted to contest the advance once again at Boonsboro, where the cavalry was once again forced to withdraw after a short but sharp fight. Richardson reached Keedysville and deployed his division into line of battle just beyond the town. Hooker discovered the reason why when he rode ahead to confer with Richardson. On the far side of Antietam Creek were thousands of enemy soldiers "ostentatiously" deployed.[10]

Meanwhile, Maj. Gen. Fitz John Porter's V Corps marched along Old Sharpsburg Road with Sykes' division. Another one of his divisions under Maj. Gen. George Morell was still at Frederick with orders to advance at 3:00 a.m. Sykes' column, with Porter accompanying it, broke camp at Middletown at 9:00 a.m. and reached Fox's Gap around noon. Porter was surprised to see that the IX Corps, which Sykes was supposed to follow, had not yet budged and showed no sign that it intended to do so any time soon. McClellan ordered Sykes to march past the tired men who had fought so hard the day before. Sykes ended the day beyond Keedysville on the left of Richardson's division.

When the IX Corps finally arrived, it went into camp to the left and rear of Sykes. Sumner's II Corps went into bivouac behind Richardson on either side of the Boonsboro Turnpike, and the I Corps slid into position on his right. After many days on the march, the Army of the Potomac was finally concentrating northeast of Sharpsburg. The only exception was Franklin's VI Corps, which was operating in Pleasant Valley despite the fact that McLaws had already vacated that place.[11]

The concentration of the bulk of the Federal army in front Lee's new position near Sharpsburg presented the Southern commander with a serious problem. His own Army of Northern Virginia was still widely separated, with fully six of his infantry divisions in or around Harpers Ferry on the morning of September 15.

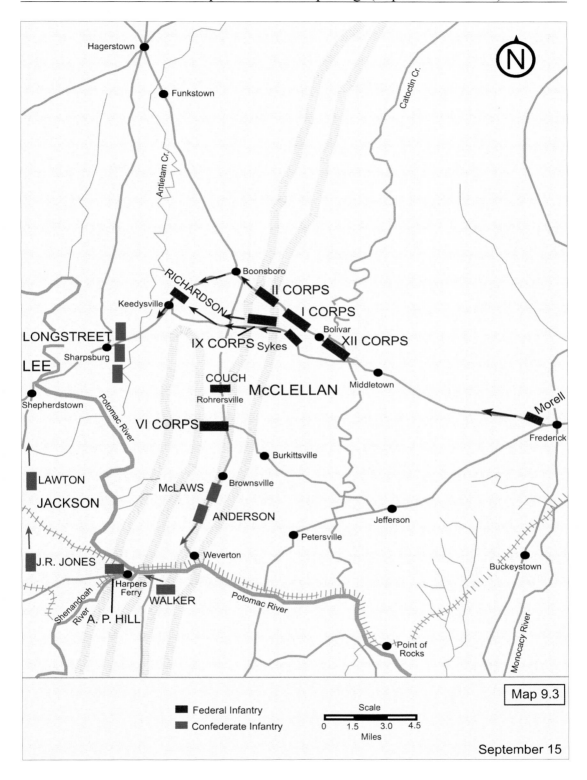

Hagerstown

Funkstown

Catoctin Cr.

N

Antietam Cr.

RICHARDSON

Boonsboro

II CORPS

Keedysville

I CORPS

LONGSTREET

Bolivar

IX CORPS Sykes

XII CORPS

LEE

Sharpsburg

Shepherdstown

COUCH

McCLELLAN

Middletown

Rohrersville

Potomac River

VI CORPS

Morell

Frederick

Burkittsville

LAWTON

McLAWS

Brownsville

JACKSON

ANDERSON

Jefferson

J.R. JONES

Petersville

Buckeystown

Harpers
Ferry

Weverton

Shenandoah
River

A. P. HILL

WALKER

Potomac River

Monocacy River

Point of
Rocks

Map 9.3

Federal Infantry

Scale

Confederate Infantry

0   1.5   3.0   4.5
Miles

September 15

Map 9.4: Jackson's Command Leaves Harpers Ferry for Sharpsburg (September 15-16)

Lafayette McLaws considered marching out of Pleasant Valley across Maryland soil to rejoin Lee's army, but Franklin's VI Corps stood in the way. Instead of risking a potentially disastrous encounter, McLaws wisely decided to cross the Potomac River near Harpers Ferry on a pontoon bridge. He sent his wagons across first, but before he could get his infantry in motion the bridge clogged with Federal prisoners trying to cross in the opposite direction. The captives were overseen by Maj. Gen. A. P. Hill, who planned to release them once in Maryland. McLaws had no choice but to wait until about 2:00 a.m. on September 16 before his men could use the bridge and march to Halltown, where they went into camp. The rear of his column did not reach the camp until 11:00 a.m. that day.[12]

Maj. Gen. John Walker's division fared little better, largely because Walker failed to reconnoiter the area on September 15 and was now forced to expend hours of precious time attempting to find a suitable ford across the Shenandoah River. In this he was unsuccessful, which forced him to backtrack. His tired infantry did not reach Halltown until after dark.[13]

Stonewall Jackson did not order his men to prepare two days' rations until 3:00 a.m. on September 15. Two brigades of Alexander Lawton's division under Cols. James Walker and Marcellus Douglass used captured Federal rations and marched immediately, but the division's remaining two brigades under Brig. Gens. Jubal Early and Harry Hays were forced to cool their heels for several hours and prepare their own rations near Harpers Ferry. These brigades began moving after dark and after a six-mile march caught up with the rest of the division in camp near Shepherdstown. J. R. Jones' division took ten hours to return to its camps southwest of Halltown, where it prepared rations and prepared to settle down for the night. Jackson had other ideas and Jones' men were on their feet marching after midnight toward Shepherdstown. Jackson must have sent the same orders to John Walker, for his two brigades were in motion during the dead of night behind

Jones. As a result, three of the Confederate divisions under Jackson's command were within nine miles of Sharpsburg by dawn. It was a tough trek, and even Jackson called it "a severe night's march." Although Jackson should have had 16,000 men with him that night, severe straggling reduced his numbers to as few as 10,000.[14]

Robert E. Lee, meanwhile, waited with some anxiety for his diminished army to reassemble. He grew more concerned when a Federal picket line appeared on the far side of meandering Antietam Creek: the enemy had arrived—or at least Richardson's vanguard division. Lee received a measure of reassurance when Fitz Lee's cavalry arrived and formed on the army's left flank near the Dunker Church. Thomas Munford's troopers deployed on the opposite right flank near the Lower Bridge.[15]

Heavy fog shrouded the low lands around Antietam Creek when dawn broke over the two armies on September 16. Both McClellan and Lee overestimated the strength of the other. McClellan thought Lee had at least 60,000 men arranged on the undulating ground around Sharpsburg, when in fact his numbers were closer to 25,000. Lee, in turn, believed McClellan had 70,000 or 80,000 Federals ready to strike his depleted force, when only some 48,000 were in position.[16]

When McClellan demonstrated unexpected aggression and broke through South Mountain on September 14, Lee had little choice but to end the campaign and cross back over the Potomac. Now that Harpers Ferry had surrendered and several divisions were about to rejoin his army, Lee determined to bend the campaign back to his advantage and reassume the initiative if at all possible. He could not determine whether Federal troops had crossed Antietam Creek on the Middle Bridge, but he suspected as much. He also believed he had at best twenty-four hours before McClellan went over to the offensive. Lee may well have remained at Sharpsburg because he considered swinging around McClellan's right flank toward Hagerstown, where he could renew his campaign and threaten Pennsylvania. He dispatched cavalry north to find out if the route was open, while sending his wagons across the Potomac to Shepherdstown, something he would not have done if he intended to fight a major engagement at Sharpsburg.[17]

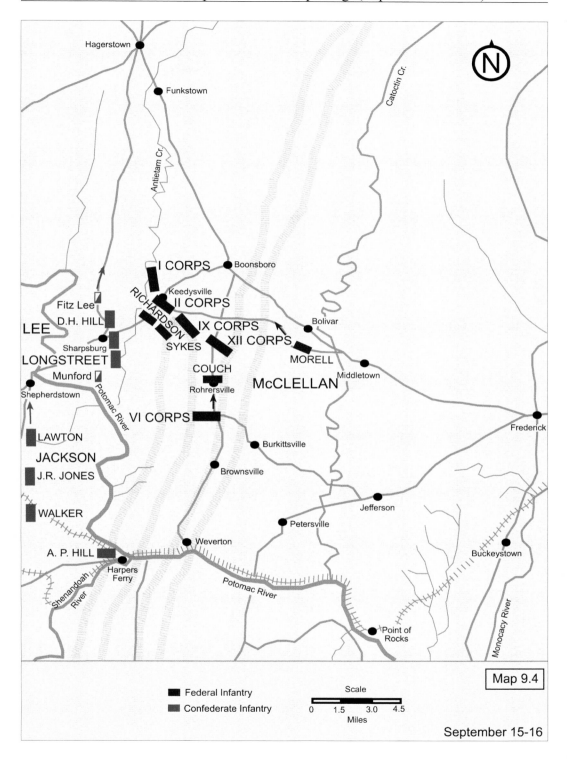

Map 9.4

■ Federal Infantry
■ Confederate Infantry

Scale

0   1.5   3.0   4.5
Miles

September 15-16

Map 9.5: Jackson and McClellan Arrive (September 16)

Most of Stonewell Jackson's command was on the road early on September 16 for the final leg of its march to reunite with the balance of Lee's army. The long roll sounded in the camps before daylight, and John R. Jones' division, which had only just reached the bivouac site about two miles from Shepherdstown, was ordered to lead the column. The exhausted men didn't say much in the darkness as they trudged the final four miles to Boteler's Ford, which they reached at daybreak. After crossing the Potomac into Maryland, they continued along the canal towpath for about two miles until they reached the Shepherdstown Road, and then marched north for three miles. The infantry camped in a grove of oaks one mile from Sharpsburg.[18]

Lawton's division trailed Jones toward Sharpsburg. Its men were in better shape because they reached their camp site earlier the evening before and rested for much of the night. Walker's division arrived at the camp near Shepherdstown just as the last of Lawton's infantry were moving out. Like Jones' men, Walker's command was also enervated after its night march, so Walker allowed them to rest a few hours before continuing their trek across the Potomac around noon. When the roughly 10,000 men in these three divisions reached Sharpsburg, Lee's numbers swelled to about 35,000 veterans.[19]

McClellan's men were also on the move, sliding into their assigned positions on either side of Antietam Creek. Hooker's I Corps was on the right (north) near the Upper Bridge between the forks of the Big and Little Antietam creeks, with Sumner's II Corps to his left. Richardson's division (Sumner's II Corps) moved toward the Middle Bridge on the right of the Boonsboro-Sharpsburg Road. The corps' other two divisions under John Sedgwick and William French were farther to the rear straddling the road. The V Corps was also in this sector, with Sykes' division deployed on Richardson's left and Morell's division farther to the rear near French's division. The IX Corps under Burnside/Cox anchored the left of the line. Just before noon, Mansfield's XII Corps arrived and rested behind French's division.[20]

Prior to the arrival of Jackson's men, Lee had three divisions in position in front of Sharpsburg. D. H. Hill's command, which had stubbornly held the vital Fox's and Turner's gaps during the battles of September 14, arrived on the 15th and deployed on the hills just north of Sharpsburg straddling a farm lane between the Boonsboro Pike and the Hagerstown Pike. George B. Anderson's brigade held the right, bisecting the pike with Roswell Ripley's brigade deployed a short distance to the rear. Alfred Colquitt's brigade was farther north on the opposite side of the line. Rodes' and McRae's brigades were in the middle. Hill's roughly 3,000 men barely covered their front. All were hungry, and many throughout the army suffered from diarrhea because green corn and apples were the staple of the day.

Longstreet's pair of divisions were farther south. When D. R. Jones' division crossed Antietam Creek about 10:00 a.m. on September 16, Longstreet placed it on the commanding ridge south of the Boonboro and Sharpsburg pike facing southeast and the Lower Bridge. The brigades were arranged in two lines: Jenkins, Drayton, and Kemper in the first and Garnett behind them. Toombs' small brigade from this same division was thrown forward to cover the Lower Bridge. Longstreet's second division under Hood, with Shanks Evans' and G. T. Anderson's brigades in tow, arrived about an hour later. They deployed just east of Sharpsburg, but Hood was soon ordered to move his two-brigade division north to the Dunker Church on the Hagerstown Pike.[21]

While Lee planned his next move, McClellan waited. "It is evident that McClellan had no idea of fighting Lee on the fifteenth; there seems to have been no intention to do it on the sixteenth," concluded campaign historian Ezra Carman. "Certainly no orders to that effect were issued, nor did he make any preparation. In fact he expected Lee to retreat during the night of the fifteenth." As a frustrated veteran from Sumner's II Corps later explained it, "If it be admitted to have been impracticable to throw the thirty-five brigades that had crossed the South Mountain . . . during the 15th . . . to undertake the attack upon Lee's fourteen brigades . . . it is difficult to see what excuse can be offered for the failure to fight the impending battle on the 16th."[22]

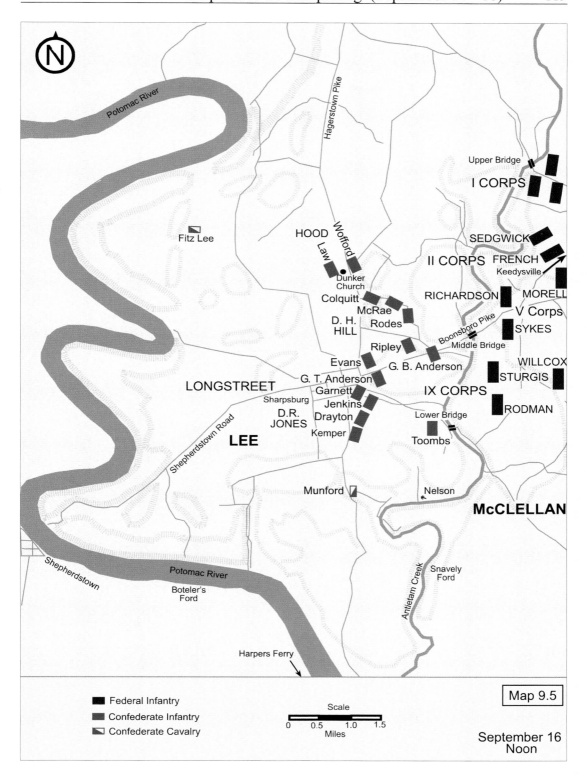

N

Potomac River

Hagerstown Pike

Upper Bridge

I CORPS

Fitz Lee

HOOD

Wofford

Law

Dunker
Church

Colquitt

McRae

D. H.
HILL

Rodes

Ripley

Evans

G. T. Anderson

LONGSTREET

Garnett

Sharpsburg

Jenkins

D.R.
JONES

Drayton

Kemper

LEE

Shepherdstown Road

SEDGWICK

II CORPS   FRENCH

Keedysville

RICHARDSON

MORELL

V Corps

SYKES

Boonsboro Pike

Middle Bridge

G. B. Anderson

WILLCOX

STURGIS

IX CORPS

RODMAN

Lower Bridge

Toombs

Munford

Nelson

McCLELLAN

Shepherdstown

Potomac River

Boteler's
Ford

Antietam Creek

Snavely
Ford

Harpers Ferry

■ Federal Infantry
■ Confederate Infantry
◨ Confederate Cavalry

Scale

0   0.5   1.0   1.5
Miles

Map 9.5

September 16
Noon

Map 9.6: The Antietam Battlefield

The area around Sharpsburg served Lee's purpose now that Harpers Ferry had fallen and his army was coalescing on solid defensive terrain. The position offered wide viewsheds in several directions. The undulating landscape provided Lee with opportunities to deploy his smaller army on ridges and bluffs, and even mask large parts of his army from view. Sharp bluffs lined many places along Antietam Creek. Lee would use this terrain, including the high ground around Sharpsburg, to good advantage.

The region was studded with good roads and a system of farm lanes that allowed Lee to use interior lines to move troops, wagons, and ordnance quickly from one end of the battlefield to the other. Five major roads radiated out of Sharpsburg. Boonsboro Pike ran northeast and crossed the creek at the Middle Bridge. The same route became the Shepherdstown Road on the west side of Sharpsburg on its way to the Potomac and Lee's only route of escape. The Hagerstown Pike ran north of town and offered Lee the option of moving in that direction should he decide to turn the Army of the Potomac's right flank. This pike was intersected by Keedysville-Williamsport Road about three miles outside Sharpsburg. This road crossed Antietam Creek at the Upper Bridge. The Smoketown Road branched off the Hagerstown Pike just north of the Dunker Church. Running roughly parallel to the Hagerstown Pike, another road made its way to Mercerville and New Industry along the Potomac River northwest of Sharpsburg. South of town, the Harpers Ferry Road connected with the once-besieged fortress. Finally, a sunken farm lane just north of the Boonsboro Pike cut along what would be the center of Lee's army. It would figure heavily in the coming battle.

Though strong in many ways, the Sharpsburg position was also fraught with peril. Although he was positioned in a giant bend of the Potomac, Lee had too few men to anchor either flank on the wide river. His army was also sandwiched between two waterways—the Potomac in his rear and Antietam Creek in his front. The 200-yard Potomac was a formidable obstacle, especially if it had to be traversed rapidly by large numbers of men, wagons, and

artillery. Shepherdstown had once boasted a good bridge, but it was destroyed the year before, so the only way across the river was a ford about one mile south of town. Jackson's men would use the crossing (variously referred to as Shepherdstown, Blackford's, and Boteler's fords) on September 16 and 17 when they rejoined Lee after the surrender of Harpers Ferry. Lee would use this ford again to retire his battered army during the night of September 18-19 after the battle ended.[23]

Antietam Creek was easier to cross because of three arched stone structures called the "Upper," "Middle," and "Lower" bridges. The Middle Bridge carried the Boonsboro-Sharpsburg Road leading to Keedysville and Boonsboro. The creek could also be forded easily in several places. Pry's Ford was about one-half mile south of the Upper Bridge. Federal engineers improved this excellent crossing point on the evening of September 15 by cutting down the creek's steep banks. Some of Hooker's I Corps would cross the creek using Pry's Ford on the afternoon of September 16, as would Sumner's II Corps the next morning. A couple of other fords were available between Pry's and the Middle Bridge, but they were more difficult to use. However, there was a fairly good ford several hundred yards north of the Lower Bridge that portions of George Crook's brigade would use about noon on September 17. Other fords straddled Antietam Creek farther south, including Snavely's, which Isaac Rodman's division would use on September 17.

Much of the area around Sharpsburg was planted in crops (mainly corn), with hayfields and meadows sprinkled across the scenic landscape. Heavily wooded areas were few in number, but three—the North Woods, East Woods and West Woods—would figure prominently in the battle.

Lee's army, concluded one historian, was in a "fairly strong position for defense in front, but entirely open to an enterprising enemy on the left. Of this Lee was well aware, and it caused him some anxiety on the afternoon of the fifteenth." To compensate, Lee sent Hood's division, reinforced by four of Stephen Lee's artillery batteries, to his left around the Dunker Church. Lee knew he was outnumbered and he had some time to develop his defenses, but "not a spadeful of earth was turned."[24]

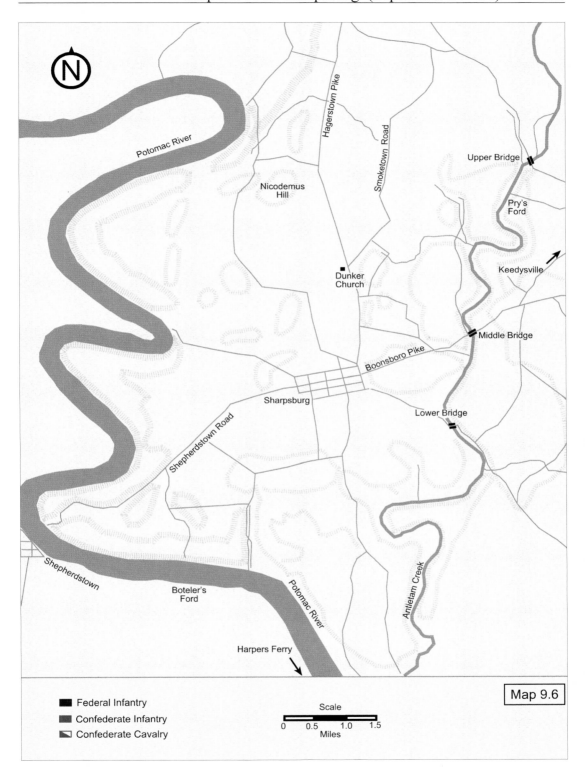

Federal Infantry
Confederate Infantry
Confederate Cavalry

Scale

0   0.5   1.0   1.5
Miles

Map 9.6

Map Set 10. The Eve of Battle
(September 16)

Map 10.1: McClellan and Lee Prepare for Battle at Sharpsburg (September 16: noon - 4:00 p.m.)

Maj. Gen. McClellan was likely surprised and dismayed when the dense fog cleared and the Army of Northern Virginia was still in position in front of Sharpsburg. He was impressed with his adversary's position on the rolling high ground to the west. "On all favorable points, the enemy's artillery was posted, and their reserves, hidden from view by the hills on which their line of battle was formed, could maneuver unobserved by our army, and, from the shortness of their line, could rapidly re-enforce any point threatened by our attack," he wrote. "Their position, stretching across the angle formed by the Potomac and Antietam, their flanks and rear protected by these streams, was one of the strongest to be found in this region of country, which is well adapted to defensive warfare."[1]

Gen. Lee deployed his artillery as well as possible, but his roster was still littered with a large number of obsolete iron pieces and small calibers. Col. John Brown's battalion guarded Light's Ford near Williamsport, Maj. William Nelson's battalion defended Boteler's Ford near Shepherdstown, and the rest of the batteries were deployed in a wide crescent along the ridges surrounding Sharpsburg. The batteries of Maj. Scipio Pierson's battalion were packed along Maj. Gen. D. H. Hill's front, while the Washington Artillery dropped trail south of the Boonsboro Road in front of D. R. Jones' division. Stephen Lee's battalion rolled north and unlimbered to the right of the Dunker Church.[2]

McClellan countered by crowning the heights on the eastern side of Antietam Creek with masses of artillery above and below the Middle Bridge. The guns opened fire whenever enemy infantry showed themselves. Rebel pieces returned fire until Maj. Gen. James Longstreet stopped it. Ammunition was in short supply and the Southern guns did not have the distance to compete, so "Old Pete" ordered the guns moved behind the high ground. D. H. Hill, never a fan of

Confederate artillery, observed that the pieces "could not cope with the superior weight, caliber, range, and number of the Yankee guns," and that the duel between the Washington Artillery and the Federal guns on the far side of the creek was "the most melancholy farce in the war." When Jackson's men arrived, the distant Federal guns maimed and killed dozens during the move north later in the day to bolster Lee's left near the Dunker Church.[3]

Unlike his past experience with Lee, it appeared to McClellan that the Southern leader was not going to attack. Still, McClellan slid his IX Corps south toward the Lower Bridge to guard his vulnerable left against a movement from Harpers Ferry and Pleasant Valley. He issued these orders about noon, but they were not carried out until 3:30 p.m. Brig. Gen. Samuel Sturgis' division faced the Lower Bridge, and Brig. Gen. Isaac Rodman's division deployed one-half mile farther south to watch the road leading from Rohersville. Georgians from Brig. Gen. Howell Toombs' brigade faced Sturgis from the high ground in front of the bridge and from behind a breastwork of rails and stone.[4]

After examining the terrain on September 15, McClellan decided his best opportunity was to swing around from the north and attack Lee's left flank. A more thorough examination was carried out the following morning. According to historian Joseph Harsh, McClellan estimated that Lee's army equaled his own in numbers, which meant a direct frontal assault was out of the question. Instead, he would probe both flanks to see which was most vulnerable. He decided to probe Lee's left first and selected the aggressive Joe Hooker to lead the way. Although Hooker's I Corps had fought long and well two days before at Turner's Gap, his corps was in position on the Union right and fully up to the task. If this failed, McClellan would probe Lee's right flank with the IX Corps. This outfit, too, had seen hard action on September 14 at Fox's Gap, but its new commander, Maj. Gen. Ambrose Burnside, was one of McClellan's closest corps leaders and Burnside's men were already in position on the army' left. McClellan husbanded his major strength, about 35,000 men—the II Corps (18,000 men), V Corps (9,000 men), and XII Corps (8,000 men)—in the center near the Middle Bridge.[5]

One distinguished historian characterized the situation this way: "The plan was a good one, but its execution, from beginning to end, was miserable, though the fighting was splendid."[6]

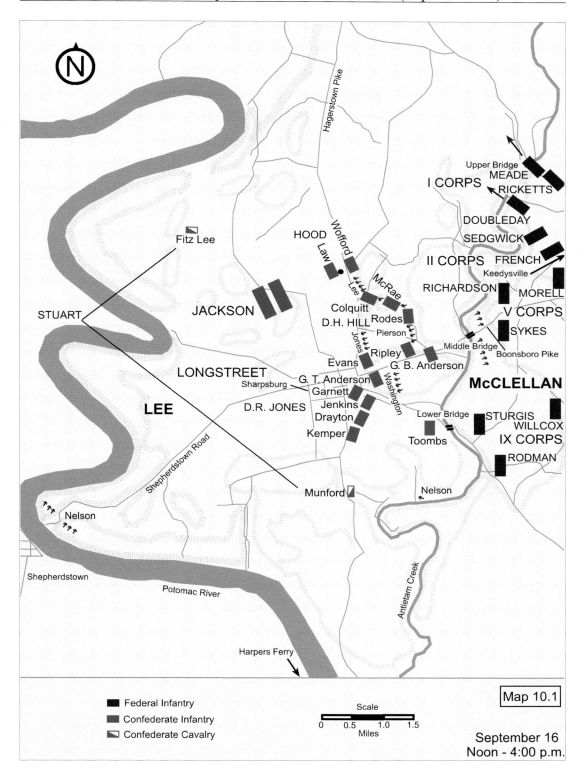

Federal Infantry

Confederate Infantry

Confederate Cavalry

Scale

0   0.5   1.0   1.5
Miles

Map 10.1

September 16
Noon - 4:00 p.m.

Map 10.2: Hooker's I Corps Crosses Antietam Creek (September 16: 4:00 - 6:30 p.m.)

McClellan gave the order for Hooker to cross Antietam Creek via the Upper Bridge and Pry's Ford about 2:00 p.m. Maj. Gen. George Meade's and Brig. Gen. James Ricketts' divisions crossed via the bridge and Brig. Gen. Abner Doubleday's via the ford. By throwing two divisions across the creek at nearly the same time, McClellan was apparently attempting to prevent Lee from turning his right flank and also ambushing Meade, whose men began crossing the bridge between 3:00 p.m. and 4:00 p.m. Hooker rode to McClellan's headquarters to get additional information and was told that once across the creek, he was to angle to the left and move south toward Sharpsburg, feeling for Lee's flank. He was also told that he could call upon other corps for reinforcements, as needed.[7]

Hooker threw two regiments out as skirmishers and, as usual, rode along with them. According to Hooker, he gave McClellan an earful when the army commander later joined him. "I said to the general that he had ordered my small corps, now numbering between 12,000 and 13,000 (as I had just lost nearly 1,000 men in the battle of South Mountain), across the river to attack the whole rebel army, and if reenforcements were not forwarded promptly, or if another attack was not made on the enemy's right, the rebels would eat me up."[8]

Before he returned to his headquarters at the Pry House, McClellan redirected Meade's column, which had been marching west along the Keedysville-Williamsport Road instead of turning left as ordered. Doubleday made good progress at Pry's Ford, moved north, and slipped left (south) when it was observed by Rebel cavalry, who rode south to the Dunker Church to inform Maj. Gen. Jeb Stuart of the crossing. Stuart passed on the unwelcome news to Gen. Lee: Federals were crossing Antietam Creek and moving toward his left—the sector Lee was the most worried about and where he was the most vulnerable.[9]

The unpleasant news arrived while Lee was meeting with his chief lieutenants, Jackson and Longstreet, at the Jacob Grove home at the southwest corner of the Sharpsburg town square. Lee moved quickly to counter the enemy threat. He ordered Longstreet to move Brig. Gen. John Hood's two brigades north to deal with the Yankees, and directed Jackson, whose three divisions were behind Hood, to move up to the left of them. Lee also had John Walker deploy his small division on Longstreet's right flank.[10]

Moving southwest, Meade's division, with Brig. Gen. Truman Seymour's brigade in the van, struck the Smoketown Road and headed south on it (No. 1). Doubleday's division continued moving west instead of joining the march on Smoketown Road, with its first brigade under Brig. Gen. Marsena Patrick crossing the road. Just then, Ricketts' division arrived on the Smoketown Road, cutting off the rest of Doubleday's remaining three brigades (No. 2), which could not cross the road behind Patrick until the last of Ricketts' men had passed. Doubleday's division reunited after nightfall at the northern edge of the Joseph Poffenberger farm. Worried about the presumed route Jackson's men might take from Harpers Ferry, Doubleday formed his men facing west along the Hagerstown Pike.[11]

When Meade's division continued marching down the Smoketown Road, Brig. Hen. Fitzhugh Lee sent the 9th Virginia cavalry east to contest its movement. Hood, whose two-brigade division occupied the sector near the Dunker Church, sent a couple of infantry companies from the 6th North Carolina and 2nd Mississippi up the Hagerstown Pike to the D. R. Miller farm. About 100 men from the 4th Texas were also thrown forward to their right, stopping just south of the East Woods. Stephen Lee also sent two howitzers from Capt. A. B. Rhett's battery to the left of the Mumma house (near the Smoketown Road) and D. H. Hill sent Capt. John Lane's battery, which deployed between the Smoketown Road and Hagerstown Pike. Three guns from Capt. William Poague's battery would later add its weight to the approaching fight.[12]

After marching about one mile, Meade moved slightly to his left to occupy high ground. When the enemy opened fire on him, Hooker ordered the 13th Pennsylvania Reserves forward to the left of the Smoketown Road as a strong skirmish line while four companies of the 3rd Pennsylvania Reserves moved cautiously southward on their right.[13]

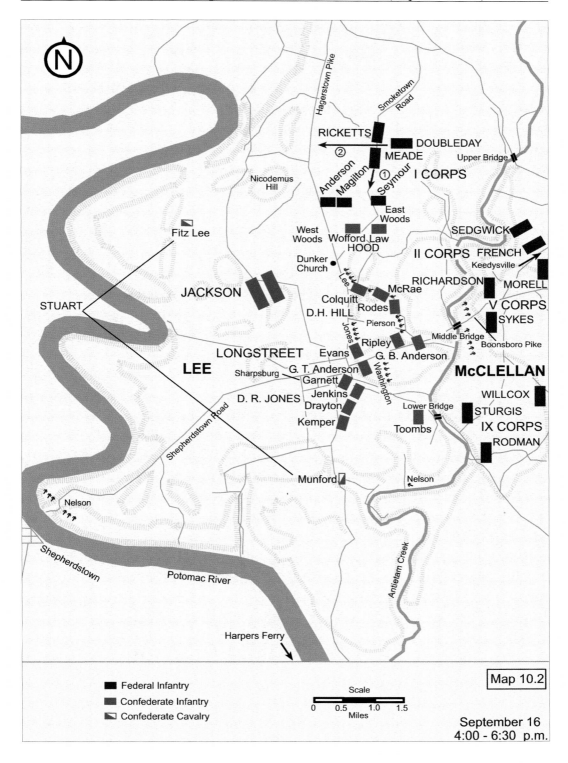

N

RICKETTS
②
DOUBLEDAY
MEADE
Upper Bridge
Anderson
Magilton
Nicodemus
Hill
①
Seymour
I CORPS
Fitz Lee
East
Woods
West
Woods
Wofford Law
HOOD
SEDGWICK
II CORPS FRENCH
Keedysville
Dunker
Church
Lee
JACKSON
RICHARDSON
MORELL
STUART
Colquitt
McRae
V CORPS
SYKES
Rodes
D.H. HILL
Pierson
Jones
Middle Bridge
Boonsboro Pike
LONGSTREET Evans
Ripley
LEE
G. T. Anderson
G. B. Anderson
Washington
McCLELLAN
Sharpsburg
Garnett
D. R. JONES
Jenkins
Drayton
WILLCOX
Lower Bridge
STURGIS
Kemper
Toombs
IX CORPS
RODMAN
Munford
Nelson
Nelson
Antietam Creek
Shepherdstown Road

Shepherdstown
Potomac River

Harpers Ferry

Federal Infantry
Confederate Infantry
Confederate Cavalry

Scale
0   0.5   1.0   1.5
Miles

Map 10.2

September 16
4:00 - 6:30 p.m.

Map 10.3: Meade Deploys his Division for Battle (September 16: 6:30 - 10:00 p.m.)

Confederate artillery and small arms fire began chipping away at Seymour's brigade, which steadily continued its southward advance as the shadows lengthened with the approach of dusk. The 13th Pennsylvania Reserves was in the lead and supported by the 3rd Pennsylvania Reserves. The former regiment, also called the "Bucktails," was reprising its role of September 14 when it was thrown out as skirmishers for the division during the approach to Turner's Gap at South Mountain. After advancing three-quarters of a mile and pushing the enemy's skirmish line before them, Col. Hugh McNeil permitted his men to rest in a plowed field west of the Samuel Poffenberger farm.[14]

Hood watched the developing fight between the two skirmish lines intensify and decided to move his two brigades forward from their positions near the Dunker Church. Col. William Wofford's brigade, which had occupied open ground east of the church, moved by its left flank, sliding about 700 yards to the Miller cornfield between the Smoketown Road and the Hagerstown Pike. Brig. Gen. Evander Law's brigade, which was in the woods surrounding the church, moved forward and took position on Wofford's right on the east side of the Smoketown Road. The East Woods loomed just in front of them. Surely some of the men recalled a similar situation just two days before, when night was settling in and they were shuttled quickly to the front to blunt the Federal attack at Fox's Gap. The situation on this evening, however, was not quite so desperate.[15]

The 13th Pennsylvania Reserves rested for about fifteen minutes at the edge of the plowed field just north of the East Woods while the remainder of Seymour's brigade approached. Meade brought up Capt. James Cooper's battery to duel with the Confederates and advanced the other two brigades of his division into the North Woods, where they supported Capt. Dunbar Ransom's guns.[16]

Now it was up and forward, as McNeil deployed his entire 13th Pennsylvania Reserves. Four companies formed on the right of the Smoketown Road and six on the left. The Bucktails could see the white Dunker Church in the distance when they moved out into the open. Confederate artillery and small arms fire raked through their lines. Shouted orders to quicken their pace toward the East Woods urged them on. Their immediate goal was the fence line at the southern end of the timber, which also harbored Evander Law's veteran Confederate infantry.[17]

The furrowed field, freshly plowed for autumn planting, impeded the Pennsylvanians' progress and the well-aligned battle line soon fell apart. When the line was about 75 yards from the woods, the intense Confederate fire convinced the Federals to fall flat on their faces to avoid being killed or maimed. McNeil's men returned fire as best they could, stood once more, and bounded over several more furrows before hitting the ground again. They repeated this tactic several times until they reached the East Woods, though they did so without Col. McNeil, who had been shot through the heart. "Forward, Bucktails, Forward!" he urged before dying. Anger propelled his men, who leaped the fence into the woods and confronted Law's troops standing firm on the far side. The combat was desperate, particularly on the right side of the Reserves' line, which battled not only Law's men in front but the 4th and 5th Texas of Wofford's brigade advancing against their vulnerable right flank. Darkness, however, ended the fighting. "[T]he enemy was driven, at dark to the farther side of the wood, toward the Antietam," reported Law."[18]

The intensive counter-artillery fire triggered a shifting of the batteries. Rhett's guns were pounded by the Federal pieces firing from near the North Woods. As Rhett pulled back, Poague's Rebel guns galloped up and unlimbered. Ransom's Federal battery also fell back to the north side of the North Woods.[19]

By 10:00 p.m. it was pitch dark and the fields fell silent. Occasional firing during that evening, however, interrupted any attempt at sound sleep.[20]

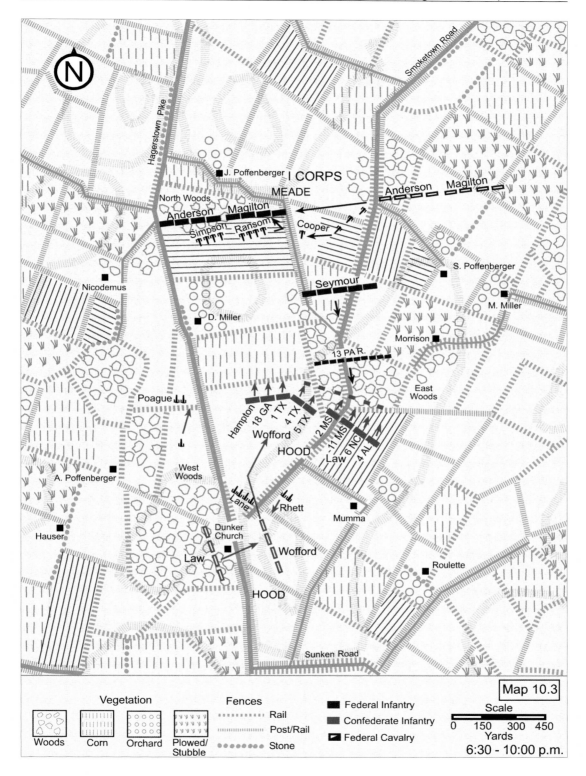

Map Set 10. The Eve of Battle (September 16)

I CORPS
MEADE

J. Poffenberger

North Woods
Anderson   Magilton
Simpson   Ransom

Anderson   Magilton

Cooper

Nicodemus

S. Poffenberger

D. Miller

Seymour

M. Miller

Morrison

13 PA R.

Poague

East
Woods

Hampton
18 GA
1 TX
4 TX
5 TX
2 MS
11 MS
6 NC
4 AL

Wofford
HOOD
Law

West
Woods

A. Poffenberger

Lane
Rhett

Mumma

Hauser

Dunker
Church

Wofford

Law

Roulette

HOOD

Sunken Road

Vegetation

Woods   Corn   Orchard   Plowed/
Stubble

Fences

Rail
Post/Rail
Stone

Federal Infantry
Confederate Infantry
Federal Cavalry

Map 10.3

Scale

0   150   300   450
Yards

6:30 - 10:00 p.m.

Map 10.4: The Night Before Antietam (September 16-17, 1862)

Both Lee and McCellan spent the night planning for the next day. Given the intensity of the fighting around the East Woods and his own observations of enemy troops being shifted to the sector, McClellan believed Lee intended to stand and fight. He was pleased that Lee was weakening other parts of his line to reinforce his left, which would leave him more vulnerable to a strong attack against his center or right. Still, McClellan worried about Hooker's I Corps being isolated and destroyed by a concentrated assault. He decided to reinforce Hooker with Brig. Gen. Joseph Mansfield's XII Corps, which was the army's reserve.

Nearly 60 years old, Mansfield was the second oldest general after Edwin Sumner in the entire Army of the Potomac. Despite his West Point pedigree, the aging warrior had never led troops in battle; to date he had spent his time as commander of the Department of Washington. Mansfield assumed command of the XII Corps on September 15—just two days before the bloodiest single day in U.S. history. Worst, he did not have confidence in his volunteer soldiers, and many of his subordinates were unimpressed with their new commander.

McClellan also sent a dispatch to Maj. Gen. William Franklin, whose VI Corps was still in Pleasant Valley, to leave one division there and march immediately north to Keedysville with the rest of his corps to be closer to the field. McClellan sent wing commander Maj. Gen. Edwin Sumner orders at 5:50 p.m. on September 16 to send Mansfield's XII Corps across Antietam Creek at once and to prepare his own II Corps for a possible move as early as an hour before sunlight.[21]

Breaking camp near Keedysville, Mansfield led his men across the Upper Bridge and allowed them to camp around 2:30 a.m. on September 17 about one and one-half miles behind Hooker's I Corps near the Hoffman and Line farms. In anticipation of renewed action in this sector, Sumner also dispatched five batteries across the Antietam, where they parked near the XII Corps. Although he was aware of the arrival of these reinforcements, Hooker chose to leave the XII Corps in the rear. Before turning in for a rest at his headquarters at the Joseph Poffenberger barn, Hooker visited his picket line in the East Woods. The enemy was so close Hooker could hear them.[22]

The troops Hooker heard did not belong to Hood's division, which had occupied this part of the field for most of the evening. Because his exhausted men had barely eaten for the past several days, Hood rode to see Lee to request permission to pull them back so they could cook their meager rations before the pending combat on the morrow. After hearing Hood explain their "extreme suffering," Lee replied that he would "cheerfully do so, but he knew of no command which could be spared for the purpose," recalled Hood. Lee suggested he discuss the matter with Stonewall Jackson. The latter agreed to help, explained Hood, but "extracted of me, however, a promise that I would come to the support of these forces the moment I was called upon." Hood of course agreed. Alexander Lawton's former brigade (under Col. Marcellus Douglass) relieved Wofford while Isaac Trimble's brigade (under Col. James Walker) filed into Law's position just south of the East Woods. Hood's men fell back beyond the Dunker Church to cook and rest. Lawton's two other brigades under Brig. Gens. Jubal Early and Harry Hays were just behind Hood in a deep reserve position. Jackson also sent John R. Jones' division to the front and deployed it on the west side of the Hagerstown Pike near the West Woods. Jones' brigade (led by Capt. John Penn) and Brig. Gen. Charles Winder's (under Col. Andrew Grigsby) occupied the first line with the brigades of Brig. Gen. William Starke and Brig. Gen. William Taliaferro (commanded by Col. J. W. Jackson of the 48th Alabama) formed behind them. To provide additional support, Lee ordered Brig. Gen. Roswell Ripley's brigade to leave D. H. Hill's main body in the center of his meandering front and move north to deploy on Walker's right near the Mumma house.[23]

Confederate cavalry guarded the yawning gap between each flank and the river beyond, with Fitz Lee's brigade on army's left flank and Thomas Munford's on the right flank. The rest of Lee's troops remained in place during the nighttime hours.

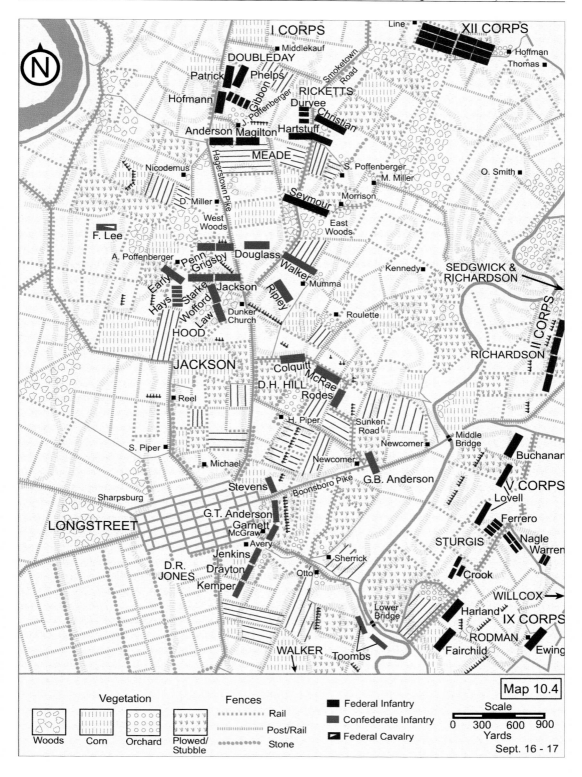

N

I CORPS

Line

XII CORPS

Middlekauf

Hoffman

DOUBLEDAY

Thomas

Patrick   Phelps

RICKETTS

Hofmann   Gibbon

Duryee

Poffenberger

Christian

Anderson Magilton   Hartstuff

MEADE

Nicodemus   S. Poffenberger

O. Smith

M. Miller

Seymour   Morrison

D. Miller

West   East
Woods   Woods

F. Lee

A. Poffenberger   Douglass

SEDGWICK &
RICHARDSON

Penn   Walker

Grigsby

Kennedy

Early

Mumma

Hays   Starke   Jackson   Ripley

Wofford

Roulette

Law   Dunker
Church

HOOD

RICHARDSON

JACKSON

Colquitt   McRae

D.H. HILL   Rodes

Reel

H. Piper   Sunken
Road

S. Piper   Newcomer

Buchanan

Michael   Newcomer

Middle
Bridge

Stevens   G.B. Anderson   V CORPS

Sharpsburg   Boonsboro Pike   Lovell

G.T. Anderson   Ferrero

LONGSTREET   Garnett
McGraw   Nagle
Warren

Avery   Sherrick   STURGIS

Jenkins

D.R.   Drayton   Otto   Crook
JONES   Kemper   WILLCOX

Lower   Harland   IX CORPS
Bridge

RODMAN

WALKER   Toombs   Fairchild   Ewing

Map 10.4

Vegetation   Fences   ▬ Federal Infantry   Scale
·········· Rail   ▬ Confederate Infantry
┅┅┅┅ Post/Rail   ◤ Federal Cavalry   0   300   600   900
Woods Corn Orchard Plowed/   ●●●●● Stone   Yards
Stubble   Sept. 16 - 17

Map Set 11. Antietam: Hooker Opens the Battle (5:15 - 7:00 a.m.)

Map 11.1: Hooker's I Corps Attacks (5:15 - 6:15 a.m.)

Even without Maj. Gen. William Franklin's large VI Corps, Maj. Gen. George McClellan had some 48,000 men on hand when dawn broke on September 17—a large advantage over Gen. Robert E. Lee's roughly 35,000. Maj. Gen. A. P. Hill's division was on the way from Harpers Ferry, but whether it would arrive in time to participate in the battle remained to be seen.

The fog that had covered the fields during the night was slowly lifting when Maj. Gen. Joseph Hooker's I Corps attacked south. Hooker intended to strike Lee's left flank and capture the high ground around the Dunker Church, which would serve as an artillery platform for further operations. From there, he would drive deeper into Lee's ranks, catching Maj. Gen. D. H. Hill on his left flank and force the Rebels from the battlefield and into a potentially disastrous retreat toward the Potomac River. Little went as planned. Hooker's first surprise came early when he learned he was not on Lee's flank. The Rebel front, or what little he could see of it, angled southeast to northwest toward the river. If Hooker attacked south as planned, he would expose his right flank to the Confederate front.[1]

The battle got underway before dawn when Brig. Gen. Truman Seymour continued moving southward as he had the night before. His Pennsylvania Reserves advanced southeast, passed through the eastern part of the D. R. Miller cornfield and the East Woods, and fell upon the 31st Georgia of Col. Marcellus Douglass' brigade. Hit in front and on the right flank, the Georgians fell back about 150 yards and joined the rest of the brigade south of the cornfield. This lower terrain was dotted with rock ledges, and his Georgians used them and fence rails to fashion crude breastworks.[2]

Within a few minutes Seymour's Federals encountered two Rebel brigades (Cols. Douglass and James Walker). The 13th Pennsylvania Reserves marched about 100 yards in front of the rest of the brigade and made an oblique movement in the East Woods so its left flank rested on the Smoketown Road. The 13th fired into Douglass' right front and Walker's left front. The 5th Pennsylvania Reserves advanced behind the 13th and to its left, made good progress through the eastern portion of the East Woods, and caught up with the 13th Pennsylvania Reserves to form a two-regiment front. The 5th's right was about 25 yards from the Smoketown Road, and it opened fire on Walker's men on the opposite side of the plowed field in front. Out in the open, Walker's men got the worst of the exchange. With their ammunition running low, the 13th Pennsylvania Reserves fell back to replenish their supply. They were not in good spirits because they had lost their commanding officer the night before and had not eaten since their noon meal the previous day.

The 2nd Pennsylvania Reserves moved up to take the 13th's place. The former unit did not occupy the same position, but instead slid farther to the right. The commander of the 5th Pennsylvania Reserves, Col. James Fisher, saw the 13th falling back but did not see the 2nd advance, and so thought it prudent to also pull his men back. He halted his men near the Samuel Poffenberger farm.[3]

Help was on the way for Seymour's men. Capt. Ezra Matthews' battery galloped up and unlimbered on the northwest corner of the East Woods to fire into Douglass' men. Federal guns on the opposite side of Antietam Creek also hammered the Rebels. Walker, whose brigade was deployed perpendicular to the Federal guns and out in the open fields, reported that his "command was exposed to full view of their gunners and had no shelter, this fire was very annoying, but less destructive than I at first apprehended it to be." Col. Stephen D. Lee tried to help out by sending two guns from Capt. Tyler Jordan's battery of his battalion to deploy between Douglass and Walker.[4]

As Seymour's Pennsylvanians struggled at the front, orders arrived for Brig. Gen. James Ricketts to move his division forward to support them. Farther to the north and west, massed Confederate artillery firing from Nicodemus Hill struck Brig. Gen. John Gibbon's brigade (Hatch's division, now under Brig. Gen. Abner Doubleday), which was bivouacked just east of the Hagerstown Pike. Gibbon moved his men to a more secure spot near the Joseph Poffenberger farm.[5]

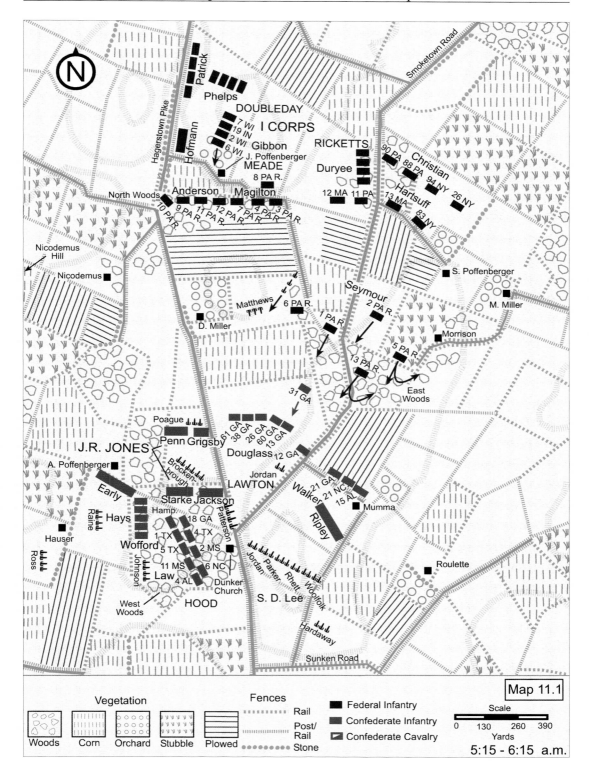

Map 11.1

Vegetation

Woods Corn Orchard Stubble Plowed

Fences
- - - - - Rail
·········· Post/Rail
●●●●●●● Stone

■ Federal Infantry
■ Confederate Infantry
◪ Confederate Cavalry

Scale
0   130   260   390
Yards

5:15 - 6:15 a.m.

Map 11.2: The Battle Spreads
(5:15 - 6:15 a.m.)

Dawn was breaking when the three brigades composing Brig. Gen. James Ricketts' division astride the Smoketown Road moved to support Seymour. Brig. Gen. George Hartsuff's brigade was deployed in front of the division west of the road, with Brig. Gen. Abram Duryee's and Col. William Christian's brigades behind it on the east and west, respectively. The division slid right and halted just east of the North Woods.

Duryee was deployed in columns; when he reached the North Woods orders arrived to move through Hartsuff's regiments. Executing this order was difficult because Col. Albert Magilton's brigade occupied the woods. Duryee's men gingerly picked their way through Magilton's ranks and continued south toward the front.

Christian's brigade, which had been deployed behind Hartsuff, moved south and halted in a plowed field west of the Samuel Poffenberger farm. Gunners with Stephen Lee's battalion of artillery near the Dunker Church saw the movement and opened fire on the Federal infantry, killing and wounding many. Capt. James Thompson's Federal battery dropped trail just south of the North Woods and opened an effective counter-fire against Capt. Tyler Jordan's Southern guns and drove them back. Thompson limbered up and advanced to the pasture just east of the D. R. Miller home to redeploy next to Capt. Ezra Matthews' guns. The two batteries concentrated their fire against Lee's battalion.[6]

Duryee continued pushing to the front and about 6:00 a.m. marched through the Miller cornfield to a fence along its southern border. Douglass' Georgians were now fully in view. The 104th and 105th New York on the left of the line moved up and opened fire on them. Ezra Carman, who not only fought at Antietam but interviewed hundreds of veterans and wrote about the campaign, observed that during this phase of the battle, "no attention was paid by either line to the rail fences in their respective fronts. Each stood and fired on the other, neither party endeavoring to advance." This mini-stalemate finally ended when mounting losses convinced those still on their feet to seek cover.

Duryee's soldiers found a measure of relief by lying on the ground. According to H. W. Burlingame of the 104th New York, dropping flat provided "a partial shelter from the awful storm of lead and iron which filled the air, during that time the stalks of corn were cut off as by a scythe."[7]

Meanwhile, the 2nd Pennsylvania Reserves (Seymour) battled the right side of Douglass' front and Walker's left front. The Pennsylvanians had to contend with heavy small arms fire, especially from the veteran 12th Georgia in front of it, and a deadly artillery shelling. It does not appear that the 2nd ever broke free from the woods. According to one of its soldiers, "we crept on our bellies to our position, and opened a heavy fire upon the enemy, both parties keeping the ground and maintaining their positions."[8]

The 2nd Pennsylvania Reserves was falling back deeper into the woods to take advantage of its protection when the 104th and 105th New York to its right arrived on scene, leveled their rifles, and pulled their triggers. Exposed to this sudden flanking fire, the 100 or so men of the 12th Georgia wheeled left and made for the protection of a rock ledge running nearly parallel with the Smoketown Road.[9]

Hooker was now well aware that the Rebel line stretched north and west beyond the Hagerstown Pike, so he directed Doubleday to move Hatch's division south to engage it. When Gibbon's "Iron Brigade" was ordered to take the lead, his Hoosiers and Badgers slipped through Magilton's troops in the North Woods and tramped south toward the enemy. The 6th Wisconsin moved along the pike and the 2nd Wisconsin moved on its left and entered the Miller cornfield. The 7th Wisconsin and 19th Indiana extended the line along and west of the pike. Doubleday's remaining brigades under Phelps and Patrick advanced behind Gibbon. Phelps' men stepped into the cornfield behind the 2nd Wisconsin; Patrick remained in reserve.[10]

Hooker's troops, especially those on the right, were all too aware that the Confederates had a number of guns atop Nicodemus Hill. At least fourteen pieces there under cavalry commander Jeb Stuart delivered a withering fire against the flank of the I Corps. This artillery was supported by Jubal Early's infantry brigade. Hooker sent twenty-six guns in five batteries north of the Joseph Poffenberger farm to counter this threat.[11]

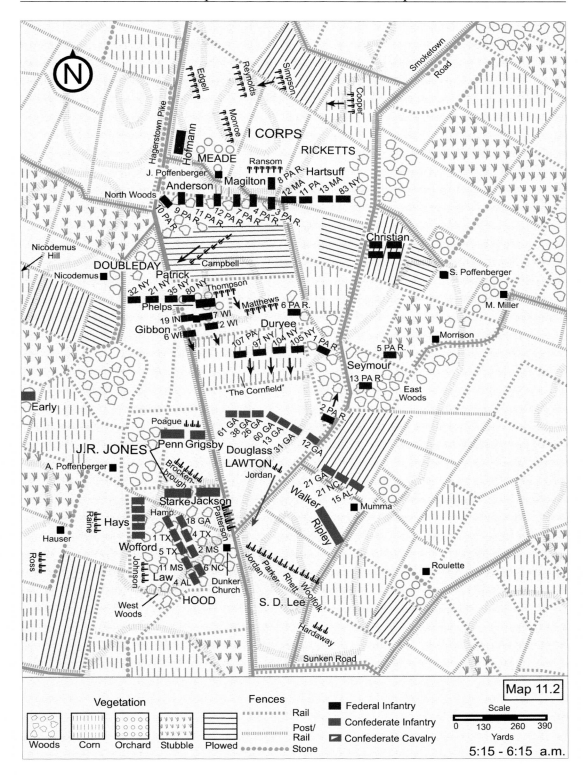

Map 11.2

5:15 - 6:15 a.m.

Map 11.3: Ricketts' Division Enters the Fight (5:15 - 6:15 a.m.)

After volleying with the Confederates in front of them across an open field, the 104th and 105th New York on the left of Duryee's line advanced into the open field (No. 1). The right side of Douglass' line of Georgians—the 60th, 13th, and 31st regiments, and 12th Georgia on the far right—held their fire until the New Yorkers stepped within 100 yards, when they poured several volleys into them. "The men went down like leaves before an autumn breeze," was how one Federal remembered the effects of the fatal blasts. Col. James Walker wheeled his 21st Georgia and 21st North Carolina regiments into line on the right of the 12th Georgia to add their weight to the firing. The impact was almost immediate and the Federal regiments fell back into the cornfield with heavy losses (No. 2).[12]

Meanwhile, the 107th Pennsylvania and the 97th New York on Duryee's right battled the left of Douglass' line composed of the 61st, 38th, and 26th Georgia regiments. The commander of the 61st Georgia slid his men left toward the Hagerstown Pike to put his men on the flank of the 107th Pennsylvania, into which they poured a terrible fire while the other regiments fired into its front. The 38th Georgia tried to advance to a rock ledge for more protection, but was driven back to its original place in line (No. 3).[13]

Reinforcements on both sides were now making their way to the chaotic front. Division commander Alexander Lawton ordered Brig. Gen. Harry Hays' small Louisiana brigade to move from its reserve position north of the Dunker Church to the open space between Douglass' left and the Hagerstown Pike. Hays was executing the order when a new directive arrived, this time from Col. Douglass, to move his troops east to support the right side of Douglass' embattled brigade (No. 4). Portions of four Federal brigades under Hartsuff, Christian, Phelps, and Gibbon were also on the move to join in the fighting.[14]

It was intended that Ricketts deliver his attack simultaneously with all three of his Federal brigades. Duryee's men moved smartly forward, but the other two brigades encountered a variety of problems. After sliding right and halting near the North Woods, Hartsuff's men waited while their commander rode ahead to reconnoiter the terrain and determine how the fighting was going between Seymour and the Rebels in front of him. Hartsuff only made it a short distance before a minie ball tore into his left hip. Col. Richard Coulter of the 11th Pennsylvania assumed command of the brigade, which halted for about thirty minutes before being ordered forward (No. 5) to reinforce Duryee's embattled men fighting in the Miller cornfield. Christian's experience was unhappier. During his approach to the North Woods, he ordered a series of what can only be described as erratic movements that exposed his brigade to a deadly crossfire from the Confederate guns on Nicodemus Hill to their right and from Stephen Lee's guns firing from near the Dunker Church. Caught in this iron rain, Christian tried to maneuver his troops to a safer area. The 90th Pennsylvania was spared this bloody confusion because it was ordered to support Matthews' battery, which was deployed in the open field just north of the Miller cornfield.[15]

Farther west, John Gibbon's Iron Brigade made good progress in its southward movement (No. 6). When he spotted Confederates from Col. Andrew Grigsby's and Capt. John Penn's brigades moving toward the exposed right flank of the 6th Wisconsin, Gibbon ordered the 19th Indiana and 7th Wisconsin to march by their right flank to a patch of woods to place them on what he hoped would be the enemy's exposed left flank.

The 2nd and 6th Wisconsin, meanwhile, moved due south following the Hagerstown Pike. Lt. James Stewart was ordered to advance with a section of guns, and Capt. Joseph Campbell's battery deployed along the Hagerstown Pike to shell the enemy. Luckily for the advancing Federals, they were spared from what would have been destructive discharges from Capt. William Poague's battery because it had been forced from its exposed forward position in front of Grigsby's Virginia brigade.[16]

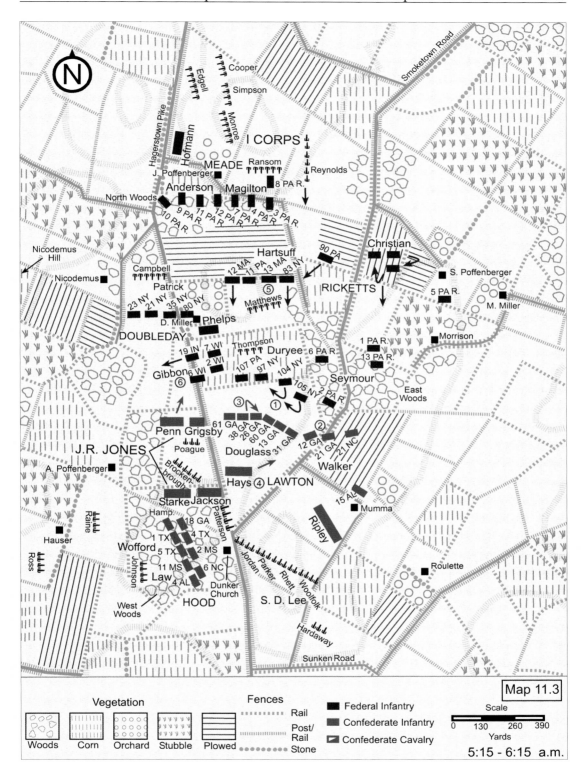

Map 11.3

5:15 - 6:15 a.m.

Vegetation

Woods | Corn | Orchard | Stubble | Plowed

Fences

Rail

Post/ Rail

Stone

■ Federal Infantry

■ Confederate Infantry

▨ Confederate Cavalry

Scale

0   130   260   390

Yards

Map 11.4: Hays and Walker Counterattack (6:15 - 7:00 a.m.)

With three fresh Federal brigades angling toward their left flank and two additional brigades moving toward the center of their line, the Confederate situation looked grim. After being pummeled on his front and flank and losing about one-third of his strength, Duryee received a report that the Rebels were infiltrating the East Woods to his left. Without checking the veracity of this intelligence, Duryee began withdrawing his men. The movement to his left was probably not the enemy but the 2nd Pennsylvania Reserves being repositioned in the East Woods in response to the realignment of two of Walker's Confederate regiments to its front. (See Map 11.3 for details.) The right side of Duryee's brigade, however, did not hear the order to withdraw and hung on a bit longer before pulling back. The men had not moved far before they saw Hartsuff's brigade sweeping toward the cornfield. The new arrivals moved through the field and took their positions behind the fence line Duryee's men had just abandoned. With their wayward movements completed, Christian's men entered the East Woods and moved south toward Hartsuff's left, led "by the gallant Capt. Williams of Rickets [sic] staff, Col. Christian commanding brigade, could not be found," recalled an officer. With the addition of Christian's brigade, the Federals had cobbled together a formidable front (No. 1). Thompson's battery pushed directly into the cornfield and dropped trail, adding additional firepower to the strengthening Federal line.[17]

Alexander Lawton ordered his Rebels after Duryee's retreating infantry. His skirmish line advanced into the cornfield but did not get far before Hartsuff's Federals appeared and drove the Southern infantry from it. Douglass' main line also advanced but was driven back to its former position by Hartsuff's infantry. The historian of the 12th Massachusetts, which occupied the right side of Hartsuff's line, described this as "the most deadly fire of the war." Col. Douglass' losses, especially in officers, were staggering. Douglass himself was killed and every regimental commander was killed or wounded (No. 2).[18]

By this time, Harry Hays' Louisiana brigade was in position on Douglass' right. With his men exposed and the enemy apparently falling back, Hays ordered his men to charge. The Louisianans angled toward the southeast corner of the cornfield with the East Woods on their right and collided directly with Hartsuff's brigade. The heavy close-quarter firing drove Hartsuff's men into the corn. The Louisiana troops tried to follow, but the Federals regrouped and, with the help of an effective artillery barrage, pushed them out of the field with heavy losses (No. 3). "[I]n very short time my command was so reduced, having lost more than half (323 killed and wounded), that . . . I was obliged to retire," reported Hays. His losses were closer to 60% and included every staff officer and regimental commander.

When Hays appeared on his left, Col. Walker also ordered his men forward. But like the Louisianans discovered, the sheets of small arms fire in front and flank, coupled with artillery rounds, were too much to bear. A shell fragment wounded Walker and killed his horse. He remained on the field, however, and when he saw Hays' men in full retreat decided to abort his own attack and his survivors tumbled rearward. "[I] tried to hold the advanced position thus gained," he wrote, "but the enemy was re-enforced, and we were compelled to fall back to our original line." The experience left him bitter, however, and he went on to incorrectly report that "[T]he fresh troops [Hays], which were advancing in such good order at first, gave way under the enemy's fire and ran off the field . . . almost before they had fired a gun." When he learned his men were running low on ammunition, Walker ordered them to scavenge from the cartridge boxes of the wounded and the dead. He had no intention of falling back any farther.[19]

Hartsuff's brigade under Col. Coulter had also suffered horrendous losses battling Hays' and Lawton's men. His 12th Massachusetts lost about 67% and the 11th Pennsylvania's losses exceeded 50%. Desperate for support, Coulter found the 90th Pennsylvania moving south to rejoin Christian's brigade and was able to bring it up to help stabilize his embattled position.

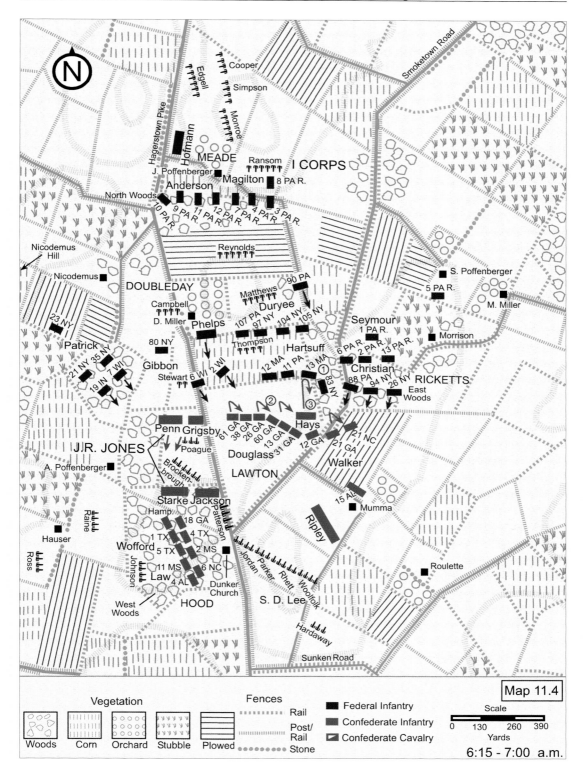

Map 11.4

Vegetation
Woods   Corn   Orchard   Stubble   Plowed

Fences
.... Rail
.... Post/Rail
●●●●●●●● Stone

■ Federal Infantry
■ Confederate Infantry
◤ Confederate Cavalry

Scale
0   130   260   390
Yards

6:15 - 7:00 a.m.

Map 11.5: Gibbon's Brigade Attacks (6:15 - 7:00 a.m.)

During this early fighting, an artillery shell exploded just above Brig. Gen. John R. Jones, commander of the Stonewall Division. Brigade leader Brig. Gen. William Starke replaced the disoriented Jones. Starke would not live long enough to enjoy his elevation to divisional command. Senior officers all across the front were cut down by bullets and artillery fire. On the Confederate right, about the time Hays went over to the attack, Alexander Lawton was severely wounded in the upper leg and had to be carried off the field. He was replaced by Brig. Gen. Jubal Early.[20]

On the opposite side of the line, when Maj. Rufus Dawes of the 6th Wisconsin (Gibbon) saw a gap between his left flank and the 2nd Wisconsin on his left, he sent orders to his three right companies that he intended to close it. When it was determined that artillery fire was too murderous to make the move, the regiment split into two parts. The right side advanced west of the Hagerstown Pike while the left companies of the 6th linked with the 2nd Wisconsin within the Miller cornfield (No. 1). Hartsuff's brigade was also in the cornfield, but farther to the left. "[A]s we appeared at the edge of the corn, a long line of men in butternut and gray rose up from the ground," recalled Dawes. The Wisconsin men had stumbled upon the advanced left regiments from Douglass' brigade (the 61st, 26th, and 38th Georgia) lying in wait in a pasture. The two sides exchanged brutal volleys at close range, and as Dawes later reported, "men, I can not say fell; they were knocked out of the ranks by the dozens." Fighting in the open, Douglass' men did their best to hold their ground while also suffering heavily. There were too many Yankees to stand indefinitely, however, and before long the bloodied Georgians began drifting to the rear, where the remnants coalesced to form a new rather disorganized line.[21]

While the 2nd and 6th Wisconsin were making their way south and east through the cornfield to engage Douglass, Gibbon's other pair of regiments—the 19th Indiana and the 7th Wisconsin—swept southeast (well west of the Hagerstown Pike) toward the West Woods. Gibbon's brigade was now fighting in two separate chunks. Patrick's brigade supported the advancing Hoosiers and Badgers (No. 2). Directly in their path stood Penn's and Grigsby's small brigades (Jones' division), deployed just east of the West Woods perpendicular to the Hagerstown Pike. The Federals, recalled a member of Stonewall Jackson's staff, were "in apparent double battle line . . . moving toward us at charge bayonets . . . and the sunbeams falling on their well-polished guns . . . gave a glamour and a show at once fearful and entrancing."[22]

Together, Penn and Grigsby probably fielded fewer than 500 men (No. 3). Much of Penn's command had been fighting on the skirmish line and some had taken position behind a rock ledge running south from the Miller barn, firing into the right flank of the 6th Wisconsin. It was this fire that had convinced Gibbon to shift the 19th Indiana and 7th Wisconsin farther right. The 19th Indiana and 7th Wisconsin were aiming for the north end of the West Woods and the vulnerable left flank of the thin Confederate line. Lt. James Stewart's section of Campbell's battery added to the Confederates' misery by throwing a devastating hail of iron against their front, while men on the right and center of the 6th Wisconsin picked off Virginia infantrymen at an alarming rate.

The Confederate veterans knew a helpless situation when they saw one and began melting to the rear. Unwilling to order a retreat, Col. Grigsby watched as the commander of the 5th Virginia did just that. Capt. Penn's small brigade tried to hold its position, but it too was forced into retreat by the unrelenting pressure being applied by Gibbon's Westerners. Penn fell during this time with a severe leg wound that would later require amputation.

According to the commander of the 5th Virginia, the retreat south to the West Woods was caused by "the heavy loss sustained, the confusion unavoidably arising from change in commanders and the protracted nature of the contest." Some of the regiments, like the 27th Virginia, maintained their cohesion. At one point, this regiment and the 49th Virginia (Grigsby) even turned and managed a sharp counterattack that forced the enemy to briefly halt the advance.[23]

The situation in this sector was critical for the Southerners, but a trio of fresh Confederate brigades was moving quickly to join the combat and stabilize Gen. Lee's fragmenting left flank.

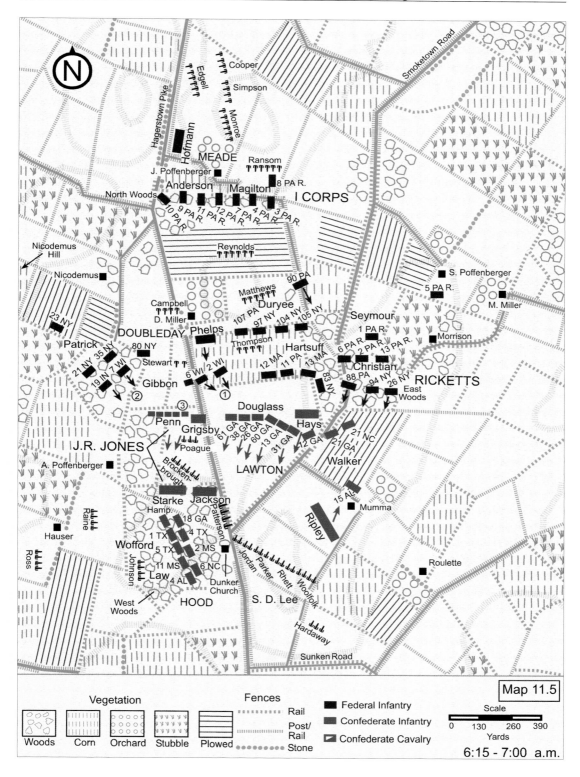

Map 11.5

6:15 - 7:00 a.m.

Map 11.6: Lee's Imperiled Left Flank (6:15 - 7:00 a.m.)

Whatever elation the men of the 2nd and 6th Wisconsin may have felt after defeating the Rebels to their front did not last long. Almost immediately, large numbers of Confederates were spotted moving on the opposite side of the Hagerstown Pike. These men belonged to J. R. Jones' "Stonewall Division," which was now under Brig. Gen. William Starke because a shell burst had disabled Jones.

Starke had watched with dismay as the paltry remnants of Grigsby's and Penn's brigades streamed toward his reserve position along the northern edge of the West Woods. All Starke had left was the 1,150 men in the division's two remaining brigades—his own Louisianans and Brig. Gen. William B. Taliaferro's Virginians and Alabamians under Col. James Jackson. Starke could see that the Confederate front left had been crushed and that Federals in large numbers were flooding into this sector. He decided to attack northeast across the Hagerstown Pike toward the southwest corner of the Miller cornfield, a decision that required an oblique movement to the right. During the early minutes of the movement confusion erupted when the right side of Starke's brigade bumped into the left side of Jackson's. With the enemy emerging from the cornfield and bearing down on the Confederate flank, there was no time to spare. Starke sorted out the lines as best and as fast as he could and pushed his infantry toward the Hagerstown Pike.[24]

When they saw this new threat, the two Wisconsin regiments obliqued to their right and opened a heavy fire that thinned the Southern ranks with every step. Starke was among the fallen. Struck three times west of the road, he would die within the hour. His men continued on, scaling the fence along the road to get into the field and at the enemy occupying it. The Federal advance ground to a halt and the hail of Southern lead forced the blueclad infantry to fall back into the cornfield. Some of the men tore down fencing to construct a rough barricade. Col. Walter Phelps brought his brigade up to within twenty-five feet of the Wisconsin line of battle and ordered his men to lie down. Phelps' 14th Brooklyn (84th New York) was ordered up

to plug gaps in the disordered Wisconsin line. "Men and officers of New York and Wisconsin are fused into a common mass, in the frantic struggle to shoot fast," recalled Rufus Dawes of the 6th Wisconsin. The 2nd U.S. Sharpshooters (Phelps) added its firepower to the right of the line. "[M]en are falling in their places or running back into the corn," continued Dawes. In some cases, only thirty yards separated the combatants.[25]

Starke's men were in serious trouble. With Phelps' reinforcements, the Federals scaled the fence or jumped the downed rails and charged. The 2nd U. S. Sharpshooters on the right of the line extended beyond Starke's left, which was also being torn apart by Stewart's Federal guns just to the north. The situation turned completely untenable with the appearance of the 19th Indiana and 7th Wisconsin of Gibbon's brigade, supported by two of Patrick's regiments, all approaching the Confederate rear from the northwest. With Starke and many other officers down (Starke's brigade went through four commanders during this brief combat), Rebel command cohesion disintegrated. The Louisianans and Jackson's men fell back to the Hagerstown Pike and then slipped beyond; the entire line disintegrated. As Dawes recalled, "the whole field before us is covered with rebels fleeing for life."[26]

Hooker's I Corps had met and crushed seven Confederate brigades within less than two hours. The Stonewall Division had been soundly defeated and so many officers had been shot down that a mere colonel (Grigsby) was in command. Farther east, Lawton's hard-fighting battered division was also falling back. Federal losses had also been very heavy.

Fresh Federal troops in the form of Lt. Col. Robert Anderson's and Col. Albert Magilton's brigades were moving south from their reserve positions in the North Woods and approaching the cornfield. The same was true on the Southern side of the field. Brig. Gen. John Hood's two-brigade division was preparing to move into action from its reserve position west of the Dunker Church. Farther northeast, Brig. Gen. Roswell Ripley's brigade, which had been in reserve behind James Walker's brigade, was moving to occupy the fence line near the Mumma farm.[27]

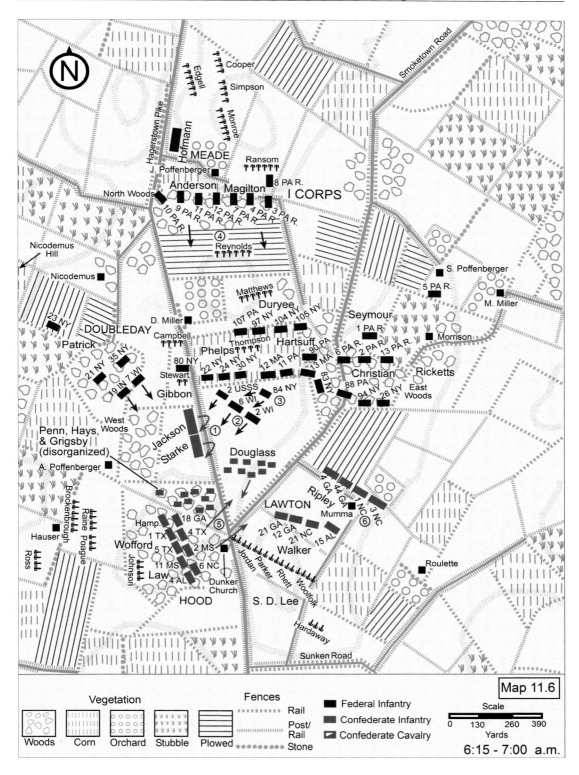

Map 11.6

Vegetation

Woods Corn Orchard Stubble Plowed

Fences
.... Rail
━━━━━━ Post/Rail
●●●●●● Stone

■ Federal Infantry
■ Confederate Infantry
◪ Confederate Cavalry

Scale
0   130   260   390
Yards

6:15 - 7:00 a.m.

Map Set 12. Antietam: Hood's Division Moves up and Attacks (6:45 - 7:45 a.m.)

Map 12.1: Hood Moves up from the Dunker Church (6:45 - 7:15 a.m.)

Shortly before 7:00 a.m., a staff officer from Brig. Gen. Alexander Lawton's division found Brig. Gen. John B. Hood and delivered a desperate plea for help. Hood's men had been on the forward line the prior evening when Hood asked Stonewall Jackson to replace them with other infantry so he could pull his men back to the Dunker Church to rest and eat. Jackson agreed—with the proviso that Hood would come quickly if called. With the front collapsing, it was time for Hood to join the battle.

Hood assembled his two brigades, one under Col. William T. Wofford (900 men) and Hood's former command under Col. Evander M. Law (1,400 men). Both were made up of battle-hardened veterans with competent field officers. The men, however, were unhappy with the orders because they were still cooking their breakfast. Many wolfed down partially cooked food and formed for action. The order to advance did not come as a complete surprise because the combat had been raging in their direction since just before daylight. In fact, the waiting was very hard on the men, as Cpl. W. D. Pritchard of the 1st Texas recalled: "Standing inactive, conscious of unseen danger, with bullets whistling over and around them, the increasing rattle of musketry in front, with now and then the ominous shriek of a shell as it tears through the ranks . . . the strain upon the men is terrible."[1]

It was about 7:00 a.m. when Hood's men filed past the Dunker Church and across the Hagerstown Pike with Law's brigade in the lead and Wofford's behind it (No. 1). Federal gunners saw them, found the range, and took out scores of men before they could fire a shot in their own defense. Law sized up the situation: "On reaching the road [Hagerstown Pike], I found but few of our troops on the field, and these seemed to be in much confusion, but still opposing the advance of the enemy's dense masses with determination." The troops Law spotted were likely survivors from Lawton's wrecked division. Law could see "dense masses" of the enemy, but did not know they were from five Federal brigades under Gibbon, Phelps, Patrick, Hartsuff (Coulter), and Christian (Lyle).[2]

After marching his men north a short distance along the Smoketown Road Law left the road and moved west into the field, where Douglass' men had fought the Federals holding the cornfield. Law deployed his regiments from left to right as follows: 2nd Mississippi, 11th Mississippi, 6th North Carolina, with the latter straddling the Smoketown Road. His last regiment, the 4th Alabama, was in the rear probably waiting for an opportunity to deploy to the front line. Given the nature of the movement, terrain, and situation, Wofford deployed his own brigade in a piecemeal manner. Hampton's Legion and the 18th Georgia on Wofford's left had room and so were able to advance in line of battle on Law's left, but the brigade's remaining three regiments (the 1st, 4th, and 5th Texas) formed a temporary reserve behind Law. Roswell Ripley's brigade, which had moved up to occupy Walker's former position (No. 2), was on Hood's right.[3]

After crushing the left side of Douglass' brigade, the 2nd and 6th Wisconsin (No. 3) obliqued right to help drive Starke's and Warren's (Jackson's) brigades from along the Hagerstown Pike. Few defenders stood between them and the Dunker Church until Hood's men made their appearance. "A long and steady line of rebel gray, unbroken by the fugitives who fly before us, comes sweeping down through the woods around the church," recalled Maj. Rufus Dawes of the 6th Wisconsin. "They raise the yell and fire. It is like a scythe running through our line." Exhausted, bloodied, and discouraged by the sudden change of circumstance, and with men falling all around them, Gibbon's survivors began streaming back toward the cornfield. James Denon of the 18th Georgia recalled he and his comrades "charged with a yell & hit the yanks in front of the corn & they fairly flew apart and fled."[4]

With the front east of the pike tumbling back, division commander Maj. Gen. George Meade ordered his remaining two brigades under Lt. Col. Robert Anderson and Col. Albert Magilton up to a fence about thirty yards north of the cornfield, where the men took cover behind rocks that had been piled up under the rails.[5]

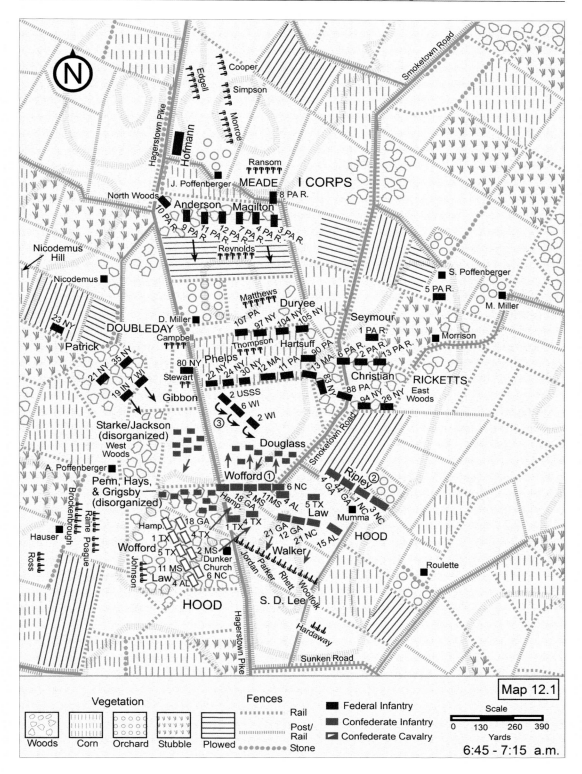

Map 12.1

Vegetation

| Woods | Corn | Orchard | Stubble | Plowed |

Fences

Rail

Post/Rail

Stone

■ Federal Infantry
■ Confederate Infantry
◪ Confederate Cavalry

Scale

0   130   260   390
Yards

6:45 - 7:15 a.m.

Map 12.2: Hood Counterattacks
(6:45 - 7:15 a.m.)

Once in the open clover field, Federal small arms fire combined with blasts of artillery (including from artillery east of Antietam Creek) killed and maimed Hood's men by the score. Scattered knots of disorganized Georgians and Louisianans from Douglass' and Hays' brigades littered the landscape in front Hood's arriving men and prevented many from firing their own weapons. Remaining in place was intolerable, so Hood passed along the order to attack into the face of the advancing enemy. Federal troops overlapped his left flank, so Wofford ordered his 18th Georgia and Hampton's Legion to oblique in that direction and aligned his brigade flank on the Hagerstown Pike (No. 1). He also ordered the 1st Texas, which was still some distance to the rear, to move up and extend the line on the right.[6]

The unexpected and strong Confederate attack knocked Phelps' regiments (including the 2nd U.S. Sharpshooters) and Gibbon's 2nd and 6th Wisconsin back into the Miller cornfield (No. 2). The two Wisconsin regiments halted and established a defensive line with the relatively few men still remaining in the ranks. On the west side of the Hagerstown Pike, Gibbon personally directed Stewart's section of Campbell's battery. All six of the battery's guns were up and in action at this time.[7]

Once deep into the field, Hood's advancing Confederates found a heavy row of dead and wounded that denoted where Douglass' left flank had made its stand. The 1st Texas finally linked up with the 18th Georgia about this point near the Miller cornfield. Hundreds of voices raised the "Rebel Yell" as the men plunged into the trampled bloody field without pause. "[T]he corn blades rose like a whirlwind," recalled one of the Rebel veterans. Some of Gibbon's Westerners were not intimidated by the screams of the advancing enemy and made a stand about fifty yards into the cornfield. When the Southerners spotted them they halted, raised their rifles, and fired. When the smoke cleared, all signs of Yankee resistance had vanished. With its infantry support breaking quickly for the rear, Thompson's Federal cannoneers—who had deployed in the cornfield—limbered their guns as fast as possible and galloped to safety.[8]

While Wofford's three regiments were driving back the Federals in their front, Law's brigade was angling toward the southeast corner of the cornfield and the adjacent portion of the East Woods (No. 3). Hartsuff's exhausted regiments under Col. Coulter, which had recently held off determined attacks by Douglass and Hays, were waiting for them. The three regiments forming Law's left (the 2nd and 11th Mississippi and 6th North Carolina) obliqued slightly to the left and advanced on Wofford's right, periodically firing as they stepped forward. The target of this attack may have been the 90th Pennsylvania (Christian), whose small arms fire was creating havoc in the Southerners' ranks. The Pennsylvanians were in a tough situation. The 12th Massachusetts and 11th Pennsylvania on their right had drifted rearward, exposing their right flank to an intense oblique fire. The troops on their left were also retreating from the East Woods.[9]

On Law's extreme right, meanwhile, the 4th Alabama continued attacking toward the East Woods along the Smoketown Road. Some or all of the 21st Georgia had not withdrawn with the rest of Walker's brigade, and many asked to join the Alabamians in their effort (No. 4). These Alabama troops formed on the right of the line and helped drive the remainder of Christian's brigade to the rear. The Rebels entered the woods and fired into the 90th Pennsylvania and the 6th Pennsylvania Reserves, hastening their retreat. According to Lt. Sam Moore of the former regiment, "the men stood up to the work as long as possible expecting reinforcements but in vain, we had to fall back a short distance and hold them at bay."[10]

Hood oversaw this part of the attack and rode to the 4th and 5th Texas to issue additional orders. He directed the latter regiment to advance toward the East Woods and extend the line to the right (it formed on the right of the 21st Georgia), and instructed the former regiment to reinforce the left side of the line just east of the Hagerstown Pike.[11]

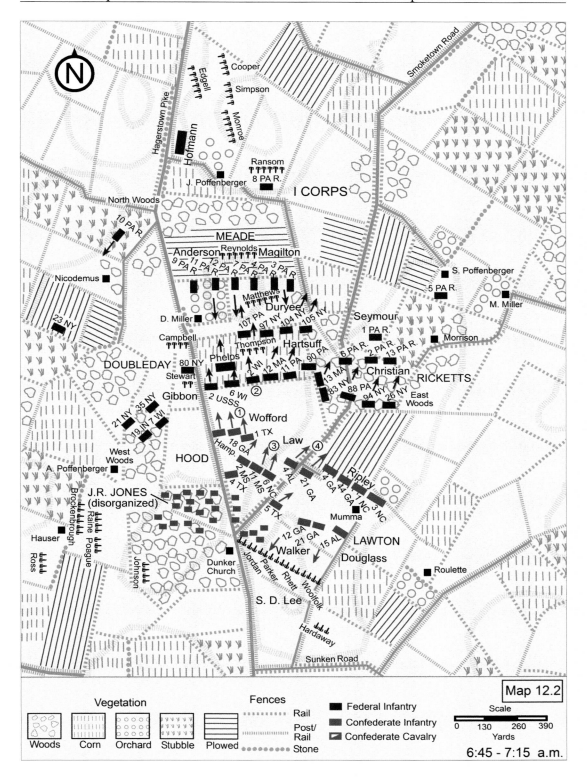

Map 12.2

6:45 - 7:15 a.m.

Vegetation

Woods | Corn | Orchard | Stubble | Plowed

Fences

Rail
Post/Rail
Stone

Federal Infantry
Confederate Infantry
Confederate Cavalry

Scale

0   130   260   390
Yards

Map 12.3: Hood Enters the West Woods and Cornfield (6:45 - 7:15 a.m.)

While much of Hooker's front line east of the Hagerstown Pike was being thrown back by Hood's determined attack, portions of Gibbon's and Patrick's brigades occupied the northern fringe of the West Woods on Hood's left, and two of Meade's fresh brigades under Anderson and Magilton were moving south toward the Miller cornfield directly in the path of the Confederate attack (No. 1).

Anderson and Magilton had occupied the North Woods since the previous night and were moving south in column of battalions in mass while Ransom's Federal battery advanced on their left. Hood's infantry (probably Law's left regiments) in the Miller cornfield leveled their rifled muskets and hit these new arrivals hard, as did Stephen Lee's guns firing from near the Dunker Church. Meade halted the two brigades behind a fence in a ravine north of the cornfield and formed a long line of battle. Worried that his right flank was exposed, he detached the 10th Pennsylvania Reserves to support it. Before he could order the rest of his men forward, Meade received a message from Hooker to send one of his brigades to reinforce the collapsing line in the East Woods. Meade selected Magilton for the task and promptly shifted his regiments to the left.[12]

Meade was maneuvering into position when Hood ordered the left side of Law's brigade, composed of the 2nd and 11th Mississippi and the 6th North Carolina, to advance (No. 2). The Mississippians and Tar Heels crashed deep into the cornfield, driving away the last remnants of the Federal defenders there. The 1st Texas (Wofford) advanced on their left on the far side of a wide gap in the line, and off to the southeast well to the right of the Texans advanced the 4th Alabama. Fighting blazed across the entire front from the Hagerstown Pike on the west to the East Woods, with the Federals getting the worst of it everywhere along the line.

Hood was watching Meade's two brigades moving into position when one of Stonewall Jackson's aides arrived to inquire about how the battle was progressing. "Tell General Jackson unless I get reinforcements I must be forced back, but I am going on while I can," replied the division commander.[13]

Somewhere in the cornfield Law's men encountered about 100 men from the 104th and 105th New York (Duryee). Rounds of small arms fire scattered them. The three Confederate regiments were approaching the fence denoting the northern boundary of the cornfield when devastating double rounds of iron canister from Matthews' battery farther north tore into their ranks. Although stunned by the deadly fire, the Mississippians and North Carolinians continued to the fence, where they spotted Magilton's men marching by the left flank across their front on their way to the East Woods. The Confederate regiments opened fire against the vulnerable enemy and threw the 3rd and 4th Pennsylvania Reserves in the center of the brigade into bloody disarray and retreat. "An infantry line appeared on the crest and engaged our line," recalled Pvt. David Love of the 11th Mississippi. "The flag of the Regiment [probably the 4th Pennsylvania Reserves] opposing [the] 11th Miss. was shot down or lowered at least a half dozen times before it disappeared behind the hill." The fire returned by the Reserves originated from higher ground, so many of the rounds flew harmlessly above Law's men. The 8th Pennsylvania Reserves on Magilton's left flank also discovered that it was difficult to reach the relative safety of the East Woods. "As we neared the grove . . . a regiment of rebels [probably the 6th North Carolina], who had lain concealed among the tall corn, arose and poured upon us the most withering volley we ever felt," admitted one Federal. "Another and another followed . . . we could not stop to reply—we could but hurry on." The well-thinned regiment finally reached the timber and opened fire on the 6th North Carolina. The 7th Pennsylvania Reserve on Magilton's right flank continued moving to the left.[14]

Although the fighting had thus far gone largely Hood's way, what he did not know was that the remainder of Gibbon's brigade (the 19th Indiana and 7th Wisconsin) and several regiments from Patrick's brigade were now in position west of the Hagerstown Pike on his exposed left flank. The Federals adjusted their orientation and bore down on the tantalizing prize (No. 3).[15]

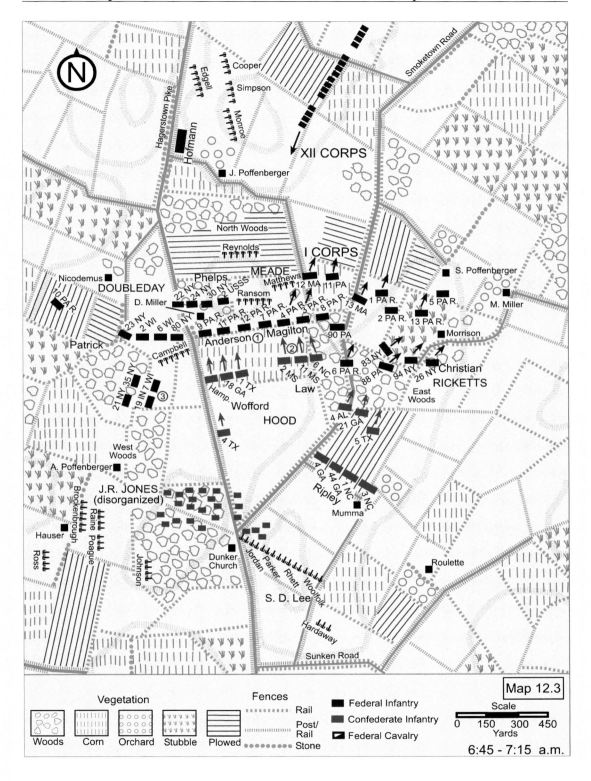

Map 12.3

6:45 - 7:15 a.m.

Vegetation

Woods · Corn · Orchard · Stubble · Plowed

Fences

Rail ·········
Post/Rail ｜｜｜｜｜｜
Stone ●●●●●●●

■ Federal Infantry
■ Confederate Infantry
◪ Federal Cavalry

Scale
0   150   300   450
Yards

Map 12.4: Federal Reinforcements Arrive (6:45 - 7:15 a.m.)

Evander Law's three regiments continued battling the 7th and 8th Pennsylvania Reserve regiments from Magilton's brigade after its other two regiments (3rd and 4th Pennsylvania Reserves) had been driven back.

The 8th Pennsylvania Reserves, which had reached the protection of the East Woods, opened an effective frontal and flank fire against the 6th North Carolina. Although it was not enough to force the Tar Heels to retreat, it did prevent them from advancing from behind the fence at the northern boundary of the Miller cornfield (No. 1). The Mississippians of the 2nd, meanwhile, scaled the fence without orders and discovered the exposed left flank of the 7th Pennsylvania Reserves, which swivelled to take on this new threat. Losses mounted quickly and the 7th retreated. Confederate small arms fire was so destructive in this area that Capt. Matthews ordered his artillerists to the rear, a decision that effectively abandoned his guns. Capt. Ransom's pieces to the southwest kept up a steady fire against Law's infantry.

When Meade realized "the gap made by the withdrawal of Magilton was soon filled by the enemy, whose infantry advanced boldly through the cornfield to the wood," he ordered Ransom to train "his guns on their advancing column." Meade's smart handling of the artillery forced the 2nd Mississippi back to the fence line. About this same time the Rebels opened fire on a Federal officer mounted on a stunning white horse. What none of them knew was that the rider was Maj. Gen. Joseph Hooker, who was actively engaged in the tactical direction of the fighting.[16]

The staunch Rebel defense and Hood's counterstroke had essentially wrecked Hooker's I Corps. "So far, we had been entirely successful and everything promised a decisive victory," Col. Law wrote in his battle report. "It is true that strong support was needed to follow up our success, but this I expected every moment." Law waited for help in vain; the only reinforcements that would arrive were clad in blue.

Timely help arrived in the form of Maj. Gen. Joseph Mansfield's XII Corps. Law and many of his men probably spotted the first six regiments of Brig. Gen. Samuel Crawford's brigade about this time advancing south toward them (No. 2). After driving away Magilton's regiments, recounted D. Love of the 11th Mississippi, "in a few minutes another line of infantry in splendid order confronted us." Behind Crawford and also possibly in view marched Brig. Gen. George Gordon's brigade, with Lt. Col. Hector Tyndale's also arriving in the sector. "At this stage of the battle, a powerful Federal force (ten times our number) of fresh troops was thrown in our front," recalled Law. Because Mansfield had pushed his regiments to the front massed in column, the units appeared larger than they really were (see below). The Rebel euphoria of driving all back the Yankees proved short-lived. With his losses mounting and his ammunition running low, Law had little choice but to order his men to fall back from the fence deeper into the devastated cornfield.[17]

The fortune of war had also turned against Wofford's regiments battling portions of Gibbon's and Phelps' brigades on the western side of the Miller cornfield (No.3). The 18th Georgia and Hampton's Legion had driven them across the Hagerstown Pike, where they formed a new defensive line. Anderson's brigade (Meade's division) arrived north of the fence marking the northern boundary of the cornfield and opened fire on the Southerners. Lt. Col. Philip Work's 1st Texas faced the entire brigade. The Texans had orders to halt at the edge of the cornfield after the Federal troops there had fled, but they either did not receive the order or, just as likely with their blood up, "slipped the bridle and got away from the command."

The 18th Georgia and Hampton's Legion wheeled left to face the approach of the 19th Indiana and 7th Wisconsin of Gibbon's brigade, and behind them the three regiments of Patrick's brigade. The 4th Texas, which had been in the rear, arrived and deployed along the Hagerstown Pike on the left of the Georgians and South Carolinians. Operating between the two wings of Gibbon's brigade, Capt. Joseph Campbell's battery sprayed canister into the Confederate ranks in an effort to keep them at a distance. One by one, however, Wofford's men picked off the gunners until two of the guns fell silent. Someone called up the battery's wagon drivers and the guns roared to life once again.[18]

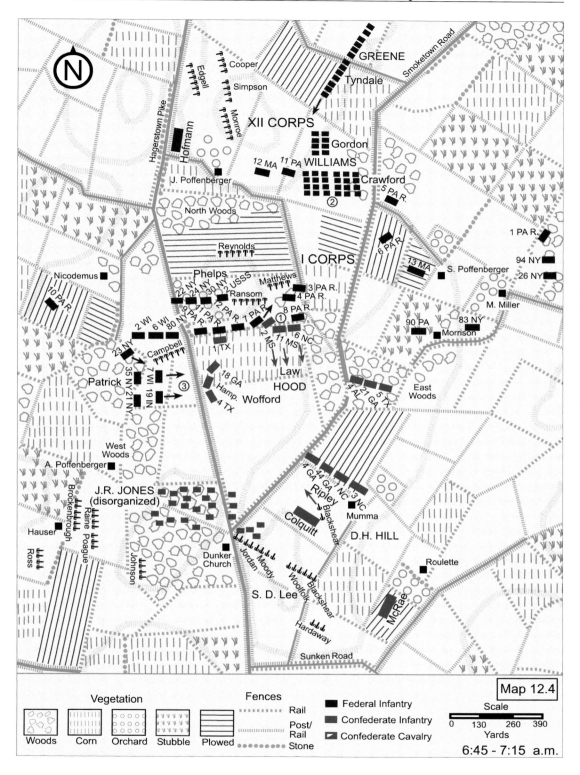

GREENE

Smoketown Road

Cooper

Edgell

Tyndale

Simpson

Monroe

Hagerstown Pike

XII CORPS

Hofmann

Gordon

12 MA   11 PA

WILLIAMS

J. Poffenberger

Crawford

5 PA R.

North Woods

1 PA R.

Reynolds

6 PA R.

13 MA

S. Poffenberger

94 NY

26 NY

I CORPS

Nicodemus

Phelps

Matthews

M. Miller

10 PA R.

22 NY 24 NY 30 NY 1 USSS

Ransom

3 PA R.

4 PA R.

2 WI   6 WI   80 NY   1 PA R.
2 PA R. 7 PA R.

8 PA R.

90 PA

83 NY

Morrison

23 NY

Campbell

1 TX

2 MS 11 MS

6 NC

Patrick

35 NY·21 NY

7 WI
19 IN

18 GA

Hamp.

Law

HOOD

4 AL 2 1 GA 5 TX

East
Woods

4 TX

Wofford

West
Woods

A. Poffenberger

Brockenbrough

J.R. JONES
(disorganized)

4 GA 44 GA 1 NC 3 NC

Ripley

Raine Poague

Mumma

Blackshear

Hauser

Colquitt

D.H. HILL

Ross

Johnson

Dunker
Church

Jordan

Moody

Roulette

Woolfolk

Blackshear

S. D. Lee

McRae

Hardaway

Sunken Road

| Vegetation | | | | | Fences | | Federal Infantry | | Map 12.4 |

Vegetation: Woods Corn Orchard Stubble Plowed

Fences: Rail Post/Rail Stone

Federal Infantry
Confederate Infantry
Confederate Cavalry

Scale
0   130   260   390
Yards

6:45 - 7:15 a.m.

Map 12.5: Hood Suffers Heavy Losses
(6:45 - 7:15 a.m.)

Four distinct actions were unfolding during this time, and all four involved Hood's embattled division. The result in each case was the same: heavy Confederate losses and deep retreat.

On Hood's left, three regiments from Wofford's brigade (the 4th Texas, 18th Georgia, and Hampton's Legion) rotated ninety degrees west to face the Hagerstown Pike to confront the renewed threat from the right wing of Gibbon's brigade (the 19th Indiana and 7th Wisconsin) on the first line and Patrick's brigade (the 21st 23rd, and 35th New York) behind it. Campbell's battery, supported by the remnants of the 2nd and 6th Wisconsin and by the 80th New York, continued sending deadly rounds of canister into the Confederate ranks. It was a reasonably strong defensive front, but Gibbon continued to worry about the potential loss of the battery. When some Southern infantry realized that Gibbon's men had taken possession of a Rebel battle flag, some fifty Texans from the 4th regiment decided to retrieve it. The short-lived effort to cross the pike was ripped apart by Federal fire and forced back. For a time both sides seemed content to stand firm and trade fire. Casualties mounted on both sides and the sights of splintered men were horrific. As one Texan recalled, "legs, arms, and other parts of human bodies were flying in the air like straw in a whirlwind. The dogs of war were loose, and 'havoc' was their cry."[19]

The stalemate broke when the five Federal regiments from Gibbon's and Patrick's brigades advanced from west to east. As a member of Hampton's Legion named E. Carson wrote after the war, "it seemed that the whole world was in arms against us. A grander sight I never witnessed. Their new, bright flags were waving in every direction." The Confederates gamely held their ground as the distance between the opposing lines narrowed. According to Carson, his regiment looked more like a skirmish line by this time, with the dead and wounded thrown about in heaps. The Georgians and Texans were no better off. The 18th Georgia on the right of Wofford's line fell back when the Federal advance reached the Hagerstown Pike. Firing into their exposed right flank, Campbell's guns

devastated the Georgians. When their withdrawal exposed Hampton's Legion's right flank (No. 1), an order was issued to "fall back and take care of the colors." The 4th Texas on the left was the last to go. All told, these three Confederate regiments left about one-half of their effective fighting strength strewn along the Hagerstown Pike.[20]

On their right and farther north, meanwhile, Lt. Col. Work's 1st Texas gamely battled it out with most or all of Anderson's Pennsylvania Reserve brigade in the northwest quadrant of the Miller cornfield (No. 2). They had entered the corn earlier on the right side of the 18th Georgia, but the Texans had bolted forward in pursuit of fleeing Yankees. What they did not see was the line of Pennsylvanians lying behind the fence with their guns propped on the bottom rail. The Federals aimed low as the Texans approached, and when they stepped within thirty feet jumped up and fired a killing volley into them. Ransom's battery blasted the Texans with lethal canister. Despite this destructive fire in front and along both flanks, the men of the 1st Texas refused to budge. It was a mismatch from the outset, but the Texans somehow stood their ground. A Federal watching the fight observed that "these brave men were mowed down like the corn surrounding them." The Texans were finally ordered to the rear when Anderson's men began lapping around their failing flanks.[21]

Farther to the right of the Texans, Col. Law reformed his 2nd and 11th Mississippi and 6th North Carolina in the southeast corner of the Miller cornfield (No. 3). They had roughly handled Magilton's Pennsylvania Reserve brigade at the northeastern corner of the cornfield, but were almost out of ammunition and facing the arrival of fresh infantry from Mansfield's XII Corps. Law pulled back to the southern edge of the corn and took stock of his losses (about one-half of his men; the 2nd Mississippi had lost almost all of its officers and was led by a second lieutenant). Given the critical situation, and with no reinforcements of his own in sight, Law ordered his regiments to withdraw to the Dunker Church.[22]

On the far Confederate right flank, Law's 4th Alabama, 21st Georgia (Walker's brigade), and 5th Texas (Wofford's brigade) held the southern edge of the East Woods after driving out Christian's brigade and the surviving remnants of Seymour's Pennsylvania Reserve Brigade (No. 4).[23]

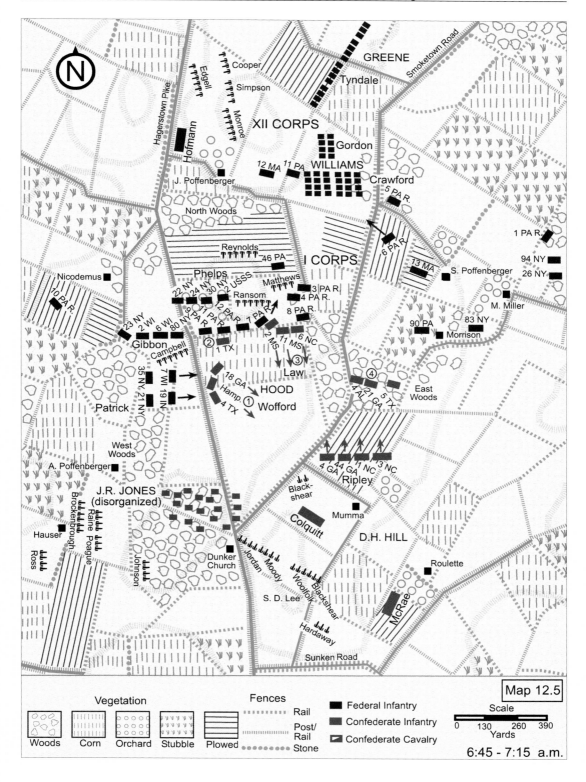

Map 12.5

6:45 - 7:15 a.m.

Map 12.6: Hood's Division Retreats
(7:15 - 7:45 a.m.)

Except for the 4th Alabama and 5th Texas in the East Woods, what was left of Hood's division was now in full retreat.

On the Confederate left, Patrick's three Federal regiments advanced to the front line on the left of the 19th Indiana and together charged across the Hagerstown Pike (No. 1). Only the 4th Texas remained near the road; its members fired a few rounds and fell back. Wofford's 4th Texas and the remnants of the 18th Georgia and Hampton's Legion reassembled in a swale east and south of the cornfield. After regrouping, the Texans—probably the most cohesive unit of the three—marched by the left flank toward the Dunker Church. The other two regiments took longer to make the trek toward the church, and many stopped to rifle through cartridge boxes of the dead and wounded (No. 2).[24]

Farther east, Law's three regiments (the 2nd and 11th Mississippi and 6th North Carolina), which had held the northeast portion of the cornfield and had driven most of Magilton's brigade to the rear, were also in full retreat through the pasture (No. 3) in the direction of the Dunker Church. On the right, a portion of the 21st Georgia, together with the 4th Alabama and 5th Texas in the East Woods watched the approach of the advance elements of Mansfield's XII Corps. This concerned them, but they still had a solid defensive front and many expected that reinforcements would soon arrive (No. 4).[25]

What all of this meant was that Lt. Col. Philip Work's 1st Texas was exposed and vulnerable in the northwest corner of the cornfield (No. 5). The regiment had battled the whole of Anderson's Pennsylvania Reserve brigade and was probably the last Confederate unit to leave the corn. Gibbon, who was watching the action unfold from across the Hagerstown Pike, could not understand why Anderson's Pennsylvanians were not following the retreating Texans. Unable to find Gen. Meade, Gibbon rode to the Pennsylvanians and ordered them forward. The Texans periodically turned to fire into their pursuers. When Lt. Col. Work could not find his regimental flag, someone told him that the banner was already safely in the rear. In fact, a volley from the Pennsylvania Reserves had knocked down many of the men in the flag detail, and the banner was lost on the field. The rare flag had been made from the silk dress of the wife of the regiment's former commander, Col. Louis Wigfall.[26]

As the 1st Texas maneuvered and fought its way south, the 19th Indiana and Patrick's brigade closed in from west of the pike, with Anderson's Pennsylvanians following from the north. Lt. Col. Work ordered his men to continue south as fast as their legs could carry them. Heading diagonally across the pasture, the Texans finally reached the Smoketown Road and halted to reform. About 75 other men from a variety of units were milling about. The Smoketown Road was somewhat sunken at this point, and the men went prone to take advantage of this bit of shelter and opened "a deadly and telling fire, every shot counting," Work recalled.[27]

Work's embattled Texans and the handful of others were organizing on the Smoketown Road when Brig. Gen. Roswell Ripley's brigade (D. H. Hill's division) finally entered the fighting (No. 6). These Georgians had been lying behind James Walker's men in a plowed field near the Mumma farm exposed to a steady shelling by the Federal artillery east of Antietam Creek. Ripley's large brigade (nearly 1,400 men) was still fresh because its inept leader had not maneuvered it into combat on South Mountain three days before. According to Ripley, when he gave the order to advance, the men "sprang to their arms with alacrity and moved forward." The brigade initially headed north for the East Woods, but D. H. Hill ordered it to change direction by the left flank into the bloody pasture south of the Miller cornfield. Work's 1st Texas fell back as Ripley moved his regiments across the road. Hood appeared and escorted the skeletal remains of the devastated 1st Texas west toward the Dunker Church.[28]

Losses on this part of the field were heavy for both sides, but for Hood's division they were simply staggering. As a whole, Hood lost 44% of his strength. Wofford lost 64% of his effectives, with the 1st Texas suffering 82% casualties. Law's total losses came in under 20%. Joe Hooker's federal I Corps was also out of the fight, but his losses (about 26%) were fewer because several of his brigades had been only lightly engaged.[29]

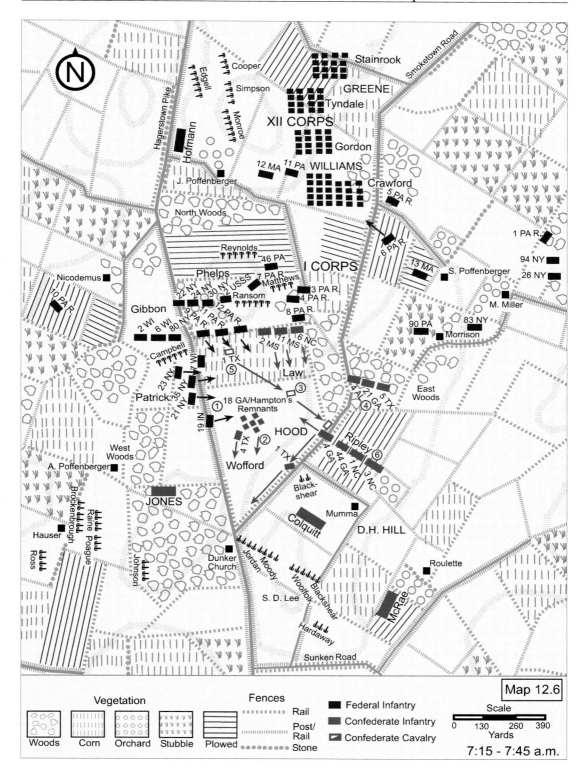

Map 12.6

7:15 - 7:45 a.m.

Map Set 13. Antietam: Mansfield's XII Corps Enters the Battle
(7:15 - 8:45 a.m.)

Map 13.1: The XII Corps Drives South
(7:15 - 7:45 a.m.)

Flushed with victory, parts of three Federal brigades—the 19th Indiana (Gibbon), the 21st and 35th New York (Patrick), and the 9th, 11th, and 12th Pennsylvania Reserves (Anderson)—advanced into the pasture south of the Miller cornfield. With the Confederates falling back across much of the front, it was time for a heavy southward push to capture the now very visible Dunker Church and the high ground surrounding it. The Rebels had other plans.

Maj. Gen. D. H. Hill had three of his division's five brigades in this sector. Roswell Ripley's brigade was moving ahead after spending the night and a terrifying early morning supporting James Walker's brigade. Hill led Ripley's Georgians and North Carolinians north into the pasture above the Smoketown Road. The 3rd North Carolina held the right flank near the southern tip of the East Woods, and the 4th Georgia manned the left flank about halfway across the pasture toward the Hagerstown Pike. Ripley's infantry opened fire on Anderson's Pennsylvanians near the cornfield. The two Georgia regiments making up the left half of Ripley's front faced the 9th Pennsylvania Reserves and likely some of Patrick's men, while the two North Carolina regiments on the right drove the 11th and 12th Pennsylvania Reserves out of the Miller cornfield. A portion of the 1st North Carolina shifted left of the 4th Georgia and formed perpendicular to it to prevent the sort of flanking attack that had driven Wofford's three regiments away from the Hagerstown Pike.

While Hill was guiding Ripley into the pasture, Jones' (Starke's) division in the West Woods (driven back earlier by Gibbon) could not resist attacking the 19th Indiana's exposed right flank as the Hoosiers advanced east across the Hagerstown Pike. The Louisianans and Virginians advanced slowly and methodically. They delivered a ripping fire into the enemy flank and rear that forced them back across the pike, where the Federals changed front to face the new

Southern threat. Patrick's regiments also turned south and, together with the Hoosiers, drove Jones' men back into the West Woods. Seeing Ripley's Georgians in the pasture, the 19th Indiana, 7th Wisconsin, and Patrick's Brigade made their way back to their original positions in the northern portion of the West Woods (No. 1).[1]

When a minie ball struck Ripley in the throat, he relinquished command to the 4th Georgia's Col. George Doles. With the pasture cleared of Yankees, the brigade angled right and moved northeast and connected with the left of the 4th Alabama in the East Woods (No. 2). According to a Georgian on the brigade's left, "we moved . . . through an open field, and took position on a ridge overlooking an immense corn field which seemed literally alive with Yankees." Once Ripley (Doles) was in position, seven Southern regiments (Ripley's four and the 4th Alabama, 21st Georgia, and 5th Texas) waited for the next onslaught, which would arrive in the form of Maj. Gen. Joseph Mansfield's XII Corps. Confederate small arms fire forced the artillerists of Ransom's battery to abandon their guns.[2]

Mansfield's small two-division XII Corps, about 7,500 men in five brigades, rested near the Hoffman and Line farms after crossing Antietam Creek at 2:00 a.m. The fifty-nine year old engineer and career Army officer had been in command just two days and had never led troops in battle. His brief tenure at the head of the corps increased his concern about how his volunteers would behave under fire. He believed in moving them into action close in mass to discourage men from breaking ranks. Massed troops, though, were vulnerable to artillery fire. Mansfield also believed he needed to direct the fighting from near the front. Mansfield had earlier caught some sleep in a fence corner near the Line house. A few hours later he would be carried to the same spot a mortally wounded man.

Mansfield's troops were straddling the Smoketown Road and grumbling about not having had breakfast or coffee when artillery opened fire on them. They did not like being under fire while packed tight, when a single round could kill and wound many. After 7:15 a.m., Hooker told Mansfield that his own I Corps was hard pressed and he needed help. Mansfield complied. Brig. Gen. Samuel Crawford's brigade (Williams' division) would go in first astride the Smoketown Road (No. 3), followed by Brig. Gen. George Gordon. George Greene's three-brigade division would bring up the rear.[3]

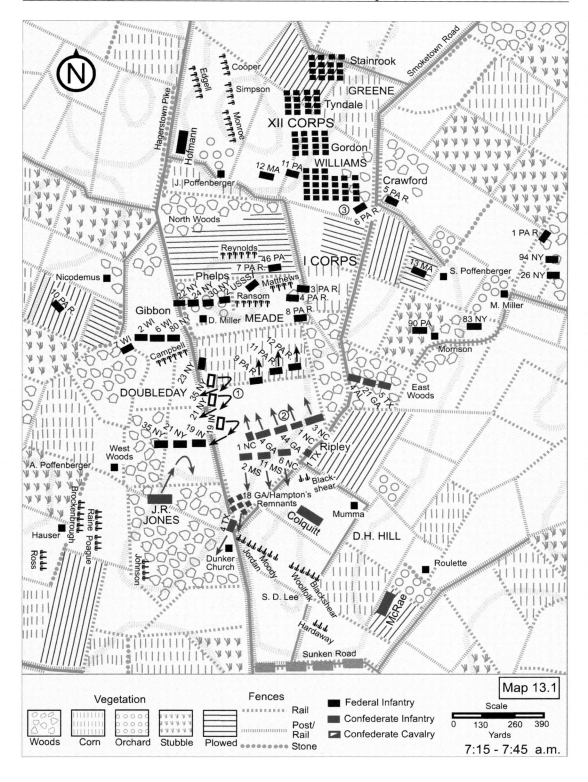

Map 13.1

7:15 - 7:45 a.m.

Map 13.2: The XII Corps Deploys
(7:15 - 7:45 a.m.)

Half of Brig. Gen. Crawford's six regiments (the 10th Maine, 46th Pennsylvania, and 28th New York) were hardened veterans, but green units (the 124th, 125th, 128th Pennsylvania) made up the balance of his brigade. Crawford's slow and cautious movements on the morning of September 17 reflected Maj. Gen. Mansfield's state of mind. Crawford halted his move in an open field east of Joseph Poffenberger's home about 6:30 a.m. to allow his men to boil their morning coffee. The brigade was deployed in massed columns with the 124th, 125th, and 128th Pennsylvania on the left and the 10th Maine, 28th New York, 46th Pennsylvania on the right. The plan called for the green regiments to be sent into action first. Division commander Brig. Gen. Alpheus Williams was deploying the regiments when Mansfield, who had ridden up to reconnoiter, countermanded Williams. As a result, a fresh set of orders reached Crawford: deploy your regiments again as a prelude to a general advance to support Joe Hooker's I Corps.[4]

Crawford deployed the large 125th Pennsylvania first and moved it cautiously south through a small cornfield to a fence connecting with the northern portion of the East Woods (No. 1). From that point the men could see the three Rebel regiments holding the southern end of the woods. Orders moved the 125th Pennsylvania into the woods a short distance before it was recalled. Crawford's three veteran regiments arrived behind the 125th, followed by the inexperienced 128th Pennsylvania. (The 124th Pennsylvania had been sent west to the North Woods.)[5]

Mansfield marched the veteran 10th Maine (still massed in columns) through the small cornfield and across the Smoketown Road north of the East Woods. According to the 10th Maine's Lt. John Gould, "we were under fire and advancing at a brisk walk, closed in mass, that is ten ranks deep (or fifteen ranks counting the file closers)." The foolish tactical situation was not lost on the lieutenant, who added that he and his comrades "were almost as good a target as a barn." When the Maine men halted and deployed

into line of battle, Mansfield obliqued the regiment left to approach the East Woods from almost due north (No. 2). After driving away a Confederate skirmish line, the men climbed a fence to get into the East Woods before opening fire on the 4th Alabama, 21st Georgia, and 5th Texas deployed in the lower fringe of the timber. The 10th Maine's right flank touched the Smoketown Road, with two companies refused on the left because there were no other Federals in that direction. The small 28th New York (about 60 men) and the 46th Pennsylvania (about 150 men) were moving south to deploy and enter the East Woods on the right flank of the 10th Maine. Crawford's arrival meant the remaining Pennsylvania Reserves to head to the rear.[6]

While Mansfield slowly moved into position on the Union left flank, farther west Brig. Gens. Meade and Gibbon raised a serious concern with I Corps commander Hooker. Unless they were reinforced, they argued, their artillery would be lost. Alpheus Williams, who was also meeting with Hooker at this time, immediately ordered the last brigade in Brig. Gen. George Greene's division (Col. William B. Goodrich) to move to the right on the west side of the Hagerstown Pike and report to Gibbon or any other officer he might find. The 124th Pennsylvania (Crawford) was also ordered to push west and enter and hold the North Woods (No. 3). At the same time, Brig. Gen. George Gordon's brigade (Williams), which had been following Crawford's brigade, was directed to continue south and form on Crawford's right to help protect the Federal batteries deployed there. Before Gordon could do so, however, new orders arrived to move south as quickly as possible to help Hooker's embattled I Corps (No. 4).[7]

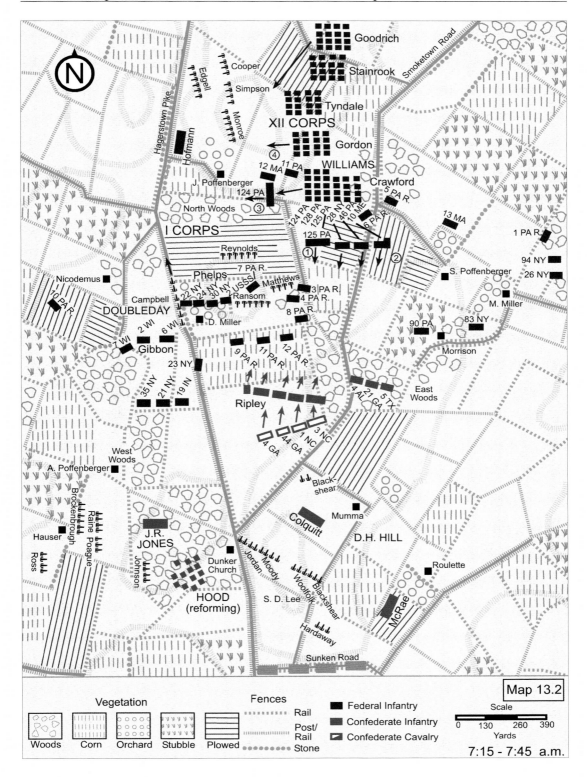

Map 13.2

7:15 - 7:45 a.m.

Map 13.3: Crawford's Brigade Enters the East Woods (7:45 - 8:15 a.m.)

Division leader Williams rode forward with the 124th Pennsylvania to the right (west) side of the Federal front. From there, the green troops headed south through the eastern portion of the North Woods, into the plowed field, and finally deployed with their right flank on the Hagerstown Pike (No. 1). Williams gave the 124th's commander orders to advance with other units as they arrived, but Hooker cancelled the orders and retained the strong Pennsylvania regiment in a reserve position to support his own retreating I Corps troops. At that point Williams returned to the rest of his division to assist in its deployment, which XII Corps commander Mansfield was already actively doing.

The 46th Pennsylvania and the small 28th New York moved as a line of battle on the right (west) side of the Smoketown Road (No. 2) toward the potentially vulnerable flank of the 10th Maine, and Mansfield brought up the large but inexperienced 128th Pennsylvania still massed in column of divisions a bit farther west. These troops were approaching the East Woods when the remaining men from Seymour's and Magilton's battered brigades left their positions and headed for the rear.[8]

When he reached the East Woods, Mansfield ordered the 128th Pennsylvania to slide behind the 46th Pennsylvania and 28th New York and deploy for battle. The XII Corps leader intended to move the novice 128th Pennsylvanians to the right of the veteran 10th Maine, 46th Pennsylvania, and 28th New York. As soon as the 128th's commander Col. Samuel Croasdale gave the order to deploy, however, he was killed and his next in command fell severely wounded. This double blow left Maj. Joel Wanner in charge of the large green regiment. Under fire for the first time and having seen their two senior field officers fall, the Pennsylvanians began to panic. Rather than perform a smooth deployment into position, the entire mass crowded right—away from the deadly fire coming from the three Confederate regiments in the lower portion of the East Woods.

Another tragedy befell Federal arms in general and the XII Corps in particular at this time. Mansfield was with the 10th Maine in the northern portion of the East Woods. He believed (mistakenly, as it turned out) that the regiment was shooting into Abram Duryee's Federal brigade and called out for the Maine troops to cease fire. When some of the soldiers pointed out the gray uniforms to the aging general, Mansfield admitted his error. Almost immediately his horse was wounded and a bullet struck Mansfield in the chest. The general was carried to the rear and died the next day. Williams assumed command of the XII Corps.[9]

Farther west the right and center of the 128th Pennsylvania under Maj. Wanner were in disarray, but the men did not break. Still, admitted Frederick Crouse, "I felt pretty streaky and a little weak in the knees." The Pennsylvanians received orders to hold their fire and aim low when the time came. Col. Joseph Knipe's small 46th Pennsylvania was on the left flank of the 128th Pennsylvania. "[S]eeing the uselessness of a regiment in that position," reported Knipe, "I took responsibility for getting it into line of battle the best way circumstances would admit." Soon thereafter the Federals were ordered to open fire. According to Crouse, "after two or three rounds . . . that nervous feeling left me, and I made up my mind that I was there to fight." Knipe returned a short time later with a suggestion that Maj. Wanner advance his troops into the cornfield in front of his position to drive away the Rebels (Ripley). "They started off in gallant style," wrote Wanner, "cheering as they moved, and penetrated the cornfield, but in consequence of the overpowering numbers of the enemy concealed, were compelled to fall back, which they did in tolerable order." Crouse noted that during the advance south into the corn "we could not see them, yet they were there and doing great damage." The men Crouse "could not see" probably belonged to the 3rd North Carolina, which also fell back in some confusion (No. 4).[10]

Rather than retreat to their original position, the Pennsylvanians moved left (east) and reformed on the right side of the 10th Maine in the East Woods (No. 5). This cleared a path for the left flank of Gordon's brigade, which had just arrived on the left side of Crawford's brigade. These men waited anxiously for their front to clear to return the fire Ripley's men and those in the East Woods were pouring into them.[11]

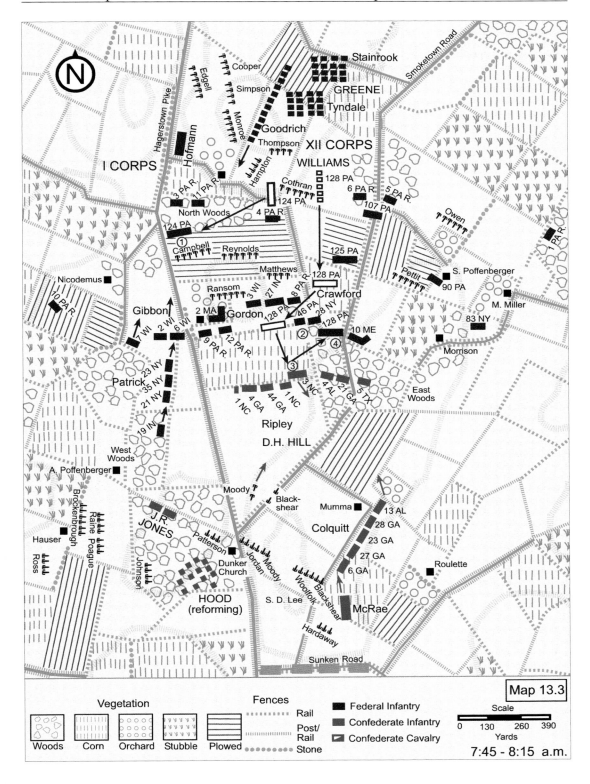

Map 13.3

7:45 - 8:15 a.m.

Vegetation

Woods   Corn   Orchard   Stubble   Plowed

Fences

Rail
Post/
Rail
Stone

■ Federal Infantry
■ Confederate Infantry
▨ Confederate Cavalry

Scale

0   130   260   390
Yards

Map 13.4: D. H. Hill's Division Moves North (7:45 - 8:15 a.m.)

Except for a few scattered units, Joe Hooker's I Corps was out of the fight. Now it was Mansfield's XII Corps' turn to crush the enemy left flank and drive southward.

On the Confederate side, most of three divisions (Lawton's, Jones' and Hood's) had been decimated during the early morning fighting, and only three small Rebel regiments (the 4th Alabama, 21st Georgia, and 5th Texas) were left holding the lower portion of the East Woods (No. 1). Directly in their front stood the 10th Maine, the anchor of the left side of Samuel Crawford's brigade line in the northern fringe of the East Woods (No. 2). From his position in the timber, the 10th Maine's Lt. John Gould could see the Confederates "dodging from tree to tree, aiming at us, yelling, and shaking their fists at times."[12]

Several brigades from Maj. Gen. D. H. Hill's division were either engaged or entering the battle. The first, under Roswell Ripley, had scored several sharp but decisive early tactical victories. Ripley advanced into the pasture south of the Miller cornfield to drive away portions of the Pennsylvania Reserves and men from John Gibbon's and Marsena Patrick's brigades before swinging northeast to repulse a disordered attack by the 128th Pennsylvania. Ripley's concentrated volleys had also forced back the 46th Pennsylvania and 28th New York (No. 3). When George Gordon's Federal brigade deployed at the fence at the northwest corner of the cornfield and dispatched heavy volleys from its three regiments (about 1,140 men), many of Ripley's men may have wondered whether driving these new fresh Federals away from the field would be as easy (No. 4). Hard pressed, D. H. Hill called up Col. Alfred Colquitt's and Col. Duncan McRae's (Samuel Garland's) brigades, which combined numbered perhaps 2,000 troops (No. 5). It was now Hill's fight to wage.

Colquitt's command, which had been resting near the center of the army's line near a sunken farm road—soon to be better known as the Bloody Lane—received its marching orders about 7:00 a.m. The 13th Alabama led the column through the plowed fields past the burning Mumma farm buildings and beyond before obliquing left across the Smoketown Road to enter the corpse-strewn pasture. A few hundred yards north, Ripley's men were barely holding their ground against mounting XII Corps pressure. Colquitt's men had helped hold the vital National Road through Turner's Gap throughout much of September 14 before being challenged heavily late in the day and being pushed back at dusk by John Gibbon's Iron Brigade. Sam Garland's command had also been heavily engaged at Fox's Gap on the morning of September 14, where it lost its commander together with hundreds of men trying to stave off a determined IX Corps division. The brigade was now under Col. McRae. The unit was in no shape for another major combat, as events would soon demonstrate.[13]

Meanwhile, the XII Corps (without Mansfield, who was mortally wounded) completed its deployment. With his First Division engaged in a line north of the Miller cornfield, temporary corps leader Alpheus Williams brought up Brig. Gen. George Greene's division. Col. William Goodrich's brigade had been dispatched west and was heading down the Hagerstown Pike to bolster the Federal right flank, which was in total disarray (No. 6). Greene's two remaining brigades under Lt. Col. Hector Tyndale and Col. Henry Stainrook (about 1,730 men) continued south toward the center and left of the Federal line. Williams ordered Greene to deploy the brigades left of the Joseph Poffenberger farm lane. Greene was to advance south and swing his left flank toward the Mumma buildings, which were easy to locate because of the billowing smoke. The intent was to catch the Confederates in a vise and drive them back with heavy losses.[14]

When Gordon's brigade arrived north of the cornfield, Capt. Dunbar Ransom's Union gunners returned to their pieces and opened with canister. Capt. George Cothran's battery deployed near the North Woods and opened fire. On the Southern side, a section from Lt. Col. Allen Cutts' battalion and another from Capt. George Moody's battery ventured forward in the direction of Ripley's line to provide additional support.

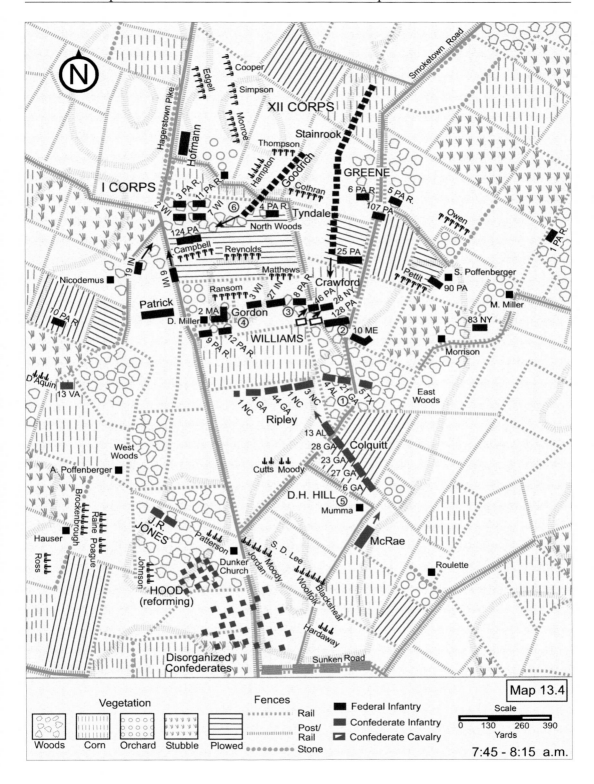

Map 13.4

Vegetation

| Woods | Corn | Orchard | Stubble | Plowed |

Fences
- Rail
- Post/Rail
- Stone

■ Federal Infantry
▬ Confederate Infantry
▱ Confederate Cavalry

Scale
0   130   260   390
Yards

7:45 - 8:15 a.m.

Map 13.5: Colquitt's Brigade Advances into the Cornfield (8:15 - 8:45 a.m.)

Moving by the left flank, Alfred Colquitt guided his brigade in front of Roswell Ripley's command (No. 1). Ripley's Georgians and North Carolinians were simply worn out after their fight with parts of Gibbon's, Phelps', Patrick's, Crawford's, and Gordon's brigades. Its men were more than willing to leave the pasture and cornfield in the hands of the new arrivals. The 13th Alabama led Colquitt's command and deployed on the left of the brigade, with the 28th, 23rd, 27th, and 6th Georgia extending the line to the right. The march forward angled north by northwest, cutting diagonally across the Miller cornfield.

Colquitt's two right-most regiments (the 6th Georgia and a portion of the 27th Georgia) reached the cornfield's northern fence line, but heavy firing from the 2nd Massachusetts, 3rd Wisconsin and 27th Indiana (Gordon) prevented the rest of the brigade from doing the same. The Hoosiers of the 27th advanced and refused their left flank so it was nearly perpendicular to the rest of the line, a smart movement that allowed it to throw an enfilade fire into Colquitt's men. Many of the Southerners lay down to avoid the hail of lead and returned the favor, inflicting serious losses on Gordon's three Federal regiments. The 3rd Wisconsin sustained the heaviest losses because it was positioned on a small hill and so was more exposed to enemy fire. For the first time that morning, an entire Rebel brigade was deployed in the devastated Miller cornfield. Ripley's 3rd North Carolina (together with part of the 1st North Carolina) remained in the field south of Colquitt's men.[15]

After about five minutes of heavy fighting Samuel Garland's North Carolina brigade under McRae crossed the Smoketown Road. Its arrival raised the hopes of the men struggling to hold the Miller cornfield. Exhausted and almost out of ammunition, the 4th Alabama, 5th Texas, and 21st Georgia in the East Woods were also excited to see the 750 North Carolinians. A host of problems plagued the unlucky brigade, which had not yet recovered from its harrowing ordeal and bloodletting at Fox's Gap just three days earlier. Many of the officers had been killed and wounded there, and inexperienced and incapable men had taken their place, including Col. Duncan McRae, who was not suited to brigade command. The orders coursing through the brigade's ranks were confused and often contradictory. One officer on the right side of the line in the 5th North Carolina spotted a large group of Yankees and panicked. The officer rushed to the regiment's commander, Capt. Thomas Garrett, and screamed, "They are flanking us!" Garrett told him to quiet himself and get back into line. "The men before this were far from being cool," admitted Garrett. According to division leader D. H. Hill, "this cry spread like an electric shock along the ranks, bringing up vivid recollections of the flank fire at South Mountain." Panic spread left down the line and eventually consumed the entire brigade. Within a few minutes it was in full retreat—much to the chagrin of the other Confederates counting on its support (No. 2).[16]

The troops who spooked McRae's men belonged to the four regiments of Lt. Col. Hector Tyndale's brigade (Greene's division). Tyndale was approaching the northern fringe of the East Woods (No. 3), with the large 28th Pennsylvania on the left (650 men) and the remaining three Ohio regiments (the 5th, 66th, and 7th) extending the line to the right. Collectively, all three Buckeye regiments mustered only 425 men. During the approach, Maj. Orrin Crane of the 7th Ohio told Lt. Col. Eugene Powell, commander of the 66th, that the troops in front of them were friendly, but Powell disagreed. Somehow the 6th Georgia fighting on the right of Colquitt's line failed to see Tyndale's advance until a captain in the 6th's right company realized the catastrophe about to befall them. He was attempting to alert the regiment's commander to the danger when both were killed by the 66th Ohio's first volley. The other Buckeye regiments also opened fire. Colquitt's men were trapped in a cauldron of fire in the open cornfield and in desperate straits.[17]

When McRae's men suddenly quit the field, D. H. Hill had no choice but to order his two other brigades under Colquitt and Ripley to follow suit. Only the 4th and 44th Georgia (Ripley) complied.[18]

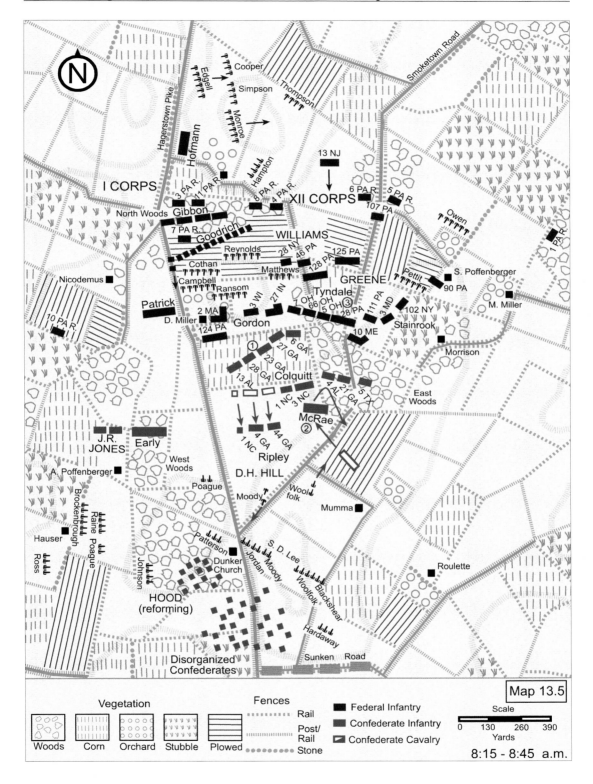

Map 13.5

8:15 - 8:45 a.m.

Map 13.6: D. H. Hill's Brigades are Defeated (8:15 - 8:45 a.m.)

The 28th Pennsylvania and 5th Ohio on the left and center of Tyndale's line were ready to go over on the offensive, but the 10th Maine blocked their path until ordered to the rear to relinquish its space to the new arrivals. Col. Henry Stainrook's brigade had followed Tyndale from its bivouac and deployed on the 28th Pennsylvania's left across the Smoketown Road. Stainrook's 111th Pennsylvania easily deployed next to the 28th Pennsylvania, but the 3rd Maryland and 102nd New York had a harder time. Soon after crossing the road, the left side of the 3rd Maryland ran into the right side of the 102nd New York while Confederate small arms fire zipped through their ranks. Once the officers sorted out the mess the two regiments fell into line (No. 1).[19]

When the 10th Maine cleared their front, the 28th Pennsylvania and 5th Ohio fired a volley through the scattered timber that was so precise it sounded like a single discharge. The sheet of lead shattered any optimism the Confederates may have harbored about being able to hold the heavily contested East Woods. Southern officers had been pleading for reinforcements, but by now it was becoming obvious only the enemy would receive additional manpower. The abrupt departure of McRae's North Carolinians did nothing to improve Southern morale. The vital woods anchored the sector's right flank, so the Texans, Georgians, and Alabamians had little choice to cling to their positions as the exchange of gunfire once again heated up.

When the 28th Pennsylvania and 5th Ohio stepped off to attack (No. 2), Stainrook's 111th Pennsylvania on their left joined the charge. The 3rd Maryland and 102nd New York were also ordered forward. When the 5th Texas men spotted the 111th Pennsylvania advancing against their front and the 3rd Maryland and 102nd New York against their right flank, they knew it was time to vacate the woods.

Meanwhile, the left flank of the large 28th Pennsylvania and the 111th Pennsylvania were already forcing the 4th Alabama and 21st Georgia out of the East Woods. R. T. Cole of the 4th Alabama described the attack as both

"terrible and overwhelming." Several hours of hard fighting had exhausted him and his comrades and their ammunition was nearly gone. They didn't need much encouragement to fall back (No. 3), and they knew where to go without having to be told: the very conspicuous Dunker Church, where Brig. Gen. John Hood met them and pointed out where to deploy to repulse an expected Federal advance. Cole recalled Hood's concern about his wounded soldiers, and that the warrior-Texan was "as sympathetic as a woman."[20]

While the left of the 28th Pennsylvania drove the enemy out of the East Woods, its right flank, along with the Ohio regiments to its right, engaged Colquitt's right wing in the Miller cornfield (No. 4). According to the 28th Pennsylvania's Sgt. William Fithian, "Tyndale . . . ordered us to move by the right flank, under cover of the hill. When we got nearly opposite them we layed low, until they were within 30 yards of us, when we [were] up and at them, cutting them up terribly." "Every stalk held a rebel," recalled another Pennsylvanian. The 6th Georgia on Colquitt's right was attacked in front, flank, and rear, and hand-to-hand fighting broke out in places where Colquitt's men refused to quit the field. Ten years later, Tyndale recalled the exchange lasting about twenty minutes. Scores of prisoners were taken and the 6th Georgia was almost wiped out.[21]

Alpheus Williams had other XII Corps troops at hand, including the 124th and 125th Pennsylvania of Crawford's brigade. The 124th had been sent to the right (west) to bolster Union positions near the Hagerstown Pike, and was now in line on Gordon's right (No. 5). The 125th Pennsylvania, together with portions of the 46th New York and 128th Pennsylvania, charged into the East Woods behind Tyndale. Two other regiments in reserve (the 13th New Jersey and 107th Pennsylvania) were also moving to the front.[22]

Unlike many of the other victorious Union troops content to stop and reform their broken ranks, some like those of the 102nd New York continued driving south, forcing the Confederates to quickly withdraw their artillery.

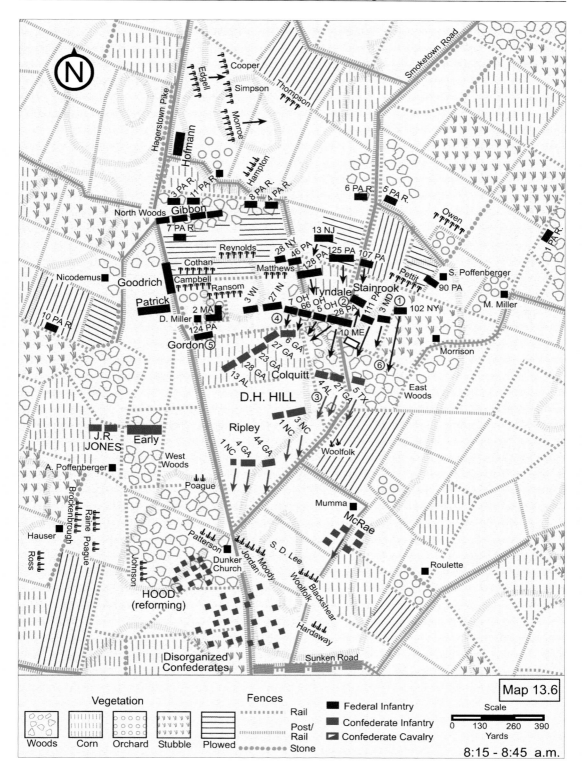

Map 13.6

8:15 - 8:45 a.m.

Map Set 14. Antietam: Sedgwick's Division Drives West
(8:15 - 9:30 a.m.)

Map 14.1: Sedgwick's Division Arrives (8:15 - 8:45 a.m.)

For the first time that day there were no organized Rebel units east of the Hagerstown Pike, and only a remnant of Brig. Gen. John R. Jones' division under Col. Andrew Grigsby (perhaps 300 men) held a position near the north end of the West Woods. Farther south, Brig. Gen. John Hood's wrecked division rested behind the Dunker Church. His 2,300 men had marched out of the woods less then two hours earlier and nearly half of them fell on the field. The only fresh brigade available was Brig. Gen. Jubal Early's (Lawton's division), which had spent the early morning on the left side of the line guarding guns on Nicodemus Hill. After leaving the small 31st Virginia to guard the guns, Early moved to the West Woods to reinforce the masses of disorganized Rebels attempting to hold it against the advancing XII Corps.[1]

The intense fighting on the northern part of the field for the first three and one-half hours (5:15 - 8:45 a.m.) knocked both combatants out of the fight. Joe Hooker's Federal I Corps lost 2,600 of the 9,438 men who marched into battle, or about 28%. Joseph Mansfield's XII Corps lost nearly 1,750, or about 24%. The outnumbered Rebels lost a higher percentage in the fields east of the Hagerstown Pike and above the Smoketown Road. Stonewall Jackson's two divisions under Jones and Lawton lost about 2,000 out of the 6,321 carried into battle, or nearly one out of every three men. D. H. Hill's losses were higher. Three of his brigades (Ripley, Colquitt, and Garland-McRae, about 3,355 men) battled in and near the Miller cornfield and East Woods, where 1,582 fell for a loss approaching 50%. This figure is all the more appalling because McRae's men never really entered the fight.[2]

After being bloodied by Ripley's and Colquitt's brigades, Brig. Gen. George Gordon moved his Federal brigade to the East Woods. With the defeat of Hill's three brigades, the path was clear for Lt. Col. Hector Tyndale's and Col. Henry Stainrook's brigades to advance toward the Dunker Church in the West Woods (No. 1). This landmark had been one of Joe Hooker's prime objectives all morning, and now it looked to be within reach. None of the Federal batteries that had fought in and around the Miller cornfield were fit for further duty, however, so two that had been engaged farther north under Capt. J. Albert Monroe and Lt. Frederick L. Edgell advanced with Tyndale and Stainrook. Only Hood's exhausted survivors were available to defend the area (No. 2). After reorganizing their ranks west of the Dunker Church, Hood moved his men back into the West Woods. According to Lt. Col. Philip Work of the 1st Texas, the division amounted to little more than a heavy skirmish line.[3]

Farther to the north, the 124th Pennsylvania marched down the Hagerstown Pike (No. 3) toward Jones' survivors under Grigsby in the northern portion of the West Woods. The rebels opened fire and forced the three companies on the west side of the pike to oblique right. The Purnell Legion of Col. William Goodrich's brigade formed behind and to the right of the 124th regiment, now pinned down by Grigsby's Virginians. The rest of Goodrich's unit advanced behind a skirmish line composed of the 3rd Delaware, followed by the 21st, 23rd, and 35th New York of Marsena Patrick's brigade (No. 4). Jubal Early brought up his brigade (No. 5) and with Grigsby's (Jones') men opened fire on Goodrich's troops, killing Goodrich and stopping the Federals in their tracks. Both sides suffered heavy losses in officers. The highest ranking officer to fall was Gen. Hooker, who suffered a painful foot wound about this time and left the front.[4]

More Federal reinforcements were arriving in the form of the large II Corps, nearly 15,000 men, under 65-year-old Edwin Sumner (No. 6). Sumner wanted to cross his II Corps over Antietam Creek the prior evening with Mansfield's XII Corps, but McClellan refused. On the morning of September 17, Sumner waited impatiently on the porch of the Pry House for McClellan to give him orders. When they arrived about 7:20 a.m., Sumner ordered his men across the stream.

On the Confederate side, Col. George T. Anderson's brigade (D. R. Jones' division) and Maj. Gen. Lafayette McLaws' division were marching to the Dunker Church sector. Just more than 4,000 Confederates were about to square off against as many as 11,000 Federals in the two II Corps divisions, and another 1,500 from the XII Corps.[5]

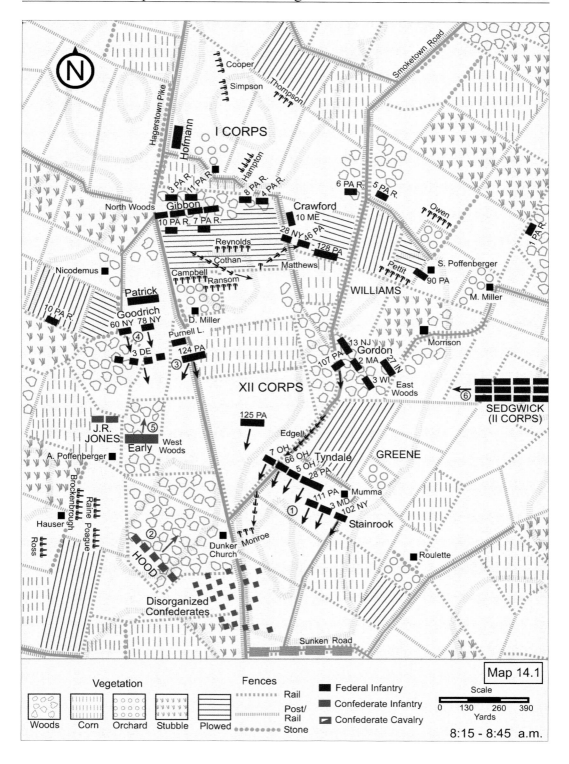

Map 14.1

8:15 - 8:45 a.m.

Vegetation

Woods Corn Orchard Stubble Plowed

Fences

Rail

Post/
Rail

Stone

Federal Infantry
Confederate Infantry
Confederate Cavalry

Scale

0   130   260   390
Yards

Map 14.2: Sedgwick Advances to the West Woods (8:15 - 8:45 a.m.)

Once across Antietam Creek, Sumner ordered Maj. Gen. John Sedgwick's division into columns by brigade. Brig. Gen. Oliver O. Howard's brigade was on the right (north), Brig. Gen. Willis Gorman's on the left (south), and Brig. Gen. Napoleon Dana's held the center. The column was moving west when Sumner met Hooker being carried from the field with his foot wound. The battle was raging in the distance and Hooker, in a semi-conscious state, told him that all was well and the battle nearly won. Sumner's orders were to push forward to the left of Hooker's line near the Mumma farm and, if not needed there, to move south toward Sharpsburg. "Use your artillery freely," urged Hooker.[6]

Sumner halted and deployed Sedgwick's division near the East Woods. The column was brought around to the right so Gorman's brigade was in the front rank, followed by Dana and Howard. Despite some Confederate artillery fire that occasionally knocked men out of the ranks, the division moved forward steadily. Riding ahead, Sumner could see two large bodies of Federal troops leaving the East Woods and moving south (the brigades of Tyndale and Stainrook). Fighting was visible beyond the open fields around the West Woods. Sumner ordered Sedgwick to march toward those woods (No. 1).[7]

Federal troops were now closing in on the Dunker Church from the north and from the east. Capt. Monroe's battery unlimbered in the open field east of the small church and opened fire. Two of its sections faced west and its canister blasts quelled any Confederate idea to mount an attack (No. 2). The remaining section faced south and fired at Alfred Colquitt's retreating men, "throwing them into great confusion." Confederate sharpshooters eased forward and silenced the battery until its gunners managed to turn their pieces and fire into them. Lt. Edgell's New Hampshire battery arrived and together with Monroe's guns silenced any visible Confederate battery still in action. Southern sharpshooters were still taking a toll, however, so Monroe ordered his gunners to reposition the battery farther to the rear just south of the East Woods, where artillery once again opened fire.

Meanwhile, the 125th Pennsylvania (Crawford's brigade), which had been in reserve, was ordered to advance and drive the enemy from the West Woods around the church (No. 3). It was a tall order for one inexperienced regiment.[8]

With the large 125th Pennsylvania sweeping toward the West Woods and two brigades of XII Corps infantry approaching in front of the Dunker Church, Col. William Wofford, commander of one of Hood's battered brigades, realized the futility of remaining in the area. "After some time the enemy commenced advancing in full force," reported Wofford. "Seeing the hopelessness and folly of making a stand with our shattered brigade and a remnant from other commands, the men being greatly exhausted and many of them without ammunition, I determined to fall back to a fence in our rear, where we met the long looked for re-enforcements." The 125th Pennsylvania entered the West Woods with its left flank only twenty yards from the Dunker Church.[9]

Jubal Early knew trouble when he saw it. He was aware that a portion of Goodrich's and Patrick's brigades were advancing south on the west side of the Hagerstown Pike, and that even more troops (three companies of the 124th Pennsylvania) were also on that side of the road. Early could also see two of George Greene's brigades (Tyndale and Stainrook) halted just east of the West Woods and the large 125th Pennsylvania driving toward the vulnerable Dunker Church. Although informed that reinforcements would arrive shortly, Early knew he could not wait. He left the remnants of Jones' division under Grigsby to hold off the threat from the north and moved his own brigade by the right flank to confront the Pennsylvanians (No. 4). Early was maneuvering into position when he spotted the head of G. T. Anderson's arriving brigade. Behind it tramped McLaws' division. Both commands had been resting in reserve south of Sharpsburg before being dispatched north to reinforce Lee's threatened left flank.[10]

What Early likely did not know was that Sedgwick's division was moving toward the northeastern portion of the West Woods and the right flank of Jones' thin handful of survivors. Gorman led the division's advance; the remaining two Federal brigades under Dana and Howard were still a good distance to the rear.[11]

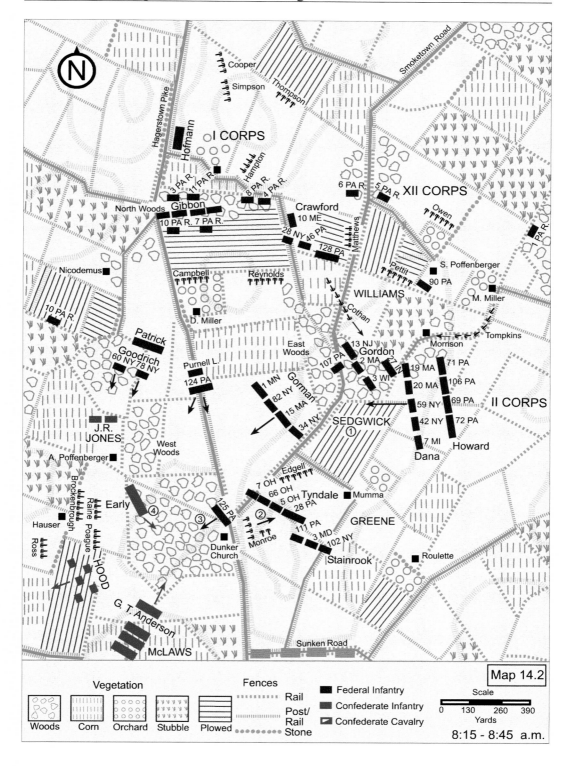

Map 14.2

8:15 - 8:45 a.m.

Map 14.3: Sedgwick's Division Drives West and McLaws' Division Arrives (8:45 - 9:15 a.m.)

Sumner remained confident that Sedgwick's division could reach the West Woods, rotate his men forty-five degrees to the left to face Lee's exposed flank, and with his overwhelming numbers drive all the way to Sharpsburg. The men, however, were apprehensive about their aggressive approach toward the West Woods.

"The total disregard of all ordinary military precaution in their swift and solitary advance was so manifest," wrote Lt. Col. Francis Palfrey of the 20th Massachusetts, "that it was observed and criticized as the devoted band moved on." One important dispatch that Sumner never received communicated the following: "General McClellan desires you to be very careful how you advance, as he fears our right is suffering." Because Sumner was riding ahead with Sedgwick, William Henry French was unsure where his division should go when he reached the East Woods (No. 1). When he spied the left side of the XII Corps off to the southwest, French decided to slide his division in that direction, perhaps because he believed the distant troops belonged to Sedgwick's division.[12]

Capt. John Pelham's Rebel horse artillery on Hauser's Ridge, together with several other batteries in action near there, struck Gorman's men as they scaled the fences flanking the Hagerstown Pike. Col. Grigsby's remnants of Jones' division, perhaps 200 to 300 men all told, swivelled to the right to meet Gorman's approaching threat.[13]

Farther south near the Dunker Church, the 125th Pennsylvania gamely held its isolated position in the West Woods for about twenty minutes (No. 2). The Pennsylvanians spotted Tyndale's and Stainrook's stationary brigades behind them and were surprised when they did not move to reinforce their lodgement. Their anxiety level increased when their skirmish line was driven in by Jubal Early's advancing brigade. Help arrived from an unexpected direction. During the approach toward the Hagerstown Pike, Gorman ordered his brigade to oblique to the right away from the Dunker Church. The 34th New York on the left of the line did not

receive these orders and continued driving toward the church (No. 3).[14]

Col. G. T. "Tige" Anderson advanced his brigade through the southwest corner of the West Woods and deployed for action. Anderson had earlier been ordered to reinforce the Confederate left flank. When he was not provided with a guide, however, Anderson followed the sounds of battle to the West Woods (No. 4). Hood was still in the sector and provided Anderson with orders when he arrived. McLaws' division was also now on the scene. Although composed of four brigades, it was soon shy of one of them. Howell Cobb's small brigade, which had been roughly handled at Crampton's Gap, was ordered to move to the right of the division. Cobb apparently misunderstood how far to the right he was to move and continued marching all the way to the Sunken Road (No. 5). McLaws deployed the rest of his division, sending Paul Semmes' brigade to the left to support Grigsby while pushing William Barksdale's and Joseph Kershaw's brigades straight ahead toward the church. These last two brigades had helped capture Maryland Heights while Semmes fought at Crampton's Gap.[15]

More Confederate reinforcements arrived. Artillerist Capt. Thomas Carter, who met Gen. Lee just north of Sharpsburg, wrote that the army leader "seemed to fear that the whole left wing, then hard pressed and losing ground, would be turned, and that the enemy would gain possession of the range of hills some three-quarters of a mile to the left of Sharpsburg." These were the same hills that stood between Lee's army and his retreat route to the Potomac River, and the same high ground that Early feared the 125th Pennsylvania would take, which in turn had prompted him to attack the Pennsylvanians.

With much anxiety, Lee mounted his horse and rode to his beleaguered left flank. Before he did so, however, he sent orders to Brig. Gen. John Walker to move his small division to the left from its position on the far right flank guarding Snavely's Ford along Antietam Creek.[16]

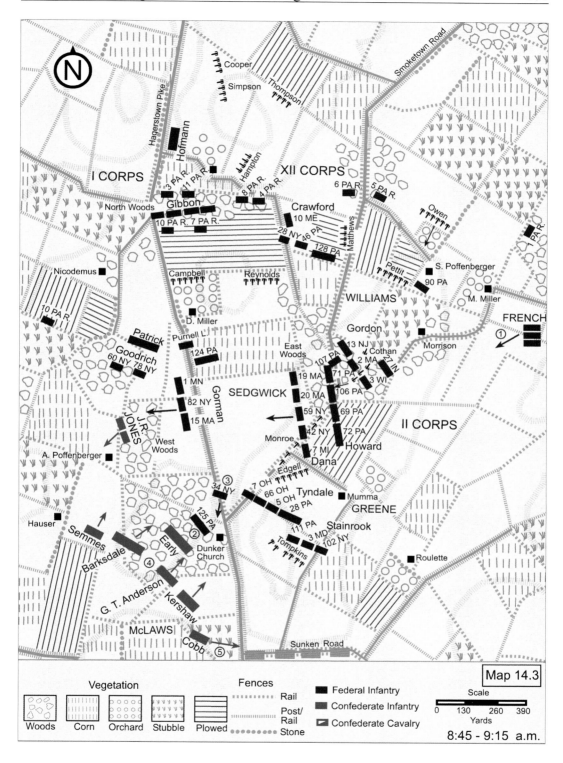

Map 14.3

8:45 - 9:15 a.m.

Map 14.4: Sedgwick's Division Drives into the West Woods (8:45 - 9:15 a.m.)

John Sedgwick's division of three brigades was marching into a trap. Worried about the right side of Sedgwick's command, Sumner rode just behind the 1st Minnesota on the right side of Gorman's brigade. From that vantage point the II Corps commander could see the fight to his front west of the Hagerstown Pike between the remnants of J. R. Jones' division (Grigsby) and Goodrich's and Patrick's brigades. When he spotted the 1st Minnesota's sheathed colors, Sumner yelled, "In God's name, what are you fighting for? Unfurl those colors!" Although they were largely veterans, many of Sedgwick's men were unnerved by the large number of dead and wounded scattered everywhere around the East Woods, near Miller's cornfield and fields to the south and around the Hagerstown Pike.[17]

As Gorman later reported, not until he had pushed his brigade into the West Woods did "the enemy's heavy lines of infantry first come into view, the front of which retired in considerable disorder before our advance" (No. 1). These Confederates, who almost certainly belonged to Jones' scattered division, reassembled near the Alfred Poffenberger farm buildings to continue the fight.

A satisfied Gorman continued pushing his men west through the timber. He would not have been as confident had he known that his 34th New York on the far left had detached itself from his line and was already well to the south approaching the Dunker Church. This mistake left a 300-yard gap between the New Yorkers and the 15th Massachusetts. As a result, the flanks of both regiments were in the air and vulnerable. A deep ravine extended through the woods between these two units.

Dana's brigade, advancing in Sedgwick's second line, moved at double-time to close the distance with Gorman, crossed the Hagerstown Pike, and continued heading west. The third brigade under Oliver Howard closed the gap with Dana and made good progress across the open fields.[18]

Once Dana's brigade crossed the Hagerstown Pike and drew near the West Woods, he reported that "a tremendous musketry fire opened on my left front, apparently perpendicular to my line of march and flanking the first line [Gorman's]." Worried that the gunfire indicated the enemy was breaking through the woods to his left, Dana detached his 7th Michigan on his left and then the 42nd New York and obliqued both regiments in that direction to counter this potential threat (No. 2). This order inadvertently helped close part of the gap between the 125th New York and the 15th Massachusetts.[19]

The Rebels were also sliding into position. Brig. Gen. Joe Kershaw threw the 2nd South Carolina forward while deploying the rest of his brigade. The regiment drew small arms fire from the 125th Pennsylvania and 34th New York behind it, forcing Kershaw to throw two more regiments, the 7th and 8th South Carolina, into the fight on the 2nd South Carolina's right flank (No. 3). His last regiment, the 3rd South Carolina, was sent to the left of the 2nd South Carolina. When the latter regiment approached the front, the commander of the 34th New York refused his left flank to face the new threat (No. 4).

Jubal Early's men, meanwhile, continued battling the Pennsylvanians west of the Dunker Church. Col. G. T. Anderson brought up his brigade and behind and slightly to the west Brig. Gen. William Barksdale did the same. The last brigade to form along this line belonged to Brig. Gen. Paul Semmes. When his men heard the orders "by company into line," followed by "forward into line," they advanced about 200 yards toward Gorman's exposed left flank (No. 5).[20]

Blissfully unaware of the mortal danger coalescing around him, Sumner breathed a sigh of relief that Sedgwick's division was nearly closed up, well ordered, and seemingly ready for anything it might face. The increasing small arms fire coming from an unseen enemy in front of the division, however, worried him.

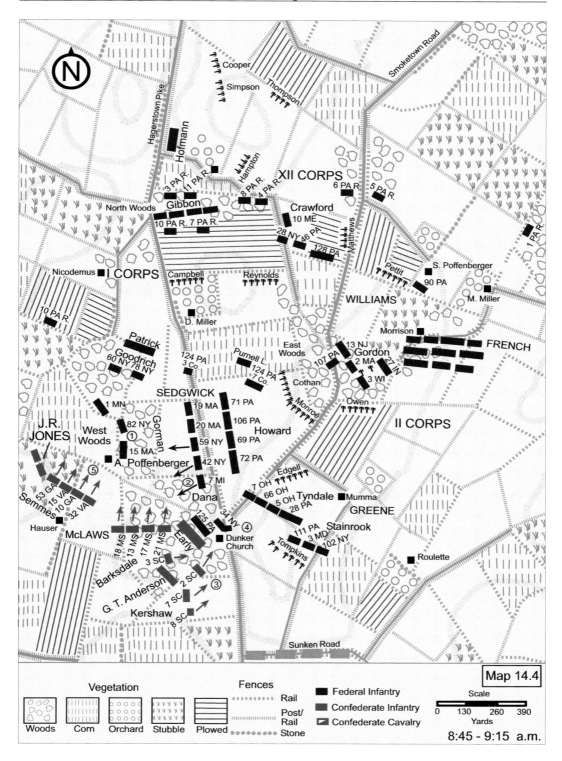

Map 14.4

8:45 - 9:15 a.m.

Vegetation
Woods | Corn | Orchard | Stubble | Plowed

Fences
Rail
Post/Rail
Stone

■ Federal Infantry
■ Confederate Infantry
▭ Confederate Cavalry

Scale
0   130   260   390
Yards

Map 14.5: The Confederates Counterattack (8:45 - 9:15 a.m.)

While many of Sedgwick's tightly packed men sought protection behind rocks, ledges, and trees, many others remained in formation, "leaning on their muskets, and some of the officers commenced smoking," recalled the historian of the 20th Massachusetts. According to Brig. Gen. Howard, "our three lines, each in two ranks were so near together that a rifle bullet would often cross them all and disable four or five men at a time." By this time the 15th Massachusetts on Gorman's left was engaged with both survivors from D. R. Jones' division and Semmes' brigade (No. 1). Both sides took advantage of the rocky ledges wherever possible as the fighting increased in its intensity. The Northerners fired about half of their eighty cartridges in the first fifteen minutes alone. Losses mounted quickly on both sides.[21]

Lt. Col. John W. Kimball, the commander of the 15th Massachusetts (Gorman's brigade), was both outraged and distressed when he learned the 59th New York of Dana's brigade directly behind him was firing into his men. When no amount of pleading could get the Bay State troops to stop pulling their triggers, Kimball turned to Sumner for help. Within a few minutes the friendly fire ended. Many of the men in the second and third lines were frustrated for another reason: their inability to engage the enemy because of the Union troops in front of them.[22]

Farther left near the Dunker Church, the 125th Pennsylvania and 34th New York behind it were being hit hard by Confederate bullets (No. 2). The two regiments were in a difficult position, attacked by Early's brigade in front and along their right flank by the 3rd South Carolina and the right wing of Barksdale's men (the 17th and 21st Mississippi). After firing about six volleys, the right side of Col. Jacob Higgins' 125th Pennsylvanians gave way in disorder. The retreat carried with it the right side of the 34th New York. The 2nd South Carolina pushed forward against the rest of the Pennsylvanians and drove them to the rear. "I held him here [the enemy] for some time, until I discovered two regiments of them moving around my right

[Barksdale's], while a brigade charged on my front [Early's]," reported Col. Higgins. "On looking around and finding no support in sight, I was compelled to retire. Had I remained in my position two minutes longer I would have lost my whole command. I fell back." The withdrawal left only part of the 34th New York in place. A veteran of the 2nd South Carolina related to Union veteran and historian Ezra Carman, "the first Union line [125th Pennsylvania] was very quickly driven, but an oblique line [34th New York], apparently of older soldiers, was not easily moved and [briefly] checked us." The New Yorkers held their ground for a while, but the crossfire from front and flanks was too much to bear for long.[23]

The 7th Michigan and the 42nd New York, meanwhile, entered the West Woods north and east of the Dunker Church (No. 3) and encountered a deep ravine running generally east to west. They could see the embattled 125th Pennsylvania on their left. The Wolverines and New Yorkers halted to realign their ranks and within a few minutes spotted troops moving in their direction through the ravine. Some officers believed that these men were friendly skirmishers returning to the main Federal line and so ordered their men to hold their fire. Their conclusion quickly changed when the strangers leveled their rifles and let loose a volley in their direction, quickly followed by another. Brigade commander Dana, who was with this wing, called the firing "the most terrific I ever witnessed."

Within minutes his men were caught in a crossfire from the left side of Barksdale's Mississippians, Kershaw's 3rd South Carolina, and the Virginians of Early's brigade. About one-half of Dana's men were killed or wounded, with Dana counted among the latter. The 7th Michigan and 42nd New York were unable to stand and gave way. Pvt. Edward Burress of the 21st Mississippi was not impressed by the Federal effort. "[T]he cowardly dogs hardly gave us a fight enough to make it interesting," Burress recalled, who boasted that he and his comrades drove the enemy "like scattered sheep."[24]

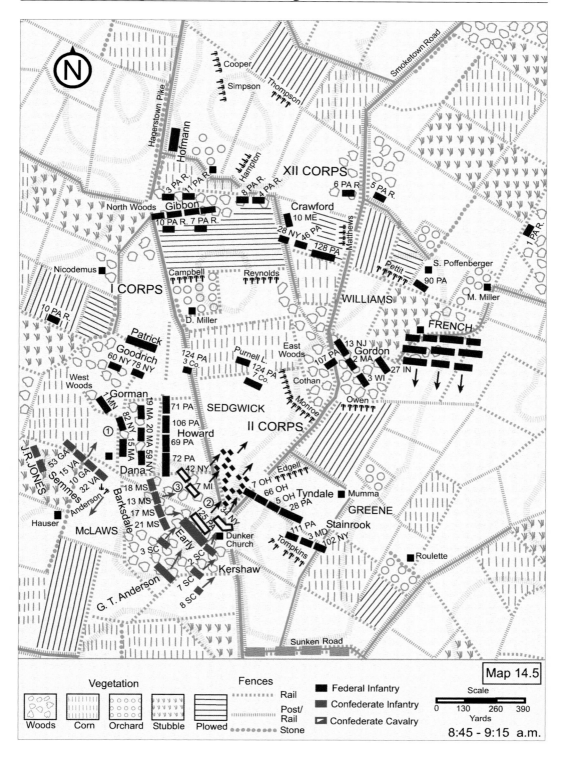

Map 14.5

Vegetation

Woods   Corn   Orchard   Stubble   Plowed

Fences
.... Rail
Post/
Rail
Stone

Federal Infantry
Confederate Infantry
Confederate Cavalry

Scale
0   130   260   390
Yards

8:45 - 9:15 a.m.

Map 14.6: The Tide Turns Against Sedgwick (8:45 - 9:30 a.m.)

The situation confronting Sedwick's division was rapidly deteriorating. The 72nd Pennsylvania advanced on the left of the division's third line, its ranks disordered by the surge of survivors from the 125th Pennsylvania sprinting for the safety of the rear (No. 1). The confusion and demoralization spread to the new arrivals, most of whom were carried to the rear without a hostile shot fired in their direction.

With the defeat of the 7th Michigan, 34th and 42nd New York, and the 125th Pennsylvania on the left of Sedgwick's main body, portions of five Rebel brigades under Semmes, Anderson, Early, Kershaw, and Barksdale stood ready to pounce on the largely unsuspecting Federal division. The latter three brigades were already pouring out of the West Woods after the fleeing Yankees.

After Early's men helped drive the 125th Pennsylvania and 34th New York from its front, his soldiers followed them without orders. The unauthorized pursuit displeased Early, who admitted that he "always found difficult to restrain" his troops following a victorious combat. Infantry on Sedgwick's left hit the surging Confederates in the flank and rear. "I succeeded in arresting my command and ordered it to retire, so that I might change front and advance on this force," Early reported. He moved his men north through the West Woods toward Sedgwick's vulnerable flank (No. 2).[25]

Barksdale's Mississippians, who had played a large role in defeating Federal troops near the Dunker Church, wheeled to the left to take on Sedgwick's left flank. Semmes' brigade, standing tall in front of Sedgwick's division, continued exchanging fire with the three regiments of Gorman's brigade in the front line (No. 3) while Early's brigade approached Sedgwick's left flank between Semmes and Barksdale. Cavalryman Jeb Stuart rushed four batteries of artillery that had been deployed on Hauser's Ridge to the area around Semmes, where they unlimbered and went to work.[26]

Sedgwick's men had advanced into the jaws of a giant gray vise, but few Federals fully realized the true nature of the danger. A member of the 59th New York would later write home that his regiment was "completely flanked on the left and in two minutes more would have been prisoners if gen Sumner himself had not rood [sic] in through the terrific fire of the enemy and brought us off." Realizing something was amiss, Sumner rode the field in search of Sedgwick but was unable to locate him. When he drew near the 59th New York, which formed the left flank of his second line (Dana's brigade) in the West Woods, Sumner was informed of a large number of Rebels off to the left. When he rode in that direction the horrified corps commander watched while hundreds of his own II Corps soldiers sprinted for the rear with the enemy in hot pursuit. "My God! We must get out of this!" he exclaimed as he rode along the line in the vain hope of redeploying his men to confront the enemy.[27]

When he reached Howard's brigade in the third line Sumner yelled, "Back boys, for God's sake move back; you are in a bad fix!" The gunfire was so loud that Sumner was forced to use hand signals to instruct Howard to pull his brigade back and reform it along a fence line, perpendicular to his current position. Before Howard could react, his regiment on the left (the 72nd Pennsylvania) broke for the rear.[28]

More Confederate reinforcements arrived in this sector in the form of Brig. Gen. John Walker's small division, which consisted of two brigades under Brig. Gen. Robert Ransom and Col. Van Manning (No. 4).

When they spotted their comrades leaving the West Woods and heading east, the 3rd South Carolina—which had fought with Barksdale's men—wheeled in that direction to rejoin its parent brigade. When these Palmetto troops came under fire from Woodruff's battery with its improvised infantry supports, they hit the ground and awaited further orders.[29]

About 9:45 a.m., a desperate plea for help from Sumner reached Alpheus Williams, the temporary XII Corps commander. Williams immediately ordered Brig. Gen. Gordon to move from the East Woods toward the Dunker Church. Gordon picked the two closest regiments, the 2nd Massachusetts and 13th New Jersey, and sent them quick-stepping to the front (No. 5).[30]

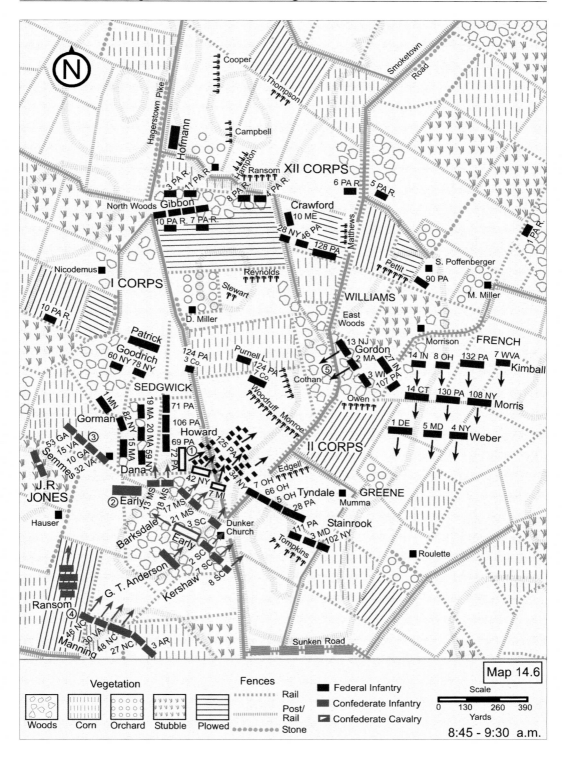

Map 14.6

Vegetation

Woods | Corn | Orchard | Stubble | Plowed

Fences

Rail
Post/Rail
Stone

Federal Infantry
Confederate Infantry
Confederate Cavalry

Scale

0   130   260   390
Yards

8:45 - 9:30 a.m.

Map 14.7: Sedgwick Retreats (8:45 - 9:30 a.m.)

The collapse of the 72nd Pennsylvania caught the attention of the rest of Howard's Philadelphia Brigade on the third line. Howard withdrew the 106th Pennsylvania (the third regiment from the left) northward to a fence on the west side of the Hagerstown Pike, where it opened an effective fire against Barksdale's men. The 69th Pennsylvania, which had been between the 72nd and 106th Pennsylvania, reformed on the left of the latter regiment just across the Hagerstown Pike (No. 1). Howard finally had an effective line to help stop the Rebel onslaught. The brigade's fourth regiment, the 71st Pennsylvania, waited until its front cleared before laying down a solid fire against the advancing Confederates. A short time later these Pennsylvanians headed up the pike toward the North Woods, as did the 69th and 106th Pennsylvania a short time later.[31]

Dana's brigade, forming Sedgwick's second line, was also under attack. Many of the men in the 59th New York and the 20th Massachusetts on the left of the line heard the cry, "The enemy is behind us!" The 20th Massachusetts attempted to turn and face the Confederates, but it was "so crowded in the centre of the division that only a few could fire without killing men on our own side," remembered one of its members. Sumner appeared about this time and ordered the survivors of both regiments to head northward (No. 2). They "retired by the right flank with arms at a shoulder and at the ordinary step." Sumner accompanied the retreat and tried to calm the men along the way. Dana's remaining regiment on the right of the line, the 19th Massachusetts, was the farthest away from the oncoming danger. Its commander calmly ordered his men to change front to the right and marched them north. The men halted several times to fire into the approaching enemy before deploying behind a stone wall.[32]

Gorman's three regiments on the front line, meanwhile, continued holding their positions and exchanging fire with Semmes. When these Federals began receiving fire from their left and rear, they discovered the other two brigades had fled and masses of Rebels were approaching.

"The attack of the enemy on the flank was so sudden and in such an overwhelming force that I had no time to lose, for my command could have been completely enveloped and probably captured," reported Gorman. He ordered a retreat but only the 1st Minnesota under Col. Alfred Sully complied, withdrawing in good order and in line of battle. The men halted periodically to fire into their pursuers before taking position next to the 19th Massachusetts behind a stone wall (No. 3). The 82nd New York to its left was probably the last to fall back when its commander realized the division's other units were already gone or in the process of retiring. It followed the 1st Minnesota north, albeit in a less-ordered fashion.[33]

The 15th Massachusetts on the left of Gorman's front line was in the most danger as it was hit squarely in the front, flank, and rear. Its survivors headed in a northeast direction toward the Miller homestead (No. 4). Gorman met and rallied the regiment near the North Woods. According to the 15th's commander, Lt. Col. John Kimball, his unit "retired slowly and in good order, bringing off our colors and a battle-flag captured from the enemy." Not all of Kimball's men agreed. According to one private, "all hands ran for dear life. I pulled to the left to get out of range of the guns. . . . The rebs chased us like the Devil for about a half or 3.4 of a mile when our batteries opened on them with grape and they give up the chase."[34]

While Semmes' and Barksdale's men chased pieces of Sedgwick's fractured division, Kershaw's 3rd South Carolina headed east. Once across the Hagerstown Pike heavy artillery fire from the massed Federal batteries, supported by the survivors of several defeated Federal regiments, ripped through the Palmetto ranks. This killing fire forced the South Carolinians to pull back (No. 5). Meanwhile, the rest of Kershaw's brigade, which had helped defeat the 125th Pennsylvania and 34th New York, headed northeast past the church and out of the West Woods (No. 6).[35]

Sedgwick's deep thrust into the West Woods and the bloody repulse of his division marked the high point of the fighting on this part of the field.

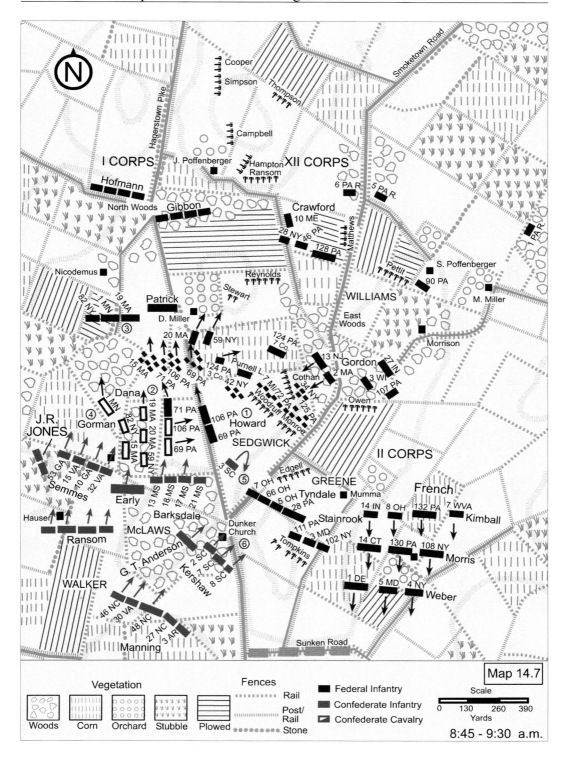

Map 14.7

8:45 - 9:30 a.m.

Vegetation

Woods   Corn   Orchard   Stubble   Plowed

Fences

∙∙∙∙∙∙∙ Rail
━━━ Post/Rail
●●●●●● Stone

■ Federal Infantry
▬ Confederate Infantry
◤ Confederate Cavalry

Scale
0   130   260   390
Yards

Map Set 15. Antietam: Final Actions on the Northern Front
(9:30 - 10:30 a.m.)

Map 15.1: Confederates Storm out of the West Woods (9:30 - 10:00 a.m.)

Joe Kershaw regrouped the three regiments with him and moved east (No. 1). According to Kershaw, he advanced to within "30 yards of one of the batteries [Tompkins'], driving the men from the guns, and only gave way when enfiladed by a new battery [probably Edgell's] . . . about this time the enemy was heavily re-enforced, and our line fell back to the wood."

What Kershaw did not know then was that he ran into Col. Henry Stainrook's Union brigade, whose concentrated fire helped throw the South Carolinians back into the West Woods with heavy losses. Stainrook's division leader, Brig. Gen. George Greene, recalled that the South Carolinians "only" advanced to within seventy yards of his command, and he described Kershaw's losses as "immense." On Kershaw's right, meanwhile, his small 8th South Carolina crested a ridge and unexpectedly stumbled upon thousands of fresh troops comprising Maj. Gen. William H. French division marching south toward the Sunken Road. The Palmetto soldiers fired into the large but green 1st Delaware on the right side of Brig. Gen. Max Weber's brigade before wisely withdrawing.[1]

Farther north, the 2nd Massachusetts and 13th New Jersey of Brig. Gen. George H. Gordon's brigade continued tramping toward the Hagerstown Pike. These Union men expected to find elements of Maj. Gen. John Sedgwick's division, but no organized friendly troops were anywhere in their front. Waiting for Gordon in the northern edge of the West Woods was Brig. Gen. Robert Ransom's newly arrived Southern brigade, together with Jubal Early's repositioned brigade on his left. Their fire ripped through the ranks of the green 13th New Jersey (No. 2) and forced the Federals to seek shelter behind low rock ledges. When they realizing the futility of fighting any longer, officers ordered the Jerseymen to retreat and rejoin the rest of the brigade back in the East Woods. The 2nd Massachusetts, which advanced behind and to

the left of the 13th New Jersey, was also hit by small arms fire and followed the New Jersey men to the rear. During the retreat the 3rd Wisconsin and 27th Indiana advanced to support them (No. 3). Gordon redeployed all four regiments in the East Woods.[2]

Flushed with an easy victory, Ransom's men rushed after the Yankees. The Tar Heels did not get far before Federal guns "poured grape shell and canister at us till we were ordered to another part of the same woods," recalled William Burgwyn of the 35th North Carolina (No. 4). Ransom had but three regiments with him because his 24th North Carolina, which had been on Ranson's left, accidently attached itself to the left side of Brig. Gen. William Barksdale's brigade. From this new position the 24th helped drive the survivors of Sedgwick's division northward before repelling part of Brig. Gen. Marsena Patrick's brigade (No. 5).[3]

About 10:00 a.m., or about fifteen minutes after its initial confrontation with Kershaw's South Carolinians, Stainrook's and Col. Hector Tyndale's brigades spotted yet another mass of Confederates advancing from the West Woods. This time it was the 46th and 48th North Carolina and 30th Virginia regiments from Col. Van Manning's brigade. Manning's other two regiments, the 3rd Arkansas and 27th North Carolina, were moving southeast to plug the gap in the Southern line between the West Woods and the Sunken Road (No. 6).

Just prior to Manning's appearance, Tyndale was ordered to fall back behind a rise. Manning, explained division commander Brig. Gen. John Walker, was "not content to hold the woods" and "dashed forward in gallant style . . . driving the enemy before him like sheep." The advance ended when Manning (who fell wounded during the movement) encountered "heavy masses of the enemy's infantry" behind a strong fence. "We poured into their advancing columns volley after volley," recalled the commander of the 7th Ohio, and "the enemy fell like grass before the mower; so deadly was the fire that the enemy retired in great disorder." A soldier in Manning's 30th Virginia agreed: "the enemy [fired] . . . volley after volley after us and it is a wonder to me that any of us escaped. I have often heard men talking of a shower of bullets, but never saw nor experienced it until yesterday." The two Federal XII Corps brigades drove after Manning's retreating men and recaptured part of the West Woods (No. 7). Manning's brigade lost more than 900 men, or about 43 percent of those carried into battle.[4]

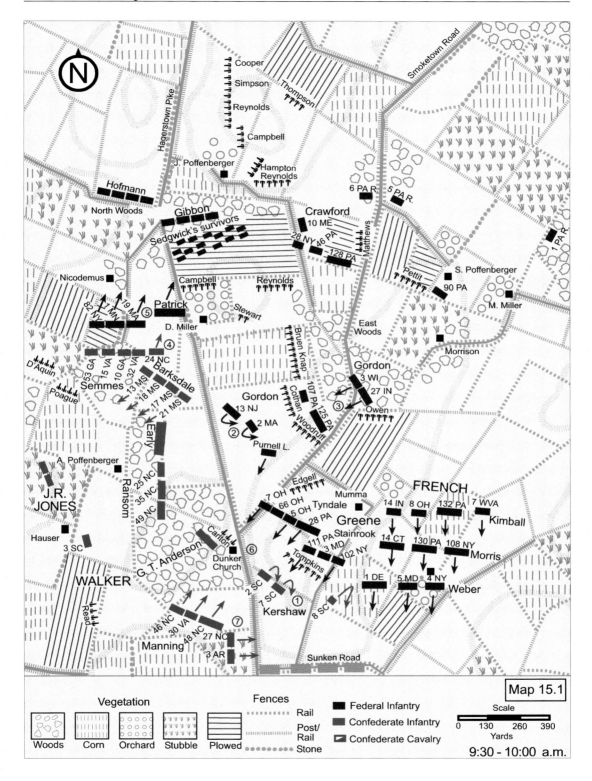

Map 15.1

9:30 - 10:00 a.m.

Map 15.2: The XII Corps Takes the West Woods (10:00 - 10:30 a.m.)

After beating back John Walker's division, Tyndale's and Stainrook's brigades charged into and through the West Woods, capturing with it one of the battlefield landmarks: the Dunker Church. "We charged them in a heavy piece of woods, driving them out of it, capturing a large number of prisoners, and made terrible havoc to their ranks, covering the ground with the slain, many of them officers," reported Maj. Orrin Crane of the 7th Ohio. The Federal line halted almost 200 yards west of the church. The 5th and 7th Ohio did not remain there long because they were nearly out of ammunition. They fell back to the high ground east of the Hagerstown Pike, where they rejoined the 66th Ohio. The 13th New Jersey of Gordon's brigade and Purnell's Legion from Col. William Goodrich's command slipped into the evacuated positions. Portions of four Federal brigades were now holding the West Woods.[5]

George Greene, the Federal division commander for most of the regiments deployed in the West Woods, considered the sector to be of critical importance. He had already requested and received reinforcements in the form of the 13th New Jersey and Purnell's Legion. The commander of the former regiment, Col. Ezra Carman, openly worried about the Federal line's vulnerable right (northern) flank and requested additional help. Greene, who was on the opposite side of the line, told the worried Carman "not to be uneasy about his flank. The whole of Sedgwick's Division was in the woods on [your] right." Greene had no idea that Sedgwick's command had been ripped apart and driven away and that only Rebels occupied the woods to the north and west of his position. Convinced that Greene was wrong, Carman sent another message to him. Greene responded by riding to the right side of his line. Although no friendly troops could be found in the deep woods beyond his right, Greene insisted that only Federal troops occupied the timber and that under no circumstances should anyone fire into the woods. Greene rode back to his left, the flank he still firmly believed was the most vulnerable. Along the way he encountered a corps-level staff officer who confirmed that Sedgwick had indeed been driven away and that the woods beyond his right were full of Rebels. The shocked Greene requested help, but none was available. A pair of guns from Capt. Joseph Knap's Pennsylvania battery was sent forward from the East Woods to reinforce Greene, despite the vigorous protest of its commander, Lt. James McGill.[6]

Confederates watched McGill's two guns arrive. One deployed near the Dunker Church and the other remained on the Hagerstown Pike. Col. John Cooke launched the 27th North Carolina and 3rd Arkansas (Manning's brigade) against the guns. About the same time, the 49th North Carolina of Ransom's brigade attacked the artillery from the northwest. What the Tar Heels found instead was the right side of Greene's line of infantry, so they moved into a nearby ravine for cover. Purnell's Legion and the 13th New Jersey saw the attacking 49th North Carolina about the same time; both sides leveled their muskets and fired. The North Carolinians had the edge because were on the flank and front of Purnell's Legion and better protected by the ravine. Before long these Federals were heading for the rear, followed by the men from New Jersey. When the leader of the next regiment in line, the 28th Pennsylvania, heard the Rebel Yell through the timber on his right and spotted the retreating enemy, he ordered a retreat. Stainrook's regiments, facing generally south in the West Woods, joined in the retreat. The Confederates drove through the woods and captured McGill's single deployed gun (the other limbered piece on the pike galloped out of harm's way). This piece under McGill from Knap's battery was the only gun lost by the Federals the entire day.[7]

A shocked Brig. Gen. Alpheus Williams, in command of the XII Corps after Maj. Gen. Mansfield's death, watched the sudden retreat with despair. Greene's men "came scampering to the rear in great confusion," he wrote, and "the Rebels followed with a yell." Dashing out of the West Woods in pursuit, Col. Cooke's 27th North Carolina and the 3rd Arkansas were exposed to massed Union artillery, a fresh VI Corps infantry division under Maj. Gen. William F. Smith, and a host of victorious regiments from Sumner's II Corps that had recently smashed the thin Confederate defensive front along the northern reaches of the Sunken Lane. (The subsequent action is recounted in Map 16.7.)[8]

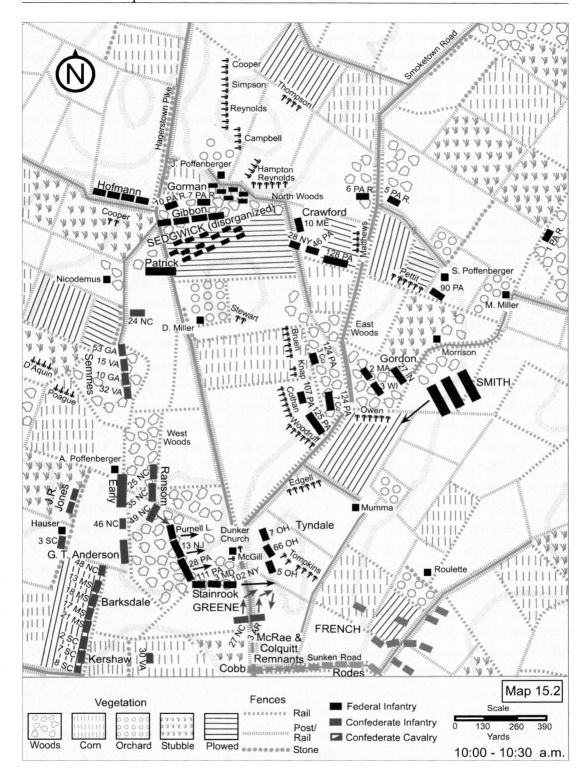

Map 15.2

Scale

| 0 | 130 | 260 | 390 |

Yards

10:00 - 10:30 a.m.

Vegetation

Woods Corn Orchard Stubble Plowed

Fences

Rail

Post/Rail

Stone

Federal Infantry

Confederate Infantry

Confederate Cavalry

Map 15.3: The Battle Transitions to the Sunken Road (10:00 - 10:30 a.m.)

Although neither side knew it, the effort to crush General Lee's left flank was over. The two sides had traded blows for more than five hours. Only heavy reinforcements and extraordinarily hard and bloody fighting had prevented a complete Confederate collapse in that sector. The stalemate was a bitter pill for George McClellan, who had thrown two corps and a division from a third into the effort (Hooker's I Corps, Mansfield's XII Corps, and Sedgwick's division, Sumner's II Corps), all told about 22,750 men. Lee countered with about 18,130. The result was a combined loss of nearly 14,000 from all causes (Federals: 6,550; Confederates: 7,307).[9]

By the time the fighting on the northern part of the field ended, the Confederates had lost at least one-half to three-quarters of a mile of ground. The organizations still in the sector had been hammered to the point that they were now barely serviceable. John Hood's division had charged out of the West Woods with some 2,300 men to save two of Thomas "Stonewall" Jackson's divisions and lost 1,025 (or roughly 45 percent). Paul Semmes' brigade, which had faced the front of John Sedgwick's division and then aggressively pursued its fleeing soldiers, left nearly half of its men (about 700) on the field, including three of its four regimental leaders. Semmes' 10th Georgia lost about 57 percent of its men and its flag was pierced by forty-six bullets and its staff twice broken. As stunning as these figures are, they do not surpass William Wofford's brigade (Hood's division), which lost 64 percent of its men (his 1st Texas alone suffering nearly 90 percent casualties).[10]

Federal losses were also heavy, but not as a comparative percentage of those engaged. While Lee lost about 40 percent of his men in the fighting north of the Sunken Road, McClellan lost about 29 percent. Sedgwick's division of the II Corps sustained the highest losses and left about one in three of its mens on the battlefield. Hooker's I Corps lost about 27 percent and Mansfield's XII Corps about 23 percent. In terms of terrain, by 10:30 a.m. the only real boast the Northerners could make was that they possessed a portion of Miller's cornfield and the East Woods. Both had witnessed heavy fighting that morning and both were now in Federal hands.

The battle for the West Woods was waning when two of Sumner's divisions angled south toward the Confederate center. Maj. Gen. D. H. Hill's Confederate division, which had gamely defended Turner's and Fox's gaps just three days before, defended his sector. Three of Hill's brigades had already been sent north to prop up the army's endangered left flank and were in no shape for further action. This left Hill with only two small brigades under Brig. Gens. Robert Rodes (850) and G. B. Anderson (1,174). Rodes and Anderson occupied a long farm road soon to be known as the "Bloody Lane." A portion of the lane was several feet lower than the surrounding fields because of heavy usage and erosion, which offered Hill's men a good defensive position. Rodes rallied some of the survivors from Alfred Colquitt's and Duncan McRae's brigades and formed them on his left, where they were joined by the remnants of Howell Cobb's brigade (357 men), which had been torn to pieces at Crampton's Gap on September 14. Cobb's command belonged to Maj. Gen. Lafayette McLaws' division, but had strayed too far to the right and did not participate in the West Woods fighting. A number of batteries helped beef up Hill's sector. No more than 2,700 infantry held Hill's weak front, which was about to face two federal divisions.[11]

Maj. Gen. William French's II Corps division marched to the field behind Sedgwick's division before halting in the East Woods about 9:15 a.m. French had orders to move to Sedgwick's left and advance into the West Woods with a two-division front. Sedgwick, however, had not waited for French and advanced into the timber on his own. When French finally moved, Greene's division (XII Corps) was in his front. French inclined southward, bypassing the burning Mumma farm buildings while marching toward the Roulette farm, where he drove away a Rebel skirmish line. It was there that the 1st Delaware on the right side of French's division encountered the 8th South Carolina (See Map 15-1). Brig. Gen. Max Weber's brigade comprised the division's front line, followed by the brigades of Col. Dwight Morris and Brig. Gen. Nathan Kimball. These 5,700 men would be soon joined by Maj. Gen. Israel Richardson's 4,300-man division (II Corps).[12]

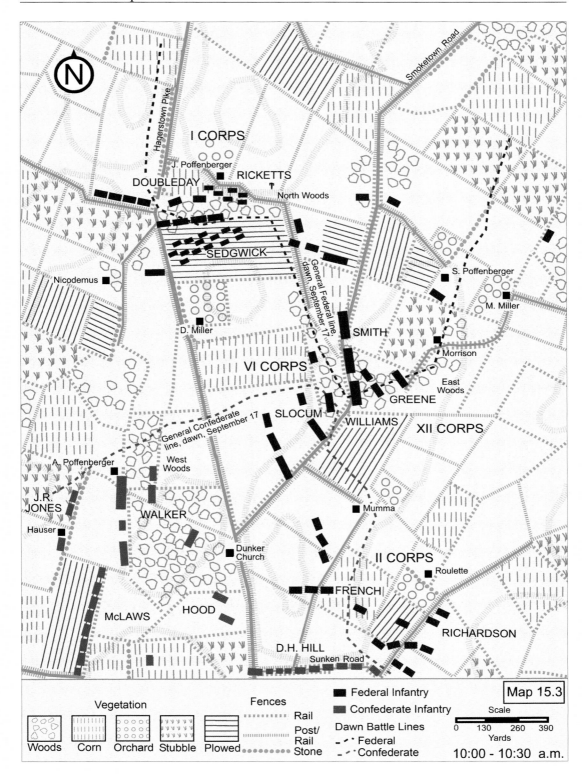

Map 15.3

10:00 - 10:30 a.m.

Map Set 16. Antietam: The Sunken Road (9:00 a.m. - 1:00 p.m.)

Map 16.1: French's Division Moves South (9:00 - 9:30 a.m.)

Brig. Gen. Robert Rodes' Rebel infantry watched the approach of William H. French's division with grim fascination. The Alabamians were still exhausted after their tough fight near Turner's Gap on September 14, and the hard marching to reach Sharpsburg after a steady diet of roasted corn only served to further weaken them. The veterans improved their position earlier in the day by piling fence rails along the lane road. The Federals, explained Rodes, "deployed in our front in three beautiful lines, all vastly outstretching ours, and commenced to advance steadily." The capable brigadier had rallied some troops on his left and could see G. B. Anderson's brigade deployed on his right. An officer serving with Anderson agreed with Rodes' description when he observed that the enemy advance was "beautiful in the extreme, and great regularity marked their column."[1]

Under orders to fix bayonets, German-born Brig. Gen. Max Weber pushed his three Federal regiments forward to a low ridge. From the crest of this ridge, which would figure prominently in the attack against Lee's center, his men could see the Rebel-held Sunken Road only fifty to eighty yards to their front. Weber ordered his men to advance down the ridge toward the position. As they did so, the entire Confederate line stood in unison and fired a volley into them. Col. John W. Andrews' 1st Delaware on Weber's right was probably aligned against Rodes' right and center, with the 5th Maryland on the left of the Delaware troops fronting Rodes' 6th Alabama and the 2nd North Carolina of Anderson's brigade. The 4th New York on the opposite side of the Roulette farm lane moved against Anderson's center.

The grand Confederate volley, recalled an officer in the 1st Delaware, was "so destructive that even veteran troops would have been repulsed." Weber's line melted away to the rear with a loss of about twenty-five percent. The 5th Maryland and 4th New York on the left and center of the brigade immediately turned and scurried back up the ridge to the safety of its reverse slope. The 1st Delaware had a longer distance to travel, rallied within fifty yards of the crest, and returned fire. Because it had approached the Sunken Road at an oblique angle, the right side of the green regiment suffered more than the left. To their credit, Weber's regiments quickly reformed their ranks and attacked again, only to suffer the same fate "with the addendum of wild confusion," added a Southern officer.[2]

Reinforcements arrived to help Weber's beleaguered command when Col. Dwight Morris' brigade reached the scene of the attack. When Southern bullets overshooting Weber's regiments leveled many of these newcomers, orders to lie down ran up and down the line. Pvt. Edward Spangler of the 130th Pennsylvania snuggled into the plowed field and lived to remember how "the bullets flew thicker than bees, and the shells exploded with a deafening roar."[3]

Weber's men were in already in bad shape, but the arrival of the 14th Connecticut of Morris' brigade only made matters worse. The 14th had never been under fire and the zipping rounds unsettled its members, who stopped to unleash a volley against the enemy. Unfortunately, the 1st Delaware was in their front when they pulled their triggers. "The supporting troops behind us, instead of charging through our line upon the enemy," reported a stunned Col. Andrews of the 1st Delaware, "halted in the cornfield and fired on us from the rear, thereby forcing the command to retire a few yards to avoid the fire from our supports." Once the move to the rear began, however, a number of the men continued their "skedaddle" all the way to the Roulette farm. This movement threw the three right companies of the 14th Connecticut into confusion.[4]

Morris' three regiments advanced to the top of the ridge, where they traded places with the remnant of Weber's brigade. Weber was rallying the 5th Maryland when a bullet struck his upper right arm and tore away three inches of bone, ending his military career. When the 108th New York on Morris' left reached the crest of the ridge, its men lurched forward to drive Anderson's Rebels from their defenses. The rash and unsupported attack met the same fate as Weber's 4th New York. The survivors fell back over the ridge crest and lay down on its opposite side as hundreds of lead rounds cut through the air just above their heads.[5]

The first effort to break Gen. Lee's center had failed.

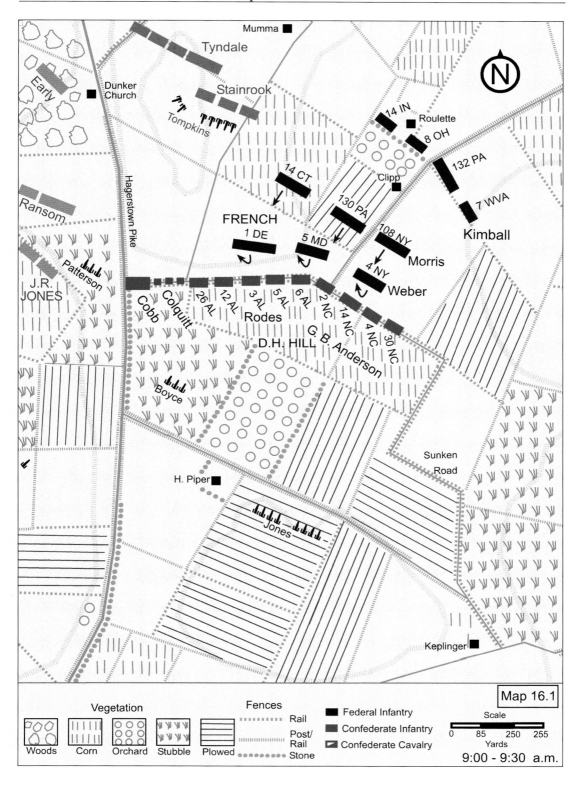

Map 16.1

9:00 - 9:30 a.m.

Map 16.2: The Confederates Counterattack (9:30 - 10:00 a.m.)

Once their initial attacks were repulsed, Maj. Gen. French's men shifted to a defensive mode. Maj. Gen. James Longstreet took advantage of the brief lull and ordered a counterattack. G. B. Anderson's Tar Heels had already launched a few small piecemeal unsuccessful counter-thrusts. Rodes, however ordered his entire line forward. Problems on both ends soon developed.

On the far left, Howell Cobb's small brigade charged ahead but quickly returned to the line when the Alabamians farther to the right aborted the attack. Alfred Colquitt's small command next to Cobb barely moved, which exposed the 26th Alabama's left flank to a deadly crossfire. On Rodes' right, the 6th Alabama never received its orders to advance and remained in the Sunken Road when the other regiments moved out. This, in turn, exposed the 5th Alabama's right flank to a raking small arms fire. By the time the 6th Alabama joined in the attack was being repulsed. Despite the disjointed nature of the assault, the 6th Alabama nearly captured the flag of the 5th Maryland before being forced to retire. Rodes, meanwhile, rode along his line first to get the attack moving and then a short time later to rally his troops in the low road so they would not retreat farther.[6]

During Rodes' offensive effort Gen. French received orders from Maj. Gen. Edwin Sumner to drive his attack ahead to take pressure off Maj. Gen. John Sedgwick's advance into the West Woods. French complied by ordering Brig. Gen. Nathan Kimball's brigade up from its reserve position and double-quicking it forward to provide support. "Charge to the front!" French ordered.[7]

When the green soldiers in Kimball's 132nd Pennsylvania reached the low ridge, however, they grew angry because the 4th New York (Weber) and 108th New York (Morris) were lying on the ground. The Pennsylvanians drove over the crest with bayonets fixed only to be "met by a terrific volley from the rebels in the sunken road down the other side, not more than one hundred yards away, and also from another rebel line in a corn-field just beyond," recorded one observer. Like the two regiments they passed

over, the 132nd Pennsylvania made its way back to the safety of the opposite side of the ridge.[8]

Unable to drive the Confederates from their defenses along the Sunken Road, the Yankees employed another tactic. As one Pennsylvanian described the technique, he and his comrades "were ordered to lie down just under the top of the hill [ridge] and crawl forward and fire over, each man crawling back, reloading his piece in this prone position and again crawling forward and firing."[9] This steady heavy fire took its toll on the defending Alabamians and North Carolinians, who piled additional fence rails and even the bodies of the dead to act as a barricade to absorb some of the deadly bullets. When ammunition ran low, men from both sides scrounged cartridges boxes of the dead and the wounded scattered around them.[10]

The Sunken Road defenders were already outnumbered more than two to one, but the situation was about to get much worse: Sumner's third and last division under Maj. Gen. Israel Richardson was up and deploying for action.

Richardson received his orders just after 9:00 a.m. that morning to leave his position south of the Pry house, cross Antietam Creek, and join the rest of Sumner's II Corps. Brig. Gen. Thomas Meagher's Irish Brigade led the column, followed by brigades under Col. John Brooke and Brig. Gen. John Caldwell. Many of these 4,300 veterans had been in the ranks since First Bull Run, including Israel Richardson, who had also seen extensive service during the Mexican War. The brigadier sat on his horse while his men crossed Antietam Creek so he could tell each regimental commander, "No straggling today, Colonel! Keep your men well up and in hand."[11]

Reinforcements also reached the embattled Sunken Road defenders. Maj. Gen. Richard H. Anderson received orders about 10:00 a.m. to move his division to support the center of Gen. Lee's position. Anderson passed to the left of Sharpsburg, picked up the Hagerstown Pike, and marched quickly north before halting near the Piper farm house. His command numbered between 3,500 and 4,000 bayonets, but all of them were worn out after their all-night march from Harpers Ferry to reach the battlefield about 7:00 a.m. Lee also ordered up at least thirty-three artillery pieces to help bolster the center of his line.[12]

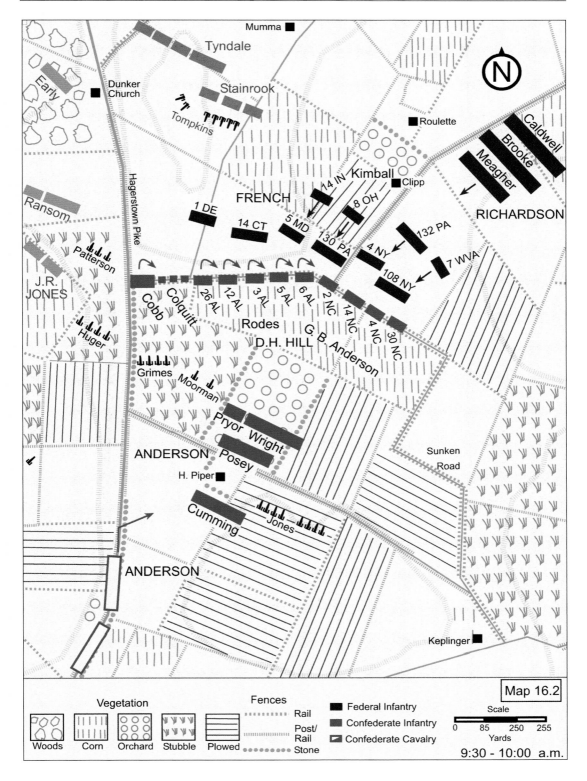

Map 16.2

Vegetation

Woods | Corn | Orchard | Stubble | Plowed

Fences
.... Rail
.... Post/ Rail
●●●●●●● Stone

■ Federal Infantry
▰ Confederate Infantry
▰ Confederate Cavalry

Scale
0   85   250   255
Yards

9:30 - 10:00 a.m.

Map 16.3: Confederate Reinforcements Approach (10:00 - 10:30 a.m.)

Prior to ordering his men forward to reinforce the rest of French's division, Brig. Gen. Kimball called them to attention as he rode along the line. "Boys," he exclaimed, "we are going in now to lick the rebels, and we will stay with them all day if necessary." His infantry stripped off their knapsacks, fixed bayonets, and headed toward the Sunken Road at the double-quick.

Kimball formed his regiments on both sides of the Roulette farm lane with the 132nd Pennsylvania and the 7th West Virginia to its left and the 8th Ohio and 14th Indiana on its right. When the latter pair of regiments encountered the 5th Maryland and 130th Pennsylvania someone yelled, "Get to the rear, you fellows!"

All was fine until Kimball's regiments topped the crest and enemy artillery fire on their right and small arms fire from Rodes' and Anderson's men in their front decimated the beautifully aligned ranks. "I found the enemy in great force," reported Kimball, who went on to describe the Confederate fire as "murderous." Some of his men crawled back to the top of the ridge, leveled their weapons, and opened fire. From their prone positions on the right side of the farm lane the 8th Ohio and 14th Indiana maintained a deadly enfilade fire against the 6th Alabama and 2nd North Carolina.[13]

The 5th Maryland also moved up and fought for a time on the right side of the farm lane. Exhausted after some two hours of fighting, the Marylanders withdrew to the Clipp homestead, where they encountered parts of the 4th New York, 108th New York, and 130th Pennsylvania of Weber's and Morris' brigades. Their comrades were still on the ridge firing toward the Sunken Road. The 1st Delaware and 14th Connecticut were in the cornfield just to their right. It was about this time on the other side of the firing line that Confederate Brig. Gen. George B. Anderson was struck in the ankle joint by a minie ball and left the field.[14]

The arrival of Richard Anderson's Confederate division could have tipped the scales in the fighting at the Sunken Road if he had attacked either Federal flank, both of which were exposed and vulnerable. Unfortunately for the Confederates, when a bullet struck Anderson in the thigh and he fell from his horse, command of his division fell to Brig. Gen. Roger Pryor, a former politician with no combat ability whatsoever. Pryor was unable to coordinate his new command, and shoved the various brigades into the fight piecemeal.

Brig. Gen. Ambrose Wright's brigade near the Piper house was the first command to advance. When a deadly artillery crossfire tore into the Georgians, they ripped down a strong oak fence surrounding a nearby orchard for protection. Ordered to their feet, Wright guided his regiments through the orchard and into the cornfield behind the Sunken Road, where a storm of lead from Yankee rifled muskets sliced through their ranks. A soldier in the 8th Ohio watched Wright's infantry approach. The Georgians, he recalled, formed "a fresh line . . . in our front . . . moved down splendidly with its colors advanced, and [was] commanded by an officer mounted on a white charger."[15]

When Wright's horse was killed beneath him, he regained his feet and rallied his men to the right of the 30th North Carolina of G. B. Anderson's brigade. Two bullets wounded Wright and his second in command also fell. Confusion spread through the ranks as officers screamed for their men to hold firm and that reinforcements were on their way. No reinforcements arrived.

From his position on the ground Wright could see the 7th West Virginia's exposed left flank. He ordered the brigade's new commander, Col. William Gibson of the 48th Georgia, to attack it. The regiments comprising the left and center of the brigade (the 24th, 44th, and 48th Georgia) made little if any attempt to advance into the hail of bullets pouring from the barrels of the 7th West Virginia, but the 3rd Georgia on Wright's right moved out as ordered. The West Virginians calmly changed their front by refusing their left flank and advancing their right. The result was a short sharp fight that drove the Georgians back to the Sunken Road.[16]

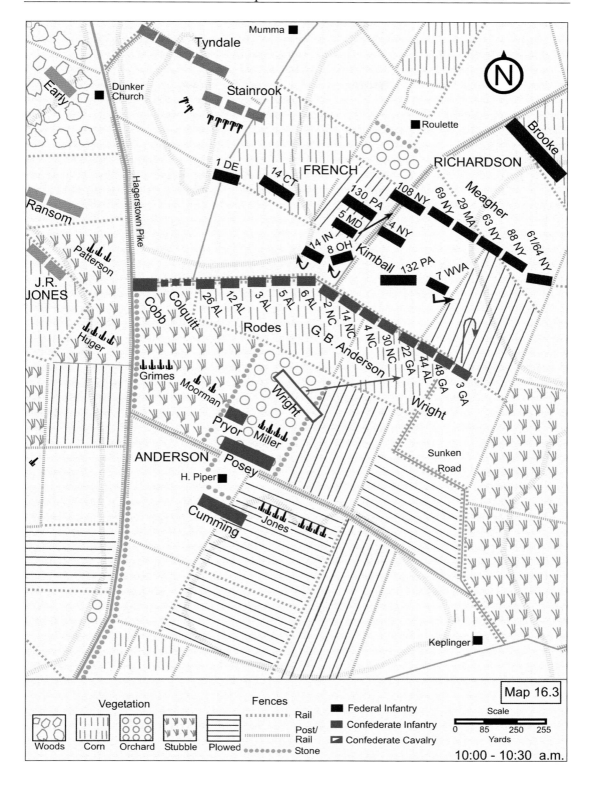

Map 16.3

10:00 - 10:30 a.m.

Vegetation

Woods   Corn   Orchard   Stubble   Plowed

Fences

Rail

Post/ Rail

Stone

Federal Infantry
Confederate Infantry
Confederate Cavalry

Scale

0   85   250   255
Yards

Map 16.4: The Attack of the Irish Brigade (10:00 - 10:30 a.m.)

By this time two Federal brigades from Isaac Richardson's division under Meagher and Caldwell had deployed left of the Roulette farm lane in preparation for assaulting the Sunken Road. Richardson kept Brooke's brigade in reserve. Thomas Meagher's Irish Brigade was on the right. Caldwell's brigade, deployed on Meagher's left, outflanked the right side of the Confederate line. A determined push combined with some tactical finesse could unravel the entire Sunken Road position and imperil Lee's entire center. Instead of tactical finesse, however, Meagher decided to use brute force. His orders were to march ahead, fire on the defenders, and charge the Sunken Road with bayonets fixed. The simple plan quickly went awry.[17]

When the Irish Brigade tramped over the ridge crest, Anderson's and Wright's men opened a punishing fire into its ranks. One of Meagher's veterans recalled it as "frightfully destructive." Fences further disrupted the uniform blue lines of battle. The Irish Brigade was about halfway into the pasture, or about 100 yards from the enemy line, when Meagher ordered his men to open fire. A short time later Meagher ordered his regiments to charge (No. 1).[18]

Riding on the right side of his long line of battle, Meagher ordered the 69th New York forward while aides spread the word to the rest of the brigade. The 69th New York's attack ground to a halt because of the debilitating loss of key line officers and the failure of the 29th Massachusetts on its left to advance. Hit on its left flank and in front, the New Yorkers retreated with heavy loss.

A similar situation unfolded on the opposite side of the brigade. The 88th New York on the far left advanced "20 or 30 paces" when its commander, Lt. Col. Patrick Kelly, looked to his right and saw that Col. John Burke's 63rd New York was not advancing with him. Kelly halted his line and rode to the New Yorkers, but no one could find Burke. The regiment's lieutenant colonel was wounded before he could assume

command, as was its major. The chaos on the left half of the Irish Brigade doomed its attack.

Meagher tried to paint his failed effort in the best light possible. "Despite a fire of musketry, which literally cut lanes through our approaching line, the brigade advanced . . . within 30 paces of the enemy," he exaggerated. "The charge of bayonets I had ordered on the left was arrested, and thus the brigade, instead of advancing and dispersing the [enemy] column with the bayonet, stood and delivered its fire."[19]

Unable to advance but unwilling to fall back, the men of the Irish Brigade held their positions as best they could as their ranks thinned and their ammunition ran short. Meagher was riding along his line shouting encouragement to his men when his horse was hit and the falling animal pinned him to the ground. The stunned general was taken to the rear and no one seems to have assumed command.[20]

Brig. Gen. Caldwell's brigade on Meagher's left fared little better (No. 2). Because of the rolling terrain most of his men could not see either the Sunken Lane or Meagher's progress. "Finding no enemy in our immediate front," explained Caldwell, "I commenced to wheel the brigade cautiously to the right." Caldwell's description was apt, for his move was slow to develop in the face of a heavy small arms fire. When one of Richardson's aides arrived and ordered him "to relieve the line of General Meagher," Caldwell moved his brigade "by right flank in the rear of General Meagher's line, and passed his line to the front in the most perfect order, under a severe fire of musketry. The brigade advanced steadily over the crest of a hill behind which the enemy were posted, receiving and returning a heavy fire" (No. 3).[21]

The Confederates were also being reinforced. Ambrose Wright's brigade was deploying on the right side of the Sunken Road line when Rodes spotted several Confederate regiments belonging to Brig. Gen. Roger Pryor's brigade in the orchard behind him. Rodes left the lane and guided his mount to Pryor's position in an effort to convince him to order his men forward to reinforce the Sunken Road line. Pryor agreed and his men advanced. Scores of them fell killed and wounded during the approach to the front (No. 4).[22]

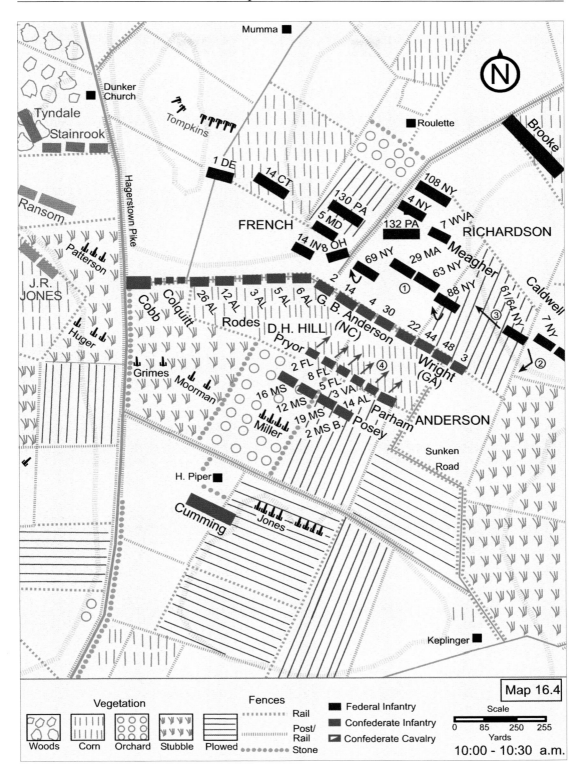

Mumma

Dunker
Church

Tyndale

Stainrook

Tompkins

Roulette

Brooke

Ransom

Hagerstown Pike

1 DE

14 CT

108 NY

4 NY

130 PA

132 PA

7 WVA

RICHARDSON

5 MD

FRENCH

14 IN 8 OH

69 NY

29 MA

Meagher

63 NY

Patterson

J.R.
JONES

Cobb

Colquitt

26 AL

12 AL

3 AL

5 AL

6 AL

2

14

4

30

88 NY

61/64 NY

Caldwell

7 NY

Huger

Rodes

G. B. Anderson
(NC)

①

22

44

48

3

③

D.H. HILL

Pryor

Grimes

Moorman

2 FL

8 FL

5 FL

3 VA

④

Wright
(GA)

②

16 MS

12 MS

14 AL

Parham

Miller

19 MS

2 MS B.

Posey

ANDERSON

Sunken
Road

H. Piper

Cumming

Jones

Keplinger

Vegetation

Woods Corn Orchard Stubble Plowed

Fences

.... Rail

.... Post/
         Rail

●●●●●● Stone

■ Federal Infantry

■ Confederate Infantry

◪ Confederate Cavalry

Map 16.4

Scale

0   85   250 255

Yards

10:00 - 10:30 a.m.

Map 16.5: The Confederates are Driven from the Sunken Road (10:30 - 11:00 a.m.)

By now, the Sunken Road line to the right of Rodes' brigade was in command chaos, jammed with men from six Confederate brigades (No. 1).

In addition to George B. Anderson's and Ambrose Wright's brigades in the front, Pryor's brigade (now under Col. John C. Hately) formed a second line, along with Brig. Gen. William Mahone's brigade (under Col. William Parham). Brig. Gen. Winfield Featherston's brigade (under Col. Carnot Posey) and Brig. Gen. Cadmus Wilcox's brigade (under Col. Alfred Cumming) also poured into the area. Each of these new arriving brigades either entered the Sunken Road or deployed along its southern lip. A few regiments from Posey's command charged beyond the Sunken Road, only to be bloodily thrown back for their impulsivity.[23]

Even though they had been reinforced, holding the line against heavy numbers for more than an hour had pushed the exhausted Rebels to their breaking point. Many units were mixed up and many officers had been shot down. The line began breaking on the right with Caldwell's renewed advance, together with a portion of the Irish Brigade (No. 2). Wright's brigade and some others from Richard Anderson's division (now under Pryor) were the first to give way.

Surprised that he had not received orders, Col. Joseph Barnes left his stationary 29th Massachusetts only to be "dismayed" to learn that the 69th New York on his right and the 63rd New York on the left had lost about half their men and were barely holding their ground. Barnes returned to his regiment and ordered a charge. Caldwell's regiments also pressed ahead. "We broke the line of the enemy along our entire front, except on the extreme right," reported Caldwell. "Here [Rodes' and G. B. Anderson's positions on the Confederate left] there was a deep road, forming a natural rifle-pit, in which the enemy had posted himself, and from which he fired on our advancing line."

Col. Francis Barlow, in command of the combined 61st and 64th New York regiments of Caldwell's brigade, "by a skillful change of front partially enveloped the enemy on his [the

enemy's] right," boasted Caldwell, "and after a destructive enfilading fire, compelled them to surrender (No. 3). Barlow's tactical excellence against Wright's exposed right flank netted some 300 men and eight commissioned officers.

Wright's collapse triggered a domino effect that spread left into G. B. Anderson's regiments, which also began peeling away from their positions. Too many exhausted, understrength, and ill-led Southern brigades had been jumbled together with no single hand to command them. The result was now unfolding along Lee's center to the detriment of the Southern army.[24]

Rodes was now back at the front with his brigade. He learned the right side of the Sunken Road line was collapsing when Lt. Col. J. N. Lightfoot of the 6th Alabama, his right-most regiment, informed him that "The right wing of his regiment was being subjected to a terrible enfilading fire, and that he had but few men left in that wing." Much of this "enfilading fire" poured into the Alabamians from Col. Barlow's New Yorkers. As Barlow later reported, "the portion of the enemy's line which was not broken then remained lying in a deep road . . . my regiments advanced and obtained an enfilading fire upon the enemy." As one of his New Yorkers recalled, "we were shooting them like sheep in a pen."[25]

Rodes ordered Lightfoot to refuse his right flank to face the enemy, but "instead of executing the order, he moved briskly to the rear of the regiment and gave the command, 'Sixth Alabama, about face, forward march,'" wrote Rodes. When he saw the 6th pulling out, the 5th Alabama's Maj. Edwin Hobson asked Lightfoot if the order was for the entire brigade. When Lightfoot confirmed it, Hobson's men retreated (No. 4). The brigade, "without visible cause to me," explained Rodes, was "retreating in confusion. . . . I found, though, that, with the exception of a few men from the Twenty-sixth, Twelfth, and Third, and a few under Major Hobson, not more than 40 in all, the brigade had completely disappeared from this portion of the field."

Division leader Maj. Gen. D. H. Hill appeared with a musket in hand to lead men through the Piper orchard against the enemy, but the Rebels were too few to alter the tide of battle. Hill and his small band of foot soldiers turned back.[26]

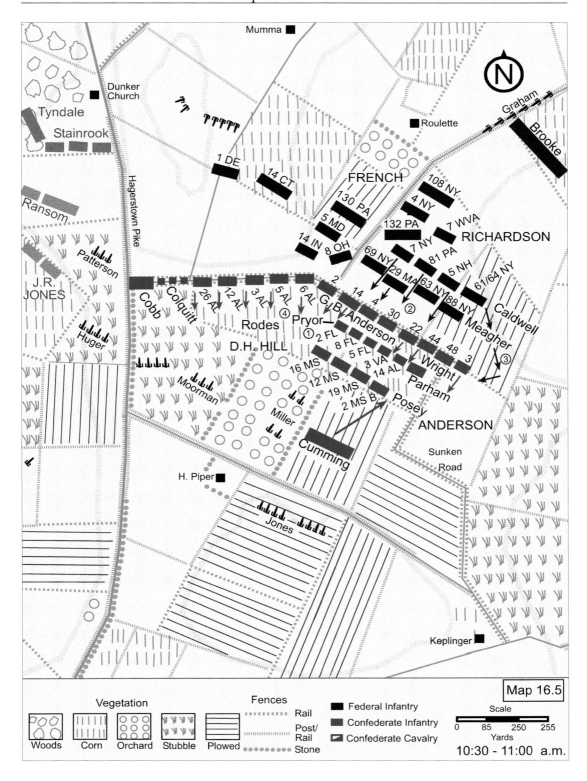

Map 16.5

10:30 - 11:00 a.m.

Map 16.6: Combat at the Piper Farm (11:00 - 11:30 a.m.)

Francis Barlow's New Yorkers and those of the 29th Massachusetts were joined at the Sunken Road by the remaining three regiments of Caldwell's brigade, which had charged toward the low lane "in an unwavering line of battle." In addition to rounding up hundreds of prisoners, the Federals also collected two battle flags. No one would ever forget what they saw there. "The dead and wounded were a horrible sight to behold," recalled one eyewitness. "This sunken road . . . was a good many rods long, and, for most of the way, there were enough dead and badly wounded to touch one another as they lay side by side. As we found in some cases, they were two and three deep." The Sunken Road had indeed earned its sobriquet "Bloody Lane."[27]

After a brief halt to reorganize his men, Caldwell ordered his three regiments forward. Small arms fire from troops rallied in the Piper orchard by D. H. Hill and Rodes peppered the advancing Federals. Capt. Merritt Miller's Confederate battery unlimbered north of the Piper house and hammered Caldwell's men, as did other batteries (Carter's, Hardaway's, and Maurin's) firing from the west side of the Hagerstown Pike. When the 7th New York on the right of Caldwell's line began to waver, Caldwell rode over to steady it while two other regiments, the 81st Pennsylvania and 5th New Hampshire, continued southwest.[28]

Earlier, when the Rebel line at the Sunken Road was about to break, Maj. Gen. Israel Richardson ordered forward his last brigade under Col. John Brooke. The colonel climbed the ridge overlooking the Confederate position and watched large gaps open between Caldwell's attacking regiments. The advancing 7th New York pulled away from Barlow's consolidated 61st and 64th New York regiments (on Caldwell's right near the intersection of the Sunken Road and the Roulette farm lane), while the same thing occurred laterally between the 81st Pennsylvania to its left and between the Pennsylvanians and 5th New Hampshire on the far left (No. 1). Whether Brooke acted alone or was ordered by Richardson is unclear, but the colonel held back the 53rd Pennsylvania on his left flank as a reserve and moved the balance of his brigade ahead to support Caldwell. The 57th and 66th New York moved forward to close the gap between the 81st Pennsylvania and 5th New Hampshire, while the 52nd New York and 2nd Delaware moved southwest to the left of the 7th New York (No. 2).

About this time Col. Barlow moved his combined command southwest to join the rest of Caldwell's brigade. Barlow was chagrined to find that in their haste to close the gaps, many of Col. John Brooke's men became intermingled with Caldwell's regiments. "[O]ur troops were joined together without much order—several regiments in front of others, and none in my neighborhood having very favorable opportunity to use their fire," complained Barlow.[29]

Barlow made a point of mentioning the inability to organize a good firing front because "quite a body of the enemy [was] moving briskly on the right of our line, at no great distance, to attack us on the flank." This often overlooked assault was organized by James Longstreet, who had witnessed the unraveling of the Sunken Road position. "Old Pete" gathered the few troops he could find and moved them briskly against the Federal right flank toward Nathan Kimball's brigade. He also ordered his artillery to zero in on Kimball's flank. These Rebel troops included Howell Cobb's small brigade and two regiments on Cobb's left (No. 3), the 27th North Carolina and 3rd Arkansas under Col. John Cooke from Col. Van Manning's brigade (Walker's division). The two Tar Heel regiments had avoided the earlier bloody repulse that had befallen their sister regiments near the Dunker Church because they had angled to the right toward the Sunken Lane. Cooke's men could not avoid the intense shelling from massed Federal artillery across Antietam Creek, however. According to one officer, the men were "eager to meet the foe upon a more equal footing." Longstreet offered them the chance to do so. With Federal small arms fire zipping through his lines, Cooke yelled to his men, "Come on boys! I am leading the charge!"[30]

Longstreet's small attack moved north from the Sunken Road a few hundred yards before turning to the northeast to strike Kimball. The only question was whether it was too little, too late.

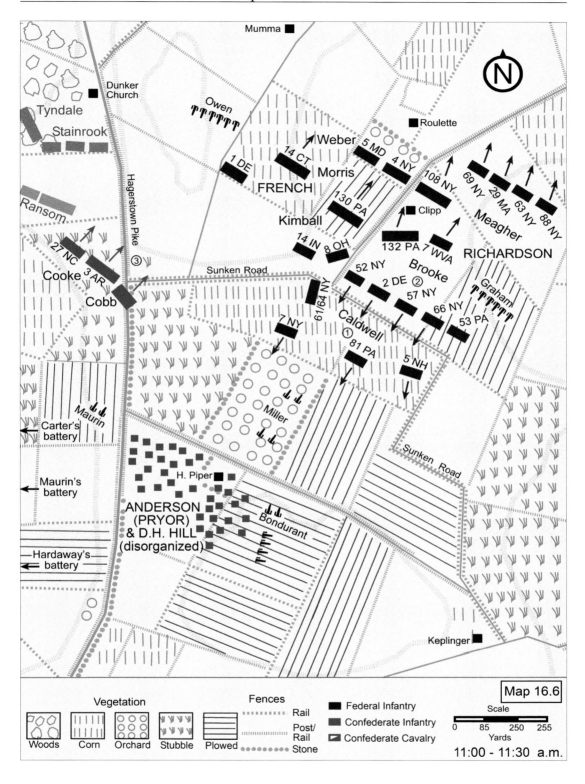

Map 16.6

11:00 - 11:30 a.m.

Vegetation

Woods Corn Orchard Stubble Plowed

Fences

.... Rail

Post/
Rail

Stone

■ Federal Infantry
■ Confederate Infantry
◤ Confederate Cavalry

Scale

0   85   250 255
Yards

Map 16.7: Longstreet's Counterattack (11:30 a.m. - noon)

The Confederates heading for the Union right flank arrayed north of the Sunken Road included Col. John Cooke's demi-brigade of the 27th North Carolina and the 3rd Arkansas on the left, and Howell Cobb's small 250-man "brigade" on the right. Cobb's command had been poorly handled and completely mauled at Crampton's Gap three days before, and his survivors were still demoralized and worn out. Because Cobb was not with his troops and Lt. Col. Christopher Sanders of the 24th Georgia was too ill to lead, Lt. Col. William MacRae of the 15th North Carolina assumed command.[31]

Cooke's pair of regiments headed for the cornfield just north (and behind) Kimball's men. The 14th Connecticut had occupied this field, but after it moved north nothing stood in the path of Cooke's men to the Federal rear. Kimball spotted the approaching threat and ordered the 14th Indiana and 8th Ohio to change front to face Cooke. The two Federal regiments reformed in a plowed field just southeast of the cornfield, where they were joined by some men of the 130th Pennsylvania (No. 1). Low on ammunition, Kimball's men fired what they had left into Cooke's onrushing Confederates and stopped the charge about halfway across the cornfield.[32]

More Federal help was on the way. Col. Brooke turned his 57th and 66th New York and 53rd Pennsylvania toward the enemy and raced them northwest. The 53rd Pennsylvania reached the Roulette barn and opened a deadly flank fire against the 27th North Carolina (No. 2). Maj. Gen. William B. Franklin's VI Corps was arriving on the field about this time. The 7th Maine from Col. William Irwin's brigade advanced to the fence line bordering the northern boundary of the cornfield and opened a deadly fire into the Tar Heels' left and rear. Realizing that he was in an untenable situation, Cooke ordered his two regiments to fall back (No. 3). The exhausted victors of the fight at the Sunken Road were content to see the backs of the Confederates, but Irwin ordered his fresh troops after the fleeing enemy infantry.[33]

Cooke's men were advancing into this cauldron of fire when Cobb's handful of troops under Lt. Col. MacRae moved northeast directly into frontal fire from the 1st Delaware (No. 4). Col. Barlow observed Cobb's advance and rotated his 61st and 64th New York to face its exposed right flank (No. 5). According to MacRae, the small brigade (which was effectively no stronger than a small regiment) held out as long as it could and even repulsed several Federal charges before being forced to retreat because of a lack of ammunition. Barlow offered a different reason. According to him, the enemy "retreated quite precipitately under the fire of the troops on our side." According to MacRae, only fifty men followed him out of the fighting.[34]

The Confederates were not yet finished with their counterattacks to retake the lost position, or at least rebuff a deeper Federal advance. Below the Sunken Road and above the Piper farm, Col. Edward Cross of the 5th New Hampshire spotted a large body of Confederates maneuvering into position on his front and left flank. This enemy gathering also threatened his rear. Cross sent aides to inform brigade commander John Caldwell about this new threat. When the enemy moved within 200 yards "advancing in line of battle and yelling awfully," Cross changed his regimental front to the rear to face the threat. The 81st Pennsylvania also changed front on Cross' right to face the enemy. The Federal volley that followed at short range, boasted Cross, "staggered and hurled them back." This Confederate advance was comprised of remnants from four brigades: the 9th Alabama (Cumming), 12th Alabama (Rodes), 5th Florida (Pryor), and 4th North Carolina (G. B. Anderson). These men absorbed the firing, rallied, and continued moving forward.

The two Federal regiments were now joined by four more (Barlow's 61st and 64th New York, and Brooke's 57th and 66th New York). These reinforcements had just repulsed Cooke and Cobb in the fields near the Roulette farm. Unable to stand in the face of this tremendous firepower, the motley collection of Confederates gave up the fight. A number of flags were captured during this sharp encounter.[35]

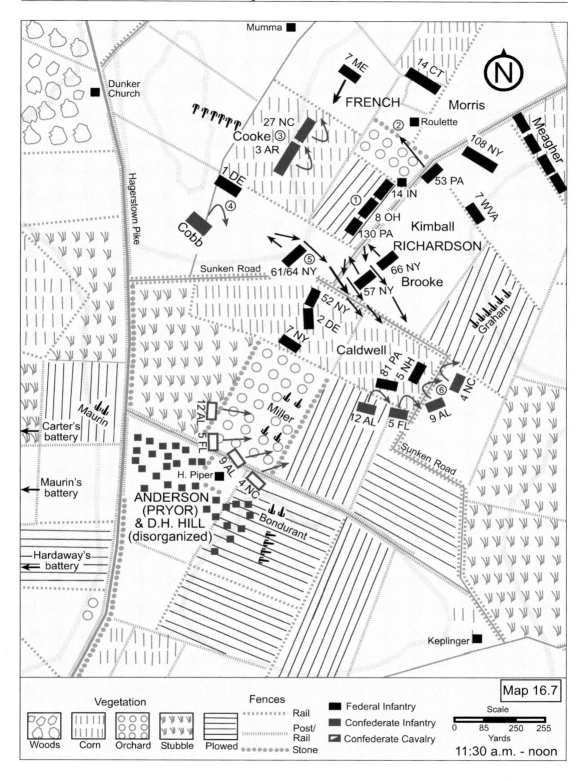

Map 16.7

11:30 a.m. - noon

Vegetation

Woods   Corn   Orchard   Stubble   Plowed

Fences

········· Rail
·········· Post/Rail
●●●●●●● Stone

■ Federal Infantry
▬ Confederate Infantry
◤ Confederate Cavalry

Scale

0   85   250   255
Yards

Map 16.8: Stalemate Along
the Sunken Road (noon - 1:00 p.m.)

Flushed with victory, Caldwell's and Brooke's intermingled units moved south to split the Confederate army in two and expand what was a solid tactical success into a decisive victory. Massed Confederate artillery and small arms fire along their front and right flank, however, prevented a deeper penetration.

Capt. Miller's four-gun Southern battery, firing from the Piper orchard, was particularly effective. During the latter part of the attack on the Sunken Road, Miller's guns unlimbered on a rise in the orchard just behind the cornfield. Intense Federal counter-battery fire forced Miller to withdraw to a more sheltered position, but as the front along the Sunken Road was being crushed, Miller deployed a section of guns closer to the cornfield and soon added a third piece, all of which opened on the advancing Federals. When he saw that there were barely enough men to work the three guns, Maj. Gen. Longstreet ordered his staff off their horses and put them to work manning the pieces. Longstreet, who was in carpet slippers because of a badly chafed heel, held the reins of their horses while directing the fire of the guns. It was a tense several minutes, for there was little standing between Miller's artillery and the open rear of Lee's broken army.

Francis Barlow's men, recalled Longstreet, "marched in steady good ranks, and the remnants before him rose to the emergency. They seemed to forget that they had known fatigue." Barlow also noted that "from these pieces, and from others still farther to our right, they had been pouring a destructive fire of shell, grape, and spherical-case shot." Barlow, who had played a key role crushing the Sunken Road line and repulsing several Rebel counterattacks, went down with a groin wound when a spherical case shot exploded near him. The grim and determined Southern stand and exhausted condition of his own troops convinced Maj. Gen. Richardson to break off the fight and he pulled his division across the Sunken Road. It was about 1:00 p.m.[36]

Richardson's withdrawal ended the battle for the Sunken Road. In all, some 10,000 Union troops from French's and Richardson's divisions

(Sumner's II Corps) battled about 7,200 Confederates, mainly from Richard Anderson's and D. H. Hill's divisions. Union losses totaled 2,920, or about 29% of those engaged (French lost 1,750, and Richardson 1,161). Although they were on the defensive for much of the fight, the Confederates lost about the same percentage (about 30%). Some units, however, lost a substantially higher number of men. Wright's brigade, for example, suffered nearly 60% losses, while G. B. Anderson's brigade lost about half its effective number. Some of the regimental losses were also exceptionally high. The 16th Mississippi of Posey's brigade, for example, lost more than 63% of its men to all causes. The Mississippians had reinforced G. B. Anderson's brigade along the Sunken Road before unsuccessfully attacking Richardson's division. Col. Van Manning's 3rd Arkansas, which had counterattacked under Col. Cooke from its position south of the West Woods, left about 61% of its men behind.

On the Union side, two regiments of the Irish Brigade lost the highest percentage of men. The 63rd New York lost 59% and the 69th New York suffered losses of 62%. Somehow, Barlow's two New York regiments managed to emerge comparatively unscathed compared to these other regiments. Although they were involved in several pivotal actions, the total for both regiments was fewer than 100 (or about 21%).[37]

The most severe loss suffered by the Federals was the mortal wounding of Maj. Gen. Israel Richardson. The intrepid division leader was standing next to Capt. William Graham's battery north of the Sunken Road when he heard a report that the battery's short-range Napoleons were no match for the Confederates' longer-ranged guns. Richardson instructed Capt. Graham to protect his battery as best he could but to be ready to go into action when Maj. Gen. Sumner ordered another advance. Just then, a shell exploded nearby and a piece of iron tore into his body. The fall of the capable Isaac Richardson may well explain why the Federals did not renew their attack.[38]

One of the best opportunities to defeat Lee's Army of Northern Virginia ended when the threat to his broken center receded.

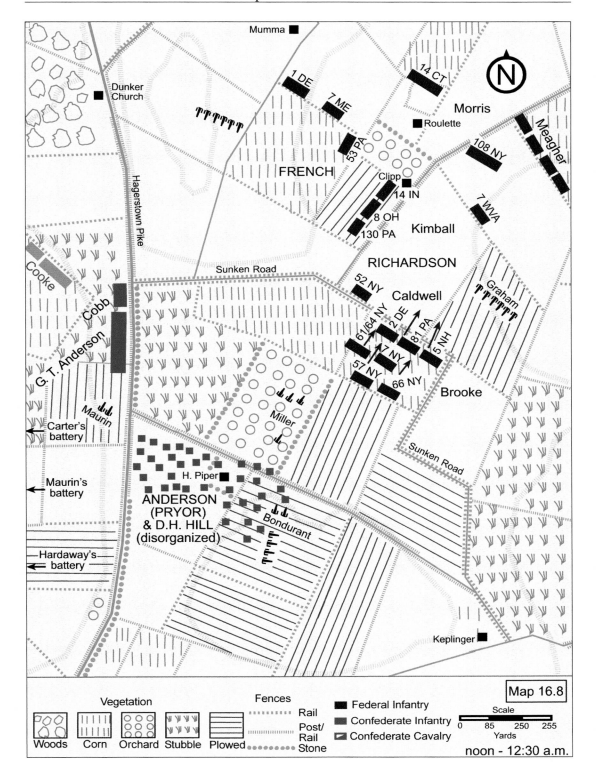

Map 16.8

noon - 12:30 a.m.

Map Set 17. Antietam: The Lower (Burnside's) Bridge
(9:00 a.m. - 2:00 p.m.)

Map 17.1: Both Sides Prepare for Battle
(9:00 - 9:30 a.m.)

Maj. Gen. George McClellan entrusted his left flank to Maj. Gen. Ambrose Burnside and the powerful IX Corps. Many of these men were still recovering from their fight at Fox's Gap at South Mountain three days earlier. McClellan visited his left flank on the eve of the battle, where he helped Burnside deploy his men and briefed him on the battle plans. Burnside learned that he would probably be called upon the next morning to force his way across a stone bridge spanning Antietam Creek in order to attack Gen. Robert E. Lee's right flank near Sharpsburg.[1]

The stone Rohrbach (or Lower) Bridge over Antietam Creek was 125 feet long but only twelve feet wide. This bottleneck would make it difficult to push large numbers of men across quickly, especially if the thrust was contested. The road leading to the bridge snaked its way along the creek before making a 90-degree turn to enter the span. Much of the route was open to enemy fire. Two hills on the Federal side of the stream overlooked the bridge. Burnside used the high ground to advantage by deploying five batteries (at least twenty-six guns) on them.[2]

The IX Corps was assigned to this sector, but relatively few troops were in the vicinity of the Lower Bridge on the morning of September 17. George Crook's brigade was on the opposite side of the Rohrbach orchard (No. 1), with two companies of the 11th Ohio in skirmish line facing the bridge. Two guns from Capt. Seth Simmonds' Kentucky battery deployed near the left flank of the skirmish line, supported by the 11th Connecticut, part of Col. Edward Harland's brigade (No. 2). The balance of the IX Corps, about 11,500 men, was resting farther east.[3]

The responsibility for defending this part of the field rested on the shoulders of Brig. Gen. Robert Toombs and his small fractured Georgia brigade (No. 3). Two of his four regiments, the 15th and 17th Georgia, were absent guarding the wagon train near Williamsport. This left Toombs with only 300 to 400 men in two understrength

regiments: the 2nd and 20th Georgia. The former unit, which counted only about 100 men, took up a position on a hill overlooking the creek with its left just south of the bridge and the rest of line following the meandering stream south for about 300 yards. To this small regiment fell the task of defending the bridge and the fords just to the south. This naturally strong position was made stronger when the Georgians reinforced it with fence rails, logs, and rocks. About 25 to 30 Georgians took advantage of a rock quarry overlooking the bridge that provided an excellent defensive position. The larger 20th Georgia deployed along the heights left (north) of the bridge, where many sought shelter behind a low stone wall. One company was thrown out almost to the bank of the stream. Farther to the right, the small 100-man 50th Georgia of Thomas Drayton's brigade guarded Snavely Ford and the right flank of the 2nd Georgia (No. 4). Toombs was given the job of commanding this entire vital sector, but Col. Henry Benning of the 17th Georgia had command of the two regiments overlooking the bridge.[4]

Rifled guns on Cemetery Hill near Sharpsburg provided long-range support. Two other batteries under Capts. John Richardson and Benjamin Eshleman deployed about 500 yards west of the bridge. Capt. John Eubank's battery also arrived and unlimbered 600 yards farther south, below the point where Antietam Creek makes its loop to the east before turning back south (No. 5).[5]

Although Burnside's IX Corps enjoyed an overwhelming numerical superiority, command issues threatened its effectiveness. Brig. Gen. Jacob Cox had assumed command of the corps on the evening of September 14 when Maj. Gen. Jesse Reno was killed on South Mountain. Burnside had been in command of the army's Right Wing (I Corps and IX Corps) during the march through Maryland, but McClellan ordered Burnside to return to his IX Corps on September 15, and the two corps were now separated on opposite sides of the battlefield. Burnside seems to have ignored the order. As one contemporary observed, "Burnside became a mere receiver and transmitter of orders to the commander of the Ninth Corps. . . . [It] might be believed that so good a soldier as Cox would have shown more activity and accomplished more, if he had felt himself really the commander. . . . [W]ith Burnside close to him, he probably felt . . . the mere tactical leader of the corps . . . simply seeing that it [the corps] executed the orders which came to him from or through Burnside."[6]

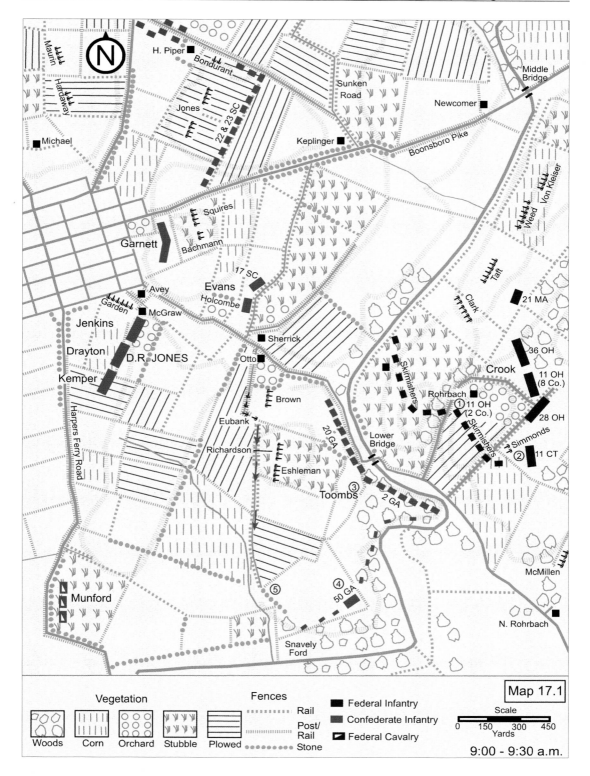

Map 17.1

Vegetation

Woods Corn Orchard Stubble Plowed

Fences

········· Rail

▪▪▪▪▪▪▪▪ Post/Rail

●●●●●● Stone

■ Federal Infantry

■ Confederate Infantry

◪ Federal Cavalry

Scale

0   150   300   450
Yards

9:00 - 9:30 a.m.

Map 17.2: The Repulse of
the 11th Connecticut Infantry
(10:00 - 10:30 a.m.)

McClellan ordered Burnside at about 7:00 a.m. to prepare to carry the Lower Bridge. Two brigades under Brig. Gens. James Nagle and Edward Ferrero (Sturgis' division) and a third under Crook (Cox's division) moved up to the vicinity of the bridge. Brig. Gen. Orlando Willcox's division followed, with Brig. Gen. Isaac Rodman's division moving ahead farther to the south (off the facing map) where Antietam Creek abruptly changes direction from slightly northeast to almost due north. Cox's remaining brigade under Col. Eliakim Scammon was also farther south, between Rodman's division and the Lower Bridge.[7]

When one of McClellan's aides reached Burnside before 10:00 a.m. with orders to commence the attack, the general ordered the 11th Connecticut infantry (Harland) to form into a skirmish line. Crook's brigade would follow, supported by Sturgis' division. After forcing their way across the bridge, the troops would form on either side of the road and drive west, forcing the enemy from the heights overlooking the creek. Once this portion of the attack was underway, Rodman's division to the south would cross Antietam Creek below Sharpsburg at an unnamed ford and flank the enemy. But as Rodman would soon discover to his dismay, the ford that McClellan's engineers selected was an unusable crossing point, and cavalry had not reconnoitered the area.[8]

The 450-man 11th Connecticut skirmish line led the way toward the bridge (No. 1). "At this time the enemy's infantry, aided by the fire of many pieces of artillery, advanced in heavy force to the attack, and soon the attack opened on our whole line as far as the bridge," remembered Col. Benning, the commander of the two defending Georgia regiments. Benning went on to describe this first assault against the bridge as "bold and persevering." By the time the enemy approached the creek, continued the Confederate colonel, the fire "not only from their infantry, but from the artillery, was incessant, the artillery being so placed that it would fire over the heads of the infantry."[9]

The right side of the 11th Connecticut dropped behind a low stone wall along the creek and opened fire at the well-hidden Georgians lining the much higher opposite bank. The low wall did not provide as much protection for the attackers as they had hoped, and many of them were hit by the return fire. (The left side of the 11th's line faced more difficult terrain and lagged behind the faster right side.) Federal shells raked the Georgians, and one Pennsylvanian watching the exchange agreed with Benning's description when he described the gunfire as "severe."[10]

Realizing that his Connecticut men could not remain in their exposed positions, Capt. John Griswold jumped on the low stone wall, waved his sword, and called for his fellow Nutmeggers to follow him as he jumped into the creek. Griswold assumed the entire right side of the regiment was behind him, but only a handful made the effort. Most of the men were still pinned down by the steady enemy fire and simply refused to join the suicidal effort. At least one bullet slammed into Griswold, who continued slogging through the shallow water (No. 2). Of those who did follow him, all were cut down or turned back. Somehow Griswold made it to the opposite side of the stream. Confederate officers ordered their men to hold their fire, but Griswold's wound was a mortal one.[11]

The left side of the 11th Connecticut under Col. Henry Kingsbury had a much harder time, marching toward the creek across open fields as the Georgia marksmen found their targets. Once they reached the stream, Kingsbury's men took cover and returned fire. Kingsbury waved his sword and ordered his men across the creek. A minie ball struck him in the foot and several more pierced his body. The colonel's men carried him off the field, but he died the next day.

The attack of the 11th Connecticut, boasted Col. Henry Benning, "was met by a rapid, well directed, and unflinching fire from our men, under which the enemy, after a vain struggle, broke and fell back." About one-third of the Connecticut troops were killed or wounded in less than thirty minutes of fighting.[12]

The first effort to cross the bridge and move against the Confederate right flank had failed.

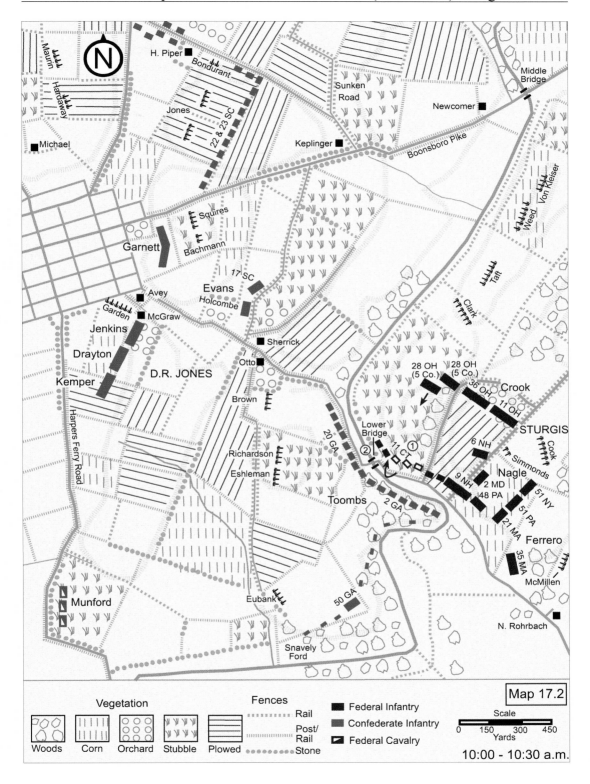

Map 17.2

Vegetation

Woods   Corn   Orchard   Stubble   Plowed

Fences

········ Rail

|||||||| Post/
         Rail

●●●●●● Stone

■ Federal Infantry
■ Confederate Infantry
◢ Federal Cavalry

Scale

0   150   300   450
         Yards

10:00 - 10:30 a.m.

Map 17.3: Crook's Attack Falters
(11:00 - 11:30 a.m.)

The steady fire of the Confederate infantry and supporting guns west of Antietam creek made a thorough reconnaissance of the bridge and its surrounding terrain impossible. As a result, many of Burnside's men had little or no idea of the severity of the task facing them.

When Col. George Crook received orders to advance his brigade to the bridge, some of his officers asked, "What bridge? Where is it?" The bridge could not be seen from their position well to the east, and no one communicated that the goal was to carry it and thrust westward. Crook did not have a guide to point out the objective, believed Sturgis had orders to attack the span before him, and seems not to have asked anyone to clarify his orders. As a result, Crook was surprised during his approach to the bridge to discover that Sturgis' men had not already secured it. In fact, Sturgis followed his orders by moving his division toward the creek and opening fire on the enemy to divert attention away from the main assault, which Crook's men were supposed to deliver. This confused state of affairs did not augur well for the second Federal effort to cross Antietam Creek.[13]

None of Crook's three large regiments were used well. The 36th Ohio remained in the Rohrbach orchard as a reserve while half of the 28th Ohio moved toward the creek in a skirmish line (No. 1). Enemy fire threw them back. These Ohioans later helped get a second section of Simmonds' battery into position. Crook moved the 11th Ohio forward to attack the bridge, supported by the other half of the 28th Ohio (No. 2). The latter got lost in the woods. When Crook got his bearings and realized the unit was too far north of the bridge, the men began grumbling about the ineptitude of their leaders. It did not help that they had not eaten breakfast that morning, nor dinner the night before.[14]

Crook decided to make the best of the situation by launching the 28th Ohio from the northeast to avoid the heavy losses Kingsbury's 11th Connecticut had sustained charging across the open ground. The 11th Ohio, meanwhile, headed directly for the bridge.[15]

Crook's men were moving toward the creek when Rebels spotted Isaac Rodman's division, supported by Col. Eliakim Scammon's brigade (Cox's division), approaching a ford about one-third of a mile south of the bridge. The ford was defended by the small 50th Georgia along with a thin skirmish line of South Carolinians. With virtually no opposition worthy of the name, these 3,000 Yankees could and should have easily crossed the shallow ford, pushed aside the handful of enemy troops, and been in a position to roll up the Confederate right flank defending the bridge. Rodman, however, had no idea what was waiting for him beyond the creek. When he learned the stream's banks were steep and rocky and his troops were under enemy infantry fire, Rodman decided to march west in search of Snavely Ford.[16]

Crook's attack on the bridge, meanwhile, was going nowhere fast. "I do not know the duty assigned [to the regiment]," admitted Maj. Lyman Jackson, who had took command of the 11th Ohio after Lt. Col. Augustus Coleman fell mortally wounded. The Buckeyes, continued Jackson, were "advancing in line across a plowed field and hill, the right and left divided, under conflicting orders, the right moving to our skirmishers forward on the right, the left moving to the base of the hill by the creek." The confused Ohioans fell back and reunited behind a hill in the rear. The fragment of the 28th Ohio farther right managed to hold its position along the creek bank and fire at the Georgians on the opposite side. Watching the assaulting Federals from across the creak, Col. Benning later reported, "This attack [of the 11th Connecticut] was succeeded by two similar ones from apparently two bodies of troops [the 11th Ohio and the five companies of the 28th Ohio], and with like results, the last of the two extending above the bridge to the upper part of the line."[17]

Meanwhile, artillery fire from both sides continued unabated. The Federal guns managed to blow out portions of the wood and stone defenses, but most of the Rebel guns well behind the bridge proved ineffective. Eubank's battery, however, had unlimbered farther south and as Benning reported, "was placed in position from which it could command at almost an enfilade the whole face of the hill occupied by our troops" (No. 3).[18]

The second effort to seize the bridge had failed as miserably as the first.

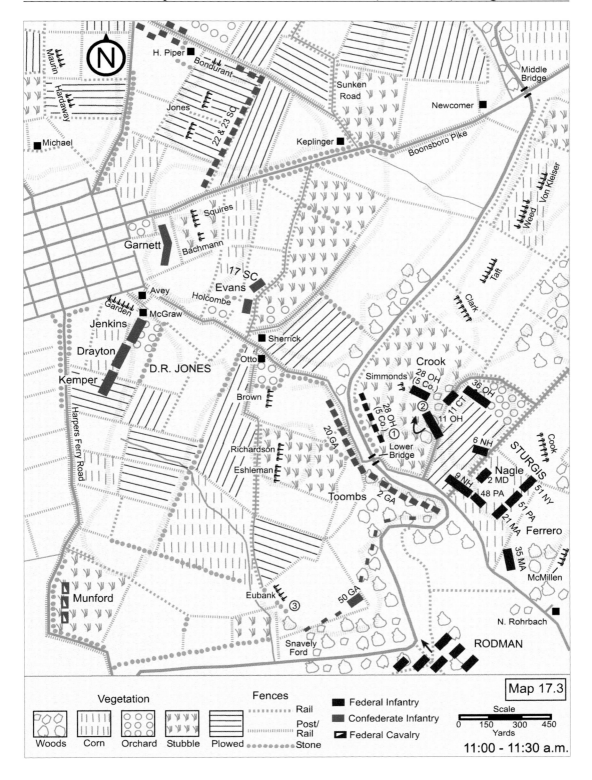

Map 17.3

Vegetation

Woods | Corn | Orchard | Stubble | Plowed

Fences
Rail
Post/Rail
Stone

Federal Infantry
Confederate Infantry
Federal Cavalry

Scale
0   150   300   450
Yards

11:00 - 11:30 a.m.

Map 17.4: Nagle's Brigade Attacks the Bridge (11:30 a.m. - noon)

The Federals had attacked the Rohrbach Bridge twice, and were easily repulsed each time. After the war, Jacob Cox related the thinking at this time circulating in the Federal IX Corps high command: "Burnside's view . . . was that the front attack at the bridge was so difficult that the passage by the ford below must be an important factor in the task, for if Rodman's division should succeed in getting across there . . . he would come up in rear of Toombs . . . [forcing him to] abandon the bridge." Both Burnside and Cox were content to wait for Rodman to cross the stream before launching another frontal attack. McClellan, however, had other ideas, explained Cox. The army commander's "sense of the necessity of relieving the right was such that he was sending reiterated orders to push the assault." Cox ordered Sturgis to force the bridge with his two brigades.[19]

Sturgis ordered Nagle's brigade to deploy first. The 48th Pennsylvania moved to its right, reforming near Simmonds' guns. The Pennsylvanians opened fire there in the vicinity of the five companies of the 28th Ohio. The 2nd Maryland, which had been waiting in a cornfield, marched to the rear and formed beside the 6th New Hampshire. Together the two regiments totaled about 300 men, all of whom fixed bayonets. Instead of launching another frontal assault, the third effort would come up from the south. Burnside correctly concluded that the Rebels would focus most of their firepower at and around the bridge, and so the best chance of success was to advance along the road leading to the bridge from the southeast. Nagle's 2nd Maryland and 6th New Hampshire would be supported by his remaining two regiments, the 48th Pennsylvania and 9th New Hampshire (No. 1). Sturgis, who understood the importance of taking the bridge, directly supervised Nagle's deployment and the movement of his regiments. His orders were simple and direct: "Over the bridge at a double quick and with bayonets fixed!" The first two regiments moved forward in column of fours.[20]

The Georgians on the opposite bank, meanwhile, patiently waited for the next enemy onslaught. They knew they occupied an almost impregnable position. However, their numbers were small, their losses were mounting, and their ammunition was running low. What they did not know was that if Nagle was not successful in taking the bridge, Cox and Burnside would throw in Ferrero's brigade and, if needed, Willcox's entire division. Given the numbers involved, seizing the bridge was just a matter of time.[21]

Officers ran ahead of the advancing regiments to help knock down the fence leading to the Rohrersvillle Road. The heavy Confederate fire, however, precluded the removal of additional fencing. The resulting bottleneck left the 2nd Maryland soldiers vulnerable to a withering fire that killed and wounded many as they tried to squeeze through the narrow opening. When those farther to the rear hesitated, officers pushed them forward and down the road toward the bridge, now just 200 yards away. By the time they reached the sharp left turn in the road leading across the span, about 40% of the Marylanders had been killed or wounded from small arms fire emanating from the quarry and along the creek bluff. The Marylanders tried to continue on, but the flank was so shattered they sought cover behind anything that could stop a bullet (No. 2). The 6th New Hampshire, advancing along the same road behind the Marylanders, suffered the same fate. One member of the Granite State regiment recalled that he and his comrades, "with fixed bayonets [at] the double quick, passed through a narrow opening in a strong chestnut fence—which there was no time to remove—and charged in the most gallant manner directly up the road to the bridge. . . . Of the first hundred men who passed through the opening in the fence, at least nine tenths were either killed or wounded. Such sweeping destruction checked the advancing column." The survivors of the two regiments huddled along the wall in front of the bridge unable to advance or retreat. The 9th New Hampshire moved up to provide assistance, but its officers wisely halted the advance before their men were similarly slaughtered.[22]

Farther downstream, meanwhile, Rodman's division continued its trek to find Snavely's Ford (No. 3). A local farmer, who seems not to have known the elusive ford's location, aided the searching Federals. The delay deeply frustrated Rodman, who knew how important it was to get over the creek.[23]

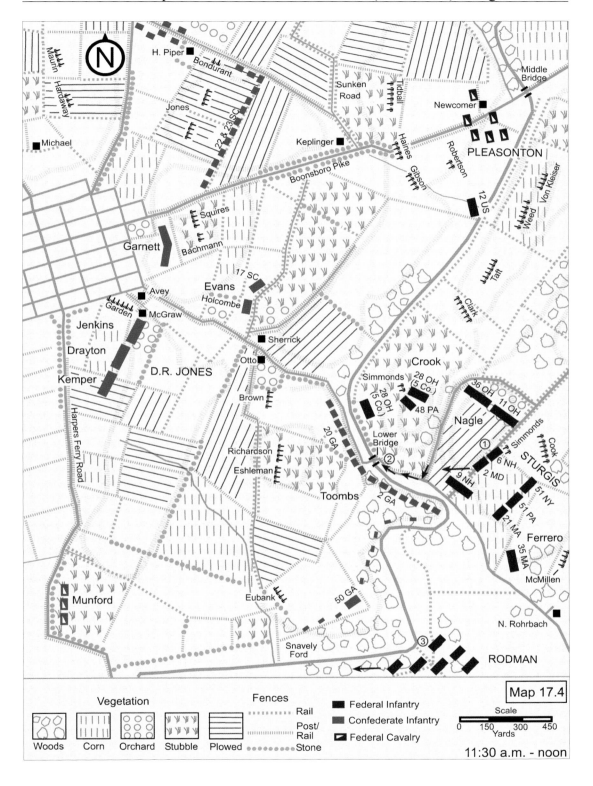

Map 17.4

11:30 a.m. - noon

Map 17.5: Ferrero's Brigade Attacks the Bridge (noon - 1:00 p.m.)

When Nagle's attack ground to a halt, Jacob Cox ordered Sturgis to throw in Ferrero's brigade. The slaughter of the 2nd Maryland and 6th New Hampshire convinced Cox that the best approach was a frontal dash against the bridge. If the men moved fast enough, he reasoned, they could overpower the defenders even though casualties would be high. In his mind, simple brute force and speed were the keys to success.[24]

To spearhead the advance Ferrero selected two crack regiments: the 51st Pennsylvania and 51st New York. Five more regiments would offer support: the 2nd Maryland, 6th and 9th New Hampshire, and the 21st and 35th Massachusetts. Knowing the difficult task awaiting his men, Ferrero offered a short inspirational speech. The soldiers, however, were more interested in their whiskey ration. Ferrero agreed to provide it if they successfully stormed the bridge. The "51's" stripped off their knapsacks, tossed them into a growing pile, and marched to the right to form near the 48th Pennsylvania. Two Federal batteries under Capt. Joseph Clark's Battery E, 4th U.S. Artillery and Capt. George Durell's Pennsylvania battery, deployed to add their weight to the effort.[25]

The two leading regiments moved by the flank to a hill that would serve as their jumping-off position. The men were not happy about the 300 yards of open ground between them and the arched bridge. Confederate artillery fire began taking its toll, killing a man here, wounding another there. Time to dwell on any misgivings was cut short when orders to charge coursed through the ranks. The tip of the spear moved through the 48th Pennsylvania, into the open, and toward the bridge (No. 1). To the surprise of many, the dreaded Confederate volleys failed to materialize as they closed the distance to their objective. The Georgians were holding their fire to preserve their precious ammunition (which by this time was running low) and to maximize the killing power of the initial volley.[26]

The strength of the small Georgia regiments ebbed with each passing minute as the steady pounding of Union artillery and small arms fire chipped away at the remaining defenders. Brig.

Gen. Toombs, who was in command of this part of the field, sent repeated requests for help to division leader Maj. Gen. D. R. Jones, whose other brigades sat idle northwest near Sharpsburg. None came, but the Yankees did. Rebel artillery firing at the oncoming Federals from across Antietam Creek was running out of fixed ammunition, and many of the gunners stuffed their tubes with anything they had collected along the way. Federal guns forced Eubank's battery, which had provided the most effective service, to abandon its position (No. 2). The remaining Confederate batteries were simply unable to compete with the enemy's longer-ranged and better handled pieces.[27]

Col. Henry Benning watched the Federal advance with a growing sense of despair. It was about noon, he reported, when "the enemy made preparations for a still more formidable attack. A battery [Simmonds] was placed in position from which it could command at almost an enfilade the whole face of the hill occupied by our troops. Soon it opened fire, and the infantry, in much heavier force than at any time before, extending far above as well as below the bridge, again advanced to the attack." A Confederate officer watching the spectacle unfold below him counted seven Federal battle flags in front of his position.[28]

Georgia rifles erupted in a splattering of fire and smoke when the 51st Pennsylvania and 51st New York moved within 200 yards of the bridge, killing and wounding men up and down the line. The men were "cheering and dropping at every step as [we] descended the plowed hill in full view of the enemy," recalled one Federal private lucky enough to survive the day. According to another, the attack column "seemed to melt away like a thread of solder before a blowtorch." William Bolton, an officer with the 51st Pennsylvania, wrote that the artillery and small arms fire "fill[ed] our faces and eyes with sand and dirt."

By this time the bridge was in view and it was obvious the frontage covered by the two regiments was too wide. The Pennsylvania attackers shifted right toward a stone wall along the creek to rectify the situation and minimize the murderous enemy fire. The 51st New York obliqued left toward a stout fence along the creek in search of protection. When he saw this movement, the commander of the 21st Massachusetts moved his men by the flank to connect with the New Yorkers.[29]

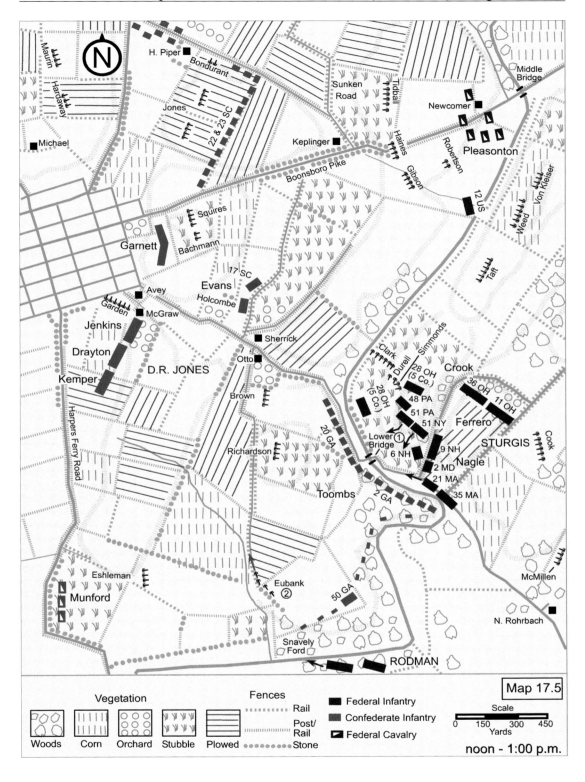

Maurin

Hardaway

Michael

H. Piper

Bondurant

Jones

22 & 23 SC

Sunken Road

Keplinger

Tidball

Haines

Gibson

Newcomer

Robertson

Pleasonton

Middle Bridge

12 US

Von Kleiser

Boonsboro Pike

Weed

Squires

Bachmann

Garnett

17 SC

Evans

Holcombe

Avey

Garden

McGraw

Jenkins

Drayton

Kemper

D.R. JONES

Sherrick

Otto

Brown

Taft

Clark

Durell

Simmonds

28 OH (5 Co.)

28 OH (5 Co.)

Crook

36 OH

11 OH

48 PA

51 PA

51 NY

Ferrero

STURGIS

Cook

Harpers Ferry Road

Richardson

20 GA

Lower Bridge ①

6 NH

9 NH

2 MD

Nagle

21 MA

35 MA

Toombs

2 GA

Eshleman

Munford

Eubank ②

50 GA

McMillen

N. Rohrbach

Snavely Ford

RODMAN

Vegetation

Woods Corn Orchard Stubble Plowed

Fences

.... Rail

Post/Rail

•••••• Stone

■ Federal Infantry

■ Confederate Infantry

◨ Federal Cavalry

Map 17.5

Scale

0   150   300   450

Yards

noon – 1:00 p.m.

Map 17.6: Rodman's Division Crosses Snavely's Ford (1:00 - 2:00 p.m.)

Even though they had repulsed every attack, the Confederates were losing the battle to hold the Lower Bridge and control that sector of the battlefield. Federal troops were descending upon the defenders from three directions: a ford north of the Lower Bridge, the Lower Bridge itself, and downriver at Snavely's Ford.[30]

Isaac Rodman's division finally began crossing the creek at Snavely Ford shortly before 1:00 p.m. (No. 1). This was hours later than Gen. McClellan expected or desired. According to historian Ezra Carman, "when Rodman's division was led to its bivouac that night [September 16], Col. Harrison Fairchild's brigade was supposed to be opposite [Snavely] ford." Rodman was expected to sweep across the creek with relative ease and roll up the Rebel right flank. Instead, precious time was wasted marching to the unsuitable ford designated by McClellan's engineers, and then trying to locate and march to the better suited Snavely's Ford.[31]

Fairchild's brigade was the first to cross Snavely's Ford. Rebels from a company of South Carolinians from Michah Jenkins' brigade and some additional troops from the 50th Georgia (Drayton) fired into the Yankees. Too few to halt the advance, the noisy nuisance was swept away and Fairchild's men climbed a bluff overlooking Antietam Creek. Eshleman's battery spotted the movement and opened fire, as did some cavalry from Thomas Munford's brigade (No. 2). Undeterred, Fairchild marched by the right flank. He would soon unite his brigade with troops forcing their way across the Lower Bridge (see below).[32]

North of the bridge, meanwhile, Col. Crook ordered the five companies of the 28th Ohio that had settled down by the creek after their aborted attack on the bridgehead to cross at a nearby ford (No. 3). When they did so successfully, Crook ordered the rest of his brigade to join the Buckeyes on the west side of the waterway. The Confederate defenders were now threatened from above and below.[33]

While Rodman and Crook slipped across the creek, the 2nd and 20th Georgia maintained their fire against the 51st Pennsylvania and 51st

New York at the Lower Bridge. Gen. Ferrero, who was watching from well to the rear, sent an aide to Col. John Hartranft, commander of the 51st Pennsylvania, demanding to know "why he didn't cross the bridge at once." Hartranft's reply was simple: accurate fire had pinned down his troops. As one officer recalled, "Never before had the [regiment] been exposed to so fearful a fire, and never will we forget it."[34]

The men on the left side of the 20th Georgia probably saw the new threat on their left posed by Crook's 28th Ohio. A few of the Georgians realized the game was up and slipped away. When their movement caught the attention of other Georgians, the rate of firing against the 51st Pennsylvania and 51st New York slackened. Col. Robert Potter of the latter regiment located Hartranft and suggested they renew their assault against the bridge. Hartranft disagreed, arguing that after the beating they had taken, he would have trouble getting his troops to leave the stone wall. Because Hartanft was his senior, Potter asked to make the charge with his regiment. Hartanft agreed. When the New Yorkers rose to prepare for the final dash across the bridge, however, the Pennsylvanians did the same thing. Both regiments closed on the bridge at the same time, with their flags crossing together (No. 4).

By this time Col. Henry Benning's Georgia defenders were in full retreat. My men, explained the officer, had held their positions "until their ammunition was quite exhausted, and until the enemy had got upon the bridge and were above and below it fording the creek. I then gave the order to fall back." Benning reassembled the remnants of his command behind a stone fence about 900 yards west of the bridge. Many Georgians were captured before they could vacate their positions, especially sharpshooters perched in trees (No. 5). A few Rebels refused to surrender or retreat. When he spotted Federal troops crossing the bridge, Lt. Col. William Holmes of the 2nd Georgia asked for volunteers and headed toward the stream. Holmes was struck by several bullets and killed while shaking his sword at the enemy. Some Federal troops were angry because of their lost comrades and the time it had taken to gain the west bank. Members of the 28th Ohio captured more than a dozen men of the 20th Georgia and were about to execute them when an officer intervened to save their lives.[35]

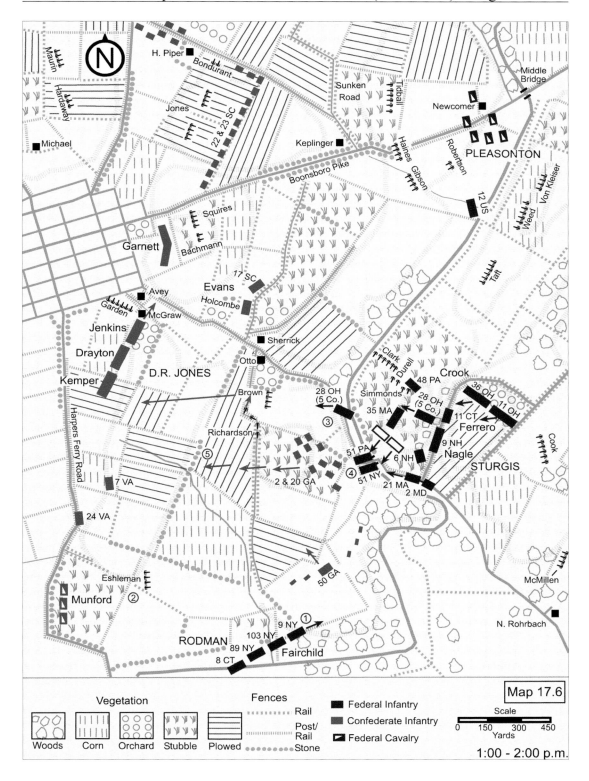

Map 17.6

1:00 – 2:00 p.m.

Map Set 18. Antietam: Burnside Advances on Sharpsburg

(Afternoon, September 17)

Map 18.1: The Federals Consolidate Their Bridgehead (2:00 - 3:30 p.m.)

It had taken several hours, but the fight for the Lower Bridge was finally over. About 500 IX Corps men lay dead or wounded on the east side of Antietam Creek, with some 120 Georgians sharing the same fate on the opposite bank. The encounter swelled the breasts of those who had held on for so long. Although eventually driven back, a proud Col. Henry Benning wrote in his report that "during that long and terrible fire not a man, except a wounded one, fell out and went to the rear—not a man." According to William Allan, an early historian of the Army of Northern Virginia, "On the Confederate side of the stream Toombs' two small regiments held their ground and threw back assault after assault with a coolness and tenacity unsurpassed in history." The Georgians still had plenty of fight left in them, and most waited for the new round behind a stone wall 900 yards west of the bridge (No.1).[1]

While the Georgians waited the Federals poured across the Lower Bridge and splashed through Antietam Creek at Snavely's Ford (No. 2). Col. Harrison Fairchild's men crossed first and filed to the right, with Col. Edward Harland's brigade behind them. Once Brig. Gen. Isaac Rodman's division was finally across Col. Eliakim Scammon's brigade, now under Col. Hugh Ewing (Scammon's division) took its turn. Capt. Benjamin Eschleman's Rebel battery tried but failed to disrupt the move.

Three Union divisions (Scammon, Sturgis, and Rodman) were now across Antietam Creek and preparing to assault Gen. Robert E. Lee's weak right flank. Brig. Gen. Jacob Cox and Maj. Gen. Ambrose Burnside, however, ordered a halt. "The ammunition of Sturgis' [division] and Crook's [brigade] men had been nearly exhausted, and it was imperative that they should be freshly supplied before entering into another engagement," explained Cox. "Sturgis also reported his men so exhausted by their efforts as to be unfit for an immediate advance." Cox asked permission to replace Sturgis' men with Brig. Gen. Orlando Willcox's fresh division (Cols. Benjamin Christ's and Thomas Welsh's brigades, positioned about three-quarters of a mile from the bridge), and to bring up the ammunition train to replenish cartridge boxes (No. 3). Cox assured Burnside that Sturgis' division would remain on the west bank of the creek to be called up if needed.[2]

"This was done as rapidly as was practicable, where everything had to pass down the steep hill road and through so narrow a defile as the bridge," Cox explained. Progress, however, was painfully slow. Burnside rode over to hasten the troops and wagons across the stone span. Christ and Welsh filed their men into position on Cox's right flank about 3:00 p.m. Three Federal batteries deployed to support the coming advance. Capts. George Durell and Joseph Clark unlimbered their guns in front of the infantry (No. 4), while Lt. Charles Muhlenburg's battery deployed farther southeast and closer to the creek. Confederate artillery on the heights to the west pounded the Federal pieces. One officer in the 9th New York of Fairchild's brigade was deployed behind Clark's battery and recorded the following: "[I]t did not appear to be able to do much in the way of firing, as it seemed to me that every time they would get fairly at work the rebels would concentrate such a fire on them as to silence them; and the men would be obliged to lie down in such shelter as they could get until the weight of the enemy's fire was directed to another part of the line."[3]

Waiting for the Federal IX Corps on the higher ground to the west was David R. Jones' division of six small brigades numbering fewer than 2,800 men, supported by some 40 guns distributed among nine batteries (No. 5). Jones had already sent two brigades under Brig. Gens. Richard Garnett and Micah Jenkins (Col. Joseph Walker) and some artillery toward the Middle Bridge after a portion of Maj. Charles Lovell's brigade (Brig. Gen. George Sykes' division), together with troopers from Brig. Gen. Alfred Pleasonton's cavalry division and several batteries crossed Antietam Creek. Jones' remaining troops were deployed on and around Cemetery Hill and a ridge running southwest toward the Harpers Ferry Road.[4]

Meanwhile, skirmishing increased as both sides prepared for what promised to be a large-scale effort to break the Confederate right flank and crush Lee's defensive position on the high ground around Sharpsburg.

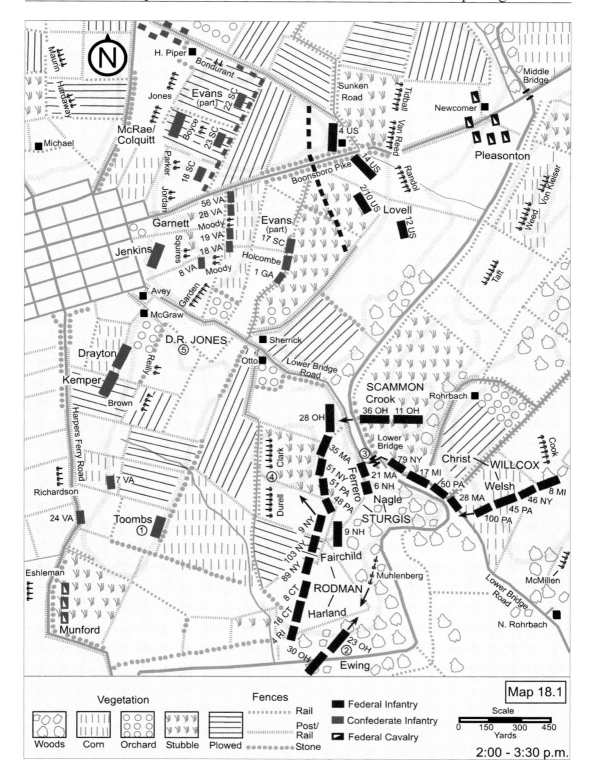

Maurin

Hardaway

McRae/
Colquitt

Michael

H. Piper

Bondurant

Jones

Evans
(part)

22 SC

Boyce

23 SC

18 SC

Parker

Jordan

Garnett

56 VA
28 VA

Moody

19 VA

Jenkins

Squires

18 VA

8 VA

Moody

Avey

McGraw

D.R. JONES
⑤

Drayton

Reilly

Kemper

Brown

Harpers Ferry Road

7 VA

Richardson

24 VA

Toombs
①

Eshleman

Munford

Sunken
Road

Tidball

Van Reed

4 US

14 US

Boonsboro Pike

2/10 US

Evans
(part)
17 SC

Holcombe

1 GA

Garden

Sherrick

Otto

Lower Bridge
Road

Clark

Durell

④

9 NY

103 NY
89 NY

8 CT

16 CT

4 RI

30 OH

Middle
Bridge

Newcomer

Pleasonton

Randol

Von Kleiser

Lovell

12 US

Weed

Taft

28 OH

SCAMMON
Crook

36 OH   11 OH

Rohrbach

Cook

Lower
Bridge

35 MA

51 NY

Ferrero

51 PA

③

48 PA

79 NY

21 MA

6 NH

Nagle

STURGIS

9 NH

Fairchild

RODMAN

Harland

23 OH
②

Ewing

Muhlenberg

17 MI

Christ

WILLCOX

50 PA

Welsh

28 MA

45 PA

100 PA

8 MI

46 NY

McMillen

Lower Bridge
Road

N. Rohrbach

Map 18.1

Vegetation

Woods   Corn   Orchard   Stubble   Plowed

Fences

Rail
Post/
Rail
Stone

■ Federal Infantry
■ Confederate Infantry
◪ Federal Cavalry

Scale

0   150   300   450
Yards

2:00 – 3:30 p.m.

Map 18.2: Both Sides Prepare
for Battle (3:30 - 4:00 p.m.)

Once Orlando Willcox's division finished deploying west of Antietam Creek, Jacob Cox was ready to order the IX Corps forward. The two sides had skirmished for several hours while the Federals resupplied and shifted troops.

Willcox deployed his two brigades with Christ on the right and Welsh on the left (No. 1). Christ's men were on the right of the Lower Bridge Road, with the 79th New York thrown out on the skirmish line and the remaining three regiments in line of battle behind it. When the men crested the high ground, Confederate artillery batteries (Capts. Squire and Garden in front and Capts. Brown and Reilly to the left) opened a deadly crossfire that forced the men to the ground to avoid the flying metal.

Willcox's second brigade under Welsh formed left of the Lower Bridge Road with the 100th Pennsylvania on the skirmish line and the 79th New York on its right. Welsh's other three regiments remained behind in line on the high ground. Welsh's 8th Michigan (one his left) connected with the right flank of the 9th New York, part of Fairchild's brigade of Rodman's division. Rodman's other brigade under Harland deployed on Fairchild's left. Rodman's brigades were deployed west of the big bend in Antietam Creek. The only remaining fresh Union brigade belonged to Col. Hugh Ewing (Cox's division), which was deployed behind Harland.

The situation facing the weak Confederate right flank was indeed grim. All that stood between the IX Corps and the high ground around Sharpsburg was David R. Jones' understrength division. The loss of the town and commanding terrain would cut vital road arteries, turn the Rebel right flank, and position the Federals to cut off the Southern army from the Potomac River ford. Two of Jones' brigades (Garnett and Jenkins) were already well to the northeast to confront the Federals opposite Middle Bridge (No. 2). Earlier that afternoon Federal batteries (16 guns) supported by Alfred Pleasonton's cavalry had rumbled across that stone span to drop trail one-half mile beyond. The 12th U.S. Regulars and the 2nd/10th U. S. Regulars (Lovell's brigade) crossed to add weight

to the bridgehead, and the remainder of the brigade did the same and deployed on both sides of the Boonsboro Pike. South of the pike, the Rebels mustered Capt. George Moody's battery, a section of Squires' battery, and three small infantry brigades (Evans, Garnett, and Jenkins). Brig. Gen. Nathan Evans' command was separated into two wings. One part was deployed north of the pike and the balance was below and well in advance along Sherrick Lane, which connected the pike with the Upper Bridge Road. About 100 men from the 1st Georgia under Capt. Hansford Twiggs (Col. G. T. Anderson's brigade) gathered on the right side of Evans' advanced wing. Brig. Gen. Richard Garnett's brigade deployed between Evans' divided command at the edge of a cornfield with its left touching the Boonsboro Pike. Jenkins' brigade (under Col. Walker) was farther west and closer to town. On paper, the defense looked reasonably strong. In reality, each brigade fielded the strength of a weak regiment with 300 or fewer men. The remnants of Maj. Gen. D. H. Hill's division extended the line left (north) of pike and the town.[5]

South of Sharpsburg (confronting the bulk of the Federal IX Corps) Jones had but three small brigades under Brig. Gen. Thomas Drayton, Col. James Kemper, and Brig. Gen. Robert Toombs (No. 3). The first two numbered not many more than 550 men in total but were protected by a ravine south of town and west of the Harpers Ferry Road. Both had been roughly handled at South Mountain, and the men were still recovering from the ordeal. The remnants of Toombs' 2nd and 20th Georgia, which had fought so long and well under Col. Henry Benning in defense of the Lower Bridge, had fallen back to far edge of a large 40-acre cornfield. When the 15th and 17th Georgia of Toombs' brigade and one-half of the 11th Georgia from G. T. Anderson's brigade arrived there, the 2nd and 20th Georgia were permitted to head to the rear to replenish their ammunition and rest. Although the Federals did not know how many Rebels were available to defend the right flank, Lee knew his front could not withstand a determined assault. Maj. Gen. A. P. Hill's division, which had remained behind at Harpers Ferry to oversee the surrender, was marching hard to reach the battlefield. The only question was whether Hill's "Light Division" would arrive in time to save the Army of Northern Virginia.[6]

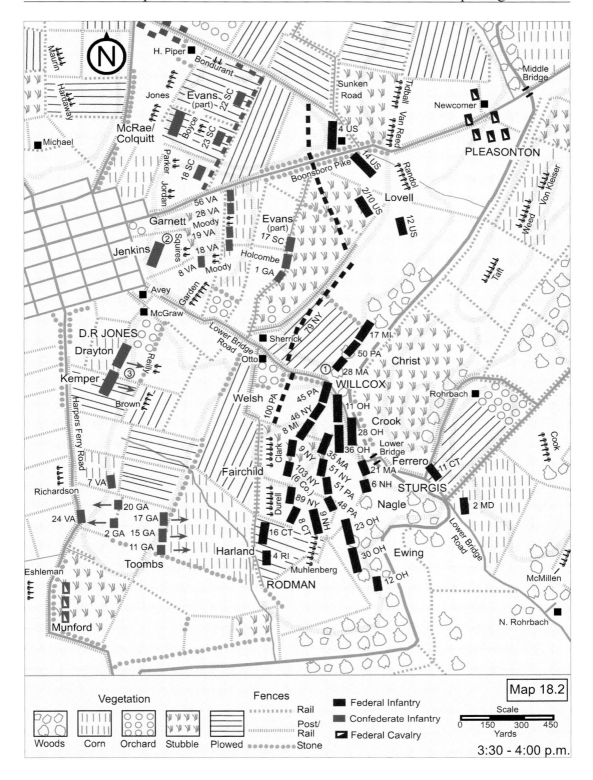

Map 18.2

Vegetation

| Woods | Corn | Orchard | Stubble | Plowed |

Fences

Rail
Post/Rail
Stone

Federal Infantry
Confederate Infantry
Federal Cavalry

Scale
0   150   300   450
Yards

3:30 - 4:00 p.m.

Map 18.3: Rodman's Division Begins its Attack (3:30 - 4:00 p.m.)

When the Federals finished deploying about 3:00 p.m., Burnside ordered Jacob Cox to open the advance with the divisions under Rodman, Willcox, and his own Kanawha Division (under Col. Eliakim Scammon). Sturgis' division would remain in reserve on the crest of the hill near the Lower Bridge. The movement was to be made en echelon, meaning the right side would advance first and troops farther left thereafter. Willcox's division on the right side of the IX Corps, supported by George Crook's brigade, would head for Sharpsburg. Rodman's division on the opposite flank, supported by Ewing's brigade, would advance on the left, clearing all troops in their front before shifting rightward to come up on Willcox's left flank.[7]

Cox gave the order to move out about 3:15 p.m. The 79th New York on Christ's skirmish line advanced with Lovell's consolidated 2nd/10th U.S. Regulars on its right against the handful of men of the 17th South Carolina and Holcombe's Legion (Evans), and a detachment of the 1st Georgia (Anderson) along the Sherrick Lane. The Union regiments brushed aside these defenders and halted in an apple orchard at the base of Cemetery Hill. Parts of three Rebel artillery batteries (Squire, Moody, and Garden) opened fire almost as soon as the Federal troops stepped into view. Undeterred, the Federals continued west toward Sharpsburg. When the commander of the 79th New York Highlanders realized the balance of Christ's brigade was not following, he ordered his men to lie down and await its arrival. Christ explained his delay in his report: "I discovered that my support on my left [Welsh's brigade] had not come up. Deeming my force alone inadequate for the attack on both artillery and infantry, I was obliged to halt until supported on my left" (No. 1).[8]

Welsh was late coming up because his brigade had farther to traverse and the terrain in his front was more difficult to negotiate (No. 2). Welsh's men moved doggedly forward on the left side of the Lower Bridge Road under a hail of artillery and small arms fire. With Crook's brigade in tow and the 100th Pennsylvania ahead on the skirmish line, Welsh's men passed the Otto farm buildings and drove the 15th South Carolina on the skirmish line back toward the main body of Drayton's brigade. The Federal brigade continued forward into a ravine, which disordered the ranks. On the right side, the 45th Pennsylvania filed right out of the ravine to straddle the Lower Bridge Road while the rest of the brigade continued straight ahead, passing through the ravine and reforming on the west side. Jenkins' Rebel brigade under Col. Joseph Walker slid to the southeast, near the Lower Bridge Road to confront the enemy advance (No. 3). The left of the brigade was north of the road along an orchard. They were joined by the 17th South Carolina, Holcombe's Legion, and the 1st Georgia detachment, which had been driven back by the 79th New York and the 2nd/10th U.S. Regulars.[9] During this phase of the Federal advance a section of guns from Cook's battery under Lt. John Coffin galloped along the Lower Bridge Road and dropped trail in the Otto orchard. According to Coffin, he was "ordered to take a position about 200 yards in advance of the column, where I was enabled to shell the enemy on our right until they were driven from their position."[10]

On the Federal left, Rodman's division (the brigades of Fairchild and Harland) prepared to advance across the hilly terrain in its front. Fairchild's infantry who would be the first to attack and they were rather anxious to do so because they were being pounded by Brown's and Reilly's Rebel batteries just southeast of Sharpsburg and by Richardson's battery firing from near the Harpers Ferry Road. When orders arrived, the troops took to their feet and set off toward the artillery that had been tormenting them from about 800 yards away (No. 4). The 7th Virginia, part of James Kemper's brigade, was deployed in the left-front of this determined Federal charge but wisely withdrew beyond the Harpers Ferry Road until they reached a depression near a fence line, where officers called a halt to rest and re-dress the lines. The accurate Confederate artillery fire had already taken out nearly one-quarter of Fairchild's brigade.[11]

Rodman's other brigade under Harland on the left side of the IX Corps also began advancing, with Ewing's brigade moving up behind it. Masses of Rebel infantry were forming well to their front, but none of the Federals understood their true significance (No. 5).[12]

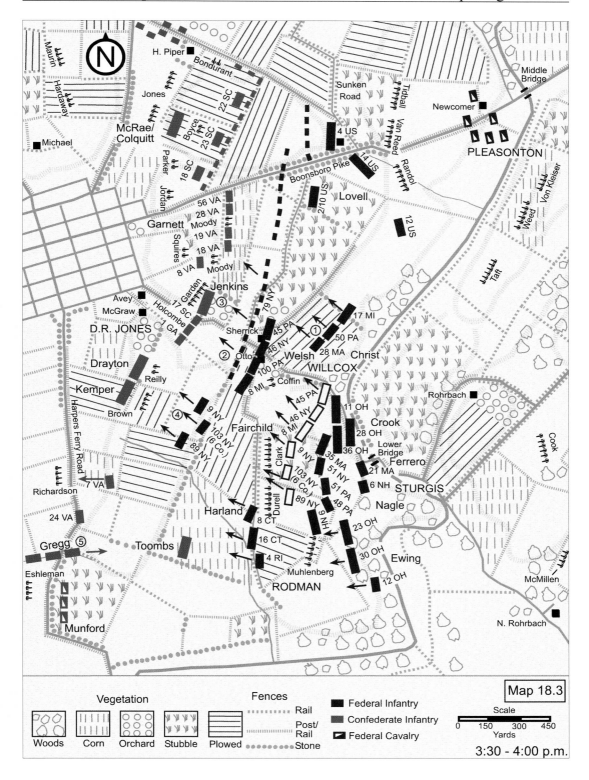

Map 18.3

Vegetation
Woods Corn Orchard Stubble Plowed

Fences
Rail
Post/
Rail
Stone

■ Federal Infantry
■ Confederate Infantry
◨ Federal Cavalry

Scale
0   150   300   450
Yards

3:30 - 4:00 p.m.

Map Set 19. Antietam: A. P. Hill's Division Arrives from Harpers Ferry (3:00 a.m. - 5:30 p.m.)

Map 19.1: Hill's March to the Battlefield (6:30 a.m. - 2:30 p.m.)

If Gen. Robert E. Lee felt any real despair at any point during the battle of Sharpsburg it was on the afternoon of September 17. His Army of Northern Virginia had been under heavy assault since dawn by the more powerful Army of the Potomac, the Potomac River was but a mile behind him, and a single ford was the only way his army could slip away. Somehow his left and center had thrown back the attackers after hours of some of the heaviest fighting the Civil War would ever witness, but the Confederates there had suffered staggering losses and were on the verge of collapse—disorganized, exhausted, and in no condition to renew the fighting. While his left was under attack, masses of Federal troops stepped into view on the far side of Antietam Creek beyond the Middle Bridge. Would they drive across in an effort to split his army in two?

By the time the Federal IX Corps forced its way across the Lower Bridge and fords opposite Lee's right flank and organized itself to renew its advance toward Sharpsburg, few troops were left to oppose them. Only David R. Jones' small and dispersed division was available to confront the powerful IX Corps. It appeared as though only fresh reinforcements could save the army, and there were only two sources from which Lee could draw.[1]

The first source was from the artillery reserve at Shepherdstown under Brig. Gen. William Pendleton. About midday, Lee sent Pendleton a desperate message for help: "If you have fifteen or twenty guns, suitable for our purpose, which you can spare, the general desires you to send them, with a sufficiency of ammunition. . . . Send up stragglers. Take any cavalry about there and send them up at the point of the sword. We want ammunition, guns, and provisions." In the end, Pendleton sent but one battery, which arrived after the fighting ended.[2]

Lee probably held out more hope that his second source of reinforcements would arrive in time to balance the scales and hold Sharpsburg. Maj. Gen. Thomas "Stonewall" Jackson left Maj. Gen. A. P. Hill's division at Harpers Ferry to process Federal prisoners and collect supplies. Shortly after the fighting began that morning, Hill received a direct order from Lee at 6:30 a.m. to move with all haste to the battlefield. Hill put five veteran infantry brigades on a northward march about 7:30 a.m., leaving Col. Edward Thomas' brigade behind to complete the tasks assigned to the division. Hill's men worried that they would miss the action. As one veteran recalled, "we believed there would be no more fighting for at least several months." Brig. Gen. Maxcy Gregg's brigade led Hill's column, followed by brigades under Brig. Gens. Lawrence O. Branch, James J. Archer, and Dorsey Pender. Field's brigade under Col. John Brockenbrough brought up the rear.[3]

The combative A. P. Hill knew the stakes were high. When he donned his worn bright red hunting shirt, which he always put on before going into battle, his troops knew what to expect. Still, they had a long seventeen miles to march just to reach the battlefield. Luckily, the winding Harpers Ferry Road along the Potomac River was a good one. Hill's column was laden with all sorts of booty, including Southern infantrymen sporting enemy clothing. One observer recalled that there were so many men wearing new blue Federal uniforms that Archer's command looked like a newly raised Union brigade.[4]

One of Gregg's South Carolinians described the day's march as "hot and dusty in the extreme." The rapid pace of the march raised clouds of dust that coated clothing and hair and choked lungs. According to some reports Hill used the flat of his sword to "encourage" men who were less than enthusiastic about the pace of the march. Hill broke his blade against the back of a young second lieutenant when he spotted the officer crouching behind a tree.[5] The march was "long and fatiguing," remembered Archer, and "many of the men fell, exhausted . . . by the way, so that when the four regiments of my brigade reached the battlefield there were only 350 men."

About 3,300 men were in the ranks when Hill's division began crossing the Potomac River at 2:30 p.m.[6]

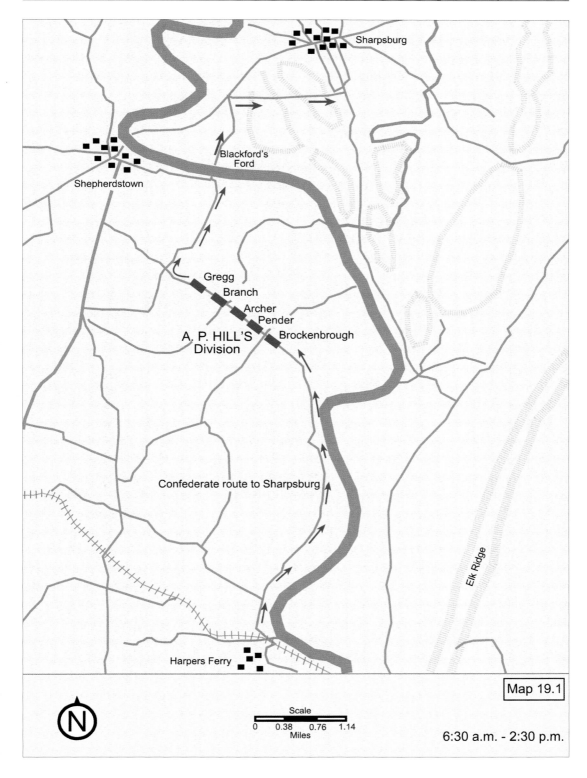

Sharpsburg

Blackford's
Ford

Shepherdstown

Gregg
Branch
Archer
Pender
A. P. HILL'S   Brockenbrough
Division

Confederate route to Sharpsburg

Elk Ridge

Harpers Ferry

Map 19.1

N

Scale
0   0.38   0.76   1.14
Miles

6:30 a.m. - 2:30 p.m.

Map 19.2: D. R. Jones
Battles Rodman's Brigades
(3:30 - 4:00 p.m.)

Some reports claim that after Hill crossed his division into Maryland outside Sharpsburg, Gen. Lee was so happy to see Hill that he embraced him. One witness claims he heard Lee exclaim, "General Hill, this is the last force we have. You must hold half in reserve and send in the other half." Whether or not Lee greeted Hill in this manner, Hill's arrival was vindication for the division leader, who had been arrested just days earlier by Jackson because of the pace of his march to Harpers Ferry. The embarrassed (and furious) Hill had been forced to march in the rear of his infantry. Now back in command and once more riding at the head of his "Light Division," he was coming onto the field exactly where needed and with no time to spare.[7]

While his men crossed the river Hill rode toward town and and found D. R. Jones. The Federal IX Corps was across Antietam Creek but had not yet launched its attack. After a brief conference Jones and Hill agreed that Hill's lead brigade under Gregg would assume Brig. Gen. Robert Toombs' advance position in the large cornfield, freeing the Georgian to move his men left to attack Col. Harrison Fairchild's exposed right flank farther north. Branch's and Archer's brigades, second and third in Hill's column, would come up and form between Toombs and Gregg. Pender's and Brockenbrough's brigades would stay in reserve. The plan went awry almost immediately when Brig. Gen. Orlando Willcox's division began attacking the Rebels defending Sharpsburg (see below). When Toombs was ordered to assist Jones' other brigades defending the town, he led his men west to the Harpers Ferry Road and then north toward Sharpsburg.[8]

Willcox's division was deployed southeast of Sharpsburg, with Col. Thomas Welsh's brigade on the left and Col. Benjamin Christ's brigade behind and to the right moving toward the Sherrick farm lane (No. 1). Welsh's 45th Pennsylvania straddled the Lower Bridge Road with the rest of the brigade extending left. Welsh led the attack and drove Micah Jenkins' brigade under Col. Joseph Walker over a hill along with portions of Brig. Gen. Nathan Evans' brigade on

its right. Once over the hill Welsh stopped to reform his brigade, which was nearly out of ammunition. To his right, Christ's 17th Michigan drove toward Capt. George Moody's battery and the 18th Virginia supporting it, forcing both to withdraw. Worried about sharpshooters deployed in his front, Christ halted his troops before they could drive forward to capture the higher ground. Moody's guns were replaced by three pieces from Capt. Thomas Carter's battery and two more from Lt. William Elliott's battery, all of which opened from just east of town on the "imposing force of Yankees" who had "advanced in fine style" against Jones' understrength division.[9]

When Welsh failed to press his advantage, Col. Walker realigned his regiments to face generally south by southwest along the Lower Bridge Road. His infantry, together with the five fresh artillery pieces, intended to use their oblique fire to knock back the Federals moving against Thomas Drayton's and James Kemper's small brigades. These Federals on Welsh's left included Col. Fairchild's three New York regiments (Rodman's division), which advanced in line of battle for about 200 yards before charging with a "wild harrah" (No. 2). Drayton's men awaited their arrival south of Sharpsburg from behind a stone wall, with Kemper's men deployed on Drayton's right. These brigades had been in a ravine just to the rear, but when Fairchild's men appeared in their front they moved up the slope to their current positions. There were not many Rebel defenders— perhaps 600 or so after their desperate fight at South Mountain and the heavy straggling during the march to Sharpsburg that followed. Fairchild probably fielded about 950 bayonets.[10]

The seventeen men of the 1st Virginia held the middle of Kemper's line (No. 3). According to Virginian John Dooley, "we were now left to oppose the numerous masses before us (the 89th New York) with a mere picket-line of musketry. . . . The Yankees, finding no batteries opposing them, approach closer and closer. . . . [W]e keep up a pretty warm fire by file upon them as they advanced." What Dooley did not realize was that the 9th New York on the right side of Fairchild's brigade was being hammered by Carter's and Elliott's five guns. Farther south, Col. Edward Harland's brigade (Rodman's division) began its move west toward the Harpers Ferry Road.[11]

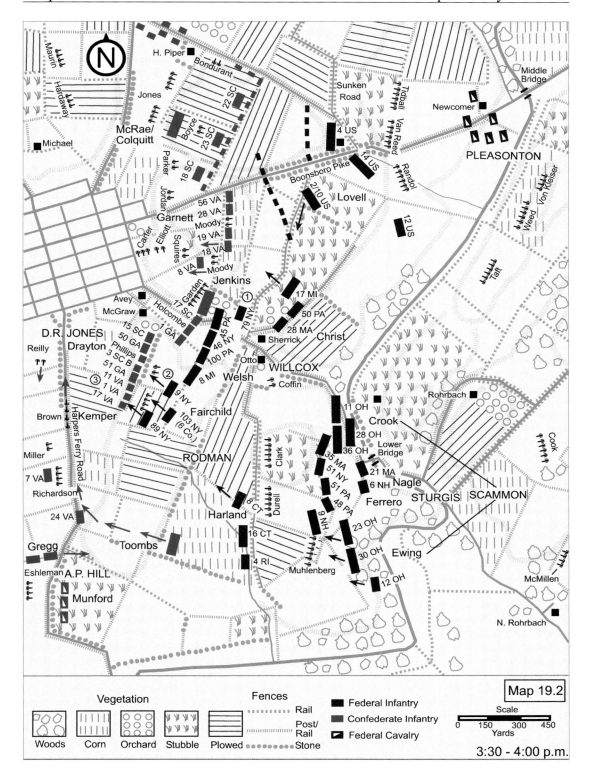

Map 19.2

3:30 – 4:00 p.m.

Vegetation

Woods | Corn | Orchard | Stubble | Plowed

Fences

Rail
Post/Rail
Stone

Federal Infantry
Confederate Infantry
Federal Cavalry

Scale

0 150 300 450
Yards

Map 19.3: Harland's Federal Brigade Advances (4:00 - 5:00 p.m.)

After driving the enemy from his immediate front, Gen. Willcox halted his men on the high ground just east of Sharpsburg. To his south, Fairchild's brigade approached Drayton's and Kemper's undersized brigades (No. 1). "Now they are at the last elevation of rising ground and whenever a head is raised we fire," remembered the 1st Virginia's John Dooley of Kemper's brigade. "Now they rise up and make a charge for our fence. Hastily emptying our muskets into their line, we fled back through the cornfield." Although the 1st Virginia retreated, the 17th Virginia next to it continued putting up quite a fight until the 89th New York overlapped the 17th's right flank. These Virginians finally fell back, but only after losing 35 of the 46 men the regiment had carried into the fighting.

Drayton's larger brigade of Georgians and South Carolinians on Kemper's left enjoyed an advantage that Kemper's men did not—a stone fence that could more easily stop Yankee bullets than the fence rails the Virginians had used to prop their guns upon. Drayton's heavy fire forced the men of the 9th New York to lie down and fight from a prone position. After a few minutes some Federal officers sprang to their feet, grabbed flags, and led the New Yorkers to the fence. After a swirling hand-to-hand combat Drayton's men joined Kemper's in full retreat.[12]

As described earlier, Jenkins' brigade under Walker farther to the north swung to face south by southwest along the Lower Bridge Road (No. 2) to fire at some distance into the exposed flank of Fairchild's advancing brigade. The five guns from Carter's and Elliott's batteries opened on Fairchild's 9th New York, which according to Capt. Carter was "was shattered and driven back without the assistance . . . of infantry" (No. 3). The usually caustic D. H. Hill admitted that the "firing was beautiful . . . this is the only instance I have ever known of infantry being broken by artillery fire at long range." What D. H. Hill and the watching Confederates did not realize was that the New Yorkers had not been "broken", but had instead moved into a ravine to shield them from the storm of shot and shell.[13]

Gen. Rodman's second brigade under Col. Harland, meanwhile, swept westward into a large forty-acre cornfield (No. 4). Unfortunately for the Federals, this advance was not well managed. When Harland gave the order to move forward, the 8th Connecticut complied by moving slightly right to avoid entering the corn. Its right flank followed the same route as had the left flank of Fairfield's 89th New York. Harland's other regiments, the 16th Connecticut and 4th Rhode Island, however, were resting in the cornfield to the left of the 8th Connecticut and did not hear the order to advance. About this time, members of Col. Hugh Ewing's brigade spotted organized Confederate troops entering the west side of the large cornfield. No one realized that A. P. Hill's division had reached the field from Harpers Ferry, and that his leading brigade under Maxcy Gregg was moving to meet the new Federal advance. As a result, the 8th Connecticut was far in advance of the rest of the brigade. When Harland suggested to Rodman that he halt the 8th Connecticut until the remainder of his brigade arrived on its left flank, the division leader disagreed; the 8th Connecticut should continue and the remaining two regiments should be ordered up (No. 5). The Nutmeggers of the 8th were hit by small arms fire from some of A. P. Hill's newly arriving troops and artillery fire from Capt. David McIntosh's battery, the first unit from Hill's division to reach the battlefield and engage the enemy.[14]

When Harland spotted Gregg's Confederates, he turned his horse (which was wounded at this time, thus delaying his arrival) and galloped back to where the 16th Connecticut and 4th Rhode Island had been resting. When he reached the 16th Connecticut, however, Harland discovered that Rodman had ordered the regiment to change front to the left and it was engaging Gregg's South Carolinians. Harland ordered the Connecticut troops to change front to gain the vulnerable right flank of the advancing 12th South Carolina. The Connecticut soldiers had only been in the service for about three weeks, and Harland's order threw them into some confusion. The tall corn, which hid portions of the regiment, did not help matters, and the bullets snaking their way into their ranks only made the situation more desperate for the green Federal troops.[15]

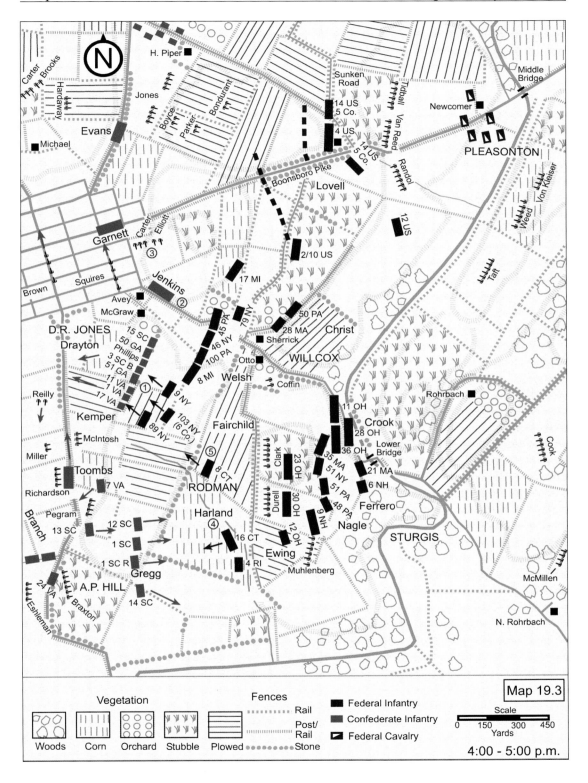

Map 19.3

Vegetation

Woods   Corn   Orchard   Stubble   Plowed

Fences
.... Rail
|||||||||||| Post/
           Rail
●●●●●● Stone

■ Federal Infantry
■ Confederate Infantry
◩ Federal Cavalry

Scale
0   150   300   450
Yards

4:00 - 5:00 p.m.

Map 19.4: Gregg's Brigade Attacks (4:00 - 5:00 p.m.)

Maxcy Gregg's brigade was deployed in line of battle and tramping east toward the Federals. The 14th South Carolina, which led A. P. Hill's column onto the battlefield, was thrown out to the right (south) behind a low stone fence well to the south and east. Its mission was to guard the division's right flank, but the Palmetto regiment ended up moving so far to the right that it never engaged the enemy. Gregg kept the 1st South Carolina Rifles in reserve and sent the 13th South Carolina, 12th South Carolina, and 1st South Carolina into the forty-acre cornfield. Gregg's four regiments (excluding the semi-detached 14th South Carolina mentioned above) totaled about 750 men, or about the size of the 16th Connecticut.

Probably because of misunderstood orders, the 13th South Carolina on the brigade's right halted at a stone fence along the edge of the cornfield. The 12th South Carolina next in line stormed into the field, faced volleys of small arms fire from the 16th Connecticut, and fell back. These South Carolinians attacked again but were forced back (No. 1). During these assaults the right side of the 12th South Carolina intermingled with the left side of the 1st South Carolina, and the jumbled group ended up retreating together. Both Palmetto regiments quickly rallied.

The 4th Rhode Island, meanwhile, came up on the 16th Connecticut's left flank, which was in some confusion after beating off the 12 South Carolina's second attack. Because the Rhode Islanders' right flank overlapped the left of the 16th Connecticut, the newly arrived regiment was forced to slide to the left. This movement disordered the Rhode Island line of battle, which was already in some disarray after its movement through the cornfield (No. 2). The arrival of the nearly 350 Rhode Islanders convinced the officers of the 12th South Carolina to reconsider launching a third charge and forced the 1st South Carolina to move farther right and refuse its right three companies in an effort to prevent any flanking maneuver.[16]

"So dense was the corn that the [opposing] lines sometimes approached within thirty or forty yards of each other before opening," recalled one of the South Carolinians. The Federal infantry was also being pounded by Capts. William Pegram's and Carter Braxton's Rebel batteries, which had arrived on the field with A. P. Hill's reinforcing column. According to their battalion commander, these artillery batteries worked "with beautiful precision and great effect." The two Federal regiments gamely held their positions in the field awaiting another charge with bayonets fixed.[17]

While the 16th Connecticut and 4th Rhode Island slugged it out with parts of Gregg's brigade in the large cornfield, the 8th Connecticut (part of Harland's brigade) continued marching northwest toward Capt. David McIntosh's battery deployed along the Harpers Ferry Road (No. 3). Federal guns firing from along Antietam Creek pounded Capt. McIntosh's battery, which was so undermanned that McIntosh himself helped work his guns. When McIntosh spotted a large part of the 8th Connecticut (Company B) approaching from his right toward his left he repositioned the guns to fire into the enemy foot soldiers. The Nutmeggers, however, were by this time too close for comfort. McIntosh ordered his men to fall back and left the guns behind. Ordinarily, infantry would have charged and captured such a tempting unmanned prize, but the 8th Connecticut was now completely isolated far ahead and to the right of the rest of Harland's brigade.

Farther right, Fairchild's brigade—which had driven Kemper's and Drayton's brigades to the rear—received orders to pull back (No. 4). Once Fairchild did so there were no Federal troops left between the 8th Connecticut's right flank and the town of Sharpsburg. The regiment's left was also unprotected because the 16th Connecticut and 4th Rhode Island had not advanced because of their fight with Gregg's South Carolinians. A heavy small arms fire from a Confederate skirmish line composed of the newly arrived 7th and 37th North Carolina of Brig. Gen. Lawrence Branch's brigade peppered the left flank of the exposed Federal regiment.[18]

About one-half mile to the southeast, the three regiments comprising Col. Ewing's brigade were moving to the support of the Federal troops in the cornfield.[19]

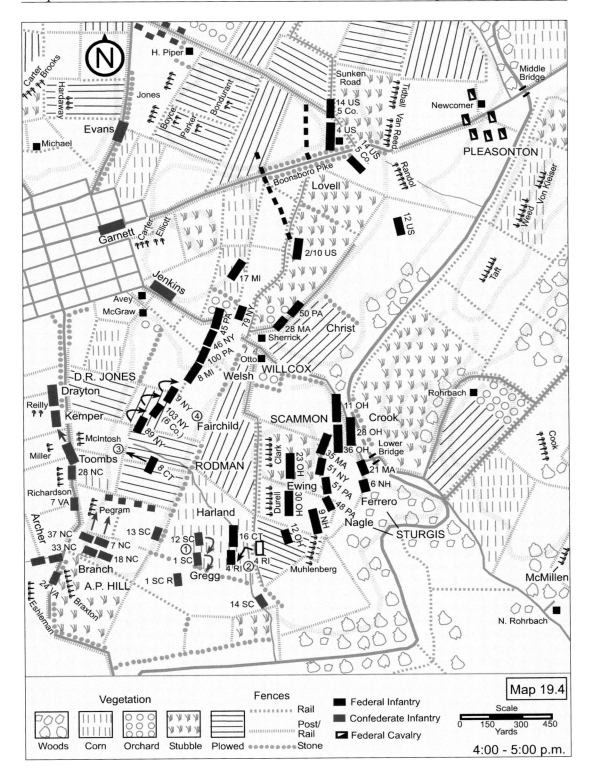

Map 19.4

Vegetation

Woods | Corn | Orchard | Stubble | Plowed

Fences

Rail
Post/Rail
Stone

Federal Infantry
Confederate Infantry
Federal Cavalry

Scale

0   150   300   450
Yards

4:00 - 5:00 p.m.

Map 19.5: Harland's Brigade Falls Back (4:00 - 5:00 p.m.)

Nearly one-half mile in front of any other Federal troops, the 8th Connecticut faced the remnants of Kemper's and Drayton's brigades along the Harpers Ferry Road (No. 1). Remnants from Robert Toombs' brigade under Col. Henry Benning joined these Southerners. All three commands enjoyed some level of cover because the road surface at this point was lower than the surrounding fields.

When the Georgians arrived on the right flank of Kemper's men Benning spotted McIntosh's abandoned guns in his front. Just beyond them was the 8th Connecticut (No. 2). Within wasting a moment Benning ordered his men to open fire because there was "no time to form." The Federals returned the favor. "The fire on both sides was very spirited but not effective—they shooting over us, we under them," reported Benning. "Very soon our fire improved and became deadly." The view from the opposite of the firing line was recorded by a member of the 8th Connecticut: "we now returned their fire and the men went to work as cooly as if on drill, but we were trapped on our left flank [by] a large corn field . . . full of rebels [and] on our right was a high hill where they were pouring in a gatling [sic] fire upon us and all this beside those in our front." The firing into the 8th Connecticut's left flank came from the 7th and 37th North Carolina of Branch's brigade. The Tar Heels were also moving rapidly north (No. 3). After ten or fifteen minutes the Connecticut troops began to waver. "I immediately ordered a charge," wrote Toombs, which was "brilliantly and energetically executed by my whole line, the enemy broke in confusion and fled." Many of the Connecticut troops insisted in separate accounts during and after the war that they did not want to abandon their position, but the pleas of their officers convinced them to do so. Accounts from the 37th North Carolina agreed. One of the Tar Heels remembered that the regiment "held ground quite stubbornly, fought splendidly, and went off very deliberately, firing back at the 37th and waving its flag."[20]

The 8th Connecticut lost about half of its men during its march toward the Harpers Ferry Road and the encounter with the Confederates they found there. Gen. Rodman, who was with Fairchild's men farther right during the advance, saw the 8th Connecticut moving forward without support and rode over to join the regiment. The Federal division leader never reached it because a Southern rifleman fired a bullet into his chest and mortally wounded him. Col. Harland assumed command of the division.[21]

Farther south the 16th Connecticut and 4th Rhode Island continued battling the 1st and 12th South Carolina in the large cornfield. The latter regiment had already attacked twice and was repulsed each time. Gregg was about to pull the 1st South Carolina out of the cornfield because its ammunition was nearly gone. Before he did so, he ordered the 1st South Carolina Rifles to come forward. Many of these new Palmetto soldiers could see that the 1st South Carolina on their left was in bad shape because the 4th Rhode Island was shredding its right flank. The Rhode Islanders were so focused on their close fight with the 1st South Carolina that no one seems to have seen the 1st South Carolina Rifles advancing toward their own exposed left flank. The Palmetto officers swung their right companies around to envelop the Rhode Islanders and opened fire, devastating the Federal regiment (No. 5). Its commander, Col. William Steere, was wounded in the hip and unable to order his men to the rear. After a short while the bloodied, disordered, and demoralized unit broke for the rear.[22]

Now fighting alone in the cornfield, the 16th Connecticut was vulnerable in front and on its left flank as enemy troops closed in around it (No. 5). According to George Merriman, who wrote home soon after the battle, "our regiment received no orders. The col . . . told us to save ourselves if we could. A skedaddle became general." He recalled that the "yells of the rebs were awful and the tune the bullets whistled by my ears is never to be forgotten." The two regiments attempted to rally near Muhlenberg's battery, which became even more active after the defeat of the Connecticut and Rhode Island troops.

By this time about half of the Federal IX Corps (the divisions of Willcox and Rodman) was in full retreat or out of the fight entirely. Now it was time for Brig. Gen. Jacob Cox's former Kanawha Division and Brig. Gen. Samuel Sturgis' division to try to turn the tide of battle.[23]

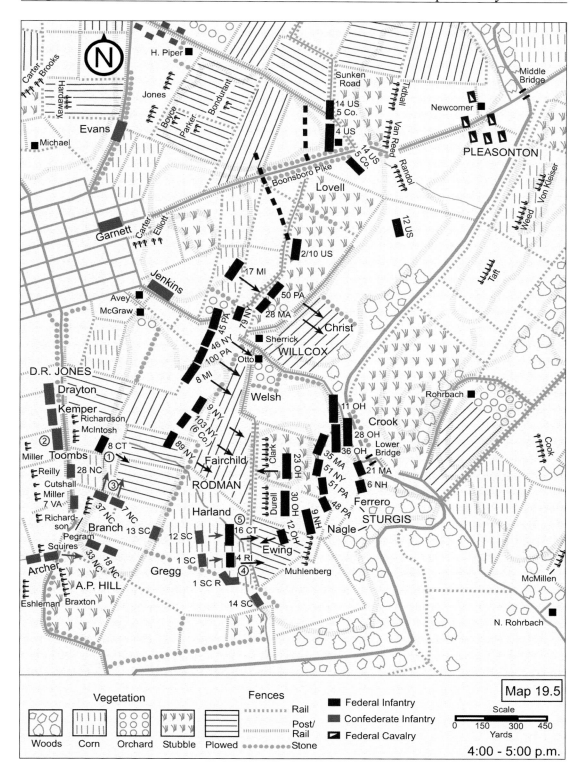

Map 19.5

Vegetation

Woods Corn Orchard Stubble Plowed

Fences

Rail
Post/Rail
Stone

■ Federal Infantry
■ Confederate Infantry
▨ Federal Cavalry

Scale
0   150   300   450
Yards

4:00 - 5:00 p.m.

Map 19.6: Archer's Brigade Strikes Ewing's Brigade (5:00 - 5:30 p.m.)

Unwilling to let the 8th Connecticut get away so easily, Gen. Toombs ordered his men and portions of Kemper's and Drayton's brigades out of the road and after the enemy. When they reached the hill where the Nutmeggers had made their stand, Toombs halted his men for a short time before ordering them to finish the climb up and then descend the reverse slope. Col. Benning, a much better leader and tactician, suggested Toombs exercise caution because the Federals could be waiting on the other side of the hill in strength. It was wise advice, and the three Confederate brigades fielded fewer than 1,000 effectives. Toombs agreed and the pursuit ended, at least for the time being. Before leaving the Harpers Ferry Road to attack, Brig. Gen. James Archer's small brigade of some 400 men arrived and formed on the right side of Toombs. Archer's was the third brigade of A. P. Hill's division to arrive and deploy for battle (No. 1).[24]

After Archer's infantry moved into the dense cornfield adjacent to the Harpers Ferry Road they heard orders to fall back (likely issued to the nearby men of the 28th North Carolina of Branch's brigade). Archer realigned his men and moved them east through corn stalks and a plowed field. Toombs (Benning) tried to keep up on Archer's right. Bullets delivered by Buckeyes of the 23rd and 30th Ohio (Ewing's brigade) crouching behind a low stone wall ripped into the Tennesseans and Georgians. The enemy, recalled a Southern private, was "posted in a heavy, dark line behind a rock fence." The attack was a desperate effort that stood little chance of success. Within minutes about one-third of Archer's men were either dead or wounded. Ewing's men were in a good defensive position, but all was not well with the Buckeye regiments. According to the commander of the 30th Ohio, "our men were at this time utterly exhausted from the effects of the double-quick step across the plowed field."[25]

Because Ewing's men were concentrating on the approach of Archer and Toombs, few noticed that the 1st and 12th South Carolina of Gregg's brigade had changed direction in the cornfield and were moving north toward the 30th Ohio's exposed left flank (No. 2). The Palmetto soldiers leveled their weapons, took aim, and pulled their triggers. The Buckeyes' commander, Lt. Col. Theodore Jones, explained what happened next: "A withering fire was directed upon us from our left flank, and from which we suffered most severely." He estimated that his men had fired twelve to fifteen rounds apiece into Archer's men before being hit in the flank.[26]

Maj. James Comly's 23rd Ohio was also behind the stone fence fighting on the right side of the battered 30th Ohio. Comly had spotted Gregg's troops moving toward the 30th's left flank but thought they were Federal reinforcements. A bit of concern swept through the major when some of the 30th Buckeyes opened fire on the unidentified arrivals. Comly thought this was a fatal mistake and so did not order his men to change direction and defend themselves. All doubt dissipated, however, when the South Carolinians stopped and opened fire on the flank and rear of the 30th Ohio. Col. Ewing ordered Comly to "change front perpendicularly to the rear" so that his men would face the South Carolinians (No. 3). Ewing ordered the 30th to do the same thing, and to form on the left of the 23rd Ohio. Ewing's order was intended to present an effective front against Gregg's attack, but it would also expose the right flank of the 23rd Ohio to Archer's and Toombs's men advancing from the west. Luckily for the Federals, only the four right companies of the 30th Ohio heard the order and moved to comply, leaving the remaining six companies at the wall on the left blazing away at approaching Confederates (No. 4). Hit in front and flank, many of the Ohioans realized that the rest of the regiment on the right was missing and broke for the rear.[27]

Some of Archer's men reached a portion of the wall and captured a number of Buckeyes, including Lt. Col. Jones, the 30th Ohio's wounded commander. Realizing now that his position was completely untenable, Ewing ordered both of his regiments to fall back.[28]

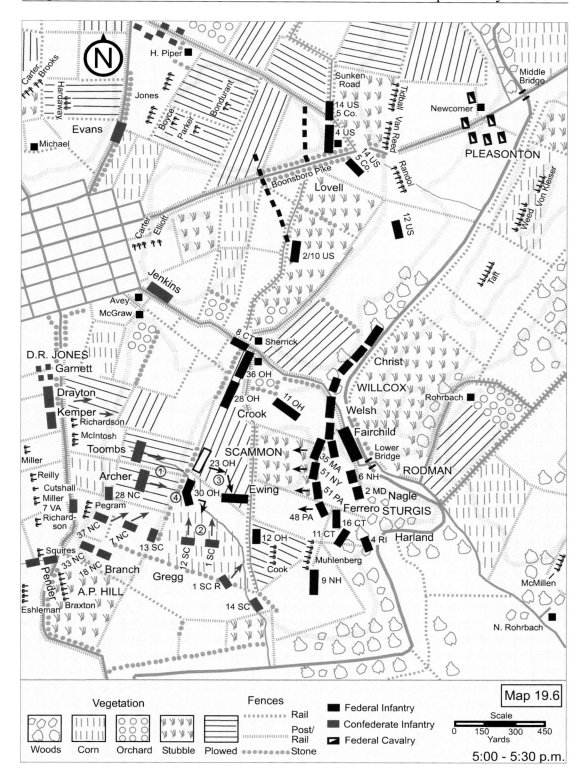

Vegetation

Woods   Corn   Orchard   Stubble   Plowed

Fences

.... Rail
Post/
Rail
•••••••• Stone

■ Federal Infantry
■ Confederate Infantry
◨ Federal Cavalry

Map 19.6

Scale
0   150   300   450
Yards

5:00 - 5:30 p.m.

Map 19.7: A. P. Hill's Division Sweeps the Field (5:00 - 5:30 p.m.)

Archer's men remained at the stone fence after helping drive back Ewing's regiments (No. 1). Archer did not have the strength to continue attacking, and waiting farther west were Brig. Gens. Edward Ferrero's and James Nagle's brigades (Sturgis' division). Meanwhile, the last brigade from Scammon's division under Crook had advanced to the same stone fence that now sheltered Archer's men, but much farther north near the Otto farmstead.[29]

While Archer's brigade was slugging it out with Ewing, other Rebel commands shuffled about to form a more cohesive front. One was Richard Garnett's, whose small brigade had been shattered at Turner's Gap and again at Sharpsburg. His Virginians were scattered about town when their commander heard of A. P. Hill's arrival and that the "fortunes of the day in that quarter [had been] "restored." Garnett gathered as many men as he could—which amounted to perhaps a few dozen—and moved south along the Harpers Ferry Road until he found the left flank of Drayton's brigade (No. 2). When the latter advanced, so too did Garnett's band.[30]

Lawrence Branch's command, the second of A. P. Hill's brigades to arrive, had experienced some success when its front line composed of the 7th and 37th North Carolina fired into the flank of the 8th Connecticut and forced its withdrawal. This initial success was cut short when they were hit by a flanking fire, probably from Ewing's regiments sheltered behind the stone wall prior to Archer's charge. A. P. Hill detached another of Branch's regiments, the 28th North Carolina, to help support a battery (probably Reilly's) near the Harpers Ferry Road. When Archer's men charged the stone fence, the 28th North Carolina was ordered forward as well and formed on Archer's right.

Branch, however, was not with his men. After positioning the 18th North Carolina in a hollow behind Archer's front, Branch guided his horse south to higher ground near the left of Maxcy Gregg's brigade to observe the Union position. As soon as he raised his field glasses a bullet entered his head through the right cheek and killed him instantly.[31]

Hill's last two brigades under Brig. Gen. Dorsey Pender and Col. John Brockenbrough moved through the fields to the right and rear of Gregg's scattered front (No. 3). During the drama unfolding on the Rebel right a rather dramatic buildup of Southern artillery took place. No fewer than nine batteries were in action during the last hour of the action. Some, like the guns under Capt. Charles Squires, had been in action near Sharpsburg but had run out of ammunition. Once replenished, the battery rumbled south along the Harpers Ferry Road, unlimbered on the high ground behind Archer's command with several other batteries, and opened fire on the Union troops attempting to cave in the Confederate right and unravel the Army of Northern Virginia.[32]

With all but Crook's brigade out of action, Jacob Cox pondered his dwindling options and decided it was best to end hostilities. "The mass of the enemy on the left continued to increase; new batteries were constantly being opened upon us, and . . . the corps would, without reinforcements, be unable to reach the village of Sharpsburg," he concluded in his battle report. "The attack having already had the effect of a most powerful diversion in favor of the center and right of the army . . . and no supports being at the time available for our exhausted corps, I ordered the troops withdrawn from the exposed ground in front to the cover of the curved hill above the bridge."[33]

Hill's "Light Division" arrived at exactly the right place and time to turn the tide of battle. "The three brigades of my division actively engaged did not number over 2,000 men, and these, with the help of my splendid batteries," Hill wrote in his report, "drove back Burnside's corps . . ."[34]

Withdrawing before an aggressive enemy is a difficult proposition. Cox pushed Ferrero's and Nagle's brigades forward to help extract his embattled units (No. 4). The rookie 35th Massachusetts moved to the fence lining the plowed field and exchanged fire with parts of Toombs' and Branch's brigades, while the rest of Ferrero's men deployed to their left and rear. They were experienced enough to know not to put themselves in harm's way unnecessarily.[35]

The two sides exchanged cannon and small arms for the next several hours until darkness put an end to the fighting. The battle of Antietam— the bloodiest day in American history—was over.

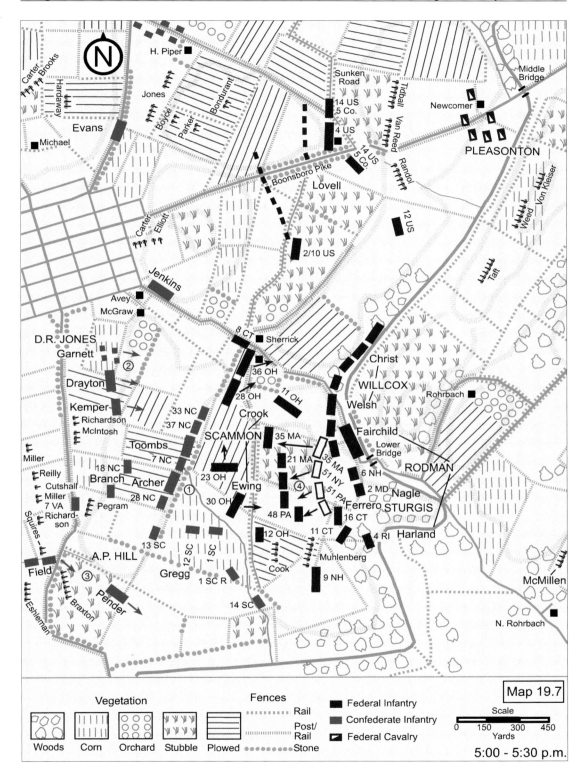

Map 19.7

5:00 - 5:30 p.m.

Map Set 20. Antietam: Evening Stalemate (September 17 - 18, 1862)

Map 20.1: Evening, September 17 & September 18, 1862

America had never experienced a single day of bloodletting like September 17, 1862, and, despite hundreds of subsequent battles in many wars, it has yet to see such a day again. For twelve long hours more than 80,000 men fought over fewer than 1,000 acres of Maryland countryside. According to Ezra Carman's careful analysis, the losses for both armies totaled 22,717. The Confederate Army of Northern Virginia lost 10,316 killed, wounded, missing, and captured, or about 28% of its available strength (including A. P. Hill's division). The Federal Army of the Potomac lost 12,401 to all causes, or about 24% of its effective fighting strength. The dead numbered 3,654 and the burials began right away. Of greater concern were the more than 17,000 wounded who needed immediate care. Many were past any human help and would soon join the ranks of the dead.[1]

The fighting shattered Lee's army. Once some 6,000 stragglers were pushed to the front, the Rebels fielded 25,000 to 30,000. Twenty of Lee's 39 infantry brigades fielded 400 or fewer bayonets by the time the fighting ended. The battle decimated the officer ranks. Three of Lee's nine division commanders, 19 of his 39 brigade leaders, and an astounding 49% of his regimental commanders had been killed or wounded. One of his divisions was led by a colonel, and only two brigades (one led by Dorsey Pender and the other by John Brockenbrough, both of A. P. Hill's division) could be considered fresh.[2]

When Maj. Gen. James Longstreet arrived to join Lee in an evening conference, recalled staff officer Moxely Sorrell, Lee put his arm around him and exclaimed, "Ah! Here is Longstreet; here's my old war-horse!" Like Lee's other lieutenants, Longstreet was frank in his appraisal about the condition of his command. My front, he explained, was manned by "little better than a good skirmish line." He strongly advised a retreat that night. Lee listened to his subordinates before announcing, "Gentlemen,

we will not cross the Potomac tonight. You will go to your respective commands [and] strengthen your forces. . . . If McClellan wants to fight in the morning, I will give him battle again."[3]

Although many writers have called Lee's decision rash and a desperate gamble (or that he somehow "understood" McClellan and "knew" he would not attack), historian Joseph Harsh disagrees. A retreat in the dark across a single ford after such a destructive battle was simply impossible to execute in a single night. With just nine hours until dawn there was not enough time for Lee to organize and withdraw his artillery, wounded, wagons, equipment, and infantry.[4]

While Lee was reorganizing his army Maj. Gen. George McClellan pondered his next move. His I, II, IX, and XII Corps had been roughly handled and were in no shape for offensive action. Only small portions of his V Corps under Maj. Gen. Fitz John Porter and the VI Corps under Maj. Gen. William Franklin had been engaged and were available. McClellan called up portions of his army that were still on the march, including Brig. Gen. Andrew Humphreys' green infantry division and Maj. Gen. Darius Couch's division, which had been left in Pleasant Valley. Some 15,000 militia who reported when the Rebels invaded Maryland were in the state, and McClellan ordered their commander, Brig. Gen. John Reynolds, to march them down to Keedysville.[5]

McClellan agreed to a plan proposed by Franklin on the evening of September 17 to use his VI Corps to capture Nicodeumus Hill on the Confederate left flank the next morning, post Federal artillery there, and drive the enemy off the fields around Sharpsburg. Franklin would then attack around the Dunker Church and West Woods. When McClellan learned that fresh troops would not arrive in time to support Franklin's attack, and that the supply of artillery shells and small arms ammunition was dangerously low, he decided against the operation.[6]

Only fitful skirmishing broke out when dawn arrived on the 18th. The two armies watched each other throughout the day while Lee's wheeled vehicles carried supplies and wounded across the ford. A general withdrawal began that evening when D. R. Jones' division and Nathan Evans' brigade left the front for Blackford (Boteler's) Ford. By 10:00 a.m. on September 19 the last of Lee's army was safely across.[7]

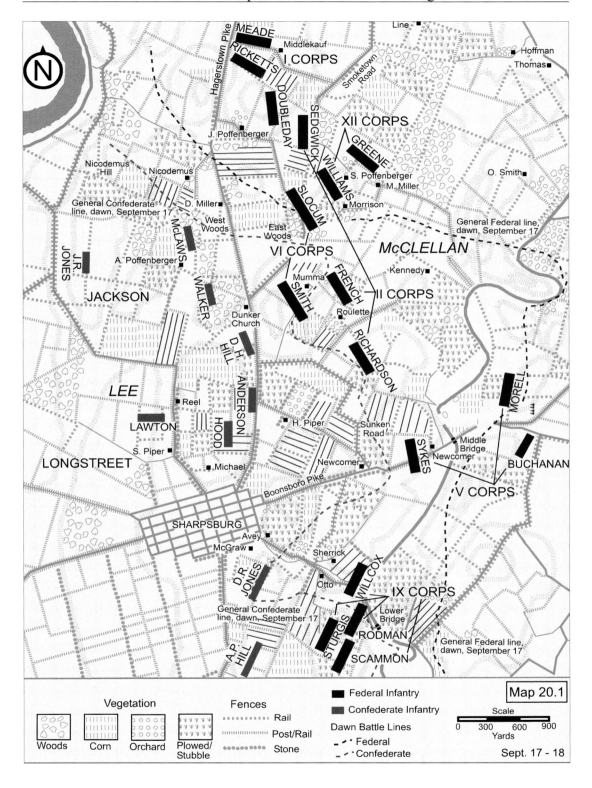

N

MEADE
RICKETTS
I CORPS

Hagerstown Pike

Line
Hoffman
Thomas

Middlekauf

Smoketown Road

DOUBLEDAY

SEDGWICK

XII CORPS

WILLIAMS

GREENE

J. Poffenberger

Nicodemus Hill
Nicodemus

SLOCUM

S. Poffenberger
M. Miller

O. Smith

General Confederate
line, dawn, September 17

D. Miller

West Woods

East Woods

McLAWS

VI CORPS

Morrison

General Federal line,
dawn, September 17

McCLELLAN

A. Poffenberger

WALKER

Mumma

FRENCH

Kennedy

J.R. JONES

JACKSON

SMITH

II CORPS

Roulette

Dunker Church

RICHARDSON

D.H. HILL

ANDERSON

LEE

Reel

HOOD

LAWTON

S. Piper

H. Piper

Sunken Road

MORELL

Michael

SYKES

Middle Bridge
Newcomer

BUCHANAN

LONGSTREET

Newcomer

V CORPS

Boonsboro Pike

SHARPSBURG

Avey
McGraw

Sherrick

WILLCOX

D.R. JONES

Otto

IX CORPS

General Confederate
line, dawn, September 17

STURGIS

Lower Bridge

RODMAN

General Federal line,
dawn, September 17

A.P. HILL

SCAMMON

Vegetation

Woods   Corn   Orchard   Plowed/ Stubble

Fences

.... Rail
|||||||||||| Post/Rail
●●●●●●●●● Stone

■ Federal Infantry
■ Confederate Infantry

Dawn Battle Lines
– ·' Federal
– ·' Confederate

Map 20.1

Scale
0   300   600   900
Yards

Sept. 17 - 18

Map Set 21. Aftermath: The Battle of Shepherdstown
(September 19 - 20, 1862)

Map 21.1: The Federal Artillery Arrives (September 19)

Brig. Gen. William Pendleton's Reserve Artillery and a handful of infantry was crowning the heights of the Potomac River overlooking Blackford's (Boteler's) Ford on the evening of September 18 as the soldiers from Gen. Robert E. Lee's Army of Northern Virginia waded across. The long line of rugged bluffs—steep, rocky, and generally barren—offered the Southern gunners a good artillery platform to cover the difficult withdrawal.

Lee assigned Pendleton the command of his rearguard on September 15, and deployment began the following day. By the time Pendleton finished about 33 guns representing a dozen batteries peppered the heights, supported by 600 exhausted infantry from Col. Marcellus Douglass' brigade (now led by Col. John Lamar of the 61st Georgia) and Brig. Gen. Lewis Armistead's brigade (now under Col. James Hodges of the 14th Virginia). Pendleton had access to another eleven guns if he needed them.[1]

The 53-year-old Pendleton was well known to the army, though few thought much of his military abilities. The West Pointer had matriculated with Lee but left the army soon after graduation for the Episcopal ministry. He joined the Confederacy at the beginning of the war and served on Joseph E. Johnston's staff at First Manassas as chief of artillery. A promotion to brigadier general followed in March of 1862. Lee inherited Pendleton when he assumed command of the primary Eastern Theater army that June. Lee appreciated his former classmate's organizational attributes, but questioned his ability to command guns in the field.[2]

Lee did not believe Maj. Gen. George McClellan would order an aggressive pursuit of his decimated army for two reasons: casualties and caution. "Gen. McClellan had been so crippled at Sharpsburg," Lee explained after the war, "that he could not follow the Confederate Army into Virginia immediately." Lee seems not to have realized that the V and VI Federal corps had only been lightly engaged during the battle. Lee also knew McClellan to be a cautious commander, and so unlikely to order a bold offensive strike—especially without extensive time to organize the operation.[3]

Still, Lee was concerned enough to give Pendleton explicit instructions on September 18, perhaps because the aging artillerist had never led a combined force of infantry and artillery. If Federal guns appeared on the opposite bank of the Potomac River and opened fire, Lee cautioned, Pendleton was to retreat the next morning. If infantry pushed forward, the retreat should begin that evening.[4]

According to a recent study of the engagement at Shepherdstown, Pendleton and his officers did a "superb job" deploying the reserve artillery. Fifteen guns were positioned downriver (below the ford), and eighteen above it. The shorter-range smoothbore pieces were unlimbered closer to the ford in a semicircle arrangement to pound with a deadly crossfire any enemy troops attempting to cross the river. Pendleton stationed his longer-ranged rifled guns on the flanks of his position.[5]

It was after 10:00 a.m. on September 19 when troopers from Brig. Gen. Alfred Pleasonton's cavalry division cautiously approached the river. When they spotted the array of artillery studding the opposite bluffs, Pleasonton deployed three batteries of horse artillery under Capts. Horatio Gibson, John Tidball, and James Robertson on Douglas Hill opposite Shepherdstown. The Union gunners opened fire on Pendleton's positions and threw some of their shells at the withdrawing Confederate infantry trudging toward the town. "It is curious how much louder guns sound when they are pointed at you than when turned the other way!" recalled one of Shepherdstown's residents. The high river banks enhanced the disheartening thunder of the guns. Two more batteries from the Federal reserve artillery under Capts. Robert Langner and Charles Kusserow arrived soon thereafter and took up a position along the ridge just to the east.[6]

Maj. Gen. Fitz John Porter's V Corps, which had seen almost no action at Antietam, followed Lee's retreating army toward the ford.[7]

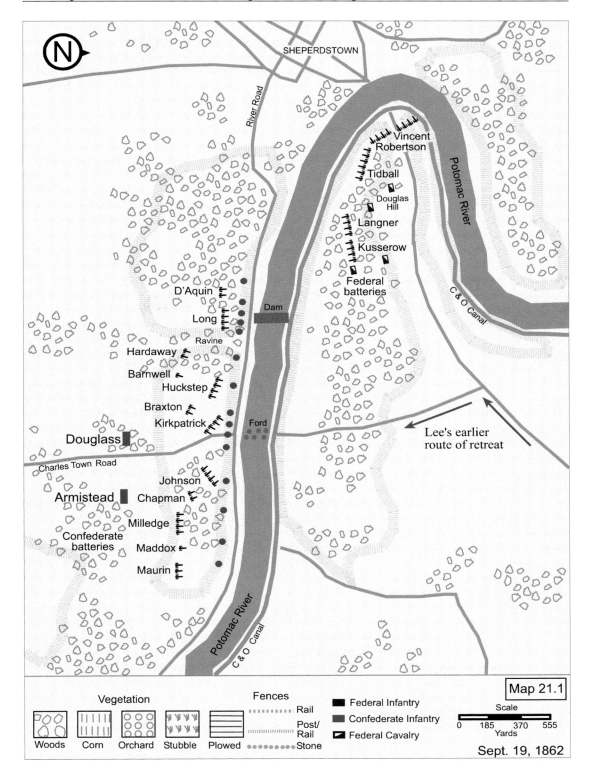

SHEPERDSTOWN

N

River Road

Vincent
Robertson

Tidball

Douglas
Hill

Langner

Kusserow

Federal
batteries

Potomac River

C & O Canal

D'Aquin

Long

Dam

Ravine

Hardaway

Barnwell

Huckstep

Braxton

Kirkpatrick

Ford

Douglass

Charles Town Road

Johnson

Armistead

Chapman

Milledge

Confederate
batteries

Maddox

Maurin

Lee's earlier
route of retreat

Potomac River

C & O Canal

Vegetation

Woods Corn Orchard Stubble Plowed

Fences

.... Rail

Post/
.... Rail
Stone

■ Federal Infantry

■ Confederate Infantry

◣ Federal Cavalry

Map 21.1

Scale

0   185   370   555
Yards

Sept. 19, 1862

Map 21.2: Pendleton is Pressed (September 19: Noon - 3:00 p.m.)

Fitz John Porter took careful note of the Confederate defensive front along the distant bank and decided to "clear the fords, and if possible, secure some of the enemy's artillery." He ordered Pleasonton to remove his cavalry from the area, thereby depriving the mounted arm of the glory their commander craved. V Corps batteries deployed once the horse artillery limbered up and moved out. In order to achieve his goal, Porter lined the banks of "the river and canal . . . with skirmishers and sharpshooters." He selected a portion of the 1st U. S. Sharpshooters and the 2nd Company of Massachusetts Sharpshooters for this task with directions to take out the Rebel artillerymen on the heights. However, they were cautioned not to open fire until the V Corps artillery was in place and in action, "unless the enemy should limber up."

When the Federal skirmishers finally began pulling their triggers, the two Confederate small infantry brigades defending the ford returned fire. Like many of their Federal counterparts, the Southern infantry was deployed along the riverbank. These outfits were woefully under-strength, almost out of ammunition, and led by inexperienced commanders. Col. Douglass had been killed at Sharpsburg and Brig. Gen. Armistead was away on provost guard duty. Of the approximately 600 men, 200 were deployed forward to guard the ford while the balance took shelter behind a hill. Pendleton ordered the colonels "to keep their force at the ford strong, vigilant, and as well sheltered as occasion allowed," and "not to fire merely in reply to shots from the other side, but only to reply any attempt at crossing, and to guard the ford."[8]

Two Federal V Corps batteries under Capt. Stephen Weed and Lt. Alanson Randol deployed directly across from the ford. Weed would later boast of driving away four Confederate batteries that day, but Randol reported that only one of his guns saw action. Porter's First and Second divisions, meanwhile, deployed in the fields behind a screen of trees east of the ford. They had arrived shortly after 1:00 p.m. and by the late afternoon held a front about one mile wide stretching from Douglas Hill on the right to well below Blackford's Ford on the left. Pendleton was only aware that his entire front was being pressed. When battery commanders on his left requested support, he sent 200 men from his reserve infantry to help guard the riverbank. Col. Thomas Munford, whose cavalry was guarding a ford farther down the Potomac River, also felt pressure and asked for infantry assistance. Pendleton sent Munford the 60-man 9th Virginia. Pendleton's entire combined command was now deployed; he had not a man in reserve.[9]

The Federal rifled guns (manned by well-trained artillerists with plenty of ammunition) engaged their counterparts throughout that afternoon. According to a gunner fighting with Capt. Charles Huckstep's Virginia battery near the middle of the Rebel line, the Yankees "brought their long range guns to bear on us and very nearly cut us to pieces while we couldn't hurt them with our little six pounders." The enemy guns, reported Pendleton, allowed Federal foot soldiers to flood the bank of the canal, which "proved to us an evil not slightly trying, since it exposed our nearer cannoneers to be picked off, when servicing their guns, by the enemy's effective infantry rifles."[10]

Under increasing Federal pressure, and with losses mounting and ammunition running low, Pendleton decided to withdraw as soon as possible. When he informed Munford of his decision, the cavalryman assured Pendleton that he would have his troopers at Blackford's Ford by dark. This reassurance allowed Pendleton to plan the withdrawal of his artillery, followed by the thin screen of infantry. The only question remaining was whether or not he could hold his position until sundown.[11]

By late that afternoon, however, Pendleton was feeling better about his prospects of holding out until sunset, but his batteries were suffering considerable damage under the iron barrage. Many of his guns were not returning fire by this time because their gunners had been driven away by the Federal long-range pieces, the sharpshooters, or a combination of both. Brig. Gen. Gouverneur Warren's brigade stationed near the canal on the left of Fitz John Porter's line was especially effective in wreaking havoc among the Rebel gunners and skirmish line.[12]

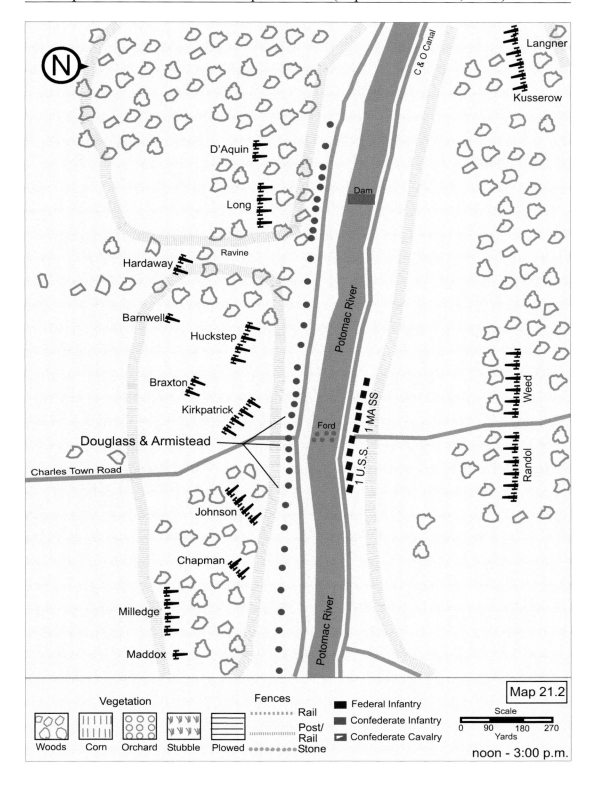

Map 21.2

noon - 3:00 p.m.

Map 21.3: Federal Infantry Crosses the River (September 19: 3:00 - 7:00 pm.)

Pleased with how well the situation was unfolding, Gen. Porter decided to push a body of infantry across the ford to seize the heights and possibly some guns. For that task he tapped Col. Jonathan W. Childs' 300-man 4th Michigan (Brig. Gen. Charles Griffin's brigade, Maj. Gen. George Morell's division). Since 60 or so men of the 1st U.S. Sharpshooters were already near the ford Porter added them as well.

The Wolverines moved down the heights to the open ground leading to the Chesapeake and Ohio Canal, but were exposed for much of the way and paid the price when the now-active Rebel gunners opened on them. When they reached the canal, Col. Childs yelled, "Boys, are you willing to cross and take that battery?" The men screamed back in the affirmative. As they waited for orders to attack, however, several had second thoughts about their mission. "Many of the men bade adieu to home, friends and kindred, concluding the time had come for them to lay down their lives for their country," one Michigander later wrote.[13]

Federal gunners redoubled their fire in preparation for the attack. Pendleton noticed the increasing hail of iron, which "became fiercer than before, and so directed as to rake most of the hollows, as well as the hills we occupied." Yankee infantry near the canal fired so fast it was described as a "continuous roll of musketry." The storm drove the Southern cannoneers from their guns and disabled two pieces.[14]

The increased enemy prompted both Rebel brigade commanders (Cols. Hodges and Lamar) to send couriers to Pendleton. According to these messages, by this time none of the Confederate guns were firing, but the enemy had "twenty-odd" shooting at them. Worse, only the thin gray skirmish line near the river, fewer than 300 men, stood between the Federals and the Southern artillery. This small number surprised Pendleton, who was under the impression that a much larger number of infantry defended the ford. He asked both officers to hold just an hour longer and he would withdraw them just after nightfall. About this same time reports flooded in from his battery commanders, who outlined

their desperate plight and requested to withdraw. Pendleton directed each to hold his position unless he could vacate without being seen.[15]

It was almost dark when the 1st U.S. Sharpshooters and 4th Michigan finally received orders to cross the river. The 5th and 10th New York of Warren's brigade on their left maintained their positions and did not advance. The Sharpshooters found the ford and crossed easily, but not the Michiganders. When they plunged into the river the water came up to the necks of many, soaking their cartridge boxes. "Tho' our guns and ammunition were wet and useless," James Vesey wrote home, "yet on the boys went struggling thro' the water over the uneven bottom." By this time most of the Southern infantry were heading for the rear, so only four Federals were hit while crossing. The Sharpshooters and 4th Michigan halted on the opposite side, formed into a line of battle, and moved up the bluff looking for Rebel guns.[16]

Knots of running Southern foot soldiers told the story, and for Pendleton it was the worst possible scenario: the infantry was retreating and leaving the artillery to its fate. According a recent historian of the battle, after hearing reports that the enemy had crossed the river, "William Nelson Pendleton, in command of every Confederate soldier for miles around him, mounted his horse and left the field with his artillery column." Another historian believed Pendleton left the area because "he did not have a basic understanding of the events at the ford."[17]

The guns under Pendleton's command were trying to make their way to safety. Somehow, most managed to get away. Four were not so lucky. A gun crew with a Parrott rifle from Capt. Victor Maurin's Louisiana battery fell behind during the retreat and got lost. With the enemy closing in the men spiked the piece and left it behind. A second gun was lost when a Federal shell took out the horses of a 6-pounder from Huckstep's battery. A third captured piece, a small howitzer belonging to Capt. Thomas Kirkpatrick's Virginia battery, was on loan from the Virginia Military Institute when lost. Federal division commander Brig. Gen. Charles Griffin was jubilant when he set eyes on the fourth captured piece. The gun had been part of his former battery and lost on the field at First Bull Run more than a year earlier.[18]

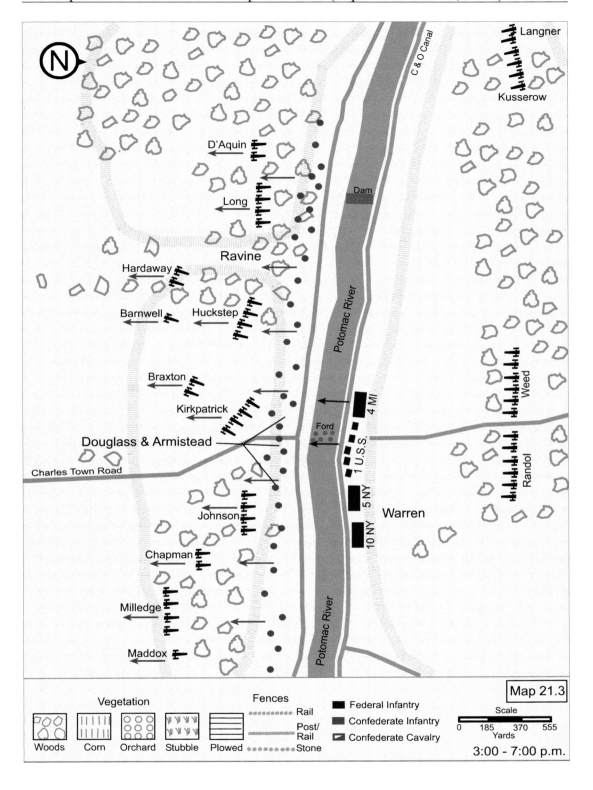

Langner

Kusserow

C & O Canal

D'Aquin

Long

Dam

Ravine

Potomac River

Hardaway

Barnwell   Huckstep

Weed

Braxton

Kirkpatrick

4 MI

Ford

1 U.S.S.

Randol

Douglass & Armistead

Charles Town Road

5 NY

Johnson

Warren

Chapman

10 NY

Milledge

Potomac River

Maddox

Vegetation

Woods   Corn   Orchard   Stubble   Plowed

Fences

········· Rail

Post/ Rail

●●●●●●●●Stone

■ Federal Infantry

■ Confederate Infantry

▨ Confederate Cavalry

Map 21.3

Scale

0   185   370   555
Yards

3:00 - 7:00 p.m.

Map 21.4: Stonewall Jackson Prepares to Attack (Sept. 20: 6:30 - 8:00 a.m.)

Pendleton eventually stumbled across the camp of Brig. Gen. Roger Pryor's brigade. "No one could inform me where Longstreet was," explained the minister-artillerist, so he struck out for army headquarters, which he reached about midnight. Pendleton woke Lee, who listened in stunned silence to the news that his Artillery Reserve had been lost at Shepherdstown.

"All?" asked Lee.

"Yes, General, I fear all," came the reply.

According to a staff officer who witnessed the sad affair, Lee "exhibited no temper, made no reproach that I could hear, either then, or afterwards." The general did tell Pendleton that nothing could be done until morning.[19]

Stonewall Jackson's reaction was quite different. "He took the matter into his own hands," wrote one of his officers, who insisted that "his staff were little out of the saddle that night." A. P. Hill's division was called to arms about 6:30 a.m. on September 20 and marched back to the Potomac. Hill's troops had saved the army just three days earlier when they came up from Harpers Ferry, and they were about to try to save a portion of it once again. Jackson also called up divisions under Jubal Early and D. H. Hill. Although he mentioned something about "Boteler's Ford" to these officers, none of them knew where to find that crossing. They knew of "Blackford's Ford" and "Shepherdstown Ford," but the name Jackson uttered was new to them. They dutifully moved their men back along the Charlestown Road, assuming they would catch sight of A. P. Hill's division and simply follow it to Jackson's desired destination. The frenetic nature of the early morning was especially troubling for Lee because when he woke a large portion of his army was missing and he didn't know where it was. Jackson had not shared his plans with the commanding general.

Jackson reconnoitered alone ahead of Hill's division. He was about a mile from the river when he saw a large Federal unit approaching. Old Jack rode back and deployed Hill's six-brigade division into two long lines. The first line was composed of three brigades, from left to right: Dorsey Pender, Maxcy Gregg, and Edward

Thomas, with three more in a supporting line, from left to right: John Brockenbrough (Field), James Lane, and James Archer. Some of Brig. Gen. Fitz Lee's cavalry protected Hill's right flank.[20]

Jackson had found Federals belonging to Maj. Charles Lovell's brigade (Brig. Gen. George Sykes' division, Porter's V Corps). They were not the first to cross the river that day. At first light, the 4th Michigan, along with the 62nd Pennsylvania and Stephen Weed's Battery I, 5th U.S., splashed across at Blackford's Ford with orders to retrieve abandoned Rebel guns and anything else of value. The troops were exploring the former Rebel positions while V Corps commander Fitz John Porter prepared for a deeper thrust into Virginia. McClellan had sent Porter orders about 10:45 p.m. the previous night that Pleasonton's cavalry was to cross the river first and Porter's infantry thereafter. McClellan ordered Pleasonton to "push your command forward after the enemy as rapidly as possible, using your artillery upon them wherever an opportunity presents, doing them all the damage in your power without incurring too much risk to your command. If great results can be obtained, do not spare your men or horses." There was one complication: Porter had ordered Pleasonton back to Keedysville and Williamsport and he would not be in position to carry out McClellan's orders at dawn. Porter waited for the cavalry to arrive before pushing an infantry brigade from each of his two divisions across the river.[21]

When 7:00 a.m. passed and Pleasonton's cavalry was not in sight, Porter began the advance into Virginia on his own. Maj. Lovell's brigade of U.S. Regulars crossed first. Lovell's command, however, was small and numbered fewer than 1,000 men. Once across the river Lovell arranged his men in a column of fours, scaled the heights, and continued inland. Within a short time the Regulars spotted horsemen in the distance. Lovell knew that Pleasonton's troopers were not up, so he wisely deployed his brigade into a line of battle. Division commander Sykes sent Lovell orders to fall back to the river—a prudent move when the size of the enemy in your front is unknown.[22]

Lovell's men were preparing to fall back when a second Federal brigade under Col. James Barnes (George Morell's division) began crossing shortly after 8:00 a.m.[23]

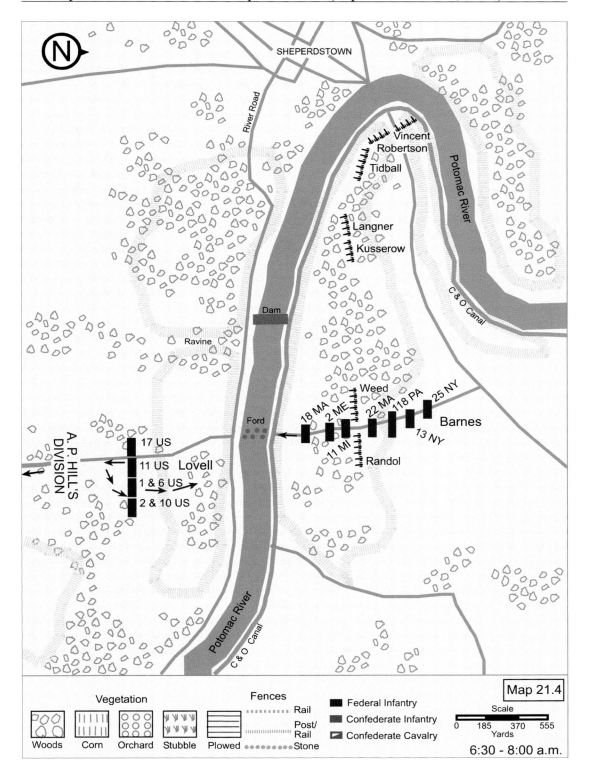

Map 21.4

6:30 - 8:00 a.m.

Map 21.5: Barnes and Lovell Move into Position (Sept. 20: 8:00 - 9:00 a.m.)

The van of Stonewall Jackson's command (A. P. Hill's division) approached the Potomac River about 8:15 a.m. and deployed into line of battle. Col. Barnes' Federal brigade was crossing the river about the same time to provide support for Maj. Lovell's brigade, which was already falling back toward the ford. By the time they reached the heights overlooking the river, all of Lovell's regiments were deployed east (left) of the Charlestown Road, with only the 17th U.S. Regulars on the opposite (west) side of the road.

When Gregg's South Carolinians advancing in the middle of A. P. Hill's first line stepped within range, the Regulars leveled their weapons and opened fire. The men of the consolidated 2nd and 10th U.S. Regulars on Lovell's left flank were told in no uncertain terms to "hold that position at all hazards" because if they lost it, the entire brigade line would be turned and thrown backward into the river or captured.[24]

Lovell welcomed Barnes' arrival when his large brigade scaled the heights behind him. Porter had originally ordered Barnes to occupy Shepherdstown. The unexpected arrival of heavy enemy infantry near the bluffs overlooking the river, however, convinced Brig. Gen. Sykes to direct Barnes to remain near the ford. When his first regiment, the 18th Massachusetts, appeared on the Virginia side of the river, Barnes ordered its commander to occupy a position "near but below the top of the ridge." This would both support Lovell's men and provide the Bay Staters with protection. The regiment used a ravine to ascend the ridge to their new position.[25]

Barnes' other regiments also made the slow and difficult climb to the top of the ridge and fell into position. The 2nd Maine formed on the far left of the brigade just to the right of Lovell's 17th U.S. Regulars and on the left of its sister regiment, the 18th Massachusetts. The balance of the regiments, the 1st Michigan, 22nd Massachusetts, 118th Pennsylvania, 13th New York, and 25th New York, extended the line to the right. The rugged terrain left gaps between the regiments. The brigade totaled nearly 1,700 effectives, with almost 800 of them in the new 118th Pennsylvania, which was also known as the

"Corn Exchange Regiment." The men were so new that they had only recently been issued Enfield rifles, which they had yet to fire.[26]

Brig. Gen. Pender commanded A. P. Hill's first line of battle of three brigades, with Brig. Gen. James Archer in charge of the second supporting line of three brigades. Pender reformed the ranks of the battle line and sent it forward across fairly open and undulating terrain. Few could have imagined what was about to transpire.

Within minutes, white clouds of smoke filled the heights on the Maryland side of the river and artillery shells screamed above the Southern infantry. A. P. Hill described the bombardment as "the most tremendous fire of artillery I ever saw." He proudly stated in his after-battle report that "too much praise cannot be awarded my regiments for their steady, unwavering step." The barrage also impressed a Federal observer, who concluded, "Their loss from our artillery fire must have been heavy, as the explosion of our shells were seen to make large gaps in their lines." A soldier in the 14th South Carolina, Gregg's brigade, confirmed the observation when he recalled that "our brave troops moved steadily on, closing up their ranks as first one comrade & then another would be stricken down." The cannonade was especially unnerving, he continued, because "it was time to put to test the mettle of the most courageous, as they had no chance to discharge a single gun." The Federal shelling killed or wounded about 300 men in Hill's first line in fewer than fifteen minutes.[27]

Most of Barnes' large brigade was hidden on the opposite side of the ridge. Lovell's command was deployed on top of the ridge and so particularly conspicuous. Gregg's brigade moved against its front and Thomas' brigade obliqued to take on its flank. About this time the large green 118th Pennsylvania moved up to the top of the ridge. For some reason Col. Charles Provost seems to have misunderstood his orders, and in doing so attracted Dorsey Pender's attention. The regiment was so large that Pender worried it would overlap his left flank. He called upon Archer to bring up the second line in close support.[28]

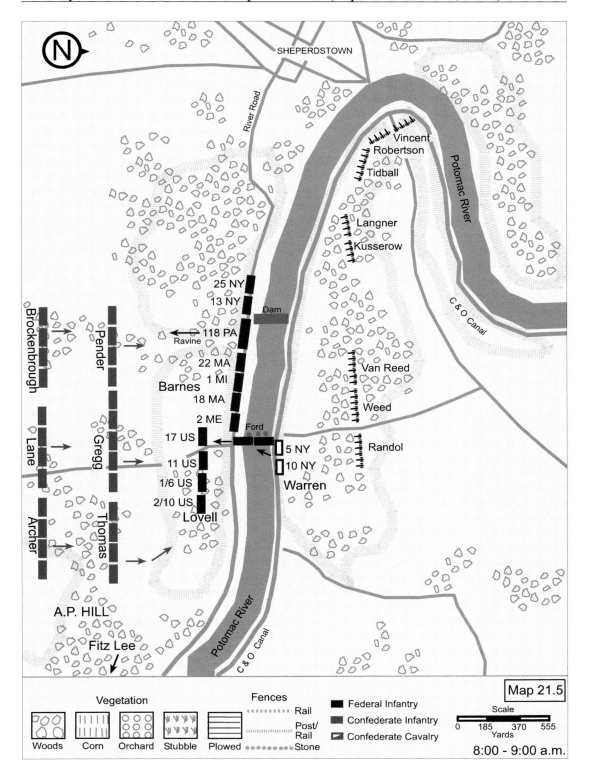

Map 21.5

8:00 - 9:00 a.m.

Map 21.6: The Federal Retreat Begins (Sept. 20: 9:00 - 9:30 a.m.)

Additional Confederate units arrived at the front in the form of Jubal Early's division. Early sent his own brigade and another under Harry Hays to the right of the Charlestown Road while James Walker's (Trimble's) moved to the left.[29]

The advancing Southern infantry in front, coupled with Federal artillery fire that was hitting some of his own men, convinced Lovell to withdraw his command to the reverse side of the ridge. Barnes' men to his right were also being pounded by errant Federal shells. Only a determined effort by various officers and men ended the friendly fire episode.

The Yankees were not the only ones who breathed a sigh of relief when the shelling finally stopped. Pender had allowed his men to take shelter against the side of the ridge to avoid the iron rain. Once the deadly artillery firing ended Pender ordered his troops forward toward the river. Federal infantry who ventured atop the ridge were exposed to a hail of gunfire from Pender's North Carolinians. When he spotted the closing enemy, Col. William Tilton of the 22nd Massachusetts ordered his men to fix bayonets and prepare to halt the advance. The Bay Staters slipped up to the top of the ridge and propped their elbows on the ground. When Pender moved within 200 yards Tilton ordered his men to open fire. The volley knocked scores of Rebels off their feet. "[W]e gave them such a shower of bullets that they had to leave us & flank off to our right, where the 118 Penn Reg . . . were," recalled a Federal. Working in tandem with the 1st Michigan on their left, Tilton's men reloaded and continued firing.[30]

With some of the pressure alleviated, the 18th Massachusetts on the left of the 1st Michigan scrambled to the top of the ridge and poured a volley into the Tar Heels as they moved to the left (possibly to fill in large gaps caused by Federal volleys). Meanwhile, Warren's small brigade (Sykes' division) composed of the 5th and 10th New York splashed across the ford and marched quickly for Lovell's exposed left flank.[31]

V Corps commander Fitz John Porter watched the action through his field glasses from the opposite side of the river as his 3,000 infantry gamely battled the enemy. Porter was especially concerned about the additional Rebel troops coming up behind Hill [Early]. There was little to gain by continuing the combat and the Potomac River immediately behind his men posed a threat to every Federal on the far bank. Porter decided to break off the action and ordered his troops to re-cross the river. This would not be easy because the troops had to descend the steep ridge and then cross the wide Potomac. It was unlikely that Hill's veteran infantry would allow them the luxury of time to do so in an orderly fashion, and would instead line the ridge and fire down upon them. Some of the Federals, like Capt. Frank Donaldson of the 118th Pennsylvania, later compared their plight to the disastrous battle of Ball's Bluff fought a year earlier.[32]

The left side of the Federal line (Lovell's and Warren's brigades) fell back first without mishap, although Gregg's South Carolinians began lining the heights and firing at the helpless Northern troops as they crossed the river at the ford. Federal batteries opened fire, driving Gregg's Palmetto troops off the ridge.

It was at this point in the fighting that many Federals began to fully appreciate just how vulnerable they were to being killed, wounded, or captured. The crossing, explained one soldier, "was done in pretty in good order . . . but . . . the enemy could have slaughtered the Regular Army of the East but they was afraid of our artillery and kept back which gave us a chance to regain the Maryland shore in safety."[33]

The withdrawing Federals were making their way across the river when Col. Thomas Stockton's brigade passed them on its way to the Virginia side. Stockton was following his orders. Half of his brigade was in the middle of the Potomac when Stockton was directed to stop his movement and return immediately to the Maryland shore. Not a single Federal soldier regretted the new orders.[34]

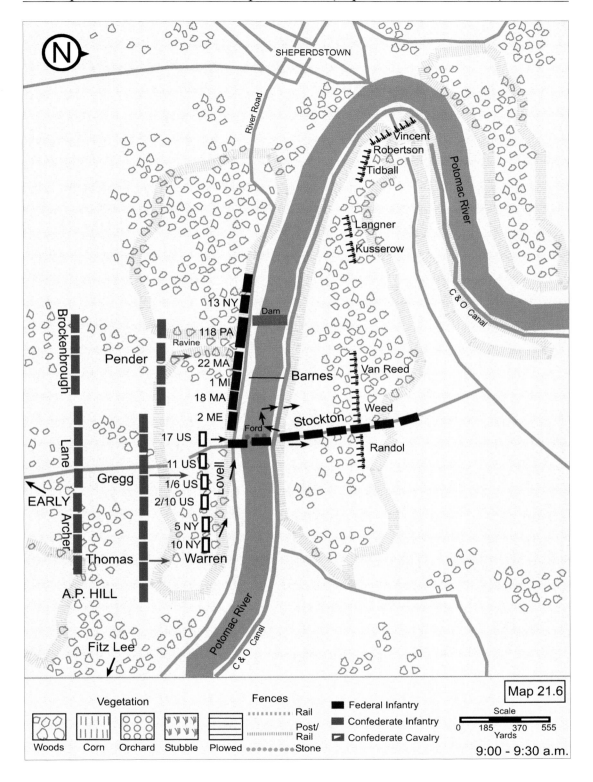

Map 21.6

9:00 - 9:30 a.m.

Map 21.7: The 118th Pennsylvania's Ordeal (Sept. 20: 9:30 – 10:30 a.m.)

As Lovell's and Warren's brigades re-crossed the Potomac River, Col. Barnes' men held their positions on the ridge between Blackford's Ford and the dam as Confederate pressure against them intensified.

When he spotted the withdrawal on his left already well underway, Lt. Col. Joseph Hayes of the 18th Massachusetts ordered one of his men to find Col. Barnes and request orders. He hoped the brigade commander would order his men to vacate their increasingly vulnerable position. One Federal wrote home that his regiment was "fighting the rebels at close quarters who were rushing down in on us in greatly superior numbers & I saw the rear of Sykes column passing up the opposite bank of the river, while I saw our brigade fighting the enemy at the same time." When it arrived, Barnes' order to vacate was especially welcomed by Hayes' 18th Massachusetts, which had just been ordered to prepare to counterattack with bayonets. Because of the protective terrain, the Bay Stater regiment had thus far lost only three killed and 11 wounded.[35]

While the regiments making up the left side of Barnes's brigade line filed down the ridge and crossed via Blackford's Ford, the 22nd Massachusetts in the center and the two regiments on the right, the 13th and 25th New York, moved down the ravine to cross over the dam. The water was very deep and swift around the dam and the bottom studded with sharp rocks and deep holes. Many of Pender's North Carolinians and Rebels from other brigades mounted the abandoned high ground to fire into the retreating enemy. Once on the Maryland side of the river the Federals used the banks of the C & O Canal as cover from the Confederate small arms fire.[36]

Unfortunately, not all of Barnes's men received the orders to retreat. The large and inexperienced 118th Pennsylvania remained exposed on top of the ridge. When the hundreds of green Pennsylvanians leveled their muskets in the direction of Pender's North Carolinians and pulled their triggers, only then did they discover that many of them were defective.[37]

Many of these Pennsylvanians would soon be dead because of the intransigence of the 118th's commmander Col. Charles Prevost. Col. Barnes sent his adjutant, Lt. Walter Davis, to the right side of his line to inform the 13th and 25th New York regiments to withdraw. When Davis saw that Prevost's 118th Pennsylvania was not pulling back, he instructed the first officer he saw, Lt. Henry Kelly, "Tell Colonel Prevost that Colonel Barnes directs that he withdraw his regiment at once," and then continued his ride to find the two New York regiments. Kelly found Prevost and gave him the orders. The news perplexed Prevost, who had recently spoken with his brigade commander, who had said nothing about a withdrawal. "From whom did you say you heard this?" asked Prevost. When Kelly responded that it was Barnes' staff officer Davis, Prevost blurted out, "I do not receive orders that way. If Colonel Barnes has any order to give me, let his aide come to me!"[38]

Within minutes Brockenbrough's (Field's) and Lane's brigades were wrapping themselves around the right flank of Prevost's 118th Pennsylvania, while Archer's brigade attacked its front. Prevost refused his right to deal with the threat. When other Pennsylvanians down the line saw the move they thought it was a retreat and headed to the edge of the ridge. Prevost intervened to rally them back into the ranks. A bullet tore into Prevost's shoulder, coming to rest near his spine. When Barnes found the wounded regimental commander at the bottom of the ridge and realized the 118th's predicament, he rode up the ridge and ordered the men to beat a hasty retreat. Many of the green soldiers of the "Corn Exchange" regiment were gunned down as they tried to make their way to safety. More than 164 were killed or wounded and another 100 captured.[39]

The return of Porter's men to the Maryland side of the river ended the sharp Shepherdstown fight. The Confederates suffered 307 killed and wounded, and the Federals counted 366. Jackson's counterattack blunted the Federal attempt to cross the Potomac and engage Lee's exhausted army.[40]

The Maryland Campaign of 1862 was finally over.

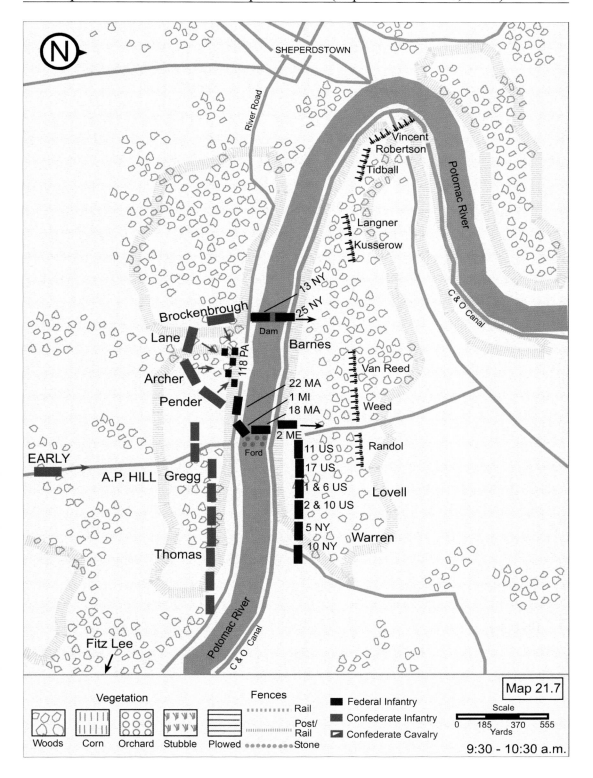

Orders of Battle

Harpers Ferry Garrison

Col. Dixon Miles

First Brigade
Col. Frederick D'Utassy

65th Illinois, Col. Daniel Cameron
39th New York, Maj. Hugo Hildebrandt
111th New York, Col. Jesse Segoine
115th New York, Col. Simeon Sammon
15th Indiana Battery, Capt. John Von Sehlen

Second Brigade
Col. William Trimble

126th New York, Col. Eliakim Sherrill
60th Ohio, Lt. Col. Noah Hixon
9th Vermont, Col. George Stannard
Ohio Battery, Capt. Benjamin Potts

Third Brigade
Col. Thomas Ford

1st Maryland Potomac Home Guard (Battalion),
Maj. John Steiner
3rd Maryland Potomac Home Guard,
Lt. Col. Stephen Downey
32nd Ohio, Col. Thomas Ford
5th New York Heavy Artillery, Co. F,
Capt. Eugene McGrath
1st Maryland Cavalry (detachment),
Capt. Charles Russell
7th Squadron, Rhode Island Cavalry, Maj. A. Corliss

Fourth Brigade
Col. William Ward

12th New York (militia), Col. William Ward
125th New York, Col. George Willard
87th Ohio, Col. Henry Banning
1st Potomac Home Guard, Col. William Maulsby
8th New York Cavalry, Col. Benjamin Davis
5th New York Heavy Artillery, Co. A, Capt. J. Graham

Indiana Battery, Capt. Silas Rigby

Unattached Commands

1st Maryland Potomac Home Guard Cavalry,
Maj. Henry Cole
12th Illinois Cavalry, Col. Hasbrouck Davis
2nd Illinois Artillery, Capt. John Phillips

Antietam Order of Battle

ARMY OF THE POTOMAC
Major General George B. McClellan

First Army Corps
Maj. Gen. Joseph Hooker
Brig. Gen. George G. Meade

First Division
Brig. Gen. Rufus King
Brig. Gen. John P. Hatch
Gen. Abner Doubleday

First Brigade
Col. Walter Phelps, Jr.

22d New York, Lt. Col. John McKie, Jr
24th New York, Capt John D. O'Brian
30th New York, Col. William M. Searing
84th New York (14th Militia), Maj. W. H. de Bevoise
2d U. S. Sharpshooters, Col. Henry A. V. Post

Second Brigade
Brig. Gen. Abner Doubleday
Col. William P. Wainwright
Lt. Col. J. William Hofmann

7th Indiana, Maj. Ira G. Grover
76th New York, Col. William P. Wainwright
95th New York, Maj. Edward Pye
56th Pennsylvania: Lt. Col. J. William Hofmann

Third Brigade
Gen. Marsena R. Patrick

21st New York, Col. William F. Rogers
23d New York, Col. Henry C. Hoffman
35th New York, Col. Newton B Lord
80th New York (20th Militia),
Lt. Col. Theodore B. Gates

Fourth Brigade
Brig. Gen. John Gibbon

19th Indiana, Col. Solomon Meredith
2d Wisconsin, Col. Lucius Fairchild
6th Wisconsin, Lt.. Col. Edward S. Bragg
7th Wisconsin, Capt. John B. Callis

Artillery
Capt. J. Albert Monroe

New Hampshire Light, First Battery,
Lt. Frederick M. Edgell
1st Rhode Island Light, Battery D,
Capt. J. Albert Monroe
1st New York Light, Battery L, Capt. John A Reynolds
4th United States, Battery B, Capt. Joseph B. Campbell

Second Division
Brig. Gen. James B. Ricketts

First Brigade
Brig. Gen. Abram Duryea
97th New York, Maj. Charles Northrup
104th New York, Maj. Lewis C. Skinner
105th New York, Col. Howard Carroll
107th Pennsylvania, Capt. James Mac Thomson

Second Brigade
Col. William A. Christian
Col. Peter Lyle

26th New York, Lt. Col. Richard H
26th New York, Lt. Col. Richard H. Richardson
94th New York, Lt. Col. Calvin Littlefield
88th Pennsylvania, Lt. Col. George W. Gile
90th Pennsylvania, Col. Peter Lyle

Third Brigade
Brig. Gen. George L. Hartsuff
Col. Richard Coulter

16th Maine, Col. Asa W. Wildes
12th Massachusetts, Maj. Elisha Burbank
13th Massachusetts, Maj. J. Parker Gould
83d New York (9th Militia), Lt.. Col. William Atterbury
11th Pennsylvania, Col. Richard Coulter

Artillery
1st Pennsylvania Light, Battery F,
Capt. Ezra W. Matthews
Pennsylvania Light, Battery C, Capt. James Thompson

Third Division
Brig. Gen. George G. Meade
Brig. Gen. Truman Seymour

First Brigade
Brig. Gen. Truman Seymour
Col. R. Biddle Roberts

1st Pennsylvania Reserves, Col. R. Biddle Roberts
2d Pennsylvania Reserves, Capt. James N. Byrnes
5th Pennsylvania Reserves, Col. Joseph W. Fisher
6th Pennsylvania Reserves, Col. William Sinclair
13th Pennsylvania Reserves (1st Rifles),
Col. Hugh W. McNeil

Second Brigade
Col. Albert Magilton

3d Pennsylvania Reserves, Lt. Col. John Clark
4th Pennsylvania Reserves, Maj. John Nyce
7th Pennsylvania Reserves, Col. Henry C. Bolinger
8th Pennsylvania Reserves, Maj. Silas M Bailey

Third Brigade
Col. Thomas F. Gallagher
Lt. Col. Robert Anderson

9th Pennsylvania Reserves, Lt. Col. Robert Anderson
10th Pennsylvania Reserves, Lt. Col. Adoniram Warner
11th Pennsylvania Reserves, Lt. Col. S. M. Jackson
12th Pennsylvania Reserves, Capt. Richard Gustin

Artillery
1st Pennsylvania Light, Battery A, Lt.. John Simpson
1st Pennsylvania Light, Battery B, Capt. James Cooper
1st Pennsylvania Light, Battery G, Lt.. Frank Amsden
5th United States, Battery C, Capt. Dunbar R. Ransom

Second Army Corps
Maj. Gen. Edwin V. Sumner

First Division
Maj. Gen. Israel B. Richardson
Brig. Gen John C. Caldwell
Brig. Gen. Winfield S. Hancock

First Brigade
Brig. Gen. John C. Caldwell

5th New Hampshire, Col. Edward E. Cross
7th New York, Capt. Charles Brestel
61st/64th New York, Col. Francis C. Barlow
81st Pennsylvania, Maj. H. Boyd McKeen

Second Brigade
Brig. Gen. Thomas F. Meagher
Col. John Burke

29th Massachusetts, Lt. Col. Joseph H. Barnes
63d New York, Col. John Burke
69th New York, Lt. Col. James Kelly
88th New York, Lt. Col. Patrick Kelly

Third Brigade
Col. John R. Brooke

2d Delaware, Capt. David L. Stricker
52d New York, Col. Paul Frank
57th New York, Lt. Col. Philip J. Parisen
66th New York, Capt. Julius Wehle
53d Pennsylvania, Lt. Col. Richards McMichael

Artillery
1st New York Light, Battery B, Capt. Rufus D. Pettit
4th U. S., Batteries A/C, Lt. Evan Thomas

Second Division
Maj. Gen. John Sedgwick
Brig. Gen. Oliver O. Howard

First Brigade
Brig. Gen. Willis A. Gorman

15th Massachusetts, Lt. Col. John W. Kimball
1st Minnesota, Col. Alfred Sully
34th New York, Col. James A. Suiter
82d New York (2d Militia), Col. Henry W. Hudson
Massachusetts Sharpshooters, 1st Co.,
    Capt. John Saunders
Minnesota Sharpshooters, 2nd Co.,
    Capt. William F. Russell

Second Brigade
Brig. Gen. Oliver O. Howard
Col. Joshua T. Owen
Col. De Witt C. Baxter

69th Pennsylvania, Col. Joshua T. Owen
71st Pennsylvania, Col. Isaac J. Wistar
72d Pennsylvania, Col. Dewitt C. Baxter
106th Pennsylvania, Col. Turner G. Morehead

Third Brigade
Brig. Gen. Napoleon J. T. Dana
Col. Norman J. Hall

19th Massachusetts, Col. Edward W. Hinks
20th Massachusetts, Col. William R. Lee
7th Michigan, Col. Norman J. Hall
42d New York, Lt. Col. George N. Bornford
59th New York, Col. William L. Tidball

Artillery
1st Rhode Island Light, Battery A, Capt. J. Tompkins
1st United States, Battery I, Lt. George A. Woodruff

Third Division
Brig. Gen. William H. French

First Brigade
Brig. Gen. Nathan Kimball

14th Indiana, Col. William Harrow
8th Ohio, Lt.. Col. Franklin Sawyer
132d Pennsylvania, Col. Richard A. Oakford
7th West Virginia, Col. Joseph Snider

Second Brigade
Col. Dwight Morris

14th Connecticut, Lt. Col. Sanford H. Perkins
108th New York, Col. Oliver H. Palmer
130th Pennsylvania, Col. Henry I. Zinn

Third Brigade
Brig. Gen. Max Weber
Col. John W. Andrews

1st Delaware, Col. John W. Andrews
5th Maryland, Maj. Leopold Blumenberg
4th New York, Lt. Col. John D. McGregor

Unattached Artillery
1st New York Light, Battery G, Capt. John D. Frank
1st Rhode Island Light, Battery B, Capt. J. G. Hazard
1st Rhode Island Light, Battery G, Capt. Charles Owen

Fourth Army Corps

First Division
Maj. Gen. Darius N. Couch

First Brigade
Brig. Gen. Charles Devens, Jr.

7th Massachusetts, Col. David A. Russell
10th Massachusetts, Col. Henry L. Eustis
36th New York, Col. William H. Browne
2d Rhode Island, Col. Frank Wheaton

Second Brigade
Brig. Gen, Albion P. Howe

62d New York, Col. David J. Nevin
93d Pennsylvania, Col. James M. McCarter
98th Pennsylvania, Col. John F. Ballier
102d Pennsylvania, Col. Thomas A. Rowley
139th Pennsylvania, Col. Frank H. Collier

Third Brigade
Brig. Gen. John Cochrane

65th New York, Col. Alexander Shaler
67th New York, Col. Julius W. Adams
122d New York, Col. Silas Titus
23d Pennsylvania, Col. Thomas H. Neill
61st Pennsylvania, Col. George C. Spear
82d Pennsylvania, Col. David H. Williams

Artillery
New York Light, Third Battery, Capt. William Stuart
1st Pennsylvania Light, Battery C, Capt. J. McCarthy
1st Pennsylvania Light, Battery D, Capt. Michael Hall
2d United States, Battery G, Lt. John H. Butler

Fifth Army Corps
Maj. Gen. Fitz John Porter

First Division
Maj. Gen. George W. Morell

First Brigade
Col. James Barnes

2d Maine, Col. Charles W. Roberts
18th Massachusetts, Lt. Col. Joseph Hayes
22d Massachusetts, Lt. Col. William S. Tilton

1st Michigan, Capt. Emory W. Belton
13th New York, Col. Elisha G. Marshall
25th New York, Col. Charles A. Johnson
118th Pennsylvania, Col. Charles M. Prevost
Massachusetts Sharpshooters, Second Co.,
    Capt. Lewis E. Wentworth

Second Brigade
Brig. Gen. Charles Griffin
2d District Of Columbia, Col. Charles M. Alexander
9th Massachusetts, Col. Patrick R. Guiney
32d Massachusetts, Col. Francis J. Parker
4th Michigan, Col. Jonathan W. Childs
14th New York, Col. James McQuade
62d Pennsylvania, Col. Jacob B. Sweitzer

Third Brigade
Col. T. B. W. Stockton
20th Maine, Col. Adelbert Ames
16th Michigan, Lt. Col. Norval E. Welch
12th New York, Capt. William Huson
17th New York, Lt.. Col. Nelson B. Bartram
44th New York, Maj. Freeman Conner
83d Pennsylvania, Capt. Orpheus S. Woodward
Michigan Sharpshooters, Brady's Co.,
    Lt. Jonas H. Titus, Jr.

Artillery
Massachusetts Light, Battery C, Capt. A. P. Martin
1st Rhode Island Light, Battery C, Capt. R. Waterman
5th United States, Battery D, Lt. Charles E. Hazlett

Sharpshooters
1st United States, Capt. John B. Isler

Second Division
Brig. Gen. George Sykes

First Brigade
Lt. Col. Robert C. Buchanan
3d United States, Capt. John D. Wilkins
4th United States, Capt. Hiram Dryer
12th United States, First Battalion, Capt. M. M. Blunt
12th United States, Second Battalion,
    Capt. T. M. Anderson
14th United States, First Battalion, Capt. W. H. Brown
14th United States Second Battalion,
    Capt. D. B. McKibbin

Second Brigade
Maj. Charles S. Lovell

1st And 6th United States, Capt. Levi C. Bootes
2d And 10th United States, Capt. John S. Poland
11th United States, Maj. De Lancey Floyd-Jones
17th United States, Maj. George L. Andrews

Third Brigade
Col. Gouverneur K. Warren

5th New York, Capt. Cleveland Winslow
10th New York, Lt. Col. John W. Marshall

Artillery
1st United States, Batteries E/G, Lt. A. M. Randol
5th United States, Battery I, Capt. Stephen H. Weed
5th United States, Battery K, Lt. William E. Van Reed

Third Division
Brig. Gen. Andrew A. Humphreys

First Brigade
Brig. Gen. Erastus B. Tyler

91st Pennsylvania, Col. Edgar M. Gregory
126th Pennsylvania, Col. James G. Elder
129th Pennsylvania, Col. Jacob G. Frick
134th Pennsylvania, Col. Matthew S. Quay

Second Brigade
Col. Peter H. Allabach

123d Pennsylvania, Col. John B. Clark
131st Pennsylvania, Lt. Col. William B. Shaut
133d Pennsylvania, Col. Franklin B. Speakman
155th Pennsylvania, Col. Edward J. Allen

Artillery
Capt. Lucius N. Robinson
1st New York Light, Battery C, Capt. Alaout Barnes
1st Ohio Light, Battery L, Capt. Lucius N. Robinson

Artillery Reserve
Lt. Col. William Hays

1st Battalion New York Light, Battery A, Lt. B. Wever
1st Battalion New York Light., Battery B,
|Lt. Alfred Von Kleiser
1st Battalion New York Light, Battery C,

Capt. Robert Langner
1st Battalion New York Light, Battery D,
Capt. Charles Kusserow
New York Light, Fifth Battery, Capt. Elijah D. Taft
1st United States, Battery K, Capt. William M. Graham
4th United States, Battery G, Lt. Marcus P. Miller

Sixth Army Corps
Maj. Gen. William B. Franklin

First Division
Maj. Gen. Henry W. Slocum

First Brigade
Col. Alfred T. A. Torbert

1st New Jersey, Lt. Col. Mark W. Collet
2d New Jersey, Col. Samuel L. Buck
3d New Jersey, Col. Henry W. Brown
4th New Jersey, Col. William B. Hatch

Second Brigade
Col. Joseph J. Bartlett

5th Maine, Col. Nathaniel J. Jackson
16th New York, Lt. Col. Joel J. Seaver
27th New York, Lt. Col. Alexander D. Adams
96th Pennsylvania, Col. Henry L. Cake
121st New York, Col. Richard Franchot

Third Brigade
Brig. Gen. John Newton

18th New York, Lt. Col. George R. Myers
31st New York, Lt. Col. Francis E. Pinto
32d New York, Col. Roderick Matheson
96th Pennsylvania, Col. Gustavus W. Town

Artillery
Capt. Emory Upton
Maryland Light, Battery A, Capt. John W. Wolcott
Massachusetts Light, Battery A, Capt. Josiah Porter
New Jersey Light, Battery A, Capt. William Hexamer
2d United States, Battery D, Lt. Edward B. Williston

Second Division
Maj. Gen. William F. Smith

First Brigade
Brig. Gen. Winfield S. Hancock
Col. Amasa Cobb

6th Maine, Col. Hiram Burnham
43d New York, Maj. John Wilson
49th Pennsylvania, Lt. Col. William Brisbane
137th Pennsylvania, Col. Henry M. Bossert
5th Wisconsin, Col. Amasa Cobb

Second Brigade
Brig. Gen. W. T. H. Brooks

2d Vermont, Maj. James H. Walbridge
3d Vermont, Col. Breed N. Hyde
4th Vermont, Lt. Col. Charles B. Stoughton
5th Vermont, Col. Lewis A. Grant
6th Vermont, Maj. Oscar L. Tuttle

Third Brigade
Col. William H. Irwin

7th Maine, Maj. Thomas W Hyde
20th New York, Col. Ernest Von Vegesack
33d New York, Lt. Col. Joseph W. Coming
49th New York, Lt. Col. William C. Alberger
77th New York, Capt. Nathan S. Babcock

Artillery
Capt. Romeyn B. Ayres

Maryland Light, Battery B, Lt. Theodore J. Vanneman
New York Light, 1st Battery, Capt. Andrew Cowan
5th United States, Battery F, Lt. Leonard Martin

Ninth Army Corps
Maj. Gen. Ambrose E. Burnside
Maj Gen. Jesse L. Reno
Brig. Gen. Jacob D. Cox

First Division
Brig. Gen. Orlando B. Willcox

First Brigade
Col. Benjamin C. Christ

28th Massachusetts, Capt. Andrew P. Caraher
17th Michigan, Col. William H. Withington
79th New York, Lt.. Col. David Morrison
50th Pennsylvania, Maj. Edward Overton

Second Brigade
Col. Thomas Welsh

8th Michigan, Lt. Col. Frank Graves
46th New York, Lt. Col. Joseph Gerhardt
45th Pennsylvania, Lt. Col. John I. Curtin
100th Pennsylvania, Lt. Col. David A. Leckey

Artillery

Massachusetts Light, Eighth Battery, Capt. A. M. Cook
2d United States, Battery E, Lt. Samuel N. Benjamin

Second Division
Brig. Gen. Samuel D. Sturgis

First Brigade
Brig. Gen. James Nagle

2d Maryland, Lt. Col. J. Eugene Duryea
6th New Hampshire, Col. Simon G. Griffin
9th New Hampshire, Col. Enoch Q. Fellows
48th Pennsylvania, Lt. Col. Joshua K. Sigfried

Second Brigade
Brig. Gen. Edward Ferrero

21st Massachusetts, Col. William S. Clark
35th Massachusetts, Col. Edward A. Wild
51st New York, Col. Robert B. Potter
51st Pennsylvania, Col. John F. Hartranft

Artillery

Pennsylvania Light, Battery D, Capt. George W. Durell
4th United States, Battery E, Capt. Joseph C. Clark, Jr.

Third Division
Brig. Gen. Isaac P. Rodman

First Brigade
Col. Harrison S. Fairchild

9th New York, Lt.. Col. Edgar A. Kimball
89th New York, Maj Edward Jardine
103d New York, Maj Benjamin Ringold

Second Brigade
Col. Edward Harland
8th Connecticut, Lt. Col. Hiram Appelman
11th Connecticut, Col. Henry W. Kingsbury

16th Connecticut, Col. Francis Beach
4th Rhode Island, Col. William H. P. Steere

Artillery

5th United States, Battery A, Lt. Charles P. Muhlenberg

Kanawha Division
Brig. Gen. Jacob D. Cox
Col. Eliakim P. Scammon

First Brigade
Col. Hugh Ewing

12th Ohio, Col. Carr B. White
23d Ohio, Lt. Col. Rutherford B. Hayes
30th Ohio, Col. Hugh Ewing
Ohio Light Artillery, First Battery, Capt. J. R. McMullin
Gilmore's Co. West Virginia Cavalry, Lt.. J. Abraham
Harrison's Co. West Virginia Cavalry, Lt.. D. Delaney

Second Brigade
Col. George Crook

11th Ohio, Lt. Col. Augustus H, Coleman
28th Ohio, Lt. Col. Gottfried Becker
36th Ohio, Lt. Col. Melvin Clarke
Schambeck's Co. Chicago Dragoons,
    Capt. Frederick Schambeck
Kentucky Light Artillery, Simmonds' Battery,
    Capt. Seth J. Simmonds

Unattached

6th New York Cavalry (Eight Companies), Col.
    Thomas C. Devin
Ohio Cavalry, Third Independant Co., Lt. J. Seamen
3d U. S Artillery, Batteries L/M, Capt. J. Edwards Jr.

Twelfth Army Corps
Maj. Gen. Joseph K. F. Mansfield
Brig. Gen. Alpheus, S. Williams

First Division
Brig. Gen. Alpheus S Williams
Brig. Gen. Samuel W. Crawford
Brig. Gen. George H, Gordon

First Brigade
Brig. Gen. Samuel W. Crawford
Col. Joseph F. Knipe

5th Connecticut, Capt. Henry W. Daboll
10th Maine, Col. George L. Beal
28th New York, Capt. William H. H. Mapes
46th Pennsylvania, Col. Joseph F. Knipe
124th Pennsylvania, Col. Joseph W. Hawley
125th Pennsylvania, Col. Jacob Higgins
128th Pennsylvania, Col. Samuel Cressdale

Third Brigade
Brig. Gen. George H. Gordon
Col. Thomas Ruger

27th Indiana, Col. Silas Colgrove
2d Massachusetts, Col. George L. Andrews
13th New Jersey, Col. Ezra A. Carman
107th New York, Col. R. B. Van Valkenburgh
Zouaves D'afrique, Pennsylvania
3d Wisconsin, Col. Thomas H. Ruger

Second Division
Brig. Gen, George S. Greene

First Brigade
Lt.. Col. Hector Tyndale
Maj. Orrin J. Crane

5th Ohio, Maj. John Collins
7th Ohio, Maj. Orrin J. Crane
29th Ohio, Lt. Theron S. Winship
66th Ohio, Lt. Col. Eugene Powell
28th Pennsylvania, Maj. Ario Pardee, Jr.

Second Brigade
Col. Henry J. Stainrook
3d Maryland, Lt. Col. Joseph M. Sudsburg
102d New York, Lt. Col. James C. Lane
109th Pennsylvania, Capt. George E. Seymour
111th Pennsylvania, Maj. Thomas M. Walker

Third Brigade
Col. William B. Goodrich
Lt. Col. Jonathan Austin

3d Delaware, Maj. Arthur Maginnis
Purnell Legion Maryland, Lt. Col. Ben L. Simpson

60th New York, Lt. Col. Charles R. Brundage
78th New York, Lt. Col. Jonathan Austin

Artillery
Capt. Clermont L. Best

Maine Light, 4th Battery, Capt. O'Neil W. Robinson
Maine Light, 6th Battery, Capt. Freeman McGilvery
1st New York Light, Battery M, Capt. G. W. Cothran
New York Light, 10th Battery, Capt. John T. Bruen
Pennsylvania Light, Battery E, Capt. Joseph M. Knap
Pennsylvania Light, Battery F, Capt. R. B. Hampton
4th United States, Battery F, Lt. E. D. Muhlenberg

Cavalry Division
Brig. Gen. Alfred Pleasonton

First Brigade
Maj. Charles J. Whiting

5th United States, Capt. Joseph H. McArthur
6th United States, Capt. William P. Sanders

Second Brigade
Col. John F. Farnsworth

8th Illinois, Maj. William H. Medill
3d Indiana, Maj. George H. Chapman
1st Massachusetts, Capt. Casper Crowninshield
8th Pennsylvania, Capt. Peter Keenan

Third Brigade
Col. Richard H. Rush

4th Pennsylvania, Col. James H. Childs
6th Pennsylvania, Lt. Col. C. Ross Smith

Fourth Brigade
Col. Andrew T. McReynolds

1st New York, Maj. Alonzo W. Adams
12th Pennsylvania, Maj. James A. Congdon

Fifth Brigade
Col. Benjamin F. Davis

8th New York, Col. Benjamin F. Davis
3d Pennsylvania, Lt. Col. Samuel W. Owen

Artillery

2d United States, Battery A, Capt. John C. Tidball
2d United States, Batteries B/L, Capt. J. M. Robertson
2d United States, Battery M, Lt. Peter C. Hains
3d United States, Batteries C/G, Capt. H. G. Gibson

Unattached
1st Maine Cavalry, Col. Samuel H. Allen
15th Pennsylvania Cavalry (Detachment),
Col. William J. Palmer

ARMY OF NORTHERN VIRGINIA
General Robert E. Lee

Longstreet's ("Wing") Command
Maj. Gen. James Longstreet

McLaws' Division
Maj. Gen. Lafayette McLaws

Kershaw's Brigade
Brig. Gen. J. B. Kershaw

2d South Carolina, Col. John D. Kennedy
3d South Carolina, Col. James D. Nance
7th South Carolina, Col. D. Wyatt Aiken
8th South Carolina, Lt. Col. A. J. Hoole

Cobb's Brigade
Brig. Gen. Howell Cobb
Lt. Col. C. C. Sanders
Lt. Col. William MacRae

16th Georgia, Lt. Col. Henry Thomas
24th Georgia, R. E. McMillan
Cobb's (Georgia) Legion, Lt. Col. L.J. Glenn
15th North Carolina, Lt. Col. William McRae

Semmes' Brigade
Brig. Gen. Paul J. Semmes
10th Georgia, Maj. Willis Holt
53d Georgia, Lt. Col. Thomas Sloan
15th Virginia, Capt. E. M. Morrison
32d Virginia, Col. E.B. Montague

Barksdale's Brigade
Brig. Gen. William Barksdale
13th Mississippi, Lt. Col. Kennon McElroy
17th Mississippi, Lt. Col. John C. Fiser

18th Mississippi, Maj. J. C. Campbell
21st Mississippi, Capt. John Sims

Artillery
Maj. S. P. Hamilton
Col. H. C. Cabell

Manly's (North Carolina) Battery, Capt. B.C. Manly
Pulaski (Georgia) Artillery, Capt. J.P. W. Read
Richmond (Fayette)Artillery, Capt. M. C. Macon
Richmond Howitzers, (1st Co.), Capt. E. S. McCarthy
Troup (Georgia) Artillery, Capt. H. H. Carlton

Anderson's Division
Maj. Gen. Richard H. Anderson

Wilcox's Brigade
Col. Alfred Cumming

8th Alabama, Maj. H. A. Herbert
9th Alabama, Maj. J. H. Williams
10th Alabama, Capt. G. C. Wheatley
11th Alabama, Maj. John Sanders

Mahone's Brigade
Col. William A. Parham

6th Virginia, Capt. John Ludlow
12th Virginia, Capt. John Llewellyn
16th Virginia, Maj. Francis Holladay
41st Virginia, Col. William A. Parham
61st Virginia, Lt. Col. William F. Neimeyer

Featherston's Brigade
Brig. Gen. Winfield S. Featherston
Col. Carnot Posey

12th Mississippi, Col. W. H. Taylor
16th Mississippi, Capt. A.M. Feltus
19th Mississippi, Col. N. W. Harris
2d Mississippi Battalion, Maj. William S. Wilson

Armistead's Brigade
Brig. Gen. Lewis A. Armistead
Col. J. G. Hodges

9th Virginia, Capt. W. J. Richardson
14th Virginia, Col. James G. Hodges
38th Virginia, Col. Edward C. Edmonds
53d Virginia, Capt. W. G. Pollard
57th Virginia, Col. David Dyer

Pryor's Brigade
Brig. Gen. Roger A. Pryor

14th Alabama, Maj. J. A. Broome
2d Florida, Col. W. D. Ballantine
5th Florida, Col. John C. Hately
8th Florida, Lt. Col. George A. Coppens
3d Virginia., Col. Joseph Mayo

Wright's Brigade
Brig. Gen. A. R. Wright

44th Alabama, Lt. Col. Charles A. Derby
3d Georgia, Capt. R. B. Nisbit
22d Georgia, Col. Robert Jones
48th Georgia, Col. William Gibson

Artillery
Maj. John S. Saunders

Donaldsonville (Louisiana) Artillery, Capt. V. Maurin
Norfolk (Virginia) Battery, Capt. Frank Huger
Lynchburg (Virginia) Battery, Capt. M. N. Moorman
Thompson's (Grimes') (Virginia), Capt. Cary F. Grimes

Jones' Division
Brig. Gen. David R. Jones

Toombs' Brigade
Brig. Gen. Robert Toombs
Col. Henry L. Benning

2d Georgia, Lt. Col. William R. Holmes
15th Georgia, Col. W. T. Millican
17th Georgia, Capt. J. A. McGregor
20th Georgia, Col. J. B. Cumming

Drayton's Brigade
Brig. Gen. Thomas F. Drayton
50th Georgia, Lt.. Col. F. Kearse
51st Georgia, ——
15th South Carolina, Col. W. D. Desaussure
3rd South Carolina Battalion, Lt. Col. George James
Phillips Legion, Lt. Col. Robert Cook

Pickett's Brigade
Brig. Gen. R. B. Garnett

8th Virginia, Col. Eppa Hunton
18th Virginia, Maj George C. Cabell
19th Virginia, Col. J. B. Strange
28th Virginia, Capt. Wingfield
56th Virginia, Col. William D. Stuart

Kemper's Brigade
Brig. Gen. James L. Kemper

1st Virginia, Capt. George Norton
7th Virginia, Maj. Arthur Herbert
11th Virginia, Maj. Adam Clement
17th Virginia, Col. M. D. Corse
24th Virginia, Col. W. R. Terry

Jenkins' Brigade
Col. Joseph Walker

1st South Carolina (Volunteers), Lt. Col. D. Livingston
2d South Carolina Rifles, Lt. Col. Robert Thompson
5th South Carolina, Capt. T. C. Beckham
6th South Carolina, Lt. Col. J. M. Steedman
4th South Carolina Battalion, Lt. W. F. Field
Palmetto (South Carolina) Sharpshooters,
　　Capt. A. H. Foster

Anderson's Brigade
Col. George T. Anderson

1st Georgia (Regulars), Col. W. J. Magill
7th Georgia, Col. G. H. Carmical
8th Georgia, Col. John Towers
9th Georgia, Lt. Col. John Mounger
11th Georgia, Maj. F. H. Little

Artillery

Fauquier (Virginia) Artillery, Capt. Robert Stribling
Loudoun (Virginia) Artillery, Capt. A. Rogers
Turner (Virginia) Artillery, Capt. W. H. Turner
Wise (Virginia) Artillery, Capt. J. S. Brown

Walker's Division
Brig. Gen. John G. Walker

Walker's Brigade
Col. Van H. Manning
Col. E. D. Hall

3d Arkansas, Capt. John W. Reedy
27th North Carolina, Col. J. R. Cooke
46th North Carolina, Col. E. D. Hall
48th North Carolina, Col. R. C. Hill
30th Virginia, ——
French's (Virginia) Battery, Capt. Thomas B. French

Ransom's Brigade
Brig. Gen. Robert Ransom Jr.

24th North Carolina, Lt. Col. John L. Harris
25th North Carolina, Col. H. M Rutledge
35th North Carolina, Col. M. W. Ransom
49th North Carolina, Lt. Col. Lee M. McAfee
Branch's Field Artillery (Virginia), Capt. Branch

Hood's Division
Brig. Gen. John B. Hood

Hood's Brigade
Col. W. T. Wofford

18th Georgia, Lt. Col. S. Z. Ruff
Hampton (South Carolina) Legion,
　　Lt. Col. M. W. Gary
1st Texas, Lt. Col. P. A. Work
4th Texas, Lt. Col. B. F. Carter
5th Texas, Capt. L N.M. Turner

Law's Brigade
Col. Evander M. Law

4th Alabama, Lt. Col. O K. McLemore
2d Mississippi, Col. J. M. Stone
11th Mississippi, Col. P. F. Liddell
6th North Carolina, Maj. Robert F. Webb

Artillery

Maj. B. W. Frobel
German Artillery (South Carolina),
　　Capt. W. K. Bachman
Palmetto Artillery (South Carolina),
　　Capt. H. R. Garden
Rowan Artillery (North Carolina), Capt. James Reilly

Evan's Brigade
Brig. Gen. Nathan G. Evans
Col. Peter F. Stevens

17th South Carolina, Col. F. W. McMaster
18th South Carolina, Col. W. H. Wallace
22d South Carolina, Lt. Col. T. C. Watkins
23d South Carolina, Capt. S. A. Durham
Holcombe (South Carolina) Legion, Col. P. F. Stevens
Macbeth (South Carolina) Artillery, Capt. R. Boyce

Artillery

Washington (Louisiana) Artillery
Col. J. B. Walton
1st Co., Capt. C. W. Squires
2d Co., Capt. J. B. Richardson
3d Co., Capt. M. B. Miller
4th Co., Capt. B. F. Eshleman

Lee's Battalion
Col. S. D. Lee
Ashland (Virginia) Artillery, Capt. P. Woolfolk Jr
Bedford (Virginia) Artillery, Capt. T. C. Jordan
Brooks (South Carolina) Artillery, Lt.. William Elliott
Eubank's (Virginia) Battery, Capt. J. L. Eubank
Madison (Louisiana) Light Artillery,
Capt. G. V. Moody
Parker's (Virginia) Battery, Capt. W. W. Parker

Jackson's ("Wing") Command
Maj. Gen. Thomas J. Jackson

Ewell's Division
Brig. Gen. A. R. Lawton
Brig. Gen. Jubal A. Early

Lawton's Brigade
Col. M. Douglass
Maj. J. H. Lowe
Col. John H. Lamar

13th Georgia, Capt. D. A. Kidd
26th Georgia, Col. Edmund N. Atkinson
31st Georgia, Lt. Col. John Crowder
38th Georgia, Capt. W. H. Battey
60th Georgia, Maj. W. B. Jones
61st Georgia, Col. John Lamar)

Early's Brigade
Brig. Gen. Jubal A. Early
Col. William Smith

13th Virginia, Capt. F. V. Winston
25th Virginia, Capt. R. D. Lilley
31st Virginia, Col. John Hoffman
44th Virginia, Capt. D. W. Anderson
49th Virginia, Col. William Smith
52d Virginia, Col. M. G. Harman.
58th Virginia, Col. Edmund Goode

Trimble's Brigade
Col. James A. Walker

15th Alabama, Capt. I. B. Feagin
12th Georgia, Capt. Rodgers
21st Georgia, Maj. Thomas C. Glover
21st North Carolina, Capt. Miller
1st North Carolina Battalion, ——

Hays' Brigade
Brig. Gen. Harry T. Hays

5th Louisiana, Col. Henry Forno
6th Louisiana, Col. H. B. Strong
7th Louisiana, ——
8th Louisiana, Lt. Col. Trevanion Lewis
14th Louisiana, Col. R. W. Jones

Artillery
Maj. A. R. Courtney

Chesapeake (Maryland) Artillery, Capt. W. D. Brown
Courtney (Virginia) Artillery, Capt. J. W. Latimer
Johnson's (Virginia) Battery, Cpt John R. Johnson
Louisiana Guard Artillery, Capt. Louis E. D'Aquin
First Maryland Battery, Capt. William F. Dement
Staunton (Virginia) Artillery, Lt.. Asher W. Garber

Hill's Light Division
Maj. Gen. Ambrose P. Hill

Branch's Brigade
Brig. Gen. L. O. Branch
Col. James H. Lane

7th North Carolina, Col. E. G. Haywood
18th North Carolina, Lt Colonel Thomas Purdie
28th North Carolina, Col. James Lane
33d North Carolina, Lt. Col. Robert Hoke
37th North Carolina, Capt. William Morris

Gregg's Brigade
Brig. Gen. Maxcy Gregg

1st South Carolina (Provisional Army),
Col. D. H. Hamilton
1st South Carolina Rifles, Lt.. Col. James M. Perrin
12th South Carolina, Col. Dixon Barnes
13th South Carolina, Col. O. E. Edwards
14th South Carolina, Lt.. Col. W.D. Simpson

Field's Brigade
Colonel John Brockenbrough

40th Virginia, Lt. Col. Fleet Cox
47th Virginia, Lt. Col. John Lyell
55th Virginia, Maj. Charles Lawson
22d Virginia Battalion, Maj. E. Poinsett Tayloe

Archer's Brigade
Brig. Gen. J. J. Archer
Col. Peter Turney

5th Alabama Battalion, Capt. Charles Hooper
19th Georgia, Maj. J. H. Neal
1st Tennessee (Provisional Army), Col. Peter Turney
7th Tennessee, Maj. S. G. Shepard
14th Tennessee, Col. William McComb

Pender's Brigade
Brig. Gen. William D. Pender
Col. R. H. Brewer

16th North Carolina, Lt. Colonel Stowe
22d North Carolina, Maj. C. C. Cole
34th North Carolina, Lt. Col. J. L. McDowell
38th North Carolina, —

Thomas' Brigade
Col. Edward L. Thomas

14th Georgia, Col. R. W. Folsom
35th Georgia, —
45th Georgia, Maj. W. L. Grice
49th Georgia, Lt. Col. S. M. Manning

Artillery
Lt. Col. R. L. Walker
Branch (North Carolina) Artillery, Capt. A. C. Latham
Crenshaw's (Virginia) Battery, Capt. W. G. Crenshaw
Fredericksburg (Virginia) Artillery, Capt. C. Braxton
Letcher (Virginia) Artillery, Capt. Greenlee Davidson

Pee Dee (South Carolina) Artillery, Capt. D. McIntosh
Purcell (Virginia) Artillery, Capt. William Pegram

Jackson's Division
Brig. Gen. John R. Jones
Brig. Gen. W E. Starke
Col. A. J. Grigsby

Winder's Brigade
Col. A. J. Grigsby
Lt. Col. R. D. Gardner
Maj. H. J. Williams

2d Virginia, Capt. R. T. Colston
4th Virginia, Lt. Col. R. D. Gardner
5th Virginia, Maj. H. J. Williams
27th Virginia, Capt. F. C. Wilson
33d Virginia, Capt. Jacob Golladay

Taliaferro's Brigade
Col. E. T. H. Warren
Col. J. W. Jackson
Col. J. L. Sheffield

47th Alabama, Col. James W. Jackson
48th Alabama, Col. James L. Sheffield
10th Virginia, Col. Edward T. Warren
23d Virginia, Col. Alexander G. Taliaferro
37th Virginia, Lt. Col. John Terry

Jones' Brigade
Col. B. T. Johnson
Capt. J. E. Penn
Capt. A. C. Page
Capt. R. W. Withers

21st Virginia, Capt. A. C. Page
42d Virginia, Capt. R. W. Withers
48th Virginia, Capt. Candler
1st Virginia Battalion, Lt. C. A. Davidson

Starke's Brigade
Brig. Gen. William E. Starke
Col. L. A. Stafford
Col. E. Pendleton

1st Louisiana, Lt. Col. M. Nolan
2d Louisiana, Col. J. M. Williams
9th Louisiana, Col. Leroy A. Stafford
10th Louisiana, Capt. H. D. Monier

15th Louisiana, Col. Edmund Pendleton
Coppens' (Louisiana) Battalion, Lt.. Col. G. Coppens

Artillery
Maj. L. M. Shumaker

Alleghany (Virginia) Artillery, Capt. John Carpenter
Brockenbrough's (Maryland) Battery,
Capt. J. B. Brockenbrough
Danville (Virginia) Artillery, Capt. G. A. Wooding
Lee (Virginia) Battery, Capt. Charles Raine
Rockbridge (Virginia) Artillery, Capt. William Poague

Hill's Division
Maj. Gen. Daniel H. Hill

Ripley's Brigade
Brig. Gen. Roswell S. Ripley
Col. George Doles

4th Georgia, Col. George Doles
44th Georgia, Capt. John Key
1st North Carolina, Lt. Col. H.A. Brown
3d North Carolina, Col. William L. De Rosset

Rodes' Brigade
Brig. Gen. Robert E. Rodes

3d Alabama, Col. C. A. Battle
5th Alabama, Maj. E. L. Hobson
6th Alabama, Col. J. B. Gordon
12th Alabama, Col. B. B. Gayle
26th Alabama, Col. E. A. O'Neal

Garland's Brigade
Brig. Gen. Samuel Garland, Jr.
Col. D. K. McRae

5th North Carolina, Col. D. K. McRae
12th North Carolina, Capt. S. Snow
13th North Carolina, Lt. Col. Thomas Ruffin, Jr.
20th North Carolina, Col. Alfred Iverson
23d North Carolina, Col. D. H. Christie

Anderson's Brigade
Brig. Gen. George B. Anderson
Col. R. T. Bennett

2d North Carolina, Col. C. C. Tew
4th North Carolina, Col. Bryan Grimes

14th North Carolina, Col. R. T. Bennett
30th North Carolina, Col. F. M. Parker

Colquitt's Brigade
Col. A. H. Colquitt

13th Alabama, Col. B. D. Fry
6th Georgia, Lt. Col. J.M. Newton
23d Georgia, Col. W. P. Barclay
27th Georgia, Col. L. B. Smith
28th Georgia, Maj. T. Graybill

Artillery
Major Pierson

Hardaway's (Alabama) Battery, Capt. R. A. Hardaway
Jeff. Davis (Alabama) Artillery, Capt. J. W. Bondurant
Jones' (Virginia) Battery, Capt. William B. Jones
King William (Virginia) Artillery, Capt. T. H. Carter

Reserve Artillery
Brig. Gen. William N. Pendleton

Brown's Battalion
Col. J. Thompson Brown

Powhatan Artillery, Capt. Willis J. Dance
Richmond Howitzers, 2d Co., Capt. D. Watson
Richmond Howitzers, 3d Co., Capt. Ben H. Smith, Jr.
Salem Artillery, Capt. A. Hupp
Williamsburg Artillery, Capt. John A. Coke

Cutts' Battalion
Lt. Col. A. S. Cutts

Blackshears' (Georgia) Battery, Capt. James Blackshear
Irwin (Georgia) Artillery, Capt. John Lane
Lloyd's (North Carolina) Battery, Capt. W. P. Lloyd
Patterson's (Georgia) Battery, Capt. George Patterson
Ross' (Georgia) Battery, Capt. H. M. Ross

Jones' Battalion
Maj. H. P. Jones

Morris (Virginia) Artillery, Capt. R. C. M. Page
Orange (Virginia) Artillery, Capt. Jefferson Peyton
Turner's (Virginia) Battery, Capt. W. H. Turner
Wimbish's (Virginia) Battery, Capt. Abram Wimbish

Nelson's Battalion
Maj. William Nelson

Amherst (Virginia) Artillery, Capt. T. J. Kirkpatrick
Fluvanna (Virginia) Artillery, Capt. John J. Ancell
Huckstep's (Virginia) Battery, Capt. C. T. Huckstep
Johnson's (Virginia) Battery, Capt. M. Johnson
Milledge (Georgia) Artillery, Capt. John Milledge

Miscellaneous

Cutshaw's (Virginia) Battery, Capt. W. E. Cutshaw
Dixie (Virginia) Artillery, Capt. G. B. Chapman
Magruder (Virginia) Artillery, Capt. T. H. Page, Jr.
Rice's (Virginia) Battery, Capt. W. H. Rice
Thomas(Virginia) Artillery, Capt. E. J. Anderson

Stuart's Cavalry Division
Maj. Gen. James E. B. Stuart

Hampton's Brigade
Brig. Gen. Wade Hampton

1st North Carolina, Col. L. S. Baker
2d South Carolina, Col. M. C. Butler
10th Virginia, Col. J. Lucius Davis
Cobb's (Georgia) Legion, Lt.. Col. P. M. B. Young
Jeff. Davis Legion, Lt. Col. W. T. Martin

Lee's Brigade
Brig. Gen. Fitz Lee

1st Virginia, Lt. Col. L. Tiernan Brien
3d Virginia, Lt. Col. John T. Thornton
4th Virginia, Col. Williams C. Wickham
5th Virginia, Col. T. L. Rosser
9th Virginia, Col. W. H. F Lee

Robertson's Brigade
Col. Thomas T. Munford

2d Virginia, Lt. Col. Burks
7th Virginia, Capt. S. B. Myers
12th Virginia, Col. A. W. Harman
17th Virginia Battalion, Maj. Thomas Massie

Horse Artillery
Capt. John Pelham

Chew's (Virginia) Battery, Capt. R. P. Chew
Hart's (South Carolina) Battery, Capt. J. F. Hart
Pelham's (Virginia) Battery, Capt. John Pelham

Appendix 2

An Interview with Author Bradley M. Gottfried

Q: Let's start with a basic question: how long have you been interested in the Civil War and how did you get interested in this period of our history?

BMG: The answer to this simple question is rather complicated. My first round of interest began when I was about 12. I started collecting books and my parents took me to a few battlefields. When I went off to college, I put the books into boxes and didn't open them again until I was about forty-three! I never had the heart to get rid of those books, and moved them from place to place as my career evolved. The urge to open those boxes hit me when I moved back to my home town of Philadelphia. That was twenty years ago. My interest was renewed as soon as I started flipping through those books.

Q: This is your ninth Civil War book. Why drives you to research and write?

BMG: I am a researcher and writer by nature, and I enjoy sharing what I learn with others. It is also a way that I can honor those who fought and died during that horrible period of American history. We owe it to them to tell their stories in a fair and balanced way.

Q: You are the president of a college with three campuses spanning three counties in Southern Maryland. How do you find the time to write?

BMG: It's all about time management and dealing with interruptions. I get up very early every morning, about 3:00 a.m., and that's when I do my writing. Sometimes I'm forced to spend that time on work-related matters, which can be frustrating. But my day job comes first. I never let more than three days pass without conducting research or writing.

Q: You began writing about the Gettysburg Campaign and have written a number of important and well-received books on that topic, including The Brigades of Gettysburg, The Roads to Gettysburg, The Artillery of Gettysburg, *and of course,* The Maps of Gettysburg. *So the obvious question: why Gettysburg?*

BMG: I get asked that a lot. It's simple: I love the topic. I've been criticized for spending so much time on Gettysburg, but any researcher knows that there is a gold mine of primary material on the subject. My philosophy is that if I am going to write, choose a topic that people are interested in learning more about, and something I have an interest in spending so much time working on.

Q: The Maps of Gettysburg was your first book in what would become the Savas Beatie Military Atlas series. How did you come up with the idea?

BMG: As odd as this might sound, I'm not really sure. It evolved over time—a realization that really took form when I was writing *The Brigades of Gettysburg*. It was then that I recognized that I was spending untold hours trying to figure out what unit was where and when. No book on the subject had enough maps to satisfy my needs, and even if they were good maps, they only covered a snapshot in time and so rarely matched the text. For the work I was doing, I needed maps—lots of maps—and they just were not available. So I settled on a concept to offer a lot of text tied to a single facing-page map. And then tell the story of the campaign that way, map by map, from beginning to end.

Q: There are not many authors who research, write, and draft their own maps. How did you learn cartography skills?

BMG: (laughing) I learned out of sheer desperation. I initially worked with a Civil War cartographer. I wrote the text to accompany each map and prepared a rough sketch map for him. It is a time-consuming process, and he decided to go in a different direction. I collaborated with a second cartographer, but we had a significant difference of opinion on the projects' direction and parted ways. It was then that it dawned on me that the only way this series was going to be realized was if I learned how to produce the maps myself. I think they are better than some, not as good as others, but they get the job done.

Q: How do you conduct your research for these atlas books?

BMG: I begin by preparing an outline of the major components of the campaign and a rough estimation of how many maps will be needed to adequately tell the story. Then I dig into the literature—primary and secondary. I also spend a lot of time visiting various repositories and battlefield libraries to review unpublished materials and visiting the battlefields to get a better sense of the topography and nature of the terrain. Once these materials are in hand I begin the writing process. I prepare the text first, and then the map

Q: Have you ever prepared a map and then thought, "That can't be right?"

BMG: Actually, I have. I look at the map and realize the text isn't quite right—that some of the literature is flawed and this event or that event could not have happened as reported. A simple example might be a soldier of one regiment claiming to have fired into a particular enemy regiment, but when you look at the terrain and walk the field, you know that could not have happened as the soldier later recalled. Visualizing the action really helps in this regard.

Q: After The Maps of Gettysburg *you turned to First Bull Run. Why?*

BMG: I have always wanted to "run the table," so to speak and complete all of the major campaigns in the Eastern Theater from first to last. Readers have certain favorites, and if I am to succeed Bull Run has to be covered, so I reached back and completed it. I am trying to concentrate on some of the most popular campaigns first. I am 62-years-old and hope one day to complete the project, but if I don't, at least the most popular campaigns will be covered.

Q: Why was Antietam the third book in the series?

BMG: After Gettysburg (and I had already completed *The Maps of First Bull Run*), I turned to the second most popular campaign for students of the war: Antietam. The invasion of Maryland in 1862 is a fascinating and rather complex affair that really needs to be visualized to be fully understood.

Q: What were some of the interesting things you learned while writing this book?

BMG: I have to say it was the fighting at South Mountain on September 14. I only knew these three major fights (Fox's, Turner's, and Crampton's gaps) in a general sense, and so I didn't fully appreciate the impact that Union victory had on the campaign. They are each quite fascinating in their own right and are now among my favorite places to visit.

Q: Any particular personalities stand out for their valor or accomplishments?

BMG: There were several. Let me pick a recognizable personality from each side. For the Confederates, I really have to say Maj. Gen. D. H. Hill's performance impresses me. With a depleted division he was assigned the task of stopping two large Federal army corps from penetrating the gaps in South Mountain. His 5,000 or so men faced upwards to 30,000 enemy troops. He had far too few men to hold the line he was assigned, but he did a good job, used the terrain as best as he could, and held off the enemy all day. It was not until after dark that the Federal I Corps captured Turner's Gap. In the end this was a Union victory, but Hill did a remarkable job given what he had to work with. Hill also held the center of Lee's line at Antietam along the Sunken Road, and he fought well there, too.

Q: And on the Union side?

BMG: I would probably say Maj. Gen. Joseph Hooker, commander of the I Corps. He fought very well at Antietam—certainly much better than did any other Federal corps leader. Hooker was visible to his troops and right out there with them, and he was outspoken in his interactions with George McClellan.

Q: Given its wide interest and its importance to the Civil War, why aren't there more books on this campaign?

BMG: That's a great question. I wish I knew the answer. Until very recently there was almost nothing of substance written about South Mountain. Only a few good overall books on Antietam exist, such as Murfin's *Gleam of Bayonets*, Sears' *Landscape Turned Red*, and essay collections edited by Gary Gallagher. Thomas Clemens has edited Ezra Carman's wonderful manuscript of the campaign, and the first volume *(The Maryland Campaign of 1862)* covers its course through South Mountain. I understand the Antietam volume will be available later in 2012. Unlike Gettysburg, which had scores of deep authoritative treatments by distinguished writers including Edwin Coddington, Harry Pfanz, David Martin, Earl Hess, Eric Wittenberg, J. D. Petruzzi—the list is a very long one—virtually nothing like it exists for Antietam. Marion Armstrong has done wonderful work on Sumner's Federal II Corps, John Hoptak on Pennsylvania troops, Kathleen Ernst on Sharpsburg-area citizens, and there is a short study about Special Orders No. 191 and several tour guides. But detailed micro-studies on the Sunken Road, for example, or on Burnside's late-afternoon assault simply do not exist. The battlefield is almost completely intact, too. I can't explain why historians have not jumped at the opportunity waiting for them.

Q: The Maps of Antietam contains 124 maps. Does it differ in any significant ways from your first two books in this series?

BMG: It really doesn't differ that much in approach. All three books begin with the onset of the campaigns and course through the major events, and then end in what I think is an appropriate place. I think my writing and cartography has matured, however. At least, I like to think so.

Q: Was Antietam a good place for Lee to offer battle?

BMG: One of the maxims of war is that you don't fight a battle with your back to a river. And that's what Lee ended up doing. Had he been defeated he almost certainly would have effectively lost his army because there was only one ford behind him. As I explain in the book, I don't think he intended to fight there, but once McClellan crossed Antietam Creek on September 16 and blocked Lee's route north, Lee had little choice because by then it was very risky to retreat from that position. From the Confederate point of view, I don't think it was a good place to wage a defensive battle given the depleted and exhausted state of Lee's army and the lay of the terrain. He didn't even have enough men to anchor his flanks.

Q: What are you working on now?

BMG: Several things. Ted Savas and I are excited about producing books to coincide with the Sesquicentennial. I am finishing an atlas book on the 1863 fall campaigns, which is as-yet unnamed. This covers the fascinating and always overlooked period after the end of the Gettysburg campaign through the turn of the year. (Ted and I are also finishing up *The Gettysburg Encyclopedia*, which we hope will be available for a Sesquicentennial release in 2013.) This post-Gettysburg atlas includes some cavalry actions, the Bristoe Station Campaign, Rappahannock Station (where two of Lee's finest infantry brigades were essentially destroyed), and the Mine Run Campaign in late November and early December. Once that is completed, I will begin work on the 1864 Overland Campaign. The first volume will include the Wilderness and Spotsylvania and related actions.

Q: I imagine you get a decent amount of feedback on these books. What do you hear?

BMG: I get quite a bit, often at book signings. I am really appreciative that people take the time and trouble to share their thoughts with me. One thing I hear a lot is that these books unlock all the other material written on the same subject, so they will read a different book on, say, Gettysburg, using my map atlas to help understand it. Even people who have a good knowledge of Gettysburg have told me that their understanding of the campaign is deeper and richer because they can now visualize it better. I have heard the same thing about *The Maps of First Bull Run*. That gives me great satisfaction. And I also hear about mistakes--this unit is misnamed, or something like that. I really welcome that, and my publisher and I work hard to correct them in subsequent printings. That just make the books better.

Endnotes

Map Set 1. The Invasion of Maryland (September 2 - 14, 1862)

1. Stephen W. Sears, *Landscape Turned Red: The Battle of Antietam* (New Haven, CT: Ticknor & Fields, 1983), 2, 4, 15-16, 35.

2. Sears, *Landscape Turned Red*, 15-16.

3. Sears, *Landscape Turned Red*, 40-41.

4. United States War Department: *The War of the Rebellion: A Compilation of the Official Records of the Union and Confederate Armies*, 128 volumes (Washington: U. S. Government Printing Office, 1880-1901), vol. 19, pt. 2, 590-1, hereafter *OR*; Joseph L. Harsh, *Taken at the Flood: Robert E. Lee and Confederate Strategy in the Maryland Campaign of 1862* (Kent, OH: Kent State University Press, 1999), 16, 18-19, 21-33; Sears, *Landscape Turned Red*, 61, 64-65.

5. *OR* 19, pt. 1, 38-39, 1019; Harsh, *Taken at the Flood*, 66-67. Maj. Gen. D. H. Hill divided his five-brigade division into four columns. G. B. Anderson's brigade marched north along the Potomac River to a point opposite the Maryland town of Berlin, where the B & O Railroad came closest to the river and was therefore vulnerable to artillery fire. Roswell Ripley's brigade crossed the river at Point of Rocks, Samuel Garland's brigade at Noland's Ferry, and Alfred Colquitt's and Robert Rodes' brigades at Cheek's Ford near the mouth of the Monocacy River. Thomas Munford's cavalry brigade (Beverly Robertson's command) screened the move by demonstrating against the western Federal forts covering the Chain Bridge. Harsh, *Taken at the Flood*, 67, 71.

6. Richard B. Irwin, "Washington Under Banks," *Battles and Leaders of the Civil War* (New York: Thomas Yoseloff, 1956), vol. 2, 542. All references to articles appearing in this series are hereafter noted as *B&L*; Harsh, *Taken at the Flood*, 34-39. Lee's men straggled for many reasons, including outright fatigue from the constant marching and fighting, the hot conditions, the stomach distress from eating green ears of corn and fruit, and later, because many refused to cross the Potomac in Northern territory because they had enlisted to defend the South and not attack the North. Lee was so concerned about the extent of the straggling that he went to extraordinary lengths to prevent it, calling stragglers, "unworthy members of an army which has immortalized itself." Lee concentrated on the officer corps because officers were the only ones who could keep the men in the ranks. Some officers were arrested. A. P. Hill, for example, was temporarily removed from the command of his division. Thomas "Stonewall" Jackson did not think Hill was marching his command as fast and well as he expected. This deprived Lee of many able officers until the fighting began. Another officer, Brig. Gen. John B. Hood, was arrested because he refused to relinquish captured wagons to Brig. Gen. Nathan Evans, his temporary division commander. James I. Robertson, Jr., *General A. P. Hill: The Story of a Confederate Warrior* (New York: Random House, 1987), 130-2.

7. *OR* 19, pt. 1, 38; pt. 2, 591-2; Harsh, *Taken at the Flood*, 70. General Orders No. 102 had several parts. It reduced the number of wagons to those carrying "the absolute necessaries of a regiment." Substandard artillery pieces were ordered to be left behind and their horses and men distributed to other units. This did not occur as planned because Lee's artillery chief, Brig. Gen. William Pendleton, fell ill. Not wishing to alienate the Marylanders, Lee firmly directed that all supplies must be purchased. *OR* 19, pt. 2, 592-3.

8. Harsh, *Taken at the Flood*, 82-83.

9. Jeffry D. Wert, *General James Longstreet: The Confederacy's Most Controversial Soldier* (New York: Simon & Schuster, 1993), 181. After crossing the Potomac River, Jackson hoped to march quickly and seize the Baltimore and Ohio Railroad bridge over the Monocacy River near Frederick, Maryland. However, the crossing took longer than Jackson anticipated and he had to delay plans to capture this vital asset. Ezra Carman, *The Maryland Campaign of September 1862, Vol 1: South Mountain*, Thomas Clemens, ed. (New York: Savas Beatie, 2010), 93. All subsequent references are to vol. 1. Ezra Carman participated in the campaign with the 13th New Jersey infantry and spent much of the balance of his life studying the Maryland Campaign and writing an authoritative manuscript of the entire operation, which has only recently been published. This two-volume edition of Carman's published manuscript, which came out in 2010, ends with the aftermath of South Mountain (vol. 1). The second volume, slated for late 2012 and so not available to me when I researched and wrote this book, includes the aftermath South Mountain, the battle of Antietam, and Lee's withdrawal. Dr. Clemens' notes are extensive and extremely helpful, and I refer to this version as often as possible. Otherwise, I refer to Joseph Pierro, ed., *The Maryland Campaign of September 1862: Ezra A. Carman's Definitive Study of the Union and Confederate*

Armies at Antietam (Routledge, 2008), 449. This single volume printing of Carman's lengthy manuscript is not nearly as helpful as the aforementioned Clemens' edition.

10. *OR* 19, pt. 1, 815, 952, 1,019. Brig. Gen. Fitzhugh Lee's brigade led Jeb Stuart's advance into Maryland. Riding ahead to Poolesville, Lee routed 100 troopers of the 1st Massachusetts Cavalry. *OR* 19, pt. 1, 815.

11. Harsh, *Taken at the Flood*, 86-87.

12. John W. Schildt, *Roads to Antietam* (Chambersburg, PA: Burd Street Press, 1997), 21-22; *OR* 19, pt. 1, 952-53; Lewis Henry Steiner, Report of Lewis H. Steiner, M.D., *Inspector of the Sanitary Commission, Containing a Diary Kept During the Rebel Occupation of Frederick, Md., and an Account of the Operations of the U.S. Sanitary Commission During the Campaign in Maryland, September 1862* (New York: Anson D. F. Randolph, 1862), 7-8. Given the fact that Lee's men had been marching and fighting almost non-stop since July, it is not surprising that they were filthy and ridden with vermin. Maj. Gen. A. P. Hill was under arrest because his new commander, Stonewall Jackson, did not like the way that his men were being supervised during the march. Douglas Southall Freeman, *Lee's Lieutenants: A Study in Command* (New York: Charles Scribner's Sons, 1943), vol. 2, 147-9.

13. Louise Porter Daly, *Alexander Cheves Haskell: The Portrait of a Man* (Norwood, MA: Plimpton Press, 1934), 76; George Michael Neese, *Three Years in the Horse Artillery* (New York: Neale Publishing Co., 1911), 112; Harsh, *Taken at the Flood*, 103-4.

14. *OR* 19, pt. 1, 814-5; Harsh, *Taken at the Flood*, 108. According to Stuart's report, Fitz Lee's brigade formed his left at New Market on the Baltimore and Ohio Railroad, Wade Hampton's brigade was in the center near Hyattstown, and Beverly Robertson's brigade (under Thomas Munford) held the right at Poolesville. *OR* 19, pt. 1, 815.

15. Schildt, *Roads to Antietam*, 1-2; Henry Kyd Douglas, I Rode with Stonewall: The War Experiences of the Youngest Member of Jackson's Staff (Chapel Hill, NC: University of North Carolina Press, 1940), 147-8; Wert, *General James Longstreet*, 182.

16. *OR* 19, pt. 1, 38; Harsh, *Taken at the Flood*, 109.

17. Sears, *Landscape Turned Red*, 80-81. The 15th New Jersey was an example of a newly formed regiment sent to an established brigade. Although they joined fellow Jerseymen, the newcomers were harassed and chastised because they had missed so much of the war. Bradley M. Gottfried, *Kearny's Own: The History of the First New Jersey Brigade in the Civil War* (New Brunswick, NJ: Rutgers University Press, 2005), 82-3.

18. Sears, *Landscape Turned Red*, 87; Harsh, *Taken at the Flood*, 112. John Walker used the ford upriver to avoid the congestion of the artillery and trains at White's Ford. He also indicated that he was joined by Brig. Gen. G. B. Anderson's brigade prior to crossing the river. The latter brigade had been detached from D. H. Hill's division to fire on Federal trains. John G. Walker, "Jackson's Capture of Harper's Ferry," *B&L*, vol. 2, 604.

19. Harsh, *Taken at the Flood*, 106, 131.

20. *OR* 19, pt. 2, 601-2.

21. Harsh, *Taken at the Flood*, 114-5; *OR* 19, pt. 1, 38.

22. George B. McClellan, "From the Peninsula to Antietam," *B&L*, vol. 2, 554; Jacob D. Cox, "Forcing Fox's Gap and Turner's Gap," *B&L*, vol. 2, 583; Carman, *The Maryland Campaign*, 170.

23. *OR* 19, pt. 2, 602-3; pt. 1, 145; Harsh, *Taken at the Flood*, 128-31.

24. Harsh, *Taken at the Flood*, 145, 147-50. According to Harsh, Lee underestimated the tenacity of the Federals defending Harpers Ferry. Lee believed that their relatively small numbers, combined with the unfavorable terrain surrounding Harpers Ferry, would convince the garrison to flee rather than put up a defense.

25. *OR* 19, pt. 2, 603-4. Maj. Gen. John Wool also wrote this to Dixon: "there must be no abandoning of a post, and shoot the first man that thinks of it, whether officer or soldier." *OR* 19, pt. 1, 523.

26. *OR* 19, pt. 1, 39.

27. *OR* 19, pt. 1, 912. Walker's men did not have adequate tools and were unable to complete their task.

28. Harsh, *Taken at the Flood*, 168. The Barbara Fritchie incident purportedly occurred as Jackson's men marched out of Frederick.

29. Harsh, *Taken at the Flood*, 173-81; *OR* 19, pt. 1, pp. 815, 852, 912; Mac Wyckoff, *A History of the 3rd South Carolina Infantry, 1861-1865* (Fredericksburg, VA: Sergeant Kirkland's Museum, 1995), 68.

30. Carman, *The Maryland Campaign*, 171-72; *OR* 19, pt. 2, 233, 234.

31. *OR* 19, pt. 2, 238; Carman, *The Maryland Campaign*, 175-76.

32. Harsh, *Taken at the Flood*, 182.

33. J. F. J. Caldwell, *History of a Brigade of South Carolina, Known first as "Gregg's" and subsequently as "McGowan's brigade"* (Marietta, GA.: Continental

Book Co., 1951), 70; *OR* 19, pt. 1, 953; Harsh, *Taken at the Flood*, 182-3.

34. Gary Gallagher, *Lee the Soldier* (Lincoln, NE: University of Lincoln Press, 1996), 8; Harsh, *Taken at the Flood*, 184-4; *OR* 19, pt. 1, 145.

35. Harsh, *Taken at the Flood*, 185; *OR* 19, pt. 1, 1019.

36. Timothy J. Reese, *Sealed with Their Lives: Battle of Crampton's Gap, Burkittsville, MD, Sept. 14, 1862* (Baltimore, MD: Butternut and Blue, 1998), 37-38; Wyckoff, *History of the 3rd South Carolina*, 68; Lafayette McLaws, *"The Maryland Campaign." An Address Delivered before the Confederate Veterans Association of Savannah, Ga.*, vol. 3, 7, 19.

37. *OR* 19, pt.1, 39-40, 432, 479; pt. 2, 263; Carman, *The Maryland Campaign*, 178-79. The Federal I Corps was dispersed. Reynolds' division ended the day at Brookeville; King's division at Lisbon, and Ricketts' at Cooksville.

38. *OR* 19, pt. 1, 524.

39. Carman, *The Maryland Campaign*, 186; *OR* 19, pt. 2, 758.

40. *OR* 19, pt. 1, 852; McLaws, "Maryland," 8-9; Reese, *Sealed with Their Lives*, 37, 39, 45; Harsh, *Taken at the Flood*, 200-3.

41. *OR* 19, pt. 1, 913, 953, 980; Harsh, *Taken at the Flood*, 198-200, 204-5.

42. Harsh, *Taken at the Flood*, 190.

43. Daniel H. Hill., "The Battle of South Mountain, or 'Boonsboro': Fighting for Time at Turner's and Fox's Gaps," *B&L*, vol. 2, 560; *OR* 19, pt. 1, 1,019, 1,031, 1,052; Harsh, *Taken at the Flood*, 207-8. Stuart's cavalry division was widely dispersed on September 12. Munford's brigade was at Jefferson just south of Burkittstown; Fitz Lee's was in Westminster, and Hampton's brigade, which had been in Frederick and had engaged the advance elements of the Federal IX Corps, was falling back to the northwest. Meanwhile, Alfred Pleasanton's Federal cavalry was moving north from Urbana to Frederick.

44. *OR* 19, pt. 1, 432, 479; pt. 2, 271; Harsh, *Taken at the Flood*, 210.

45. *OR* 19, pt. 1, 432, 479; Schildt, *Roads to Antietam*, 73-4, 80.

46. *OR* 19, pt. 1, 140; Harsh, *Taken at the Flood*, 212-4.

47. *OR* 19, pt. 1, 816-17, 823, 1019; Harsh, *Taken at the Flood*, 230-37; Carman, *The Maryland Campaign*, 345-46; Communication from Brad Coker to Steve Stotelmyer. On the right, Stuart sent Munford's brigade to Jefferson, while his center brigade under Hampton rode to Hagen's Gap on the National Turnpike. Munford had only two regiments with him, less 300 men

detached to guard Lafayette McLaws' rear. Detachments from Pleasanton's cavalry division would press Munford from three directions and force him to fall back slowly to Burkittsville, and then to Crampton's Gap. Meanwhile, the main portion of Pleasonton's division, supported by Federal infantry, forced Hampton to withdraw from the pass and retreat through Middletown.

48. Silas Colgrove, "The Finding of Lee's Lost Order," *B&L*, vol. 2, 603. It appears that the orders were found by a group of soldiers that included Sgt. John Bloss, Pvt. David Vance, and Cpl. Barton Mitchell. The latter was severely wounded at Antietam a few days later and died within four years. After reading Special Orders 191, McClellan is said to have thrown his hands in the air and exclaimed, "Now I know what to do!" Gallagher, *Lee The Soldier*, 26. For an in-depth examination about the Lost Orders controversy, see Wilbur D. Jones Jr., "Who Lost Lee's Lost Orders? Stonewall Jackson, His Courier, and Special Orders No. 191," in *Antietam: The Maryland Campaign of 1862*, a special issue of *Civil War Regiments: A Journal of the American Civil War*, vol. 5, no. 3 (Savas Publishing Company, 1997), 1-26, hereafter *CWR*. Jones offers a compelling case that Henry Kyd Douglas lost Special Orders No. 191.

49. *OR* 19, pt. 1, 45-46.

Map Set 2. Preparing for the Battle: The South Mountain Gaps (September 13 - 14)

1. Carman, *The Maryland Campaign*, 198-9; *U. S. Congress, Joint Committee on the Conduct of the War* (Washington: U. S. Printing Office, 1863), pt. 1, 451-2.

2. Harsh, *Taken at the Flood*, 242-48; *OR* 19, pt. 1, 817; Gallagher, *Lee the Soldier*, 26; James Longstreet, *From Manassas to Appomattox: The Civil War in America* (Bloomington, IN: University of Indiana Press, 1960), 219-20. D. H. Hill was Thomas "Stonewall" Jackson's brother-in-law. Hill had a reputation as being "cross, impulsive, and often gives offence," and this from a colleague who liked him. Robert K. Krick, "It Appeared as Though Mutual Extermination Would Put a Stop to the Awful Carnage," in *The Antietam Campaign*, Gary W. Gallagher, ed. (Chapel Hill, NC: University of North Carolina Press, 1999), 225.

3. Carman, *The Maryland Campaign*, 281; Sears, *Landscape Turned Red*, 117-19.

4. Hill, "The Battle of South Mountain," 560-61; Jacob D. Cox, "Forcing Fox's Gap and Turner's Gap," 585.

5. D. Scott Hartwig, "'My God Be Careful!', The Morning Fight at Fox's Gap," *CWR*, vol. 5, No. 3, 27; Cox, "Forcing Fox's Gap and Turner's Gap," 585-86. Because of the friendship between Alfred Pleasonton and George Crook, Cox decided to let the latter's brigade accompany Pleasonton's troopers. Col. Eliakim Scammon objected because it was his brigade's turn to lead the march. Cox reluctantly agreed, but Pleasonton was not happy with the change in orders. Jacob D. Cox, *Military Reminiscences of the Civil War* (New York: Charles Scribner's and Sons, 1900), 277-78.

6. Stephen W. Sears, *The Civil War Papers of George B. McClellan: Selected Correspondence, 1860-1865* (New York: Ticknor & Fields, 1989), 455n5; *OR* 19, pt. 1, 881-2; Reese, *Sealed with Their Lives*, 40-45.

7. *OR* 19, pt. 1, 1019-22; Harsh, *Taken at the Flood*, 257. Apparently unhappy with how Stuart was handling the defense of the National Road, Gen. Lee ordered D. H. Hill to ride to Turner's Gap from his headquarters at Boonsboro on the morning of September 14. Hill has been criticized for putting too much reliance on Stuart to guard the gaps prior to his orders to ride to oversee the sector. Some authors believe Hill should have accompanied his two brigades to Turner's Gap to ascertain their deployment and learn more about the terrain features in the area. D. H. Hill., "The Battle of South Mountain," 560; Carman, *The Maryland Campaign*, 373.

8. Longstreet, *From Manassas to Appomattox*, 220; *OR* 19, pt. 1, 839; Harsh, *Taken at the Flood*, 254.

9. *OR* 19, pt. 1, 853, 872-3; Reese, *Sealed with Their Lives*, 45-46; George S. Barnard, *War Talks of Confederate Veterans* (Petersburg, VA: Fenn & Owen, Publishers, 1892), 302. Col. William Parham of the 41st Virginia commanded the brigade in Brig. Gen. William Mahone's absence. Mahone was wounded during the Second Manassas Campaign, and Parham was still suffering from a severe wound he received on July 1 at Malvern Hill. Although he would serve throughout the conflict, often in limited capacities, Parham "died of wounds" (Malvern Hill injury) apparently near the end of the war. Robert K. Krick, *Lee's Colonels: A Biographical Register of the Field Officers of the Army of Northern Virginia*, 3rd Edition (Morningside, 1991), 298.

10. Cox, "Forcing Fox's Gap and Turner's Gap," 584-85; Sears, *Landscape Turned Red*, 129.

Map Set 3. South Mountain: Fox's Gap (Morning)

1. Cox, *Reminiscences*, 280; Cox, "Forcing Fox's Gap and Turner's Gap," 586.

2. James L. Speicher, "The Sumter Artillery," *CWR*, vol. 3, No. 2, 13-14. Lane's battery was composed of two 3-inch Ordnance Rifles, three 10-pounder Parrotts, and one 12-pounder Napoleon. According to Josephus Strother, one of Lane's gunners, the Parrotts were on the heights north of the turnpike while the other pieces accompanied Alfred Colquitt. Steven Stotelmyer, "Bloody Sabbath."

3. Cox, *Reminiscences*, 280-81; Cox, "Forcing Fox's Gap and Turner's Gap," 586.

4. Cox, *Reminiscences*, 281; *OR* 19, pt. 1, 458, 463-64; Steven Stotelmyer, "Bloody Sabbath"; Hartwig, "The Morning Fight at Fox's Gap," 34; J. Horton and S. Teverbaugh, *A History of the Eleventh Regiment, Ohio Volunteers* (Dayton, OH.: W. A. Shuey, Printer, 1866), 71; Curt Johnson and Richard C. Anderson Jr., *Artillery Hell: The Employment of Artillery at Antietam* (College Station, TX: Texas A&M University Press, 1995), 35-38. The actual route is the subject of some debate. For example, Ezra Carman believed Col. Scammon's column left Bolivar, took the National Pike, and turned left on a side road. Carman, *The Maryland Campaign*, 318.

5. Hill, "The Battle of South Mountain," 561. D. H. Hill's account of South Mountain, published after the war in B&L, must be used with caution. After it appeared in print, Hill wrote a letter to his son claiming the article was "badly mutilated" and "quite unsatisfactory to me." Hal Bridges, *Lee's Maverick General: Daniel Harvey Hill* (New York: McGraw Hill, 1961), 292.

6. *OR* 19, pt. 1, 1,019; Hill, "The Battle of South Mountain," 562. Stotelmyer, "Bloody Sabbath," makes a convincing case that Colquitt's brigade was not at the base of the mountain, as represented by Hill in his Battles and Leaders piece, but bivouacked higher up near the D. Beachely house. The two leaders probably moved the unit farther up the hill to its final defensive position.

7. Harsh, *Taken at the Flood*, 257-58.

8. *OR* 19, pt. 1, 1,019-20; Hartwig, "The Morning Fight at Fox's Gap," 29-30; Harsh, *Taken at the Flood*, 256-57. Orr's Pass lies between Bartman's Hill and Pine Knob. It is sometimes referred to as Hamburg Pass.

9. Hill, "The Battle of South Mountain," 562.

10. Hill, "The Battle of South Mountain," 561-62; George D. Grattan, "The Battle of Boonsboro

Gap or South Mountain, *Southern Historical Society Papers*, 52 vols. (Broadfoot Publishing Company, 1990), vol. 39, 37-8, hereafter *SHSP*.

11. Stotelmyer, "Bloody Sabbath;" Hartwig, "The Morning Fight at Fox's Gap," 34.

12. Hartwig, "The Morning Fight at Fox's Gap," 38-9; Stotelmyer, "Bloody Sabbath;" Thomas Rosser to D. H. Hill July 10, 1883 (cited in Stotelmyer's manuscript). Capt. J. W. Bondurant's battery was composed of a pair of 3-inch Ordnance Rifles and two 12-pounder howitzers.

13. Carman, *The Maryland Campaign*, 323-24; *OR* 19, pt. 1, 1,040; Hartwig, "The Morning Fight at Fox's Gap," 39-40.

14. Rutherford B. Hayes, *Diary and Letters of Rutherford B. Hayes* (Freemont, OH: Ohio Historical Center, 1998), 199; Hartwig, "The Morning Fight at Fox's Gap," 40-1. According to Stotelmyer, a close examination of Col. Duncan McRae's official report, *OR* 19, pt. 1, 1,040, indicates the right side of the 5th North Carolina was the first to retreat.

15. Hayes, *Diary and Letters*, 356; Carman, *The Maryland Campaign*, 325. While he was lying wounded on the ground, Lt. Col. Hayes engaged in a convivial talk with a wounded North Carolinian nearby. Hayes, Diary and Letters, 356.

16. Walter Clark, ed., *Histories of the Several Regiments & Battalions From North Carolina in the Great War, 1861-1865*, 5 vols. (Raleigh: E. M. Uzzell, Printer and Binder, 1901), vol. 1, 627, hereafter *North Carolina Regiments*; OR, 19, pt. 1, 1,040-41; John Purifoy, "History of the Jeff Davis Artillery," Alabama Department of Archives and History.

17. *OR* 19, pt. 1, 462; Hartwig, "The Morning Fight at Fox's Gap," 42-3.

18. *OR* 19, pt. 1, 462, 464; Stotelmyer, "Bloody Sabbath." Col. Scammon reported that the 12th Ohio advanced as a skirmish line to limit casualties during its charge against the 23rd North Carolina. The Buckeye's commander, Col. Carr White, is silent on this issue. OR 19, pt. 1, 462, 464.

19. *OR* 19, pt. 1, 269, 461, 469; Lawrence R. Laboda, *From Selma to Appomattox: The History of the Jeff Davis Artillery* (Shippensburg, PA: White Mane Publishing Company, 1994), 45-6; Wayne Jacobs Diary, in Stotelmyer, "Bloody Sabbath."

20. Hartwig, "The Morning Fight at Fox's Gap," 44; *OR* 19, pt. 1, 469, 1,046; Hill, "Battle of South Mountain," 563-64.

21. *OR* 19, pt. 1, 469, 1,046; Hartwig, "The Morning Fight at Fox's Gap," 45.

22. *OR* 19, pt. 1, 1,041.

23. Hartwig, "The Morning Fight at Fox's Gap," 45-6; *OR* 19, pt. 1, 459, 462, 464; J. E. D. Ward, *The Twelfth Ohio Volunteer Infantry* (Ripley, OH: np, 1864), 59. Ezra Carman suggested that Crome's section of McMillan's battery was in front of the 12th Ohio. This is a reasonable assumption because men from that infantry regiment helped place the guns. However, a careful reading of Alfred Iverson's correspondence and a walk over the battlefield with Steve Stotelmyer have convinced the author that Crome's section was farther north near the 36th Ohio.

24. Hartwig, "The Morning Fight at Fox's Gap," 46; Stotelmyer, "Bloody Sabbath." Ezra Carman placed the 36th Ohio on the right of the 30th Ohio. Carman, *The Maryland Campaign*, 327-28. My research, discussions with various historians, and a careful examination of terrain have convinced me that Stotelmyer and Hartwig are correct.

25. *OR* 19, pt. 1, 1041, 1,048-49. Seeking to free himself from the crushing responsibility of commanding Garland's brigade in such a precarious position, McRae ascertained Col. Tew's seniority status. When he discovered that Tew outranked him, McRae offered the brigade to him, but Tew wisely refused and requested orders from McRae on where and how to place the 450 men he had just marched onto the field.

26. Horton and Teverbaugh, *A History of the Eleventh Regiment, Ohio Volunteers*, 71-72; Stotelmyer, "Bloody Sabbath."

27. Clark, *North Carolina Regiments*, vol. 2, 220-21; *OR* 19, pt. 1, 1,041, 1,046, 1,049; Carman, *The Maryland Campaign*, 328-29.

28. Hartwig, "The Morning Fight at Fox's Gap," 48; Cox, "Forcing Fox's Gap and Turner's Gap," 587; *OR* 19, pt. 1, 1042. One of the soldiers wrote home, "With bayonets fixed we stealthily crawled to the summit of the hill, when the order was given, 'Up and at them!' At the word, every man promptly sprang to his feet and with a deafening shout rushed forward." *Youngstown Morning Register*, October 9, 1862.

29. Hartwig, "The Morning Fight at Fox's Gap," 48-9; *OR* 19, pt. 1, 1042; Horton and Teverbaugh, *A History of the Eleventh Regiment, Ohio Volunteers*, 72. According to Daniel H. Hill, the Buckeyes were so close to Garland's line at the start of the charge that the North Carolinians only had time to fire one volley before they were overwhelmed. Hill, "Battle of South Mountain," 566. Steve Stotelmyer, an authority on Fox's Gap, believes the Ohio troops were especially motivated

to do well at this battle because they had been so roughly handled at Second Bull Run. Col. Duncan McRae ordered the new commander of the 5th North Carolina, Capt. Thomas Garrett, to rally his troops on Ridge Road. Waving his flag, the flagbearer gathered a number of men around the banner but a bullet drilled into him, knocking down the flag and causing the men to scatter into the woods. Their fight was over for the day. *OR* 19, pt. 1, 1,041.

30. Carman, *The Maryland Campaign*, 328-29; Hartwig, "The Morning Fight at Fox's Gap," 49, 51; *OR* 19, pt. 1, 1,042. Col. Crook was with the 36th Ohio during this period. According to a Federal veteran, "Colonel Crook, his hat held aloft in one hand, and his sword in the other, shouted to the command, '36th, charge!' Away they went, yelling like demons incarnate." Ohio Antietam Battlefield Commission, *Antietam, Report of the Ohio Antietam Battlefield Commission* (Springfield, OH: Springfield Publishing Co., 1904), 88. The fighting at the wall was intense. One Union soldier described it as "a carnival of death," adding it was "hell itself turned loose" and "there was no more desperate battle during the whole campaign." Sol R. Smith, "South Mountain," *National Tribune*, January 17, 1895. The Ohio soldiers followed the fleeing Tar Heels for about 300 yards into the deep woods on the opposite side of Ridge Road. Stotelmyer, "Bloody Sabbath."

31. Hill, "Battle of South Mountain," 564; *OR* 19, pt. 1, 1,046; Carman, *The Maryland Campaign*, 328; George Gorman, "Memoirs of a Rebel," *Military Images Magazine* (November-December, 1981), 4-5; *OR* 19, pt. 1, 1,049.

32. *OR* 19, pt. 1, 465, 1,046; Carman, *The Maryland Campaign*, 329-30; Hill, "Battle of South Mountain," vol. 2, 564.

33. Stotelmyer, "Bloody Sabbath."

34. Cox, "Forcing Fox's Gap and Turner's Gap," vol. 2, 587; Hartwig, "The Morning Fight at Fox's Gap," 53-4. Cox later wrote: "Our own losses had not been trifling, and it seemed wise to contract our lines a little, so we might have some reserve and hold the crest we had won till the rest of the Ninth Corps should arrive." Cox, "Forcing Fox's Gap and Turner's Gap," 587.

Map Set 4. South Mountain: Fox's Gap (noon - 8:00 p.m.)

1. Carman, *The Maryland Campaign*, 331; Cox, "Forcing Fox's Gap and Turner's Gap," 587. Lt. Daniel Glassie's guns were soon out of action, not because of Bondurant's accurate artillery fire but because the cannoneers ran out of water to swab the hot cannon barrels. Joe Baker and Steve Stotelmyer, "The Battle of the South Mountain," in *A Gap in Time: Proceedings of the Appalachian Train Conference*, Joe Baker, ed. (February 2003), 16.

2. *OR* 19, pt. 1, 1,020; Carman, *The Maryland Campaign*, 332.

3. *OR* 19, pt. 1, 428; Carman, *The Maryland Campaign*, 333.

4. Lewis Crater, *History of the Fiftieth Penn. Vet. Vols., 1861-1865* (Reading, PA: Coleman Printing House, 1884), 32-33; Carman, *The Maryland Campaign*, 336; *OR* 19, pt. 1, 428.

5. Crater, *History of the Fiftieth Penn. Vet. Vols.*, 32; Pennsylvania at Antietam (Harrisburg, PA: Harrisburg Printing Company, 1906), 77. According to Crater, "amid the shrieking of the bursting shells, there comes rushing down the mountainside a confused mass of men, with blanched faces, terror depicted upon their very countenances, nothing could stop them."

6. Carman, *The Maryland Campaign*, 336; Samuel P. Bates, *History of Pennsylvania Volunteers* (Harrisburg, PA: B. Singerley, State Printer, 1870), vol. 1, 1,060, 1,279; *OR* 19, pt. 1, 439-40. The evidence is unclear, but the 45th Pennsylvania and 46th New York were apparently supported at this time by a regrouped 8th Michigan on their left.

7. *OR* 19, pt. 1, 428; Carman, *The Maryland Campaign*, 336-37; William Todd, *The Seventy-Ninth Highlanders, New York Volunteers in the War of Rebellion, 1861-1865* (New York: Brandow, Barton & Co., 1886), 232. According to a history of Bondurant's battery, the unit redeployed in a field northeast of the Wise cabin in a semi-circular deployment facing south and southeast. Laboda, *From Selma to Appomattox*, 46, 48-9.

8. *OR* 19, pt. 1, 434; William G. Gavin, *Infantryman Pettit* (Shippensburg, PA: White Mane Publishing Company, 1990), 16.

9. Kurt Graham, "Death of a Brigade: Drayton's Brigade at Fox's Gap, September 14, 1862," www.angelfire.com/ga2/PhillipsLegion/deathofabrigade.html.

10. Stewart Sifarkis, *Who was Who in the Civil War* (New York: Facts on File Publications, 1988), 545-6; Carman, *The Maryland Campaign*, 340.

11. Kurt Graham, "Death of a Brigade"; Augustus Dickert, *History of Kershaw's Brigade* (Dayton, OH: Morningside House, 1976), 174.

12. Baker and Stotelmyer, "The Battle of the South Mountain," 68; Graham, "Death of a Brigade."

13. *OR* vol. 19, pt. 1, 428, 441; Allen D. Albert, *History of the Forty-Fifth Regiment Pennsylvania Veteran Volunteer Infantry, 1861-1865* (Williamsport, PA: Grit Publishing Company, 1912), 53.

14. Hill, "The Battle of South Mountain," 571; Carman, *The Maryland Campaign*, 337-38; *Antietam Battlefield Memorial Commission of Pennsylvania, Pennsylvania at Antietam* (Harrisburg, PA: Harrisburg Publishing Company, 1906), 53. Years after this engagement D. H. Hill wrote with unveiled frustration that he had ordered Lane's battery to open fire on the Federals assailing Drayton's position. "His firing was wild, not a shot hitting the mark," complained Hill, who is not known for his accurate assessment of what transpired that day at Fox's Gap or his love for the artillery branch. Hill, "The Battle of South Mountain," 571.

15. Hill, "The Battle of South Mountain," 571; Charles A. Cuffel, *History of Durell's Battery in the Civil War: A Narrative of the Campaigns and Battles of . . . in the War of the Rebellion* (Philadelphia: Craig Finley and Co., 1904), 74; Todd, *The Seventy-Ninth Highlanders*, 232.

16. *OR* 19, pt. 1, 922.

17. Carman, *The Maryland Campaign*, 336-37; Edward O. Lord, ed., *History of the Ninth Regiment New Hampshire Volunteers* (Concord, NH: Republican Free Press Association, 1895), 72.

18. Thomas H. Parker, *History of the 51st Regiment of P.V.* (Philadelphia: King and Baird Publishers, 1869), 225; Carman, *The Maryland Campaign*, 336-37; *OR* 19, pt. 1, 442; Lord, *History of the Ninth Regiment in the War of the Rebellion*, 73.

19. Baker and Stotelmyer, "The Battle of the South Mountain," 68.

20. Carman, *The Maryland Campaign*, 338; Cuffel, *History of Durell's Battery*, 73; Graham, "Death of a Brigade"; Bates, *History of the Pennsylvania Volunteers*, vol. 1, 1,060; John Michael Priest, *Captain James Wren's Civil War Diary* (New York: Berkley Books, 1991), 84-5. Graham, "Death of a Brigade"; Dickert, *History of Kershaw's Brigade*, 174-5.

22. *OR* 19, pt. 1, 443; Oliver Christian Bosbyshell, *The 48th in the War. Being a Narrative of the Campaigns of the 48th Regiment, Infantry, Pennsylvania Veteran Volunteers, During the War of the Rebellion* (Philadelphia: Avil Printing Company, 1895), 75-76.

23. Graham, "Death of a Brigade: Drayton's Brigade at Fox's Gap, September 14, 1862," *Savannah Republican*, October 16, 1862. Drayton had long been considered unsuitable for field command and owed his position to a longtime friendship with President Jefferson Davis. Drayton was a poor organizer, and most of his superiors complained about him. In an extremely sharp rebuke of Drayton, Gen. Robert E. Lee explained to President Davis in late 1862 that he and his brigade had been "a source of delay and embarrassment from the time the army left Richmond," was slow at Second Manassas, routed at South Mountain and Sharpsburg, and lacked discipline. "He is a gentleman," concluded Lee, "but seems to lack the capacity to command." William C. Davis, "Thomas Fenwick Drayton," in William C. Davis, ed., *The Confederate General*, 6 vols. (National Historical Society, 1991), vol. 2, p. 77. The West Point graduate left Lee's army on November 26, 1862, for a variety of minor administrative posts in the Trans-Mississippi Theater. Sifakis, *Who Was Who in the Civil War*, 191; Ezra J. Warner, *Generals in Gray: The Lives of the Confederate Commanders* (Baton Rouge, LA: LSU Press, 1959), 75-6.

24. *OR* 19, pt. 1, 186-7.

25. *OR* 19, pt. 1, 922.

26. *OR* 19, pt. 1, 909; Carman, *The Maryland Campaign*, 339-40.

27. Carman, *The Maryland Campaign*, 339-40; *OR* 19, pt. 1, 909, 922.

28. Clark, *North Carolina Regiments*, vol. 2, 245-6; *OR* 19, pt. 1, 1046; Calvin Leach Diary, Southern Historical Collection, University of North Carolina. In his official account of the actions of his 3rd North Carolina (Ripley's brigade) Col. Stephen Thruston noted: "we advanced in line of battle up the side of a steep and rugged mountain covered by an almost impenetrable growth of ivy, advancing along half a mile, my line of skirmishers came in contact with a similar line from General George [Burgwyn] Anderson's Brigade, deployed in a direction nearly perpendicular to my line and masking my entire right." Janet Hewett, ed., *Supplement to the Official Records of the Union and Confederate Armies* (Wilmington, N.C.: Broadfoot Pub. Co., 1994), vol. 3, 585. William DeRosset of the same regiment (3rd North Carolina) was very concerned about how Ripley's men would be viewed after the war, particularly since their former commander did not actively involve himself in the defense of his actions. "If Ripley had any regard for his own reputation he would answer Genl. [D. H.] Hill's charge himself," complained DeRosset, "but it is not in him and we must look after the reputation of our men ourselves." William DeRosset to S. D. Thruston, July 12, 1886, copy in the 3rd North Carolina file, Antietam NMP.

29. Carman, *The Maryland Campaign*, 342-43; A Committee of the Regimental Association, *History of the Thirty-Fifth Regiment, Massachusetts Volunteers 1862-1865: With A Roster* (Boston: Mills, Knight & Co., 1884), 27-30.

30. Carman, *The Maryland Campaign*, 340-41; Hill, "The Battle of South Mountain," 569; OR 19, pt. 1, 1,032, 1,046.

31. OR 19, pt. 1, 450; Carman, *The Maryland Campaign*, 339; Charles F. Johnson, *The Long Roll* (East Aurora, NY: Roycrofters Printers, 1881), 186. The 16th Connecticut did not join Harland's brigade until September 16. OR 19, pt. 2, 197.

32. Carman, *The Maryland Campaign*, 341-42; Clark, *North Carolina Regiments*, vol. 2, 245-6; OR 19, pt. 1, 1046; Matthew J. Graham, *History of the Ninth New York Volunteers* (New York: E. P. Coby & Co., 1900), 272-72; Charles Crofut to Mira, September 28, 1862 (copy in Steve Stotelmyer's collection); Crater, *History of the Fiftieth Regiment, Penna. Vet. Vol.*, 34; *Pennsylvania at Antietam*, 76.

33. Carman, *The Maryland Campaign*, 342.

34. *The Lynn Weekly Reporter*, October 18, 1862; Albert Pope Journal, copy in the 35th Massachusetts file, Antietam NMP.

35. Carman, *The Maryland Campaign*, 342; OR 19, pt. 1, 922; Richard Sauers, *The Civil War Journal of Colonel William J. Bolton* (Conshohocken, PA.: Combined Books, 2000), 82.

36. William R. McConnell, *Remember Reno: A Biography of Major General Jesse Lee Reno* (Shippensburg, PA: White Mane Publishing Co., 1996), 81-2; A. H. Wood, "Reno's Death," *National Tribune*, July 6, 1883; Joseph Gould, *The Story Of The Forty-Eighth: A Record Of The Campaigns Of The Forty-Eighth Regiment, Pennsylvania Veteran Volunteer Infantry* (Mt. Carmel, PA: Regimental Association, 1908), 78-79; Carman, *The Maryland Campaign*, 343-44. Reno's biographer, William R. McConnell, believed the general was killed by friendly fire. According to this hypothesis, a soldier from the 35th Massachusetts saw a horsemen, thought he was the enemy, and screamed "Rebel cavalry!" before firing a bullet into Reno. Most other sources discount this story and believe one of Hood's men fired the fatal shot. In his report of his division's actions on the evening of September 14, Hood noted, "I gave instructions . . . to order their men to fix bayonets; and, when the enemy came within 75 to 100 yards, I ordered the men to front and charge. They obeyed promptly, with a genuine Confederate yell, and the Federals were driven back, pell mell, over and beyond the mountain, at a much quicker pace than they had descended." McConnell, *Remember Reno*, 81-2; OR 19, pt. 1, 922.

37. Carman, *The Maryland Campaign*, 375-8.

Map Set 5. South Mountain: Frosttown Plateau (2:00 - 9:00 p.m.)

1. E. M. Woodward, *Our Campaigns: or, The Marches, Bivouacs, Battles, Incidents of Camp Life and History of our Regiment During Its Three Year Term of Service* (Shippensburg, Pa.: Burd Street Press, 1994), 149-52; Carman, *The Maryland Campaign*, 345-7; OR 19, pt. 2, 182. Maj. Gen. Ambrose Burnside sent three messages for Joseph Hooker's I Corps to continue marching to South Mountain. When he reached the corps, Burnside encountered Hooker, who was just returning from his reconnaissance. D. Scott Hartwig, "It Looked Like a Task to Storm," *North and South Magazine*, vol. 5, no. 7, 39.

2. Hartwig, "It Looked Like a Task to Storm," 39; Josiah R. Sypher, *History of the Pennsylvania Reserve Corps* (Lancaster, PA: Elias Barr & Co.: 1865), 368.

3. Edwin A. Glover, *Bucktailed Wildcats: A Regiment of Civil War Volunteers* (New York: Thomas Yoseloff, 1960), 145; Carman, *The Maryland Campaign*, 347-48; OR 19, pt. 1, 273-4. According to historian Scott Hartwig, Seymour's regiments were initially deployed in column of regiments behind the 13th Pennsylvania Reserve skirmish line. Hartwig, "It Looked Like a Task to Storm," 41.

4. OR 19, pt. 1, 1034; Darrell L. Collins, *Major General Robert E. Rodes of the Army of Northern Virginia* (New York: Savas Beatie, 2008), 157-8.

5. Carman, *The Maryland Campaign*, 349-50; OR 19, pt. 1, 267; Bates, *History of Pennsylvania*, vol. 1, 918. The 13th Pennsylvania Reserves was a crack outfit armed with breech-loading Sharps rifles. Glover, *Bucktailed Wildcats*, 148.

6. Collins, *Rodes*, 159; Carman, *The Maryland Campaign*, 348-49; Swisher, *Warrior in Gray: General Robert Rodes of Lee's Army* (White Mane, 2001), 59.

7. Collins, *Rodes*, 160; Carman, *The Maryland Campaign*, 350. Gallagher entered the battle with a painful case of kidney stones. Joseph Gibbs, *Three Years in the Bloody Eleventh* (College Park, PA: Penn State University Press, 2002), 175.

8. Bates, *History of the Pennsylvania Volunteers*, vol. 1, 369; 549; OR 19, pt. 1, 272.

9. Robert E. Park, *Sketch of the Twelfth Alabama Infantry* (Richmond, VA: William Ellis Jones, 1906), 89; Robert E. Park, "Anniversary of the Battle of

Boonsboro, Maryland," *SHSP*, vol. 33 (1905), 278-7.

10. Memoir of William Olcott, 10th Pennsylvania Reserves folder, Antietam NMP; Carman, *The Maryland Campaign*, 359-50.

11. Carman, *The Maryland Campaign*, 352; Bates, *History of Pennsylvania*, vol. 1, 584.

12. Brandon Beck, *Third Alabama! The Civil War Memoir of Brigadier General Cullen Andrews Battle, CSA* (Tuscaloosa, AL: University of Alabama Press, 2000), 56; Collins, *Rodes*, 160.

13. *OR* 19, pt. 1, 1,035.

14. Carman, *The Maryland Campaign*, 351.

15. *OR* 19, pt. 1, 267.

16. DeWitt Boyd Stone, Jr., *Wandering to Glory: Confederate Veterans Remember Evans's Brigade* (Columbia, SC: U. of South Carolina Press, 2002), 60; Carman, *The Maryland Campaign*, 355.

17. *OR* 19, pt. 1, 1,035.

18. *OR* 19, pt. 1, 941-2; Anonymous letter to parents, September 29, 1862 (copy in the 7th Pennsylvania Reserves folder, Antietam NMP). According to Ezra Carman, the right side of Stevens' line provided a "stout defense" and as a result, it took longer for Magilton's brigade to reach the summit than the rest of Meade's division. By the time it finally reached its destination it was "quite dark." Carman, *The Maryland Campaign*, 353. The 17th South Carolina's gallant initial stand held the left of Magilton's brigade at bay until the Federals moved around the Palmetto regiment's left flank. A non-commissioned officer serving in the 8th Pennsylvania Reserves recalled this part of the fight: "We were within twenty or thirty steps of them, directly on their left, and they did not see us; then we mowed them down. Poor fellows! I almost pitied them, to see them sink down by dozens at every discharge!" Civil War Diary of Griffin Lewis Baldwin, copy in the 7th Pennsylvania Reserves folder, Antietam NMP; Isaac Andrew Moore, "Eighth Pennsylvania Reserves," 126, copy in the 8th Pennsylvania Reserves folder, Antietam NMP. Author Michael Priest estimated that the South Carolinians were on the mountain for about an hour; it is possible the actual time was much less. John Michael Priest, *Before Antietam: The Battle for South Mountain* (Shippensburg, PA: White Mane Publishing Co., 1992), 243.

19. *OR* 19, pt. 1, 1,021, 1,035-6; Collins, *Rodes*, 161. Meade's division lost about 392 men, or about ten percent of its effective strength. *OR* 19, pt. 1, 185-6.

Map Set 6. South Mountain: Turner's Gap (3:30 - 8:30 p.m.)

1. Marsena R. Patrick, *Inside Lincoln's Army: The Diary of Marsena Rudolph Patrick, Provost Marshal General, Army of the Potomac* (New York: Thomas Yoseloff, 1964), 143; Harrison J. Mills, *Chronicles of the Twenty-First Regiment, New York State Volunteers: Embracing A Full History of the Regiment* (Buffalo: 21st Regiment Veteran Association, 1887), 279; *OR* 19, pt. 1, 241; Carman, *The Maryland Campaign*, 359.

2. Mills, *Chronicles of the Twenty-First Regiment New York Volunteers*, 280.

3. Carman, *The Maryland Campaign*, 357-58.

4. Joseph T. Durkin, ed., John Dooley, *Confederate Soldier: His War Journal* (Notre Dame, IN: University of Notre Dame Press, 1963), 35-6.

5. *OR* 19, pt. 1, 220, 241-2.

6. *OR* 19, pt. 1, 894; Roger U. Delauter, *18th Virginia Infantry* (Lynchburg, VA: H. E. Howard, 1985), 16.

7. *OR* 19, pt. 1, 894-5; William A. Young and Patricia C. Young, *56th Virginia Infantry* (Lynchburg, VA: H. E. Howard, 1990), 57-58. A veteran from the 18th Virginia recalled that the enemy's main body "sheltered themselves among trees, rocks, &c." The Virginians responded with "spirit and vigor for some time." Delauter, *18th Virginia*, 16.

8. *OR* 19, pt. 1, 232, 242.

9. Hill, "The Battle of South Mountain," 571, 572.

10. Carman, *The Maryland Campaign*, 362; *OR* 19, pt. 1, 220, 221, 231.

11. *OR* 19, pt. 1, 232; Thomas Clemens, "A Brigade Commander's First Fight: The Letters of Colonel Walter Phelps Jr. During the Maryland Campaign," *CWR*, vol. 5, no. 3, 65.

12. Carman, *The Maryland Campaign*, 359; *OR* 19, pt. 1, 220, 232.

13. *OR* 19, pt. 1, 232; Henry T. Owen, "Annals of the War—Chapters of Unwritten History: South Mountain," *Philadelphia Weekly Times*, July 31, 1880.

14. Owen, "South Mountain"; *OR* 19, pt. 1, 895.

15. Owen, "South Mountain"; *OR* 19, pt. 1, 895; Robert T. Bell, *11th Virginia Infantry* (Lynchburg, VA: H. E. Howard, 1985), 30. A veteran of the 18th Virginia described the regiment's new position in the rear this way: "the ground being uneven, rocky, and covered with bushes and briars, the regiment became a good deal scattered." Delauter, *18th Virginia*, 18.

16. *OR* 19, pt. 1, 895.

17. Mills, *Chronicles of the Twenty-First Regiment New York Volunteers*, 281.

18. *OR* 19, pt. 1, 904.

19. *OR* 19, pt. 1, 220.

20. Abram P. Smith, *History of the Seventy-Sixth Regiment New York Volunteers: What it Endured and Accomplished; Containing Descriptions of its Twenty-Five Battles; its . . . a Complete Record of the Enlisted Men* (Courtland, NY: Truair, Smith and Miles, Printers, 1867), 152; Edward L. Barnes, "The 95th New York at South Mountain." *National Tribune*, January 7, 1886.

21. Diary of Mathew Hurlenger, Copy in 56th Pennsylvania file, Antietam NMP.

22. Smith, *History of the Seventy-Sixth Regiment, New York Volunteers*, 154; "The 95th New York" *National Tribune*, January 7, 1886. A soldier in the 76th New York wrote to his father after the battle, "I must confess I felt a little squeamish as it was getting most dark, and the idea of going into the woods, filled with rebels who were acquainted with every rock and hole, while we knew nothing of their whereabouts, but it was too late now to stop and think, so the order was given to "fix bayonets." *Cherry Valley Gazette*, October 1, 1862.

23. John E. Devine, *8th Virginia Infantry* (Lynchburg, VA: H. E. Howard, 1983), 12.

24. Carman, *The Maryland Campaign*, 362-63; *OR* 19, pt. 1, 906.

25. *OR* 19, pt. 1, 184-5; Pierro, ed., *The Maryland Campaign*, 449.

26. *OR* 19, pt. 1, 247; Carman, *The Maryland Campaign*, 364; Alan T. Nolan and Marc Storch, "The Iron Brigade Earns its Name," *Blue and Gray Magazine*, vol. XXI, no. 6 (2004), 11. The 2nd Wisconsin was in column of divisions, two companies wide and five deep. Nolan and Storch, "The Iron Brigade Earns its Name," 13.

27. Carman, *The Maryland Campaign*, 365; Grattan, "The Battle of Boonsboro Gap or South Mountain," 36; *OR* 19, pt. 1, 1053, Hewett, ed., *OR Supplement.*, vol. 3, 581; Frank Haskell diary, September 14, 1862, State Historical Society of Wisconsin. Patterson's and Ross' batteries were no longer in position, having been pulled out of action between 4:00 and 5:00 p.m. Brad Coker personal communication.

28. *OR* 19, pt. 1, 1053; Nolan and Storch, "The Iron Brigade Earns its Name," 12.

29. *OR* 19, pt. 1, 250; *Milwaukee Sunday Telegraph*, January 26, 1895; August 26, 1886.

30. Nolan and Storch, "The Iron Brigade Earns its Name," 15-6.

31. Rufus Dawes, *Service with the Sixth Wisconsin Volunteers* (Dayton, OH: Morningside Press, 1984), 81-2; *OR* 19, pt. 1, 249; Nolan and Storch, "The Iron Brigade Earns its Name," 16; Alan T. Nolan, *The Iron Brigade: A Military History* (Bloomington, IN: Indiana University Press, 1961), 125. After firing a volley, the 7th Wisconsin crouched down to reload while the 6th Wisconsin behind fired over their heads.

32. Nolan, *The Iron Brigade*, 125-6.

33. Craig L. Dunn, *Iron Men, Iron Will: The Nineteenth Indiana Regiment of the Iron Brigade* (Indianapolis: Guild Press, 1995), 95-96; *OR* 19, pt. 1, 250.

34. *OR* 19, pt. 1, 252-3.

35. *OR* 19, pt. 1, 1,053.

36. *OR* 19, pt. 1, 1,053.

37. *OR* 19, pt. 1, 184-6, 1,036. Rodes' brigade lost 61 killed, 157 wounded, and 204 missing. *OR* 19, pt. 1, 1,036.

38. *OR* 19, pt. 1, 1,021-2.

Map Set 7. South Mountain: Crampton's Gap (11:00 a.m. - 7:00 p.m.)

1. Henry Boyer, "Ninety-Sixth at Crampton's Pass," *Philadelphia Weekly Times*, September 30, 1871; Carman, *The Maryland Campaign*, 296; *OR* 19, pt. 1, 393. McClellan gave Franklin explicit orders not to wait for Darius Couch, but Franklin waited nonetheless. Carman, *The Maryland Campaign*, 296n.

2. Barnard, *War Talks of Confederate Veterans*, 25; John W. H. Porter, *A Record of Events in Norfolk County, Virginia . . . with a History of the Soldiers and Sailors of Norfolk County, Norfolk City* (Portsmouth, VA: W. A. Fiske, 1892), 128; *OR* 19, pt. 1, 826, 873; Reese, *Sealed with Their Lives*, 50-1. Chew lost one of his guns early in the fight when a couple of bolts snapped and put it out of action. George Neese, *Three Years in the Confederate Horse Artillery* (New York: Neale Press, 1911), 121-2.

3. Reese, *Sealed with Their Lives*, 72-75, 85; *OR* 19, pt. 1, 375, 380, 826, 836, 873, 876, 881; Barnard. *War Talks of Confederate Veterans*, 26-27; Ethan S. Rafuse, *McClellan's War: The Failure of Moderation in the Struggle for the Union* (Bloomington, IN: Indiana University, 2005), 296. Companies A and B of the 16th Virginia were deployed to the right of West Main Street; the rest were deployed on the left side of it. Chew's and Grimes' batteries could not depress their barrels enough to be effective and were withdrawn to the summit of the mountain. Historian Earl Hess believed that Munford should have taken advantage of the steep terrain of South Mountain, rather than aligning his thin line along

its base. Hess reasoned that the stone wall at the base trumped the lack of defensive features at the top of the heights. Earl Hess, *Field Armies and Fortifications in the Civil War* (Chapel Hill, NC: U. of North Carolina Press, 2005), 145.

4. Joseph J. Bartlett, "Crampton's Pass, The Start of the Great Maryland Campaign," *National Tribune*, December 19, 1889.

5. Reese, *Sealed with Their Lives*, 80.

6. OR 19, pt. 1, 388-9; Carman, *The Maryland Campaign*, 302-3.

7. Carman, *The Maryland Campaign*, 302-4; Bates, *History of Pennsylvania Volunteers*, vol. 3, 385.

8. OR 19, pt. 1, 382; Gottfried, *Kearny's Own*, 71-2.

9. Reese, *Sealed with Their Lives*, 80.

10. Sifarkis, *Who Was Who in the Civil War*, 130, 579.

11. Carman, *The Maryland Campaign*, 303-4; OR 19, pt. 1, 389.

12. OR 19, pt. 1, 826-7, 852-4, 870-3; Atlanta Southern Confederacy, October 10, 1862; Clark, *North Carolina Regiments*, vol. 1, 739-40. Cobb has been widely criticized for not immediately riding to Crampton's Gap to take command of the units there. Instead, he waited about an hour before departing. Carman, *The Maryland Campaign*, 306-7. Tom Munford graduated from V.M.I. and fought at First Manassas and throughout the war in a variety of capacities and with considerable skill. For some reason Gen. Lee did not recommend Munford for promotion to brigadier general until March of 1865 (to date from November 1864). There is no record that this recommendation was acted upon before the war ended. Munford himself claims he never received his general's commission. Bruce S. Allardice, *More Generals in Gray* (Baton Rouge, LA: LSU Press, 1995), 171-2.

13. Reese, *Sealed with Their Lives*, 125-8; OR 19, pt. 1, 827, 852-4, 870.

14. Gottfried, *Kearny's Own*, 56-7, 70-1.

15. OR 19, pt. 1, 382; Gottfried, *Kearny's Own*, 71-2; Porter, *A Record of Events in Norfolk County, Virginia*, 127-8.

16. Gottfried, *Kearny's Own*, 71-2. According to George Barnard of the 12th Virginia, *War Talks of Confederate Veterans*, 28, the officers yelled "Fix bayonets, men! Fix bayonets!" as the enemy troops closed the distance. Seeing the futility of the defense, the officers then ordered "Fall back, men! Fall back!"

17. Boyer, "Ninety-Sixth at Crampton's Pass;" OR 19, pt. 1, 39; Priest, *Before Antietam*, 285-6.

18. Carman, *The Maryland Campaign*, 303-4; OR 19, pt. 1, 390, 391, 396, 398; Barnard, *War Talks of Confederate Veterans*, 43.

19. OR 19, pt. 1, 827, 852-4, 870; Reese, *Sealed with Their Lives*, 125-8.

20. OR 19, pt. 1, 408.

21. Gottfried, *Kearny's Own*, 72-7; Reese, *Sealed with Their Lives*, 140-2; OR 19, pt. 1, 382-7; John P. Beech, "Crampton's Pass: And the Part Taken by the 4th New Jersey in That Engagement," *National Tribune*, May 8, 1884; John P. Beech, "The 1st New Jersey Brigade at Crampton's Pass," *Grant Army Scout and Soldiers' Mail*, October 4, 1884; William B. Styple, *Writing and Fighting from the Army of Northern Virginia: A Collection of Confederate Soldier Correspondence* (Kearny, NJ: Belle Grove Publishing Co., 2003), 148. Samuel Burney of Cobb's Legion was one of the few survivors. He wrote home after the battle, "I guess you have heard before now of the sad fate of Cobb's Legion. They were cut to pieces on Sunday the 14th. They were ordered down a rough rocky mountain side where right before them were three lines of Yankee troops, one just behind the other. They say that fifty of the Legion fell [at] the first volley." Nat Turner, ed., *A Southern Soldier's Letters Home* (Macon, GA: Mercer University Press, 2002).

22. OR 19, pt. 1, 870.

23. OR 19, pt. 1, 398, 399.

24. OR 19, pt. 1, 872-3, 881-2; Reese, *Sealed with Their Lives*, 151. It is tempting to hypothesize what might have been had these three regiments struck the rear of the Vermont and New Jersey troops.

25. Reese, *Sealed with Their Lives*, 151-2; Bates, *History of Pennsylvania Volunteers*, vol. 3, 385. Lt. George Hooker fought through the war until he was wounded in June 1864 at the Battle of Cold Harbor. He was discharged soon thereafter.

26. Walter F. Beyer, *Deeds of Valor: How America's Heroes Won the Medal of Honor* (Detroit: Perrien-Keydel Co., 1903), vol. 1, 73-4; Elizabeth Whitley Roberson, *In Care of Yellow River* (Gretna, LA: Pelican Press, 1994), 97.

27. Reese, *Sealed with Their Lives*, 153.

28. Clark, *North Carolina Regiments*, vol. 1, 739-40; Reese, *Sealed with Their Lives*, 156-8.

29. OR 19, pt. 1, 871; Reese, *Sealed with Their Lives*, 158-9.

30. Reese, *Sealed with Their Lives*, 159-61.

31. Reese, *Sealed with Their Lives*, 162-5.

32. OR 19, pt. 1, 384-5, 387-88, 391, 392-3, 395, 398-401, 403-4, 408-9; Reese, *Sealed with Their Lives*, 158-65; Bartlett, "Crampton's Pass," December 19, 1889.

33. *OR* 19, pt. 1, 400-1, 408; Bates, *History of Pennsylvania Volunteers*, vol. 3, 336.

34. On the Confederate side, Howell Cobb's brigade sustained the highest losses: 660 out of 1,310 or 48%. Parham's brigade lost 177 of its 520 men, or 34%. The total losses from all causes for the Federal brigades were as follows: Torbert lost 144, Barlett 192, and Newton 95. Reese, *Sealed with Their Lives*, 297-303. This view differs from that of historian Benjamin Cooling who noted that "the fighting on September 14 proved a disaster for the Confederate arms." Although Southern losses at Fox's Gap, the Frosttown Plateau, Turner's Gap, and Crampton's Gap were horrendous, the Confederates who fought there largely accomplished what was asked of them: delay the Federal move beyond South Mountain for as long as possible. Benjamin Cooling, *Counter-Thrust: From the Peninsula to the Antietam* (Lincoln, NE: University of Nebraska Press, 2008), 217.

Map Set 8. The Capture of Harpers Ferry (September 12 - 15)

1. *OR* 19, pt. 2, 519, 532, 594; pt. 1, 757; Dennis E. Frye, "Through God's Blessing," *North and South Magazine*, vol. 5, no. 7 (2002), 67; Harsh, *Taken at the Flood*, 267-8.

2. Frye, "Through God's Blessing," 69; Hess, *Field Armies and Fortifications in the Civil War*, 140.

3. *OR* 19, pt. 1, 852; McLaws, "Maryland," 8-9; Harsh, *Taken at the Flood*, 200-3.

4. Julius White, "The Capitulation of Harpers Ferry," *B&L*, vol. 2, 612; *OR* 19, pt. 1, 913, 953, 980; Harsh, *Taken at the Flood*, 198-200, 204-5; Sears, *Landscape Turned Red*, 122. White's decision to abdicate command to Miles turned out to be a blessing for his career. While Miles and others would be chastised for their actions at Harpers Ferry, White's reputation emerged relatively unscathed. He ultimately rose to the rank of brevet major general and commanded a division in the IX Corps.

5. Frye, "Through God's Blessing," 69. Charcoal roads had been cut through the forest during the 1840s. By the time of the battle, these trees had been replaced by dense vegetation. Hess, *Field Armies and Fortifications in the Civil War*, 141.

6. Wayne Mahood, "Some Very Hard Stories Were Told: The 126th New York at Harpers Ferry," *CWR* (1991), vol. 1, no. 4, 18-9. The cavalry units consisted of a squadron of Rhode Island cavalry and two companies of the First Maryland Cavalry. Capt. Eugene McGrath's battery was also present. *OR* 19, vol. 1, 542.

7. Arabella M. Willson, *Disaster, Struggle and Triumph: The Adventure of 1000 Boys in Blue* (Albany, NY: The Argus Company Printers, 1870), 97; Mahood, "Some Very Hard Stories Were Told," 16, 20-1; *OR* 19, pt. 1, 519, 532, 542, 608, 788-791; Frye, "Through God's Blessing," 69; Harsh, *Taken at the Flood*, 224-5. McGrath's battery consisted of two 9-inch naval Dahlgren rifles, one 50-pounder Parrott Rifle, and four 12-pounder smoothbore Napoleons. *OR* 19, pt. 1, 542. According to one Federal officer, the barricade-breastwork was composed of "logs, fallen trees, timbers, which lay right across the ridge." *OR* 19, pt. 1, 614.

8. *Geneva Gazette*, September 19, 1862; Carman, *The Maryland Campaign*, 233-4; Mahood, "Some Very Hard Stories Were Told," 23-4; *OR* 19, pt. 1, 608, 614, 863; *Recollections and Reminiscences 1861-1865* (n.p.: United Daughters of the Confederacy, 1998), vol. 9, 263, vol. 12, 347; Hewett, ed., *OR Supplement*, vol. 3, 565. A South Carolinian in Joseph Kershaw's brigade noted that climbing the mountain and getting into position was, "the hardest work I have ever done. The mountain was high and steep and the laurel and ivy bushes were so thick and closely matted together that it was almost impossible to pass through them." William Barksdale's men had the added difficulty of having to climb over large boulders "piled one above the other in careless confusion." Guy R. Everson and Edward W. Simpson, Jr., eds., *"Far, Far from Home": The Wartime Letters of Dick and Tally Simpson, Third South Carolina Volunteers* (New York: Oxford University Press, 1994), 149; *Voices of the Civil War: Antietam* (Richmond, VA: Time Life Books, 1996), 44. Col. Ford estimated that his men fought in front of the breastworks for about two hours before occupying them. *OR* 19, pt. 1, 543.

9. William H. Nichols, *The Siege and Capture of Harpers Ferry by the Confederates, September, 1862* (Providence, RI: Rhode Island Soldiers and Sailors Historical Society, 1889), 26; Carman, *The Maryland Campaign*, 238-9; *OR* 19, pt. 863.

10. *OR* 19, pt. 1, 537. Col. S. W. Downey of the 3rd Maryland was incredulous when told to retreat. He testified at a Congressional inquiry that he told the orderly, "If we lose this position [the barricade] we lose everything; we can hold this position unless the enemy press heavier than they do now." *OR* 19, pt. 1, 614.

11. Carman, *The Maryland Campaign*, 238-9; *OR* 19, pt. 1, 543, 614-5.

12. *OR* 19, pt. 1, 544, 576; Frye, "Through God's Blessing," 71; Mahood, "Some Very Hard Stories Were Told," 32.

13. Harsh, *Taken at the Flood*, 200-01, 209-11; Rafuse, *McClellan's War*, 293.

14. Walker, "Jackson's Capture of Harper's Ferry," 608-9; *OR* 19, pt. 1, 913. Gen. John Walker reported that his two regiments reached the top of the heights at 2:00 p.m., but the historian of the 27th North Carolina reported that it was 5:00 p.m. Clark, *North Carolina Regiments*, vol. 2, 432.

15. Harsh, *Taken at the Flood*, 228-29; *OR* 19, pt. 1, 953.

16. Carman, *The Maryland Campaign*, 242-3; Frye, "Through God's Blessing," 72; Sears, *Landscape Turned Red*, 133.

17. *OR* 19, pt. 1, 854, 913, 958; pt. 2, 607; Ronald H. Bailey, *The Bloodiest Day: The Battle of Antietam* (Alexandria, VA: Time Life Books, 1984), 56; James Dinkins, *1861 to 1865, by an Old Johnnie: Personal Recollections and Experiences in the Confederate Army* (Dayton, OH: Morningside Bookshop, 1975), 54. James Dinkins (18th Mississippi) helped haul the cannon up Maryland Heights. "The mountain was very steep," wrote Dinkins. "We carried up the wheels and axles one at a time, and a hundred or more men would pull the guns up with ropes."

18. Carman, *The Maryland Campaign*, 243-5; *OR* 19, pt. 1, 741.

19. *OR* 19, pt. 1, 854, 913, 958; *OR* 19, pt. 2, 607; Harsh, *The Maryland Campaign*, 270-71, 273.

20. Dennis Frye, "Drama between the Rivers: Harpers Ferry in the 1862 Maryland Campaign," in *Antietam: Essays on the 1862 Maryland Campaign*, Gary Gallagher, ed (Kent, OH: Kent University Press: 1989), 27; *Voices of the Civil War: Antietam*, 46.

21. Carman, *The Maryland Campaign*, 247-8.

22. *OR* 19, pt. 1, 954, 959; Carman, *The Maryland Campaign*, 245-7.

23. *OR* 19, pt. 1, 953.

24. Carman, *The Maryland Campaign*, 249-50; *OR* 19, pt. 1, 980.

25. *OR* 19, pt. 1, 951, 954, 966, 980, 1007, 1111; Harsh, *The Maryland Campaign*, 273-4.

26. Carman, *The Maryland Campaign*, 254; Bailey, *The Bloodiest Day*, 43.

27. White, "The Capitulation of Harpers Ferry," 613; Carman, *The Maryland Campaign*, 254.

28. Carman, *The Maryland Campaign*, 249-251; *OR* 19, pt. 1, 980.

29. Clark, *North Carolina Regiments*, vol. 2, 156; *OR* 19, pt. 1, 962; Harsh, *Taken at the Flood*, 316-7.

30. White, "The Capitulation of Harpers Ferry," 613. Col. Benjamin Davis was born in Mississippi and served in the army prior to the war. He remained with the Union after Fort Sumter capitulated. Sears, *Landscape Turned Red*, 151.

31. White, "The Capitulation of Harpers Ferry," 613.

32. William M. Luff, "March of the Cavalry from Harpers Ferry September 14, 1862," *Illinois MOLLUS* (Chicago: A. C. McClurg and Co., 1894), vol. 2, 33-4, 40-1.

33. Luff, "March of the Cavalry from Harpers Ferry September 14, 1862," 40-1.

34. Carman, *The Maryland Campaign*, 257.

35. Luff, "March of the Cavalry from Harpers Ferry September 14, 1862," 43-5.

36. Carman, *The Maryland Campaign*, 258-59; "March of the Cavalry from Harpers Ferry September 14, 1862," 43-5.

37. *OR* 19, pt. 1, 829-30. According to historian Thomas Clemens, everything related to the mission is subject to debate, including the route, the number of wagons captured (forty to ninety-six) and the number of Confederates captured (200 to 600). Carman, *The Maryland Campaign*, 259-60.

38. *OR* 19, pt. 1, 955, 980-1; Frye, "Through God's Blessing," 74.

39. Douglas, *I Rode With Stonewall*, 162.

40. *OR* 19, pt. 1, 855, 955, 980-1; Harsh, *Taken at the Flood*, 317.

41. Henry Kyd Douglas, "Stonewall Jackson in Maryland," *B&L*, vol. 2, 627; *OR* 19, pt. 1, 700.

42. Frye, "Through God's Blessing," 68.

43. *OR* 19, pt. 2, 608; pt. 1, 856, 951; *OR* 51, pt. 2, 618-9.

Map Set 9. To Sharpsburg (September 14 - 16)

1. *OR* 19, pt. 1, 855; Carman, *The Maryland Campaign*, 434-8.

2. George B. McClellan, *Report on the Organization of the Army of the Potomac, and its Campaigns in Virginia and Maryland* (Washington: U. S. Government Printing Office, 1864), 193, 194; *OR* 19, pt. 1, 47; *OR* 51, pt. 1, 836; William B. Franklin, "Notes on Crampton's Gap and Antietam," *B&L*, vol. 2, 596; Carman, *The Maryland Campaign*, 434-5.

3. *OR* 19, pt. 1, 1,036; Carman, *The Maryland Campaign*, 387. The cavalry probably belonged to Col. Grimes Davis' command, which had broken out of Harpers Ferry.

4. Carman, *The Maryland Campaign*, 387; *OR* 19, pt. 1, 1022.

5. Carman, *The Maryland Campaign*, 388.

6. OR 19, pt. 1, 906, 909, 922, 939; Carman, *The Maryland Campaign*, 389.

7. Carman, *The Maryland Campaign*, 389.

8. George W. Whitman, *Civil War Letters of George Washington Whitman*, Jerome M. Loving, ed. (Durham, N.C.: Duke University Press, 1975), 67; Charles F. Walcott, *History of the Twenty-First Regiment Massachusetts Volunteers in the War for the Preservation of the Union, 1861-1865* (Boston: Houghton Mifflin, 1882), 194. One wrote that, "in some parts of the field the enemys [sic] dead lay in heaps and in a road for nearly a quarter of a mile they lay so thick that I had to pick my way carefully to avoid stepping on them." Another wrote, "it was a sad sight, and in the woods they could be counted by the hundreds."

9. OR 51, pt. 1, 834-35; Carman, *The Maryland Campaign*, 403-4.

10. Carman, *The Maryland Campaign*, 397-8.

11. George B. McClellan, *McClellan's Own Story: The War for the Union* (New York: Charles L. Webster & Co., 1887), 586; OR 51, pt. 1, 832; Carman, *The Maryland Campaign*, 408-10. The IX Corps had marched toward Fox's Gap on September 14 without rations. Burnside decided to wait for the food to arrive before beginning his march on September 15.

12. OR 19, pt. 1, 855-6.

13. Harsh, *Taken at the Flood*, 321; OR 19, pt. 1, 914.

14. OR 19, pt. 1, 955, 967, 1,007, 1011; Harsh, *Taken at the Flood*, 328-9.

15. Harsh, *Taken at the Flood*, 325.

16. Harsh, *Taken at the Flood*, 330.

17. Harsh, *Taken at the Flood*, 330-33.

18. OR 19, pt. 1, 955, 1,007; Harsh, *Taken at the Flood*, 334. Gen. John Walker recalled Gen. Lee's appearance on the morning of September 16. Contrary to his thought that the army's commander would look anxious and careworn, "he was calm, dignified, and even cheerful. If he had had a well-equipped army of a hundred thousand veterans at his back, he could not have appeared more composed and confident." John G. Walker, "Sharpsburg," *B&L*, vol. 2, 675. Walker's recollections of this campaign are rife with inconsistencies and outright mistakes, and must be used with caution.

19. OR 19, pt. 1, 967, 978; Harsh, *Taken at the Flood*, 334.

20. Carman, *The Maryland Campaign*, 411.

21. OR 19, pt. 1, 907, 923, 1,032, 1,036, 1,043; Collins, *Rodes*, 164; Pierro, ed., *The Maryland Campaign*, 172, 173. Historian Jerry Holsworth

explained the condition of Hood's troops and all they had done since early July 1862, when they had last received clothing: "they had fought two major battles and numerous skirmishes. They had marched 250 miles, climbed the mountains, waded countless streams, and scrambled through tangled forests and underbrush. All this had reduced their uniforms to rags and their shoes to sandals, if the men were not already barefoot." Jerry Holsworth, "Uncommon Valor: Hood's Texas Brigade in the Maryland Campaign," *Blue and Gray Magazine*, vol. xiii, no. 6, (1996), 12.

22. Pierro, ed., *The Maryland Campaign*, 202; Francis A. Walker, *History of the Second Army Corps in the Army of the Potomac* (New York: Charles Scribner's Sons, 1887), 97.

23. Harsh, *Taken at the Flood*, 302-4.

24. Pierro, ed., *The Maryland Campaign*, 195-9.

Map Set 10. The Eve of Battle (September 16)

1. Pierro, ed., *The Maryland Campaign*, 205.

2. Pierro, ed., *The Maryland Campaign*, 174, 197; Johnson and Anderson, *Artillery Hell*, 48.

3. OR 19, pt. 1, 1,026. Most of the damage was done by the 1st New York Artillery, which was also called the "German Battalion." The unit was composed of Taft's, Langner's, von Kleiser's and Wever's 20-pounder Parrotts that could easily reach most areas of the battlefield. These guns were joined by Weed's battery of three-inch Ordnance Rifles and Benjamin's 20-pounder Parrotts. Paul Chiles, "Artillery Hell: The Guns of Antietam," *Blue and Gray Magazine*, December 1998), 24.

4. Harsh, *Taken at the Flood*, 349-50; OR 19, pt. 1, 418-9.

5. Harsh, *Taken at the Flood*, 347-9. A very odd situation existed within command of the IX Corps. Burnside, who commanded a wing of the Army of the Potomac during the march through Maryland, assigned Maj. Gen. Jesse Reno to command his IX Corps. When Reno was killed at Fox's Gap, Brig. Gen. Jacob Cox assumed command of the corps. The wing structure was not used when the army reached the battlefield, but Burnside continued to allow Cox to command the IX Corps and, according to Burnside, "my orders were to a great extent given directly to him." OR 19, pt. 1, 157, 418.

6. Pierro, ed., *The Maryland Campaign*, 205.

7. OR 19, pt. 1, 217; Harsh, *Taken at the Flood*, 350; Pierro, ed., *The Maryland Campaign*, 205.

8. OR 19, pt. 1, 217.

9. Pierro, ed., *The Maryland Campaign*, 205-6; OR 19, pt. 1, 819.

10. OR 19, pt. 1, 148, 955.

11. Harsh, *Taken at the Flood*, 351.

12. OR 19, pt. 1, 927; Pierro, ed., *The Maryland Campaign*, 206; E. E. Stickley, "Battle of Sharpsburg," *Confederate Veteran*, 40 vols. (Broadfoot Publishing Co., 1987), vol. 23, no. 2 66.

13. OR 19, pt. 1, 223, 268-69; Pierro, ed., *The Maryland Campaign*, 206-07.

14. Bates, *Pennsylvania Volunteers*, vol. 1, 918; Pierro, ed., *The Maryland Campaign*, 206.

15. OR 19, pt. 1, 925, 927, 937.

16. OR 19, pt. 1, 269; Bates, *History of Pennsylvania Volunteers*, vol. 1, 918.

17. "History of the 'Bucktails': The Maryland Campaign," 13th Pennsylvania File, Antietam National Military Park.

18. Glover, *Bucktailed Wildcats*, 154, 156; "History of the 'Bucktails': The Maryland Campaign;" OR 19, pt. 1, 937; George E. Otott, "Clash in the Cornfield: The 1st Texas Volunteer Infantry in the Maryland Campaign," in *CWR*, vol. 5 (no. 3), 84-85.

19. Pierro, ed., *The Maryland Campaign*, 208.

20. *National Tribune*, July 16, 1891.

21. Sifakis, *Who Was Who in the Civil War*, 432; Harsh, *Taken at the Flood*, 352-4; OR 19, pt. 1, 376. According to Ezra Carman, Joseph Mansfield was "of venerable appearance, white haired, yet fresh and vigorous, with an open, intelligent countenance . . . he insisted on leading his regiments into action closed in mass, contending that if deployed, they would run away." Pierro, ed., *The Maryland Campaign*, 235.

22. OR 19, pt. 1, 218; Harsh, *Taken at the Flood*, 353-4.

23. John B. Hood, *Advance and Retreat: Personal Experiences in the United States and Confederate States Armies* (The Blue and Grey Press: Edison, NJ, 1985), 42; Pierro, ed., *The Maryland Campaign*, 210; OR 19, pt. 1, 1008; F. Ray Sibley, Jr., *The Confederate Order of Battle: The Army of Northern Virginia* (Shippensburg, PA: White Mane Publishing Co., 1996), 30; Stickley, "Battle of Sharpsburg," 66. General Lee did not feel comfortable replacing Hood's troops with fresh troops, so he sent him to see Stonewall Jackson. Hood found Jackson asleep. After some discussion he convinced him to send in replacements, but with the understanding that Hood would move to their support if they were attacked. Pierro, ed., *The Maryland Campaign*, 210. While Carman's first map of the series covering

September 17 shows Ripley facing northeast, Carman's text clearly notes that his brigade was aligned "forming nearly a right angle with Trimble and fronting the Antietam." The latter seems more accurate, given the potential for an attack from the east. Pierro, ed., *The Maryland Campaign*, 210.

Map Set 11. Antietam: Hooker Opens the Battle (5:15 - 7:00 a.m.)

1. James V. Murfin, *The Gleam of Bayonets: The Battle of Antietam and the Maryland Campaign, September 1862* (New York: Thomas Yoseloff, 1965), 211; Harsh, *Taken at the Flood*, 330.

2. Letter of J. T. Baynes to Lizzie Miles, September 25, 1862, copy in the 5th Pennsylvania Reserve File; Pierro, ed., *The Maryland Campaign*, 215-6. The precise time of Seymour's movement is not known, but it was probably between 5:30 and 6:00 a.m. Firing on the skirmish line began as early as 3:00 a.m. Murfin, *Gleam of Bayonets*, 211.

3. Woodward, *Our Campaigns*, 160; OR 19, pt. 1, 976-7; Pierro, ed., *The Maryland Campaign*, 216; "History of the Bucktails;" James Smith to Friends, September 20, 1862 (copy in the 5th Pennsylvania Reserves fold, Antietam NMP).

4. OR 19, pt. 1, 844, 976. The alignment of Lee's artillery battalion is described in Robert K. Krick, *Parker's Virginia Battery*, C.S.A. (Wilmington, NC: Broadfoot Publishing Co., 1989), 56-57.

5. Pierro, ed., *The Maryland Campaign*, 217, 221; Nolan and Storch, "The Iron Brigade Earns its Name," 20.

6. OR 19, pt. 1, 259; Pierro, ed., *The Maryland Campaign*, 217. To make Thompson's battery serviceable, men from the 105th New York were used to operate the guns. Pierro, ed., *The Maryland Campaign*, 217. Brig. Gen. Hartsuff was severely wounded during this movement. OR 19, pt. 1, 259.

7. Franklin B. Hough, *History of Duryee's Brigade During the Campaign in Virginia Under Gen. Pope, and in Maryland Under Gen. McClellan, in the Summer and Autumn of 1862* (Albany, NY: J. Munsell, 1864), 119; Pierro, ed., *The Maryland Campaign*, 217; H. W. Burlingame, *Personal Reminiscences of the Civil War* (copy in the 104th New York file, Antietam National Military Park); OR 19, pt. 1, 262. Abram Duryee's name is also spelled Duryea. Duryee's men were pounded by Southern artillery when they were out in the open. According to the commander of the 107th Pennsylvania, Capt. James MacThomson, "Advancing half way across the field to within easy supporting distance of the battery, we halted for about five minutes, the enemy's shell and round shot flying about us like

hail, killing and wounding some of our poor fellows, but not injuring the morale of the regiment in the least." *OR* 19, pt. 1, 262. According to Pvt. Isaac Bradwell of the 31st Georgia, "Colonel Douglass, fearing the result of an attack by so large a force on his weak brigade, ran from regiment to regiment exhorting the men not to fire until the enemy had reached the fence and began to get over it—to shoot low and make every bullet count." Pharris D. Johnson, ed., *Under the Southern Cross: Soldier Life with Gordon Bradwell and the Army of Northern Virginia* (Macon, GA: Mercer University Press, 1999), 89-90.

8. Pierro, ed., *The Maryland Campaign*, 217; Woodward, *Our Campaigns*, 160.

9. Pierro, ed., *The Maryland Campaign*, 217; Bates, *History of Pennsylvania Volunteers*, vol. 1, 584.

10. Pierro, ed., *The Maryland Campaign*, 221; *OR* 19, pt. 1, 233, 243, 247. Although in the rear, the men of Phelps' brigade went to ground periodically to avoid the rain of bullets and other projectiles being thrown at them by the Confederates. Joseph Pettiner to Carrie, September 20, 1862, copy in the 84th New York folder, Antietam NMP.

11. OR 19, pt. 1, 819-20; Robert E. L. Krick, "Defending Lee's Flank," in Gallagher, ed., *The Antietam Campaign*, 200-1.

12. Burlingame, *Personal Reminiscences of the Civil War; Columbus Enquirer*, October 8, 1862; James Cooper Nisbet, *Four Years on the Firing Line* (Wilmington, NC: Broadfoot Pub. Co., 1987), 102-03; Dave Pridgeon, "The 21st Georgia at Sharpsburg (21st Georgia file, Antietam NMP); Clark, *North Carolina Regiments*, vol. 2, 157. The small 12th Georgia lost 59 killed and wounded out of the 100 or so men in the ranks that morning. Pierro, ed., *The Maryland Campaign*, 218. The 15th Alabama of James Walker's brigade remained in position because its men had run out of ammunition and reluctant to advance without an adequate supply. J. Gary Laine and Morris M. Penny, *Law's Alabama Brigade in the War between the Union and the Confederacy* (Shippensburg, PA: White Mane Publishing Company, 1996), 24.

13. Pierro, ed., *The Maryland Campaign*, 218. Bullets and shells were not the only cause of death. Several soldiers in Christian's brigade recalled that some of their comrades were killed by tree limbs knocked down by Confederate shells. John Vautier's Diary, copy in the 88th Pennsylvania file, Antietam NMP; Lt. Samuel Moore's Diary, copy in the 90th Pennsylvania file, Antietam NMP.

14. *OR* 19, pt. 1, 977, 978.

15. *OR* 51, pt. 1, 140; Pierro, ed., *The Maryland Campaign*, 218-9; Bates, *History of Pennsylvania Volunteers*, vol. 1, 253; P. A. Dunton to Friend Byron, September 24, 1862, copy in the 13th Massachusetts file, Antietam NMP. The bullet entered Hartsuff's pelvic cavity. Despite several painful and deep probes by various surgeons, the ball was never found. Antietam marked the end of Hartsuff's career in the field. Jack D. Welsh, M.D., *Medical Histories of Union Generals* (Kent State, 1996), 156. As one Federal veteran in Christian's brigade recalled, "We did a lot of unnecessary drilling, I think, going into action. First it was 'forward,' then by the 'left flank,' then 'forward,' then by the 'right flank,' 'forward,' 'left oblique,' etc., until we thought they were making a show of us for the benefit of the Rebel artillery." The men could easily see Col. Christian's discomfort when he suddenly dismounted and hurried to the rear, muttering that he had a great fear of this form of shelling. "He would duck and dodge his head, and go crouching along," noted one of the men. Col. Christian resigned his commission two days after the battle. John Vautier's Diary; Sears, *Landscape Turned Red*, 187-8.

16. *OR* 19, pt. 2, 248; Nolan, *The Iron Brigade*, 138.

17. Pierro, ed., *The Maryland Campaign*, 218; Lieut. Sam Moore's Diary; John D. Vautier, *History of the 88th Pennsylvania Volunteers in the War for the Union* (Philadelphia: J. B. Lippincott, 1894), 75. Although Meade singled Seymour out in his after-battle report for his "judgment and military skill," it appears that only three of Seymour's five regiments saw any significant combat. His 1st and 6th Pennsylvania Reserves were barely engaged, and should have been thrown forward when the 13th Pennsylvania Reserves ran out of ammunition and the 5th Pennsylvania Reserves abruptly retreated. Although not on the front lines, the 6th Pennsylvania sustained the highest casualties in the entire brigade. None of its enlisted men commented on ever being on the front line, and it appears that this regiment's losses were largely the result of artillery shells when the regiment was out in the open. OR 19, pt. 1, 191, 270; 51, pt. 1, 147-8, 153; Diary of Capt. Samuel Waters, Civil War Misc. Collection, U.S. Army War College Library; Wellington Ent to father, September 18, 1862, copy in 6th Pennsylvania Reserve folder, Antietam NMP; Doug Kauffmann, "Tobias's Story: The Life and Civil War Career of Tobias B. Kaufmann," copy in 1st Pennsylvania Reserve folder, Antietam NMP.

18. Benjamin F. Cook, *History of the Twelfth Massachusetts Volunteers, Webster Regiment* (Boston: Privately printed, 1882), 73; *Columbus Inquirer*, October 8, 1862. Col. Douglass purportedly fell while leading a charge toward the cornfield. One witness recalled that Douglass yelled out as he fell, "Pour it to them, my brave boys." Source Book on the Early History of Cuthbert and Randolph Co., copy in 13th Georgia file, Antietam NMP, 183.

19. *OR* 19, pt. 1, 977, 979; Terry L. Jones, *Lee's Tigers: The Louisiana Infantry in the Army of Northern Virginia* (Baton Rouge, LA: LSU Press, 1987), 129-130; Diary of George Wren, Woodruff Library, Emory University; Pierro, ed., *The Maryland Campaign*, 219; Welsh, *Medical Histories of Confederate Generals*, 223. According to the report of Lt. Col. Richard Richardson, when the 26th New York of Christian's brigade arrived in its position in the East Woods, "I gave the command to commence firing by file, and the battalion continued firing evenly and carefully for some 30 rounds, average, when the command ceased firing, saving ammunition. This cessation brought the enemy out more plainly in view on the open ground, and we again opened fire, driving the enemy again behind the fence, and under cover of the corn-field." The men were probably firing at the right flank of Marcellus Douglass' line. *OR* 19, pt. 1, 263. The disposition of Harry Hays' Brigade is unclear. It appears that the 6th Louisiana was second from the right. The famous post-battle photo of the dead white horse near the East Woods belonged to the 6th's commander Col. Henry B. Strong, who was also killed in action there. James P. Gannon, *Irish Rebels Confederate Tigers: A History of the 6th Louisiana Volunteers, 1861-1865* (Savas Publishing, 1998), 133, 138.

20. Allen Wright, "The 42nd Virginia Infantry" (copy in the 42nd Virginia file, Antietam NMP); Pierro, ed., *The Maryland Campaign*, 226; "Reminiscences of Jackson's Old Division by Captain James M. Garnett and Alexander Hunter, with Comments by Alex. Robert Chisholm," *SHSP*, vol. 31 (1903), 34. Welsh, *Medical Histories of Confederate Generals*, 130. Lawton's leg wound did not heal properly and he did not return to duty until May 1863. When he did return it was to manage various administrative assignments. Lawton never led troops in the field again.

21. Dawes, *Service with the Sixth Wisconsin Volunteers*, 90; T. Baynes to Miss Lizzie Miles, September 25, 1862 (copy in the 5th Pennsylvania Reserves file, Antietam NMP); Pierro, ed., *The Maryland Campaign*, 222-23; *OR* 19, pt. 1, 254-5; 975; Nolan, *The Iron Brigade*, 139. James Wood of the 2nd Wisconsin noted that the men "had come upon the enemy in force . . . the Second [moved] forward by the left oblique, thus bringing the regiment up to the line of battle of the Sixth and joining their left." Report of Acting Adj. James Wood, Lucius Fairchild Papers, State Historical Soc. of Wisconsin. The difficulty Union troops experienced reaching and crossing the Miller cornfield was described by Joseph Pettinger of the 84th New York: "As we advanced over a ploughed field we were obliged to lay down to escape the round shot and bomb shells, and when in the corn had to lay down every few steps, and you may try to imagine us laying there the balls going whiz, whiz, whiz within a step of us and over our heads and seeing the round shot tear up everything around a few steps off." Joseph Pettinger to Carrie, September 20, 1862, copy in the 84th New York file, Antietam NMP. According to one Rebel survivor in Douglass' brigade, the losses were so great that there was a gap of about ten feet between each man. Johnson, ed., *Under the Southern Cross*, 90. After the battle a member of the 13th Georgia wrote home, "in one short hour our Regt was literally decimated . . . Oh, our loss is terrific and irreparable. I can scarcely keep from weeping as I write." Shatt Meitchell to his wife, September 19, 1862, Shatt Meitchell Papers, University of Georgia.

22. John D. Chapla, *48th Virginia Infantry* (Lynchburg, VA: H.E. Howard, 1989), 38-9; W. Withers to E. A. Carman, March 14, 1895 (copy in the 42nd Virginia file, Antietam NMP); B. R. Maryniak, "A Rough Morning Near Sharpsburg," in *The Famous Long Ago* (Buffalo Civil War Round Table Newsletter), July, 1986, 26, 27.

23. James I. Robertson, *4th Virginia Infantry* (Lynchburg, VA: H.E. Howard, 1982), 20, 22; Lowell Reidenbaugh, *33rd Virginia Infantry* (Lynchburg, VA: H.E. Howard, 1987), 48-9; Lowell Reidenbaugh, 27th Virginia (Lynchburg, VA: H.E. Howard, 1993), 70. The deployment of the regiments in Penn's and Grigsby's brigades is not known. According to Ezra Carman, most of the former brigade was on the skirmish line. The 27th Virginia apparently formed the left flank of Grigsby's brigade and the 21st Virginia formed the left of Penn's. Pierro, ed., *The Maryland Campaign*, 222; "The 21st Virginia at the Battle of Sharpsburg," in the 21st Virginia folder, Antietam NMP. John Penn was severely wounded during this action. He was eventually captured and his leg

amputated. Personal correspondence with historian John Hoptak.

24. Pierro, ed., *The Maryland Campaign*, 223; Memoir of Pvt. William Snakenberg, copy in 14th Louisiana file, Antietam NMP; John Worsham, *One of Jackson's Foot Cavalry: His Experience and What he Saw During the War 1861-1865, Including a History of "F Company," Richmond, Va., 21st Regiment . . . Jackson's Division, Second Corps, A. N. Va.* (NY: Neale Publishing Company, 1912), 146-7.

25. Hewett, ed., *OR Supplement*, vol. 3, 541; Dawes, *Service with the Sixth Wisconsin Volunteers*, 90-1; *OR 19*, pt. 1, 233; Pierro, ed., *The Maryland Campaign*, 223. The disposition of Taliaferro's, Warren's, Jackson's, and Starke's brigades is not known. According to Ezra Carman, the 1st Louisiana was on Starke's left flank. Pierro, ed., *The Maryland Campaign*, 223. According to Welsh, *Medical Histories of Confederate Generals*, 204, Starke was hit by three minie balls and lived less than an hour. His body was retrieved and he was buried in Hollywood Cemetery in Richmond. Ironically, the 6th Wisconsin and the 84th New York would fight side by side at the next Confederate invasion of the North in 1863 when the two regiments took on Joe Davis' brigade along the unfinished railroad cut west of Gettysburg on July 1, 1863.

26. Dawes, *Service with the Sixth Wisconsin Volunteers*, 91. Both of the Wisconsin regimental commanders were also wounded during this portion of the battle.

27. Gibbs, *Three Years in the Bloody Eleventh*, 183.

Map Set 12. Antietam: Hood's Division Moves up and Attacks (6:45 - 7:45 a.m.)

1. Hood, *Advance and Retreat*, 42; *OR 19*, pt. 1, 930, 935, 937; W. D. Pritchard, "Civil War Reminisces," copy in the 1st Texas file, Antietam NMP; "The Texans at Sharpsburg," *CV*, vol. 22, no. 12 (December, 1914), 555. Hood's men had eaten very little during the past three days. After getting his men to the rear, Hood's next challenge was to find rations. When the wagons were finally found that night, the men were chagrined to learn they only contained flour. Still, flour was better than nothing and it was doled out about dawn. With no utensils to cook the bread, the men used their ramrods. Most of the bread was not fully cooked by the time the men were ordered to move immediately to the front.

Many gobbled down the half-cooked pads during the short march to the firing line. As one lieutenant in the 18th Georgia recalled when the men could not fully cook and then comfortably consume their rations, "I have never seen a more disgusted bunch of boys and mad as hornet." Pierro, ed., *The Maryland Campaign*, 226; "The Texans at Sharpsburg," 555; Holsworth, "Uncommon Valor," 18.

2. *OR 19*, pt. 1, 937; Hood, *Advance and Retreat*, 42; Pierro, ed., *The Maryland Campaign*, 227; Holsworth, "Uncommon Valor," 17-18. Some of the men Law mentioned may also have belonged to Brig. Gen. Harry Hays' brigade. Hood recalled meeting and talking with Hays during this period.

3. Otott, "The 1st Texas in the Maryland Campaign," 93; *OR 19*, pt. 1, 923, 1033; Pierro, ed., *The Maryland Campaign*, 227. Hood complained after the battle that Ripley's 1,350 men did not adequately support his attack. Hood was correct: Ripley did not move forward from his position until later that morning.

4. Dawes, *Service with the Sixth Wisconsin Volunteers*, 91; Diary of James L. Denon, 18th Georgia file, Antietam NMP.

5. *OR 51*, pt. 1, 148-50, 153, 155.

6. *OR 19*, pt. 1, 928, 930, 932; Styple, *Writing and Fighting from the Army of Northern Virginia*, 153. According to Ezra Carman, Hood wanted Wofford's entire brigade to oblique to the left, but only the Hampton Legion and 18th Georgia received these orders. Pierro, ed., *The Maryland Campaign*, 231.

7. Dawes, *Service with the Sixth Wisconsin Volunteers*, 91; *OR 19*, pt. 1, 229. Gibbon, a trained artilleryman, manned the gun because the cannoneers were not aiming their piece properly and the rounds were flying harmlessly over the enemy lines. Gibbon, *Personal Recollections of the Civil War*, 83.

8. *Autobiography of L. A. Daffin*, in Katie Daffan, *My Father as I Remember Him* (n.p., United Daughters of the Confederacy, 1906), 44-5; *OR 19*, pt. 1, 931, 932.

9. Steven H. Stubbs, *Duty-Honor-Valor; The Story of the Eleventh Mississippi Infantry Regiment* (Philadelphia, MS: Dancing Rabbit Press, 2000), 305-7; *OR 19*, pt. 1, 928, 937-8. According to Capt. Neill Ray of the 6th North Carolina, Hood ordered the men to fix bayonets as they entered the fight. According to Ray, this was done "for the first time in the war." Clark, *North Carolina Regiments*, vol. 1, 308.

10. Otott, "The 1st Texas in the Maryland Campaign," 97; Pierro, ed., *The Maryland Campaign*,

227-8; Lt. Samuel Moore's Diary; "What Confederate Troops Fought the 10th Me. in the East Woods," *National Tribune*, August 25, 1892. According to this *National Tribune* account, Capt. William Robbins told a former Union soldier that as his 4th Alabama approached the East Woods, it encountered five companies of the 21st Georgia, whose men asked if they could join them. James Cooper Nisbet, who was in command of the 21st Georgia by this time, makes no reference to the issue of having joined up with the 4th Alabama.

11. *OR 19*, pt. 1, 929, 935.

12. *OR 19*, pt. 1, 269-70; Adoniram Judson Warner, "The Ordeal of Adoniram Judson Warner: His Minutes of South Mountain and Antietam," *Civil War History*, vol. 28, number 3 (September, 1982), 226-7.

13. Susan P. Lee, *Memoirs of William Nelson Pendleton* (Philadelphia: J. B. Lippincott, 1893), 216; Billy Ellis, Tithes of Blood (Murfreesboro, TN: Southern Heritage Press, 1997), 77-8.

14. Pierro, ed., *The Maryland Campaign*, 229; Stubbs, *Duty-Honor-Valor*, 308; Steven R. Davis, "'Like Leaves in an Autumn Wind:' The 11th Mississippi Infantry in the Army of Northern Virginia," *CWR* (vol. 2, no. 4, 1992), 288; Moore, "Eighth Pennsylvania Reserves," 131.

15. B. R. Maryniak, "A Rough Morning Near Sharpsburg," 27.

16. "The Civil War Diary of Griffin Lewis Baldwin," 7th Pennsylvania Reserve folder, Antietam NMP; Pierro, ed., *The Maryland Campaign*, 229-30; *OR 19*, pt. 1, 270.

17. *OR 19*, pt. 1, 938; D. C. Love Recollections, Mississippi Department of Archives and History. Three Confederate brigades from D. H. Hill's division (Ripley's, Garland's under McRae, and Colquitt's) were just to the rear and could have been thrown into the combat.

18. W. R. Hamby, "Hood's Texas Brigade at Sharpsburg," *CV*, vol. 16, no. 1 (January 1908), 19; Pierro, ed., *The Maryland Campaign*, 231-32; Dunn, *Iron Men, Iron Will*, 109-110. Pvt. Lawrence Daffan of the 4th Texas recalled, "as we passed where Lawton's [Douglass'] Brigade had stood, there was a complete line of dead Georgians as far as I could see." *Voices of the Civil War: Antietam*, 72.

19. Theodore B. Gates, *The Ulster Guard, Twentieth N.Y. State Militia and the War of the Rebellion; Embracing a History of the Early Organization of the Regiments in its Service, Etc.* (New York: Benj. Tyrrel, 1879), 317; Edward Welch to parents, September 22, 1862, Edward Stephen Welch Papers, Library of Congress; "The Texans at Sharpsburg," 555. Campbell was wounded and his battery was now under Lt. James Stewart.

20. E. Scott Carson, "Hampton's Legion and Hood's Brigade," *CV*, vol. 16, no. 7 (July, 1908), 342; Hamby, "Hood's Texas Brigade at Sharpsburg," 19.

21. P. A. Work, "The 1st Texas Regiment of the Texas Brigade of the Army of Northern Virginia at the Battles of Boonsboro Pass or Gap and Sharpsburg or Antietam, MD in September 1862 (copy in 1st Texas file, Antietam NMP); *OR 19*, pt. 1, 932; T. J. Marshall, "The Pennsylvania Reserves at Antietam," *National Tribune*, April 11, 1907; Otott, "The 1st Texas in the Maryland Campaign," 102; "The Sharpsburg Fight," *Tri-Weekly Telegraph*, October 15, 1862. Because of the confusion, the 1st Texas was divided in half. When the commander of the right side of the regiment appeared to give a report to the regiment's commander, the noise was so ear-splitting that he had to yell into his ear. Work, "The First Texas at Sharpsburg."

22. Otott, "The 1st Texas in the Maryland Campaign," 98; Pierro, ed., *The Maryland Campaign*, 230-1.

23. Johnston, J. S. "Reminiscences of Sharpsburg," *SHSP*, vol. 8, no. 10-12 (1880), pp. 527.

24. Otott, "The 1st Texas in the Maryland Campaign," 104; J. R. Putnam, "Patrick's Brigade," *National Tribune*, April 30, 1908; *OR 19*, pt. 1, 244, 258.

25. Jeffrey D. Stocker, ed., *From Huntsville to Appomattox: R. T. Coles's History of 4th Regiment, Alabama Volunteer Infantry, C.S.A., Army of Northern Virginia* (Knoxville, TN: University of Tennessee Press, 1996), 68-9; Clark, *North Carolina Regiments*, vol. 1, 308.

26. Val C. Giles, "The Flag of First Texas, A. N. Virginia," *CV*, vol. 15, no. 9 (September 1907), 417. The silk flag was carried in a silk oilcloth case to protect it and was seldom removed, except for parades and battle.

27. Work, "The First Texas at Sharpsburg."

28. *OR 19*, pt. 1, 1,032-3; Henry Walter Thomas, *History of the Doles-Cook Brigade* (Atlanta: The Franklin Printing and Publishing Co., 1903), 69. Col. S. D. Thruston recalled the brigade's change in direction: "this change of front was admirable, though executed under a heavy fire of infantry and artillery." According to Thruston, this change in front occurred about 7:30 a.m. Clark, *North Carolina Regiments*, vol. 1, 185.

29. William F. Fox, *Regimental Losses in the American Civil War* (Albany, NY: Albany Publishing Company, 1893), 556, 558; Pierro, ed., *The Maryland Campaign*, 469. In addition to the horrendous losses to the 1st Texas, which were the highest of any regiment on either side during the Civil War, Hampton's Legion lost 69%, the 18th Georgia lost 57%, 4th Texas lost 54%, and the 5th Texas lost 47%. Holsworth, "Uncommon Valor," 54. Joe Hooker was among the wounded, hit in the foot by a bullet as he rode in the pasture south of the Miller cornfield. Sears, *Landscape Turned Red*, 215.

Map Set 13. Antietam: Mansfield's XII Corps Enters the Battle (7:15 - 8:45 a.m.)

1. B. R. Maryniak, "A Rough Morning Near Sharpsburg," 28; Pierro, ed., *The Maryland Campaign*, 233; OR 19, pt. 1, 244, 251-2; Otott, "The 1st Texas in the Maryland Campaign," 108; Zack Waters, "The Fourth Georgia at Antietam," copy in 4th Georgia folder, Antietam NMP; The Countryman, October 6, 1862; Alan D. Gaff, *On Many a Bloody Field: Four Years in the Iron Brigade* (Bloomington, IN: Indiana University Press, 1996), 186-7. Capt. Algar Wheeler of the 21st New York estimated that he lost about 40% of his men during the counterattack of Starke's division and Ripley's brigade. Algar Monroe Wheeler, "Reminiscences of the Battle of Antietam," copy in the 21st New York file, Antietam NMP.

2. Thomas, *History of the Doles-Cook Brigade*, 69. Welsh, *Medical Histories of Confederate Generals*, 184-5. Ripley's wound would have been fatal had it not first struck his thick neckband. Once his wound was dressed, he returned to the front, but left soon after because of "exhaustion." Ripley never returned to the Army of Northern Virginia. He spent most of the rest of the war defending Charleston, South Carolina, under Gen. P. G. T. Beauregard, who described Ripley as "an excellent officer" and recommended him for promotion. Ripley left Charleston near the end of the war and temporarily led a division under Gen. Joseph E. Johnston at Bentonville in North Carolina in March of 1865. Lawrence L. Hewitt, "Roswell Sabine Ripley," in *The Confederate General*, vol. 5, 89-90.

3. John M. Gould, *History of the First-Tenth-Twenty-ninth Maine Regiment, in Service of the United States from May 3, 1861 to June 21, 1866* (Portland, ME: Stephen Berry, 1871), 232-33; Pierro, ed.,

The Maryland Campaign, 235; Alpheus Williams, *From the Cannon's Mouth: The Civil War Letters of General Alpheus S. Williams* (Lincoln, NE: Bison Books, 1995), 123-4, 125. Brig. Gen. Alpheus Williams called Mansfield "fussy," and of a "very nervous temperament and a very impatient manner."

4. OR 19, pt. 1, 484, 487; Pierro, ed., *The Maryland Campaign*, 235.

5. Robert M. Green, *History of the One hundred and Twenty-Fourth Regiment, Pennsylvania Volunteers in the War of the Rebellion, 1862-1863* (Philadelphia: Ware Brothers Company, 1907), 30; OR 19, pt. 1, 484, 491.

6. Pierro, ed., *The Maryland Campaign*, 235-7; Gould, *History of the First-Tenth-Twenty-ninth Maine Regiment*, 237; OR 19, pt. 1, 484, 486, 489; "Letter from the 10th ME Regiment," *Lewiston Journal*, October 2, 1862.

7. Charles Greene to Susan Dana, Civil War Misc. Collection, U.S. Army Military History Center; OR 19, pt. 1, 475, 494, 514; Pierro, ed., *The Maryland Campaign*, 239.

8. Pierro, ed., *The Maryland Campaign*, 236, 238; Bates, *History of Pennsylvania Volunteers*, vol. 4, 90. In the confusion, no one thought to inform Crawford that one of his larger regiments was being sent far to the right. As he wrote in his report, "The One hundred and twenty-fourth Pennsylvania . . . was detached from my brigade by some superior order unknown to me." OR 19, pt. 1, 484.

9. Gould, *History of the First-Tenth-Twenty-ninth Maine Regiment*, 240-1; Hewett, ed., *OR Supplement*, vol. 3, 562-4. According to Welsh, *Medical Histories of Union Generals*, 219-220, no one saw Mansfield receive his wound. The general tried to jump his wounded mount over a low rail fence, but when the animal refused, the general climbed down and walked the horse over. Only when the wind or some other movement opened his coat did aides discover the general's chest soaked in blood. Too weak to mount another horse, the general asked to be carried to the rear, and men fashioned a rough litter of rifles and hauled him some distance until a blanket was procured.

10. OR 19, pt. 1, 487, 493; Frederick Crouse, "An Account of the Battle of Antietam," copy in the 128th Pennsylvania folder, Antietam NMP; David to Father, September 22, 1862, copy in the 128th Pennsylvania folder, Antietam NMP; Pierro, ed., *The Maryland Campaign*, 238. Map 6 of the Cope-Carman set clearly shows the 128th Pennsylvania in front of the 46th Pennsylvania and 28th New York. Yet, most first-person accounts place the latter two regiments on the front line

between the novice regiment and the 10th Maine.

11. Pierro, ed., *The Maryland Campaign*, 240.

12. Gould, *History of the First-Tenth-Twenty-ninth Maine Regiment*, 238, 239. The men of the 10th Maine were using "combustible envelope cartridges," which allowed them to load their muskets without first biting off their ends. This led to a faster rate of fire.

13. *OR* 19, pt. 1, 1,043; 1,053-4; Mills, *Chronicles of the Twenty-First New York*, 291-2. Roswell Ripley's two regiments of Georgians were equipped with smoothbore muskets firing "buck and ball," which was deadly at this close range. Among the casualties in the 27th Indiana were two of the men who found Lee's Special Order No. 191 four days earlier. Cpl. Barton Mitchell and Sgt. John Bloss were wounded and Capt. Peter Kop, the officer to whom they delivered the correspondence, was killed outright. Sears, *Landscape Turned Red*, 208. Maj. Gen. D. H. Hill ordered the Mumma house burned because it could be occupied by Yankee sharpshooters. Kathleen A. Ernst, *Too Afraid to Cry: Maryland Civilians in the Antietam Campaign* (Mechanicsville, PA: Stackpole Books, 1999), 131.

14. *OR* 19, pt. 1, 511-2.

15. Edwin E. Bryant, *History of the Third Regiment of Wisconsin Veteran Volunteer Infantry* (Madison, WI: 3rd Wisconsin Veterans Association, 1891), 126-8; Alonzo H. Quint, *The Record of the Second Massachusetts Infantry* (Boston: J. P. Walker, 1867), 136; *OR* 19, pt. 1, 1054; Lyman Richard Comey, ed., *A Legacy of Valor: The Memoirs and Letters Of Captain Henry Newton Comey* (Knoxville, TN.: University of Tennessee Press, 2004), 77; Pierro, ed., *The Maryland Campaign*, 240-1.

16. *OR* 19, pt. 1, 1,023, 1,044; Clark, *North Carolina Regiments*, vol. 1, 627. Except for the disposition of the 5th North Carolina, the deployment of the remainder of McRae's brigade is unknown.

17. Eugene Powell, "Recollections of the Eastern Campaigns of the Fall of 1862," *National Tribune*, June 27, 1901; Pierro, ed., *The Maryland Campaign*, 242-3; *The Jeffersonian Democrat*, October 3, 1862; *OR* 19, pt. 1, 506, 508, 509; David Cunningham and Wells Miller, *Antietam. Report of the Ohio Antietam Battlefield Commission* (Springfield, OH: Springfield Publishing Company, 1904), 33-4; *Reunion of the 28th & 147th Regiments, Pennsylvania Volunteers* (Philadelphia: Pawson and Nicholson, 1872), 8.

18. Clark, *North Carolina Regiments*, vol. 1, 141-2; William L. DeRosset, "Battle of Sharpsburg— A Correction," *CV*, vol. IX (1901), 265.

19. Pierro, ed., *The Maryland Campaign*, 243-44.

20. Diary of John Foering, Historical Society of Pennsylvania; Stocker, *From Huntsville to Appomattox*, 68-70; Randall Allen and Keith S. Bohannon, eds., *Campaigning with "Old Stonewall": Confederate Captain Ujanirtus Allen's Letters to His Wife* (Baton Rouge, LA: Louisiana State University Press), 1998, 165.

21. William H. H. Fithian Diary, September 17, 1862, Alexander R. Chamberline Collection, U.S. Military History Institute; Pierro, ed., *The Maryland Campaign*, 243; John McLaughlin, *Memoir of Hector Tyndale* (Philadelphia: Collins, 1882), 54; *OR* 19, pt. 1, 508, 509, 1,054; Matthew R. Beer, "The Scene of a Battlefield: 28th Pennsylvania Volunteers at Antietam," copy in the 28th Pennsylvania folder, Antietam NMP, 5-7; James Madison Folsom, *Heroes and Martyrs of Georgia: Georgia's Record in the Revolution of 1861* (Baltimore, MD: Butternut and Blue, 1995), 25. According to the commander of the 3rd North Carolina, Col. Stephen Thruston, once "forced to retire, we did so in good order, the men turning and firing as they chanced to find a cartridge lying on the field." Hewett, ed., *OR Supplement*, vol. 3, 587. Maj. Orrin Crane of the 7th Ohio recalled it differently, writing in his report, "the enemy gave way in confusion and disorder before the furious onset of our troops. We pursued them rapidly, capturing many prisoners, and strewing the ground with their dead and wounded." *OR* 19, pt. 1, 506. According to Sgt. William Fithian of the 28th Pennsylvania, "they [Colquitt's men] did a good bit of damage to us. They fought well, in fact they seemed to know no fear, dareing [sic] men." The left side of George Gordon's Federal brigade was masked during this attack, and so forced to hold its fire.

22. *OR* 19, pt. 1, 501, 502-03, Pierro, ed., *The Maryland Campaign*, 244; Col. R. B. Van Valkenburg Recollections, copy in the 107th New York folder, Antietam NMP; Samuel Toombs, *Reminiscences of the War, Comprising a Detailed Account of the Experiences of the Thirteenth Regiment New Jersey Volunteers* (Orange, NJ: Journal Office, 1878), 19.

Map Set 14. Antietam: Sedgwick's Division Drives West (8:15 - 9:30 a.m.)

1. Pierro, ed., *The Maryland Campaign*, 453-54, 459, 462-4, 469-73; *OR* 19, pt. 1, 967-9; "The 21st Virginia at the Battle of Sharpsburg."

2. Pierro, ed., *The Maryland Campaign*, 453-4, 459, 462-64, 469-73.

3. Work, "The 1st Texas at Sharpsburg"; OR 19, pt. 1, 928; "107th New York," copy in 107th New York folder, Antietam NMP.

4. Sparks, *Inside Lincoln's Army*, 149; OR 19, pt. 1, 514-5, 969; Pierro, ed., *The Maryland Campaign*, 248-9, 250; Lee A. Wallace, Fifth Virginia (Lynchburg, VA: H. E. Howard, 1988), 42; John E. Olson, *21st Virginia Infantry* (Lynchburg, VA: H. E. Howard, 1989), 23-25. When Monroe's battery deployed and opened fire on Grigsby's and Early's men to the northwest, the Virginians initially thought it was "friendly fire." The guns soon changed direction to face Sharpsburg. Chapla, *48th Virginia Infantry*, 39-40.

5. Walker, *History of the Second Army Corps in the Army of the Potomac*, 101; OR 19, pt. 1, 275. McClellan told Sumner he would cross Antietam Creek with only two of his three divisions because Richardson's command would have to wait until the V Corps could relieve it.

6. U. S. Congress, *Joint Committee on the Conduct of the War*, pt. 1, 581-2; Marion V. Armstrong, *Unfurl Those Colors!: McClellan, Sumner, and the Second Army Corps in the Antietam Campaign* (Tuscaloosa, AL: The University of Alabama Press, 2008), 170-1.

7. Pierro, ed., *The Maryland Campaign*, 254; Walker, *History of the Second Army Corps*, 101; Armstrong, *Unfurl Those Colors!*, 178. Both Ezra Carman and Francis Walker were highly critical of Sumner's handling of his corps during this period of the battle. Sumner, they argued, refused to listen to Gen. Williams' summary of the fight and was so confident that Sedgwick's men would carry the West Woods that he did not give specific orders to French on what he was expected to do. When French eventually went in, his division veered south (left) and struck the Sunken Road, where he could not off any support to Sedgwick's embattled command. Pierro, ed., *The Maryland Campaign*, 254; Walker, *History of the Second Army Corps*, 101. However, modern historian, Marion Armstrong, offers convincing counterarguments to this general thesis, explaining that the battlefield was quiet at this time, which meant that the enemy were either pulling back or regrouping. He also noted that Federal troops had entered the southern portion of the West Woods without incident. Marion Armstrong, *Unfurl Those Colors!*, 178.

8. OR 19, pt. 1, 227-8; Bates, *History of Pennsylvania Volunteers*, vol. 4, 108-9.

9. OR 19, pt. 1, 487, 491-2, 928.

10. Pierro, ed., *The Maryland Campaign*, 256. The disposition of Jubal Early's brigade is not clear. It appears the 25th Virginia formed the brigade's left flank and the 49th Virginia formed its right flank. Pierro, ed., *The Maryland Campaign*, 263, 265.

11. Ernest L. Waitt, *History of the Nineteenth Regiment Massachusetts Volunteer Infantry* (Salem, MA: Salem Press, Co., 1906), 134; OR 19, pt. 1, 311, 319; Gibbon, *Recollections*, 87-8. Dana's men emerged from the East Woods to find a line of battle lying on the ground. Believing these prone soldiers represented Gorman's, Dana ordered his men into a prone position behind them. A staff officer appeared, corrected Dana, and ordered him forward. The men were probably from Gordon's brigade of Mansfield's XII Corps, and not Gorman's. Oliver Howard's brigade received contradictory orders that delayed its move forward. Armstrong, *Unfurl Those Colors!*, 181-2; Pierro, ed., *The Maryland Campaign*, 261-2.

12. George B. Davis, "The Antietam Campaign," in *Campaigns in Virginia, Maryland, and Pennsylvania, Papers of the Military Historical Society of Massachusetts* (Boston: Griffith-Stillings Press, 1903), vol. 3, 62; OR 51, pt. 1, 842; Francis W. Palfrey, *Antietam and Fredericksburg* (New York: Scribner's, 1882), 84. Palfrey's account, of course, was written after Sedgwick's division was slaughtered in the West Woods. What Palfrey apparently did not know was that French's division may not have been so far behind Sedgwick. Also see Armstrong, *Unfurl Those Colors!*, 207-8.

13. OR 19, pt. 1, 971; Pierro, ed., *The Maryland Campaign*, 263-4.

14. Pierro, ed., *The Maryland Campaign*, 260.

15. OR 19, pt. 1, 858-9, 909; W. H. Andrews, "'Tige' Anderson's Brigade at Sharpsburg," *CV*, vol. 16 (1908), 578; Dinkins, *By an Old Johnnie*, 59. Like so many of Lee's divisions on September 17, Lafayette McLaws' command was in poor shape when it entered the combat. Straggling had significantly reduced its strength, and those still in the ranks were hungry and exhausted. McLaws' division arrived from Pleasant Valley, where it had confronted the Federal VI Corps on the morning of September 16. Most of the men marched that day without provisions of any sort, and those who did had no time to cook them. None slept during the night of September 15, but managed some rest early on September 16. The column marched that day until it was too dark to see the road and halted about two miles from the Shepherdstown ford. When urgent orders arrived to keep moving, McLaws roused his men and continued marching. The head of his column reached Sharpsburg on the

morning of September 17, where the troops finally rested a few hours before being ordered to their feet once more and rushed to the left to try and rescue Lee's collapsing left flank. *OR* 19, pt. 1, 857-8; Pierro, ed., *The Maryland Campaign*, 257-8.

16. *OR* 19, pt. 1, 914, 1030.

17. Pierro, ed., *The Maryland Campaign*, 261; Armstrong, *Unfurl Those Colors!*, 180-1.

18. *OR* 19, pt. 1, 311; Armstrong, *Unfurl Those Colors!*, 183-4; Pierro, ed., *The Maryland Campaign*, 262.

19. *OR* 19, pt. 1, 320.

20. Mac Wyckoff, *A History of the 2nd South Carolina Infantry, 1861-1865* (Fredericksburg, VA: Sgt. Kirkland's Museum and Historical Society, 1994), 45; Pierro, ed., *The Maryland Campaign*, 261-3; John T. Parham, "Thirty-Second at Sharpsburg," *SHSP*, vol. 34, (1906), 252; *Recollections and Reminiscences, 1861-1865*, vol. 12, 349-50; *OR* 19, pt. 1, 316, 865, 874, 883, 874, 910; Armstrong, *Unfurl Those Colors!*, 189; Col. E. M. Morrison, "Fifteenth Virginia Infantry," *SHSP*, vol. 33 (1905), 103-4. The 2nd South Carolina was thrown into the fight first because it had not participated in the combat on Maryland Heights. Robert Shand, "Incidents in the Life of a Private Soldier," 34-35, copy in 2nd South Carolina folder, Antietam NMP. According to one soldier, Semmes' 53rd Georgia attacked with unusual fierceness because its members were enraged because their commanding officer, Lt. Col. Thomas Sloan, had been mortally wounded. John W. Lynch, *The Dorman-Marshbourne Letters* (Senoia, GA: Down South Publishing Company, 1995), 31. Krick, *Lee's Colonels*, 348, however, quotes a member of the regiment who wrote just a few weeks earlier that "[Sloan] treats the boys very tyrannically and has got the ill will of all the regt. I don't suppose he has a friend in the whole regt."

21. Waitt, 19th Massachusetts, 137; George A. Bruce, *The Twentieth Regiment of Massachusetts Volunteer Infantry, 1861-1865* (Boston: Houghton, Mifflin and Company, 1906), 169; Oliver Otis Howard, *Autobiography of Oliver Otis Howard, Major General United States Army* (New York: Baker and Taylor Col, 1907), vol. 1, 296; Armstrong, *Unfurl Those Colors!*, 188.

22. *OR* 19, pt. 1, 313; Armstrong, *Unfurl Those Colors!*, 188; Henry Ropes to Father, September 20, 1862, copy in 20th Massachusetts folder, Antietam NMP. According to Ezra Carman, Sumner "cussed them out by the right flank." Pierro, ed., *The Maryland Campaign*, 267. The men

in Sedgwick's second line (Dana's brigade) were frustrated by the way the battle was going. An officer in the 59th New York explained, "A charge over the space in front was impossible, and the men were obliged to stand up and fire, every part of their persons exposed to the deadly aim of the enemy, who was partially concealed behind a stone fence breast high, and the houses and out-houses of the farm upon which this portion of the battle was fought." Plattsburg *Express & Sentinel*, October 11, 1862.

23. T. Harry Williams, "The Civil War Letters of William L. Cage," *Civil War History*, vol. 39, no. 1 (January, 1956), 122; *OR* 19, pt. 1, 492, 971; Pierro, ed., *The Maryland Campaign*, 263-4. Col. Jacob Higgins of the 125th Pennsylvania watched the Southerners approach "in solid columns like an avalanche that threatened to sweep all before it." Jacob Higgins, "At Antietam: The Gallant Services of the 125th Pennsylvania," *National Tribune*, June 3, 1886. William Andrews of the 1st Georgia noted that "after the second volley our men fired, they charged. The enemy's line giving away, it then became almost a tree-to-tree fight. W. H. Andrews, *Footprints of a Regiment: A Recollection of the 1st Georgia Regulars, 1861-1865* (Atlanta: Longstreet Press, 1992), 80.

24. *OR* 19, pt. 1, 320; Edward Burruss Memoirs, copy in 21st Mississippi folder, Antietam NMP.

25. *OR* 19, pt. 1, 971; Andrews, *Footprints of a Regiment*, 79-80.

26. Pierro, ed., *The Maryland Campaign*, 266-67.

27. Armstrong, *Unfurl Those Colors!*, 191; Bruce, *Twentieth Massachusetts*, 169; Pierro, ed., *The Maryland Campaign*, 266; Bradley M. Gottfried, *Stopping Pickett: The History of the Philadelphia Brigade* (Shippensburg, PA: White Mane Publishing Co., 1999), 116.

28. Pierro, ed., *The Maryland Campaign*, 266; Gottfried, *Stopping Pickett: The History of the Philadelphia Brigade*, 116.

29. Wyckoff, *A History of the 3rd South Carolina Infantry*, 75-6; Pierro, ed., *The Maryland Campaign*, 272; *OR* 19, pt. 1, 868-9.

30. *OR* 19, pt. 1, 477, 501-2; Comey, *A Legacy of Valor*, 77.

31. *OR* 19, pt. 1, 307, 318; Isaac Jones Wistar, *Autobiography of Isaac Jones Wistar* (Philadelphia: Wistar Institute of Anatomy and Biology, 1937), 404-5.

32. Bruce, *Twentieth Massachusetts*, 169; Catherine Drinker Bowen, *Yankee from Olympus: Justice Holmes and his Family* (Boston: Little Brown and Co., 1944), 172; John G. B. Adams, *Reminiscences of the Nineteenth Massachusetts Regiment* (Boston: Wright &

Porter Printing Company, 1899), 44-5; Waitt, *19th Massachusetts*, 138-9.

33. OR 19, pt. 1, 311, 314, 317; Richard Moe, *The Last Full Measure: The Life and Death of the First Minnesota Volunteers* (New York: Henry Holt, 1993), 184-5.

34. OR 19, pt. 1, 313; Gregory Coco, ed., *From Ball's Bluff to Gettysburg . . . and Beyond: The Civil War Letters of Private Roland E. Bowen, 15th Massachusetts Infantry 1861-1864* (Gettysburg: Thomas Pub., 1994), 135.

35. OR 19, pt. 1, 869. Ezra Carman makes a convincing argument that Early's brigade did not participate in the pursuit of Sedgwick's shattered division. He based this on the fact that Early spent very little ink on this part of the fighting in his after-action report, and the relatively low numbers of casualties the brigade sustained. Pierro, ed., *The Maryland Campaign*, 272.

Map Set 15. Antietam: Final Actions on the Northern Front (9:30 - 10:30 a.m.)

1. OR 19, pt. 1, 505, 865; Robert Shand, "Incidents in the Life of a Private Soldier," 37. J. J. McDaniel of the 7th South Carolina recalled that his regiment charged out of the woods and scaled a hill. "No sooner did we gain the top of the hill than they opened a most murderous fire of grape and shells . . . of all the cannonading I have ever experienced, this was the most destructive. It seemed almost whole lines would melt away at once." *Recollections and Reminiscences, 1861-1865*, vol. 12, 350. Although the 8th South Carolina fielded but forty trigger-pullers, when it reached the rise overlooking the Roulette cornfield these men fired a volley that disordered the large 1st Delaware. According to Gen. French, it was a "sudden and terrible fire." Recognizing the mismatch, however, the South Carolinians wisely fell back a couple of minutes later. OR 19, pt. 1, 323-4; Pierro, ed., *The Maryland Campaign*, 279.

2. Pierro, ed., *The Maryland Campaign*, 273-5; OR 19, pt. 1, 495; Toombs, *Reminiscences of the War*, 20; Alonzo Quint, *The Record of the Second Massachusetts Infantry, 1861-65*, 137-8; Comey, *A Legacy of Valor*, 78.

3. Herbert M. Schiller, *A Captain's War: The Letters and Diaries of William H. S. Burgwyn, 1861-1865* (Shippensburg, PA: White Mane, 1994), 18; OR 19, pt. 1, 920; Beer, "The Scene of a Battlefield," 12; Clark, *North Carolina Regiments*, vol. 2, 603. Gen. John Walker, whose two brigades were now up and engaging or ready to engage the enemy, were hit by a tremendous storm of iron from the Federal batteries in front of them. As Walker later reported, his men "lay upon the ground, taking advantage of such undulations and shallow ravines as gave promise of partial shelter, while this fearful storm raged a few feet above their heads, tearing the trees asunder, lopping off huge branches, and filling the air with shrieks and explosions." OR 19, pt. 1, 916. Federal Brig. Gen. George H. Gordon noted in his report: "these [Confederate] regiments were received with a galling fire, which they sustained and returned for a brief period, then fell back upon their supports." A soldier in the 13th New Jersey also recalled the "galling" fire, which "astonished the boys, and made it so hot that it would have been madness to remain. Acting on the principle of discretion being the better part of valor, the regiment broke and moved in pretty lively style to the rear, halting within the protection of a piece of woods. OR 19, pt. 1, 495; n.a., *Historical Sketch of Company D, Thirteenth Regiment, N. J. Volunteers* (Newark, NJ: D. L. Gildersleeve and Co., 1875), 16.

4. OR 19, pt. 1, 506, 915; Pierro, *The Maryland Campaign*, 275, 462, 471; Clark, *North Carolina Regiments*, vol. 2, 434; Patriot (Greensborough, North Carolina), October 23, 1862; *Voices of the Civil War: Antietam*, 102; Robert K. Krick, *30th Virginia Infantry* (Lynchburg, VA: H.E. Howard, Inc., 1983), 26-7. Col. Van Manning's losses for this brief charge are substantially higher when taking into account that only three regiments participated in the attack. Calvin L. Collier, *They'll Do to Tie To! The Story of the Third Regiment, Arkansas Infantry C.S.A.* (Little Rock, AK: Democrat Litho and Printing Co., 1995), 94-5.

5. OR 19, pt. 1, 506; Pierro, *The Maryland Campaign*, 299; Beer, "The Scene of a Battlefield," 13-16; Toombs, *Reminiscences of the War*, 21.

6. Pierro, *The Maryland Campaign*, 301-2.

7. Pierro, *The Maryland Campaign*, 304; OR 19, pt. 1, 515, 505, 506, 509; William H. H. Fithian Diary; n.a., *Historical Sketch of Company D, Thirteenth Regiment N. J. Volunteers*, 18.

8. Williams, *From the Cannon's Mouth*, 129.

9. Pierro, *The Maryland Campaign*, 454, 456, 459, 463, 464, 469, 471, 472, 473; OR 19, pt. 1, 191,193, 199.

10. Pierro, *The Maryland Campaign*, 263. Other divisional losses were as follows: McLaws: 38%; Hill: 36%; Lawton: 32%; J. R. Jones: 31%; and Walker: 28%.

11. Pierro, *The Maryland Campaign*, 461, 465; T. D. Bell, "Reminiscences about Sharpsburg," *CV*, vol. 1, no. 8 (1893), 246. Robert Rodes' brigade was

ordered to reinforce Alfred Colquitt to the north about 9:00 a.m., but when Rodes reached the Roulette farm lane, Colquitt's beaten infantry was already falling back. Rodes' brigade was ordered to move back to the Sunken Road. *OR* 19, pt. 1, 1036-37. Historian Robert K. Krick questioned whether Colquitt's brigade even occupied the western portion of the Sunken Road, noting that "an extensive collection of manuscript accounts . . . by veterans . . . includes not a word about standing in the leftward extension of the Bloody Lane." A number of disorganized troops from Colquitt's regiments, however, may indeed have rallied there. Krick, "It Appeared as Though Mutual Extermination Would Put a Stop to the Awful Carnage," 229-230.

12. Armstrong, *Unfurl Those Colors!*, 208-9; Pierro, *The Maryland Campaign*, 278-9. French's division was essentially a new unit. It was formed on September 16, and many of its men had never been in combat. Krick, "It Appeared as Though Mutual Extermination Would Put a Stop to the Awful Carnage," 230.

Map Set 16. Antietam: The Sunken Road (9:00 a.m. - 12:30 p.m.)

1. *OR* 19, pt. 1, 1037, 1047.

2. William P. Seville, *History of the First Regiment, Delaware Volunteers, From the Commencement of the "Three Months' Service" to the Final Muster-out at the Close of the Rebellion* (Baltimore: Longstreet House, 1986), 47-8; Armstrong, *Unfurl Those Colors!*, 210; *OR* 19, pt. 1, 1,047. Capt. Edwin Osborne of the 4th North Carolina recalled that Weber's men advanced "in magnificent style, with mounted officers in full uniform, swords gleaming . . . on they came with steady tramp and confident men. They did not see our single line of hungry jaded and dusty men, who were lying down, until within good musket shot, when we rose and delivered our fire with terrible effect." *Voices of the Civil War: Antietam*, 112-3.

3. Edward Spangler, *My Little War Experience, with Historical Sketches and Memorabilia* (York, PA: York Daily Publishing Company, 1904), 34.

4. *OR* 19, pt. 1, 332, 333; Charles D. Page, *History of the Fourteenth Regiment, Connecticut Vol. Infantry* (Meriden, CT: Horton Publishing Co., 1906), 37-8; Seville, *History of the First Delaware*, 48.

5. George Washburn, *A Complete Military History and Record of the 108th Regiment, N.Y. Vols.* (Rochester, NY: Press of E. R. Andrews, 1894),

24-5; Henry S. Stevens, *Souvenir of Excursion to Battlefields by the Society of the Society of the Fourteenth Connecticut Regiment and Reunion at Antietam, September 1891* (Washington: Gibson Brothers, Printers, 1893), 52; *OR* 19, pt. 1, 334, 336; The Maryland Campaign, 280.

6. *OR* 19, pt. 1, 1037 Collins, *Rodes*, 168; Pierro, *The Maryland Campaign*, 280-1.

7. *OR* 19, pt. 1, 334.

8. Frederick L. Hitchcock, *War from the Inside: The Story of the 132nd Regiment Pennsylvania Volunteer Infantry in the War for the Suppression of the Rebellion* (Philadelphia: Press of J. B. Lippincott, 1904), 59, 66; Armstrong, *Unfurl Those Colors!*, 216.

9. Hitchcock, *War from the Inside*, 59.

10. Franklin Sawyer, *A Military History of the 8th Regiment, Ohio Vol. Infantry* (Cleveland, OH: Fairbanks & Co., Printers, 1881), 78-9.

11. William H. Osborne, *The History of the Twenty-Ninth Regiment of the Massachusetts Vounteer Infantry in the Late War of the Rebellion* (Boston: Albert J. Wright, Printer, 1877), 184-5; Armstrong, *Unfurl Those Colors!*, 220-1; Walter Holden, William E. Ross, and Elizabeth Slomba, eds., *Stand Firm and Fire Low: The Civil War Writings of Colonel Edward E. Cross* (Hanover, NH: University of New Hampshire, 2003), 46-7.

12. Carman-Cope Map, Number 9; Krick, "It Appeared as Though Mutual Extermination Would Put a Stop to the Awful Carnage," 239.

13. David W. Mellott, "The 7th West Virginia Infantry's Assault on Bloody Lane," *CWR*, vol. 5, no. 3 (1997), 136-7; Pierro, *The Maryland Campaign*, 281; *OR* 19, pt. 1, 327; *Pennsylvania at Antietam*, 163. Col. John Gordon of the 6th Alabama watched as the first Federal wave (probably composed of the 130th Pennsylvania) approached his position. "So far as I could see," recalled Gordon, "every soldier wore white gaiters around his ankles. The banners above them had apparently never been discolored by the smoke and dust of battle. Their gleaming bayonets flashed like burnished silver in the sunlight. With the precision of step and perfect alignment of a holiday parade, this magnificent array moved to the charge, every step keeping time to the tap of the deep-sounding drum." General John B. Gordon, *Reminiscences of the Civil War* (New York: Scribners, 1903), 85-86. Lying in front of the Sunken Road, the men of Kimball's brigade hugged the ground. As Sgt. Thomas Galwey recalled, "our men are falling by the hundreds. . . . General Kimball passes, muttering, 'God save my poor boys' . . . the din is frightful. Alas, no words can depict the horrors of a great battle as they appear to the men unaccustomed to them."

Thomas F. Galway, *The Valiant Hours: Narrative of "Captain Brevet," an Irish-American in the Army of the Potomac* (Harrisburg, PA: Stackpole Press, 1961), 41-42.

14. Pierro, *The Maryland Campaign*, 282; Bates, *History of Pennsylvania Volunteers*, vol. 4, 205. G. B. Anderson was struck on a small rise behind his men. The severe wound was not thought to be life-threatening, and no bullet was initially located. The wound became infected and his foot was amputated, but Anderson died on October 16, 1862, at the age of 32. Welsh, *Medical Histories of Confederate Generals*, 6. Two other officers took command of the brigade during the battle, but both were quickly struck down, essentially rendering the brigade leaderless for much of the fighting. A. M. Waddell, "General George Burgwyn Anderson: The Memorial Address, May 11, 1885," *SHSP*, vol. 14, 395; Krick, "It Appeared as Though Mutual Extermination Would Put a Stop to the Awful Carnage," 236-7.

15. Krick, "It Appeared as Though Mutual Extermination Would Put a Stop to the Awful Carnage," 239; Franklin Sawyer, *A Military History of the 8th Regiment Ohio Vol. Inf'y: Its Battles, Marches and Army Movements* (Nabu Press, 2010), 79-80; Pierro, *The Maryland Campaign*, 283. Welsh, *Medical Histories of Confederate Generals*, 9.

16. Hewett, ed., *OR Supplement*, vol. 3, 569; Pierro, *The Maryland Campaign*, 283-84; Mellott, "The 7th West Virginia Infantry's Assault on Bloody Lane," 137-8.

17. Armstrong, *Unfurl Those Colors!*, 221-2, 227.

18. *OR* 19, pt. 1, 294-5; David Power Conyngham, *The Irish Brigade and its Campaigns* (New York: Fordham University Press, 1994), 305; Armstrong, *Unfurl Those Colors!*, 223-4.

19. *OR* 19, pt. 1, 294-5, 298; R. L. Murray, "The Irish Brigade at Antietam," in *New Yorkers in the Civil War*, R. L. Murray, ed., 10 vols. (2006), vol. 6, 23-5. Meagher specifically mentioned in his battle report that he personally ordered the 69th New York's charge and sent aides to have the 63rd and 88th New York to join in the attack. Nowhere, however, did he indicate that he ordered the 29th Massachusetts, which was not manned by Irish soldiers, to also advance. Armstrong, *Unfurl Those Colors!*, 225-6.

20. Conyngham, *The Irish Brigade*, 306; Armstrong, *Unfurl Those Colors!*, 227-8.

21. *OR* 19, pt. 1, 285; Charles Augustus Fuller, *Personal Recollections of the War of 1861* (Sherburne, NY: News Job Printing House, 1906), 58-59; Walker, *The Second Corps*, 114.

22. *OR* 19, pt. 1, 1037; Pierro, *The Maryland Campaign*, 286-7; Collins, *Rodes*, 168-9; Zack C. Waters and James C. Edmonds, *A Small but Spartan Band: The Florida Brigade in Lee's Army of Northern Virginia* (Tuscaloosa, AL: University of Alabama Press, 2010), 33-6. William Mahone's brigade, commanded by Lt. Col. William A. Parham, numbered a mere 82 men. It was consolidated into a regiment and attached to Roger Pryor's brigade. Pierro, *The Maryland Campaign*, 283.

23. Austin C. Dobbins, *Grandfather's Journal: Company B, Sixteenth Mississippi Infantry Volunteers, Harris' Brigade, Mahone's Division, Hill's Corps, ANV* (Dayton, OH: Morningside Books, 1988), 105; *OR* 19, pt. 1, 884; William W. Chamberlaine, *Memoirs of the Civil War: Between the Northern and Southern Sections of the United States of America 1861 to 1865* (Washington: Bryon S. Adams, 1912), 32. It appears there were several instances of friendly fire when Confederate reinforcements approached the Sunken Road and mistook their own comrades for the enemy. Ambrose Wright's and G. B. Anderson's brigades both seem to have suffered as a result of this deadly confusion. Krick, "It Appeared as Though Mutual Extermination Would Put a Stop to the Awful Carnage," 242, 244; *OR* 19, pt. 1, 285. Moving beyond the Irish Brigade to take position on the front line was no small feat for Caldwell's Brigade. While under enemy fire its members had to knock down several fences and undertake a complex maneuver best attempted on a parade ground. Holden, Ross, and Slomba, *Stand Firm and Fire Low*, 47; Mark Pride and Mark Travis, *My Brave Boys: To War with Colonel Cross and the Fighting Fifth* (Hanover, NH: University Press of New England, 2001), 134.

24. Osborne, *The History of the Twenty-Ninth Massachusetts*, 186-7; *OR* 19, pt. 1, 289.

25. *OR* 19, pt. 1, 289, 1037; Fuller, *Personal Recollections*, 59; Newsom Jenkins, "Recollections of a Sergeant," copy in the 14th North Carolina file, Antietam NMP. According to William Osborne, the 29th Massachusetts approached the Sunken Road firing destructive volleys into the Rebels from a few paces away. However, only Francis Barlow's New Yorkers maneuvered to enfilade the remainder of the Southern line. Barlow apparently moved his companies by the left flank toward the front and then reformed his line of battle perpendicular to the Sunken Road. Osborne, *The History of the Twenty-Ninth Massachusetts*, 187; Fuller, *Personal Recollections*, 59; Armstrong, *Unfurl Those Colors!*, 229.

26. *OR* 19, pt. 1, 1037-8; Collins, *Rodes*, 169. There is considerable disagreement with regard to

which unit was the last to leave the Sunken Road position. Rodes insisted that it was his brigade, but division commander D. H. Hill claimed Rodes' position collapsed before G. B. Anderson's did. Pierro, *The Maryland Campaign*, 290. Hill's assertion is hard to square given how the Federals assaulted the position. When his brigade did unravel, Rodes was distracted for a short time and unable to prevent its collapse, as he noted in his report: "I did not see their retrograde movement until it was too late for me to rally them, for this reason: Just as I was moving on after Lightfoot, I heard a shot strike Lieutenant Birney, who was immediately behind me. Wheeling, I found him falling, and found that he had been struck in the face. He found that he could walk after I raised him, though he thought a shot or piece of shell had penetrated his head just under the eye. I followed him a few paces, and watched him until he had reached a barn, a short distance to the rear, where he first encountered someone to help him in case he needed it. As I turned toward the brigade, I was struck heavily by a piece of shell on my thigh. At first I thought the wound was serious, but, finding, upon examination, that it was slight, I again turned toward the brigade, when I discovered it, without visible cause to me, retreating in confusion. I hastened to intercept it at the Hagerstown road." OR 19, pt. 1, 1,038.

27. Thomas Livermore, *Days and Events, 1860-1866* (Boston: Houghton, Mifflin Company, 1920) 134-5; Fuller, *Personal Recollections*, 59; OR 19, pt. 1, 285.

28. OR 19, pt. 1, 285, 288; Armstrong, *Unfurl Those Colors!*, 232-4; William Child, *A History of the Fifth Regiment, New Hampshire Volunteers in the American Civil War* (Bristol, NH: R. W. Musgrove, Printer, 1893), 132. According to some sources, Caldwell did not order the brigade forward. When Richardson rode up to the brigade and could not find Caldwell, he issued the order himself. Pride and Travis, *My Brave Boys*, 133-4. A number of men in the 5th New Hampshire questioned Caldwell's bravery during the battle. One went so far as to write that they had seen him "under the hill behind the haystack out of harm's way." Livermore, *Days and Events*, 133; Holden, Ross, and Slomba, *Stand Firm and Fire Low*, 47-48. Historian Marion Armstrong reviewed the information and concluded there was no evidence upon which to question Caldwell's whereabouts, which was near the 7th New York on the right of his line. Armstrong, *Unfurl Those Colors!*, 341.

29. OR 19, pt. 1, 290; Armstrong, *Unfurl Those Colors!*, 335-6.

30. OR 19, pt. 1, 290, 872; Pierro, *The Maryland Campaign*, 292; Clark, *North Carolina Regiments*, vol. 2, 434; Collier, *They'll Do to Tie To!*, 98.

31. Pierro, *The Maryland Campaign*, 293; Clark, *North Carolina Regiments*, vol. 2, 434.

32. OR 19, pt. 1, 326; Pierro, *The Maryland Campaign*, 293.

33. OR 19, pt. 1, 299; Pierro, *The Maryland Campaign*, 293; Clark, *North Carolina Regiments*, vol. 2, 435.

34. OR 19, pt. 1, 290, 872. Ezra Carman believed that Cobb's men fired about twenty rounds before being forced back. Pierro, *The Maryland Campaign*, 293.

35. OR 19, pt. 1, 290; Pierro, *The Maryland Campaign*, 293-4; Pride and Travis, *My Brave Boys*, 136-7. Ezra Carman believed the attack was made by masses of Confederate troops from different commands. Caldwell, who apparently remained with the 7th New York, did not oversee the activities of the rest of his brigade. Indeed, Ezra Carman noted that "the colonels of the regiments of Caldwell's brigade fought the battle pretty nearly at their own discretion in the absence of direction from the brigade commander, so that the regiments were not in continuous line much of the time. They faced in varying directions and at varying intervals from each other and sometimes were interspersed with regiments of the other brigades." Pierro, *The Maryland Campaign*, 293-294. Cross' men captured the 4th North Carolina's flag, G. B. Anderson's Brigade; the 57th New York captured the 12th Alabama's flag (Rodes' brigade); the 66th New York captured the 5th Florida's banner (Pryor's brigade).

36. Longstreet, *From Manassas to Appomattox*, 250; OR 19, pt. 1, 290.

37. Pierro, *The Maryland Campaign*, 297-98; OR 19, pt. 1, 191-93; Krick, "It Appeared as Though Mutual Extermination Would Put a Stop to the Awful Carnage," 246-7.

38. Armstrong, *Unfurl Those Colors!*, 247. Richardson lingered from more than six weeks before dying of pneumonia on November 3, 1862. Welsh, *Medical Histories of Union Generals*, 278.

Map Set 17. Antietam: The Lower (Burnside's) Bridge (9:00 a.m. - 2:00 p.m.)

1. George B. McClellan, *McClellan's Own Story*, 589; Pierro, *The Maryland Campaign*, 329-30.

2. OR 19, pt. 1, 31.

3. Carman-Cope Map 8; OR 19, pt. 1, 419.

4. Phillip Thomas Tucker, *Burnside's Bridge: The Climactic Struggle of the 2nd and 20th Georgia at Antietam Creek* (Mechanicsville, PA: Stackpole Books, 2000), 50-3; Pierro, *The Maryland Campaign*, 332, 458; OR 19, pt. 1, 889; James W. Parrish, *Wiregrass to Appomattox: The Untold Story of the 50th Georgia Infantry Regiment, CSA* (Winchester, VA: Angle Valley Press, 2009), 56-7. While Ezra Carman believed the 2nd and 20th Georgia fielded a total of 400 men, a more recent analysis puts the figure between 280 and 290. Pierro, *The Maryland Campaign*, 332; Tucker, *Burnside's Bridge*, 62. Brig. Gen. John Walker's division occupied the area near Snavely Ford before being ordered north to help repel Federal attacks near the Dunker Church.

5. OR 19, pt. 1, 889-90.

6. OR 19, vol. 2, 297; Palfrey, *Antietam and Fredericksburg*, 117; William Marvel, *Burnside* (Chapel Hill, NC: University of North Carolina Press, 1991), 129.

7. Carman-Cope Map 10; OR 19, pt. 1, 419; John Cannan, *Burnside's Bridge: Antietam* (Da Capo, 2000), 46.

8. Pierro, *The Maryland Campaign*, 333; OR 19, pt. 1, 419.

9. Tucker, *Burnside's Bridge*, 83; Dave Dameron, *Benning's Brigade. Vol. 1: A History and Roster of the Fifteenth Georgia* (Spartanburg, SC: The Reprint Company, 1997), 24. Col. Harland did not know what happened to the 11th Connecticut until he stumbled upon it by the bridge after the battle. The regiment had been left behind to guard a battery and that was all that was ever communicated to Harland. OR 19, pt. 1, 452-53. A section of Simmonds battery was in this sector; the other section was attached to Benjamin's battery.

10. Tucker, *Burnside's Bridge*, 84-5.

11. Walter J. Yates, *Souvenir of Excursion to Antietam and Dedication of Monuments of the 8th, 11th, 14th, and 16th Regiments of Connecticut Volunteers* (New London, CT: 1894), 37-38; Tucker, Burnside's Bridge, 85-6.

12. Pierro, *The Maryland Campaign*, 333; Tucker, *Burnside's Bridge*, 86-7. Dameron, *Benning's Brigade*, 24. Kingsbury's son was born three months after his death.

13. John W. Schildt, *The Ninth Corps at Antietam* (Chewsville, MD: 1988), 103; Pierro, *The Maryland Campaign*, 333; OR 19, pt. 1, 471-2.

14. Pierro, *The Maryland Campaign*, 333-4; Tucker, *Burnside's Bridge*, 89.

15. OR 19, pt. 1, 471-472; Pierro, *The Maryland Campaign*, 334.

16. OR 19, pt. 1, 452; Tucker, *Burnside's Bridge*, 92.

17. OR 19, pt. 1, 473; Dameron, *Benning's Brigade*, 24.

18. Dameron, *Benning's Brigade*, 24.

19. Jacob Cox, "The Battle of Antietam," *B&L*, vol. 2, 650.

20. Tucker, *Burnside's Bridge*, 95-96; Pierro, *The Maryland Campaign*, 335.

21. Tucker, *Burnside's Bridge*, 99.

22. Pierro, *The Maryland Campaign*, 335; Lyman Jackman, *History of the Sixth New Hampshire in the War for the Union* (Concord, NH: Republican Press Assoc., 1891), 104.

23. Sears, *Landscape Turned Red*, 263-4. McClellan ordered his cavalry to remain close to his headquarters for most of the battle.

24. Cox, "The Battle of Antietam," 652; John W. Hudson, "Tired Soldiers Don't Go Very Fast," *Civil War Times, Illustrated*, January-February, 1992, 39.

25. OR 19, pt. 1, 444; Whitman, *Civil War Letters of George Washington Whitman*, 67; Gould, *The Story of the Forty-Eighth*, 82; "Fighting Them Over: How the 51st Pennsylvania took the Bridge," *National Tribune*, copy in the 51st Pennsylvania folder, Antietam NMP.

26. Pierro, *The Maryland Campaign*, 335.

27. Tucker, *Burnside's Bridge*, 104, 105.

28. OR 51, pt. 1, 162-63; Tucker, *Burnside's Bridge*, 118.

29. Pierro, *The Maryland Campaign*, 335-36; Tucker, *Burnside's Bridge*, 114; Sauers, *The Civil War Journal of Colonel William J. Bolton*, 86; Henry W. Brown to Parents, October 2, 1862, copy at Antietam NMP.

30. OR 51, pt. 1, 163.

31. Pierro, *The Maryland Campaign*, 338.

32. Pierro, *The Maryland Campaign*, 338-9.

33. OR 19, pt. 1, 472.

34. Tucker, *Burnside's Bridge*, 118.

35. Pierro, *The Maryland Campaign*, 336-7; "Notes by General H. L. Benning on the Battle of Sharpsburg," *SHSP*, vol. 16 (1888), 393.

Map Set 18. Antietam: Burnside Advances on Sharpsburg (Afternoon, September 17)

1. OR 51, pt. 1, 163; William Allan, *The Army of Northern Virginia in 1862* (Boston: Houghton, Mifflin, and Co., 1892), 429-30; Pierro, *The Maryland Campaign*, 338.

2. Cox, "The Battle of Antietam," 653; Pierro, *The Maryland Campaign*, 340.

3. Cox, "The Battle of Antietam," 653-4; Cope-Carman Map #12; *OR* 19, pt. 1, 435; Matthew J. Graham, *The Ninth Regiment New York Volunteers (Hawkins' Zouaves): Being a History of a Regiment and Volunteer Association from 1860 to 1900* (New York: E. P. Coby & Co., 1900), 292-3.

4. Pierro, *The Maryland Campaign*, 340-1; Delauter, *18th Virginia Infantry*, 16.

5. *OR* 19, pt. 1, 438; Pierro, *The Maryland Campaign*, 318-23.

6. Pierro, *The Maryland Campaign*, 340-1, 348-49; *OR* 19, pt. 1, 912.

7. Cox, "The Battle of Antietam," 654-5; Pierro, *The Maryland Campaign*, 342.

8. *OR* 19, pt. 1, 438; Pierro, *The Maryland Campaign*, 342.

9. Pierro, *The Maryland Campaign*, 342; *Pennsylvania at Antietam*, 54.

10. *OR* 19, pt. 1, 435.

11. Graham, *The Ninth Regiment New York Volunteers*, 294; Pierro, *The Maryland Campaign*, 344-5.

12. Pierro, *The Maryland Campaign*, 347.

Map Set 19. Antietam: A. P. Hill's Division Arrives from Harpers Ferry (3:00 a.m. - 5:30 p.m.)

1. *OR* 19, pt. 1, 148-50.

2. *OR* 19, pt. 2, 610; Pierro, *The Maryland Campaign*, 341.

3. *OR*, pt. 1, 981; Felix Motlow, "Campaigns in Northern Virginia," *CV*, vol. 11, no. 10 (1903), 310; Pierro, *The Maryland Campaign*, 354-5; Cope-Carman Map #13. Col. John Brockenbrough was in temporary command of Brig. Gen. Charles Field's brigade. Field had been badly wounded at Second Manassas and would miss about one year of action before returning to the field.

4. Randy Bishop, *The Tennessee Brigade* (Bloomington, IN: AuthorHouse, 2005), 130; Sgt. Robert T. Mockbee, "The 14th Tennessee Infantry Regiment," *CWR*, vol. 5, no. 1, 21; Martin Schenck, *Up Came Hill: The Story of the Light Division and Its Leaders* (Harrisburg: Stackpole, 1958), 198.

5. *OR* 19, pt. 1, 987; Caldwell, *Gregg's-McGowan's Brigade*, 44; Freeman, *Lee's Lieutenants*, vol. 2, 222.

6. *OR* 19, pt. 1, 1000; Col. W. Allan, "First Maryland Campaign," *SHSP*, vol. 14, 116.

7. Schenk, *Up Came Hill*, 190; Freeman, *Lee's Lieutenants*, vol. 2, 222.

8. Freeman, *Lee's Lieutenants*, vol. 2, 222; Pierro, *The Maryland Campaign*, 349.

9. *OR* 19, pt. 1, 439, 440; Pierro, *The Maryland Campaign*, 343; Gavin, ed., *Infantryman Pettit*, 20; Stone, Jr., *Wandering to Glory*, 65.

10. Pierro, *The Maryland Campaign*, 345, 458.

11. Durkin, ed., *John Dooley, Confederate Soldier*, 46.

12. *OR* 19, pt. 1, 1025, 1031; Durkin, ed., *John Dooley, Confederate Soldier*, 46; Alexander Hunter, *Johnny Reb & Billy Yank* (New York: Smithmark, 1996), 290-3; Alexander Hunter, "A High Private's Sketch of Sharpsburg: Conclusion," *SHSP*, vol. 11 (1883), 18-9; Graham, *The Ninth Regiment New York Volunteers*, 296; Hewett, ed., *OR Supplement*, vol. 3, 557-8. Pvt. Alexander Hunter of the 17th Virginia (Kemper's brigade) related how the brigade's first volley drove back the advancing Federal troops. "We had barely loaded and capped the muskets when the blue line came with a rush and we fired now without orders. . . . The Federals, now commingled as one solid bank of men, poured a volley into us that settled the matter. It killed or wounded every officer and man in the regiment except five." Alexander Hunter, "The Battle of Antietam or Sharpsburg," *SHSP*, vol. 31 (1903), 42.

13. *OR* 19, pt. 1, 1025, 1031.

14. *OR* 19, pt. 1, 453; Pierro, *The Maryland Campaign*, 347-48; Jennie Porter Arnold, "At Antietam," *National Tribune*, October 18, 1888; J. L. Napier, "M'Intosh's battery at Sharpsburg," *CV*, vol. 19, no. 9 (1911), 429.

15. Lesley J. Gordon, "All Who Went Into That Battle Were Heroes," in Gallagher, ed., *The Antietam Campaign*, 175-6; Pierro, *The Maryland Campaign*, 350-1.

16. *OR* 19, pt. 1, 988; Caldwell, *Gregg's-McGowan's Brigade*, 45-6; Pierro, *The Maryland Campaign*, 350-51; Henry J. Spooner, "The Maryland Campaign with the Fourth Rhode Island," *Rhode Island MOLLUS*, vol. 3, 232; Susan Williams Benson, *Berry Benson's Civil War Book* (Athens, Georgia: University of Georgia Press, 1991), 28.

17. Caldwell, *Gregg's-McGowan's Brigade*, 46; *OR* 19, pt. 1, 984; George Merriman to Mary, September 24, 1862, copy in Antietam NMP; Sgt. Jacob Bauer to wife, September 20, 1862, Antietam NMP; Anonymous, *Sixteenth Regiment Connecticut Volunteers Excursion and Reunion at Antietam Battlefield* (Hartford, CT: Carr, Lockwood & Brainard Co., 1889), 20.

18. Pierro, *The Maryland Campaign*, 348; Henry Clay Hall to Sister, October 5, 1862, Antietam

NMP; *OR* 19, pt. 1, 455, 984; Napier, "M'Intosh's battery at Sharpsburg," 429.

19. Pierro, *The Maryland Campaign*, 348.

20. Tucker, *Burnside Bridge*, 145-6; Wolcott Marsh to Anna, September 24, 1862, Antietam NMP; *OR* 51, pt. 1, 164; 19, pt. 1, 891; Henry Clay Hall to Sister; Rodman's Brigade at Antietam," *National Tribune*, December 9, 1886; Pierro, *The Maryland Campaign*, 352. Col. Henry Benning was in command of the brigade because Brig. Gen. Robert Toombs was in command of the Lower Bridge sector.

21. Pierro, *The Maryland Campaign*, 349. Sgt. Jacob Bauer wrote home to his wife, "our conel [sic] is now a General and commands our division. He is too ugly a man for even a bullet to touch him." Sgt. Jacob Bauer to wife, September 20, 1862, Antietam NMP. According to Welsh, *Medical Histories of Union Generals*, 282-3, the bullet that killed Rodman struck him in a lung. He lingered for nearly two weeks before dying on September 30 at a field hospital established on the Rohrbach farm.

22. Pierro, *The Maryland Campaign*, 351; Spooner, "The Maryland Campaign with the Fourth Rhode Island," 232-33; Robert Grandchamp, "Our men fell like sheet at the slaughter: The 4th Rhode Island Volunteers in Otto's Cornfield," Antietam NMP.

23. George Merriman to Mary.

24. *OR* 51, pt. 1, 164; *OR* 19, pt. 1, 1,001; Pierro, *The Maryland Campaign*, 352-3; Bishop, *The Tennessee Brigade*, 130-1. Although a tough fighter, Brig. Gen. James Archer had a weak constitution and made the trip to the battlefield in an ambulance before mounting his horse. *OR* 19, pt. 1, 1,000. Archer fell to the Federals as a prisoner at Gettysburg on July 1, 1863, the first of Lee's generals to be captured in battle. Exposure to the elements on Johnson's Island on the shore of Lake Erie weakened him considerably. Archer was exchanged in the summer of 1864, led his brigade for a brief time, and died that October.

25. Bishop, *The Tennessee Brigade*, 130-1; Mockbee, "The 14th Tennessee Infantry Regiment," 21-2; *OR* 19, pt. 1, 470; Motlow, "Campaigns in Northern Virginia," 311. The 12th Ohio of Ewing's brigade was not up on the front line with the 23rd and 30th Ohio because of reports that the enemy, probably Maxcy Gregg's brigade, was attempting to move around the brigade's left flank. The regiment was ordered to form at right angles along the eastern side of the forty acre cornfield. *OR* 19, pt. 1, 466.

26. *OR* 19, pt. 1, 470; J. E. Walton, "The 30th Ohio: Some Reminiscences of the Battle of Antietam," *National Tribune*, December 31, 1885.

27. Pierro, *The Maryland Campaign*, 353; *OR* 19, pt. 1, 467. Ezra Carman hypothesized that some of Archer's losses may have been inflicted by the 12th South Carolina, which was firing through portions of the cornfield whose stalks had not been destroyed, and therefore could not see that Ewing's men had retreated and that Archer's were at the wall. Pierro, *The Maryland Campaign*, 353-4.

28. Pierro, *The Maryland Campaign*, 353. Archer's Tennesseans took advantage of the situation. One member noted that he and his comrades "picked them off with unerring aim by the score before they got out of range." Motlow, "Campaigns in Northern Virginia," 311.

29. Cope-Carman Map 14.

30. Pierro, *The Maryland Campaign*, 354; *OR* 19, pt. 1, 897; Frank E. Fields, *28th Virginia Infantry* (Lynchburg, Va.: H. E. Howard, Inc., 1985), 19.

31. Cope-Carman Map 14; Pierro, *The Maryland Campaign*, 354-5; Clark, *North Carolina Regiments*, vol. 2, 434-5. According to Welsh, *Medical Histories of Confederate Generals*, 24, there are two versions of how Branch's died. The first has him killed while on the hill looking at the Union positions during a consultation with A. P. Hill, Maxcy Gregg, and James Archer. The second version of his demise has Branch killed while leading his men into battle.

32. *OR* 19, pt. 1, 1,004; Pierro, *The Maryland Campaign*, 355.

33. *OR* 19, pt. 1, 426.

34. *OR* 19, pt. 1, 981.

35. Pierro, *The Maryland Campaign*, 357; Clipton Blanchard to F. B. Fay, September 20, 1862, copy in the Antietam NMP; E. Couillard to the Editor of the *Telegraph and Pioneer*, September 22, 1862, copy in the Antietam NMP.

Map Set 20. Antietam: Evening Stalemate (September 17 - 18)

1. Harsh, *Taken at the Flood*, 423; Pierro, *The Maryland Campaign*, 469-74.

2. Harsh, *Taken at the Flood*, 432-3. A member of the venerable Stonewall Brigade summed up the battle when he wrote home on September 21, 1862, "Some parts of the battle field we repulsed the Yankees, whilst in others they repulsed us, neither party can claim much of a victory in my opinion. We captured a good many prisoners they also done the same." Harlan R. Jessup, *The Painful News I Have to Write* (Baltimore, MD: Butternut and Blue, 1998), 119.

3. S. D. Lee, "New Lights on Sharpsburg," *Richmond Dispatch*, December 20, 1896.

4. Harsh, *Taken at the Flood*, 426-8. Dr. Harsh puts Lee's achievements in perspective: In eighty-three days, the army had driven the enemy's large army from the gates of Richmond to fight a decisive battle on Northern soil. In that time, the army had fought numerous battles and engagements, usually outnumbered and certainly under-equipped and underfed. Harsh, *Taken at the Flood*, 433.

5. *OR* 19, pt. 1, 368-74; pt. 2, 332; 51, pt. 1, 843-4, 847.

6. Harsh, *Taken at the Flood*, 437-8.

7. Harsh, *Taken at the Flood*, 446-8.

Map Set 21. The Battle of Shepherdstown (September 19 - 20)

1. *OR* 19, pt. 1, 830-1; Peter S. Carmichael, "We Don't Know What on Earth to Do with Him," in Gallagher, ed., *The Antietam Campaign*, 266.

2. Thomas A. McGrath, *Shepherdstown: The Last Clash of the Antietam Campaign, September 19-20, 1862* (Schroeder Publications, Lynchburg, VA: 2007), 50; Carmichael, "We Don't Know What on Earth to Do with Him," 266-7. As a captain, Pendleton led the Rockbridge Artillery, a four-gun battery whose pieces he had named Matthew, Mark, Luke, & John after the Gospel writers. When Lee assumed command of the army after Johnston fell wounded at Seven Pines, Pendleton was a brigadier general in charge of the army's reserve artillery (roughly one-quarter of all guns), with the balance of the pieces distributed to individual infantry commands. Lee utilized Pendleton's solid organizational abilities (Pendleton's reorganization of the Army of Northern Virginia's long-arm in May 1863 brought it to the peak of its efficiency). Other officers, however, often performed his tasks in the field during active operations. "William Nelson Pendleton," by Lawrence L. Hewitt, in Davis, *The Confederate General*, vol. 5, 12-17.

3. Robert E. Lee to Mrs. Thomas J. Jackson, January 25, 1866, Jedediah Hotchkiss Papers, Library of Congress; Carmichael, "We Don't Know What on Earth to Do with Him," 266-7; Mark A. Snell, "The 118th ("Corn Exchange") Pennsylvania at the Battle of Shepherdstown," *CWR*, vol. 6, no. 2 (1998), 126.

4. *OR* 19, pt. 1, 612; Freeman, *Lee's Lieutenants*, vol. 2, 228.

5. McGrath, *Shepherdstown*, 52.

6. Mary Bedinger Mitchell, "A Woman's Recollections of Antietam," *B&L*, vol. 2, 692; *OR* 19, pt. 1, 342.

7. Sifakis, *Who was Who in the Civil War*, 515-6. Although an accomplished and highly respected commander, Fitz John Porter was one of the scapegoats for the Federal defeat at Second Bull Run the previous month. Porter was arrested on November 25, 1862, and court-martialed. His close relationship with McClellan, who was by this time no longer in command of the army, coupled with his sharp and public criticism of Maj. Gen. John Pope, played a major role in his conviction in January 1863. Shepherdstown was Porter's final Civil War engagement.

8. *OR* 19, 1, 831-32; Carmichael, "We Don't Know What on Earth to Do with Him," 268.

9. McGrath, *Shepherdstown*, 69, 71; *OR* 19, 1, 354-54; Carmichael, "We Don't Know What on Earth to Do with Him," 268. Pendleton claimed that he did not realize the depleted state of Douglass' and Armistead's brigades. Had he known, he continued, he would not have dispatched troops north and south of the vital ford. Of course, it was Pendleton's responsibility to determine the actual condition and number of the men under his command. *OR* 19, pt. 1, 833, 832.

10. David G. Martin, *Fluvanna Artillery* (Lynchburg, VA: H. E. Howard, Inc., 1992), 51, 52; Freeman, *Lee's Lieutenants*, vol. 2, 229.

11. McGrath, *Shepherdstown*, 71; *OR* 19, pt. 1, 833, 835.

12. McGrath, *Shepherdstown*, 72.

13. Henry McGee letter, November 1862, 4th Michigan folder, Antietam NMP; James Vesey Letter, October 1862, 4th Michigan folder, Antietam NMP; Carmichael, "We Don't Know What on Earth to Do with Him," 269.

14. *OR* 19, pt. 1, 354, 832; J. B. Moore, "Sharpsburg: Graphic Description of the Battle and its Results," *Richmond Times*, May 28, 1899.

15. *OR* 19, pt. 1, 832; McGrath, *Shepherdstown*, 73-4.

16. McGrath, *Shepherdstown*, 76-8; Carmichael, "We Don't Know What on Earth to Do with Him," 269-270; James Vesey letter.

17. McGrath, *Shepherdstown*, 79-80; Carmichael, "We Don't Know What on Earth to Do with Him," 270-71.

18. McGrath, *Shepherdstown*, 81-3; Francis Parker, *The Story of the 22nd Massachusetts Infantry* (Boston: Regimental Association, 1887), 198.

19. Douglas, *I Rode With Stonewall*, 181; McGrath, *Shepherdstown*, 86-7; Freeman, *Lee's Lieutenants*, vol. 2, 232-23.

20. *OR* 19, pt. 1, 957, 982, 1,001; Douglas, *I Rode With Stonewall*, 181; Berry Benson Memoir, Robert Brake Collection, United States Army Military Historical Institute.

21. *OR* pt. 1, 340; pt. 2, 331; 51, pt. 1, 853; McGrath, *Shepherdstown*, 92-3.

22. *OR* 19, pt. 1, 351, 361.

23. *OR* 19, pt. 1, 346; McGrath, *Shepherdstown*, 99, 101.

24. *OR* 19, pt. 1, 361, 363, 366.

25. McGrath, *Shepherdstown*, 110-11; *OR* 19, pt. 1, 346.

26. McGrath, *Shepherdstown*, 99, 112; Mark Snell, "The 118th ("Corn Exchange") Pennsylvania at the Battle of Shepherdstown," 127.

27. *OR* 19, pt. 1, 982; *New York Times*, September 22, 1862; Andrew B. Wardlaw Diary, September 20, 1862, Civil War Misc. Collection, United States Army Military History Institute; McGrath, *Shepherdstown*, 117-9; Pierro, *The Maryland Campaign*, 374.

28. McGrath, *Shepherdstown*, 112, 117; *OR* 19, pt. 1, 346, 1,001; John L. Smith, *History of the Corn Exchange Regiment, 118th Pennsylvania Volunteers, from their first engagement at Antietam to Appomattox* (Philadelphia: J. L. Smith, 1905), 59, 81.

29. *OR* 19, pt. 1, 361, 973.

30. McGrath, *Shepherdstown*, 120-2; Edwin C. Bennett, *With Musket and Sword: or The camp, march, and firing line in the Army of the Potomac* (Boston: Coburn Publishers, 1900), 99-100; "Newton Bibbins to Ones at Home," Bentley Historical Library.

31. *OR* 19, pt. 1, 367.

32. *OR* 19, pt. 1, 340; Gregory Acken, ed., *Inside the Army of the Potomac: The Civil War Experience of Captain Francis Adams Donaldson* (Mechanicburg, PA: Stackpole Books, 1998), 133. At the Battle of Ball's Bluff on October 21, 1861, Federal troops were defeated with the Potomac River at their back. The route that followed killed and wounded hundreds of men. For a complete look at this fascinating early-war battle and is ramifications, see James A. Morgan, III's revised and expanded *A Little Short of Boats: The Fights at Ball's Bluff and Edwards Ferry, October 21-22, 1861* (Savas Beatie, 2011).

33. McGrath, *Shepherdstown*, 124, 125; Amaziah Barber to family, September 28, 1862, United States Army Military History Institute.

34. McGrath, *Shepherdstown*, 126, 128.

35. John J. Hennessy, ed., *Fighting with the Eighteenth Massachusetts: The Civil War Memoir of Thomas H. Mann* (Baton Rouge, LA: Louisiana State University Press, 2000), 104; McGrath, *Shepherdstown*, 128-9; *OR* 19, pt. 1, 347.

36. McGrath, *Shepherdstown*, 128-30. One soldier wrote home that after getting into the water, "it was impossible to keep in line: so it was each one for himself and get across as soon as we could: had there not been so many balls flying among us it would have been highly amusing to see the men stumble and go in all over." Lewis Wentworth Diary, September 20, 1862 entry, Massachusetts Historical Society.

37. *History of the 118th Pennsylvania Volunteers*, 61, 82; *OR* 19, pt. 1, 340, 348; Snell, "The 118th Pennsylvania Infantry," 129. Gen. Fitz John Porter knew about the condition of the rifles, for he wrote in his report: "these defective arms had been reported to the General-in-Chief, but all efforts to replace them had failed." *OR* 19, pt. 1, 340.

38. Smith, *History of the 118th Pennsylvania Volunteers*, 60-1.

39. *OR* 19, pt. 1, 347; *History of the 118th Pennsylvania Volunteers*, 64; McGrath, *Shepherdstown*, 183.

40. McGrath, *Shepherdstown*, 217.

Bibliography

Archival Sources

Alabama Department of Archives and History
  John Purifoy, "History of the Jeff Davis Artillery"

Antietam National Military Park
  "The Civil War Diary of Griffin Lewis Baldwin"
  Sgt. Jacob Bauer to wife, September 20, 1862
  Matthew R. Beer, "The Scene of a Battlefield: 28th Pennsylvania Volunteers at Antietam."
  J. T. Baynes to Lizzie Miles, September 25, 1862
  Clipton Blanchard to F. B. Fay, September 20, 1862
  Henry W. Brown to Parents, October 2, 1862
  H. W. Burlingame, Personal Reminiscences of the Civil War
  Edward Burruss Memoirs
  Henry Clay Hall to Sister, October 5, 1862
  Frederick Crouse, "An Account of the Battle of Antietam"
  James L. Denon Diary
  William DeRosset to S. D. Thurston, July 12, 1886
  P. A. Dunton to Friend Byron, September 24, 1862
  Wellington Ent to father, September 18, 1862
  Robert Grandchamp, "Our men fell like sheep at the slaughter: The 4th Rhode Island Volunteers in
      Otto's Cornfield"
  History of the 'Bucktails': The Maryland Campaign
  Mathew Hurlenger Diary
  Newsom Jenkins, "Recollections of a Sergeant"
  Doug Kauffmann, "Tobias's Story: The Life and Civil War Career of Tobias B. Kaufmann"
  Henry McGee letter, November 1862
  Wolcott Marsh to Anna, September 24, 1862
  George Merriman to Mary, September 24, 1862
  Isaac Andrew Moore Diary
  Samuel Moore Diary
  William Olcott Memoir
  "107th New York"
  Joseph Pettiner to Carrie, September 20, 1862
  Albert Pope Journal
  Pridgeon, Dave. "The 21st Georgia at Sharpsburg"
  W. D. Pritchard, "Civil War Reminisces"
  Robert Shand, "Incidents in the Life of a Private Soldier"
  James Smith to Friends, September 20, 1862
  Memoir of Pvt. William Snakenberg
  Source Book on the Early History of Cuthbert and Randolph Co.
  "The 21st Virginia at the Battle of Sharpsburg"
  Col. R. B. Van Valkenburg Recollections
  John Vautier Diary
  James Vesey Letter, October, 1862
  Waters, Zack, "The Fourth Georgia at Antietam"

Wheeler, Algar Monroe, "Reminiscences of the Battle of Antietam"

Withers W. to E. A. Carman, March 14, 1895

Work, P. A. "The 1st Texas Regiment of the Texas Brigade of the Army of Northern Virginia at the Battles of Boonsboro Pass or Gap and Sharpsburg or Antietam, MD., in September 1862"

Wright, Allen, "The 42nd Virginia Infantry"

Bentley Historical Library (Massachusetts)
  Newton Bibbins Letters

Robert Brake Collection, United States Army Military Historical Institute.
  Berry Benson Memoir

Alexander R. Chamberline Collection, U.S. Military History Institute
  William H. H. Fithian Diary

Civil War Misc. Collection, U.S. Army War College Library
  Amaziah Barber Letters
  Charles Greene Letters
  Andrew B. Wardlaw Diary
  Samuel Waters Diary

Historical Society of Pennsylvania
  Diary of John Foering

  Library of Congress
  Edward Stephen Welch Papers
  Jedediah Hotchkiss Papers

Massachusetts Historical Society
  Lewis Wentworth Diary

Mississippi Department of Archives and History
  D. C. Love Recollections

University of Georgia (Shatt Meitchell Papers)
  Shatt Meitchell to wife, September 19, 1862

Woodruff Library, Emory University
  George Wren Diary

Southern Historical Collection, University of North Carolina
  Calvin Leach Diary

Steve Stotelmyer's Collection
  Charles Crofut to Mira, September 28, 1862

State Historical Society of Wisconsin
  Frank Haskell Diary, September 14, 1862
  Report of Acting Adj. James Wood

Newspapers

Atlanta Southern Confederacy, October 10, 1862
Cherry Valley Gazette, October 1, 1862
Columbus (Georgia) *Inquirer*, October 8, 1862
Milwaukee Sunday Telegraph, August 26, 1886 and January 26, 1895
New York Times, September 22, 1862
Plattsburg Express & Sentinel, October 11, 1862
Savannah Republican, October 16, 1862
Telegraph and Pioneer, September 22, 1862
The Countryman, October 6, 1862
The Jeffersonian Democrat, October 3, 1862
The Lynn Weekly Reporter, October 18, 1862

Official Documents

Hewett, Janet, ed. *Supplement to the Official Records of the Union and Confederate Armies*. 100 vols. Wilmington, N.C.: Broadfoot Pub. Co., 1994.

United States Congress. *Joint Committee on the Conduct of the War*. Washington: U. S. Printing Office, 1863.

United States War Department. *The War of the Rebellion: A Compilation of the Official Records of the Union and Confederate Armies*. 128 vols. Washington: U. S. Government Printing Office, 1880-1901.

Books

Acken, Gregory, ed., *Inside the Army of the Potomac: The Civil War Experience of Captain Francis Adams Donaldson*. Mechanicburg, PA: Stackpole Books, 1998.

Adams, John G. B. *Reminiscences of the Nineteenth Massachusetts Regiment*. Boston: Wright & Porter Printing Company, 1899.

Albert, Allen D. *History of the Forty-Fifth Regiment Pennsylvania Veteran Volunteer Infantry, 1861-1865*. Williamsport, PA: Grit Publishing Company, 1912.

Allardice, Bruce S. *More Generals in Gray*. Baton Rouge, LA: LSU Press, 1995.

Allan, William. *The Army of Northern Virginia in 1862*. Boston: Houghton, Mifflin , and Co., 1892.

Allen, Randall and Keith S. Bohannon, eds., *Campaigning with "Old Stonewall": Confederate Captain Ujanirtus Allen's Letters to His Wife*. Baton Rouge, LA: Louisiana State University Press, 1998.

Andrews, W. H. *Footprints of a Regiment: A Recollection of the 1st Georgia Regulars, 1861-1865*. Atlanta: Longstreet Press, 1992.

Antietam Battlefield Memorial Commission of Pennsylvania. Pennsylvania at Antietam. Harrisburg, PA: Harrisburg Publishing Company, 1906.

Armstrong, Marion V. *Unfurl Those Colors!: McClellan, Sumner, and the Second Army Corps in the Antietam Campaign*. Tuscaloosa, AL: The University of Alabama Press, 2008.

Bailey, Ronald H. *The Bloodiest Day*. Alexandria, VA: Time Life Books, 1984.

Barnard, George S. *War Talks of Confederate Veterans*. Petersburg, VA: Fenn & Owen, Publishers, 1892.

Bates, Samuel P. *History of Pennsylvania Volunteers*. 5 volumes. Harrisburg, PA: B. Singerley, State Printer, 1870.

Beck, Brandon. *Third Alabama!* Tuscaloosa, AL: University of Alabama Press, 2000.

Bell, Robert T. *11th Virginia Infantry*. Lynchburg, VA: H. E. Howard, 1985.

Bennett, Edwin C. *With Musket and Sword*. Boston: Coburn Publishers, 1900.

Benson, Susan Williams. *Berry Benson's Civil War Book*. Athens, Georgia: University of Georgia Press, 1991.

Beyer, Walter F. *Deeds of Valor: How America's Heroes Won the Medal of Honor*. Detroit: Perrien-Keydel Co., 1903.

Bishop, Randy. *The Tennessee Brigade*. Bloomington, IN: AuthorHouse, 2005.

Bosbyshell, Oliver Christian. *The 48th in the war. Being a Narrative of the Campaigns of the 48th Regiment, Infantry, Pennsylvania Veteran Volunteers, During the War of the Rebellion*. Philadelphia: Avil Printing Company, 1895.

Bowen, Catherine Drinker. *Yankee from Olympus*. Boston: Little Brown and Co., 1944.

Bowen, Roland E. *From Ball's Bluff to Gettysburg*. Gettysburg: Thomas Publications, 1994.

Bridges, Hal. *Daniel Harvey Hill: Lee's Maverick General*. New York: McGraw Hill, 1961.

Bruce, George A. *The Twentieth Regiment of Massachusetts Volunteer Infantry, 1861-1865*. Boston: Houghton, Mifflin and Company, 1906.

Bryant, Edwin E. *History of the Third Regiment of Wisconsin Veteran Volunteer Infantry*. Madison, WI: 3rd Wisconsin Veterans Association, 1891.

Caldwell, J. F. J. *History of a Brigade of South Carolinians*. Marietta, GA: Continental Book Co., 1951.

Carman, Ezra. *The Maryland Campaign of September 1862, Vol 1: South Mountain*. New York: Savas Beatie, 2010.

Child, William. *A History of the Fifth Regiment, New Hampshire Volunteers in the American Civil War*. Bristol, NH: R. W. Musgrove, Printer, 1893.

Chamberlaine, William W. *Memoirs of the Civil War*. Washington: Bryon S. Adams, 1912.

Chapla, John D. *48th Virginia Infantry*. Lynchburg, VA: H.E. Howard, 1989.

Clark, Walter. *Histories of the Several Regiments And Battalions From North Carolina in the Great War 1861-65*. 5 vols. Raleigh: E. M. Uzzell, Printer and Binder, 1901.

Collier, Calvin. *They'll Do to Tie To! The Story of the Third Regiment, Arkansas Infantry C.S.A* Little Rock, AK: Democrat Litho and Printing Co., 1995.

Collins, Darrell L. *Major General Robert E. Rodes of the Army of Northern Virginia*. New York: Savas Beatie, 2008.

Comey, ed., Lyman Richard. *A Legacy of Valor*. Knoxville, TN: University of Tennessee Press, 2004.

Conyngham, David Power. *The Irish Brigade and its Campaigns*. New York: Fordham University Press, 1994.

Cook, Benjamin F. *History of the Twelfth Massachusetts Volunteers*. Boston: Privately printed, 1882.

Cooling, Benjamin. *Counter-Thrust: From the Peninsula to the Antietam*. Lincoln, NE: University of Nebraska Press, 2007.

Cox, Jacob D. *Military Reminiscences of the Civil War*. New York: Charles Scribner's and Sons, 1900.

Crater, Lewis. *History of the Fiftieth Penn. Vet. Vols., 1861-1865*. Reading, PA: Coleman Printing House, 1884.

Cuffel, Charles A. *History of Durell's Battery in the Civil War: A Narrative of the Campaigns and Battles in the War of the Rebellion*. Philadelphia: Craig Finley and Co., 1904.

Cunningham, David and Wells, Miller. *Antietam. Report of the Ohio Antietam Battlefield Commission*. Springfield, OH: Springfield Publishing Company, 1904.

Daffan, Katie. *Autobiography of L. A. Daffin: My Father as I Remember Him*. n.p., United Daughters of the Confederacy, 1906.

Daly, Louise Porter. *Alexander Cheves Haskell: The Portrait of a Man*. Norwood, MA: Plimpton Press, 1934.

Dameron, Dave. *Benning's Brigade. Vol. 1: A History and Roster of the Fifteenth Georgia*. Spartanburg, SC: The Reprint Company, 1997.

Dawes, Rufus. *Service with the Sixth Wisconsin Volunteers*. Dayton, OH: Morningside Press, 1984.

Delauter, Roger U. *18th Virginia Infantry*. Lynchburg, VA: H. E. Howard, 1985.

Devine, John E. *8th Virginia Infantry*. Lynchburg, VA: H. E. Howard, 1983.

Dickert, Augustus. *History of Kershaw's Brigade*. Dayton, OH: Morningside House, 1976.

Dinkins, James. *1861 to 1865, by an Old Johnnie: Personal Recollections and Experiences in the Confederate Army*. Dayton, OH: Morningside Bookshop, 1975.

Dobbins, Austin C. *Grandfather's Journal: Company B, Sixteenth Mississippi Infantry Volunteers, Harris' Brigade, Mahone's Division, Hill's Corps, ANV*. Dayton, OH: Morningside Books, 1988.

Douglas, Henry Kyd. *I Rode With Stonewall: The War Experiences of the Youngest Member of Jackson's Staff*. Chapel Hill, NC: University of North Carolina Press, 1940.

Dunn, Craig L. *Iron Men, Iron Will: The Nineteenth Indiana Regiment of the Iron Brigade*. Indianapolis: Guild Press, 1995.

Durkin, Joseph T., ed., *John Dooley, Confederate Soldier: His War Journal*. Notre Dame, IN: University of Notre Dame Press, 1963.

Ellis, Billy. *Tithes of Blood*. Murfreesboro, TN: Southern Heritage Press, 1997.

Ernst, Kathleen A. *Too Afraid to Cry: Maryland Civilians in the Antietam Campaign*. Mechanicsville, PA: Stackpole Books, 1999.

Everson, Guy R. and Edward W. Simpson, Jr., eds. *Far, Far from Home: The Wartime Letters of Dick and Tally Simpson, Third South Carolina Volunteers*. New York: Oxford University Press, 1994. New York: Oxford University Press, 1994.

Fields, Frank E. *28th Virginia Infantry*. Lynchburg, VA: H. E. Howard, Inc., 1985.

Folsom, James Madison. *Heroes and Martyrs of Georgia*. Baltimore, MD: Butternut and Blue, 1995.

Fox, William F. *Regimental Losses in the American Civil War*. Albany, NY: Albany Publishing Company, 1893.

Freeman, Douglas Southall. *Lee's Lieutenants: A Study in Command*. New York: Charles Scribner's Sons, 1943.

Fuller, Charles Augustus. *Personal Recollections of the War of 1861*. Sherburne, NY: News Job Printing House, 1906.

Gaff, Alan D. *On Many a Bloody Field: Four Years in the Iron Brigade*. Bloomington, IN: Indiana University Press, 1996.

Galway, Thomas F. *The Valiant Hours*. Harrisburg, PA: Stackpole Press, 1961.

Gallagher, Gary. *Lee the Soldier*. Lincoln, NE: University of Lincoln Press, 1996.

———. *The Antietam Campaign*. Chapel Hill, NC: University of North Carolina Press, 1999.

Gannon, James P. *Irish Rebels Confederate Tigers: A History of the 6th Louisiana Volunteers, 1861-1865*. Mason City, IA: Savas Publishing, 1998.

Gates, Theodore B. *Ulster Guard, Twentieth N.Y. State Militia and the War of the Rebellion; Embracing a History of the Early Organization of the Regiments*. New York: Benj. Tyrrel, 1879.

Gavin, William G. *Infantryman Pettit*. Shippensburg, PA: White Mane, 1990.

Gibbs, Joseph. *Three Years in the Bloody Eleventh*. College Park, PA: Penn State University Press, 2002.

Glover, Edwin A. *Bucktailed Wildcats: A Regiment of Civil War Volunteers*. New York: Thomas Yoseloff, 1960.

Gordon, John B. *Reminiscences of the Civil War*. New York: Scribners, 1903.

Gottfried, Bradley M. *Stopping Pickett: The History of the Philadelphia Brigade*. Shippensburg, PA: White Mane, 1999.

———. *Kearny's Own: The History of the First New Jersey Brigade in the Civil War*. New Brunswick, NJ: Rutgers University Press, 2005.

Gould, John M. *History of the First-Tenth- Twenty-ninth Maine Regiment, in Service of the United States from May 3, 1861 to June 21, 1866*. Portland, ME: Stephen Berry, 1871.

Gould, Joseph. *The Story of the Forty-Eighth: A Record of the Campaigns of the Forty-Eighth Regiment, Pennsylvania Veteran Volunteer Infantry*. Mt. Carmel, PA: Regimental Association, 1908.

Graham, Matthew J. *The Ninth Regiment New York Volunteers (Hawkins' Zouaves): Being a History of a Regiment and Volunteer Association from 1860 to 1900*. New York: E. P. Coby & Co., 1900.

Green, Robert M. *History of the One Hundred and Twenty-fourth Regiment Pennsylvania Volunteers*. Philadelphia: Ware Brothers Company, 1907.

Harsh, Joseph L. *Taken at the Flood: Robert E. Lee and Confederate Strategy in the Maryland Campaign of 1862*. Kent, OH: Kent State University Press, 1999.

Hayes, Rutherford B. *Diary and Letters of Rutherford B. Hayes*. Freemont, OH: Ohio Historical Center, 1998.

Hess, Earl. *Field Armies and Fortifications in the Civil War*. Chapel Hill, NC: U. of North Carolina Press, 2005.

Historical Sketch of Company D, Thirteenth Regiment, N. J. Volunteers. Newark, NJ: D. L. Gildersleeve and Co., 1875.

History of the Thirty-Fifth Regiment, Massachusetts Volunteers. Boston: Mills, Knight & Co., 1884.

Hitchcock, Frederick L. *War from the Inside: The Story of the 132nd Regiment Pennsylvania Volunteer Infantry in the War for the Suppression of the Rebellion*. Philadelphia: Press of J. B. Lippincott, 1904.

Holden, Walter, William E. Ross, and Elizabeth Slomba, eds. *Stand Firm and Fire Low: The Civil War Writings of Colonel Edward E. Cross*. Hanover, NH: University of New Hampshire, 2003.

Hood, J. B. *Advance and Retreat*. The Blue and Grey Press: Edison NJ, 1985.

Horton, J. and S. Teverbaugh. *A History of the Eleventh Regiment, Ohio Volunteers*. Dayton, OH.: W. A. Shuey, Printer, 1866.

Hough, Franklin B. *History of Duryee's Brigade*. Albany, NY: J. Munsell, 1864.

Howard, Oliver Otis. *Autobiography of Oliver Otis Howard, Major General United States Army*. New York: Baker and Taylor Co., 1907.

Hunter, Alexander. *Johnny Reb & Billy Yank*. New York: Smithmark, 1996.

Jackman, Lyman. *History of the Sixth New Hampshire in the War for the Union*. Concord, NH: Republican Press Assoc., 1891.

Livermore, Thomas. *Days and Events, 1860-1866*. Boston: Houghton, Mifflin Company, 1920.

Jessup, Harlan R. *The Painful News I Have to Write*. Baltimore, MD: Butternut and Blue, 1998.

Johnson, Charles F. *The Long Roll*. East Aurora, NY: Roycrofters Printers, 1881.

Johnson, Curt and Richard C. Anderson, *Artillery Hell: The Employment of Artillery at Antietam*. College Station, TX: Texas A & M Press, 1998.

Johnson, Pharris D. ed. Under the Southern Cross: *Soldier Life with Gordon Bradwell and the Army of Northern Virginia*. Macon, GA: Mercer University Press, 1999.

Jones, Terry L. *Lee's Tigers: The Louisiana Infantry in the Army of Northern Virginia*. Baton Rouge, LA: LSU Press, 1987.

Kent, Jack D. *Medical Histories of Confederate Generals*. Kent, OH: Kent State University Press, 1995.

——. *Medical Histories of Union Generals*. Kent, OH: Kent State University Press, 1996.

Krick, Robert K. *30th Virginia Infantry*. Lynchburg, VA: H.E. Howard, Inc., 1983.

——. *Parker's Virginia Battery*. Wilmington, NC: Broadfoot Publishing Co., 1989.

Laboda, Lawrence R. *From Selma to Appomattox: The History of the Jeff Davis Artillery*. Shippensburg, PA: White Mane, 1994.

Laine, J. Gary and Morris M. Penny. *Law's Alabama Brigade in the War Between the Union and the Confederacy*. Shippensburg, PA: White Mane, 1996.

Lee, Susan P. *Memoirs of William Nelson Pendleton*. Philadelphia: J. B. Lippincott, 1893.

Longstreet, James. *From Manassas to Appomattox: The Civil War in America*. Bloomington, IN: University of Indiana Press, 1960.

Lord, Edward O., ed., *History of the Ninth Regiment New Hampshire Volunteers*. Concord, NH: Republican Free Press Association, 1895.

Lynch, John W. *The Dorman-Marshbourne Letters*. Senoia, GA: Down South Publishing Company, 1995.

McClellan, George B. *Report on the Organization of the Army of the Potomac, and its Campaigns in Virginia and Maryland*. Washington: U. S. Government Printing Office, 1864.

——. *McClellan's Own Story: The War for the Union*. New York: Charles L. Webster & Co., 1887.

McConnell, William R. *Remember Reno*. Shippensburg, PA: White Mane, 1996.

McGrath, Thomas A. *Shepherdstown: The Last Clash of the Antietam Campaign, September 19-20, 1862.* Schroeder Publications, Lynchburg, VA: 2007.

McLaughlin, John. *Memoir of Hector Tyndale.* Philadelphia: Collins, 1882.

McLaws, Lafayette. "The Maryland Campaign." In Address Delivered before the Confederate Veterans Association of Savannah, Georgia." Savannah, GA: George N. Nichols, 1896.

Mann, Thomas H., Hennessy, John J. ed. *Fighting with the Eighteenth Massachusetts: The Civil War Memoir of Thomas H. Mann.* LSU Press, Baton Rouge: 2000.

Martin, David G. *Fluvanna Artillery.* Lynchburg, VA: H. E. Howard, Inc., 1992.

Marvel, William. *Burnside.* Chapel Hill, NC: University of North Carolina Press, 1991.

Mills, Harrison J. *Chronicles of the Twenty-First Regiment New York Volunteers.* Buffalo: 21st Regiment Veteran Association, 1887.

Moe, Richard. *The Last Full Measure. The Life and Death of the First Minnesota Volunteers.* New York: Henry Holt, 1993.

Morgan, James A. III. A *Little Short of Boats: The Fights at Ball's Bluff and Edwards Ferry, October 21–22, 1861.* New York: Savas Beatie, 2011.

Murfin, James V. *The Gleam of Bayonets: The Battle of Antietam and the Maryland Campaign, September 1862.* New York: Thomas Yoseloff, 1965.

Neese, George Michael. *Three Years in the Horse Artillery.* New York: Neale Publishing Co., 1911.

Nisbet, James Cooper. *Four Years on the Firing Line.* Wilmington, NC: Broadfoot Publishing Company, 1987.

Nichols, William H. *The Siege and Capture of Harpers Ferry by the Confederates, September, 1862.* Providence, RI: Rhode Island Soldiers and Sailors Historical Society, 1889.

Nolan, Alan T. *The Iron Brigade. A Military History.* Bloomington, IN: Indiana University Press, 1961.

Ohio Antietam Battlefield Commission. Antietam, Report of the Ohio Antietam Battlefield Commission. Springfield, OH: Springfield Publishing Co., 1904.

Olson, John E. *21st Virginia Infantry.* Lynchburg, VA: H. E. Howard, 1989.

Osborne, William H. *The History of the Twenty-Ninth Regiment of the Massachusetts Volunteer Infantry in the Late War of the Rebellion.* Boston: Albert J. Wright, Printer, 1877.

Page, Charles D. *History of the Fourteenth Regiment, Connecticut Vol. Infantry.* Meriden, CT: Horton Publishing Co., 1906.

Palfrey, Francis Winthrop. *Antietam and Fredericksburg.* New York: Charles Scribner's Sons, 1882.

Park, Robert E. *Sketch of the Twelfth Alabama Infantry.* Richmond, VA: William Ellis Jones, 1906.

Parker, Francis. *The Story of the 22nd Massachusetts Infantry.* Boston: Regimental Association, 1887.

Parker, Thomas H. *History of the 51st Regiment of Pennsylvania Volunteers.* Philadelphia: King and Baird Publishers, 1869.

Parrish James W. *Wiregrass to Appomattox: The Untold Story of the 50th Georgia Infantry Regiment, CSA.* Winchester, VA: Angle Valley Press, 2009.

Patrick, Marsena R. *Inside Lincoln's Army: The Diary of Marsena Rudolph Patrick, Provost Marshal General, Army of the Potomac.* New York: Thomas Yoseloff, 1964.

Pierro, Joseph ed., *The Maryland Campaign.* New York: Routledge, 2008.

Porter, John W. H. *A Record of Events in Norfolk County, Virginia . . . with a History of the Soldiers and Sailors of Norfolk County, Norfolk City.* Portsmouth, VA: W. A. Fiske, 1892.

Pride, Mark and Mark Travis. *My Brave Boys: To War with Colonel Cross and the Fighting Fifth.* Hanover, NH: University Press of New England, 2001.

Priest, John Michael. *Antietam: The Soldiers' Battle.* White Mane, 1989.

——. Captain James Wren's Civil War Diary. New York: Berkley Books, 1991.

——. *Before Antietam. The Battle of South Mountain.* Shippensburg, PA: White Mane, 1992.

Quint, Alonzo. *The Record of the Second Massachusetts Infantry, 1861-65.* Boston: James P. Walker, 1867.

Rafuse, Ethan S. *McClellan's War. The Failure of Moderation in the Struggle for the Union.* Bloomington, IN: Indiana University, 2005.

Recollections and Reminiscences 1861-1865. n.p.: United Daughters of the Confederacy, 1998. 12 volumes.

Reidenbaugh, Lowell. *33rd Virginia Infantry*. Lynchburg, VA: H.E. Howard, 1987.

———. *27th Virginia Infantry*. Lynchburg, VA: H.E. Howard, 1993.

Reese, Timothy J. *Sealed with Their Live: Battle of Crampton's Gap*. Burkittsville, MD, Sept. 14, 1862. Baltimore, MD: Butternut and Blue, 1998.

Reunion of the 28th & 147th Regiments, Pennsylvania Volunteers. Philadelphia: Pawson and Nicholson, 1872.

Roberson, Elizabeth Whitley. *In Care of Yellow River*. Gretna, LA: Pelican Press, 1994.

Robertson, James I. *4th Virginia Infantry*. Lynchburg, VA: H.E. Howard, 1982.

———. *General A. P. Hill: The Story of a Confederate Warrior*. New York: Random House, 1987.

Sauers, Richard. *The Civil War Journal of Colonel William J. Bolton*. Conshohocken, PA.: Combined Books, 2000.

Sawyer, Franklin. *A Military History of the 8th Regiment, Ohio Vol. Infantry*. Cleveland, OH: Fairbanks & Co., Printers, 1881.

Schenck, Martin. *Up Came Hill: The Story of the Light Division and Its Leaders*. Harrisburg: Stackpole, 1958.

Schildt, John W. *The Ninth Corps at Antietam*. Chewsville, MD: n.p., 1988.

———. *Roads to Antietam*. Shippensburg, PA: Burd Street Press, 1997.

Schiller, Herbert M. *A Captain's War. The Letters and Diaries of William H. S. Burgwyn, 1861-1865*. Shippensburg, PA: White Mane, 1994.

Sears, Stephen W. *Landscape Turned Red: The Battle of Antietam*. New Haven, CT: Ticknor & Fields, 1983.

———. *The Civil War Papers of George B. McClellan: Selected Correspondence, 1860-1865*. New York: Ticknor & Fields, 1989.

Seville, William P. *History of the First Regiment Delaware Volunteers*. Hightstown, NJ: Longstreet House, 1986.

Sibley, F. Ray, Jr. *The Confederate Order of Battle*. Shippensburg, PA: White Mane, 1996.

Sifarkis, Stewart. *Who Was Who in the Civil War*. New York: Facts on File Publications, 1988.

Sixteenth Regiment Connecticut Volunteers Excursion and Reunion at Antietam Battlefield. Hartford, CT: Carr, Lockwood & Brainard Co., 1889.

Smith, Abram P. *History of the Seventy-Sixth Regiment New York Volunteers: What it Endured and Accomplished; Containing Descriptions of its Twenty-Five Battles; its . . . a Complete Record of the Enlisted Men*. Courtland, NY: Truair, Smith and Miles, Printers, 1867.

Spangler, Edward. *My Little War Experience, with Historical Sketches and Memorabilia*. York, PA: York Daily Publishing Company, 1904.

Steiner, Lewis Henry. *Report of Lewis H. Steiner, M.D., Inspector of the Sanitary Commission, Containing a Diary Kept During the Rebel Occupation of Frederick, Md., and an Account of the Operations of the U.S. Sanitary Commission During the Campaign in Maryland, September 1862*. New York: Anson D. F. Randolph, 1862.

Stevens, Henry S. *Souvenir of Excursion to Battlefields by the Society of the Society of the Fourteenth Connecticut Regiment and Reunion at Antietam, September 1891*. Washington: Gibson Brothers, Printers, 1893.

Stocker, Jeffrey D. ed. *From Huntsville to Appomattox: R. T. Coles's History of 4th Regiment, Alabama Volunteer Infantry, C.S.A., Army of Northern Virginia*. Knoxville, TN: University of Tennessee Press, 1996.

Stone, DeWitt Boyd, Jr., *Wandering to Glory: Confederate Veterans Remember Evans's Brigade*. Columbia, SC: U. of South Carolina Press, 2002.

Stubbs, Steven H. *Duty-Honor-Valor; The Story of the Eleventh Mississippi Infantry Regiment*. Philadelphia, MS: Dancing Rabbit Press, 2000.

Styple, William B. *Writing and Fighting from the Army of Northern Virginia: A Collection of Confederate Soldier Correspondence*. Kearny, NJ: Belle Grove Publishing Co., 2003.

Survivor's Association. *History of the 118th Pennsylvania Volunteers*. Philadelphia: J. L. Smith, 1905.

Sypher, Josiah R. *History of the Pennsylvania Reserve Corps*. Lancaster, PA: Elias Barr & Co., 1865.

Thomas, Henry Walter. *History of the Doles-Cook Brigade.* Atlanta: The Franklin Printing and Publishing Co., 1903.

Todd, William. *The Seventy-Ninth Highlanders, New York Volunteers in the War of Rebellion, 1861-1865.* New York: Brandow, Barton & Co., 1886.

Toombs, Samuel. *Reminiscences of the War, Comprising a Detailed Account of the Experiences of the Thirteenth Regiment New Jersey Volunteers.* Orange, NJ: Journal Office, 1878.

Tucker, Phillip Thomas. *Burnside's Bridge: The Climactic Struggle of the 2nd and 20th Georgia at Antietam Creek.* Mechanicsville, PA: Stackpole Books, 2000.

Turner, Nat, ed. *A Southern Soldier's Letters Home.* Macon, GA: Mercer University Press, 2002.

Vautier, John D. *History of the 88th Pennsylvania Volunteers in the War for the Union.* Philadelphia: J. B. Lippincott, 1894.

Voices of the Civil War: Antietam. Richmond, VA: Time Life Books, 1996.

Waitt, Ernest L. *History of the Nineteenth Regiment Massachusetts Volunteer Infantry.* Salem, MA: Salem Press, Co., 1906.

Walcott, Charles F. *History of the Twenty-First Regiment Massachusetts Volunteers in the War for the Preservation of the Union, 1861-1865.* Boston: Houghton Mifflin, 1882.

Walker, Francis A. *History of the Second Army Corps in the Army of the Potomac.* New York: Charles Scribner's Sons, 1887.

Wallace, Lee A. *5th Virginia Infantry.* Lynchburg, VA: H. E. Howard, 1988.

Waters, Zack C. and James C. Edmonds. *A Small but Spartan Band: The Florida Brigade in Lee's Army of Northern Virginia.* Tuscaloosa, AL: University of Alabama Press, 2010.

Ward, J. E. D. *The Twelfth Ohio Volunteer Infantry.* Ripley, OH: np, 1864.

Warner, Ezra J. *Generals in Gray: Lives of the Confederate Commanders.* Baton Rouge, LA: LSU Press, 1959.

———. *Generals in Blue: Lives of the Union Commanders.* Baton Rouge, LA: LSU Press, 1959.

Washburn, George. *A Complete Military History and Record of the 108th Regiment, N.Y. Vols.* Rochester, NY: Press of E. R. Andrews, 1894.

Wert, Jeffry D. *General James Longstreet: The Confederacy's Most Controversial Soldier.* New York: Simon & Schuster, 1993.

Whitman, George W. *Civil War Letters of George Washington Whitman.* Durham, N.C.: Duke University Press, 1975.

Williams, Alpheus. *From the Cannon's Mouth: The Civil War Letters of General Alpheus S. Williams.* Lincoln, NE: Bison Books, 1995.

Willson, Arabella M. *Disaster, Struggle and Triumph: The Adventure of 1000 Boys in Blue.* Albany, NY: The Argus Company Printers, 1870.

Wistar, Isaac Jones. *Autobiography of Isaac Jones Wistar.* Philadelphia: Wistar Institute of Anatomy and Biology, 1937.

Woodward, E. M. *Our Campaigns: or, The Marches, Bivouacs, Battles, Incidents of Camp Life and History of our Regiment During its Three Year Term of Service.* Shippensburg, PA: Burd Street Press, 1994.

Worsham, John. *One of Jackson's Foot Cavalry: His Experience and What he Saw During the War 1861-1865, Including a History of "F Company," Richmond, Va., 21st Regiment . . . Jackson's Division, Second Corps, A. N. VA.* New York: Neale Publishing Company, 1912.

Wyckoff, Mac. *A History of the 2nd South Carolina Infantry, 1861-1865.* Fredericksburg, VA: Sgt. Kirkland's Museum and Historical Society, 1994.

———. *A History of the 3rd South Carolina Infantry, 1861-1865.* Fredericksburg, VA: Sergeant Kirkland's Museum, 1995.

Yates, Walter J. *Souvenir of Excursion to Antietam and Dedication of Monuments of the 8th, 11th, 14th, and 16th Regiments of Connecticut Volunteers.* New London, CT: n.p., 1894.

Young, William A., and Patricia C. Young. *56th Virginia Infantry.* Lynchburg, VA: H. E. Howard, 1990.

Articles and Essays

Allan, W. "First Maryland Campaign." *Southern Historical Society Papers*, vol. 14, pp. 102-118.

Andrews, W. H. "Tige Anderson's Brigade at Sharpsburg." *Confederate Veteran*, vol. XVI (1908), 578.

Arnold, Jennie Porter. "At Antietam." *National Tribune*, October 18, 1888.

Baker, Joe and Steve Stotelmyer. "The Battle of the South Mountain," Joe Baker, ed. *A Gap in Time: Proceedings of the Appalachian Train Conference*, February 2003.

Barnes, Edward L. "The 95th New York at South Mountain." *National Tribune*, January 7, 1886.

Bartlett, Joseph J. "Crampton's Pass, The Start of the Great Maryland Campaign." *National Tribune*, December 19, 1889.

Beech, John P. "Crampton's Pass: And the Part Taken by the 4th New Jersey in That Engagement." *National Tribune*, May 8, 1884.

——. "The 1st New Jersey Brigade at Crampton's Pass." *Grant Army Scout and Soldiers' Mail*, October 4, 1884.

Bell, T. D. "Reminiscences about Sharpsburg." *Confederate Veteran*, vol. 1, no. 8 (1893), 246.

Benning, H. L. "Notes by General H. L. Benning on the Battle of Sharpsburg." *Southern Historical Society Papers*, vol. 16 (1888), 393- 395.

Boyer, Henry. "Ninety-Sixth at Crampton's Pass." *Philadelphia Weekly Times*, September 30, 1871.

Carmichael, Peter S. "We Don't Know What on Earth to Do with Him," in Gallagher, ed. *The Antietam Campaign*. Chapel Hill, NC: University of North Carolina Press, 1999.

Carson, E. Scott. "Hampton's Legion and Hood's Brigade." *Confederate Veteran*, vol. 16, no. 7 (July, 1908), 342-3.

Chiles, Paul. "Artillery Hell: The Guns of Antietam," *Blue and Grey Magazine*, December 1998, 10-56.

Clemens, Thomas, "A Brigade Commander's First Fight." *Civil War Regiments*, vol. 5, no. 3 (1997), 59-72.

Colgrove, Silas. "The Finding of Lee's Lost Order," in Johnson and Buell, eds. *Battles and Leaders of the Civil War*, 4 vols., New York: Thomas Yoseloff, 1956, vol. 2, 603.

Cox, Jacob D. "Forcing Fox's Gap and Turner's Gap," in Johnson and Buell, eds. *Battles and Leaders of the Civil War*, 4 vols., New York: Thomas Yoseloff, 1956, vol. 2, 583-590.

——. "The Battle of Antietam," in Johnson and Buell, eds. *Battles and Leaders of the Civil War*, 4 vols., New York: Thomas Yoseloff, 1956, vol. 2, 650.

Davis, George B. "The Antietam Campaign," in *Campaigns in Virginia, Maryland, and Pennsylvania, Papers of the Military Historical Society of Massachusetts*. Boston: Griffith-Stillings Press, 1903, vol. 3, 27-72.

Davis, Steven R. "'Like Leaves in an Autumn Wind:' The 11th Mississippi Infantry in the Army of Northern Virginia." *Civil War Regiments*, vol. 2, no. 4 (1992), 269-312.

DeRosset, William L. "Battle of Sharpsburg: A Correction." *Confederate Veteran*, vol. 9 (1901), 265.

Douglas, Henry Kyd. "Stonewall Jackson in Maryland," in Johnson and Buell, eds. *Battles and Leaders of the Civil War*, 4 vols., New York: Thomas Yoseloff, 1956, vol. 2, 620-629.

Franklin, William B. "Notes on Crampton's Gap and Antietam," in Johnson and Buell, eds. *Battles and Leaders of the Civil War*, 4 vols., New York: Thomas Yoseloff, 1956, vol. 2, 591-597.

Frye, Dennis. "Drama between the Rivers," in Gary Gallagher, ed. *The Antietam Campaign*. Chapel Hill, NC: University of North Carolina Press, 1999.

——. "Through God's Blessing." *North and South Magazine*, vol. 5, no. 7 (2002), 66-75.

Garnett, James M. and Alexander Hunter, "Reminiscences of Jackson's Old Division by Captain James M. Garnett and Alexander Hunter, with Comments by Alex Robert Chisholm." *Southern Historical Society Papers*, vol. 31 (1903), 34.

Giles, Val C. "The Flag of First Texas, A. N. Virginia." *Confederate Veteran*, vol. 15, no. 9 (September 1907), 417.

Gordon, Lesley J. "All Who Went Into That Battle Were Heroes," in Gary Gallagher, ed. *The Antietam Campaign*. Chapel Hill, NC: University of North Carolina Press, 1999.

Gorman, George. "Memoirs of a Rebel." *Military Images Magazine* (November-December, 1981), 4-5.

Graham, Kurt. "Death of a Brigade: Drayton's Brigade at Fox's Gap, September 14, 1862." www.angelfire.com/ga2/phillipslegion/deathofabrigade.html.

Grattan, George D. "The Battle of Boonsboro Gap or South Mountain." *Southern Historical Society Papers*, vol. 39 (1914), pp. 39-44.

Hamby, W. R. "Hood's Texas Brigade at Sharpsburg." *Confederate Veteran*, vol. 16, no. 1 (January 1908), 19.

Hartwig, D. Scott. "'My God Be Careful!' The Morning Fight at Fox's Gap." *Civil War Regiments* (1997), Vol. 5, No. 3, pp. 27-58.

———. "It Looked Like a Task to Storm." *North and South Magazine*, vol. 5, no. 7 (2002), 36-53.

Higgins, Jacob. "At Antietam: The Gallant Services of the 125th Pennsylvania." *National Tribune*, June 3, 1886.

Hill, D. H. "The Battle of South Mountain, or 'Boonsboro': Fighting for Time at Turner's and Fox's Gaps," in Johnson and Buell, eds. *Battles and Leaders of the Civil War*, 4 vols., New York: Thomas Yoseloff, 1956. vol. 2, pp. 559-581.

Holsworth, Jerry. "Uncommon Valor: Hood's Texas Brigade in the Maryland Campaign." *Blue and Gray Magazine*, vol. xiii, no. 6, (1996), 6-55.

Hudson, John W. "Tired Soldiers Don't Go Very Fast." *Civil War Times Illustrated*, January-February, 1992, 36-40.

Hunter, Alexander. "A High Private's Sketch of Sharpsburg: Conclusion." *Southern Historical Society Papers*, vol. XI (1883), 10-21.

———. "The Battle of Antietam or Sharpsburg." *Southern Historical Society Papers*, vol. 31 (1903), 37-43.

Irwin, Richard B. "Washington Under Banks," in Johnson and Buell, eds. *Battles and Leaders of the Civil War*, 4 vols., New York: Thomas Yoseloff, 1956, vol. 2, 541-544.

Johnston, J. S. "Reminiscences of Sharpsburg." *Southern Historical Society Papers*, vol. 8, no. 10-12 (1880), pp. 526-529.

Krick, Robert E. L. "Defending Lee's Flank," in Gary Gallagher, ed. *The Antietam Campaign*. Chapel Hill, NC: University of North Carolina Press, 1999.

Krick, Robert K. "It Appeared as Though Mutual Extermination Would Put a Stop to the Awful Carnage," in Gary Gallagher, ed. *The Antietam Campaign*. Chapel Hill, NC: University of North Carolina Press, 1999.

Lee, S. D. "New Lights on Sharpsburg." *Richmond Dispatch*, December 20, 1896.

"Letter from the 10th Me. Regiment." *The Lewiston Journal*, October 2, 1862.

Luff, William M. "March of the Cavalry from Harper's Ferry, September 14, 1862," in *Military Essay and Recollections: Papers Read before the Commandery of the State of Illinois, Military Order of the Loyal Legion of the United States*. Chicago: A. C. McClurg and Co., 1894. 39-45.

McClellan, George B. "From the Peninsula to Antietam," in Johnson and Buell, eds. *Battles and Leaders of the Civil War*, 4 vols., New York: Thomas Yoseloff, 1956, vol. 2, 545-555.

Mahood, Wayne. "Some Very Hard Stories Were Told: The 126th New York at Harpers Ferry," *Civil War Regiments*, vol. 1, no. 4 (1991), 7-41.

Marshall, T. J. "The Pennsylvania Reserves at Antietam." *National Tribune*, April 11, 1907.

Maryniak, B. R. "A Rough Morning Near Sharpsburg." *The Famous Long Ago*. Buffalo Civil War Round Table Newsletter (July 1986), 26-27.

Mellott, David W. "The 7th West Virginia Infantry's Assault on Bloody Lane." *Civil War Regiments*, vol. 5, no. 3 (1997), 124- 150.

Mitchell, Mary Bedinger "A Woman's Recollections of Antietam," in Johnson and Buell, eds. *Battles and Leaders of the Civil War*, 4 vols., New York: Thomas Yoseloff, 1956, vol. 2, 686-693.

Mockbee, Robert T. "The 14th Tennessee Infantry Regiment." *Civil War Regiments*, vol. 5, no. 1, (1997), 1-44.

Moore, J. B. "Sharpsburg: Graphic Description of the Battle and its Results." *Richmond Times*, May 28, 1899.

Morrison, Col. E. M. "Fifteenth Virginia Infantry." *Southern Historical Society Papers*, vol. XXXIII (1905), 103-104.

Motlow, Felix. "Campaigns in Northern Virginia." *Confederate Veteran*, vol. 11, no. 10 (1903), 310.

Murray, R. L. "The Irish Brigade at Antietam," in R. L. Murray, ed., *New Yorkers in the Civil War*, 10 vols. (2006), vol. 6, 1-39.

Napier, J. L. "M'Intosh's Battery at Sharpsburg." *Confederate Veteran*, vol. XIX, no. 9 (1911), 429.

Nolan, Alan T. and Marc Storch, "The Iron Brigade Earns its Name." *Blue and Gray Magazine*, vol. 21, no. 6 (2004), 6-50.

"Notes by General H. L. Benning on the Battle of Sharpsburg." *Southern Historical Society Papers*, vol. XVI (1888), 393.

Otott, George E. "Clash in the Cornfield: The 1st Texas Volunteer Infantry in the Maryland Campaign." *Civil War Regiments*, vol. 5, no. 3 (1997), 73-123.

Owen, Henry T. "Annals of the War: Chapters of Unwritten History: South Mountain." *Philadelphia Weekly Times*, July 31, 1880.

Parham, John T. "Thirty-Second at Sharpsburg." *Southern Historical Society Papers*, vol. 34 (1906), 250-53.

Park, Robert E. "Anniversary of the Battle of Boonsboro, Maryland," *Southern Historical Society Papers*, vol. 33 (1905), 278-7.

Powell, Eugene. "Recollections of the Eastern Campaigns of the Fall of 1862." *National Tribune*, June 27, 1901.

Putnam, J. R. "Patrick's Brigade." *National Tribune*, April 30, 1908.

"Rodman's Brigade at Antietam." *National Tribune*, December 9, 1886.

Smith, Sol R. "South Mountain." *National Tribune*, January 17, 1895.

Snell, Mark A. "The 118th ("Corn Exchange") Pennsylvania at the Battle of Shepherdstown." *Civil War Regiments*, vol. 6, no. 2 (1998), 119-142.

Speicher, James L. "The Sumter Artillery." *Civil War Regiments* (1993), vol. 3, no. 2, pp. 1-60.

Spooner, Henry J. "The Maryland Campaign with the Fourth Rhode Island." *Rhode Island MOLLUS*, vol. III, 211-235.

Stickley, E. E. "Battle of Sharpsburg." *Confederate Veteran*, vol. 22, no. 2 (1914), 66-67.

"The Sharpsburg Fight," *Tri-Weekly Telegraph*, October 15, 1862.

"The Texans at Sharpsburg." *Confederate Veteran*, vol. 22, no. 12 (December, 1914), 555.

Waddell, A. M. "General George Burgwyn Anderson: The Memorial Address, May 11, 1885," *Southern Historical Society Papers*, vol. 14, 387-397.

Walker, John G. "Jackson's Capture of Harper's Ferry," in Johnson and Buell, eds. *Battles and Leaders of the Civil War*, 4 vols. New York: Thomas Yoseloff, 1956, vol. 2, 604-611.

———. Walker, John G. "Sharpsburg," in Johnson and Buell, eds. *Battles and Leaders of the Civil War*, 4 vols. New York: Thomas Yoseloff, 1956, vol. 2, 675-682.

Walton, J. E. "The 30th Ohio: Some Reminiscences of the Battle of Antietam." *National Tribune*, December 31, 1885.

Warner, Adoniram Judson. "The Ordeal of Adoniram Judson Warner: His Minutes of South Mountain and Antietam." *Civil War History*, vol. 28, number 3 (September, 1982). 213-236.

"What Confederate Troops Fought the 10th Me. in the East Woods?" *National Tribune*, August 25, 1892.

White, Julius. "The Capitulation of Harpers Ferry," in Johnson and Buell, eds. *Battles and Leaders of the Civil War*, 4 vols. New York: Thomas Yoseloff, 1956. vol. 2, 612-615.

Williams, T. Harry, "The Civil War Letters of William L. Cage." *Civil War History*, vol. 39, no. 1 (January, 1956), 113-130.

Wood, A. H. "Reno's Death." *National Tribune*, July 6, 1883.

Index

About the Author

Bradley M. Gottfried holds a Ph.D. in Zoology from Miami University. He has worked in higher education for more than three decades as a faculty member and administrator and is currently the President of the College of Southern Maryland.

An avid Civil War historian, Dr. Gottfried is the author of nine books, including *The Battle of Gettysburg: A Guided Tour* (1998); *Stopping Pickett: The History of the Philadelphia Brigade* (1999); *Brigades of Gettysburg* (2002); *Roads to Gettysburg* (2002); *Kearny's Own: The History of the First New Jersey Brigade* (2005), *The Maps of Gettysburg* (2007), *The Artillery of Gettysburg* (2008), and *The Maps of First Bull Run* (2009). He is currently (with co-editor Theodore P. Savas) completing *The Gettysburg Campaign Encyclopedia*.

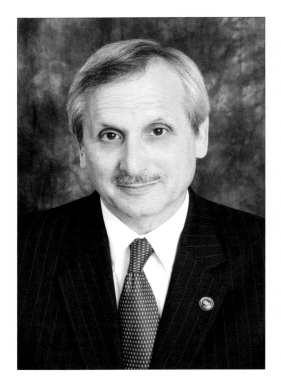